Microsoft® ASP.NET 4
Step by Step

George Shepherd

PUBLISHED BY
Microsoft Press
A Division of Microsoft Corporation
One Microsoft Way
Redmond, Washington 98052-6399

Library of Congress Control Number: 2010925074

Printed and bound in the United States of America.

1 2 3 4 5 6 7 8 9 WCT 5 4 3 2 1 0

Distributed in Canada by H.B. Fenn and Company Ltd.

A CIP catalogue record for this book is available from the British Library.

Microsoft Press books are available through booksellers and distributors worldwide. For further information about international editions, contact your local Microsoft Corporation office or contact Microsoft Press International directly at fax (425) 936-7329. Visit our Web site at www.microsoft.com/mspress. Send comments to mspinput@microsoft.com.

Microsoft, Microsoft Press, Access, ActiveX, DirectX, Expression, Expression Blend, Hotmail, IntelliSense, Internet Explorer, MS, MSDN, MS-DOS, MSN, SharePoint, Silverlight, SQL Server, Visual Basic, Visual C#, Visual Studio, Win32, Windows, Windows Live, Windows NT, Windows Server and Windows Vista are either registered trademarks or trademarks of the Microsoft group of companies. Other product and company names mentioned herein may be the trademarks of their respective owners.

The example companies, organizations, products, domain names, e-mail addresses, logos, people, places, and events depicted herein are fictitious. No association with any real company, organization, product, domain name, e-mail address, logo, person, place, or event is intended or should be inferred.

This book expresses the author's views and opinions. The information contained in this book is provided without any express, statutory, or implied warranties. Neither the authors, Microsoft Corporation, nor its resellers, or distributors will be held liable for any damages caused or alleged to be caused either directly or indirectly by this book.

Acquisitions Editor: Ben Ryan
Developmental Editor: Maria Gargiulo
Project Editor: Melissa von Tschudi-Sutton and Maria Gargiulo
Editorial Production: Waypoint Press, www.waypointpress.com
Technical Reviewer: Kenn Scribner; Technical Review services provided by Content Master, a member of
                        CM Group, Ltd.
Cover: Tom Draper Design

Body Part No. X16-61997

Dedicated to Sally Bronson Harrison and Gene Harrison, my second mom and dad.

Contents at a Glance

Table of Contents

What do you think of this book? We want to hear from you!

Microsoft is interested in hearing your feedback so we can continually improve our books and learning resources for you. To participate in a brief online survey, please visit:

www.microsoft.com/learning/booksurvey/

What do you think of this book? We want to hear from you!

Microsoft is interested in hearing your feedback so we can continually improve our books and learning resources for you. To participate in a brief online survey, please visit:

www.microsoft.com/learning/booksurvey/

Acknowledgments

The last time I wrote the acknowledgments for this book, I mentioned how my son, Ted, had written a Father's Day card for me in HTML. Ted is in college now, and I can remember his searching out and applying for schools during the last couple of years of high school. He did it almost entirely online, over the Web. How different that was from my experience applying to schools!

The Web permeates our social infrastructure. Whether you're a businessperson wanting to increase the visibility of your business, an avid reader trying to find an out-of-print book, a student fetching homework assignments from a school Web site, or any other producer or consumer of information, you touch the Internet.

Publishing a book is a huge effort. My name is on the lower right corner of the cover as the author, but I did only some of the work. I have so many people to thank for helping get this book out.

Thank you, Claudette Moore, for hooking me up with Microsoft Press again. Claudette has acted as my agent for all my work with Microsoft Press, handling the business issues so I can be free to write. Thank you, Maria Gargiulo, for managing the project. It's been great working with you. Thank you, Charlotte Twiss, for getting the code samples onto the CD. Thank you, Steve Sagman, for composing the pages so beautifully. Thank you, Christina Yeager, for copyediting the pages and making it appear that I can actually write coherent sentences, as well as for indexing the project. You all did a wonderful job on the editing, production, and layout. Thank you, Kenn Scribner, for providing the best technical objective eye I've ever worked with. Thank you, Ben Ryan, for accepting the book proposal and hiring me to create the book.

Thank you, Jeff Duntemann, for buying and publishing my first piece ever for *PC Tech Journal*. Thank you, JD Hildebrand, for buying my second writing piece ever, and for the opportunity to work with you all at Oakley Publishing. Thank you, Sandy Daston, for your support and guidance early in my writing career. Thank you to the folks at DevelopMentor for being an excellent group of technical colleagues and a great place for learning new technology. Thanks to my buds at Schwab Performance Technologies.

Thanks to my evil Java twin, Pat Shepherd, and his family, Michelle, Belfie, and Bronson. Thank you, Ted Shepherd, you're the best son ever. Thank you, George Robbins Shepherd and Betsy Shepherd. As my parents, you guided me and encouraged me to always do my best. I miss you both dearly.

Finally, thank you, reader, for going through this book and spending time learning ASP.NET. May you continue to explore ASP.NET and always find new and interesting ways to handle HTTP requests.

—George Shepherd
Chapel Hill, NC
March, 2010

Introduction

This book shows you how to write Web applications using Microsoft ASP.NET 4, the most current version of the Microsoft HTTP request processing framework. Web development has come a long way since the earliest sites began popping up on the Internet in the early 1990s. The world of Web development offers several choices of development tools. During the past few years, ASP.NET has evolved to become one of the most consistent, stable, and feature-rich frameworks available for managing HTTP requests.

ASP.NET, together with Microsoft Visual Studio, includes a number of features to make your life as a Web developer easier. For example, Visual Studio offers several project templates that you can use to develop your site. Visual Studio also supports a number of development modes, including using Microsoft Internet Information Services (IIS) directly to test your site during development, using a built-in Web server, and developing your site over an FTP connection. With the debugger in Visual Studio, you can run the site and step through the critical areas of your code to find problems. With the Visual Studio Designer, you can develop effective user interfaces by dropping control elements onto a canvas to see how they appear visually. And when you are ready to deploy your application, Visual Studio makes it easy to create a deployment package. These are but a few of the features built into the ASP.NET framework when paired with Visual Studio.

The purpose of this book is to tell the story of ASP.NET development. Each section presents a specific ASP.NET feature in a digestible format with examples. The stepwise instructions yield immediate working results. Most of the main features of ASP.NET are illustrated here using succinct, easily duplicated examples. The examples are rich to illustrate features without being overbearing. In addition to showing off ASP.NET features by example, this book contains practical applications of each feature so that you can apply these techniques in the real world. After reading this book and applying the exercises you'll have a great head start into building real Web sites that include such modern features as AJAX, WCF services, custom controls, and master pages.

This book is organized so that you can read each chapter independently for the most part. With the exception of Chapter 1, "Web Application Basics," and the three chapters on server-side controls (Chapters 3 to 5), which make sense to tackle together, each chapter serves as a self-contained block of information about a particular ASP.NET feature. In addition, for the sake of completeness, Chapter 1 also includes information about how IIS and ASP.NET interact together.

Who This Book Is For

This book is targeted at several types of developers:

- **Those starting out completely new to ASP.NET**   The text includes enough back story to explain the Web development saga even if you've developed only desktop applications.

- **Those migrating from either ASP.NET 1.*x*, 2.0, 3.*x,* or even classic ASP**   The text explains how ASP.NET 4 is different from earlier versions of ASP.NET. It also includes references explaining differences between ASP.NET and classic ASP.

- **Those who want to consume ASP.NET how-to knowledge in digestible pieces**   You don't have to read the chapters in any particular order to find the book valuable. Each chapter stands more or less on its own (with the exception of the first chapter, which details the fundamentals of Web applications—you might want to read it first if you've never ventured beyond desktop application development). You might find it useful to study the chapters about server-side controls (Chapters 3 to 5) together, but it's not completely necessary to do so.

Getting Started

If you've gotten this far, you're probably ready to begin writing some code.

> **Important** Before beginning, make sure that:
> - Visual Studio 2010 is installed on your computer.
>
>   As long as you've installed the development environment, you can be sure the .NET run-time support is installed as well.
> - You have Administrator permissions on your computer.
>
>   See "Installing the C# Code Samples" later in this Introduction for more information.
> - IIS is installed and running on your computer.
>
>   IIS is required to run the code samples for Chapters 1, 2, 9, and 26. To install IIS in Windows 7, click Start, and click Control Panel. In Control Panel, click Programs and Features, and click Turn Windows Features On or Off. In the Windows Features dialog box, expand Internet Information Services, select the checkboxes next to Web Management Tools and World Wide Web Services, and click OK.

If you attempt to install the code without IIS running, you will see an error message like the following. To bypass this error message, click Ignore to continue installation.

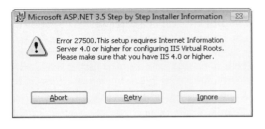

The first few code examples require nothing but a text editor and a working installation of IIS. To start, you can begin with some basic examples to illustrate the object-oriented nature and compilation model of ASP.NET. In addition to seeing exactly how ASP.NET works when handling a request, this is a good time to view the architecture of ASP.NET from a high level. Next, you progress to Web form programming and begin using Visual Studio to write code—which makes things much easier!

After learning the fundamentals of Web form development, you can see the rest of ASP.NET through examples of ASP.NET features such as server-side controls, content caching, custom handlers, output and data caching, and debugging and diagnostics, all the way to ASP.NET support for Web Services.

Finding Your Best Starting Point in This Book

This book is designed to help you build skills in a number of essential areas. You can use this book whether you are new to Web programming or you are switching from another Web development platform. Use the following table to find your best starting point in this book.

If you are	Follow these steps
New to Web development	1. Install the code samples.
	2. Work through the examples in Chapters 1 and 2 sequentially. They ground you in the ways of Web development. They also familiarize you with ASP.NET and Visual Studio.
	3. Complete the rest of the book as your requirements dictate.
New to ASP.NET and Visual Studio	1. Install the code samples.
	2. Work through the examples in Chapter 2. They provide a foundation for working with ASP.NET and Visual Studio.
	3. Complete the rest of the book as your requirements dictate.

If you are	Follow these steps
Migrating from earlier versions of ASP.NET	1. Install the code samples. 2. Skim the first two chapters to get an overview of Web development in the Microsoft environment and with Visual Studio 2010. 3. Concentrate on Chapters 3 through 26 as necessary. You might already be familiar with some topics and might need only to see how a particular current feature differs from earlier versions of ASP.NET. In other cases, you might need to explore a feature that is completely new in ASP.NET 4.
Referencing the book after working through the exercises	1. Use the index or the table of contents to find information about particular subjects. 2. Read the Quick Reference section at the end of each chapter to find a brief review of the syntax and techniques presented in the chapter.

Conventions and Features in This Book

This book uses conventions designed to make the information readable and easy to follow. Before you start the book, read the following list, which explains conventions you'll see throughout the book and points out helpful features in the book that you might want to use.

Conventions

- Each chapter includes a summary of objectives near the beginning.

- Each exercise is a series of tasks. Each task is presented as a series of steps to be followed sequentially.

- "Tips" provide additional information or alternative methods for completing a step successfully.

- "Important" reader aids alert you to critical information for installing and using the sample code on the companion CD.

- Text that you type appears in bold type, like so:

```
class foo
{
    System.Console.WriteLine("HelloWorld");
}
```

- The directions often include alternative ways of accomplishing a single result. For example, you can add a new item to a Visual Studio project from either the main menu or by right-clicking in Solution Explorer.

- The examples in this book are written using C#.

Other Features

- Some text includes sidebars and notes to provide more in-depth information about the particular topic. The sidebars might contain background information, design tips, or features related to the information being discussed. They might also inform you about how a particular feature differs in this version of ASP.NET from earlier versions.

- Each chapter ends with a Quick Reference section that contains concise reminders of how to perform the tasks you learned in the chapter.

Prerelease Software

This book was reviewed and tested against the Visual Studio 2010 release candidate one week before the publication of this book. We reviewed and tested the examples against the Visual Studio 2010 release candidate. You might find minor differences between the production release and the examples, text, and screenshots in this book. However, we expect them to be minimal.

Hardware and Software Requirements

You need the following hardware and software to complete the practice exercises in this book:

 Important The Visual Studio 2010 software is *not* included with this book! The CD-ROM packaged in the back of this book contains the code samples needed to complete the exercises. The Visual Studio 2010 software must be purchased separately.

- Windows 7; Windows Server 2003; Windows Server 2008; or Windows Vista

- Internet Information Services (included with Windows). You will need IIS 5.1 or later. IIS 7.5 is the latest release at the time of this writing.

- Microsoft Visual Studio 2010 Ultimate, Visual Studio 2010 Premium, or Visual Studio 2010 Professional

- Microsoft SQL Server 2008 Express (included with Visual Studio 2010) or SQL Server 2008 (SQL Server 2008 R2 is the latest release at the time of this writing)

- 1.6-GHz Pentium or compatible processor

- 1 GB RAM for x86

- 2 GB RAM for x64

- An additional 512 MB RAM if running in a virtual machine

- DirectX 9–capable video card that runs at 1024 × 768 or higher display resolution
- 5400-RPM hard drive (with 3 GB of available hard disk space)
- DVD-ROM drive
- Microsoft mouse or compatible pointing device
- 5 MB of available hard disk space to install the code samples

You also need to have Administrator access to your computer to configure Microsoft SQL Server 2008 Express.

Code Samples

The companion CD inside this book contains the code samples, written in C#, that you use as you perform the exercises in the book. By using the code samples, you won't waste time creating files that aren't relevant to the exercise. The files and the step-by-step instructions in the lessons also help you learn by doing, which is an easy and effective way to acquire and remember new skills.

Digital Content for Digital Book Readers

If you bought a digital-only edition of this book, you can enjoy select content from the print edition's companion CD. Visit *http://go.microsoft.com/fwlink/?LinkId=186954* to get your downloadable content. This content is always up-to-date and available to all readers.

Installing the C# Code Samples

Follow the steps here to install the C# code samples on your computer so that you can use them with the exercises in this book.

Important   Before you begin, make sure that you have

- Administrator permissions on your computer.
- IIS installed and running on your computer.

Chapters 1, 2, 9, and 26 include information about using IIS, and their companion code samples require IIS. The code sample installer modifies IIS. Working with IIS requires that you have administration privileges on your machine. If you are using your own computer at home, you probably have Administrator rights. If you are using a computer in an organization and you do not have Administrator rights, please consult your computer support or IT staff.

To install IIS in Windows 7, click Start, and click Control Panel. In Control Panel, click Programs and Features, and click Turn Windows Features On or Off. In the Windows Features dialog box, expand Internet Information Services, select the checkboxes next to Web Management Tools and World Wide Web Services, and click OK.

If you attempt to install the code without IIS running, you will see an error message like the following. To bypass this error message, click Ignore to continue installation.

1. Remove the companion CD from the package inside this book and insert it into your CD-ROM drive.

 Note A menu screen for the CD should open automatically. If it does not appear, open Computer on the desktop or the Start menu, double-click the icon for your CD-ROM drive, and then double-click StartCD.exe.

2. In the companion CD UI, select Code from the menu on the left. The InstallShield Wizard will guide you through the installation process.

3. Review the end-user license agreement. If you accept the terms, select the accept option, and then click Next.

4. Accept the default settings to install the code.

The code samples are installed to the following location on your computer:

\C*Microsoft Press\ASP.NET 4 Step by Step*\

Additionally, if you have IIS running and you open the Internet Information Services conole, you will see that the installer creates a virtual directory named *aspnet4sbs* under the Default Web Site. Below the aspnet4sbs virtual directory, various Web applications are created.

Using the Code Samples

Each chapter in this book explains when and how to use any code samples for that chapter. When it's time to use a code sample, the book lists the instructions for how to open the files. Many chapters begin projects completely from scratch so that you can understand the entire development process. Some examples borrow bits of code from previous examples.

Here's a comprehensive list of the code sample projects:

Project	Description	
Chapter 1		
HelloWorld.asp, Selectnoform.asp, Selectfeature.htm, Selectfeature2.htm, Selectfeature.asp	Several Web resources illustrating different examples of raw HTTP requests	
WebRequestor	A simple application that issues a raw HTTP request	
Chapter 2		
HelloWorld, HelloWorld2, HelloWorld3, HelloWorld4, HelloWorld5, partial1.cs, partial2.cs	Web resources illustrating compilation models and partial classes in ASP.NET	
Chapter 3		
BunchOfControls.htm, BunchOfControls.asp, BunchOfControls.aspx	Web resources illustrating rendering control tags	
ControlsORama	Visual Studio–based project illustrating Visual Studio and server-side controls	
Chapter 4		
ControlsORama	Extends the example begun in Chapter 3. Illustrates creating and using rendered server-side controls	
Chapter 5		
ControlsORama	Extends the example used in Chapter 4. Illustrates creating and using composite server-side controls and user controls	
Chapter 6		
ControlPotpourri	Illustrates control validation, the *TreeView*, the *Image*, the *ImageButton*, the *ImageMap*, and the *MultiView/ View* controls	
Chapter 7		
MasterPageSite	Illustrates developing a common look and feel throughout multiple pages in a single Web application using master pages, themes, and skins	

Project	Description
Chapter 8	
ConfigORama	Illustrates configuration in ASP.NET. Shows how to manage the web.config file, how to add new configuration elements, and how to retrieve those configuration elements.
Chapter 9	
SecureSite	Illustrates Forms Authentication and authorization in a Web site
Login.aspx, OptionalLogin.aspx, Web.Config, Web.ConfigForceAuthentication, Web.ConfigForOptionalLogin	Web resources for illustrating Forms Authentication at the very barest level
Chapter 10	
DataBindORama	Illustrates data binding to several different controls, including the *GridView*. Illustrates the *DataSource* controls. Also illustrates loading and saving data sets as XML and XML schema
Chapter 11	
NavigateMeSite	Illustrates ASP.NET navigation features
Chapter 12	
MakeItPersonal	Illustrates ASP.NET personalization features
Chapter 13	
UseWebParts	Illustrates using Web Parts in a Web application
Chapter 14	
SessionState	Illustrates using session state in a Web application
Chapter 15	
UseDataCaching	Illustrates caching data to improve performance
Chapter 16	
OutputCache	Illustrates caching output to improve performance
Chapter 17	
DebugORama	Illustrates debugging and tracing Web applications
Chapter 18	
UseApplication	Illustrates using the global application object and HTTP modules as a rendezvous point for the application. Illustrates storing globally scoped data and handling application-wide events

Project	Description	
Chapter 19		
CustomHandlers	Illustrates custom HTTP handlers, both as separate assemblies and as ASHX files	
Chapter 20		
DynamicDataLinqToSQLSite	Illustrates how ASP.NET Dynamic works to create data-driven sites	
Chapter 21		
XAMLORama	Illustrates how to use loose XAML in a site	
XBAPORama	Illustrates how to create an XAML-based Browser Application (XBAP)	
Chapter 22		
MVCORama	Illustrates how to create and manage an MVC-based site, complete with a database	
Chapter 23		
AJAXORama	Illustrates using AJAX to improve the end user experience	
Chapter 24		
SilverlightSite	Illustrates how to include Silverlight content in an ASP.NET site	
SilverlightLayout	Shows how Silverlight layout panels work	
SilverlightAnimations	Illustrates using animations in Silverlight	
SilverlightAndWCF	Shows how a Silverlight component can communicate to a Web site via WCF	
Chapter 25		
WCFQuotesService	Illustrates how to create and consume an ASP.NET WCF service	
Chapter 26		
DeployThisApplication	Illustrates the new ASP.NET Packaging system, which facilitates deployment	

All these projects are available as complete solutions for the practice exercises (in case you need any inspiration).

Uninstalling the Code Samples

Follow these steps to remove the code samples from your computer:

1. In Control Panel, open Add Or Remove Programs.
2. From the list of Currently Installed Programs, select Microsoft ASP.NET 4 Step by Step.
3. Click Remove.
4. Follow the instructions that appear to remove the code samples.

Support for This Book

Every effort has been made to ensure the accuracy of this book and the contents of the companion CD. As corrections or changes are collected, they will be added to a Microsoft Knowledge Base article. Microsoft Press provides support for books and companion CDs at the following Web site:

http://www.microsoft.com/learning/support/books/

If you have comments, questions, or ideas regarding the book or the companion CD, or questions that are not answered by visiting the sites previously mentioned, please send them to Microsoft Press by sending an e-mail message to *mspinput@microsoft.com.*

Please note that Microsoft software product support is not offered through the preceding address.

We Want to Hear from You

We welcome your feedback about this book. Please share your comments and ideas through the following short survey:

http://www.microsoft.com/learning/booksurvey

Your participation helps Microsoft Press create books that better meet your needs and your standards.

> **Note** We hope that you will give us detailed feedback in our survey. If you have questions about our publishing program, upcoming titles, or Microsoft Press in general, we encourage you to interact with us using Twitter at *http://twitter.com/MicrosoftPress*. For support issues, use only the e-mail address shown earlier.

Part I
Fundamentals

Chapter 1
Web Application Basics

After completing this chapter, you will be able to

- Interpret HTTP requests.
- Use the Microsoft .NET Framework to make HTTP requests without a browser.
- Interpret HTML.
- Work with Internet Information Services (IIS).
- Produce dynamic Web content without using Microsoft ASP.NET yet.

This chapter covers the fundamentals of building a Web-based application. Unlike the development of most desktop applications, in which many of the parts are available locally (as components on the user's hard disk drive), developing a Web application requires getting software parts to work over a widely distributed network using a disconnected protocol. The technologies underlying ASP.NET have been around for a long time, but ASP.NET puts them together in a way that makes Web development very approachable.

This chapter covers three topics necessary for you to understand to work with ASP.NET:

- How HTTP requests work
- How HTML works
- How HTTP requests are handled on IIS, the Microsoft production Web server

Even though ASP.NET makes developing Web applications far easier than it was earlier, having a solid understanding of how the individual components actually work is important and can help you make sense of all parts of Web application development. For example, when you are tracking down a stray HTTP request or trying to figure out why a section of your page is appearing in the wrong font in a client's browser, it's helpful to know how HTTP and HTML work together to deliver the page to the client. And when you write a custom control for a Web page, because custom controls often require that you write the rendering code manually and ensure that the HTML tags emitted by the control occur in exactly the right order, you need to understand HTML.

Understanding of the three technologies underlying ASP.NET frames the rest of the system. As you study ASP.NET, these pieces will undoubtedly fall into place.

Important To install the code samples for this book, you must have Administrator rights on your computer. If you are using your own computer, you probably have Administrator rights. If you are using a computer in an organization and you do not have Administrator rights, please consult your computer support or IT staff. See the "Code Samples" section in the Introduction for more information.

 Important The code samples for this chapter on the companion CD require IIS support to execute. See the "Code Samples" section in the Introduction for important information on running the examples for this chapter.

HTTP Requests

The communication mechanism with which Web browsers talk to Web sites is named *Hypertext Transfer Protocol* (HTTP). The World Wide Web as we know it today began as a research project at CERN in Switzerland. In those days, the notion of hypertext—documents linked together arbitrarily—was becoming increasingly popular. Applications such as Hypercard from Apple Computer introduced hypertext applications to a wider audience. If documents could then be linked over a network, that would revolutionize publishing. That's the reason for the development of HTTP, which lies on top of TCP/IP as an application layer.

In its original form, HTTP was meant to transfer hypertext documents. That is, it was originally intended simply to link documents together without consideration for anything like the Web-based user interfaces that are the staple of modern Web sites. The earliest versions of HTTP supported a single GET request to fetch the named resource. It then was the server's job to send the file as a stream of text. After the response arrived at the client's browser, the connection terminated. The earliest versions of HTTP supported only transfer of text streams and did not support any other sort of data transfer.

The first formal specification for HTTP was version 1.0 and was published in the mid-1990s. HTTP 1.0 added support for more complex messaging beyond a simple text transfer pro-tocol. HTTP grew to support different media (specified by the Multipurpose Internet Mail Extensions). The current version of HTTP is version 1.1.

As a connection protocol, HTTP is built around several basic commands. The most important ones you see in developing ASP.NET applications are GET and POST, but other important HTTP commands not as commonly used within ASP.NET include HEAD and PUT.

GET retrieves the information identified by the Uniform Resource Identifier (URI) specified by the request. The HEAD command retrieves only the header information identified by the URI specified by the request (that is, it does not return a message body). You use the POST method to make a request to the server that might cause side effects, such as when you send information to the server for it to process. PUT is also used to send information to the server, but in the sense of documents and records versus request parameters, as is typically the case for POST when related to HTML page requests. You make most initial contacts to a page using a GET command, and you commonly handle subsequent interactions using POST commands.

HTTP Requests from a Browser

For example, look at the request that is sent from a browser to fetch the helloworld.htm resource from the virtual directory aspnet4sbs running on localhost. (I cover the concept of a virtual directory later; for now just imagine a virtual directory as the location of a Web application that everyone can access.) Here is a sample (fictitious) HTTP server request:

```
GET /aspnet4sbs/helloworld.htm HTTP/1.1
Accept: image/gif, image/x-xbitmap, image/jpeg, image/pjpeg, ... , */*
Accept-Language: en-us
Accept-Encoding: gzip, deflate
User-Agent: Mozilla/4.0 (compatible; MSIE 7.0; Windows NT 5.1; ... .NET CLR 3.0.04506.30)
Host: localhost:80
Connection: Keep-Alive
```

If you would like to see the actual data going back and forth, several TCP monitors are available. A good one is TcpTrace, found at *http://www.pocketsoap.com/tcptrace/.* You can find instructions for its use there as well.

To issue a request to a Web server, the browser creates the HTTP request using the URI along with other information (such as header information and the requested file name). The header information in the request includes details about the operating environment of the browser and some other information that is useful to the server. It then sends the request to the server identified by the host HTTP header. When the server receives this request, it returns the requested resource as a text stream. The browser then parses it and formats the contents. The following code shows the response provided by the server when asked for a simple HelloWorld.htm file. Typically, you don't see all the header information when viewing the resource through a browser, but a good TCP tracing utility such as TcpTrace shows it to you. When you look at the tracing facilities of ASP.NET later on, this header information is visible.

```
HTTP/1.1 200 OK
Server: Microsoft-IIS/5.1
X-Powered-By: ASP.NET
Date: Thu, 01 Nov 2007 23:44:04 GMT
Content-Type: text/html
Accept-Ranges: bytes
Last-Modified: Mon, 22 Oct 2007 21:54:20 GMT
ETag: "04e9ace185fc51:bb6"
Content-Length: 130
<html>
    <body>
        <h1> Hello World </h1>
        Nothing really showing here yet, except some HTML...
    </body>
</html>
```

The first line indicates the protocol (HTTP version 1.1) and the return code (200, meaning "OK"). The rest of the response (until the first <html> tag) is information about the time of the request, the last time the file was modified, and what kind of content is provided. This information is useful later when you examine such issues as page caching and detecting browser capabilities. The content following the response header information is literally the HTML file sent by the server.

Making HTTP Requests Without a Browser

In addition to being a framework for building Web applications, the .NET development environment includes classes for making HTTP requests in the raw. The *WebRequest* class includes a member named *GetResponse* that sends a request to the address specified by the Uniform Resource Locator (URL). To get a feeling for how to make direct requests to a Web server without a browser, try compiling and then running this short program that fetches the home page for Microsoft.com.

Building a simple HTTP requestor

1. Start Visual Studio .NET by clicking New, Project on the main menu. In the New Project dialog box, click Console Application and name the application *WebRequestorApp*, as shown in the following graphic:

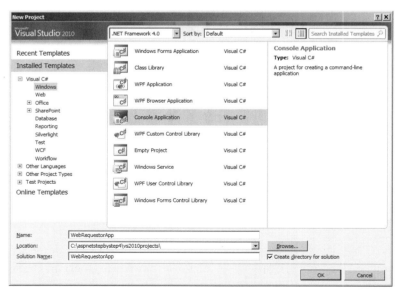

Visual Studio generates a blank Console program for you.

2. Add the code necessary to make a Web request to the program. Visual Studio places the entry point of the Console application in a file named Program.cs. (This file is the code that appears in the code window by default.) The code you add for making a Web request is shown in bold type in the following lines of code:

```
using System;
using System.Collections.Generic;
using System.Linq;
using System.Text;
using System.Net;
using System.IO;
namespace WebRequestorApp
{
    class Program
    {
        static void Main(string[] args)
        {
            WebRequest req =
                WebRequest.Create
                    ("http://www.microsoft.com");
            WebResponse resp = req.GetResponse();
            StreamReader reader =
                new StreamReader(resp.GetResponseStream(),
                    Encoding.ASCII);
            Console.WriteLine(reader.ReadToEnd());
        }
    }
}
```

3. Run the application by clicking Debug, Start Without Debugging on the main menu. Visual Studio starts a Console for you and runs the program. After a couple of moments, you will see some HTML on your screen.

Of course, the HTML isn't meant for human consumption. That's what a browser is for. However, this example does show the fundamentals of making a Web request—and you can see exactly what comes back in the response.

In this case, the request sent to the server is much smaller than a POST request would be. *WebRequest.GetResponse* doesn't include as much information in the request—just the requisite GET followed by the URI, host information, and connection type:

```
GET /aspnet2sbs/helloworld.htm HTTP/1.1
Host: localhost:80
Connection: Keep-Alive
```

The fundamental jobs of most browsers are (1) to package a request and send it to the server represented in the URI, and (2) to receive the response from the server and render it into a useful form. The response usually comes back as a text stream marked up with HTML tags. The next section discusses HTML.

Hypertext Markup Language

In the course of looking at ASP.NET, you see quite a bit of HTML. Most of it is generated by the ASP.NET server-side controls. Some of it you write yourself just to create the basic page you're looking for. However, it's also important to understand HTML because you might want to write your own server-side control from scratch, and at other times you might need to tweak or debug the output of your ASP.NET application.

Most HTTP requests result in a stream of text returning to the program issuing the request. The world has pretty much agreed that HTML is the language to use for formatting documents, and all browsers understand HTML.

The first release of HTML worth using was version 2.0. Version 3.2 introduced new features, such as tables, text flow, applets, and superscripts and subscripts, while providing backward compatibility with the existing HTML 2.0 standard.

The bottom line is that a competent browser and well-structured HTML form the basis of a user interface development technology. And because HTML is understood by browsers running on a variety of platforms, the door was open for implementing a worldwide interactive computing platform. The other key besides a mature version of HTML that made this happen was the ability of servers to adapt their output to accommodate the requests of specific users at run time.

For example, the following HTML stream renders an HTML page containing a button and a selection list filled with options. (This file is named SelectNoForm.htm in the collection of examples for this chapter.)

```html
<html>
 <body>
   <h2>Hello there. What's your favorite .NET feature?</h2>
   <select name='Feature'>
    <option> Type-Safety</option>
    <option> Garbage collection</option>
    <option> Multiple syntaxes</option>
    <option> Code Access Security</option>
    <option> Simpler threading</option>
    <option> Versioning purgatory</option>
   </select>
   <br/>
   <input type=submit name='Lookup' value='Lookup'></input>
   <br/>
 </body>
</html>
```

Note You actually surf to an HTML file that you write in subsequent chapters. Getting to that point is a bit involved, so for now, you can trust that the HTML renders in this fashion.

Figure 1-1 shows how the page looks when rendered by the browser.

FIGURE 1-1 A simple HTML page showing a selection tag (rendered here as a Windows selection list) and a submission button.

This is a static page. Even though it has a selection list and a button, they don't do anything worthwhile. You can pull down the selection list and work with it inside the browser. You can click the button, but all the action happens locally. That's because the server on the other end needs to support dynamic content.

Dynamic Content

The earliest Web sites were built primarily using static HTML pages. That is, you could surf to some page somewhere and read the HTML document living there. Whereas at that time the ability to do this was pretty amazing, HTML eventually evolved to be capable of much more than simply formatting text.

For example, HTML includes tags such as <select>and </select> that browsers interpret as a Windows selection list control, called a *drop-down list* in ASP.NET. The first tag, <select>, is called the *opening* tag while the second, </select>, is called the *closing* tag. Tags can contain other tags, as you saw earlier with the <option></option> tags that provide content for the drop-down list. Tags also can have *attributes*, which are used to modify or tailor the behavior of the tag. Various attributes applied to the <input></input> tags cause browsers to draw text boxes and buttons. HTML provides a special tag, <form>, that groups other tags designed to return information to the server for processing.

HTML Forms

HTML includes the <form></form> opening and closing tags for notifying the browser that a section of HTML includes tags representing controls the user will interact with to eventually return information to the server. You use the <form> tag to specify how a Web document will handle input from the end user (not just output). The contents of the form, which is to say the data contained in the input controls, are "posted back" to the server for processing. This action is commonly called a *postback*. This is why the typical HTTP use case for an HTML document is GET, which initially retrieves the document, and then POST (or a modified form of GET), which returns data to the server, if necessary.

The <form> tag usually sandwiches a set of tags specifying user input controls. The following shows the same feature selection page you saw earlier but with the <form> tag added (the code is from the file named SelectFeature2.htm in sample code on the book's companion CD):

```
<html>
 <body>
   <form action="http://localhost/HttpHandlers/selectfeature2.htm"
     method="get">
      <h2>Hello there. What's your favorite .NET feature?</h2>
      <select name='Feature'>
         <option> Type-Safety</option>
         <option> Garbage collection</option>
         <option> Multiple syntaxes</option>
         <option> Code Access Security</option>
         <option> Simpler threading</option>
         <option> Versioning purgatory</option>
      </select>
   <br/>
   <input type=submit name='Lookup' value='Lookup'></input>
   <br/>
   </form>
 </body>
</html>
```

If you'd like to see this work right away, type this code into a file named SelectFeature2.htm and save it to the directory c:\inetpub\wwwroot. Surf to the file by typing **http://localhost/ selectfeature2.htm** in your browser's address bar.

The <form> tag includes several attributes that you can set to control how the page behaves. In the preceding example, notice that the <form> tag sets the *action* attribute, which indicates which server receives the form's contents. In the absence of the *action* attribute, the current document URL is used.

The other attribute used in the HTML is the *method* attribute. The *method* attribute specifies the HTTP method used when submitting the form and therefore dictates how the form data is returned to the server. The method employed in the example is GET because it's the first request to the server. If you select the last option (Versioning Purgatory), and then click Lookup, the form's GET method causes the form's input control contents to be appended to the URL, like so:

```
http://localhost/SelectFeature2.htm?Feature=Versioning+purgatory&Lookup=Lookup
```

This modified URL, often called a *query string*, is then sent to the server.

The form's POST method causes the form contents to be sent to the server in the body of a returned HTTP packet, as you see here:

```
POST /SelectFeature2.htm HTTP/1.1
Accept: image/gif, image/x-xbitmap, image/jpeg, image/pjpeg, ... , */*
Accept-Language: en-us
Content-Type: application/x-www-form-urlencoded
Accept-Encoding: gzip, deflate
User-Agent: Mozilla/4.0 (compatible; MSIE 7.0; Windows NT 5.1; ... .NET CLR 3.0.04506.30)
Host: localhost:80
Content-Length: 42
Connection: Keep-Alive
Cache-Control: no-cache

Feature=Versioning+purgatory&Lookup=Lookup
```

Adding the <form> tag to the body of the document gets you part of the way to having an HTTP application that actually interacts with a user. Now you need a little more support on the server end. When you click the Lookup button, the browser actually forces another round-trip back to the server (although in this case, it only performs an HTTP GET command to refetch the document because you specified this in the form's *method* attribute).

At this point, a normal HTTP GET command returns only the document. In a truly interactive environment, the server on the other end modifies the content as requests go back and forth between the browser and the server.

For example, imagine that the user makes an initial GET request for the resource, selects a feature from the selection list, and then clicks the Lookup button. In an interactive application, the browser must make a second round-trip to the server with a new request that includes for processing the user's inputs. The server must examine the request coming from the browser and figure out what to do about it. This is when the server begins to play a much more active role. Depending on the platform involved, a server can handle the postback in several different ways—through such programs as the Common Gateway Interface or IIS.

Common Gateway Interface: Very Retro

The earliest Web servers supporting dynamic Web content did so through the Common Gateway Interface (CGI). CGI was the earliest standard for building Web servers. CGI programs execute in real time and change their output based on the state of the application and the requests coming in. Each request coming into a Web server running CGI runs a separate instance of a program to respond. The application can run any sort of operation, including looking up data in a database, accepting credit card numbers, and sending out formatted information.

The Microsoft Environment as a Web Server

When using Microsoft operating systems to host Web content, it's too expensive to start up a new process for each request (as does CGI). Microsoft's solution is to have a single daemon process (which in the Windows operating system is called a *service*) monitor port 80 for incoming network packets and load dynamic-link libraries (DLLs) to handle separate requests when the content needs to change. Microsoft's standard Web platform is based on Internet Information Services (IIS).

> **Note** When you create and edit Web applications using Microsoft Visual Studio 2010, you can load them from the file system and from IIS (as well as by a few other means). If you load your Web application using IIS, IIS acts as the Web server, as you'd expect. But when you load a Web application from the file system, which application serves HTML (or ASP.NET) documents? As it happens, starting with Visual Studio 2005, you can use a special development Web server to simplify debugging and administration. Based on a Web server named Cassini, the development server can serve HTML and ASP.NET pages just as effectively as IIS can for development purposes. However, keep in mind that for robustness and security IIS is Microsoft's professional-grade Web server and is the intended target for your ASP.NET Web application. And although the development Web server rather faithfully mimics IIS, it isn't an exact duplicate and some differences do arise when moving Web applications between the two. Most often those differences are related to security and permissions.

Internet Information Services

Fundamentally, all Web application environments work the same way. No matter what hardware/software platform you use, some piece of software is required on the server to monitor port 80 (typically) for incoming HTTP requests. When a request arrives, it's the server's job to somehow respond to the request in a meaningful way. In Microsoft operating systems, IIS is by far the most widely used watchdog intercepting HTTP requests on port 80, the usual inbound port for HTTP requests. Internet servers use other ports as well. For example, HTTPS (Secure HTTP) uses port 443. However, right now you are mostly interested in normal Internet traffic over port 80.

When a browser makes a call to a server running on the Microsoft platform, IIS intercepts that request and searches for the resource identified by the URL. IIS divides its directory space into manageable chunks called *virtual directories*. For example, imagine someone tries to get to a resource on your server using this URL:

http://www.northwind.com/products/showfeatures.htm

The domain northwind is fictitious and is used here for illustration. However, if there were a server registered using this name, the URL would identify the entire resource. In this URL, *http://www.northwind.com* identifies the server and directs the request through a maze of routers. Once the request reaches the server, the server looks for the showfeatures.htm resource in some directory-type entity named products. If the server is running IIS, *products* refers to a virtual directory.

IIS divides its working space into multiple virtual directories. Each virtual directory typically refers to a single application and is used to map a physical directory on your server's hard drive to an Internet URL. Using virtual directories, one per application, IIS can serve multiple applications. Each virtual directory includes various configuration properties, including such items as security options, error-handling redirections, and application isolation options. The configuration parameters also include mappings between file name extensions and op-tionally configured IIS extension DLLs, called *ISAPI DLLs* (ISAPI stands for Internet Services Application Programming Interface). (In versions of IIS prior to version 7.0, ASP.NET itself is handled by one of these ISAPI DLLs!) Moving forward, ASP.NET becomes a first-class citizen in IIS.

Although it's not initially critical to writing ASP.NET applications, knowing a bit about how IIS works is tremendously important when you need to debug, test, and deploy your Web appli-cations fully. The built-in Visual Studio Web server (Cassini) is fine for most tasks, but it lacks much that IIS offers. True ASP.NET developers understand this and often become quite adept at administering IIS. If you want to get going writing applications straightaway, you can skip the following section on IIS, but I discuss various aspects of IIS operations and administration throughout the book. To begin, here's a brief look at ISAPI and how it extends IIS.

Internet Services Application Programming Interface DLLs

With Microsoft operating systems, creating a process space is an expensive proposition in terms of system resources and clock cycles. Imagine trying to write a server that responds to each request by starting a separate program. The poor server would be bogged down very quickly, and your e-commerce site would stop making money.

In the Microsoft environment, DLLs are used to respond to requests. DLLs are relatively inexpensive to load, and running code in a DLL executes very quickly. Historically, the DLLs handling Web requests were named *ISAPI DLLs*. Prior to IIS 7, IIS would intercept requests and hand them off to specific ISAPI DLLs to process the request. ASP (before ASP.NET) was actually handled by a single ISAPI DLL named ASP.DLL. In fact, earlier versions of ASP.NET relied on an ISAPI DLL named ASPNET_ISAPI.DLL. However, the ASP.NET pipeline is now actually part of IIS.

Internet Information Services

The user interface to IIS is available in Control Panel. To get a feel for how to administer IIS, take a short tour. It's important to have some facility with IIS because ASP.NET relies on it to service Web requests in real Web applications. IIS 7.0 and earlier versions work similarly as far as dividing the server's application space into virtual directories. IIS 6.0 and IIS 7.0 include many other features such as application isolation and recycling to help control runaway requests and limit memory consumption if something untoward happens during a request.

Running IIS

1. To get to IIS, first go to Administrative Tools. In the Windows 7 operating system, in Control Panel, double-click Administrative Tools, and then select Internet Information Services. You should see the IIS user interface on your screen. The following graphics show the Features View and the Content View—both running under Windows 7.

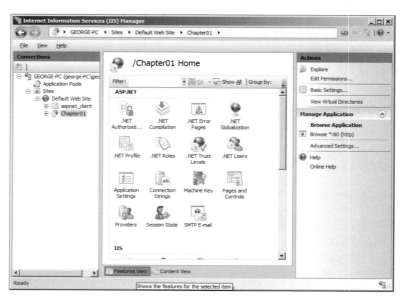

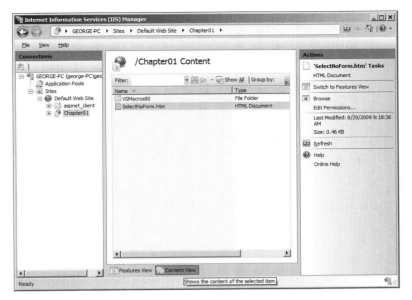

On the left side of the screen is an expandable tree showing the Web sites and virtual directories available through IIS on your computer. IIS 5.*x* and IIS 6.0 show the virtual directories in the left pane, with the directory contents on the right side. The IIS 7 management console (shown here) includes two views: the Features View and the Content View. The Features View includes various icons for managing specific aspects of IIS for the items in the list in the left pane. The Content View shows the files contained in the selected item.

2. View the configuration of a specific virtual directory. In the Features View, you can see how a specific virtual directory is configured. To find out more about the directory's configuration, try clicking the various icons in the Features View. For example, to see how IIS figures out the correct default file to show in the absence of a specific file name extension, double-click the Default Document icon. The following figure shows the list of default file names that IIS will try to load.

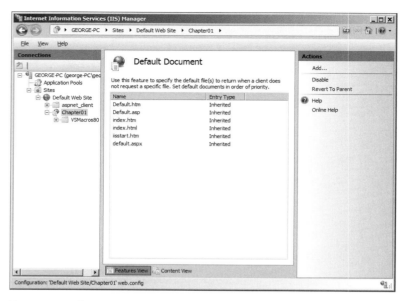

You can configure a number of features in IIS, and they are all represented by the icons presented in the Features View. The feature set is fairly extensive, covering all aspects of how the directory is accessed from the outside world. You need not spend a lot of time here because ASP.NET takes care of most of these issues (rather than leaving them up to IIS).

3. View module mappings for a virtual directory. Static file types such as .htm files are transmitted directly back to the client. However, dynamic pages whose contents can change between posts require further processing, so they are assigned to specific handlers. As you'll see in a moment, IIS 7.0 prefers to handle most requests through managed code, which is code that executes within the context of the .NET Common Language Runtime (CLR). For those developers who wish to write native code, IIS 7.0 includes a new C++/native core server application programming interface (API). This new API works with IIS 7.0 through the *IsapiModule* to expose classic ISAPI extension DLLs. Another module, the *IsapiFilterModule*, replaces the traditional ISAPI filter API from earlier versions of IIS. To view the IIS 7.0 module mappings, double-click the Modules icon in the Features View. You should see a listing of the IIS 7.0 modules that intercept requests.

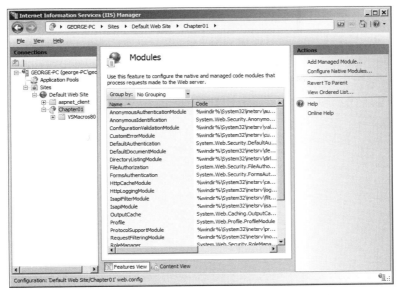

4. For those applications that handle requests using managed code, IIS pipes them through the handlers listed on the Handler Mappings page. To view the file mappings for a specific virtual directory, double-click the Handler Mappings icon in the Features View. IIS responds by listing the handler mappings for the directory:

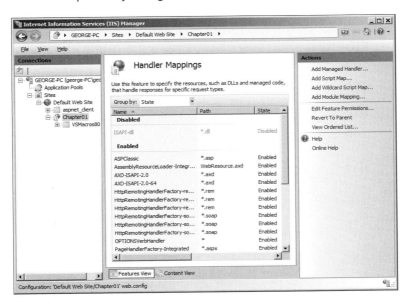

These mappings tell IIS how to handle specific requests. As you can see, most requests are handled through managed code by ASP.NET. Notice at the top of the list the handler for classic ASP files named *ASPClassic*. This handler takes care of requests bearing the .asp extension (earlier versions of IIS piped these requests directly to the ASP.DLL handler).

Note If for some reason you find yourself needing to run classic ASP, note that IIS 7.0 does not install *ASPClassic* by default—you must add this feature deliberately.

1. In Control Panel, double-click Programs And Features from the list.
2. Select Turn Windows Features On And Off.
3. Select Internet Information Services in the dialog box that appears.
4. Expand the World Wide Web Services node, and then the Application Development Features node.
5. Click the ASP box to install classic ASP handling, as shown here:

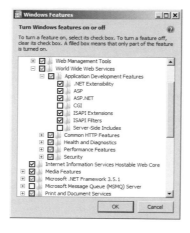

Classic ASP: Putting ASP.NET into Perspective

Although this book is really about ASP.NET, understanding classic ASP can be helpful. By comparing classic ASP and ASP.NET, you get a good idea about why things are the way they are in ASP.NET. You can also gain an appreciation for all that ASP.NET does for you.

Microsoft originally developed Active Server Pages (ASP) to encourage a larger number of developers than just those using C++ to undertake Web development. When IIS became available, it was certainly a feasible environment for developing Web sites in the Microsoft environment compared to other environments. In fact, you can still see some sites today deployed as pure ISAPI DLL sites (eBay for one); just look in the query strings going between the browser and the server for clues. For example, you might see a file name such as *ACMEISAPI.DLL* embedded in the query string.

However, writing an entire site using ISAPI DLLs can be daunting. Writing ISAPI DLLs in C or C++ gives you complete control over how your site will perform and makes the site work. However, along with that control comes an equal amount of responsibility because developing software using C or C++ presents numerous challenges.

So, in delivering ASP, Microsoft provides a single ISAPI DLL named *ASP.DLL*. ASP Web developers write their code into files tagged with the extension .asp (for example, somefile. asp). These files often contain a mixture of static HTML and executable sections (usually written in a scripting language) that emit output at run time. For example, the code in Listing 1-1 shows an ASP program that renders the HelloWorld page, which contains both static HTML and text generated at run time. (The file name is HelloWorld.asp in the book's accompanying examples.)

LISTING 1-1 A classic ASP file

```
<%@ Language="javascript" %>
<html>
 <body>
   <form>
    <h3>Hello world!!! This is an ASP page.</h3>

    <% Response.Write("This content was generated ");%>
    <% Response.Write("as part of an execution block");%>
   </form>
 </body>
</html>
```

The code shown in Listing 1-1 renders the following page. IIS monitored port 80 for requests. When a request for the file HelloWorld.asp came through, IIS recognized the .asp extension and asked ASP.DLL to handle the request (that's how the file mapping was set up). ASP.DLL simply rendered the static HTML as the string "Hello world!!! This is an ASP page." Then, when ASP.DLL encountered the funny-looking execution tags <% and %>, it executed those blocks by running them through a JavaScript parser (note the language tag in the first line of code). Figure 1-2 shows how the page renders in Windows Internet Explorer.

FIGURE 1-2 The results of a request made to the ASP program from Listing 1-1.

This book is about developing ASP.NET software, so it focuses most of the attention there. However, before leaving the topic of classic ASP, Listing 1-2 shows the SelectFeature.htm page rewritten as a classic ASP page. This simple ASP application presents some of the core issues in Web development and illustrates why Microsoft rewrote its Web server technology as ASP.NET. (The accompanying file name is SelectFeature.asp.)

LISTING 1-2 The SelectFeature.htm page rewritten as a classic ASP page

```
<%@ Language="javascript" %>
<html>
 <body>
   <form>
      <h2>HelloWorld<h2>

      <h3>What's your favorite .NET feature?</h3>
      <select name='Feature'>
         <option> Type-Safety</option>
         <option> Garbage collection</option>
         <option> Multiple syntaxes</option>
         <option> Code Access Security</option>
         <option> Simpler threading</option>
         <option> Versioning purgatory</option>
      </select>
      </br>
      <input type=submit name="Submit" value="Submit"></input>
      <p>
         Hi, you selected <%=Request("Feature") %>
      </p>
   </form>
 </body>
</html>
```

Much of the text in SelectFeature.asp looks very similar to SelectFeature.htm, doesn't it? The differences are mainly in the first line (that now specifies a syntax for executable blocks) and the executable block marked by <% and %>. The rest of the static HTML renders a selection control in a form.

Take note of the executable blocks and how the blocks use the *Response* object (managed by the ASP infrastructure) to push text out to the browser. The executable block examines the *Feature* control (specified by the <select> tag) and prints out the value selected by the user.

Figure 1-3 shows how SelectFeature.asp renders in Internet Explorer.

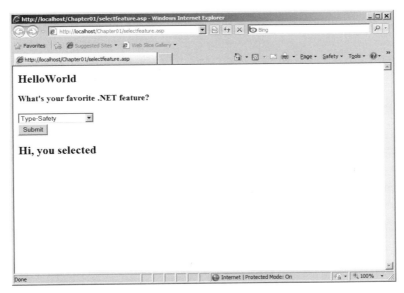

FIGURE 1-3 The code from Listing 1-2 as viewed in Internet Explorer.

The screen in Figure 1-3 might look a bit odd because the drop-down list box shows "Type-Safety" whereas the rendered text shows "Simpler Threading." Without doing anything extra, the drop-down list box will always rerender with the first element as the selected element. You can see how ASP.NET fixes this later in the discussion of server-side controls. That's enough background information to begin to look at specific Web development concepts outlined in the next section.

Web Development Concepts

In the end, developing Web applications forces you to deal with two significant issues— managing user interfaces (UIs) using HTML over a disconnected protocol and managing the state of your application. These fundamental activities separate Web development from other types of application development.

In many ways, the programming model has gone back to the form that dominated in the mid-1970s, when large mainframes served output to terminals connected directly to them. Users submitted jobs to the mainframe and got output to their terminals. So, what's changed here? First, the terminal is a lot fancier—it's a powerful computer running a browser that interprets HTML. The endpoint to which the browser connects is a Web server (or perhaps a server farm). Finally, the connection protocol used by the client and the server is indirect (and a request can quite literally cross the globe before the user sees a result).

In Web application development, the program's primary job is to receive requests from "out there" and provide meaningful responses to the requestors. That often means generating complex HTML that renders in a form humans can read on the client's browser. That can be fairly involved, for example, in a modern commercial Web site supporting commerce. Customers will undoubtedly ask about current pricing, request inventory levels, and per-haps even order items or services from the Web site. The process of generating meaningful HTML for the client suddenly means accomplishing such tasks as making database accesses, authenticating the identity of the client, and keeping track of the client's product order. Imagine doing all this from scratch!

Although frameworks such as classic ASP go a long way toward making Web develop-ment more approachable, developers are still left with many features to create on their own (mostly related to the two issues mentioned at the beginning of this section). For example, building a secure but manageable Web site in classic ASP usually meant writing your own security subsystem (or buying one). Managing the state of the UI emitted by your Web site was often a tedious chore as well.

ASP.NET

All of this brings us to ASP.NET. A common theme you'll see throughout this book is that ASP.NET takes features usually implemented (over and over again) by developers and rolls them into the ASP.NET framework.

ASP.NET has been evolving steadily since it was first released. ASP.NET 1.0 introduced a well-defined pipeline, a viable extensibility model, a server-side control rendering model, and numerous other features to make developing Web sites very doable. ASP.NET 2.0 took ASP.NET 1.x to the next level and pushed even more commonly implemented features into the framework. For example, ASP.NET 2.0 improved upon earlier versions of ASP.NET in the area of authentication and authorization services. ASP.NET 1.x included a reasonable and easy-to-manage authentication model. However, developers were often left with the task of creating their own authentication systems and manually incorporating those systems into their Web sites. ASP.NET 2.0 adds an authorization subsystem. (Chapter 9, "Logging In," covers ASP.NET Forms Authentication and other security features in depth.)

ASP.NET 2.0 has been in use for more than two years. Even with all the improvements provided by the release of version 2.0, there's still room for more. ASP.NET 3.5 delivers a couple of significant new features. The first one is support for asynchronous Java and XML-style programming (commonly known as AJAX). The second main feature is support for Windows Communication Foundation application hosting through IIS/ASP.NET. In the now available version 4, you see features such as enhanced AJAX support, support for dynamic data, an implementation of the Model-View-Controller pattern, and support for Microsoft Silverlight.

The following chapters in this book cover the most important ASP.NET features. By the end of the last chapter, you will be well equipped to develop a Web site based on ASP.NET.

Chapter 1 Quick Reference

To	Do This
Start Internet Information Services management console	Go to Control Panel. Select Administrative Tools. Select Internet Information Services.
Create a new virtual directory	Open the IIS management console. Open the Web Sites node. Open the Default Web Site node. Right-click the Default Web Site node and select New Virtual Directory. Then, follow the wizard.
Surf to a resource from IIS	Right-click the resource and click Browse.
See what file types are supported in an IIS virtual directory	Select the virtual directory. Select the Features View. Browse the Handler Mappings and the Module Mappings pages.

Chapter 2
ASP.NET Application Fundamentals

After completing this chapter, you will be able to

- Create Internet Information Services (IIS) virtual directories.

- Develop an HTML page into an ASP.NET application.

- Mix HTML with executable code and work with server-side script blocks.

- Locate and view the assembly compiled by ASP.NET from an .aspx file.

- Work with code-behind and code-beside execution models.

- Use Microsoft Visual Studio 2010 to create Web projects.

This chapter covers the fundamentals involved in building an ASP.NET application. From a syntactical point of view, writing .NET code is similar to writing the classic ASP code that you might have seen during the late dot-com era. Many of the key symbols remain the same, and even some of the syntax survives directly. However, the entire underlying execution model changed dramatically between classic ASP and ASP.NET. Whereas executing classic ASP pages was primarily an exercise in rendering HTML, interpreting script code, and calling Component Object Model (COM) code, ASP.NET introduces an entirely new object-oriented execution model. ASP.NET execution centers around Common Language Runtime (CLR) classes that implement an interface named *IHttpHandler*. ASP.NET includes a number of classes that already implement *IHttpHandler*, and you can actually write your own implementation from scratch. Typically, though, you'll write ASP.NET pages that, under the covers, are generated by an ASP. NET-provided *IHttpHandler*.

This chapter examines the ASP.NET execution model to see how ASP.NET enables its features. It takes a bottom-up approach, showing how the simplest ASP.NET page executes. Along the way, it introduces various ASP.NET programming techniques, including code behind. You will see how ASP.NET's compilation model works. Finally, you can observe how ASP.NET's Web Form architecture operates and how it's all nicely wrapped up by Microsoft Visual Studio 2010.

You can start by studying a simple page to discover how you can evolve it using ASP.NET's programming techniques.

 Important This chapter's code samples on the companion CD require IIS support to execute. See the "Code Samples" section in the Introduction for important information on running the examples for this chapter.

The Canonical Hello World Application

Nearly all programming texts start by using the technology at hand to present the classic string "Hello World" to the end user. This time, your job is to send the statement "Hello World" to the awaiting browser.

To see how ASP.NET works, you will take the simplest Web page and develop it into an ASP.NET Web application. You won't use Visual Studio quite yet. Visual Studio is such a rich development environment that building and running Web applications with it seems almost like magic. This is a bare-bones example built from scratch so that you can see exactly what's going on before bringing Visual Studio's full capabilities into the picture. You then can examine each iteration along the way to see what ASP.NET is doing.

Building the HelloWorld Web Application

1. Create a directory to hold the Web application files. Using either a command shell or Windows Explorer, create a new folder to hold the Web application files. Although the name of the directory is unimportant to Internet Information Services (IIS), call it something meaningful. This example uses c:\aspnetstepbystepexamples.

2. Create an application/virtual directory to hold the files. To start, you need a virtual directory in which to hold the source code. As you saw earlier when examining the Web Application architecture imposed by the Microsoft Windows environment, IIS divides the applications on your server using virtual directories. In addition to providing application management features, IIS creates a mapping between requests coming in over port 80 and some real directory on your computer. Virtual directories show IIS where to find the code you want to execute in your application.

   Open Control Panel, and then go to Administrative Tools and start Internet Information Services. Expand the nodes in the tree on the left side to expose the Default Web Site node under the Sites node, as shown in the following illustration:

Then, right-click the Default Web Site node and click Add Application on the shortcut menu. (The illustration shows how to perform this operation in IIS 7.5. If you're using earlier versions of IIS, the screen will look slightly different—though you can add new virtual directories in the same way.) IIS will ask you to provide a name for the application/virtual directory:

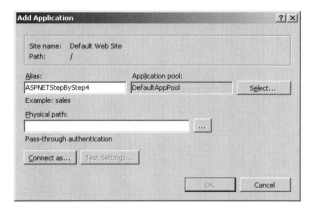

Name the Web site *ASPNETStepByStep*. This is the name by which your Web application will be known to the world. For example, when Internet users surf to your Web site, they'll use the following URL:

http://www.contoso.com/ASPNETStepByStep

The name *contoso.com* is a fictitious site, only used here for illustration. When you surf to this site on this computer, the server name will be *localhost*.

The wizard will ask you to provide a physical path for the virtual directory. Either browse to the physical directory you just created or type the name of the directory. Leave the IIS administration tool open; you use other features in the following steps.

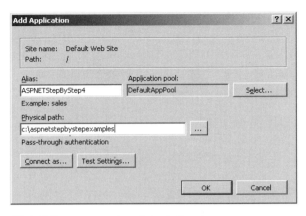

Click OK to create the virtual directory.

3. Start with a simple HTML page. The easiest way to do this is to store some text in an HTML file and browse to it.

Notepad works fine for creating a simple HTML file, or you can use Visual Studio to create the HTML file. If you use Visual Studio, start Visual Studio and select File, New, and then click File. Select Text File as the file type, and then click Open. A new, blank file will open in the Visual Studio editor.

Type the following HTML text between the opening and closing <body> tags. Save the file as HelloWorld.htm in your new physical directory (the one that you mapped to a virtual directory in the previous step).

```
<html xmlns="http://www.w3.org/1999/xhtml">
  <head>
    <title>Untitled Page</title>
  </head>

  <body>
    <h1> Hello World </h1>
    Nothing really showing here yet, except some HTML...
  </body>
</html>
```

4. Browse to the page. There are two ways to do this. First, you can browse to the page by selecting the file from within IIS. Navigate to the directory in IIS (the IIS control panel should still be open if you haven't closed it). Click the Content View tab near the bottom of the main pane. You'll see the files in the directory. Right-click the

HelloWorld.htm file and click Browse. Alternatively, you can type the entire URL into the browser navigation bar:

http://localhost/ASPNETStepByStep/helloworld.htm

The browser will send an HTTP request to the server. On the Microsoft platform, IIS will see the HTM extension and simply return the contents of the file to the browser. Because the text is marked using standard HTML tags, the browser understands it and displays it correctly.

Here's how the file appears to the end browser:

5. Convert the HTML file to an ASP.NET application. Take the HelloWorld.htm file that you were working on and convert it into a file type that will invoke the ASP.NET runtime. Turning this file into an ASP.NET application involves two small steps: adding a single line to the top of the file (the *Page* directive) and renaming the file from HelloWorld.htm to HelloWorld.aspx. This text represents an implementation of HelloWorld that works within the ASP.NET framework (be sure to save the file as HelloWorld.aspx by clicking Save HelloWorld.htm As on the File menu):

```
<%@ Page Language="C#" %>
<html xmlns="http://www.w3.org/1999/xhtml">
  <head>
    <title>Untitled Page</title>
  </head>

  <body>
    <h1> Hello World </h1>
    Nothing really showing here yet, except some HTML...
  </body>
</html>
```

When you fire up your browser and surf to this file in the virtual directory on your computer, you'll see the following in your browser:

Admittedly, it might seem a small feat to simply show some text in a browser. However, it shows how a simple ASP.NET application works when using IIS.

6. View the HTML source that the browser is interpreting. While viewing the content from the previous step in your browser, use the View, Source menu to show the HTML source text being processed by the browser. It should look like this:

```
<html xmlns="http://www.w3.org/1999/xhtml" >
<head>
    <title>Untitled Page</title>
</head>
<body>
     <h1> Hello World </h1>
     Nothing really showing here yet, except some HTML...
</body>
</html>
```

Notice that this text is almost identical to the text in HelloWorld.aspx (without the *Page* directive: *<%@ Page Language="C#" %>*). In this case, you can see that the page-processing logic is fairly simple. That is, the ASP.NET runtime is simply spitting out the text within the file.

The *Page* directive appearing at the top of the code is used by the ASP.NET runtime as it compiles the code. The *Page* directive shown earlier is fairly simple—it tells the runtime to compile this code and base it on the *Page* class and to treat any code syntax it encounters as C# code. ASP.NET supports integrating .aspx files with assemblies, which you see shortly.

In subsequent examples, you can see how ASP.NET compiles code on the fly and stores the assemblies in a temporary directory. There's no C# code in HelloWorld.aspx, so you should add some now.

A Note About Application Pools

In addition to mapping incoming HTTP requests to actual physical directories, IIS 6.*x* and IIS 7.*x* support a feature called application pooling. One of the primary purposes behind application pooling is to support application isolation. For example, imagine you want to isolate the Web applications running in the same computer from other software managed by IIS. By creating a separate application pool for each Web application, you tell IIS to run each application in its own worker process. If anything bad happens in one application pool, the other applications can continue to run unaffected.

With application pooling, you also can govern the security aspects of a Web application. Some applications might need a higher degree of security than do others.

IIS 5.*x* runs the ASP.NET worker process as LocalSystem. LocalSystem has system administrator rights. This has interesting implications because the account can access virtually any resource on the server. In IIS 6.*x* and IIS 7.*x*, you can set the identity of the worker process to be the same as that of the application pool level. Application pools operate under the NetworkService account by default—which does not have as many access rights as LocalSystem does.

Mixing HTML with Executable Code

Classic ASP had an interesting way of marking code segments within a page. ASP always supported the classic script tags (<script> </script>) where anything found between the <script> tags was treated as executable code. However, in classic ASP, the script blocks were sent to the browser, and it became the browser's job to run the script. In addition to client-side script blocks, a classic ASP Web page could define script blocks to be interpreted on the server. These methods often performed tasks such as database lookups. Causing code to execute on the server involved marking executable segments with angle brackets and percent signs like this:

```
<% ExecuteMe() %>
```

ASP.NET also supports server-side code execution. To write code that executes inline, simply mark it with the <% %> tags as well. When ASP.NET parses the file to manufacture the run-time class representing the page (more on that shortly), it will insert whatever code it finds between the execution tags as executable code. The only requirement is that the code between the execution tags is valid C# (because that's the language specified in the *Page* directive).

Adding executable code inline

1. Add executable code to the Web application. Create a new blank text file from within Visual Studio. Type the following code into the text file and save it as HelloWorld2.aspx.

```
<%@ Page Language="C#" Debug="true" %>
<html>
    <body>
        <h1>Hello World!!!</h1>
        <%
            // This block will execute in the Render_Control method
            Response.Write("Check out the family tree: <br/> <br/>");
            Response.Write(this.GetType().ToString());
            Response.Write(" which derives from: <br/> ");
            Response.Write(this.GetType().BaseType.ToString());
            Response.Write(" which derives from: <br/> ");
            Response.Write(this.GetType().BaseType.BaseType.ToString());
            Response.Write(" which derives from: <br/> ");
            Response.Write(
              this.GetType().BaseType.BaseType.BaseType.ToString());
            Response.Write(" which derives from: <br/> ");
            Response.Write(
              this.GetType().BaseType.BaseType.BaseType.BaseType.ToString());
        %>
    </body>
</html>
```

This code is almost exactly identical to code you see in a classic ASP application—including references to the *Response* object. In classic ASP, the *Response* object was one of those intrinsic objects, perennially available to the page's execution block. For the sake of a complete explanation, the *Response* object in classic ASP was a *COM* object that hung off the thread managed by the lower-level components (the Internet Services Application Programming Interface DLL, or the ISAPI DLL). Notice that ASP.NET also has a *Response* object. However, this *Response* object is part of the *HttpContext* managed by the ASP.NET pipeline and is in no way related to the classic ASP object except in name.

2. Browse to the ASP.NET page using Windows Internet Explorer. The page should look like this in the browser:

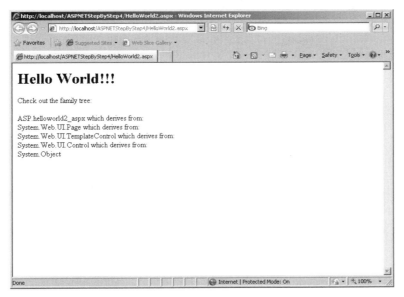

The output produced by HelloWorld2.aspx shows a very important aspect of the ASP.NET execution model. Before moving on, take a look at the inline code listed in the previous exercise and compare it to the output appearing in the browser. Notice that the code includes statements such as

```
Response.Write(this.GetType().BaseType.ToString());
```

Of course, the C# *this* keyword specifies an instance of a class. The code that's executing is clearly part of a member function of a class instance. The output shown by the browser indicates the class rendering the HTML to the browser is named *ASP.helloworld2_aspx*, and it derives from a class named *System.Web.UI.Page*. You learn more about this later in the chapter.

Server-Side Executable Blocks

ASP.NET also supports server-side code blocks (not just inline execution tags). ASP.NET adds a new *runat* attribute to the script tag that tells ASP.NET to execute the code block at the server end.

Adding executable code using a script block

1. Add an executable script block to the page. Create a new text file in Visual Studio. Type the following code into the Visual Studio editor. Note that the code separates rendered HTML from the script block that runs at the server. Save the file as HelloWorld3.aspx in your virtual directory.

```
<%@ Page Language="C#" Debug="true" %>
<script runat="server">
    void ShowLineage()
    {
        Response.Write("Check out the family tree: <br/> <br/>");
        Response.Write(this.GetType().ToString());
        Response.Write(" which derives from: <br/> ");
        Response.Write(this.GetType().BaseType.ToString());
        Response.Write(" which derives from: <br/> ");
        Response.Write(this.GetType().BaseType.BaseType.ToString());
        Response.Write(" which derives from: <br/> ");
        Response.Write(
           this.GetType().BaseType.BaseType.BaseType.ToString());
        Response.Write(" which derives from: <br/> ");
        Response.Write(
           this.GetType().BaseType.BaseType.BaseType.BaseType.ToString());
    }
</script>
<html>
    <body>
        <h1>Hello World!!!</h1>
        <%
            ShowLineage();
        %>
    </body>
</html>
```

    As with the inline execution blocks, the most important criterion for the contents of the script block is for its syntax to match that of the language specified in the *Page* directive. The preceding example specifies a single method named *ShowLineage()*, which is called from within the page.

2. Surf to the page. Notice that the output of HelloWorld2.aspx and HelloWorld3.aspx is identical.

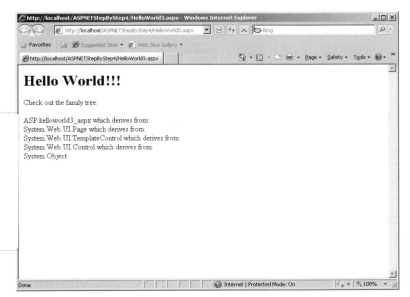

Marking the <script> tag containing the *ShowLineage* method with the *runat=server* attribute causes ASP.NET to execute the code on the server. But although classic ASP interprets the script block using the designated script language, ASP.NET has an entirely different execution model—the whole page is actually compiled into a class that runs under the Common Language Runtime (CLR). Here's how the ASP.NET compilation model works.

A Trip Through the ASP.NET Architecture

When it arrives on the Web server, the HTTP request/response is routed through many server-side objects for processing. Once a request ends up at the server, it winds its way through the IIS/ASP.NET pipeline. The best way to understand the path of an HTTP request through ASP.NET is to follow a request as it originates in the browser and is intercepted by Internet Information Services and your Web application.

When an end user presses the Return key after typing in a URL, the browser sends an HTTP GET request to the target site. The request travels through a series of routers until it finally hits your Web server and is picked up on port 80. If your system has software listening to port 80, the software can handle the request. On the Microsoft platform, the software most often listening to port 80 is IIS. For the time being, ASP.NET works with three versions of IIS: version 5.*x* (if you are using the Windows XP Professional operating system), version 6.*x* (if you are using the Windows Server 2003 operating system), and version 7.*x* (if you are using the Windows Vista, Windows 7, or Windows Server 2008 operating systems).

The general flow of the requests is the same, regardless of which version of IIS you choose. IIS maintains a mapping between file extensions and binary components capable of interpreting the request (you see more about the binary components later). When a request comes in, IIS reads the file name identified in the request and routes the request to the appropriate component.

Earlier versions of IIS (prior to version 7.*x*) implement such features as client authentication and output caching independently of ASP.NET. That is, IIS and ASP.NET each implement their own versions of these features. IIS 7.*x* integrates the ASP.NET versions of these features (some of which you see in future chapters). As far as the ramifications of IIS 7.*x* to ASP.NET developers, running in Integrated mode makes .NET functionality part of the core pipeline. Features such as Forms Authentication can now be applied to a wide range of content—not just ASP.NET forms. For example, this helps when trying to secure an entire Web site using a uniform authentication method.

For the purposes of illustration, the following graphics show how IIS 7.*x* routes requests of various types. The following shows the IIS 7.*x* module mappings when running in Integrated mode:

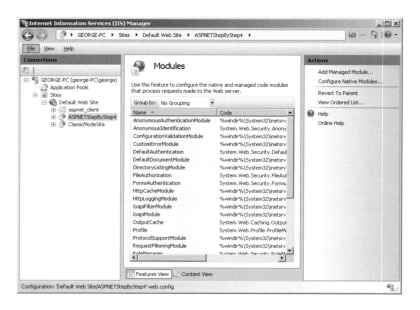

Also for illustration purposes, the following shows IIS 7.*x* handler mappings when running in Integrated mode:

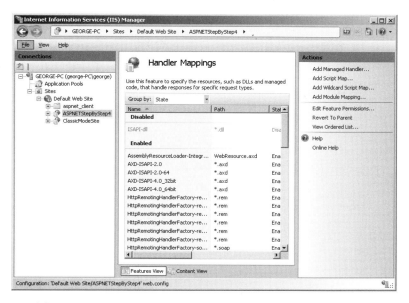

In addition to running in Integrated mode, IIS 7.*x* also runs in Classic mode to support backward compatibility. When running in Classic mode, IIS 7.*x* uses the module and handler architecture to pass processing to specific traditional binary components (that is, ISAPI DLLs).

To illustrate how mappings work in Classic mode, the following graphic shows IIS 7.*x* module mappings running in Classic mode:

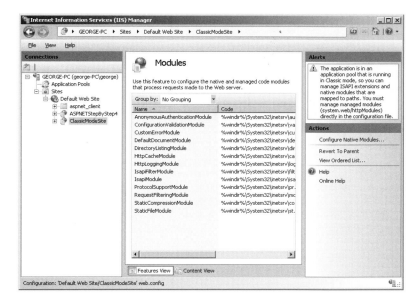

The following graphic shows IIS 7.*x* running in Classic mode and its handlers mappings:

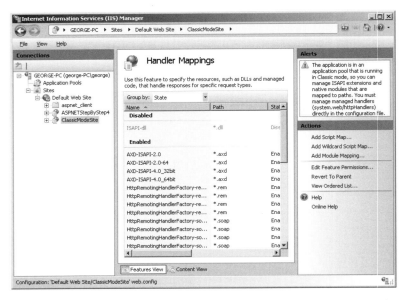

Once IIS intercepts the request and maps it to the worker process, the request follows a very specific path through the pipeline. Later sections in look at each part of the pipeline in more detail. The outline of the request's path through versions of IIS earlier than 7.*x* is this:

1. The request lands in IIS.

2. IIS routes the request to aspnet_isapi.dll.

   a. If IIS 5.*x* is running, IIS asp_isapi.dll routes the request through a pipe to aspnet_wp.exe.

   b. If IIS 6.*x* is running, the request is already in the worker process.

3. ASP.NET packages the request context into an instance of *HttpContext*.

4. ASP.NET pipes the request through an instance of an *HttpApplication* object (or an *HttpApplication*-derived object).

5. If the application object is interested in receiving any of the request preprocessing events, *HttpApplication* fires the events to the application object. Any *HttpModules* that have subscribed to these events will receive the notifications as well.

6. Runtime instantiates a handler and handles the request.

Figure 2-1 shows how IIS version 5.*x* and ASP.NET work together to handle HTTP requests. Figure 2-2 shows how IIS version 6.*x* works with ASP.NET to handle requests.

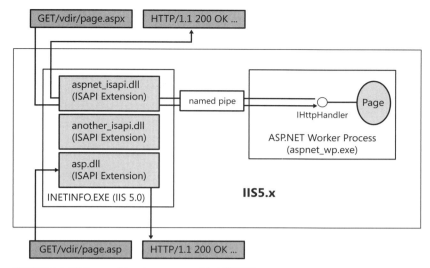

FIGURE 2-1 IIS 5.*x* working in concert with ASP.NET.

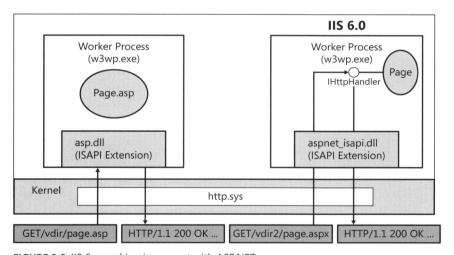

FIGURE 2-2 IIS 6.*x* working in concert with ASP.NET.

By contrast, the request path through IIS 7.*x* is slightly different. Here's a request's path through IIS 7.*x*:

1. The browser makes a request for a resource on the Web server.

2. HTTP.SYS picks up the request on the server.

3. HTTP.SYS uses the WAS to find configuration information to pass on to the WWW Service.

4. WAS passes the configuration information to the WWW Service, which configures HTTP.SYS.

5. WAS starts a worker process in the application pool for which the request was destined.

6. The worker process processes the request and returns the response to HTTP.SYS.

7. HTTP.SYS sends the response to the client.

Figure 2-3 shows the relationship between IIS 7.x and ASP.NET.

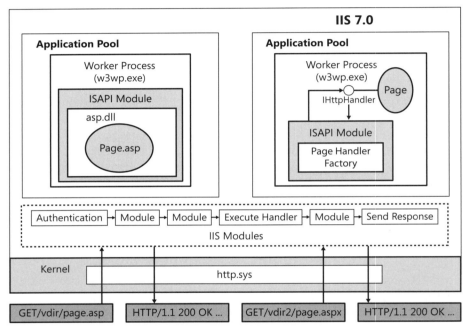

FIGURE 2-3 ASP.NET and IIS 7.x.

Throughout the forthcoming chapters, you follow a request through the ASP.NET pipeline. You can plug into the ASP.NET pipeline at a number of distinct points to deal with various aspects of handling the requests. For example, if you'd like to do any preprocessing, you can either override event handlers in the *HttpApplication* class or you can write HTTP modules and plug them into the pipeline. Whereas the *System.Web.UI.Page* class provides a great amount of functionality for building Web-based user interfaces, the pipeline is flexible enough that you can easily write your own custom handlers.

The ASP.NET Compilation Model

One of the most important improvements Microsoft has made to the ASP development environment is to build the Web request handling framework out of classes. Pushing request processing into a class-based architecture allows for a Web-handling framework that's compiled. When ASP.NET pages are first accessed, they are compiled into assemblies.

This is advantageous because subsequent access loads the page directly from the assembly. Whereas classic ASP interpreted the same script code over and over, ASP.NET applications are compiled into .NET assemblies and ultimately perform better and are safer. Because the code is compiled, it runs more quickly because it doesn't have to be interpreted. In addition, the managed runtime is a type-safe environment; you won't see the same sorts of errors and anomalies that you'd encounter in a scripting environment (as was the case for classic ASP).

In addition, compiling the Web request framework allows for more robust and consistent debugging. Whenever you run an ASP.NET application from Visual Studio, you can debug it as though it were a normal desktop application.

ASP.NET compiles .aspx files automatically. To get an .aspx page to compile, you simply need to surf to the .aspx file containing the code. When you do so, ASP.NET compiles the page into a class. However, you won't see that assembly containing the class anywhere near your virtual directory. ASP.NET copies the resulting assemblies to a temporary directory.

The .NET versions of Visual Studio have always included a tool named Intermediate Language Disassembler (ILDASM) that uses reflection to reverse compile an assembly so that you can view its contents. The result is an easily negotiated tree view you can use to drill down to the contents of the assembly. Right now, that's the important thing. (If you want to peer any more deeply into the assembly and see the actual Intermediate Language, ILDASM will show you that as well.)

Here's how to view the assemblies generated by ASP.NET.

Viewing the ASP.NET assemblies

1. To run ILDASM, open the Visual Studio .NET 2010 command prompt and type **ILDASM**.

2. Select File, Open.

3. Find the assembly compiled by the ASP.NET runtime. Go to C:\WINDOWS\ Microsoft.NET\Framework\v2.0.50727\Temporary ASP.NET Files\aspnetstepbystep4\ (on a 64-bit computer, the subdirectory will be "Framework64"). The subdirectory is named v2.0.50727 at the time of this writing. The final subdirectory might be slightly different. You'll see some oddly named directories underneath. For example, on my computer, the subdirectory names generated by ASP.NET are 4076b23e and ac422a67. The directory name(s) will most likely be different on your computer. There's no easy way to figure out which directories have the code that just executed (though looking at the

dates and times of the file creation might help), so you need to follow the path into the directories until you unearth some .dll files. Depending on how many times you've run the application, you might see several files. Open the files one at a time until ILDASM displays something similar to what's shown in Figure 2-4.

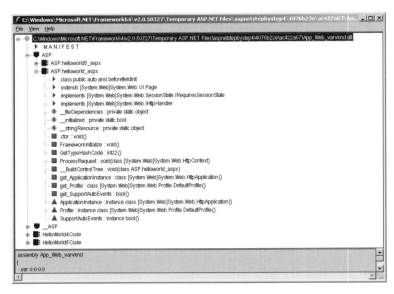

FIGURE 2-4 ILDASM showing the contents of the assembly generated by ASP.NET after surfing to HelloWorld.aspx.

ASP.NET has used this temporary directory strategy since version 1.0. The reason ASP.NET copies these files to a temporary directory is to solve a long-standing problem that plagued classic ASP. Classic ASP Web sites often depended on *COM* objects to do complex operations such as database lookups and transactions. When you deploy a classic ASP site and clients begin accessing it, those files become locked. Of course, that's not really a problem—until you decide to upgrade or modify part of the Web site.

Classic ASP locked files during execution, meaning you couldn't copy new files into the virtual directory without shutting down the Web site. For many Web deployment scenarios, this is a bad option. Because ASP.NET copies the files and the components to the temporary directory and *runs them from there*, they're not locked. When it is time to update a component, you can simply copy the new assembly into the virtual directory. You can do that because it's not locked.

Coding Options

In addition to supporting inline code (that is, including executable code directly inside a server-side script block), modern ASP.NET offers two other distinct options for managing code: ASP.NET 1.*x* code behind, and modern ASP.NET code beside. ASP.NET supports code behind for backward compatibility. Code beside is the style employed by Visual Studio 2010. The following subsections look at these.

ASP.NET 1.*x* Style

ASP.NET continues to support ASP.NET 1.*x* style code behind. This can be important to understand if you ever run into any legacy code from that era. Using the code-behind directives in the .aspx file, you provide the code to run behind the page in a separate class and use the *Page* directive to tell ASP.NET which class to apply to the page. Then, you tell ASP.NET the name of the file containing the source code for the class. For example, imagine this code is placed in a file named HelloWorld4Code.cs:

```
using System.Web;
public class HelloWorld4Code : System.Web.UI.Page
{
    public void ShowLineage()
    {
        Response.Write("Check out the family tree: <br/> <br/>");
        Response.Write(this.GetType().ToString());
        Response.Write(" which derives from: <br/> ");
        Response.Write(this.GetType().BaseType.ToString());
        Response.Write(" which derives from: <br/> ");
        Response.Write(this.GetType().BaseType.BaseType.ToString());
        Response.Write(" which derives from: <br/> ");
        Response.Write(
          this.GetType().BaseType.BaseType.BaseType.ToString());
        Response.Write(" which derives from: <br/> ");
        Response.Write(
          this.GetType().BaseType.BaseType.BaseType.BaseType.ToString());
    }
}
```

An ASP.NET page that uses the *HelloWorld4Code* class to drive the page might then look like this:

```
<%@ Page Language="C#" Inherits="HelloWorld4Code"
    Src="HelloWorld4Code.cs" Debug="true" %>
<html>
    <body>
        <h1>Hello World!!!</h1>
        <%
            this.ShowLineage();
        %>
    </body>
</html>
```

With the ASP.NET 1.*x* style of code behind, ASP.NET sees the *Src* attribute in the directives and compiles that file. ASP.NET reads the *Inherits* attribute to figure out how to base the class that runs the page. In the previous example, ASP.NET uses the *HelloWorld4Code* class to drive the page.

By using the *Src* attribute, you tell the ASP.NET runtime to compile the file named by the *Src* attribute value. The ASP.NET runtime will compile it into the temporary directory. Alternatively, you can also precompile the file into an assembly containing the *HelloWorld4Code* class. For this to work, the precompiled assembly must appear in the bin directory of your virtual directory. If you precompile the page class and put the assembly in the bin directory, you don't even need to mention the source code file. In the absence of an *Src* attribute, the ASP.NET runtime will search the assemblies in the bin directory looking for the class specified in the *Inherits* attribute.

Modern ASP.NET Style

The other coding option for ASP.NET is new starting with version 2.0. This model is sometimes referred to as code beside. Consider the following ASP.NET page:

```
<%@ Page Language="C#" CodeFile="HelloWorld5Code.cs"
    Inherits="HelloWorld5Code" %>
<html>
    <body>
        <h1>Hello World!!!</h1>
        <%
            // This block will execute in the RenderControl method
            ShowLineage();
        %>
    </body>
</html>
```

It references the code found in the HelloWorld5Code.cs file:

```
using System.Web;
public partial class HelloWorld5Code : System.Web.UI.Page
{
    public void ShowLineage()
    {
        Response.Write("Check out the family tree: <br/> <br/>");
        Response.Write(this.GetType().ToString());
        Response.Write(" which derives from: <br/> ");
        Response.Write(this.GetType().BaseType.ToString());
        Response.Write(" which derives from: <br/> ");
        Response.Write(this.GetType().BaseType.BaseType.ToString());
        Response.Write(" which derives from: <br/> ");
        Response.Write(
        this.GetType().BaseType.BaseType.BaseType.ToString());
```

```
        Response.Write(" which derives from: <br/> ");
        Response.Write(
        this.GetType().BaseType.BaseType.BaseType.BaseType.ToString());
    }
}
```

In this case, ASP.NET looks to the *CodeFile* directive to figure out what code to compile. ASP.NET expects to find a partial class to implement the page's logic. Partial classes let you split the definition of a type (*class, struct,* or *interface*) between multiple source files, with a portion of the class definition living in each file. Compiling the source code files generates the entire class. This is especially useful when working with generated code, such as that generated by Visual Studio. You can augment a class without going back and changing the original code. Visual Studio .NET 2010 prefers the code-beside/partial class code representation.

The following short listings, Listing 2-1 and Listing 2-2, show two files that implement a singular class named *SplitMe*.

LISTING 2-1 Partial1.cs

```
// Partial1.cs
using System;

public partial class SplitMe
{

    public void Method1()
    {
        Console.WriteLine("SplitMe Method1");
    }
}
```

LISTING 2-2 Partial2.cs

```
// Partial2.CS
using System;

public partial class SplitMe
{
    public static void Main()
    {
        SplitMe splitMe = new SplitMe();
        splitMe.Method1();
        splitMe.Method2();
    }

    public void Method2()
    {
        Console.WriteLine("SplitMe Method2");
    }
}
```

To compile the code you see in Listings 2-1 and 2-2, you build the project with Visual Studio, or you can use the following command line in the Visual Studio Command Prompt (if these are just loose files):

```
csc /t:exe Partial1.cs Partial2.cs
```

This generates an executable file named Partial2.exe.

After working with ASP.NET source code in the raw, it's time to look at how Visual Studio and ASP.NET work together. Visual Studio .NET 2010 brings many new features for creating and developing Web applications, as you can see when working through subsequent examples.

The ASP.NET HTTP Pipeline

As soon as ASP.NET 1.0 was released, it offered a huge improvement over classic ASP by introducing well-defined code processing modules that together form the *ASP.NET HTTP pipeline*. Classic ASP was patched together from several disparate components (IIS, the Web Application Manager, and the ASP ISAPI DLL). The *Request* and *Response* objects were *COM* objects hanging off the threads owned by IIS. If you wanted to do any processing outside the context of ASP, you needed to write an ISAPI filter. If you wanted to write code to execute during processing, it had to occur within a *COM* object implementing *IDispatch* (severely limiting the available types of data you could use and negatively affecting performance). If you wanted to write any request-handling code (outside the context of ASP), you had to write a separate ISAPI DLL. The ASP.NET HTTP pipeline includes the facilities to do these things, but in a much more manageable way.

In ASP.NET, your application has the opportunity to perform preprocessing and postprocessing within *HttpModules*. If you use IIS 5.*x* or IIS 6.*x* as your Web server, the ASP.NET pipeline stands by itself, and requests are processed completely by ASP.NET as soon as aspnet_isapi. dll hands control off to the ASP.NET worker process. If you're using IIS 7.*x* as your Web server, the ASP.NET pipeline is integrated into the server so that you can apply most ASP.NET services to non-ASP.NET content. In any case, your application also has the opportunity to process application-wide events using the *HttpApplication* object. Because of the ASP.NET object model, the need for separate *COM*-based scripting objects on the server disappears. The endpoint of all requests is an implementation of *IHttpHandler*. ASP.NET already includes some useful implementations of *IHttpHandler* (that is, *System.Web.UI.Page* and *System.Web. Services.WebService*). However, you can easily write your own (as you see later).

The IIS 5.*x* and IIS 6.*x* Pipeline

Once a request comes into the *AppDomain* managed by the ASP.NET runtime, ASP.NET uses the *HttpWorkerRequest* class to store the request information. Following that, the runtime wraps the request's information in a class named *HttpContext*. The *HttpContext* class includes all the information you'd ever want to know about a request, including references to the current request's *HttpRequest* and *HttpResponse* objects. The runtime produces an instance of *HttpApplication* (if one is not already available), and then fires a number of application-wide events (such as *BeginRequest* and *AuthenticateRequest*). These events are also pumped through any *HttpModules* attached to the pipeline. Finally, ASP.NET figures out what kind of handler is required to handle the request, creates one, and asks the handler to process the request. After the handler deals with the request, ASP.NET fires a number of postprocessing events (such as *EndRequest*) through the *HttpApplication* object and the *HttpModules*.

Figure 2-5 illustrates the structure of the ASP.NET pipeline inside the ASP.NET worker process using IIS 6.*x* (the only difference from IIS 5.*x* is the name of the worker process).

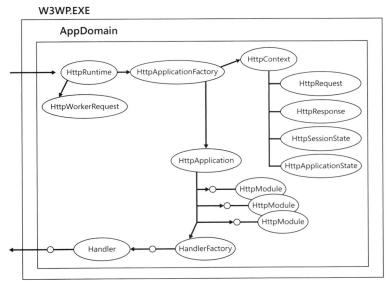

FIGURE 2-5 Main components of the HTTP pipeline in ASP.NET.

The IIS 7.*x* Integrated Pipeline

The integrated IIS 7.*x* pipeline is very similar to the ASP.NET HTTP pipeline that's been around since ASP.NET was first released (shown in Figure 2-5). As you can see from earlier investigations using the IIS 7.*x* management console, the IIS 7.*x* integrated pipeline employs modules and handlers just like earlier versions of the ASP.NET HTTP pipeline did. However, whereas the ASP.NET HTTP pipeline runs entirely within the ASP.NET worker process, IIS 7.*x* runs the pipeline as directed by IIS. The integrated pipeline in IIS 7.*x* works in very much the same way as the ASP.NET pipeline, so the application-wide events exposed through the *HttpApplication* events work just as before (application-wide events are discussed in detail later). When running your application through IIS 7.*x* in Integrated mode, your request no longer passes through aspnet_isapi.dll. IIS 7.*x* pushes the request through the modules and handlers directly.

Tapping the Pipeline

Although some of the parts in the pipeline are unavailable to you as a developer, several parts are available directly and provide a useful means of managing your request as it goes through the pipeline. The most important parts of the pipeline that you can touch include the *HttpApplication*, the *HttpContext*, the *HttpModule*, and the *HttpHandler*.

The following sections supply some details about these critical sections in the HTTP request path.

The *HttpApplication*

At this point, you understand the nature of a Web application as being very different from that of a normal desktop application. The code that you're writing is responsible for returning some HTML response to a client. In many ways, the model relates back to the terminal–mainframe model prevalent during the mid-1970s. In ASP.NET, the endpoint of a request is an implementation of *IHttpHandler* (even if that handler ultimately forms a Web page based on your ASP.NET Web Forms code).

HTTP handlers live for a very short period of time. They stick around long enough to handle a request, and then they disappear. For very simple applications, this model might be just fine. However, imagine the requirements of even a modest commercial-grade application. If all you had to work with was these ephemeral handlers, you'd have no way to achieve application-wide functionality. For example, imagine you want to cache data to avoid round-trips to the database. You'd need to store that data in a place where all the HTTP handlers could get to it.

The *HttpApplication* class exists for that purpose—to act as a rendezvous point for your request processing. During the lifetime of a Web application, the *HttpApplication* objects serve as places to hold application-wide data and handle application-side events.

The *HttpContext*

The *HttpContext* class acts as a central location in which you can access parts of the current request as it travels through the pipeline. In fact, every aspect of the current request is available through *HttpContext*. Even though the *HttpContext* components are really just references to other parts of the pipeline, having them available in a single place makes it much easier to manage the request.

Here is an abbreviated listing of *HttpContext*, showing the parts you'll use most frequently in developing Web applications. The members are exposed as properties.

```
class HttpContext
{
    public static HttpContext Current {...};
    public HttpRequest Request {...};
    public HttpResponse Response {...};
```

```
public HttpSessionState Session {...};
public HttpServerUtility Server {...};
public HttpApplicationState Application {...};
public HttpApplication ApplicationInstance {...};
public IDictionary Items {...};
public IPrincipal User {...};
public IHttpHandler CurrentHandler {...};
public Cache Cache {...};
...
}
```

The static *Current* property gives you a means of getting to the current request at any time. Many times, the *HttpContext* is passed as a method parameter (as in the method *IHttpHandler.RequestProcess(HttpContext ctx)*); however, there might be times when you need the context even though it hasn't been passed as a parameter. With the *Current* property, you can grab the current process out of thin air. For example, this is how you might use *HttpContext.Current*:

```
public void DealWithRequest()
{
    HttpContext thisRequest = HttpContext.Current;
    thisRequest.Response.Write("<h3> Hello World</h3>");
}
```

As you can see from the previous snippet of the *HttpContext* object, the properties within *HttpContext* include such nuggets as these:

- A reference to the context's *Response* object (so that you can send output to the client)

- A reference to the *Request* object (so that you can find information about the request itself)

- A reference to the central application itself (so that you can get to the application state)

- A reference to a per-request dictionary (for storing items for the duration of a request)

- A reference to the application-wide cache (to store data and avoid round-trips to the database)

You'll see a lot more of the context—especially when you write a custom *HttpHandler*.

HttpModules

Although the *Application* object is suitable for handling application-wide events and data on a small scale, sometimes application-wide tasks need a little heavier machinery. *HttpModules* serve that purpose.

ASP.NET includes a number of predefined *HttpModules*. For example, session state, authentication, and authorization are handled by *HttpModules*. Writing *HttpModules* is pretty straightforward and is a great way to handle complex application-wide operations. For example, if you want to write some custom processing that occurs before each request, using *HttpModules* is a good way to do it. You can see *HttpModules* up close later.

HttpHandlers

The last stop a request makes in the pipeline is at an *HttpHandler*. Any class implementing the interface *IHttpHandler* qualifies as a handler. When a request finally reaches the end of the pipeline, ASP.NET consults the configuration file to see whether the particular file name extension is mapped to an *HttpHandler*. If it is, ASP.NET loads the handler and calls the handler's *IHttpHandler.ProcessRequest* method to execute the request.

Visual Studio and ASP.NET

Visual Studio .NET 2010 expands your options for locating your Web sites during development. The Visual Studio .NET 2010 wizards define eight separate Web site project deployment locations: local IIS Web sites, file system–based Web sites, FTP Web sites, and remote Web sites.

Here's a rundown of the different types of Web sites available using the Project Wizard. Each is useful for a particular scenario, and having these options makes it much easier to develop and deploy an ASP.NET application with Visual Studio 2010 than it was to do with earlier versions.

Local IIS Web Sites

Creating a local IIS Web site is much like creating a Web site using the older versions of Visual Studio .NET specifying a local virtual directory. This option creates sites that run using IIS installed on your local computer. Local IIS Web sites store the pages and folders in the IIS default directory structure (that is, \Inetpub\wwwroot). By default, Visual Studio creates a virtual directory under IIS. However, you can create a virtual directory ahead of time and store the code for your Web site in any folder. The virtual directory just needs to point to that location.

One reason to create a local Web site is to test your application against a local version of IIS, for example, if you need to test such features as application pooling, ISAPI filters, or HTTP-based authentication. Even though a site is accessible from other computers, it's often much easier to test these aspects of your application when you can see it interact with IIS on your computer. To create a local Web site, you need to have administrative rights. For most developers, this is not an issue.

File System–Based Web Sites

File system–based Web sites live in any folder you specify. The folder can be on your local computer or on another computer sharing that folder. File system–based Web sites do *not* require IIS running on your computer. Instead, you run pages by using the Visual Studio Web server.

Visual Studio Web Server

Until Visual Studio 2005, the development environment used IIS directly to serve up pages. That meant that developers needed to have IIS fully enabled on their computers to be able to develop effectively. This created a possible security compromise. Visual Studio 2010 includes its own built-in Web server. This lets you develop Web applications effectively even if you don't have IIS installed on your development computer.

File-system Web sites are useful for testing your site locally but independently of IIS. The most common approach is to create, develop, and test a file-system Web site. Then, when it is time to deploy your site, simply create an IIS virtual directory on the deployment server and move the pages to that directory.

Because file-system Web sites employ the Visual Studio Web server rather than IIS, you can develop your Web site on your computer even when logged on as a user without administrative rights.

This scenario is useful for developing and testing application-specific features of your site. Because IIS is out of the picture, you won't be able to work with (or have to deal with) such IIS features as ISAPI filters, application pooling, or authentication (though in many cases you won't need to worry about that sort of thing during development).

FTP Web Sites

In addition to creating HTTP-based sites, you can use Visual Studio to manage Web sites available through an FTP server. For example, if you use a remote hosting company to host your Web site, an FTP server offers a convenient way to move files back and forth between your development location and the hosting location.

Visual Studio connects to any FTP server for which you have read and write access. Once connected, you then use Visual Studio to manage the content on the remote FTP server.

You would use this option to deploy your Web site to a server that lacks Microsoft FrontPage 2002 Server Extensions.

Remote Web Sites

The final option for developing and managing Web sites through Visual Studio is to use the remote Web sites option. Remote Web sites use IIS on another computer that is accessible over a network. In addition to running IIS, the remote computer must have IIS installed and needs to have FrontPage 2002 Server Extensions installed. Pages and folders on a remote site become stored under the default IIS folder on the remote computer.

This option is useful if you decide you want to move the Web site to its actual deployment server. In addition, the entire development team can work on the site simultaneously. The downside of this approach is that debugging and configuring a Web site remotely can sometimes be tricky because the process is slow and it's hard to control the site as a whole.

Hello World and Visual Studio

To get started, use Visual Studio to generate the HelloWorld Web application.

Generating the HelloWorld Web application

1.   Start Visual Studio in Administrative mode by clicking the Windows Start button and typing **Visual Studio** in the Search box. When Visual Studio appears in the list of programs, right-click the menu and click Run As Administrator. Create a new Web site by clicking File, New, and then Web Site. Visual Studio will display a dialog box like this one:

So that you can compare this site to the previous IIS-based examples in this chapter, make this an HTTP site. Select HTTP from the Web Location drop-down list. Give the Web site a useful name such as *ASPNETStepByStepExamples*. Even though this is the same directory name used for the previous IIS examples, you can use it because Visual Studio will create the subdirectory under the IIS default subdirectory \inetpub\wwwroot.

Notice that several different kinds of sites are showing in the dialog box. Select Empty Web Site for this example, which causes Visual Studio to generate an ASP.NET solution file in a directory named Visual Studio 2010\Projects in your normal My Documents directory. Visual Studio also creates a new directory in your inetpub\wwwroot directory and maps it as an IIS virtual directory. However, the virtual directory is devoid of any files.

One of the other project templates available is ASP.NET Web Site. By contrast, selecting ASP.NET Web Site causes Visual Studio to generate a directory structure similar to the one generated by Empty Web Site. However, Visual Studio includes a default Web form and source code (default.aspx and default.aspx.cs). You also get an App_Data directory that might contain data pertinent to your site (for example, a database file containing ASP.NET security information could be contained here).

2. Choose the language syntax. At this point, you have the option of choosing a syntax to use within your code. Choose among Visual Basic, C#, and J#. For this example, select C#.

3. Create a local Web site. For this example, select HTTP from the Location combo box to run this Web site locally on your computer. The Visual Studio default option is to create a Web site on your local computer's file system. By using the HTTP project type, clients trying to access your Web site will have their requests directed through IIS. This is the best option to choose when learning how ASP.NET works with IIS because it gives you the chance to work with your Web site as an entire system, and you can use tracing and debugging on your local computer. Later examples that focus on specific ASP.NET features use the more convenient file system–style project.

4. Add a HelloWorld page by selecting Website, Add New Item to open the Add New Item dialog box:

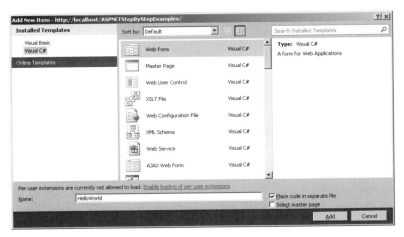

This dialog box lists all the various pieces you can add to your Web site. Topping the list is an item named *Web Form*. Select this option, and then type **HelloWorld.aspx** into the Name text box. Leave the other defaults the same.

Visual Studio will provide you with the pure ASP.NET code from the HelloWorld.aspx file.

Notice that the code generated by Visual Studio includes directives near the top of the markup file connecting HelloWorld.aspx to the accompanying source file HelloWorld.aspx.cs (using the *CodeFile* and *Inherits* attributes in the *Page* directive). Following the directive is some initial HTML produced by Visual Studio:

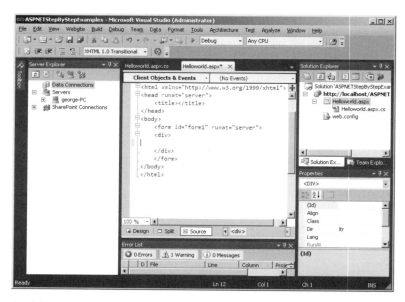

At this point, take a moment to explore the layout of Visual Studio. Along the top of the window, you can see a number of toolbar buttons and menu options. You visit most of them throughout the course of this text. Directly beneath the code window, you can see three tabs labeled Design, Split, and Source (the Source tab is selected by default). If you click the Design tab, you can see what the page will look like in a browser. Right now, the page has no visible HTML tags or ASP.NET Web Forms controls, so the design view is blank.

To the right of the Source window, you'll see Solution Explorer, which lists the components of your application that Visual Studio will compile into an executable code base. Along the top of Solution Explorer, you'll find a number of buttons. By resting your mouse pointer on the buttons, you can see what they do. The following graphic shows how each button functions when an .aspx file is selected.

View Code

Nest Related Files

Refresh

View Designer

Copy Web Site

Properties

ASP.NET Configuration

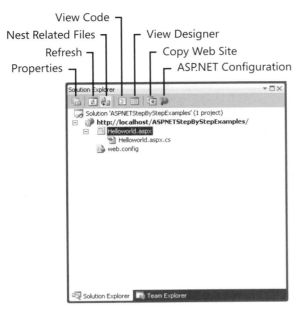

5. Write some code into the page. Select the HelloWorld.aspx file in Solution Explorer, and then click the View Code button. This shows the C# code in the Source code window, like so:

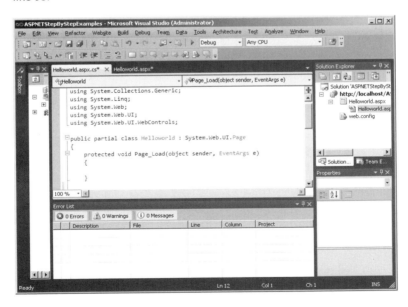

Add the following code to show the page's lineage (it's the same code from HelloWorld5 shown previously). The code you add should follow the *Page_Load* method:

```
public void ShowLineage()
{
    Response.Write("Check out the family tree: <br/> <br/>");
    Response.Write(this.GetType().ToString());
    Response.Write(" which derives from: <br/> ");
    Response.Write(this.GetType().BaseType.ToString());
    Response.Write(" which derives from: <br/> ");
    Response.Write(this.GetType().BaseType.BaseType.ToString());
    Response.Write(" which derives from: <br/> ");
    Response.Write(
    this.GetType().BaseType.BaseType.BaseType.ToString());
    Response.Write(" which derives from: <br/> ");
    Response.Write(
    this.GetType().BaseType.BaseType.BaseType.BaseType.ToString());
}
```

The HelloWorld.aspx.cs file should look like the following:

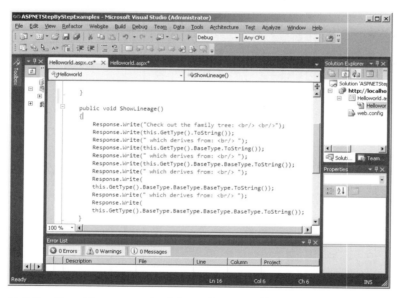

6. Call the *ShowLineage* method from the .aspx file. Click the HelloWorld.aspx tab at the top of the editor window to return to the visual designer, and then click the Source tab near the bottom of the screen. With the HTML content showing, insert the following markup in the page. It should be placed between the opening and closing <div> tags:

```
<h2> Hello World!!!</h2>
<%
ShowLineage();
%>
```

The HelloWorld.aspx markup then would appear like the following:

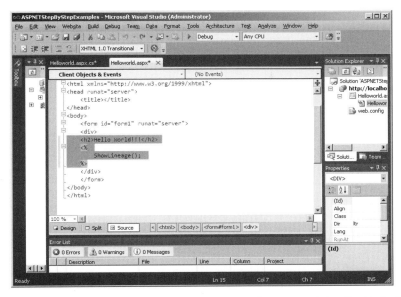

7. Now build the project and run the Web site from Visual Studio. To build the application, select Build, Solution from the main menu. If the source code has any errors, they'll appear in the Errors window in the bottom pane.

   To run the application, select Debug, Start Without Debugging (or press Ctrl+F5). Visual Studio will start up a copy of an Internet browser (Internet Explorer by default) and browse the page. You should see a page like this (make sure the HelloWorld.aspx page is highlighted in Solution Explorer):

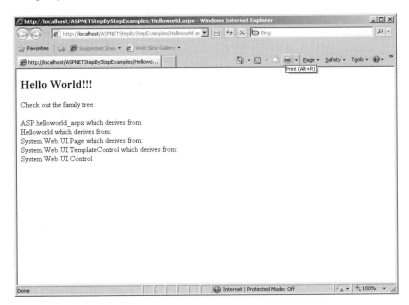

When you run this application, Visual Studio compiles the HelloWorld.aspx and its code-beside file, HelloWorld.aspx.cs, and moves them to the temporary ASP.NET directory. IIS is then called to activate the ASP.NET HTTP pipeline, which loads the compiled files (DLLs) and renders the page you just created.

Chapter 2 Quick Reference

To	Do This
Create an FTP Web site in Visual Studio 2010	Select File, New, Web Site from the main menu. Select FTP in the Locations combo box.
	This option is useful for creating sites that will eventually be deployed by sending the bits to the site's host over FTP.
Create an HTTP Web site in Visual Studio 2010	Select File, New, Web Site from the main menu. Select HTTP in the Locations combo box.
	This option is useful for creating sites that use IIS as the Web server throughout the entire development cycle.
Create a file-system Web site in Visual Studio 2010	Select File, New, Web Site from the main menu. Select File System in the Locations combo box.
	This option creates sites that use Visual Studio's built-in Web server. That way, you can develop your own site even if you don't have IIS available on your computer.

Chapter 3
The Page Rendering Model

After completing this chapter, you will be able to

- Work directly with server-side control tags.

- Work with Web Forms and server-side controls using Microsoft Visual Studio.

- Work with postback events using Visual Studio.

- Understand the ASP.NET page rendering model.

This chapter covers the heart of the ASP.NET Web Forms rendering model: controls. As you will see here, *System.Web.UI.Page* works by partitioning the rendering process into small components known as server-side controls.

The entire tour of the ASP.NET control model includes the fundamental control architecture. This chapter starts by looking at the HTML required to render controls in the browser. Then, it examines the classic Active Server Pages (ASP) approach to displaying controls. Although you might never use classic ASP in your career, seeing it in this context can help you appreciate some of the problems ASP.NET has solved. This lays the groundwork for subsequent chapters that look at how controls can provide custom rendering, user controls, some of the standard user interface (UI) controls, and some of the modern, more complex controls. This chapter starts with the ASP.NET rendering model.

Rendering Controls as Tags

As you saw in basic HTML Web Forms, developing a Web-based UI is all about getting the right tags out to the browser. For example, imagine you want to have your application's UI appear in the client's browser as shown in Figure 3-1.

Getting this to appear in a client's browser means populating an HTML stream with the correct tags so that the browser renders the screen using client-side controls. Listing 3-1 shows some HTML that does the job. If you would like to run this page, the file is named BunchOfControls.htm and is included in the sample code for this chapter. To run the page, save the file in a virtual directory and browse to it.

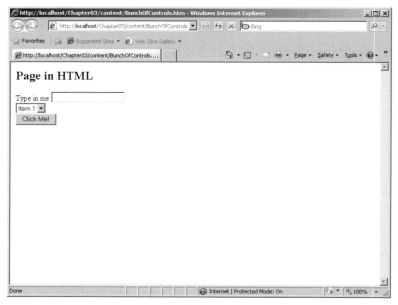

FIGURE 3-1 Some HTML tags rendered as controls in Internet Explorer.

LISTING 3-1 Initial HTML markup from BunchOfControls.htm

```
<html>
<body>
<h2> Page in HTML </h2>
<form method="post" action="BunchOfControls.htm" id="Form1">
    <label>Type in me</label>
    <input name="textinfo" type="text" id="textinfo" />
    <br/>
    <select name="selectitems" id="ddl">
    <option value="Item 1">Item 1</option>
    <option value="Item 2">Item 2</option>
    <option value="Item 3">Item 3</option>
    <option value="Item 4">Item 4</option>

    </select>
    <br/>
    <input type="submit" name="clickme" value="Click Me!" id="clickme" />
</form>
</body>
</html>
```

Of course, using controls on a page usually implies dynamic content, so getting this HTML to the browser should happen dynamically, in a programmatic way. Classic ASP has facilities for rendering dynamic content. However, classic ASP generally relies on raw HTML for rendering its content. For example, a page like the BunchOfControls.htm page shown in Listing 3-1 might look something like Listing 3-2 in classic ASP. Figure 3-2 shows how the ASP page renders in Windows Internet Explorer.

LISTING 3-2 Source for BunchOfControls page using classic ASP

```
<%@ Language="javascript" %>
<h2> Page in Classic ASP </h2>
<form>

    <label>Type in me</label>
    <input name="textinfo" type="text" id="textinfo" />
    <br/>
    <select name="selectitems" id="ddl">
    <option value="Item 1">Item 1</option>
    <option value="Item 2">Item 2</option>
    <option value="Item 3">Item 3</option>
    <option value="Item 4">Item 4</option>

</select>
    <br/>
    <input type="submit" name="clickme" value="Click Me!" id="clickme" />
<p>
    <% if (Request("textinfo") != "") { %>
        This was in the text box: <%=Request("textinfo") %> <br/>
        And this was in the selection control: <%=Request("selectitems") %>
      <% } %>
</p>

</form>
```

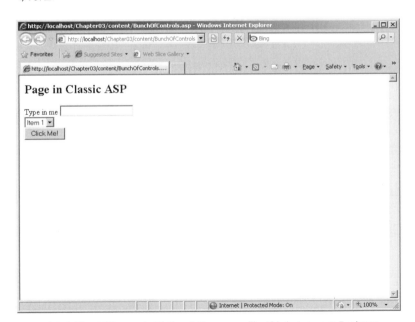

FIGURE 3-2 The ASP page in Listing 3-2 appears like this in Internet Explorer.

When you select an item from the selection control, notice that the page responds by telling you what you selected. This demonstrates ASP support for dynamic content.

Notice that even though classic ASP offers a way to decide your page's content at run time, you still have to create much of the content using raw HTML. Also, the state of the controls is always reset between posts. (I discuss this topic later in the examination of the ASP.NET *ViewState*.) ASP.NET adds a layer of indirection between the raw HTML and the rendered page—that layer of indirection is provided by the collection of ASP.NET server-side controls. Server-side controls eliminate much of the tedium necessary to develop a Web-based UI in classic ASP.

Packaging the UI as Components

Being able to assemble the UI from component parts is one of the most-cited benefits of producing components. The earliest methods for building components in the Windows operating system were to write custom Windows procedures, to use the owner draw capabilities of controls such as list boxes or buttons, and to subclass an existing window. In the early 1990s, Windows employed Microsoft Visual Basic Controls (VBXs) as a viable UI technology. Of course, that was more than a decade ago. Throughout the mid- and late 1990s and early 2000s, ActiveX controls represented the graphical user interface (GUI) componentization technology of the day. Windows Forms controls are the current standard for modular GUIs for writing rich client applications.

In the late 1990s, ActiveX controls also emerged as a way to render a Web-based GUI as components. The idea was that by using an ActiveX control in a page, the control would be downloaded as users surfed to the page. During the mid-1990s, Java applets also gained some popularity as a way to package GUI components for distribution over the Web. However, both of these techniques depend on some fairly extensive infrastructure on the client computer (the Component Object Model infrastructure to support ActiveX and a Java Virtual Machine to support Java applets). When you're developing a Web site, you might not be able to count on a specific infrastructure being available on the client computer to support your GUI. To support the greatest number of clients, represent your GUI using only HTML. That means GUI componentization must happen on the server side.

Now that modern client platforms are becoming more homogeneous, Web UIs are beginning to lean increasingly toward the Asynchronous Java and XML programming model (AJAX). You see how AJAX works a bit later in this book. AJAX tends to push more intelligence back up to the browser. However, AJAX applications still have plenty of rendering to do. The ASP.NET UI componentization model makes developing AJAX applications very approachable. The AJAX programming model includes a lot of underlying plumbing code that fits perfectly in the server-side control architecture of ASP.NET.

As you saw earlier, ASP.NET introduces an entirely new model for managing Web pages. The infrastructure of ASP.NET includes a well-defined pipeline through which a request flows. When a request ends up at the server, ASP.NET instantiates a handler (an implementation of *IHttpHandler*) to deal with the request. As you see in Chapter 19, "HTTP Handlers," the handling architecture is extraordinarily flexible. You can write any code you wish to handle the request. The *System.Web.UI.Page* class implements *IHttpHandler* by introducing an object-oriented approach to rendering. That is, every element you see on a Web page emitted by an ASP.NET page is somehow generated by a *server-side control*. Let's see how this works.

The Page Using ASP.NET

Try turning the previous Web page into an ASP.NET application. Doing so introduces some canonical features of ASP.NET, including server-side controls and server-side script blocks.

1. Create a file named *BunchOfControls.aspx*. Follow the steps from Chapter 2, "ASP.NET Application Fundamentals," to create a basic text file. Because all of the code will be in a single file, do not create a full-fledged ASP.NET file for this step using the wizard.

2. Add the source code in Listing 3-3 to the file.

   LISTING 3-3 Source code for the BunchOfControls page using ASP.NET

   ```
   <%@ Page Language="C#" %>

   <script runat="server">
     protected void Page_Load(object sender, EventArgs ea)
     {
        ddl.Items.Add("Item 1");
        ddl.Items.Add("Item 2");
        ddl.Items.Add("Item 3");
        ddl.Items.Add("Item 4");
     }
   </script >
   <h2> Page in ASP.NET </h2>

   <form id="Form1" runat="server" >
     <asp:Label Text="Type in me" runat="server" />
     <asp:TextBox id="textinfo" runat="server" />
     <br/>
     <asp:DropDownList id="ddl" runat="server" />
     <br/>
     <asp:Button id="clickme" Text="Click Me!" runat="server" />
   </form>
   ```

3. Save the file in a virtual directory (either create one or use the one from Chapter 2).

Many of the same elements in the classic ASP page also appear here; for example, there is a top-level *Page* directive. The *Language* attribute is new for ASP.NET, stipulating that any code encountered by the ASP.NET runtime should be interpreted as C# code. There's a server-side script block that handles the *Page_Load* event. Following the script block is an HTML <form> tag. Notice that the <form> tag has an attribute named *runat*, and the attribute is set to *server*. The *runat=server* attribute tells the ASP.NET runtime to generate a server-side control to handle that UI element at the server. You see this in detail throughout the rest of this chapter.

When the *runat=server* attribute is included in page control tags, the ASP.NET runtime implicitly creates an instance of the control in memory. The resulting assembly includes a member variable of the same type and name (tied to the control's ID value) as the control listed on the page. Notice that the ASP.NET code specifies the *DropDownList* named *ddl* to run at the server. To access the control programmatically, the code block (expressed inline in this case) simply needs to refer to the *DropDownList* as *ddl*. The preceding example accesses the member variable to add items to the drop-down list.

If you need to access the control using code beside, you can explicitly declare the *DropDownList* variable as *ddl* in the associated code file. This is required because ASP.NET derives the code-beside class from *System.Web.UI.Page*. Microsoft Visual Studio does this for you automatically, as you see shortly.

Farther down the ASP.NET code, you can see that the other elements (the label, the text box, the selection control, and the button) are also represented as server-side controls. The job of each of these controls is to add a little bit of HTML to the response. Each time you add a server-side control to the page, ASP.NET adds an instance of the control to a control tree that the page maintains in memory. The control tree acts as a container that collects every single element encapsulated by one of these server-side controls—including the title text that seems to be floating near the top of the page even though there is no explicit *runat=server* attribute associated with the <h2> tag.

The Page's Rendering Model

To get a good idea of how the ASP.NET *Page* model works, you can run the page again, but this time turn on the tracing mechanism. (You examine tracing in more detail later when you look at the diagnostic features of ASP.NET.) For now, you simply need to know that ASP.NET dumps the entire context of a request and a response if you set the page's *Trace* attribute to *true*. Here's the *Page* directive with tracing turned on:

```
<%@ Page Language="C#" Trace="true" %>
```

Figure 3-3 shows what the page looks like with tracing turned on.

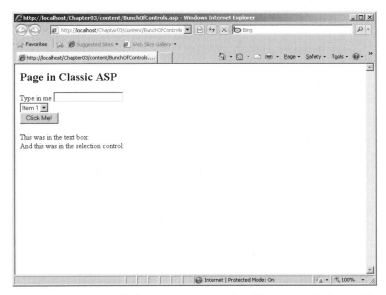

FIGURE 3-3 The .aspx file from Listing 3-3 rendered in Internet Explorer with tracing turned on.

If you look at the raw text of the response (click Page, View Source in Internet Explorer), you can see that ASP.NET responds with pretty straightforward, ordinary HTML. There's a bit extra near the top—the hidden *_VIEWSTATE* field, which is covered later in Chapter 4, "Custom Rendered Controls." After that, the rest is familiar HTML describing a form. Listing 3-4 shows the raw HTML emitted by the ASP.NET code from Listing 3-3. Be sure to turn tracing off first before surfing to the page!

LISTING 3-4 Raw HTML produced by the BunchOfControls.aspx file

```
<h2> Page in ASP.NET </h2>
<form method="post" action="BunchOfControls.aspx" id="Form1">
<div>
<input type="hidden" name="__VIEWSTATE" id="__VIEWSTATE"
value="/wEPDwUJODQ1ODEz ... " />
</div>

    <span>Type in me</span>
    <input name="textinfo" type="text" id="textinfo" />
    <br/>
    <select name="ddl" id="ddl">
    <option value="Item 1">Item 1</option>
    <option value="Item 2">Item 2</option>
    <option value="Item 3">Item 3</option>
    <option value="Item 4">Item 4</option>

</select>
    <br/>
    <input type="submit" name="clickme" value="Click Me!" id="clickme" />
</form>
```

You don't see any of the *runat=server* attributes anywhere in the rendered page. That's because the *runat=server* attributes are there to instruct ASP.NET how to construct the page's control tree.

The Page's Control Tree

After you set the page's *Trace* property to *true*, ASP.NET spews a ton of information your way in the form of a page trace. If you scroll down just a bit in the trace information, you can see that part of the ASP.NET page trace includes the page's control tree. Figure 3-4 shows what the BunchOfControls.aspx page's trace looks like, with the focus on the control tree.

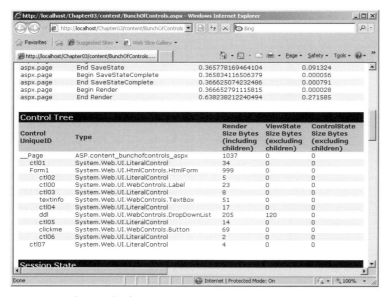

FIGURE 3-4 The BunchOfControls.aspx page's control tree shown in the page trace.

The first line in the page's control tree trace is an item named __*Page*. This is in fact the *System.Web.UI.Page* object running in memory. Beneath that is a whole host of other items. You might recognize some of their names because they are named in the ASP.NET source code. Notice the *Form1*, *textinfo*, and *clickme* items. Those names come from the tags in the original .aspx file.

What's happening here is that ASP.NET is breaking down the page rendering architecture into small, easily managed pieces. Every item in the control tree shown in Figure 3-4 derives from the *System.Web.UI.Control* class. Every time the *System.Web.UI.Page* needs to render the page, it simply walks the control tree, asking each control to render itself. For example, when the ASP.NET runtime asks the *TextBox* server-side control to render itself, the *TextBox* control adds the following HTML to the output stream heading for the browser:

```
<input name="textinfo" type="text" id="textinfo" />
```

This works similarly for the other controls. For example, the *DropDownList* is responsible for emitting the <select> and <option> tags (the <option> tags represent the collection of items held by the *DropDownList* control).

```
<select name="ddl" id="ddl">
    <option value="Item 1">Item 1</option>
    <option value="Item 2">Item 2</option>
    <option value="Item 3">Item 3</option>
    <option value="Item 4">Item 4</option>
</select>
```

Now that you see how these tags work, you can learn how to manage them in Visual Studio.

Adding Controls Using Visual Studio

Visual Studio (in concert with ASP.NET) can easily fool you about the real nature of Web-based development. As you saw in earlier chapters, Web-based development dates back to the old terminal–mainframe days of the mid-1970s. However, now the terminal is a sophisticated browser, the computing platform is a Web server (or perhaps a Web farm), and the audience is worldwide. When a client browser makes a round-trip to the server, it's really getting only a snapshot of the state of the server. That's because Web user interfaces are built using a markup language over a disconnected protocol.

When you build Web applications in Visual Studio, it's almost as if you are developing a desktop application. With Visual Studio, you don't have to spend all your time typing ASP-style code. The Designer is a great environment in which to design a Web-based UI visually.

To learn how to work with Visual Studio, you can develop a simple page that uses server-side controls. The page will look roughly like the ones you have seen so far in this chapter.

Building a page with Visual Studio

1. In Visual Studio, create a new Empty ASP.NET Web site project to experiment with controls. Call the Web site ControlsORama, as shown here:

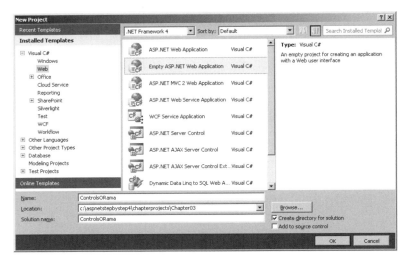

2. Add a default page by right-clicking the project node, and selecting Add, New Item. Select WebForm from the available templates shown by Visual Studio, and make sure the form is named Default.aspx. Visual Studio starts you off editing the markup in the Default.aspx file. If you don't see the page layout in Design mode, switch to the Design view as shown here by clicking the Design tab near the bottom of the editing window:

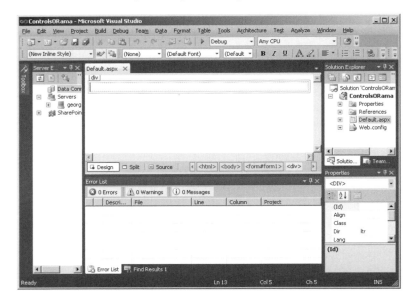

The ASP.NET code generated by Visual Studio includes an HTML <div> tag in the body of the page. To see the code generated by Visual Studio as you modify elements in the Designer, click the Source tab near the bottom of the design window. Visual Studio also now includes a handy Split tab that you can use to see both the Design and Source views at the same time.

If you simply start typing text into the Design view pane, you will see some text at the top of the page. The following graphic illustrates the Design view with some text inserted. To insert the text, click inside the box with the dashed blue border and type **Page in Visual Studio**.

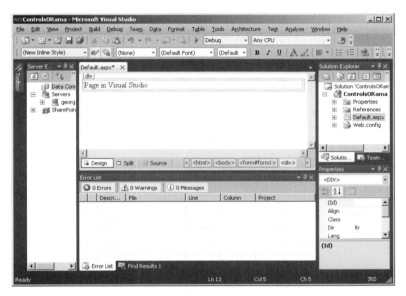

3. To edit the format of the text on the page, you need to view the page's properties. Highlight the text, right-click the text, and click Properties. Then, highlight the *Style* property in the Properties pane. A small button with an ellipsis (. . .) appears in the *Property* field. Click the button to open the Modify Style dialog box. The Modify Style dialog box is where you can set the attributes for the <div> tag including the font style and size. The following graphic shows the Modify Style dialog box. Select the Font-Family, Font-Size, and Font-Weight values that you see in the graphic, and then click OK.

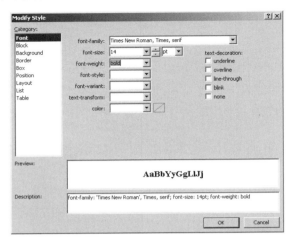

4. Click the Toolbox tab on the far left side of the Visual Studio window to open the Toolbox, as shown in the following graphic:

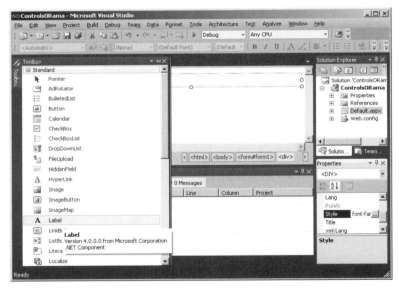

5. Insert a line break tag (<br/>), drag a label from the Toolbox onto the page, and then select it as shown in the following graphic. (Notice how the Visual Studio 2010 Designer adorns the label with a small tag right above it, which helps you identify the label in the Designer when you select it.)

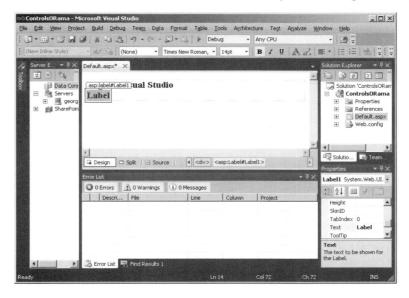

6. To edit the content of the label, you need to view the properties of the control. If the properties aren't showing, right-click the label and click Properties on the shortcut menu. The following graphic shows the Properties pane:

You can now manipulate the appearance of the label to your liking. The example label here uses a small Times New Roman font, and the text in the label is **Type in me:**.

7. Add a text box next by dragging a *TextBox* from the Toolbox and positioning it next to the *Label*. After the *TextBox*, insert a line break tag (<br/>).

8. Next, add a *DropDownList* box by dragging it out of the Toolbox and placing it on the page. The following graphic illustrates the drop-down list as it appears in the Designer:

As soon as you drop the control on the page, Visual Studio offers you the opportunity to add items to the *DropDownList* by using the shortcut menu that appears. Click Edit Items on the DropDownList Tasks menu to open the ListItem Collection Editor dialog box, as shown in the following graphic:

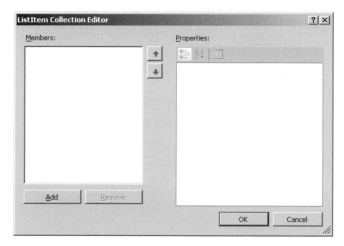

Each time you click the Add button, the ListItem Collection Editor adds a new item to the *DropDownList* item collection. After adding and selecting an item, you can edit the display name (the *Text* property). You can add a corresponding value to associate with the text as well. For example, in an inventory-tracking application, you might include a product name as the *Text* property and an enterprise-specific product code in the *Value* field. You can retrieve either or both aspects of the item at run time.

Add several of these items to the *DropDownList*, as shown in the following graphic. After you have added several, click OK.

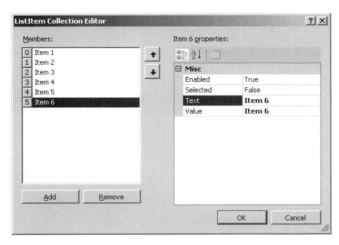

9. Add a button to the page. First, add a line break (<br/>) after the *DropDownList*. Then, drag a *Button* from the Toolbox onto the page. The following graphic shows the controls in place:

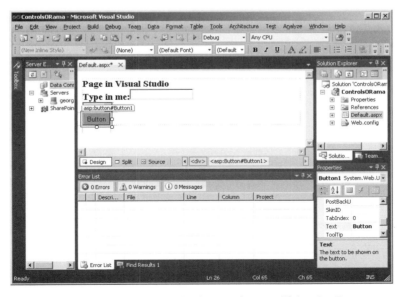

Add some meaningful text to the button by modifying its *Text* property.

Before moving on, take a minute to look at the source code generated by Visual Studio. For a *Label* control, a *TextBox* control, a *DropDownList* control, and a *Button* control, Visual Studio adds four new member variables to your code (implied through the *runat=server* attributes placed in the control tags). At this point, the contents of the .aspx file (starting with the <form> tag) look something like the code in Listing 3-5.

LISTING 3-5 Final Default.aspx markup

```
<form id="form1" runat="server">
<div style=
   "font-family: 'Times New Roman', Times, serif; font-size: 14pt; font-weight: bold">
   Page in Visual Studio<br />
   <asp:Label ID="Label1" runat="server" Text="Type in me:"></asp:Label>
   <asp:TextBox ID="TextBox1" runat="server"></asp:TextBox>
   <br />
   <asp:DropDownList ID="DropDownList1" runat="server">
     <asp:ListItem>Item 1</asp:ListItem>
     <asp:ListItem>Item 2</asp:ListItem>
     <asp:ListItem>Item 3</asp:ListItem>
     <asp:ListItem>Item 4</asp:ListItem>
     <asp:ListItem>Item 5</asp:ListItem>
     <asp:ListItem>Item 6</asp:ListItem>
   </asp:DropDownList>
   <br />
   <asp:Button ID="Button1" runat="server" Text="Click Me" />
   </div>
\</form>
```

Notice that each ASP.NET tag that runs at the server has an *ID* attribute. This is the identifier by which the control is known at run time. You use it shortly.

10. Finally, to make the button do something, you need to add an event handler to the page so that it responds when the button is clicked. The easiest way to add an event handler is to double-click the button in Design view. Visual Studio generates a handler function for the button click, and then shows that code in the Source view. At this point, you can add some code to respond to the button click.

11. Add the source code in Listing 3-6 to the file.

LISTING 3-6 Button handling code

```
protected void Button1_Click(object sender, EventArgs e)
{
    Response.Write("Hello. Here's what you typed into the text box: <br/>");
    Response.Write(this.TextBox1.Text);

    Response.Write("<br/>");
    Response.Write("And the selected item is: <br/>");
    Response.Write(this.DropDownList1.SelectedItem.Text);
}
```

The code shown here responds to the button click by sending some text to the output stream using the *Response* object. The text coming through *Response.Write* is the first text the client browser sees, so it appears at the top of the page.

Notice that the response code uses the *TextBox1* member variable in the page's class, showing that the controls are available programmatically at run time. Here's how the page appears to the client browser. Notice how the text emitted by *Response.Write* is inserted before any of the controls are.

To test the controls on the page, browse to the page by clicking the Debug menu, and then clicking Start Without Debugging. To see the HTML generated by all the server-side controls, you can view the source sent to the browser. (If your browser is Internet Explorer, click Page, View Source.) When you view the source, you should see something like that shown in Listing 3-7. Notice how the text emitted by *Response.Write* appears at the very top of the listing.

LISTING 3-7 HTML resulting from running Default.aspx

```
Hello. Here's what you typed into the text box: <br/>Hello world<br/>
And the selected item is: <br/>Item 4
```

```
    <!DOCTYPE html PUBLIC "-//W3C//DTD XHTML 1.0 Transitional//EN"
     "http://www.w3.org/TR/xhtml1/DTD/xhtml1-transitional.dtd">


    <html xmlns="http://www.w3.org/1999/xhtml">
    <head><title>
    </title></head>
    <body>
      <form name="form1" method="post" action="Default.aspx" id="form1">
    <div>
    <input type="hidden" name="__VIEWSTATE" id="__VIEWSTATE"
    value="/wEPDwUKMTcOODY5OTM3N2RkvlciIj/EgelYYjZ7ti51iSLFZ6g=" />
    </div>
    <div>
      <input type="hidden" name="__EVENTVALIDATION" id="__EVENTVALIDATION"
    value="/wEWCQLi6ca/AgLsObLrBgKTmtqTCAKTmsaTCAGBhPVvUl6OSn5X9GuTKtorQF1aF3r" />
    </div>
    <div style="font-family: 'Times New Roman', Times, serif; font-size: 14pt; font-
    weight: bold">
    Page in Visual Studio<br />
    <span id="Label1">Type in me:</span>
    <input name="TextBox1" type="text" value="Hello world" id="TextBox1" />
      <br />
        <select name="DropDownList1" id="DropDownList1">
          <option value="Item 1">Item 1</option>
          <option value="Item 2">Item 2</option>
          <option value="Item 3">Item 3</option>
          <option selected="selected" value="Item 4">Item 4</option>
          <option value="Item 5">Item 5</option>
          <option value="Item 6">Item 6</option>
        </select>
      <br />
      <input type="submit" name="Button1" value="Click Me" id="Button1" />
      </div>
    </form>
    </body>
    </html>
```

Notice that the browser displays just pure HTML—ASP.NET generated it using its page rendering model, but the browser is none the wiser.

Layout Considerations

You might have noticed when building the last page that the layout of the page flowed. That is, every time you dropped a control onto the page, the Designer forced it up against the placement of the previous control. If you've worked with earlier versions of Visual Studio, you know that this is different default behavior. Visual Studio 2003 uses absolute positioning for elements on a page (which is what you're used to if you've done rich client or standard Windows development).

Although today Visual Studio 2010 does not let you set positioning styles directly in the Designer, you can apply different positioning options using a style that applies to the whole page or to single elements in the page. To add a new style to the page, make sure the Designer is showing in the window and click Format, New Style from the main Visual Studio menu. The New Style dialog box opens:

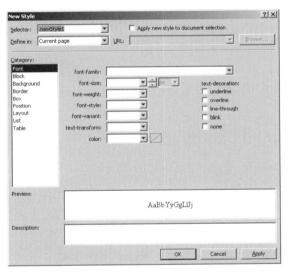

To change the layout options using the style, select Position in the Category list on the left side of the dialog box. Notice the combo selection for setting positions. Once you've set up a style, you can apply it to various elements on the page by referring to the class name through the element's *CssClass* property.

By changing the positioning options, you can apply various kinds of layout assignments to the page. Play around with them a bit because that's the only way to get a feel for how they work. You explore styles in greater depth later in the discussion of master pages in Chapter 7, "A Consistent Look and Feel."

Chapter 3 Quick Reference

To	Do This
Switch between ASPX Source code mode and Designer mode	Click the Design or Source tab, which both usually appear near the bottom left side of the editor window. You can also use the Split tab to see both the Source and Design views at once.
Add a server-side control to a page	Open the Toolbox if it's not already showing by clicking View, Toolbox on the main menu. (You can use the key combinations Ctrl+W and Ctrl+X also.) Click the control in the Toolbox. Drag the control onto the page.
Change the properties of controls on a page	Make sure the page editor is in Design mode. Highlight the control whose property you want to change. Select the property to edit in the Properties pane.
Turn on tracing	In Source code editing mode, edit the *Page* directive to include the attribute *Trace="true"*. Or Select the *Document* element from the combo box near the top of the Properties pane. Set the *Trace* property to *true*.
Change the size of a server-side control	Click the control to highlight it. Click one of the handles appearing on the border of the control and drag the mouse until the control is the correct size.
Add a handler for a control's default event	Double-click the control for which you want to handle the event. The code editor will appear, allowing you to add the code necessary to handle the specific event.
Change the layout characteristics of a page	Add a new style to the page by clicking Format, New Style on the main menu. Click Layout on the main menu and develop a style (defining a style also includes other elements in addition to the layout options, such as font face, size, and margins). Apply the style to the page or to single elements.

Chapter 4
Custom Rendered Controls

After completing this chapter, you will be able to

- Add a new project to the existing project in a Microsoft Visual Studio solution file.
- Create a server-side control that renders custom HTML.
- Add a server-side control to the Visual Studio Toolbox.
- Place a server-side control on a Web Form.
- Manage events in the control.
- Use ASP.NET to detect differences in client browsers and apply that information.

Chapter 3, "The Page Rendering Model," describes the fundamental architecture behind the ASP.NET rendering model. *System.Web.UI.Page* manages a list of server-side controls, and it's the job of each server-side control to render a particular portion of the page. ASP.NET broadly classifies server-side controls into two categories:

- Rendering controls (controls that completely manage the rendering process)
- Composite controls (multiple server-side controls bundled into a single unit)

This chapter focuses on the first type: custom rendered controls. In this chapter, you will see how the control works once it's part of a Web page. Along the way, the chapter covers topics such as how controls manage events and how they detect the differences in client browsers.

First, start by looking at the heart of the ASP.NET server-side control architecture—the *System.Web.UI.Control* class.

The *Control* Class

ASP.NET server-side controls derive from a class named *System.Web.UI.Control*. In fact, the *Control* class is the core of almost every user interface (UI) element in ASP.NET. Even *System.Web.UI.Page* is derived from the *Control* class. Table 4-1 shows a small sampling of the *System.Web.UI.Page* class.

TABLE 4-1 Sampling of the Page's Properties, Methods, and Events

Member	Description
Application	Reference to the *HttpApplicationState* object associated with the current request
Cache	Reference to the application's cache—an in-memory dictionary of application-wide state (usually for optimization)
Controls	The control collection maintained by *Page*
CreateChildControls	Virtual method during which the page constructs its control tree
Init	Event indicating the page has initialized
IsPostBack	Distinguishes the request as either a new request or a POST
Load	Event indicating the page has been loaded
RenderControl	Virtual method during which the page renders its contents
Request	Reference to a stateful object representing the incoming request
Response	Reference to a stateful object representing the outgoing response
Session	Reference to a stateful object representing information specific to the current request
Unload	Event indicating the page has unloaded

The entries in Table 4-1 show a small cross section of the functionality available in *System.Web.UI.Control*. Later you visit all these members while investigating ASP.NET Web Forms. Remember from the last chapter that ASP.NET Web Forms manage a collection of controls as part of their internal structure. As you add controls to a Web page, they're placed in the collection. When it comes time for a page to render its content back to the client, *System.Web.UI.Page* iterates the collection of controls and asks each one to render itself. If a control contains subcontrols (just as a page includes controls), ASP.NET walks down those collections as well. You can see the *RenderContents* method in Table 4-1. *RenderContents* takes a single argument of type *HtmlTextWriter*. You examine that class later in this chapter. Right now, think of it as the conduit through which you send the page's response back to the client.

Other elements of the *Control* class include items such as the following:

- Properties for managing the control's view state
- Properties for managing skins (to accommodate a consistent look and feel across multiple pages in a site)
- Properties for getting the parent control (in the case of composite controls) and the parent page
- Event handlers for the *Init*, *Load*, *PreRender*, and *Unload* events

- Methods for raising the *Init*, *Load*, *PreRender*, and *Unload* events
- Methods for managing child controls

In this chapter, you visit the most important topics while examining both rendered controls and composite controls. Although the *Page* class is sizable, it uses straightforward logic and unfolds nicely in practice. The easiest way to start is to jump into building a custom control.

Visual Studio and Custom Controls

In this section, you build a simple control (the default control Visual Studio generates for you) and see how it fits on a Web Form. Visual Studio creates a simple control that contains a single *Text* property, and it renders that *Text* property to the end browser. It's a good way to discover how server-side controls work.

Creating a custom control

1. Begin by opening the ControlsORama project from Chapter 3, as shown in the following graphic. Note: If you want to preserve the current state of ControlsORama, make a copy of the whole project directory and work on the copy. This example is built over this chapter and the next chapter to demonstrate the different approaches to developing controls.

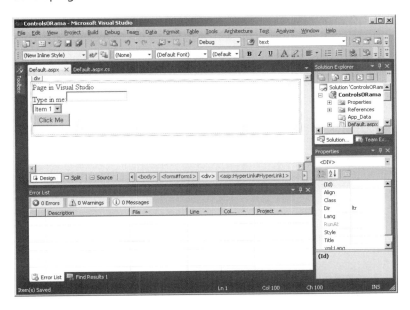

2. Add a new project to ControlsORama by right-clicking the Solution node in Solution Explorer, and clicking Add, New Project on the shortcut menu. Name the new project *CustomControlLib*. Select ASP.NET Server Control as the template, as shown here:

Visual Studio gives you a simple Web control named *ServerControl1* to start with. Listing 4-1 shows the default code generated by Visual Studio for a Web Control Library.

LISTING 4-1 Default custom control implementation

```
using System;
using System.Collections.Generic;
using System.ComponentModel;
using System.Linq;
using System.Text;
using System.Web;
using System.Web.UI;
using System.Web.UI.WebControls;

namespace CustomControlLib
{
    [DefaultProperty("Text")]
    [ToolboxData("<{0}:ServerControl1 runat=server></{0}:ServerControl1>")]

    public class ServerControl1 : WebControl
    {
        [Bindable(true)]
        [Category("Appearance")]
        [DefaultValue("")]
        [Localizable(true)]
        public string Text
        {
            get
            {
                String s = (String)ViewState["Text"];
```

```
            return ((s == null) ? "[" + this.ID + "]" : s);
        }
        set
        {
            ViewState["Text"] = value;
        }
    }

    protected override void RenderContents(HtmlTextWriter output)
    {
        output.Write(Text);
    }
  }
}
```

The code generated by Visual Studio includes a simple class derived from *System.Web.UI.WebControl.WebControl* (which derives from the standard *Control* class) with some standard properties added along the way. Notice that the code has a single property named *Text* that overrides the *Control RenderContents* method. This is a real, functioning control (although all it really does is act very much like a *Label*).

3. Build the project by selecting Build, Build Solution on the main menu.

4. Visual Studio makes the control available to your main project as soon as you compile it. You can also see that it has been added to your project another way: On the Tools menu, click Choose Toolbox Items, click the Browse button in the Choose Toolbox Items dialog box, navigate to the ControlsORama project directory, and then go to the CustomControlLib directory. Next, open the Bin\Debug directory. (Visual Studio builds debug versions by default.) Select the *CustomControlLib.DLL* assembly and click the Open button.

   SeverControl1 appears in the Choose Toolbox Items dialog box. The check box shows it as selected.

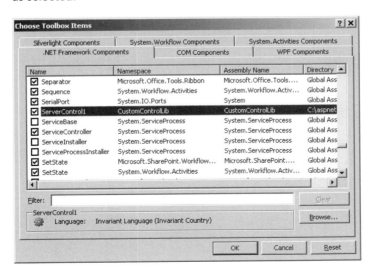

As soon as you click the OK button in the Choose Toolbox Items dialog box, the new *ServerControl1* will appear in the Toolbox. To make it easier to find the control, right-click the Toolbox and click Sort Items Alphabetically. Here is the *ServerControl1* as it appears in the Toolbox:

5. To see how the control works, you need to give it a home. Add a new page to the Web site. Select the ControlsORama project in Solution Explorer. Select Web Site, Add New Item, and add a Web Form. Name the Web Form *UseCustomControl.aspx*.

To place the control on the page, switch to Design mode. Drag the *ServerControl1* from the Toolbox onto the UseCustomControl Design view. You can see it appear as a rectangle in the upper left corner of the design surface:

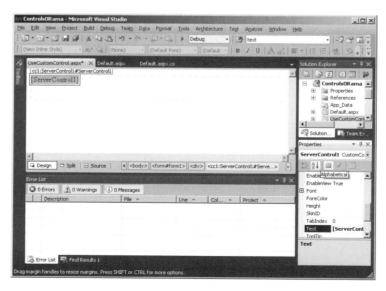

Some text in the control identifies it. Also, some text right above the control identifies the entire class name. Although the control is already selected, you might need to select it later whenever you switch to another page and then back to this one. You can select the new control using the drop-down list in the Properties pane in the lower right corner of the Visual Studio window. Change the *Text* property in the control and watch it show up in the Designer.

The Text property is rendered by the control. You can modify it here.

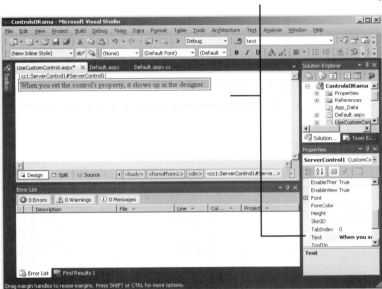

Take a look at the source code for the control again—specifically, look at the *RenderContents* method. Notice that the method simply uses the parameter (an *HtmlTextWriter*) to send the *Text* property to the browser. That's why the *Text* property shows after you change it in the Designer.

The following lines of code are what Visual Studio adds to the .aspx file to accommodate the control. You can see it by clicking the Source tab at the bottom of the code window in Visual Studio. The *Register* directive tells the ASP.NET runtime where to find the custom control (which assembly) and maps it to a tag prefix.

```
<%@ Register
Assembly="CustomControlLib, Version=1.0.0.0,
Culture=neutral,
PublicKeyToken=null"
Namespace="CustomControlLib" TagPrefix="cc1" %>
```

Listing 4-2 shows how the control is declared on the page when you set the control's *Text* property to the string value "When you set the control's property, it shows up in the designer."

LISTING 4-2 UseCustomControl.aspx markup with the custom Web control

```
<form id=form1 runat=server>
<div>
<cc1:ServerControl1 ID="ServerControl11"
   runat="server"
   Text="When you set the control's property,
       it shows up in the designer..." />

</div>
</form>
```

Now take a moment to change a few of the control's properties and see what happens in the Designer (for example, changing the font is always very noticeable). The properties you see in the Properties pane are all standard, and they show up because the control is derived from *System.Web.UI.WebControl*.

6. Now add a text box and a button to the Web page, separated by breaks (<br />). After you drop them on the page, Visual Studio adds the code shown in Listing 4-3.

LISTING 4-3 Revised UseCustomControl.aspx markup

```
    <form id=form1 runat=server>
    <div>
<cc1:ServerControl1 ID="ServerControl11"
   runat="server"
   Text="When you set the controls property,
       it shows up in the designer..." />
       <br />
       <br />
       <asp:Label ID="Label1"
       runat="server"
       Text="Type something here:">
       </asp:Label>
       <asp:TextBox ID="TextBox1" runat="server">
       </asp:TextBox>


       <br />
       <asp:Button ID="Button1"
       runat="server"           Text="Set Control Text" />
       </div>
    </form>
```

Notice that the standard ASP.NET controls (the button, the text box, and the label) all begin with the *asp:* prefix whereas the new custom control uses the prefix *cc1:*. Visual Studio made up the tag *cc1:* when you dropped the control into the Designer, although you could change this for this page by modifying the *TagPrefix* attribute in the *Register* directive.

7. Add an event handler for the button by double-clicking the button in the Designer. After Visual Studio adds the event handler for you, have the button pull the text from the *TextBox* and use it to set your custom control's *Text* property. To do this, type in the code you see in boldface type:

```
protected void Button1_Click(object sender, EventArgs e)
{
    this.ServerControl11.Text = this.TextBox1.Text;
}
```

Now press Ctrl+F5 to surf to the new page with the control. When you type something into the text box and click the button, the browser sends your request to the server. The server responds by taking the text from the *TextBox* and using it to set the *Text* property of the *ServerControl1*.

Notice how the new control appears in the control tree with tracing turned on. (You can turn on page tracing by setting the page's *Trace* property to *true*, as you did in Chapter 3.)

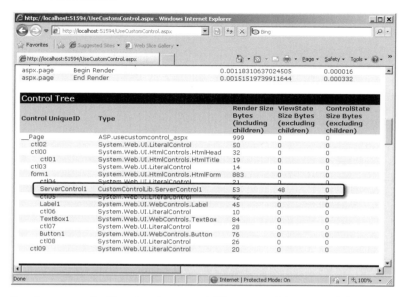

You have now built a simple control. The control framework is pretty flexible, and you can send out anything you want using the *RenderContents* method. Next, you develop a more sophisticated control that demonstrates more advanced control rendering.

A Palindrome Checker

The preceding exercise shows the fundamentals of writing a simple server-side control that renders client-side markup. However, ASP.NET already delivers a perfectly good *Label* control. Do you really need another one? To further illustrate rendered server-side controls, here's a simple control that checks to see whether the string typed by the client is a palindrome. In this exercise, you can observe some more advanced rendering techniques as well as how control events work.

Creating the *Palindrome Checker* control

1. To create the *Palindrome Checker* control, in Solution Explorer, right-click the CustomControlLib node, and click Add, New Item on the shortcut menu. Under Installed Templates, be sure the Web category is selected, and then highlight the ASP.NET Server Control node. Enter **PalindromeCheckerRenderedControl** in the Name text box, and click Add to generate the code.

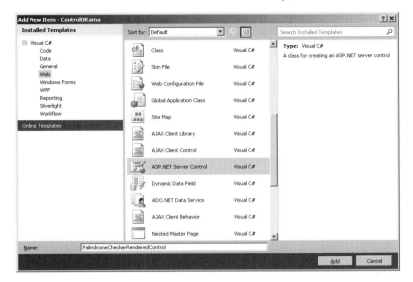

2. Add a method to the *PalindromeCheckerRenderedControl* class to test for a palindrome.
A *palindrome* is a word, sentence, or phrase that reads the same forward as it does
backward (for example, "radar"). Add a method to the control that checks to see
whether the internal text is a palindrome. This is a simple test for a palindrome that
converts the text to uppercase, reverses it, and then compares the result to the original
text. You should also strip out nonalphanumeric characters. Listing 4-4 shows some
code that does the trick. (This example uses some outdated font tags; you will replace
them with modern style font tags shortly.)

LISTING 4-4 Stripping alphanumerics

```
protected string StripNonAlphanumerics(string str)
{
    string strStripped = (String)str.Clone();
    if (str != null)
    {
        char[] rgc = strStripped.ToCharArray();
        int i = 0;
        foreach (char c in rgc)
        {
            if (char.IsLetterOrDigit(c))
            {
                i++;
            }
            else
            {
                strStripped = strStripped.Remove(i, 1);
            }
        }
    }
    return strStripped;
}
```

```
protected bool CheckForPalindrome()

{
   if (this.Text != null)
   {
      String strControlText = this.Text;
      String strTextToUpper = null;
      strTextToUpper = Text.ToUpper();
      strControlText =
              this.StripNonAlphanumerics(strTextToUpper);
      char[] rgcReverse = strControlText.ToCharArray();
      Array.Reverse(rgcReverse);
      String strReverse = new string(rgcReverse);
      if (strControlText == strReverse)
      {
         return true;
      }
      else
      {
         return false;
      }
   }
   else
   {
      return false;
   }
}
```

3. Change the rendering method to print palindromes in blue and nonpalindromes in red.
The *RenderContent* method takes a single parameter of type *HtmlTextWriter*. In addition to allowing you to stream text to the browser, *HtmlTextWriter* is full of other very
useful features you will see shortly. For now, you can treat it very much like *Response.
Write*. Whatever you send through the *Write* method ends up at the client's browser.

```
protected override void RenderContent(HtmlTextWriter output)
{

   if (this.CheckForPalindrome())
   {
      output.Write("This is a palindrome: <BR/>");
      output.Write("<FONT size=5 color=blue>");
      output.Write("<B>");
      output.Write(this.Text);
      output.Write("</B>");
      output.Write("</FONT>");
   } else {
      output.Write("This is NOT a palindrome <BR/>");
      output.Write("<FONT size=5 color=red>");
      output.Write("<B>");
      output.Write(this.Text);
      output.Write("</B>");
      output.Write("</FONT>");
   }}
```

4. Build the project by selecting Build, Build Solution on the main menu.

5. Visual Studio should add the *PalindromeCheckerRenderedControl* to the Toolbox. If not, you can add it manually by right-clicking the Toolbox and clicking Choose Item. Use the Browse button to find the *CustomControlLib.DLL* assembly, and then select it. Visual Studio loads the new control in the Toolbox.

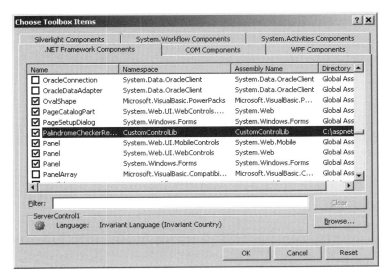

6. Add a page to use the palindrome checker control by adding a new Web Form to the ControlsORama project and naming it UsePalindromeCheckerControls.aspx. Drag the *PalindromeCheckerRenderedControl* to the page. Add a *TextBox* and a button so that you can add a palindrome to the control and check it.

7. Add a handler for the button by double-clicking the button. Visual Studio will add a handler to the page. In the handler, set the *Text* property of the *PalindromeCheckerRenderedControl* to the *TextBox.Text* property.

```
public partial class UsePalindromeCheckerControls : System.Web.UI.Page
{
    protected void Button1_Click(object sender, EventArgs e)
    {
        this.PalindromeCheckerRenderedControl1.Text = this.TextBox1.Text;
    }

}
```

8. Run the page and test for a palindrome. Palindromes should appear in blue and nonpalindromes in red.

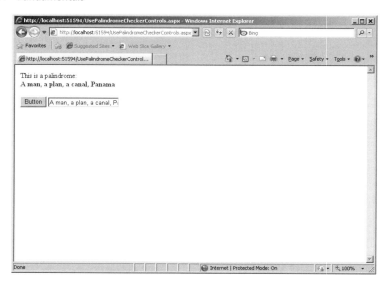

Controls and Events

The *PalindromeCheckerRenderedControl* shows how to render control content depending on the state of the *Text* property. Although that's useful in itself, it's often helpful to alert the host page to the fact that a palindrome was found by exposing an event from the control.

Most of the ASP.NET standard server-side controls already support events. You've already seen how the *Button* control sends an event to the host page when it is clicked. You can actually do this type of thing with any control. Next, you add a *PalindromeFound* event to the *PalindromeCheckerRenderedControl*.

Adding a *PalindromeFound* event

1. Open the PalindromeCheckerRenderedControl.cs file. To add a *PalindromeFound* event, type in the following line:

```
public class PalindromeCheckerRenderedControl : WebControl
{
    public event EventHandler PalindromeFound;
            // Other palindrome control code goes here
}
```

2. Once hosts have subscribed to the event, they'll want to know when the event fires. To do this, fire an event on detecting a palindrome. The best place to do this is in the *Text* property's setter. Add the following bold type lines of code to the palindrome's *Text* property and rebuild the project:

```
[Bindable(true)]
[Category(Appearance)]
[DefaultValue("")]
```

```
[Localizable(true)]
public string Text
{
    get
    {
        string s = (string)ViewState[Text];
        return ((s == null) ? String.Empty : s);
    }

    set
    {
        ViewState[Text] = value;
        if (this.CheckForPalindrome())
        {
            if (PalindromeFound != null)
            {
                PalindromeFound(this, EventArgs.Empty);
            }
        }
    }
}
```

Notice that the code generated by Visual Studio 2010 stores the value found in the *Text* property in the control's *ViewState*. That way, the property retains its value between posts. You examine *ViewState* more closely later in this chapter.

3. Now wire the event in the host page by remove the current instance of the *PalindromeCheckerRenderedControl* from the page and drop a new instance on the page. This refreshes the *CustomControlLib.DLL* assembly so that the changes (the new event) appear in Visual Studio. Select the *PalindromeCheckerRenderedControl* on the page and click the Events button (the little lightning bolt) in the Properties pane in Visual Studio. Double-click the text box next to the *PalindromeFound* event. Visual Studio creates an event handler for you.

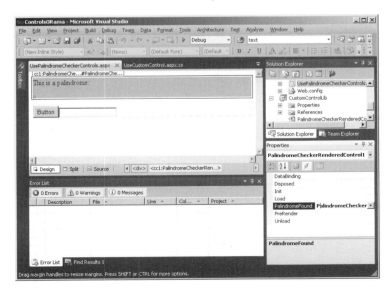

4. Respond to the *PalindromeFound* event. The example here simply prints some text out to the browser using *Response.Write.*

```
public partial class UsePalindromeCheckerControls : System.Web.UI.Page
{
    protected void Page_Load(object sender, EventArgs e)
    {
    }
    protected void Button1_Click(object sender, EventArgs e)
    {
        this.PalindromeCheckerRenderedControl1.Text =
                this.TextBox1.Text;
    }
    protected void PalindromeCheckerControl1_PalindromeFound(
        object sender, EventArgs e)
    {
        Response.Write("The page detected a PalindromeFound event");
    }
}
```

Run the page. You should see something like the following when you type a palindrome:

Now that the control renders palindromes correctly and has an event, look more closely at the parameter passed in during the call to *Render: HtmlTextWriter.*

HtmlTextWriter and Controls

Go back and briefly review the control's *RenderContents* method. Notice that the *RenderContents* method places literal font tags to change the color of the palindrome text. Although this is certainly effective, this technique has a couple of downsides. For example, HTML is defined by multiple standards. That is, browsers running both HTML version 3.2 and version 4.0 occur in nature. Certain HTML elements have changed between version 3.2 and version 4.0. If you render all your HTML directly expecting requests from a certain kind of browser, your users might be surprised if they browse to your page with a new browser that interprets HTML differently.

Note The .NET Framework includes multiple versions of the *HtmlTextWriter* class: *Html32TextWriter*, *HtmlTextWriter*, *XhtmlTextWriter*, and *ChtmlTextWriter*. When a request comes from a browser, it always includes some header information indicating what kind of browser made the request. These days, most browsers are capable of interpreting the current version of HTML. In this case, ASP.NET passes in a normal *HtmlTextWriter* to the *RenderControl* method. However, if you happen to get a request from a browser that understands only HTML 3.2, ASP.NET passes in an *Html32TextWriter*. The classes are similar as far as their use and they can be interchanged. *Html32TextWriter* emits certain tags (such as table tags) in HTML 3.2 format, whereas *HtmlTextWriter* emits the same tags in HTML 4.0 format. Information in *machine.config* and the browser capabilities configuration help ASP.NET figure out what kind of *HtmlTextWriter* to use. The browser capability information deduced by the ASP.NET runtime can be used for more than simply selecting the correct *HtmlTextWriter*. The *Request* property (available as part of the *HttpContext* and the *Page*) includes a reference to the *Browser* object. This object includes a number of flags indicating various pieces of information, such as the type of browser making the request, whether the browser supports scripting, and the name of the platform the browser is running on. This information comes down as part of the headers included with each request. The ASP.NET runtime runs the headers against some well-known regular expressions in the configuration files to figure out the capabilities. For example, here's a short listing that illustrates how ASP.NET figures out whether the browser making the request supports frames:

```
public class TestForFramesControl : Control
{
    protected override void RenderContents(HtmlTextWriter output)
    {
        if (Page.Request.Browser.Frames)
        {
            output.Write(
                This browser supports Frames);
        }
        else
        {
            output.Write(No Frames here);
        }
    }
}
```

To get a feel for using the more advanced capabilities of *HtmlTextWriter*, replace the hard-coded font tags in the *RenderContents* method of the *PalindromeCheckerRenderedControl* with code that uses the *HtmlTextWriter* facilities.

Using the *HtmlTextWriter*

1. Open the PalindromeCheckerRenderedControl.cs file.

2. Update the *RenderContents* method to use the *HtmlTextWriter* methods. Use *HtmlTextWriter.RenderBeginTag* to start a font tag and a bold tag. Use *HtmlTextWriter.AddStyleAttribute* to change the color of the font to blue.

```
protected override void RenderContents(HtmlTextWriter output)
{
    if (this.CheckForPalindrome())
    {
        output.Write("This is a palindrome: <br/>");
        output.RenderBeginTag(HtmlTextWriterTag.Font);
        output.AddStyleAttribute(HtmlTextWriterStyle.Color, "blue");
        output.RenderBeginTag(HtmlTextWriterTag.B);
        output.Write(Text);
        output.RenderEndTag(); // bold
        output.RenderEndTag(); // font
    } else {
        output.Write("This is not a palindrome: <br/>");
        output.RenderBeginTag(HtmlTextWriterTag.Font);
        output.AddStyleAttribute(HtmlTextWriterStyle.Color, "red");
        output.RenderBeginTag(HtmlTextWriterTag.B);
        output.RenderBeginTag(HtmlTextWriterTag.B);
        output.Write(Text);
        output.RenderEndTag(); // bold
        output.RenderEndTag(); // font
    }
}
```

The *HtmlTextWriter* class and the enumerations include support to hide all the oddities of switching between HTML 3.2 and 4.0. Listing 4-5 shows how a table would be rendered using an HTML 4.0–compliant response. Listing 4-6 shows how a table would be rendered using an HTML 3.2–compliant response.

LISTING 4-5 HTML 4.0 rendered control

```
<span id="PalindromeCheckerRenderedControl1">
This is a palindrome:
<br/>
<font><b style="color:blue;">Radar</b></font>
</span>
```

LISTING 4-6 HTML 3.2 rendered control

```
<span id="PalindromeCheckerRenderedControl1">
This is a palindrome:
<br/>
<font color=blue><b>Radar</b></font>
</span>
```

Controls and *ViewState*

Before leaving the topic of rendered controls, take a look at the issue of view state managed by controls. If you go back to some of the classic Active Server Pages (ASP) examples in earlier chapters, you might notice something disconcerting about the way some of the controls rendered after posting back. After you select something in the combo box and make a round-trip to the server, by the time the response gets back, the controls (especially selection controls) have lost their state. Recall that the basic Web programming model is all about making snapshots of the server's state and displaying them using a browser. It essentially tries to perform stateful user interface (UI) development over a disconnected protocol.

ASP.NET server-side controls include a facility for holding onto a page's visual state—it's a property in the Page named *ViewState*, and you can easily access it any time you need it. *ViewState* is a dictionary (a name/value collection) that stores any serializable object.

Most ASP.NET server-side controls manage their visual state by storing and retrieving items in the *ViewState*. For example, a selection control might maintain the index of the selected item between posts so that the control knows which item has its *selected* attribute assigned and can render the appropriate markup to show that item as selected in the user's browser.

The entire state of a page is encoded in a hidden field between posts. For example, if you browse to an .aspx page and view the source code coming from the server, you'll see the *ViewState* come through as a BASE 64–encoded byte stream.

To get a feel for how *ViewState* works, add some code to keep track of the palindromes that have been viewed through the control.

Using *ViewState*

1. Open the PalindromeCheckerRenderedControl.cs file.

2. Add *System.Collections* to the list of using directives.

   ```
   using System;
   using System.Collections.Generic;
   using System.ComponentModel;
   using System.Text;
   using System.Web.UI;
   using System.Web.UI.WebControls;
   using System.Collections
   ```

3. Add an *ArrayList* to the control to hold the viewed palindromes. Update the *Text* property's setter to store text in the view state if the text is a palindrome:

   ```
   public class PalindromeCheckerRenderedControl : WebControl


   {
       public event EventHandler PalindromeFound; // public event
       ArrayList alPalindromes = new ArrayList();
   ```

```
[Bindable(true)]
[Category(Appearance)]
[DefaultValue("")]
[Localizable(true)]
public string Text
{
    get
    {
        String s = (String)ViewState[Text];
        return ((s == null) ? String.Empty : s);
    }
    set
    {
        ViewState[Text] = value;
        string text = value;
        this.alPalindromes =
            (ArrayList)this.ViewState["palindromes"];
        if (this.alPalindromes == null)
        {
            this.alPalindromes = new ArrayList();
        }
        if (this.CheckForPalindrome())
        {
            if (PalindromeFound != null)
            {
                PalindromeFound(this, EventArgs.Empty);
            }
            alPalindromes.Add(text);
        }
        ViewState.Add("palindromes", alPalindromes);
    }
}
```

4. Add a method to render the palindrome collection as a table, and update the *RenderContents* method to render the viewed palindromes:

```
protected void RenderPalindromesInTable(HtmlTextWriter output)
{
    output.AddAttribute(HtmlTextWriterAttribute.Width, "50%");
    output.AddAttribute(HtmlTextWriterAttribute.Border, "1");
    output.RenderBeginTag(HtmlTextWriterTag.Table); //<table>

    foreach (string s in this.alPalindromes)
    {
        output.RenderBeginTag(HtmlTextWriterTag.Tr); // <tr>
        output.AddAttribute(HtmlTextWriterAttribute.Align, "left");
        output.AddStyleAttribute(HtmlTextWriterStyle.FontSize, "medium");
        output.AddStyleAttribute(HtmlTextWriterStyle.Color, "blue");
        output.RenderBeginTag(HtmlTextWriterTag.Td); // <td>
        output.Write(s);
        output.RenderEndTag(); // </td>
        output.RenderEndTag(); // </tr>

    }
```

```
      output.RenderEndTag(); // </table>
}

protected override void RenderContents (HtmlTextWriter output)
{
   if (this.CheckForPalindrome())
   {
      output.Write(This is a palindrome: <br>);
      output.RenderBeginTag(HtmlTextWriterTag.Font);
      output.AddStyleAttribute(HtmlTextWriterStyle.Color, blue);
      output.RenderBeginTag(HtmlTextWriterTag.B);
      output.Write(Text);
      output.RenderEndTag(); // bold
      output.RenderEndTag(); // font
   } else {
      output.Write(This is NOT a palindrome: <br>);
      output.RenderBeginTag(HtmlTextWriterTag.Font);
      output.AddStyleAttribute(HtmlTextWriterStyle.Color, red);
      output.RenderBeginTag(HtmlTextWriterTag.B);
      output.Write(Text);
      output.RenderEndTag(); // bold
      output.RenderEndTag(); // font
   }

   output.Write("<br>");
   RenderPalindromesInTable(output);
}
```

5. Build and run the application. When you surf to the page holding the palindrome checker, you should see the previously found palindromes in the table.

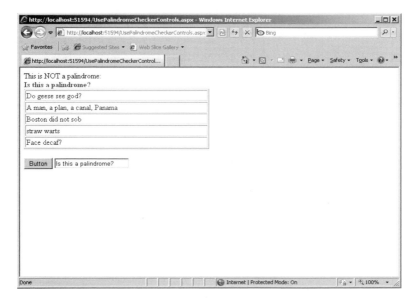

Now that the control stores more information in the *ViewState*, the HTML response resulting from postbacks increases in size as the _VIEWSTATE field in the response grows. Add a few more palindromes to the page and view the source that's sent to the browser each time. You'll see the VIEWSTATE hidden field grow in size with each postback. The caveat here is that introducing controls that use view state increases the size of the HTTP payload coming back to the browser. Use the view state judiciously because overuse can bog down a site's performance.

Chapter 4 Quick Reference

To	Do This
Create a custom control that takes over the rendering process	Derive a class from *System.Web.UI.Control*. Override the *RenderContents* method. Visual Studio includes a project type, ASP.NET *ServerControl*, that fits the bill.
Add a custom control to the Toolbox	Open the Toolbox if it's not already showing by selecting View, Toolbox on the main menu. Right-click anywhere in the Toolbox, and click Choose Items on the shortcut menu. Choose a control from the list, or browse to the assembly containing the control.
Change the properties of controls on a page	Make sure the page editor is in Design mode. Highlight the control whose property you want to change. Select the property to edit in the Properties pane.
Manage events fired by controls on a page	Make sure the page editor is in Design mode. Highlight the control containing the event you want your page to handle. Select the event in the event window (you can highlight it by clicking the lightning bolt button in the Properties pane). Double-click in the combo box next to the event to have Visual Studio insert the given handler for you, or insert your own event handler name in the field next to the event name.
Store view state information that lives beyond the scope of the page	Use the *ViewState* property of the control (a name/value dictionary) that contains serializable types. Just be sure to use the same index to retrieve the information as you do to store the information.
Write browser version–independent rendering code	Use the *HtmlTextWriter* tag-rendering methods for specific tags instead of hard-coding them. The *RenderContents* method uses the correct *HtmlTextWriter* based on header information coming down from the browser.

Chapter 5
Composite Controls

After completing this chapter, you will be able to

- Create a binary composite custom control.

- Create a composite *User* control.

- Use both kinds of controls in an application.

- Recognize when each kind of control is appropriate.

Chapter 4, "Custom Rendered Controls," covers the details of controls that do custom rendering, whereas this chapter covers the other kind of control: composite controls. ASP.NET defines two broad categories of composite controls—binary custom controls and user custom controls. Each type of composite control has advantages and disadvantages, which this chapter discusses. First, we'll explore the primary differences between rendered controls and composite-style controls.

Composite Controls versus Rendered Controls

Recall that custom rendered controls completely form and tailor the HTML returned to the client by using the *System.Web.UI.Control.RenderControl* method. Custom rendered controls take over the entire rendering process. With custom rendered controls, you have extraordinary flexibility and power over the HTML emitted by your Web site—all the way down to the individual HTML tag level.

However, with that power and flexibility also comes the need to keep track of an enormous amount of detail. For example, if you were to add an input button to a custom rendered control, you'd need to insert the correct HTML to describe the button in the response stream heading back to the client. Things get even more difficult when you decide to add more complex controls such as selection controls that might need to track collections of items. Even though input buttons and selection controls are easy to describe in HTML, you have seen that ASP.NET already includes server-side control classes that render the correct tags. The standard ASP.NET controls greatly simplify user interface (UI) programming for Web Forms.

Composite controls take advantage of these server-side controls that have already been written. Composite controls are *composed* from other controls. To illustrate the utility of composite controls, imagine you're working on a number of projects with login screens that require a similar look and feel. On the one hand, you know that it's fairly easy to build Web Forms in Microsoft Visual Studio. However, if you run into a situation that requires the same group of controls to appear together in several instances, it's pretty tedious to re-create those pages repeatedly. ASP.NET solves this problem with composite controls.

If you need common login functionality to span several Web sites, you might group user name/password labels and text boxes together in a single control. Then, when you want to use the login page on a site, you simply drop the controls *en masse* on the new form. The controls (and the execution logic) instantly combine, so you don't need to keep writing the same HTML over and over.

 Note Beginning with version 2.0, ASP.NET includes a set of login composite controls, so you don't need to write new ones from scratch. However, they are mentioned here because they represent an excellent illustration of the power of composite controls.

We'll begin by looking at custom composite controls.

Custom Composite Controls

Chapter 4 shows how binary custom controls render custom HTML to the browser. The factor most distinguishing this kind of control is that these controls override the *RenderContents* method. Remember, the *System.Web.UI.Page* class manages a list of server-side controls. When ASP.NET asks the whole page to render, it goes to each control on the page and asks it to render. In the case of a rendering control, the control simply pushes some text into the stream bound for the browser. Likewise, when the page rendering mechanism encounters a composite-style control, the composite control walks its list of child controls, asking each one to render—just as the *Page* walks its own list of controls.

Composite controls can contain an arbitrary collection of controls (as many children as memory will accommodate), and the controls can be nested as deeply as necessary. Of course, there's a practical limit to the number and depth of the child controls. Adding too many controls or nesting them too deeply adds complexity to a page, and it can become unsightly. In addition, adding too many nested controls can greatly inhibit the performance of the application—it takes time to walk the control collection and have each one render.

In Chapter 4, you created a control that checks for palindromes. When the control's *Text* property is set to a palindrome, the control renders the palindrome in blue text, adds it to an *ArrayList*, and then renders the contents of the palindrome collection as a table. Here, you build a similar control; however, this time it is a composite control.

Building the palindrome checker as a composite custom control

1. Open the ControlsORama project. Highlight the CustomControlLib project in Solution Explorer. Right-click the project node and click Add, New Item. Create an ASP.NET Server Control and name it *PalindromeCheckerCompositeControl.cs*. Use the ASP.NET Server Control template (as you did with the PalindromeCheckerRenderedControl in Chapter 4).

2. After Visual Studio creates the code, do the following:

   a. Edit the code to change the derivation from *WebControl* to *CompositeControl*. Deriving from the *CompositeControl* also adds the *INamingContainer* interface to the derivation list. (*INamingContainer* is useful to help ASP.NET manage unique IDs for the control's children.)

   b. Add the *PalindromeFound* event that the host page can use to listen for palindrome detections (just as you did in the last chapter).

   c. Remove the *RenderContents* method.

   d. Add four fields to the control—a *TextBox*, a *Button*, a *Label*, and a *LiteralControl*.

   The code should look something like this when you're finished:

```
public class PalindromeCheckerCompositeControl :
        CompositeControl
{
    protected TextBox textboxPalindrome;
    protected Button buttonCheckForPalindrome;
    protected Label labelForTextBox;
    protected LiteralControl literalcontrolPalindromeStatus;
    public event EventHandler PalindromeFound;
...
// RenderContents method removed.
}
```

   Leave the *Text* property intact. You still need it in this control.

   The control is very much like the one in Chapter 4. However, this version includes the palindrome *TextBox* and the *Button* to invoke palindrome checking, and it contains a literal control to display whether the current property is a palindrome.

3. Borrow the *StripNonAlphanumerics* and *CheckForPalindrome* methods from the *PalindromeCheckerRenderedControl*:

```
protected string StripNonAlphanumerics(string str)
{
    string strStripped = (String)str.Clone();

    if (str != null)
    {
    char[] rgc = strStripped.ToCharArray();
```

```
        int i = 0;

        foreach (char c in rgc)
        {
            if (char.IsLetterOrDigit(c))
            {
                i++;
            }

            else
            {
                strStripped = strStripped.Remove(i, 1);
            }
        }
    }

    return strStripped;
}

protected bool CheckForPalindrome()
{
    if (this.Text != null)
    {
        String strControlText = this.Text;
        String strTextToUpper = null;

        strTextToUpper = Text.ToUpper();

        strControlText = this.StripNonAlphanumerics(strTextToUpper);

        char[] rgcReverse = strControlText.ToCharArray();
        Array.Reverse(rgcReverse);
        String strReverse = new string(rgcReverse);
        if (strControlText == strReverse)
        {
            return true;
        }
        else
        {
            return false;
        }
    }
    else
    {
        return false;
    }
}
```

4. Add an event handler to be applied to the *Button* (which you install on the page soon).
   Because this is a binary control without Designer support, you need to add the event
   handler using the text wizard (that is, you need to type it by hand).

```
public void OnCheckPalindrome(Object o, System.EventArgs ea)
{
    this.Text = this.textboxPalindrome.Text;
    this.CheckForPalindrome();
}
```

5. Add an override for the *CreateChildControls* method. Overriding the *CreateChildControls* method is what really distinguishes composite controls from rendered controls. In the method, you need to create each *UI* element by hand, set the properties you want to appear in the control, and add the individual control to the composite control's list of controls.

```
protected override void CreateChildControls()
{
    labelForTextBox = new Label();
    labelForTextBox.Text = "Enter a palindrome: ";
    this.Controls.Add(labelForTextBox);

    textboxPalindrome = new TextBox();
    this.Controls.Add(textboxPalindrome);

    Controls.Add(new LiteralControl("<br/>"));

    buttonCheckForPalindrome = new Button();
    buttonCheckForPalindrome.Text = "Check for Palindrome";
    buttonCheckForPalindrome.Click += new EventHandler(OnCheckPalindrome);
    this.Controls.Add(buttonCheckForPalindrome);

    Controls.Add(new LiteralControl("<br/>"));

    literalcontrolPalindromeStatus = new LiteralControl();
    Controls.Add(literalcontrolPalindromeStatus);

    Controls.Add(new LiteralControl("<br/>"));

    this.ChildControlsCreated = true;
}
```

Although the preceding code is pretty straightforward, a couple of lines deserve special note. First is the use of the *LiteralControl* to render the line breaks. Remember, every element on the page (or in this case, the control) is rendered using a server-side control. If you want any literal text rendered as part of your control, or if you need HTML markup that isn't included as a provided ASP.NET control (such as the <br/> element), you need to package it in a server-side control. The job of a *LiteralControl* is to take the contents (the *Text* property) and simply render it to the outgoing stream.

The second item to notice is how the event handler is hooked to the *Button* using a delegate. When you use Visual Studio Designer support, you can usually wire up event handlers by clicking a UI element in the Designer—at which point Visual Studio adds the code automatically. However, because there's no Designer support here, you need to handle the event hookup manually.

6. Show the palindrome status whenever the *Text* property is set by modifying the *Text* property to match the following bit of code. The *Text* property's setter checks for a palindrome and renders the result in the *LiteralControl* you added in step 2. The setter should instantiate the palindrome list if it is not in the view state. It should also raise the *PalindromeFound* event.

```
private string text;

public string Text
{

  get
  {
    return text;
  }
  set
  {
    text = value;
    this.alPalindromes = (ArrayList)this.ViewState["palindromes"];
    if (this.alPalindromes == null)
    {
      this.alPalindromes = new ArrayList();
    }

    if (this.CheckForPalindrome())
    {
      if (PalindromeFound != null)
      {
        PalindromeFound(this, EventArgs.Empty);
      }

        literalcontrolPalindromeStatus.Text =
          String.Format(
          "This is a palindrome <br/><FONT size=\"5\" color=\"blue\"><B>{0}</B></
FONT>",
          text);
    }
    else
    {
        literalcontrolPalindromeStatus.Text =
          String.Format(
          "This is NOT a palindrome <br/><FONT size=\"5\" color=\"red\"><B>{0}</B></
FONT>",
          text);
      }
  }
}
```

7. Show the palindromes in a table, just as the rendered version of this control did, by first adding an *ArrayList* and a *Table* control to the *PalindromeCheckerCompositeControl* class.

```
using System.Collections;

public class PalindromeCheckerCompositeControl :
CompositeControl
{

    protected Table tablePalindromes;
    protected ArrayList alPalindromes;

}
```

8. Add a method to build the palindrome table based on the contents of the *ArrayList*. Check to see whether the array list is stored in the *ViewState* (it is created within the property setter). If it's not, populate it. Iterate through the palindrome collection and add a *TableRow* and a *TableCell* to the table for each palindrome found:

```
protected void BuildPalindromesTable()
{
    this.alPalindromes = (ArrayList)this.ViewState["palindromes"];
    if (this.alPalindromes != null)

    {
        foreach (string s in this.alPalindromes)
        {
            TableCell tableCell = new TableCell();
            tableCell.BorderStyle = BorderStyle.Double;
            tableCell.BorderWidth = 3;
            tableCell.Text = s;
            TableRow tableRow = new TableRow();
            tableRow.Cells.Add(tableCell);
            this.tablePalindromes.Rows.Add(tableRow);
        }
    }
}
```

9. Update the *Text* property's setter to manage the table. Add palindromes to the *ArrayList* as they're found, and build the palindrome table each time the text is changed:

```
public string Text
{
  get
  {
    return text;
  }
  set
  {
    text = value;
```

```
        this.alPalindromes = (ArrayList)this.ViewState["palindromes"];
        if (this.alPalindromes == null)
        {
          this.alPalindromes = new ArrayList();
        }

        if (this.CheckForPalindrome())
        {
          if (PalindromeFound != null)
          {
            PalindromeFound(this, EventArgs.Empty);
          }

          alPalindromes.Add(text);

           literalcontrolPalindromeStatus.Text =
              String.Format(
              "This is a palindrome <br/><FONT size=\"5\" color=\"blue\"><B>{0}</B></
FONT>",
              text);
        }
        else
        {
           literalcontrolPalindromeStatus.Text =
              String.Format(
              "This is NOT a palindrome <br/><FONT size=\"5\" color=\"red\"><B>{0}</B></
FONT>",
              text);
         }


        this.ViewState.Add("palindromes", alPalindromes);
        this.BuildPalindromesTable();

    }
}
```

10. Build the project and add the *PalindromeCheckerCompositeControl* control to the
ControlsORama UsePalindromeCheckerControls.aspx page. If you are extending the
example from the last chapter, add a line break (<br/>) after the rendered control from
the last chapter. Add a *label* or some text preceding the control to indicate that the
next control is the composite control and add one more line break. Then, drag the
PalindromeCheckerCompositeControl control directly from the Toolbox to the page.
When you run the page, this control checks for palindromes and keeps a record of
the palindromes that have been found, as shown in the following graphic. (Tracing
is turned on in this example so that you can see the control tree later.) Note that this
example extends the previous chapter's example and the page includes the controls
added from the previous chapter.

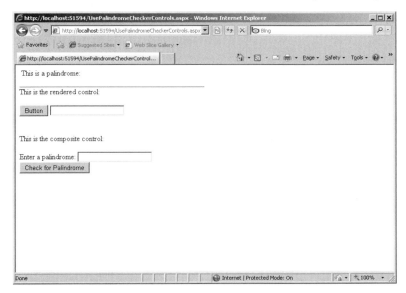

With tracing turned on, you can look farther down and see the control tree. Notice how the *PalindromeCheckerCompositeControl* acts as a main node on the tree and that the composite control's child controls are shown under the PalindromeCheckerCompositeControl node.

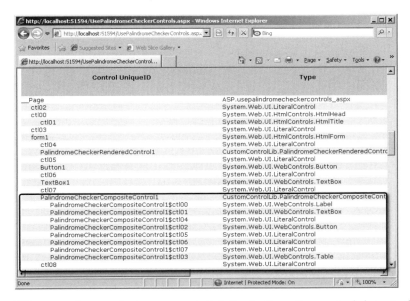

When you type palindromes and click the button, the control detects them. The control displays the current *Text* property in red if the entered text is *not* a palindrome and in blue if it *is* a palindrome. You can also see the table rendering, showing the currently found palindromes:

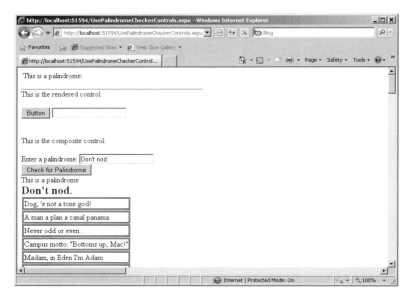

The palindrome checker is a good example of a binary composite control. The composite control lives entirely within the *CustomControlLib* assembly and does not have any Designer support at present. (You could add code to support high-quality design time support, but that's beyond the scope of this chapter.) The next section discusses an alternative to coding a composite control entirely by hand: The second way to create composite controls is by using a *User* control.

User Controls

User controls are composite controls that contain child controls very much like binary composite controls do. However, instead of deriving from *System.Web.UI.CompositeControl*, they derive from *System.Web.UI.UserControl*. Perhaps a better description is that they're very much like miniature Web Forms. They have a UI component (an .ascx file) that works with the Visual Studio Designer, and they employ a matching class to manage the execution. However, unlike a Web Form, you can drag them onto the Toolbox and drop them into a Web Form.

To get a good idea of how Web *User* controls work, you can build the palindrome checker as a *User* control.

Building the palindrome checker as a *User* control

1. Open the ControlsORama project (if it's not already open). Highlight the ControlsORama Web site in Solution Explorer (*not* the CustomControlLib project as in

earlier steps). Right-click the site and click Add New Item. Select the Web User Control template and name the control *PalindromeCheckerUserControl.ascx*, as shown in the following graphic:

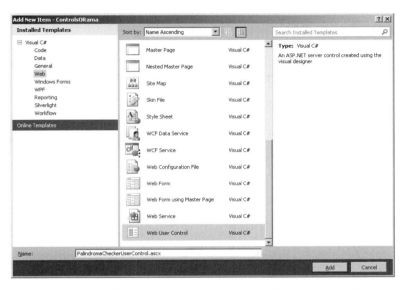

2. In this step, you add new controls. Notice that Visual Studio might drop you into the Designer. (If instead you are in code view, switch to the Design view by clicking the Design tab.) *User* controls are Designer friendly. Drag a *Label*, a *TextBox*, a *Button*, and another *Label* from the Toolbox onto the *User* control. Delete the *Text* property from the second label so that it shows its identifier. Format them as shown in the following graphic:

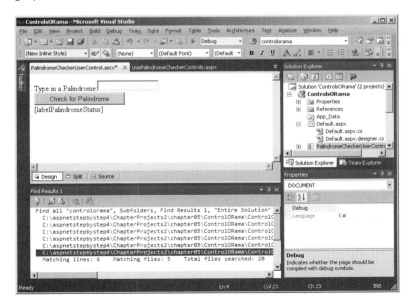

Name the second label *labelPalindromeStatus* to make it easier to use from within the code beside.

3. Borrow the *StripNonAlphanumerics* and *CheckForPalindrome* methods from the *PalindromeCheckerCompositeControl* class by opening the source code file PalindromeCheckerCompositeControl.cs and copying these methods into the *PalindromeCheckerUserControl* class in the PalindromeCheckerUserControl.ascx.cs file. Note that this code depends on a *Text* property, which you've not added quite yet. The program will compile after step 5.

```
protected string StripNonAlphanumerics(string str)
{
    string strStripped = (String)str.Clone();
    if (str != null)
    {
        char[] rgc = strStripped.ToCharArray();
        int i = 0;
        foreach (char c in rgc)
        {
            if (char.IsLetterOrDigit(c))
            {
                i++;
            }
            else

            {
                strStripped = strStripped.Remove(i, 1);
            }
        }
    }

    return strStripped;
}

protected bool CheckForPalindrome()
{
    if (this.Text != null)
    {
        String strControlText = this.Text;
        String strTextToUpper = null;

        strTextToUpper = Text.ToUpper();

        strControlText = this.StripNonAlphanumerics(strTextToUpper);

        char[] rgcReverse = strControlText.ToCharArray();
        Array.Reverse(rgcReverse);
        String strReverse = new string(rgcReverse);
        if (strControlText == strReverse)
        {
            return true;
        }
        else
        {
            return false;
```

```
      }
    }
    else
    {
      return false;
    }
  }
```

4. Add the *PalindromeFound* event to the control class:

```
public event EventHandler PalindromeFound; // public event
```

5. Open the code file and add a text member variable and a *Text* property, very much like the other composite control implemented. Unlike binary composite controls, *User* controls aren't generated with default properties. (There are some minor changes, such as the use of a *Label* control instead of the *Literal* control for accepting the palindrome status, so be sure to make the necessary adjustments if you copy and paste code from the previous control.)

```
private String text;

public string Text
{
  get
  {

    return text;
  }
  set
  {
    text = value;

    if (this.CheckForPalindrome())
    {
      if (PalindromeFound != null)
      {
        PalindromeFound(this, EventArgs.Empty);
      }

      this.labelPalindromeStatus.Text =
          String.Format(
          "This is a palindrome <br/><FONT size=\"5\" color=\"blue\"><B>{0}</B></
FONT>",
          text);
    }
    else
    {
      this.labelPalindromeStatus.Text =
          String.Format(
          "This is NOT a palindrome <br/><FONT size=\"5\" color=\"red\"><B>{0}</B></
FONT>",
          text);
    }
  }
}
```

6. Now add support for keeping track of palindromes by adding an *ArrayList* to the control class (be sure to include a *using* statement for *System.Collections* at the top of the PalindromeCheckerUserControl.ascx.cs file to resolve the *ArrayList*):

```
ArrayList alPalindromes;
```

7. Add a *Table* to the control by switching to the *PalindromeCheckerUserControl* Design view and dragging a *Table* onto the form.

8. Add a method to build the table of palindromes. It's very much like the one in the *PalindromeCheckerCompositeControl*, except the name of the table is different: Visual Studio automatically names the table *Table1* in this case.

```
protected void BuildPalindromesTable()
{
    this.alPalindromes = (ArrayList)this.ViewState["palindromes"];
    if (this.alPalindromes != null)
    {
        foreach (string s in this.alPalindromes)
        {
            TableCell tableCell = new TableCell();
            tableCell.BorderStyle = BorderStyle.Double;
            tableCell.BorderWidth = 3;
            tableCell.Text = s;
            TableRow tableRow = new TableRow();
            tableRow.Cells.Add(tableCell);
            this.Table1.Rows.Add(tableRow);
        }
    }
}
```

9. Add support for keeping track of the palindromes in the *Text* property's setter and call *BuildPalindromesTable*:

```
public string Text
{
  get
  {
    return text;
  }

  set
  {
    text = value;

    this.alPalindromes =
            (ArrayList)this.ViewState["palindromes"];
    if (this.alPalindromes == null)
```

```
    {
      this.alPalindromes = new ArrayList();
    }

    if (this.CheckForPalindrome())
    {
      if (PalindromeFound != null)
      {
        PalindromeFound(this, EventArgs.Empty);
      }

      alPalindromes.Add(text);

      this.labelPalindromeStatus.Text =
          String.Format(
          "This is a palindrome <br/><FONT size=\"5\" color=\"blue\"><B>{0}</B></
FONT>",
          text);
    }
    else
    {
      this.labelPalindromeStatus.Text =
          String.Format(
          "This is NOT a palindrome <br/><FONT size=\"5\" color=\"red\"><B>{0}</B></
FONT>",
          text);
    }

    this.ViewState.Add("palindromes", alPalindromes);
    this.BuildPalindromesTable();

  }
}
```

10. Add a *Click* handler to the button by double-clicking the button in the Designer. This generates a handler in the associated code file. In the handler, grab the control's *Text* property from the *TextBox.Text* property and call the method *CheckForPalindrome*. This sets the control's *Text* property and builds the table of palindromes:

```
protected void Button1_Click(object sender, EventArgs e)
{
    this.Text = this.TextBox1.Text;
    CheckForPalindrome();
}
```

11. Now add the control to the page by dragging the .ascx file from Solution Explorer onto the UsePalindromeCheckerControls.aspx page. Alternatively, you could drag the control onto the Toolbox, and then drag it into the page from there. Finally, you can add a line break between the last control on the page and this one to improve the layout.

12. Build and run the project. When you type palindromes into the
PalindromeCheckerUserControl, it should look something like this:

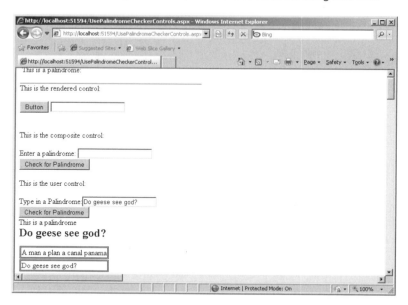

Before leaving this project, run the page by pressing F5 from within Visual Studio. Take a look
at the page with tracing turned on. Here, you can see how the page/control hierarchy is laid
out in memory:

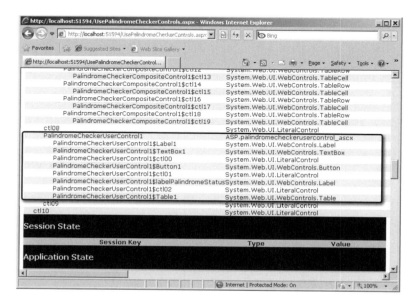

Notice how similar the *User* control is to the binary composite control. Both composite-style controls nest multiple single controls. They're very convenient ways of grouping rich Web-based user interface functionality into single units.

When to Use Each Type of Control

Binary composite controls and *User* controls are similar, so there seems to be some redundancy in the framework. Because *User* controls have such an affinity for the Designer, perhaps it seems you don't need custom composite controls at all. However, each style of composite control has distinct advantages and disadvantages.

The major advantage of binary composite controls is that they are deployed as individual assemblies. Because binary composite controls are packaged in distinct assemblies, you can sign them and deploy them across the enterprise. You also can install them in the global assembly cache. Signing and deploying global assemblies is an advanced topic—but I mention it here because this is one of the main reasons to choose a binary control over a *User* control. The primary downside to using binary composite controls is that they require you to pay more attention to detail in the coding process (there's no Designer support as you write them because they are created entirely from code).

The primary advantage of *User* controls is that they *do* include Designer support, which makes them very easy to design visually. However, *User* controls have a downside in their deployment: They go with the project in which they were created, and they are deployed that way. You can include them as part of other projects, but that requires copying the .ascx and the .cs files to the new project. They are not deployed as signed, secure assemblies.

Chapter 5 Quick Reference

To	Do This
Create a binary control composed of other server-side controls that lives in its own assembly	Derive a class from *System.Web.UI.Control*. Override the *CreateChildControls* method. Visual Studio includes a project type, ASP.NET Server Control, that meets your requirements.
Add controls to a binary composite control	Instantiate the child control. Add the child control to the composite control's *Control* collection.
Add a custom control to the Toolbox	Show the Toolbox if it's not already showing by selecting View, Toolbox on the main menu. Right-click anywhere in the Toolbox. Click Choose Items from the shortcut menu and choose a control from the list. OR Browse to the assembly containing the control.

To	Do This
Tell ASP.NET to assign unique IDs to the child controls in either type of composite control	Derive the binary composite control from the ASP.NET *CompositeControl* class. If you're creating a *User* control, this functionality is built in.
Raise events in either type of composite control	Expose the (public) events using the *event* keyword.
Create composite (*User*) controls using the Visual Studio Designer	In a Visual Studio Web Site project, select Web Site, Add New Item from the main menu. Select the Web User Control template.

Chapter 6
Control Potpourri

After completing this chapter, you will be able to

- Use ASP.NET validation controls.

- Use the *Image, ImageButton,* and *ImageMap* controls.

- Use the *TreeView* control.

- Use the *MultiView* control.

ASP.NET has evolved with the goal of reducing the effort developers must expend to get their Web sites up and running. One theme you might notice as you tour ASP.NET is that Microsoft has done a great job of anticipating what the developer needs and putting it in the framework. The three previous chapters describe the architecture behind ASP.NET Web Forms and controls. With an understanding of this architecture, you can easily extend the framework to do almost anything you want it to do.

ASP.NET versions 1.0 and 1.1 took over much of the functionality developers were building into their sites with classic ASP. For example, server-side controls handled much of the arduous coding that went into developing Web sites displaying consistent user interfaces (such as selection lists that always showed the last selection that was chosen).

Later versions of ASP.NET extend that theme by introducing new server-side controls that insert commonly desired functionality into the framework. This chapter discusses support provided by ASP.NET for validating the data represented by controls. It also examines a few other controls that are very useful: various flavors of the *Image* control, the *MultiView* control, and the *TreeView* control.

First, start with the validation controls.

Validation

One of the primary goals of ASP.NET is to provide functionality to cover the most used scenarios. For example, later you will see that authorization and authentication are commonly required on Web sites. Most sites won't let visitors get to the real goodies until the visitors authenticate as valid users. ASP.NET now includes some login controls and an entire security infrastructure with which those controls work to make authorization and authentication easier.

Another scenario you often find when surfing Web sites is that most sites include a page onto which users are to enter various types of information. For example, to enter a Web site, a user might need to enter a user name and password. If the user wants to have something e-mailed to him or her, the user might have to enter an e-mail address.

When the owner of a Web site requests information from visitors, the Web site program logic needs to ensure that it receives valid information. Although it can't guarantee that user input is 100 percent accurate, it can at least have a fighting chance of getting useful information by validating the fields the user enters. For example, some fields might be required, and the Web site ensures that data is entered in them. The site might require users to enter a phone number in a certain format, and then it applies a regular expression to validate that the information entered is at least formatted correctly. If the user is asked to change a password, the site might require the user to enter the new password twice for validation purposes.

ASP.NET includes a host of validation controls that accompany standard controls (such as a *TextBox*) on a Web Form. The validation controls work in concert with the standard controls and emit error messages (and alerts if configured to do so) if the user enters information that might be incorrect.

ASP.NET includes six validator controls:

- **RequiredFieldValidator**   Ensures that a field is filled in
- **RangeValidator**   Ensures that the value represented by a control falls within a certain range
- **RegularExpressionValidator**   Validates that data in a control matches a specific regular expression
- **CompareValidator**   Ensures that the data represented by a control compares to a specific value or another control
- **CustomValidator**   Provides an opportunity to specify server-side and client-side validation functions
- **ValidationSummary**   Shows a summary of all the validation errors on a page

All the validation controls work the same way. First, you define a regular control on the page. Then, you place the accompanying validators wherever you want the error messages to appear on the page. The validator controls include a property named *ControlToValidate*, which you point to the control that needs validation, and the rest works automatically. Of course, the validator controls have a number of properties you can use to customize the appearance of the error messages coming from the controls.

The ASP.NET validator controls work with the following server-side controls:

- *TextBox*
- *ListBox*
- *DropDownList*

- *RadioButtonList*
- *HtmlInputText*
- *HtmlInputFile*
- *HtmlSelect*
- *HtmlTextArea*
- *FileUpload*

To see how they work, follow the next example, which applies validation controls to a Web Form.

Creating a page that employs validation controls

1. Begin by creating a new Web site named ControlPotpourri.

2. Add a new Web Form named ValidateMe.aspx. This form will hold the regular server-side controls and their accompanying validation controls. The form will resemble a sign-in form such as is common on Web sites. It's the canonical example for employing user input validation.

3. Add a *TextBox* to hold the user's first name. Name the control *TextBoxFirstName*. It's important to give the controls meaningful names because they are attached to the validators by their names. If you use the defaults produced by Microsoft Visual Studio (that is, TextBox1, TextBox2, TextBox3, and so forth), you'll have a difficult time remembering what the validators represent. For each of the following steps, "adding a text box" also means adding an associated label and a <br/> element to make the form look nice. In this case, the label that precedes the *TextBoxFirstName* should be First Name:. The other labels should be self-evident. Note that you should also set the label's *ControlToAssociate* property to the text box the label precedes. This ties the label and text box together (actually the label renders using the <label> element rather than as simple text).

4. Add a last name *TextBox*. Name the control *TextBoxLastName*.

5. Add an address *TextBox*. Name the control *TextBoxAddress*.

6. Add a postal code *TextBox*. Name the control *TextBoxPostalCode*.

7. Add a phone number *TextBox*. Name the control *TextBoxPhone*.

8. Add two more *TextBox* controls to hold a password and a password confirmation. Name them *TextBoxPassword* and *TextBoxPasswordAgain*, respectively. Set the *TextMode* property for both of them to *Password* so that they don't display the text being typed by the user. Using a secondary (or confirmative) *TextBox* ensures that the user types the password correctly two times. (Setting the *TextMode* property to *Password* on the *TextBox* prevents the user from seeing the characters as they are keyed.)

9. Add a *TextBox* to hold the user's age. Name the control *TextBoxAge*.

10. Add a *Button* to submit the form. Add the text **Submit Information**.

The form should look something like this when you're done:

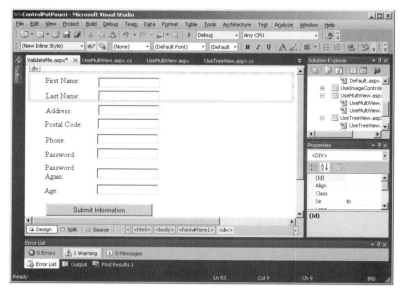

11. Now start adding validators. Add a *RequiredFieldValidator* control for the first name by dragging an instance of *RequiredFieldValidator* on the page just to the right of the *TextBoxFirstName*. In the properties for the first name validator control, find the *ControlToValidate* property and select the *TextBoxFirstName* control. Set the *ErrorMessage* property to a useful error message such as *Please give your first name*.

12. As with the first name text box, add a *RequiredFieldValidator* control for the last name. In the properties for the last name validator control, again find the *ControlToValidate* property and select the *TextBoxLastName* control. Set the *ErrorMessage* property to a useful error message such as *Please give your last name*.

13. Add *RequiredFieldValidator* controls for the address, postal code, the phone number, the password, and the age text boxes.

14. In the properties for the postal code validator control, and as before, find the *ControlToValidate* property and select the *TextBoxPostalCode* control. Set the *ErrorMessage* property to a useful error message such as *Please give your postal code*.

15. In the properties for the phone validator control, click the combo box in the *ControlToValidate* property and select the *TextBoxPhone* control. Set the *ErrorMessage* property to a useful error message such as *Please give your phone number so that we can call you at dinner time.*

16. In the properties for the first password validator control, click the combo box in the *ControlToValidate* property and select the *TextBoxPassword* control. Set the *ErrorMessage* property to a useful error message such as *Please make up a password.*

17. In the properties for the second password validator control, click the combo box in the *ControlToValidate* property and select the *TextBoxPasswordAgain* control. Set the *ErrorMessage* property to a useful error message such as *Please confirm your password.*

18. In the properties for the age required field validator control, click the combo box in the *ControlToValidate* property and select the *TextBoxAge* control. Set the *ErrorMessage* property to a useful error message such as *Please give your age.*

19. Add a *ValidationSummary* to the form. This shows any errors occurring at once. If you want an alert to appear, set the *ValidationSummary.ShowMessageBox* property to *true*. After you have added all the validators, the page in the Designer should look something like the following graphic. The example here uses absolute positioning for the controls so that they can be moved around freely:

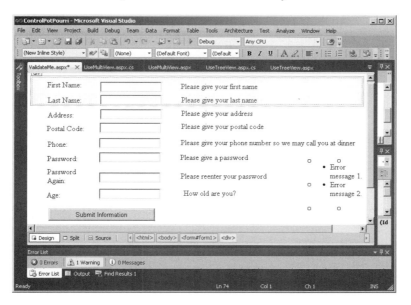

20. Compile the site and view the page. At first, all you can see is a collection of input boxes. Before entering any fields, click the Submit Information button. Watch the error messages appear, as shown in the following graphic:

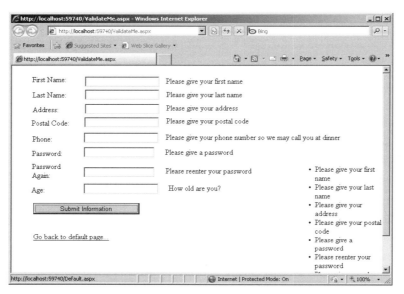

21. Type a first name, and then press the Enter key. This invokes the client-side JavaScript validation script. Watch what happens. The ASP.NET validator controls have inserted some JavaScript into the HTML sent to the browser (if the browser understands JavaScript, which the majority today do). With the client-side script in place, required field validators can manage their error messages without a round-trip to the server, as shown in the following graphic:

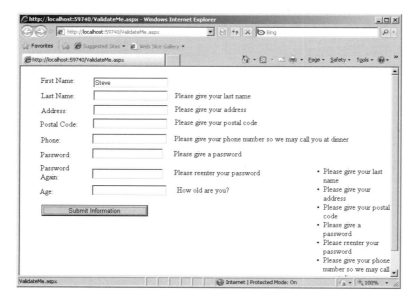

Before adding more validation controls, take a look at how ASP.NET user input validation works.

How Page Validation Works

ASP.NET page validation is very clever—and it's all based on the page *server-side control ar-chitecture*. As with many other features in ASP.NET, the validation mechanism solves the most common use cases you encounter during Web site development. Most sites include both client-side and server-side validation. By supporting client-side validation, users are spared a round-trip when validating data input to the page. In addition to client-side validation, most sites also support server-side validation for two reasons: to make sure no data is garbled or modified during transmission and to support clients unable to support client-side scripting (perhaps the client browser doesn't support JavaScript). First, consider client-side validation.

Client-Side Validation

If you looked at the ASPX source code generated by Visual Studio as you placed controls on the page, you probably noticed the page became littered with tags, such as server-side control tags to support text boxes and selection controls. In addition, each validator control placed on the page corresponds to a separate tag. Validators are server-side controls, too. They render standard browser-interpretable code—similar to regular server-side controls.

ASP.NET validator controls support client-side validation by including references to JavaScript utilities that are included with the HTML sent to the browser. The file contains the client-side validation functions necessary to support client-side validation.

When the validation controls render to the browser, they add to the rendered HTML span elements with custom attributes. The validation handlers are hooked up when the HTML document is loaded in the browser.

Because client-side validation requires JavaScript support in the client, clients without JavaScript support must rely on server-side validation. If you want, you can disable the client-side script for each control by setting the *EnableClientScript* property on the validator to *false*.

Server-Side Validation

After the client passes the client-side validation tests, the request is posted back to the server and the server-side validation starts. Server-side validation is managed by infrastruc-ture in the *Page* class. As you add validator controls to the page, they're added to a collec-tion of validators managed by the page. Each validation control implements an interface named *IValidator*. The *IValidator* interface specifies a *Validate* method, an *ErrorMessage* property, and an *IsValid* property. Of course, each validator has its own custom logic to determine the validity of the data held in the control it is validating. For example, the *RequiredFieldValidator* checks to see that data is entered in the control it is associated with. The *RegularExpressionValidator* compares the data in a control to a specific regular expression.

During the postback sequence for a page, validation occurs just after the *Page_Load* event fires. The page checks each validator against its associated control. If validation fails, the server-side validation controls that failed render themselves as visible span elements.

The page itself has a property named *IsValid* that you can check to increase your confidence in the data passed in from the client before you actually start using the data in the controls. In addition, the *Page* class implements a method named *Validate()*. *Validate* walks the list of validation controls, running each control's *Validate* method.

After you ensure that users fill the required fields, it's important to make sure that the data coming from users is likely to be correct. For example, you might not be able to ensure the veracity of the user's phone number, but at least you can make sure it is in the right format and doesn't contain garbage characters that could not possibly form a phone number. In the following procedure, you add a validator that uses regular expressions to validate patterns. Then, you add a couple of new validators to the page.

Adding finer-grained validation

1. Close the browser and go back to the Designer window in Visual Studio. Now that you have controls that show error messages when the user forgets to type something, you can add some finer-grained validation. The fields present on the form offer a couple more opportunities for the user to enter bad data.

2. There's not much you can do for the first name, last name, and address fields except hope that the users type what they really mean to type. However, you might want to ensure that users type only numbers into the Postal Code field by using a *RegularExpressionValidator* for the *TextBoxPostalCode* control. Drop a *RegularExpressionValidator* on the page. Set the *ControlToValidate* property so that it points to the postal code control. For an error message, set the *ErrorMessage* property to *The postal code you provided is invalid*. Click the button associated with its *ValidationExpression* property, and in the Regular Expression Editor, select U.S. ZIP Code as the validation expression, as shown in the following graphic:

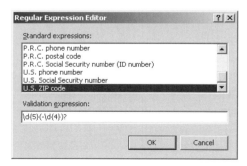

3. Add a regular expression validator for the *TextBoxPhone* control by setting the *ControlToValidate* property to *TextBoxPhone*. Assign its *ErrorMessage* property to be *The phone number you typed is invalid*. Open the Regular Expression Editor, and select U.S. Phone Number as the regular expression to validate, as shown in the following graphic:

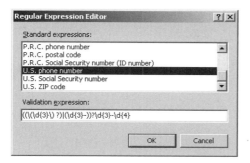

4. Add a *CompareValidator* for the *TextBoxPasswordAgain* control. In the properties for the password confirmation validator control, look for the *ControlToValidate* property and select the *TextBoxPasswordAgain* control. Set the *ControlToCompare* property to *TextBoxPassword*. Set the *ErrorMessage* property to a useful error message such as *The passwords provided do not match*.

5. Add another *CompareValidator* for the *TextBoxAge* control. Enter **30** for *ValueToCompare* and **Integer** as the data type to compare (the *Type* property). A possible error message here could be *You must be younger than 30 to submit data*. The *operator* property should be *LessThanEqual*.

6. Build and run the program. Enter some erroneous data. See what happens. You should see the error messages emitted by the validator controls. For example, if you type **33** as the age, the *CompareValidator* for the *TextBoxAge* control should emit an error message because the validator is looking for values less than or equal to 30.

Other Validators

In addition to the validators mentioned previously, ASP.NET includes three other validators: the *RangeValidator*, the *CustomValidator*, and the *DynamicValidator*. This section takes a quick look at each.

The *RangeValidator* is similar to the *CompareValidator* in that you can use it to check the data in a control against a value. However, the purpose of the *RangeValidator* is to report an error if the data held in a control is out of a range. The validator specifies a minimum and a maximum value and reports an error if the value in the control falls outside these thresholds.

You can try to fit any other kind of validation you might encounter into the *CustomValidator*. The *CustomValidator* fits on the page in the same way the other validators do. However, rather than predefining validation methods (on the server and in the client script), these pieces are left open. When you put a *CustomValidator* on a page, you assign it an associated control. Then, you refer to a validation function (that you write into the page). You can also specify a validation script block to be shipped to the client and run along with the other client-side validation script.

Finally, ASP.NET includes a new validator to support its Dynamic Data model: the *DynamicValidator*. You learn more about Dynamic Data in Chapter 20, "Dynamic Data." The ASP.NET Dynamic Data model supports data-driven application development. The *DynamicValidator* control catches any exceptions thrown during data binding and validation, forwarding the exception as a validation event on the Web page.

Validator Properties

You can see that validator controls contain the standard properties available to the other standard ASP.NET controls. For example, there's a *Text* property, a *Font* property, and various coloring properties. In addition, a couple of other properties useful for managing the error output sent to the browser are available.

The value of the *Display* property can be either static or dynamic. This property manages the client-side rendering of the error message. *Static* (the default value) causes the span element emitted by the control to take up layout space in the HTML bound for the client, even when hidden. When the *Display* property is *Dynamic*, the span element emitted by the control changes the layout and dynamically expands when displayed.

ASP.NET has the ability to group validation controls. That is, each validation control can belong to a named group. The *ValidationGroup* property controls the name of the group. When a control belongs to a group, controls in that group validate only when one of the other validators in the group fires. This gives you a "multiple forms" effect in a single page.

The following sections look at a few other interesting controls: the *Image* control and image-based controls, the *TreeView* control, and the *MultiView* control.

Image-Based Controls

Graphic images are often used in Web pages. HTML includes an image tag that tells the browser to fetch an image file (for example, a .gif, .jpg, or .png file) and display it. When you need to set an image on a page, the HTML <img /> tag is the one to use. Naturally, ASP.NET wraps the <img /> tag using a server-side control—the *Image* control.

Using the *Image* control is fairly straightforward. You select it in the Toolbox like any other control and drop it on the page. The ASP.NET *Image* control generates an <img /> tag complete with the correct *src* attribute.

In addition to the normal *Image* control, ASP.NET includes an *ImageButton* control and an *ImageMap* control. The *ImageButton* control wraps the <input type=image /> tag so that you can use an image as the background of a button. The *ImageMap* control shows a bitmap with hot spots on it that users can click.

The following exercise illustrates how the various ASP.NET image-based controls work.

Using image controls in a page

1. Add a new Web Form to the project to hold some image controls. Call the page UseImageControls.aspx.

2. Drag an *Image* control from the Toolbox to the page.

3. Go to the Properties pane and add a valid path to an image to the *ImageUrl* property. The image file can be on your own computer, or you can point the *ImageUrl* property to a valid URL for an image on the Web. To use an image on the Web, right-click an image in the browser and click Properties. Then, copy the URL from the Properties pane and paste it in the *ImageUrl* in the property explorer. If the file is on your computer, you need to add it to your Web project by dragging the image file from your local drive to the ControlPotpourri solution in Solution Explorer. If you'd like to organize your images in separate folders, simply create a new folder and drag the images there. If you want to use an image from the Web, you need to edit the *ImageUrl* property manually in Source view. Needless to say, no matter which image URL you use, if the image cannot be found (with a resulting error in the <img/> tag), you'll get the standard "image not found" message in your browser. In Microsoft Internet Explorer, this message takes the form of a box with a red *X* in the center.

4. Run the site and see what the ASP.NET *Image* control produces. (Note that your image URL will undoubtedly differ from the example that follows.)

   ```
   <img id="Image1" src="Images/sandiego.jpg" />
   ```

5. Now add an *ImageButton* to the page. With *ImageButton*, you can decorate a normal input button so that it shows a graphic. You can direct your application to react to an *ImageButton* in one of three ways. First, the *ImageButton* can behave like a typical button to which you can attach a typical *Click* event handler on the server. Second, you can define a client-side script block and point the *ImageButton OnClientClick* property to the script. When you click the button, the button press runs the script on the browser. Finally, you can tell the *ImageButton* to redirect the next request to a specific page by using the *ImageButton PostBackUrl* property.

6. Run the page and examine the HTML produced by the *ImageButton*. It should look something like this (keep in mind that your image URL will be different):

   ```
   <input type="image" name="ImageButton1" id="ImageButton1"
   src="Images/goldengatebridge.jpg" style="border-width:0px;" />
   ```

7. Finally, add an *ImageMap* to the page. The *ImageMap* is useful for defining clickable areas on a bitmap. Pick an image available to you (download one from somewhere, or use one you have floating around on your hard drive). Set the *ImageMap ImageUrl* property to the image file.

8. Open the image that you have decided to use for the *ImageMap* using a picture editor such as Microsoft Paintbrush or the Visual Studio bitmap editor. The *ImageMap* in this example defines a hot spot that can be used to zoom in to a portion of the image used in the map. Mark out a rectangular portion of the picture and make a new graphic file using the selected portion. Make a note of the coordinates defining the section of the graphic you cut out. Enlarge the new image and save it to a new file.

9. Next, you can define some hot spots on the *ImageMap*. Among the *ImageMap* properties is one named *HotSpots*. Click the button in the property field to open the HotSpot Collection Editor, as shown in the following graphic:

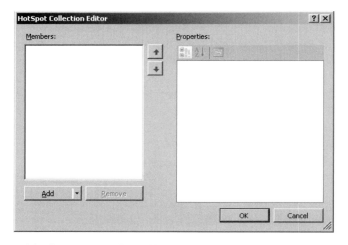

10. Add a hot spot to the collection by clicking the Add button. Notice that you can define circular, rectangular, or polygonal hot spots by clicking the drop-down list on the Add button. Create a rectangular hot spot using the coordinates of the portion of the image you just defined. Add some text to the *AlternateText* property—this is the text that shows in the tooltip. Set the *HotSpotMode* property to *Navigate*, and use the NavigateUrl editor to set the *NavigateUrl* property to point to the new image file you just created (you might have to add the new image file to the project explicitly using the Add Existing Item menu after right-clicking the project node in Solution Explorer). The following graphic shows a hot spot being edited:

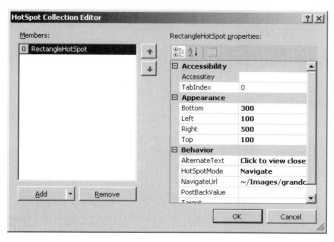

11. After adding the hot spot, run the new page. You should see something similar to the following graphic—the example here shows the Grand Canyon, and the hot spot is outlined in the image with a rectangle. (Note that the rectangle was added to the image manually—the hot spot doesn't draw the rectangle for you.) Notice how the tooltip appears.

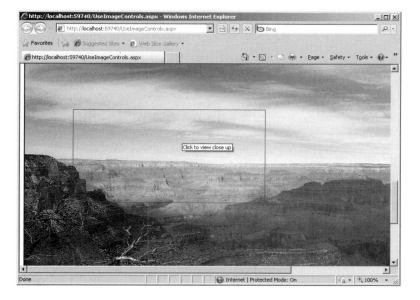

12. Click the hot spot and notice how the application redirects to the "enlarged" image, as shown in the next graphic:

This section only scratches the surface of working with the image controls. However, you can see that you have much flexibility in defining how images look and behave.

TreeView

One of the most common user interface conventions in modern software is a hierarchy represented by expandable nodes. For example, whenever you browse for a file using Windows Explorer, you need to expand and collapse various folders (subdirectories) to see what's inside. This type of control is generically known as a *tree control*.

With tree controls, users can navigate hierarchies represented by expandable and collapsible nodes. For example, when you explore your C drive using Windows Explorer and the Classic Windows theme, the directories appear as closed folders with small plus signs next to them. When you click a plus sign, Windows Explorer displays an open folder and then shows the subdirectories listed under that folder. If there are nested subdirectories, you can open them the same way. Other themes use slightly different means of expanding and collapsing nodes.

ASP.NET provides this functionality through the *TreeView*. It's useful any time you want to represent a nested data structure and have a way of drilling down into it.

The following exercise explains the *TreeView* control by showing a hierarchical, expandable list of 1970s bands that are still around today. The example illustrates the hierarchical nature of the bands by showing the name of the band followed by a list of roles performed by each particular member.

Using the *TreeView* control

1. Begin by adding a new Web Form to the ControlPotpourri Web site. Name it *UseTreeView*.

2. Drag a *TreeView* from the Toolbox to the default page. You can find it under the Navigation controls.

3. Format your tree view by using the options Visual Studio presents. Right-click the *TreeView* control, and under TreeView Tasks, click the Auto Format option. A dialog box showing a number of styles for the *TreeView* opens. Browse through a few of them, highlighting them to see what the styles look like. The following graphic shows the TreeView Tasks menu with the Auto Format link:

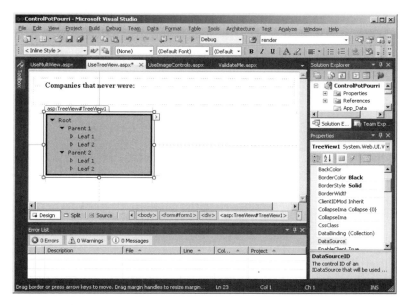

4. You can edit the nodes by right-clicking the *TreeView* control and clicking the Edit Nodes link. In the TreeView Node Editor, you can edit each of the nodes. The leftmost button adds new root nodes. In this example, the bands are represented as root nodes. The next button to the right is for adding child nodes. You can nest nodes as deeply as necessary. In this example, the second layer of nodes represents the members of

the bands, and the third layer represents their roles. The following graphic shows the TreeView Node Editor:

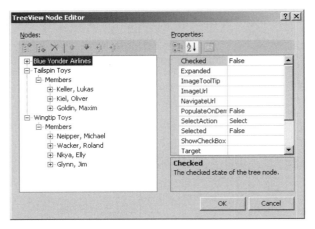

5. Add a border around the *TreeView* using the *BorderStyle* and *BorderColor* properties. Set the style to solid and the color to black. Of course, this is for visual aesthetics.

6. Build the project and browse to the page. If you selected a theme such as the Arrow theme, you should be able to expand and collapse the nodes. After running the page, take a quick look at the ASPX source code to see how the *TreeView* manages its nodes. The following graphic shows how the *TreeView* appears in the browser:

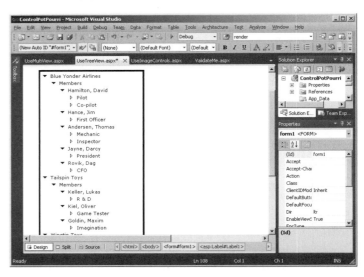

7. To make it a bit more interesting, add some functionality to handle some of the tree node events. First, add a label to show the selected node. Name the label *LabelSelectedNode* so that you have programmatic access to it. Add a *TextBox* to show information about the selected node. Name it *TextBoxInfo*. Make the *TextBox* multiline.

Then, add an event handler for the *TreeView SelectedNodeChanged* event. Add the following code to interrogate the selected node to list information about the child nodes. Don't forget to add a *using* statement for *System.Text* (to identify *StringBuilder*):

```
protected void TreeView1_SelectedNodeChanged(object sender, EventArgs e)
{
    this.LabelSelectedNode.Text = String.Format("Selected Node changed to: {0}",
        this.TreeView1.SelectedNode.Text);
    TreeNodeCollection childNodes = this.TreeView1.SelectedNode.ChildNodes;
    if (childNodes != null)


    {
        this.TextBoxInfo.Text = String.Empty;
        StringBuilder sb = new StringBuilder();
        foreach(TreeNode childNode in childNodes)
        {
            sb.AppendFormat("{0}\n", childNode.Value);
        }
        this.TextBoxInfo.Text = sb.ToString();
    }

}
```

The following graphic shows how the selected details appear in the *ListBox*:

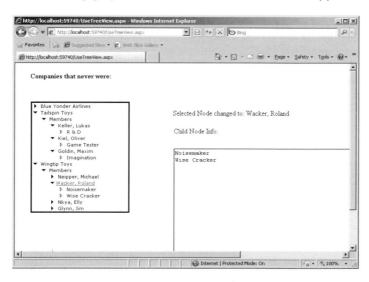

This is just a small illustration of what *TreeView* is capable of doing. In addition to building nodes using the Designer, you can build them programmatically. You can expand and collapse nodes as well. Finally, *TreeView* supports data binding so that you can throw a hierarchical data structure at the control so that it renders properly for you.

Finally, take a look at the ASP.NET *MultiView* and *View* controls.

MultiView

From time to time, it's useful to gather controls together in several panes and give the user the opportunity to page through the panes. During the lifetime of ASP.NET 1.0, Microsoft released several rich dynamic (though officially unsupported) controls that emitted dynamic HTML (DHTML) instead of regular HTML. A trio of these controls—*TabStrip*, *MultiView* (an older version), and *PageView*—worked together to form essentially a set of tabbed panes.

These exact controls aren't available in later versions of ASP.NET; however, two controls— *MultiView* and *View*—go a long way toward providing similar functionality. *MultiView* acts as a container for *Panel*-like controls (*View* controls) and includes support for paging through the various *Views* held within it. The *MultiView* shows a single *View* at a time.

The following exercise provides an example that shows how the *MultiView* and the *View* controls work together.

Using the *MultiView* and *View* controls

1. Add a new Web Form to the ControlPotpourri site. Name it *UseMultiview.aspx*.

2. Add a *MultiView* control to this Web Form.

3. The main purpose of the *MultiView* is to manage a set of *Views*. To add a *View* to a *MultiView*, drag a *View* instance from the Toolbox and drop it *inside* the *MultiView*. Add three *Views* to the Web Form like so. You might need to tweak the size of the container manually to get the views to fit:

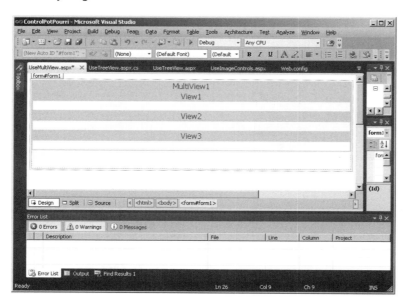

4. Add some content to each of the *Views*. You can think of the *Views* very much like panes. In this example, the views include labels that distinguish them. The following graphic illustrates how the *Views* look in the Designer:

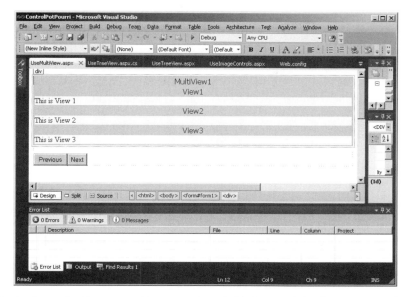

5. Activate the first pane. To cause the *MultiView* and the first *View* to show up, set the *MultiView ActiveViewIndex* property to **0** to show the first pane.

6. Add some controls to navigate between the *Views* in *MultiView* by adding two buttons to the bottom of the form. Call them *ButtonPrev* and *ButtonNext*—they'll be used to page through the *Views*.

7. Add event handlers for the buttons by double-clicking each of them.

8. Add code to the page through the *Views*. This code responds to the button clicks by changing the index of the current *View*.

```
protected void ButtonPrev_Click(object sender, EventArgs e)
{
    if (MultiView1.ActiveViewIndex == 0)
    {
        MultiView1.ActiveViewIndex = 2;
    }
    else
    {
        MultiView1.ActiveViewIndex -= 1;
    }
}
protected void ButtonNext_Click(object sender, EventArgs e)
{
    if (MultiView1.ActiveViewIndex == 2)
```

```
    {
        MultiView1.ActiveViewIndex = 0;
    }
    else
    {
        MultiView1.ActiveViewIndex += 1;
    }
}
```

9. Compile the project and browse to the Web page. Clicking the navigator buttons causes postbacks to the server, which render the individual views. The following graphic shows how the *MultiView* and *View* number 2 appear in a browser:

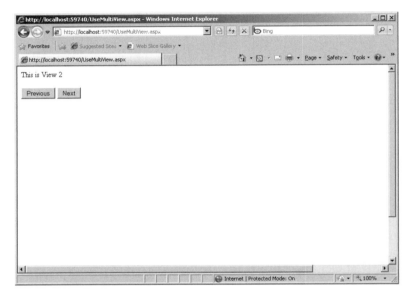

As you can see, the *MultiView* and the *View* classes act as panes that you can swap in and out. They are a great way to manage the surface area involved in collecting large amounts of data. Another version of this kind of control is the *Wizard* control used in conjunction with the session state.

Chapter 6 Quick Reference

To	Do This
Validate form input	ASP.NET includes a number of validator controls that check data entered via server-side controls. These controls include
	CompareValidator
	RangeValidator
	RequiredFieldValidator
	RegularExpressionValidator
	ValidationSummary
	CustomValidator
	To validate the input of a server-side control, drag the appropriate validator control onto the page and set the *ControlToValidate* property to the target control.
	Set the other validator properties appropriately.
Display hierarchical data sets in an intuitive way	Use the *TreeView* control.
	Either add items by hand or bind the *TreeView* control to a hierarchical data source. We'll see *TreeViews* again when we look at navigation controls in Chapter 12.
Swap between several pages of information on the same Web page	Use the *MultiView* and *View* controls.
	You can think of the *View* control as a miniature page managing controls.
	The *MultiView* manages a collection of *Views*.
	The *MultiView* supports swapping between *Views*.
Add an image to a Web page	Drop an *Image* control onto the Web page.
	Set the *Image* control's *ImageUrl* property to the URL of the image you'd like to show.
Add an image with clickable regions to the Web page	Drop an *ImageMap* onto the Web page.
	Use the hot spot editor to define clickable regions.

Part II
Advanced Features

Chapter 7
A Consistent Look and Feel

After completing this chapter, you will be able to

- Use master pages to develop a consistent look and feel for your entire Web site.
- Use themes to apply styles to controls and pages across an entire Web site.
- Use skins to apply styles to custom controls.

A distinguishing characteristic of most well-designed modern Web sites is the consistent look and feel of each page in a site. For example, many sites incorporate a specific color scheme and font set. Also, the way a well-designed site frames information and provides navigation tools is consistent from one page to the next. Can you imagine visiting a site where each page was radically different in appearance from the previous page? At the very least, you'd be confused. At the very worst, you might even be repulsed.

This chapter covers one of the most useful features of ASP.NET for developing a consistent look and feel across a site—master pages. Master pages help you make the appearance of your site consistent for visitors. ASP.NET also provides a way you can apply specific styles to controls. This chapter examines how these features work.

 Important To install the code samples for this book, you must have Administrator rights on your computer. If you are using your own computer, you probably have Administrator rights. If you are using a computer in an organization and you do not have Administrator rights, please consult your computer support or IT staff. See the "Code Samples" section in the Introduction for more information.

Managing User Interface Consistency

Getting to the point where Web development tools support creating a common look and feel for all the pages in a site has been a long process. Classic ASP provided a very crude way of applying a common look and feel to a site through a file inclusion mechanism that pulled one .asp file into another wholesale. It was brute force to say the least. Although it worked to a certain degree, you had very little control over the nuances of your site while clumping files together.

ASP.NET 1.0 went quite a bit further by composing the whole page-rendering mechanism out of smaller server-side controls and user controls. You saw this in Chapter 2, "ASP.NET Application Fundamentals," and Chapter 3, "The Page Rendering Model." However, even though you could package portions of a Web application's user interface (UI) into separate modules, you still had some work to do to implement a common look and feel among the pages in your application. For example, user controls could be made to support developing a common look and feel. You can create a user control with specific navigation controls and links and use it in the same place on every page in your site. That in itself creates a common look and feel, but it's up to you to write that functionality into your site as well as make sure the control's use is consistent for each and every page in your Web application.

Although using the custom control/user control approach to break apart a site's user interface is useful for developing a consistent UI, it falls short of being an ideal solution in a couple of ways. First, all the pages in an application need to include the surrounding code. That means that you have to apply the controls in the same way to *each page* as just mentioned. If you decide to change the placement of the controls (or some other aspect not governed by the controls), you have to change each page. Second, every page using a custom control needs a *Register* directive—and more code that needs to be copied. As a reuse model it went much further than earlier approaches (that is, classic ASP). But what you really want is a single place in the site where you can lay out the look and feel of the page *once* and have it propagate across the site.

One way to accomplish this goal and avoid building pages one at a time is to build a primary class from which all the pages in your application derive. Because ASP.NET is built on an object model based on the *Page* class, why not simply add a new layer to your application? Figure 7-1 is a diagram illustrating how you might build a set of pages from a single base page.

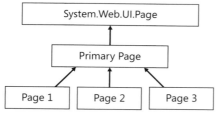

FIGURE 7-1 A base class to implement functionality common among several pages.

All the .aspx pages inherit from the same code-behind class deriving from the primary class (which in turn derives from *System.Web.UI.Page*). The primary class takes responsibility for loading the controls necessary for the site's look and feel. Then, each separate page is responsible for managing the rest.

This approach works, as long as you don't mind doing a lot of coding. In addition, there was no design support in ASP.NET 1.*x* for this sort of thing, and changing the *Page* class hierarchy in Microsoft Visual Studio sometimes would break the project.

ASP.NET 2.0 introduced *master pages* to support developing a common look and feel across your entire site, and now they are a staple among many developers for keeping Web sites consistent across all the different pages.

ASP.NET Master Pages

Master pages represent a sort of metapage. They have much the same structure as typical pages. However, they live in files that use the .master extension. A master page serves as a template that renders a common appearance to all pages based on it. Master pages use XHTML document tags (such as <html>, <head>, and <body>), which apply only to the master page. When a visitor surfs to a page that has a master page applied to it, the request and response are filtered through the master page. The master page cannot be served by itself. Instead, it ensures that each page has a common look and feel by (logically) acting as the "primary page" shown in Figure 7-1. ASP.NET merges the master page and the .aspx page (the content page) into a single class. At that point, the class processes requests and renders output like any other *System.Web.UI.Page*-derived class.

Because master pages are similar to typical .aspx pages, they can contain the same sort of content and functionality as typical pages. That is, they can contain server-side controls, user controls, and markup. In addition to markup and controls, a master page can contain instances of the *System.Web.UI.WebControls.ContentPlaceHolder* control. As its name implies, the content placeholder stands in place of the real content that will eventually appear in pages based on the master page. A master page renders all the elements it contains—that is, those elements not contained within a *System.Web.UI.WebControls.ContentPlaceHolder* control.

Because master pages play a part in how the final page handler is synthesized, they work a bit differently from the straight inheritance technique described previously (that is, writing a base class to implement common functionality through inheritance). As the page executes, the master page injects its own content into the .aspx page. Specifically, the master content ends up being represented by a control that is added to the .aspx page's *Controls* collection, where it is rendered in the same way as all other controls are rendered.

Like usual page attributes and functionality, master pages can contain the following attributes in their *MasterPage* directive:

- *AutoEventWireup*
- *ClassName*
- *CompilerOptions*
- *Debug Description*
- *EnableViewState Explicit*
- *Inherits*
- *Language*
- *Strict*

- *Src*
- *WarningLevel*
- *Master*

The following exercise illustrates developing a site around a master page.

Using a master page

1. Create a new Empty Web site named *MasterPageSite*. Typically, you'd simply create a new site project. However, in this case be sure to use the "empty" Web site template so that you can add the master and derived pages by hand. This will give you a little more experience using master pages by creating one from scratch instead of using one created by Visual Studio.

2. Add a new item to the page. Select Master Page from the available templates. Name the page *MasterPage.master*. The following graphic shows how to add a master page template:

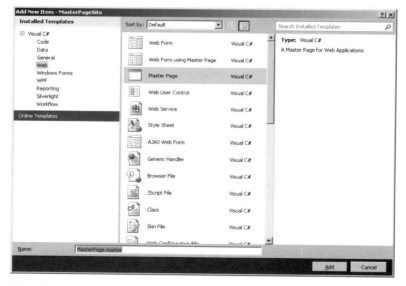

Visual Studio pumps out code like the following in a file named MasterPage.master. Notice the *ContentPlaceholder* controls generated by Visual Studio.

```
<%@ Master Language="C#"
AutoEventWireup="true"
CodeFile="MasterPage.master.cs"
Inherits="MasterPage" %>
<!DOCTYPE html PUBLIC "-//W3C//DTD XHTML 1.0 Transitional//EN"
"http://www.w3.org/TR/xhtml1/DTD/xhtml1-transitional.dtd">
<html xmlns="http://www.w3.org/1999/xhtml">
  <head runat="server">
```

```
    <title></title>
    <asp:ContentPlaceHolder id="head" runat="server">
    </asp:ContentPlaceHolder>
  </head>
  <body>
    <form id="form1" runat="server">
    <div>
      <asp:ContentPlaceHolder id="ContentPlaceHolder1" runat="server">
      </asp:ContentPlaceHolder>
    </div>
  </form>
</body>
</html>
```

This is what the master page looks like in Design mode:

Notice how the master page looks similar to a typical .aspx page. In fact, you can work with a master page in very much the same way you work with a typical .aspx page.

3. Look for the <body> tag in the MasterPage.master file. Edit the background color of the body to show a different color:

```
<body style="background-color: #bbbbbb;">
  <form id="form1" runat="server">
    <div>
      <asp:ContentPlaceHolder ID="ContentPlaceHolder1" runat="server">
      </asp:ContentPlaceHolder>
    </div>
  </form>
</body>
```

The example here uses light gray. By updating the background color, you can see that the master page is really used in subsequent .aspx files.

4. Right-click the project node and click Add New Item. Create a new form using the Web Form Using Master Page template, as shown in the following graphic. Name it *UseMasterPage.aspx*. Be sure to select the Select Master Page option.

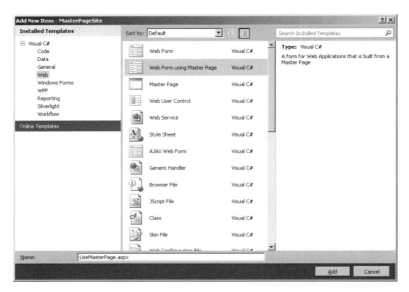

Visual Studio will ask you to select a master page, as shown in this graphic:

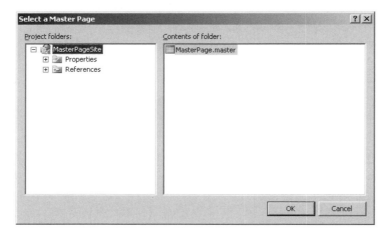

When you view UseMasterPage.aspx in the Designer, it looks like the MasterPage. master file. Notice the grayish hue applied to the page, as shown in the following graphic. This lets you know the master page is really being applied here.

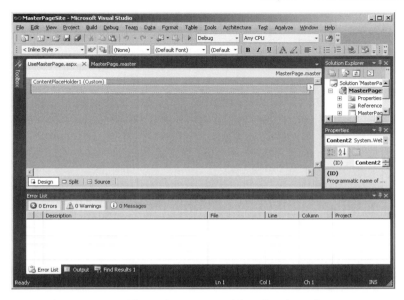

This is the page-specific code generated by Visual Studio to support using the master page:

```
<%@ Page Title="" Language="C#"
MasterPageFile="~/MasterPage.master"
AutoEventWireup="true" CodeFile="UseMasterPage.aspx.cs"
Inherits="UseMasterPage" %>

<asp:Content ID="Content1"
  ContentPlaceHolderID="head" Runat="Server">
</asp:Content>

<asp:Content ID="Content2"
  ContentPlaceHolderID="ContentPlaceHolder1"
  Runat="Server">
</asp:Content>
```

5. Now add some content to UseMasterPage.aspx. Add a label to the content placeholder and type in text so that you can distinguish this as a separate page.

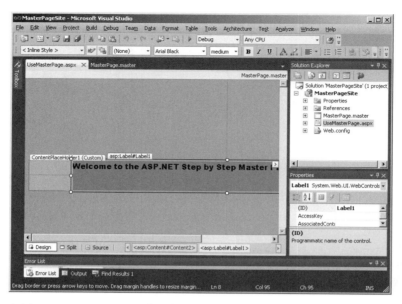

6. Add two more pages to the site. The example here includes a page describing the chapter content of this book and a second page describing the projects. You can use these or add your own content. Add some content to the two pages in the content placeholders so that you can distinguish the pages (you add navigation support later).

The important point is to add two more pages and apply the master page to them (that is, create the Web Forms with the Select Master Page option selected).

The following two graphics show the example site's pages containing a *ListBox* to select the topic and a *TextBox* to hold information about the topic. Setting the positioning of the items to *absolute* can make it easier to arrange items on the page. The examples here use absolute positioning. In addition, the examples here populate the *ListBox* with project names (on the Projects page) and chapter names (on the Chapters page). Each page has a *ListBox* selection change handler that fills the *TextBox* with information about the projects and chapters. This is so that you can actually see that the pages have functionality in addition to the consistent look and feel from the master page.

Here's how to add elements to the *ListBox* by hand. (You see another technique—data binding—in Chapter 10, "Data Binding.") First, select the *ListBox* in the Designer. Click the small arrow on the right side of the *ListBox* to open a dialog box in which you can add item/value pairs. The example here uses two *ListBox*es—one holds project information for this book and the other holds chapter information for this book. Here's what the Chapters page might look like:

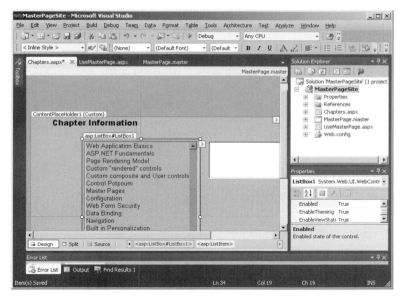

Here's what the Projects page might look like:

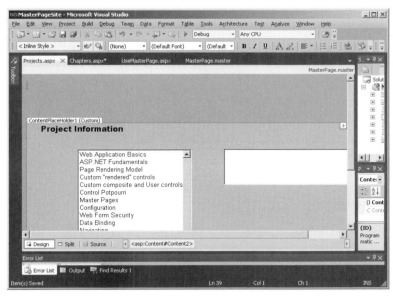

7. Go back to the MasterPage.master page and update it so that it includes a bit more content. Click Table, Insert Table to insert a table immediately above the content pane on the master page. Give the table one row and two columns. Size it so that the left cell is narrow and the right cell is wide. It should look something like this:

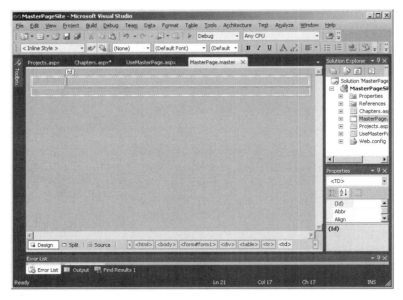

8. Add a menu to the leftmost cell in the table. To customize the menu, add an *AutoFormat* style to it. The example here uses the *Classic* style. Add three items to the menu for navigating to the three pages in this site—the Home page, the Chapters page, and the Projects page. To add the menu items, select the menu in the Designer, click the small arrow in the control, and click Edit Menu Items. The following dialog box appears. Add the menu items here.

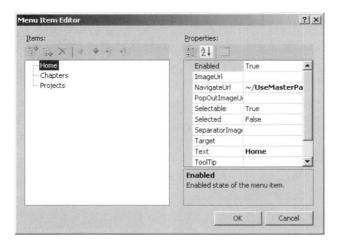

Set up the appropriate navigation for each menu option. That is, set the Home menu item to navigate to the UseMasterPage.aspx page. Set the Chapters menu item to navigate to the Chapters.aspx file. Finally, set the Projects menu item to navigate to the Projects.aspx file. You can set up the navigation URLs individually here by clicking the navigation button in the *NavigateUrl* field of the *Property* page. (You look at using ASP.NET site map support shortly.)

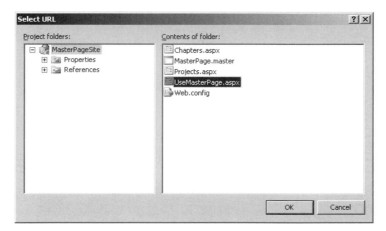

Open one of the master pages (for example, UseMasterPage.aspx). You should end up with something like this:

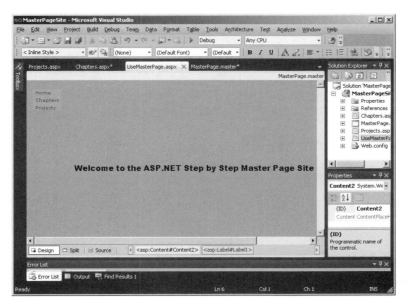

9. Finally, add a banner. In my opinion, no master page is complete without a banner. Use the bitmap editor (or Paintbrush—mspaint.exe) to draw a banner. The one in this

example is approximately 1000 pixels wide by 90 pixels high. Drop the banner into the table cell on the right. Your master page should look something like this now:

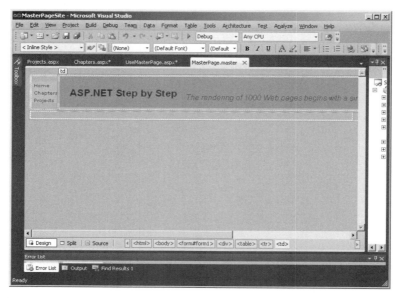

Because you created the UseMaster.aspx, Chapters.aspx, and Projects.aspx files using the master page, they have the menu and banner built in automatically. Surf to the UseMaster.aspx file and browse through the menu items. You should see that each page has a common look and feel, and includes the correct content. Here is the Chapters page:

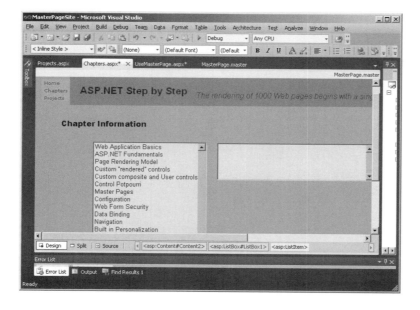

And here is the Projects page:

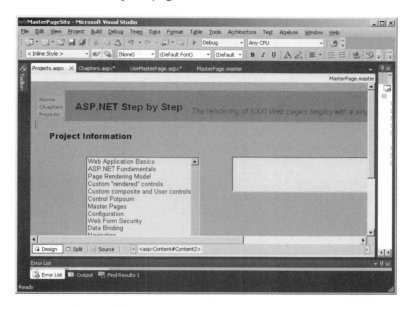

Master pages offer significant improvements over earlier versions of classic ASP and ASP.NET for developing a common look and feel across all the pages in your application. Of course, you can use multiple master pages in a project, and you can also nest them.

A second way to help manage the look and feel of your application is by using ASP.NET themes.

Themes

Master pages control the general layout of a series of pages in an application. However, you might like other elements (such as those that are subject to change between pages) to remain constant. Themes provide a means of applying common styles to the elements on each page in your site.

If you're familiar with Cascading Style Sheets (CSS), you will feel very at home with themes. The two techniques are similar because with both you can define the visual styles for your Web pages. Themes go a step beyond CSS, however. You can use themes to specify styles, graphics, and even CSS files in the pages of your applications. When available, you can apply ASP.NET themes at the application, page, or server control level.

Themes are represented as text-based style definitions in ASP.NET. Straight out of the box ASP.NET includes a number of themes. You can find them at C:\WINDOWS\Microsoft.NET\ Framework\v*xxxxx*\ASP.NETClientFiles\Themes (where v*xxxxx* indicates the version of the .NET Framework you're using). ASP.NET includes some predefined themes. In addition, you can define and use your own themes.

The following exercise shows how to create and use a theme.

Creating and using a theme

1. Add a new form to the MasterPagesSite project. Make this a regular form that *doesn't* use master pages. Name the page *UseThemes.aspx*.

2. Add a theme folder to your project by right-clicking the Web Site node in Solution Explorer, and clicking Add ASP.NET Folder. Select Theme. This creates an App_Themes directory for you.

3. Right-click the App_Themes folder, click Add Folder, and then click Theme Folder. Rename the Theme1 folder *Default*.

4. Add a new style sheet to the Default folder. Right-click the project node in Solution Explorer and click Add New Item. Select the style sheet Template, as shown in the following graphic, and name the style sheet Default.css. Drag the Default.css file into the Themes\Default folder. This is now the style sheet that will apply when the page uses the style named Default.

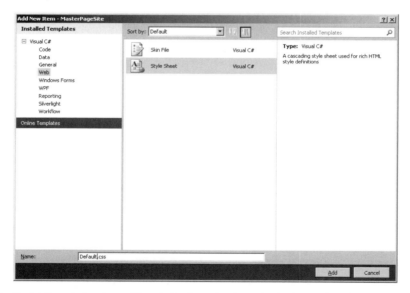

5. Build the style sheet. The default style sheet includes only a *body* tag. When the style sheet is open in Visual Studio, select Add Style Rule from the Styles menu. You can right-click the Elements node to modify the style for the node. For example, if you want to change the style of the <h1> tag, right-click the Elements node and click Add Style Rule. To add a style for the <h1> tag, select the style from the list of elements and move it into the Style Rule Hierarchy area by clicking the > button, as shown in the following graphic. Then, click OK.

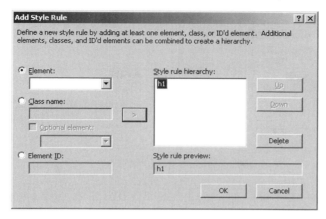

To modify the style, click the H1 node in the CSS outline page and select Style in the Properties pane. Click the ellipsis button (...) to open the Modify Style dialog box, shown in the following graphic, and change the size and weight of the font (or any other aspects). Then, click OK.

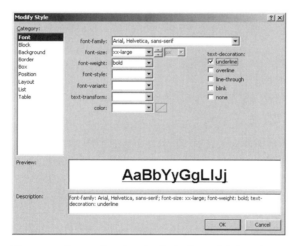

The sample application included on this book's accompanying CD sets the font to Arial Black, xx-large, bold, and with an underscore.

If you look in the CSS file, you'll see that the style has been modified:

```
body
{
}
h1
{
  font-family: Arial, Helvetica, sans-serif;
  font-size: xx-large;
  font-weight: bold;
  text-decoration: underline;
}
```

6. Now test the theme by declaring it in the page by adding the *Theme* directive and then by typing a heading with <h1> tags:

```
<%@ Page Language="C#" AutoEventWireup="true"
  Theme="Default"
CodeFile="UseThemes.aspx.cs"
Inherits="UseThemes" %>

<!DOCTYPE html PUBLIC "-//W3C//DTD XHTML 1.0 Transitional//EN"
"http://www.w3.org/TR/xhtml1/DTD/xhtml1-transitional.dtd">

<html xmlns="http://www.w3.org/1999/xhtml">
<head runat="server">
<title></title>
</head>
<body>
<form id="form1" runat="server">
<div>
  <h1> How does this look? </h1>
</div>
</form>
</body>

</html>
```

Here's how the themed page appears in the browser with the new theme applied (the <h1> tag set to the new font and to use underlining in this example):

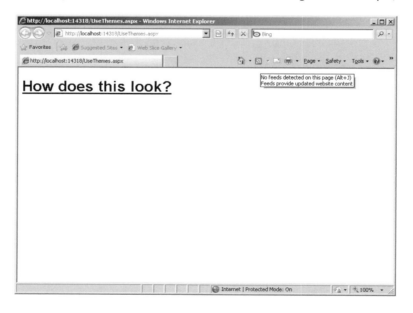

7. Add another theme to the project and name the theme *SeeingRed*. That is, create a new theme folder and add a new style sheet called SeeingRed. Set the <h1> tag font color to red this time. Then, change the theme used by the page to SeeingRed (you can also set the theme in the Properties pane in Visual Studio):

```
<%@ Page Language="C#" AutoEventWireup="true"
CodeFile="UseThemes.aspx.cs"
Theme="SeeingRed"
trace="false" Inherits="UseThemes" %>
```

Surf to the page to see the <h1> tag printed in red.

This is just a taste of the kinds of things you can do by using themes in a page. Once you have defined a theme, you can apply it by declaring it as part of the *Page* declaration or by intercepting the *PreInit* event and changing the *Theme* property in the page to a valid theme.

Skins, described in the next section, go hand in hand with themes.

Skins

Skins complement master pages and themes as a way to manage the style of your Web site. Using skins is almost like combining *WebControl*-based controls with CSS. You can also think of skins as a way of setting certain properties of a control as a group. For example, you might want to define different color schemes for a particular control, for example, the *TextBox* control or the *Calendar* control, which has extensive capabilities and customizable properties. By providing skins for controls, you can make available a number of different appearance options for various controls without having to go into detail and manage the control properties one by one for each instance of the control used in your site.

Actually, you have used skins already. Many server-side controls support style templates. For example, when you worked with the *TreeView* in an earlier chapter, you saw that you could apply one of several styles to it. Earlier in this chapter, you applied a set of color attributes to the *Menu* control when you chose the "classic" style from the *AutoFormat* control option menu. This section discusses how skins work and how to apply them.

Skin files define specific controls and the attributes that apply to them. That is, a .skin file contains server-side control declarations. The skin file's job is to preset the style properties for the control. Skin files reside in named theme folders for an application, accompanied by any necessary CSS files.

The following exercise illustrates how to create skins for some controls on your Web site.

Creating a skin

1. Create a skin file by right-clicking the SeeingRed folder in the App_Theme node in Solution Explorer and clicking Add New Item. Choose Skin File from the templates. Name the file *SeeingRed.skin*.

2. In the SeeingRed.skin file, predeclare some controls for which you'd like to have default property values set. For example, the following SeeingRed.skin file declares default properties for some controls. These controls have their various colors default to assorted shades of red.

```
<asp:Label runat="server" ForeColor="red"
Font-Size="14pt" Font-Names="Verdana" />

<asp:button runat="server" borderstyle="Solid"
borderwidth="2px" bordercolor="#ff0000" backcolor="#cc0000"/>

<asp:CheckBoxList runat=server ForeColor="#ff0000" />

<asp:RadioButtonList runat=server ForeColor="#ff9999" />
```

3. Add the controls for which you've predeclared attributes in the skin file to the UseThemes.aspx page to see how the SeeingRed.skin file applies. In the following graphic, the red colored controls appear as a lighter gray color. You can see this effect when you run the sample application.

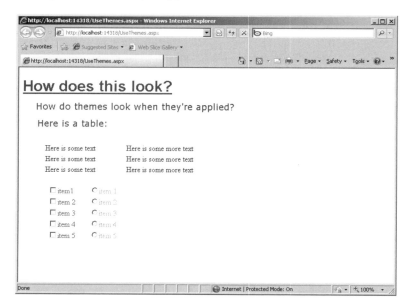

You can automatically apply the SeeingRed.skin file by declaring the SeeingRed theme within the page. You can also prescribe different skins at run time in the page's *PreInit* handler, and you can apply separate skins to each control.

Chapter 7 Quick Reference

To	Do This
Enable a Web page to use *WebPart* controls	Add a *WebPartManager* to the page on which you wish to use *WebPart* controls.
Add various editing capabilities to a Web Parts page	Add an *EditorZone* to the page.
Add a place in which to position server-side controls to be managed by the Web Part architecture	Add a *WebZone* to the page.
Allow users to dynamically add controls from a collection of controls	Add *CatalogZone* to the page. Add controls to the catalog while in Edit Templates mode.
Create a Web Part	Derive a class from *System.Web.UI.WebControls.WebParts. WebPart* and Render some HTML in the Web Part's *Render* method or Create ASP.NET child controls and add them to the Web Part's *Controls* collection for automatic rendering.

Chapter 8
Configuration

After completing this chapter, you will be able to

- Understand the way the Microsoft .NET Framework handles configuration.
- Apply configuration settings to ASP.NET applications.
- Manage ASP.NET configuration using the ASP.NET Administration tool.
- Manage ASP.NET configuration using the Microsoft Management Console (MMC) snap-in.

This chapter introduces how ASP.NET manages its configuration information. It gives a taste of how ASP.NET configuration works. You revisit ASP.NET configuration in later chapters. ASP.NET is a feature-rich system for developing and deploying Web sites. The features you see in more detail as you examine ASP.NET further include some of the following:

- Session state
- Caching content to help optimize your Web site's responses
- Tracing requests
- Mapping specific file extensions to custom handlers
- Authenticating users

Each of these features is controlled by a number of separate configurable parameters. For example, when you enable session state for your application, you can choose where to locate your application's session state (in process, on a separate computer using a Windows Service, or using Microsoft SQL Server). You can also configure the lifetime of your session state and how your application tracks the session state (using a cookie or some other method).

A second feature the configuration file controls is caching output. When you cache the content of your site, you can vary the lifetime of your cached content and where it is cached (on the server, on the client, or on the proxy).

For both these features (and others), the configuration options are governed by configuration files. This chapter first examines the nature of Windows configuration and then looks specifically at how ASP.NET handles configuration. In ASP.NET 1.*x*, modifying the configuration of your application meant editing the XML-based configuration file by hand. Fortunately, more recent versions of ASP.NET (2.0 and later) offer two tools that make configuration a much easier task. One tool is the ASP.NET Configuration tab available through the Internet Information Services (IIS) 7.*x* configuration panel. The second tool is the Web Site Administration Tool, available through the Web Site, ASP.NET Configuration menu in Microsoft Visual Studio. This chapter discusses both these tools as well.

Windows Configuration

Every computing environment needs a configuration mechanism to control its behavior. A number of parameters can govern how the operating system and programs operate. You often need to modify the parameters, perhaps to tune performance or tailor security or even just to control typical operation. For example, the Windows operating system provides an environment variable named *PATH* that controls the search path for executable programs. Other environment variables include *TEMP* (controls the location of temporary files) and *USERPROFILE* (identifies the location of the current user's profile information).

In addition to operating system variables, individual applications might require different settings specific to that program. For example, many applications require a specific version of the Windows operating system or that specific dynamic-link libraries (DLLs) be available. These actions vary from one installation to the next, and it's not a good idea to hard-code the settings into your application. Instead, you store values in a secondary file that accompanies the application.

During the early days of Windows, you could use initialization files (.ini files) to configure individual applications and the Windows operating system itself; there is even a set of Windows application programming interface (API) functions for managing configuration parameters. The files contain a name/value pair that dictates a property and its associated setting. For example, the name/value pair in Win.INI that turns on Object Linking and Embedding (OLE) messaging looks like

```
OLEMessaging=1
```

Now, in this new millennium, XML is the way to go. .NET depends on XML files (machine.config< web.config, and various trust alternatives) for its configuration.

> **Note**   In the past, the other way that you could configure applications was through the registry. The registry is a centralized database that applications can use to store name/value pairs. The reason ASP.NET doesn't use the registry for configuration information is because the global nature of the registry is in direct conflict with the need for ASP.NET to be flexible during deployment. Settings stored in the registry would need to be copied through the Registry API, whereas configuration files can simply be copied. In addition, the account that runs most ASP.NET sites is specifically configured to be opted out of the registry to secure the site from hacks and attacks.

.NET Configuration

.NET configuration files are well-formed XML files whose vocabulary is understood by the .NET runtime. You can see a list of all the configuration files by looking in the configuration directory (which you explore just a little later).

The .NET runtime reads these configuration files into memory as necessary to set the various .NET run-time parameters, and these parameters are cumulative. For example, web.config is loaded when ASP.NET applications are started, but the first configuration file the server examines is machine.config.

Machine.Config

The default .NET configuration for your computer is declared in a file named machine.config. You can find machine.config in the directory C:\Windows\Microsoft.NET\Framework\v*xxxxx*\ Config (where *xxxxx* is the .NET version; the current release at the time of this writing is 4 and the directory name of the beta version at the time of this writing is v4.0.21006). Machine.config sets the default .NET application behaviors for the entire computer.

Recent .NET versions have improved the machine.config arrangement. Versions 1.*x* of .NET lumped all of machine.config into a single file—even comments and configuration information for systems not in use on the specific computer (browser information, for example, even though the computer might not have been hosting ASP.NET). With version 2.0, machine. config was trimmed down substantially. The comments were moved to a separate file named machine.config.comments, and separate browser definition capability files were moved to separate configuration files. This is important to know because the machine.config comments are sometimes more useful as documentation for configuring .NET than the regular online documentation is. As you configure various ASP.NET applications, the machine.config comments should be the first place you look for information. Version 4.0 of the machine.config file is only a little bit larger than its 3.0 predecessor.

Configuration Section Handlers

At the top of machine.config you can see a number of configuration section handlers. Each handler understands a specific vocabulary for configuring .NET (and ultimately ASP.NET). Whereas machine.config controls the settings for the entire computer, ASP.NET applications rely on files named web.config to manage configuration. You see much more about web.config shortly. However, for now here is an example of what you might find in a web.config file for a specific application:

```xml
<?xml version="1.0" encoding="utf-8"?>
<configuration>
    <system.web>
        <authentication mode="Forms" />
        <sessionState mode="SQLServer" cookieless="UseUri" timeout="25" />
    </system.web>
</configuration>
```

This small segment tells the ASP.NET runtime to use Forms Authentication (one of the ASP.NET authentication options) to authenticate users of this site. The configuration information also tells ASP.NET to use SQL Server to manage session state, to allow session state information to expire after 25 minutes, and to track session information using a session ID embedded in the request Uniform Resource Identifier (URI). Chapter 14, "Session State," examines session state in detail—for now, it's a good example to illustrate some of the parameters ASP.NET configuration manages.

You can see from this example that configuring ASP.NET relies on the ability of the runtime to understand some keywords. In this case, the keywords *authentication*, *mode*, and *Forms* tell ASP.NET how to manage authentication. ASP.NET must correctly interpret *sessionState*, *mode*, *SQLServer*, *cookieless*, *UseURI*, and *timeout* to know how to manage an application's session state.

The .NET components that understand these vocabularies are listed near the top of machine.config.

```
<configuration>
  <configSections>
    <section name="appSettings"
     type="{entire strong assembly name here...}"
        restartOnExternalChanges="false" />
    <section name="connectionStrings"
      type="{entire strong assembly name here...}" />
    ...
    <sectionGroup name="system.web"
      type="{entire strong assembly name here...}">
      <section name="authentication"
        type="{entire strong assembly name here...}"
          allowDefinition="MachineToApplication" />
      <section name="sessionState"
        type="{entire strong assembly name here...}"
          allowDefinition="MachineToApplication" />
    ...
    </sectionGroup>
  </configSections>
</configuration>
```

The preceding code is necessarily abbreviated. Go ahead and take a look at machine.config and you'll see the section handlers in their full glory. (On most computers, machine.config is located at C:\Windows\Microsoft.NET\Framework\v*xxxxx*\Config.) When you look at the configuration handlers, you can see that the *sessionState* configuration settings are interpreted by an assembly with the strong name *System.Web.Configuration.SessionStateSection, System.Web, Version=4.0.0.0, Culture=neutral, PublicKeyToken=b03f5f7f11d50a3a*. A *strong name* fully specifies the name of an assembly, including a version (to ensure version compatibility) and a public token (to ensure the assembly has not been tampered with).

Web.Config

Machine.config lays out the default settings for your computer (and ultimately for your applications). The default settings are generally targeted toward the most common use cases you will encounter rather than some special configuration you might need to apply to a specific application. For example, *sessionState* is configured to be handled in process by default. That's fine when you're developing but almost certainly is not appropriate for a commercial-grade application that services many diverse clients.

Because all your .NET applications depend on machine.config to configure them, making changes to machine.config could potentially affect multiple applications. It's a bad idea to update machine.config directly.

To configure themselves, stand-alone .NET applications depend on configuration files named after the application. For example, an application named MyApp.EXE would have a configuration file named MyApp.EXE.config. Of course, ASP.NET applications do not follow that naming convention. Instead, the ASP.NET runtime expects configuration information to be declared in a file named web.config.

Microsoft Visual Studio 2010 introduces a new feature: separate configurations for debug and release versions of your application. Earlier versions of Visual Studio provided only a single web.config file, and the debug and release versions of the application shared the same settings. In Visual Studio 2010, when you generate a Web application, Visual Studio provides three configuration files: web.config, web.debug.config, and web.release.config. Settings shared by the debug and release versions go in web.config. Settings specific to the debug or release version (such as the *Trace* setting) go in the respective web.config files.

To override the default settings, you simply need to include a file named web.config in the application's virtual directory. For example, the following code sets up the Web application to which it applies. The configuration file turns on Forms Authentication and tracing, for example.

```xml
<?xml version="1.0" encoding="utf-8"?>
<configuration>
    <system.web>
        <authentication mode="Forms" />
        <trace enable=true/>
    </system.web>
</configuration>
```

The configuration settings your application actually sees have been inherited from a (potentially) long line of other web.config files. The machine.config file sets up the default .NET configuration settings. The top-level web.config file (in the .NET configuration directory) sets up the initial ASP.NET configuration. Then, you can use subsequent child web.config files in the request path to tweak folder-specific settings for a single application.

This way of managing configuration information works well. Many of the usual defaults apply in most situations, and you sometimes need to tweak only a few items. When you do, you just drop a web.config in your virtual directory and/or subdirectory.

However, managing settings by littering your hard disk with web.config files can get a bit unwieldy if many separate configurations are necessary. The ASP.NET configuration schema includes a *location* element for specifying different settings for different directories—but all the settings can all go in a master configuration file for your application.

For example, the following configuration section removes the ability of the AppSubDir directory to process standard ASP.NET Web Services. The *remove* instruction causes ASP.NET to have amnesia about all files with the extension .asmx.

```
<configuration>
  <location path="AppSubDir">
    <system.web>
      <httpHandlers>
        <remove verb="*" path="*.asmx" />
      </httpHandlers>
    </system.web>
  </location>
</configuration>
```

You could also apply other specific settings to the subdirectory, such as for security purposes. (Chapter 9, "Logging In," explores security in depth.) You might not find it surprising that ASP.NET configuration files include terms to manage authorization and authentication. This is a perfect use for the *location* element. The following configuration code allows all users into the main (virtual) directory but requires that users who want to access the PagesRequiringAuth subdirectory be authenticated:

```
<configuration>
  <system.web>
    <authorization>
      <allow users="*" />
    </authorization>
  </system.web>
  <location path="PagesRequiringAuth">
    <system.web>
      <authorization>
       <deny users="?" />
      </authorization>
    </system.web>
  </location>
</configuration>
```

Managing Configuration in ASP.NET 1.*x*

In ASP.NET 1.*x*, you configured settings manually by typing changes into a target web.config file. For example, if you wanted your application to use *SQLServer* as a session state database, you had to insert the correct verbiage into the application's web.config file, keystroke by keystroke. Unfortunately, there was no configuration compiler to help ensure that the syntax was correct. If you typed something wrong, you usually wouldn't know about it until you ran the application, at which point ASP.NET would display a cryptic error message.

Managing Configuration in Later Versions of ASP.NET

ASP.NET 2.0 introduced some major improvements to the process of managing ASP.NET applications, and these improvements carry through to the current version of ASP.NET. Although you can still type configuration information into the web.config file manually, ASP.NET 2.0 and later versions provide some new configuration utilities, including the Web Site Administration Tool (WSAT) available in Visual Studio and the ASP.NET configuration facilities available through IIS 7.*x*.

In this exercise, you change settings in an application's configuration and see how they are reflected in web.config.

Configuring your application

1. Begin by creating a new Visual Studio ASP.NET Web Application project named *ConfigORama*.

2. After Visual Studio generates the application, click Project, ASP.NET Configuration to open the ASP.NET Web Site Administration Tool, which is shown in the following graphic:

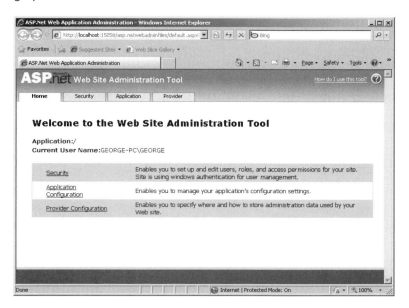

The Other Administration Tabs

Notice that the Web Site Administration Tool includes four tabs: Home, Security, Application, and Provider. The Security tab manages authentication and authorization settings. That is, you can use the Security tab to add users and assign roles to them. You explore that process in detail in the next chapter.

The Application tab is for maintaining various settings related to your application. You can control basic configuration settings here, including maintaining key/value pairs specific to your application, Simple Mail Transfer Protocol (SMTP) settings for defining how the site manages e-mail, and turning debugging and tracing on and off. You can also use the Application tab to take an application offline to perform maintenance.

Finally, you can use the Provider tab to manage various data providers. In ASP.NET 2.0, Microsoft introduced the concept of a provider designed to make data access for a given ASP.NET subsystem easier and more standardized. For example, users might have personalized settings, and the *Membership* provider retrieves them for your code to display to the user or otherwise manage. The *Roles* provider provides the roles your user might be assigned when using your Web application. You can configure the various providers individually using the Provider tab. Although you will most likely use the built-in ASP.NET providers that access a database for data archival and retrieval, you could use custom providers that you create, third-party providers, or mix and match the two types. Provider configuration in the Provider tab includes which provider to use (if you have more than one available) and database connection string settings if a database is to be used.

With the Web Site Administration Tool, you can manage parts of web.config without having to type settings manually. The tool is accessible from Visual Studio. Visual Studio 2010 creates a web.config file by default. But if for some reason one is not created, the Web Site Administration Tool can create a web.config file for you. When you manage authentication and roles, the tool also creates a database suitable for consumption by SQL Server Express in the App_Data folder of your Web site for storing application data. (You see more about that later in the discussion of ASP.NET features such as personalization and authorization.)

3. Click the Application tab and add a couple of application settings by clicking the Create Application Settings link. Add a setting named *Copyright* and one named *CompanyName*, as shown in the following graphics. In this exercise, it doesn't matter what you type as the corresponding value. First, go to the Application tab.

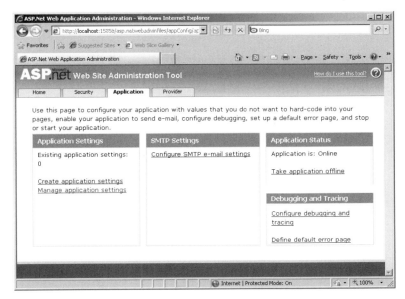

Then, click the Create Application Settings link to add some settings:

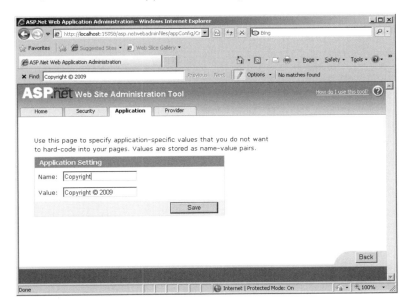

When you return to the Application tab, it shows how many application settings there are in the config file:

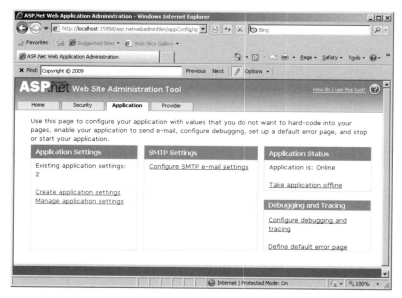

4. Open the application's web.config file. You should see entries for *Copyright* and *CompanyName*.

Web.config should look like this now (some entries inserted by Visual Studio have been omitted):

```xml
<?xml version="1.0" ?>
<configuration >

    <appSettings>
        <add key="Copyright" value="Copyright © 2009 " />
        <add key="Company" value="ThisIsACompanyName" />

    </appSettings>

    <connectionStrings/>
</configuration>
```

5. Now write some code to access the application settings you just added, which are available through a class named *ConfigurationManager*. Add a drop-down list to the Default.aspx form to hold the application settings keys (with an ID of *DropDownListApplicationSettings*) and a label to display the values (with the ID *LabelSetting*). Add a button with the ID *ButtonLookupSetting* so that users can look up the value associated with the application settings key. In the *Page_Load* handler, interrogate the *ConfigurationManager* for all the application settings:

```
using System.Configuration

public partial class _Default : System.Web.UI.Page
{
    protected void Page_Load(object sender, EventArgs e)
    {


        if (!this.IsPostBack)
        {
            foreach (String strKey
                in ConfigurationManager.AppSettings.AllKeys)
            {
                this.
                    DropDownListApplicationSettings.
                    Items.Add(strKey);
            }
        }

    }
    protected void ButtonLookupSetting_Click(object sender, EventArgs e)
    {

        string strSetting;
        strSetting =
            ConfigurationManager.AppSettings[this.
                DropDownListApplicationSettings.
                SelectedItem.Text];
        this.LabelSetting.Text = strSetting;

    }
}
```

6. Compile the program and run the site. When you start the page, it loads the drop-down list so that it contains all the keys from the *ConfigurationManager.AppSettings* collection. When you select application settings by clicking a key in the drop-down list, the code you inserted in the previous step looks up the value of the application setting and displays it in the label:

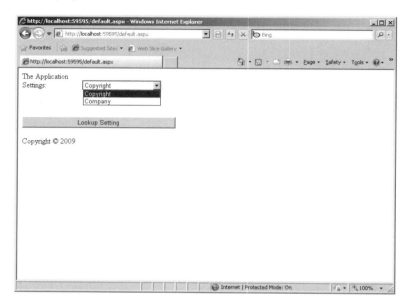

In ASP.NET, you can also manage application settings using the Configuration tab for your site when it is hosted in IIS.

Configuring ASP.NET from IIS

If your site is running from within a virtual directory (through IIS), you can use the features view in IIS to edit configuration information. To do so, your site must be managed by IIS.

Although you can configure ASP.NET applications from IIS only on the computer that hosts the site, the level of configuration you control is much more extensive than it is when using the Web Site Administration Tool from within Visual Studio. Your configuration changes also have an immediate operational effect on your Web application.

Following is an exercise to help you become familiar with the ASP.NET Configuration tab in IIS.

Using IIS to configure ASP.NET

1. Before creating this new Web site, be sure to execute Visual Studio as an administrator
   (that is, right-click Visual Studio on the Start menu and select Run As Administrator. This
   is necessary when creating (or editing) Web sites hosted directly by IIS. Create a new
   Web site called *ConfigORamaIIS*.

To host the Web site directly within IIS, click the Browse button to open the dialog box
that lets you choose the location. Choose your own computer (*localhost*). Visual Studio
will create a virtual directory for you and point itself to the virtual directory:

Create New Web Application button

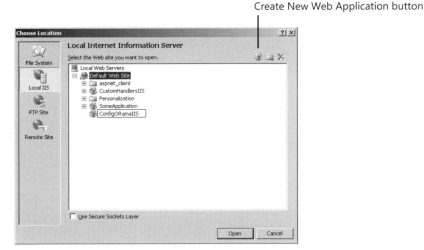

2. Open the IIS management console. To do so, open Control Panel and then Administrative Tools. If you are using Windows Vista or Windows 7, you can access Administrative Tools through the System And Security settings option. There, you should be able to open the Internet Information Services (IIS) Manager. Look for the ConfigORamaIIS site in the Connections pane. Click the ConfigORamaIIS virtual directory, and you'll see the ASP.NET-related settings appear in the Features View pane:

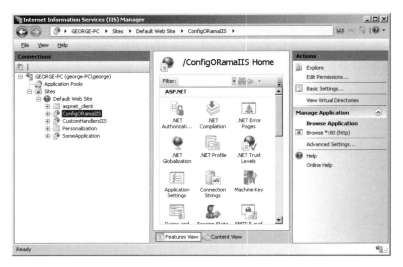

3. Double-click one or two of the features to view their configuration screens. For example, click the Connection Strings icon to open the Connection Strings pane:

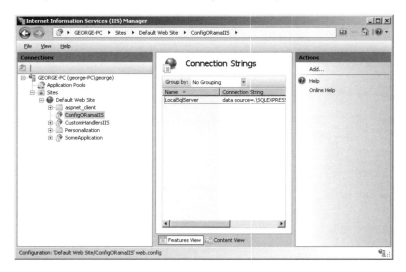

4. Right-click the Connection Strings pane, and then click Add to add a new connection string using the Add Connection String dialog box. The Add Connection String dialog box is a user-friendly place in which to enter connection string information (the following entry is a fictitious database name):

In addition to managing connection strings from the Features View, you can also manage application settings. In the Features View pane, click Application Settings to view the Application Settings pane, as shown in the following graphic:

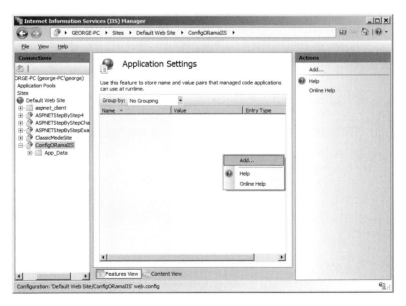

In the Application Settings pane, right-click in the middle of the pane, and then click Add to open the Add Application Setting dialog box where you can add application settings—just as you did using the ASP.NET Web Site Administration Tool. Add a key/value pair like so:

5. Open web.config in your application. It should now include an entry for *Copyright*.

```
<?xml version="1.0" encoding="UTF-8"?>
<configuration >
    <appSettings>
        <add key="Copyright" value="Copyright © 2009" />
    </appSettings>
</configuration>
```

6. Use the IIS ASP.NET configuration editor to add a setting named *BackgroundColor* with a value of *#00FF00*. This exposes a setting that administrators can use to change the background color of Default.aspx (after support for changing the background color is built into the code). That is, anyone having access to the web.config file will be able to modify the background color.

7. Return to Visual Studio and add a property to the Default page (Default.aspx.cs) to retrieve the background color. (If you created a site using a master page, do this in the master page code file rather than in Default.aspx.cs.) It should be available from the *ConfigurationManager.AppSettings* collection.

```
using System.Configuration;

public partial class SiteMaster : System.Web.UI.MasterPage
{
    protected string BackgroundColor    {
        get { return
          ConfigurationManager.AppSettings["BackgroundColor"]; }
    }

    protected void Page_Load(object sender, EventArgs e)
    {
    }
}
```

8. By default, Visual Studio will include a master page with your application. Open the Site.master page in Source view and update the <p> tag to retrieve the background color from the application settings. Use the <% and %> braces to mark executable code. Also add a line to the .aspx file to display the background color value.

```
<%@ Master Language="C#" AutoEventWireup="true"
  CodeFile="Site.master.cs" Inherits="SiteMaster" %>

  <!DOCTYPE html PUBLIC "-//W3C//DTD XHTML 1.0 Strict//EN"
  "http://www.w3.org/TR/xhtml1/DTD/xhtml1-strict.dtd">
  <html xmlns="http://www.w3.org/1999/xhtml" xml:lang="en">

  <head runat="server">
    <title></title>
    <link href="~/Styles/Site.css" rel="stylesheet" type="text/css" />
    <asp:ContentPlaceHolder ID="HeadContent" runat="server">
    </asp:ContentPlaceHolder>
  </head>
  <body style="background-color: <%=BackgroundColor%>">

  <!-- other content is here... -->
  </body>
</html>
```

9. Compile the program and run the page. The value #00FF00 translates to a bright green, so the background for the master page should now appear bright green:

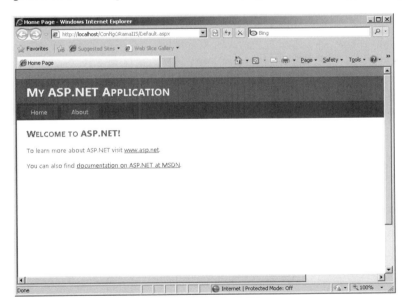

   10. Browse through some of the other icons in the ASP.NET Configuration Settings pane
   in IIS. You will encounter many of these settings as you explore ASP.NET in the coming
   chapters:

   - The Authentication page is for setting up users and assigning them roles in your
     application.

   - The .NET Globalization page manages globalization issues.

   - The Session State management feature is for managing session state. You can
     tell ASP.NET to store session state in any of a number of places, including in pro-
     cess on the host computer, out of process using a dedicated state server, or in a
     dedicated SQL Server database.

   - The Pages And Controls page allows you to manage the UI of your application
     such as themes and master pages.

ASP.NET relies on web.config for almost all of its settings. The configuration story doesn't end
here, however. This chapter describes only a couple of settings, and you will see most of them
as well as many others throughout the book. You revisit configuration when you encounter
features such as security, session state, error messages, and HttpHandlers/HttpModules.

Chapter 8 Quick Reference

To	Do This
View global configuration files	Look in the Windows directory under Microsoft.NET\Framework\v*xxxxx*\ config, where *xxxxx* is the version of .NET your ASP.NET site uses.
Change configuration settings in a specific ASP.NET application	Place a web.config file in the application's directory and modify the settings.
Change configuration settings for a specific subdirectory under a virtual directory	Place a separate web.config file in the subdirectory OR Use the *location* element in the virtual directory's web.config file.
Modify a Web application's settings using the Web Site Administration Tool (WSAT)	In Visual Studio, click Web Site, ASP.NET Configuration from the main menu.
Modify a Web application's settings using the IIS ASP.NET Configuration tool	Open the IIS control panel. Highlight the virtual directory for your Web application. In the Features View pane for the virtual directory, double-click the icon that represents the settings you want to view/modify.
Retrieve settings from the configuration file	Use the ASP.NET *ConfigurationManager* class.

Chapter 9
Logging In

After completing this chapter, you will be able to

- Manage Web-based security.

- Implement Forms Authentication.

- Work with Forms Authentication in the raw.

- Work with ASP.NET login controls to make writing login pages painless.

- Work with ASP.NET role-based authorization.

This chapter covers managing access to your ASP.NET application. Web site security is a major concern for most enterprises. Without any means of securing a site, a Web site can expose areas of your enterprise that you might not want exposed to the general public. In this chapter, you take a quick look at what security means in relation to Web applications. Then, you look at various services available in ASP.NET for authenticating and authorizing users.

Note *Authenticating users* means determining that users really are who they say they are (verifying the identity of a user). This is often accomplished by using a shared secret such as a password. *Authorizing users* means allowing or restricting access for specific users who have identified themselves based on permissions or *roles* assigned to them. For example, clients in an administrative role are often granted more access than are clients in simple user roles.

This chapter also describes the new login controls, which greatly reduce the amount of development effort you might otherwise expend securing your site. Finally, the chapter examines ASP.NET support for authorization (assigning users to roles).

Important This chapter's code samples on the companion CD require IIS support to execute. See the "Code Samples" section in the Introduction for important information on running the examples for this chapter.

Web-Based Security

Software security is a prominent topic these days, especially with ever increasing public awareness of security issues such as privacy. When a Web application runs in the Microsoft environment, several security issues arise immediately: (1) the security context of Internet Information Services (IIS), (2) being sure your clients are who they say they are, and (3) specifying what those clients may and may not do with your application.

Managing Web-based security is similar to managing typical network security in that you still need to manage the authentication and authorization of users. However, Web-based security involves managing clients running different platforms in an open system. That is, programming for a Web-based platform involves servicing requests from a client browser over which you have much less control in a closed network (such as a Windows operating system–based office network).

Although not quite a trivial problem, Windows security is at least a solved problem. Anyone who has configured a Windows network knows there are myriad issues involved in setting up all users appropriately. But a Windows network is a closed system, and everyone on the network is connected and has a baseline level of trust among them (that is, they're all on the network). When you log on to a Windows network, you prove who you are (you *authenticate*) by providing your user name and password. If the security subsystem believes you are who you say you are, it issues a security token to your Windows session, and every application you start runs using that security token.

The resources (files, folders, drives, applications, and so forth) on your computer and on your network are associated with discretionary access control lists (DACLs). If the security context under which your application runs belongs to a resource's DACL, you can use it. Otherwise, the system prevents you from using the resource. This is known as *authorization*.

In a closed system such as a Windows network, an administrator can effectively survey the whole system and grant users access to various resources. Because it's a closed system, the system can determine very easily whether a user belongs in the system and what that user may do.

Contrast this with a Web application: The range of users of your application is quite wide and users are not necessarily part of your local network. This means that you need another way (outside of the Windows infrastructure) to authenticate and authorize the users of your Web application. Or, put another way, Windows authentication doesn't scale well to the general Internet.

Securing IIS

The first security issue you encounter in programming Web applications in the Windows environment is understanding the security context of IIS. Virtually all access to your Web site is directed through IIS. As with all Windows applications, IIS runs under a specific context. When you install IIS on your computer, the install process creates a separate security identity specifically for IIS.

You can see the identity under which your version of IIS runs by starting IIS in Control Panel, opening Internet Information Services (IIS) Manager, selecting a virtual directory, viewing the Features pane, double-clicking the Authentication item to open the Authentication page, right-clicking Anonymous Authentication, and then clicking Edit. On my computer, the name of the user is IUSR, as shown in Figure 9-1.

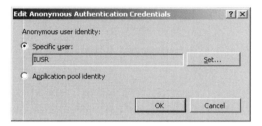

FIGURE 9-1 Managing authentication settings in IIS.

By default, IIS runs the virtual directories using Anonymous Authentication. When this mode is specified, IIS uses the principal identified in the Specific User field as its security principal. That is, IIS runs with access to the resources available to IUSR.

IIS supports other types of authentication, including Windows authentication. In this case, you need to give all potential clients a Windows user name and password. This only works when the clients are running on Windows-based platforms. Users logging on to your site are *challenged*, meaning they are asked to authenticate themselves. They will see a Windows login dialog box when they log on to your Web site (perhaps you've run into this type of site before). Windows authentication does work well for enterprise-wide sites when you can count on your audience running Windows-based browsers. However, for a Web site with a wider audience that uses operating systems other than Windows, you'll want to use other means of authentication because the underlying security mechanism available to Windows users is not present in other operating systems, so those users could not authenticate.

Fortunately, ASP.NET includes *Forms Authentication,* a straightforward means of authenticating clients. The Forms Authentication subsystem in ASP.NET 1.0 and 1.1 was a huge improvement over having to write your own authentication subsystem. Later versions of ASP.NET include and improve on the Forms Authentication model by adding an Authorization subsystem as well.

First, look at Forms Authentication in the raw.

Basic Forms Authentication

ASP.NET 1.0 and 1.1 introduced a straightforward means of authenticating users. Forms Authentication is driven by an application's web.config file. In addition to controlling such aspects as session state, tracing and debugging, and application key/value pairs, web.config includes authentication and authorization nodes.

To require users of your site to authenticate, you simply need to place some instructions in the web.config file. You can edit the file directly, or you can use a tool such as the Web Site Administration Tool available through Microsoft Visual Studio. (Chapter 8, "Configuration," discusses the Web Site Administration Tool in some detail.)

Web.config includes a section for specifying how your site should deal with authentication and authorization. In the absence of the authentication and authorization elements, ASP.NET allows unrestricted access to your site. However, once you add these elements to your web.config file, ASP.NET forces a redirect to a URI dedicated to authentication. Most of the time, the file is some sort of login page in your Web application where users must do something to authenticate, such as type in a user name and password.

Before you look at the code, look at Figure 9-2, which illustrates how control flows on your Web site when you turn on Forms Authentication using web.config.

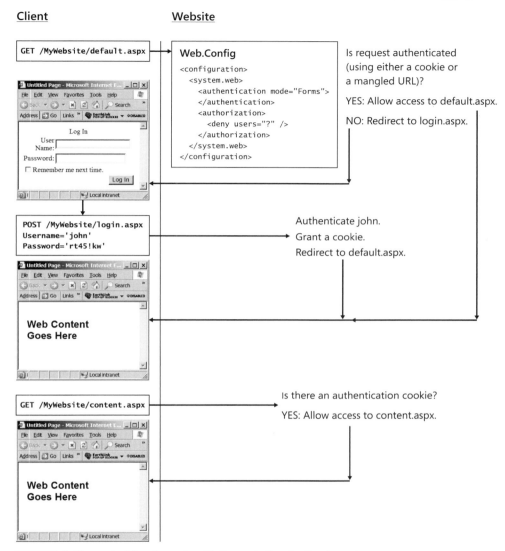

FIGURE 9-2 The control flow for a site with Forms Authentication turned on.

This book's accompanying CD includes this login page. To see an example of the most basic authentication you can use in your application, look at the files Login.aspx and web.config. The web.config file includes the *Authentication* and *Authorization* elements to support Forms Authentication for the site. Listing 9-1 shows the web.config settings necessary to force authentication.

LISTING 9-1 A basic web.config file requiring authentication

```
<configuration>
  <system.web>
    <authentication mode="Forms">
      <forms loginUrl="login.aspx" />
    </authentication>

    <authorization>
      <deny users="?" />
    </authorization>
  </system.web>
</configuration>
```

The login page that goes with it is shown in Listing 9-2.

LISTING 9-2 A basic ASP.NET login page

```
<%@ Page language="C#" %>
<%@ Import namespace="System.Web.Security" %>

<html>
  <script runat="server">

  protected bool AuthenticateUser(String strUserName,
                                  String strPassword) {
    if (strUserName == "Gary") {
      if(strPassword== "K4T-YYY") {
        return true;
      }
    }
    else if(strUserName == "Jay") {
      if(strPassword== "RTY!333") {
        return true;
      }
    }
    else if(strUserName == "Susan") {
      if(strPassword== "erw3#54d") {
        return true;
      }
    }
    return false;
  }

  public void OnLogin(Object src, EventArgs e) {
    if (AuthenticateUser(m_textboxUserName.Text,
                         m_textboxPassword.Text)) {



        FormsAuthentication.RedirectFromLoginPage(
            m_textboxUserName.Text, m_bPersistCookie.Checked);
    } else {
        Response.Write("Invalid login: You don't belong here...");
    }
  }
  </script>
```

```
<head>
  <title>Login Page</title>
</head>
<body>
  <form runat="server">
    <h2>A most basic login page</h2>
    User name:
    <asp:TextBox id="m_textboxUserName" runat="server"/><br/>
    Password:
    <asp:TextBox id="m_textboxPassword"
        TextMode="password" runat="server"/>
    <br/>
    Remember password and weaken security?:
    <asp:CheckBox id="m_bPersistCookie" runat="server"/>
    <br/>
    <asp:Button text="Login" OnClick="OnLogin"
              runat="server"/>
    <br/>
  </form>
</body>
</html>
```

This is a simple login page that keeps track of three users—Gary, Jay, and Susan.

In this scenario, when users try to surf to any page in the virtual directory, ASP.NET stops them and forces them to pass the login page shown in Figure 9-3.

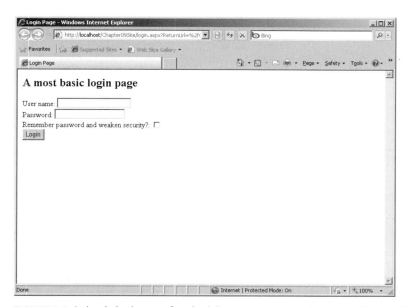

FIGURE 9-3 A simple login page for obtaining a user name and password from a client.

This simple login page authenticates the user (out of a group of three possible users). In a real Web site, the authentication algorithm would probably use a database lookup to see whether the user is included in the database and whether the password matches. Later in this chapter, you see the ASP.NET authentication services. The login page then issues an authentication cookie using the *FormsAuthentication* utility class, which is found in the *System.Web.Security* namespace.

Figure 9-4 shows what the Web page looks like in the browser with tracing turned on. Here, you can see the value of the authentication cookie in the Request Cookies Collection.

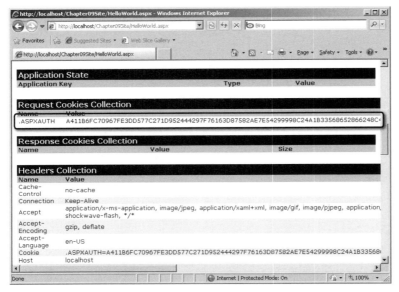

FIGURE 9-4 Tracing turned on reveals the authentication cookie for a page using Forms Authentication.

The following example shows how to employ Forms Authentication on your site.

Running the Forms Authentication example

1. To run the Forms Authentication example, create an IIS application to hold the site. This example is intended to be simple—ASP.NET requires some target and version info—so this site is configured for ASP.NET version 2.0. Right-click the directory in the IIS Connections window, and click Manage Application, Advanced Settings. Select A Classic Mode Application Pool for the application pool property. Add an HTML file to the directory that simply displays a banner text of "Hello World." Name the file Default.htm. You must have a target file to surf to for Forms Authentication to work.

2. Copy the Login.aspx page from the Chapter 9 examples on the accompanying CD into the virtual directory for which you want to apply Forms Authentication.

3. Copy the Web.ConfigForceAuthentication file from the Chapter 9 examples on the accompanying CD into the virtual directory for which you want to apply Forms Authentication. Make sure to rename the configuration file *web.config* after you copy it.

4. Try to surf to a page in that virtual directory. ASP.NET should force you to complete the Login.aspx page before moving on.

5. Type in a valid user name and password. (You can find valid user names and passwords by examining the Login.aspx page from step 2.) Subsequent access to that virtual directory should work just fine because now there's an Authentication ticket associated with the request and response.

Although you might build your own authentication algorithms, ASP.NET includes a number of new features that make authenticating users a straightforward and standard process. You examine those in a moment.

Briefly, ASP.NET allows two other types of authentication: Passport authentication and Windows authentication. There's not much talk about Passport anymore. Passport authentication has evolved into Windows Live ID and requires a centralized authentication service provided by Microsoft. If you've ever used Hotmail.com, you've used Windows Live ID. The advantage of Windows Live ID authentication is that it centralizes login and personalization information at one source. Although this is not a free service, your users can use a single user ID to log in to many Web sites, providing convenience and easing your own development efforts because you don't need to manage user authentication yourself.

The other type of authentication supported by ASP.NET is Windows authentication. If you specify Windows authentication, ASP.NET relies on IIS and Windows authentication to manage users. Any user making his or her way through IIS authentication (using basic, digest, or Integrated Windows Authentication as configured in IIS) is authenticated for the Web site. These other forms of authentication are available when configuring IIS. However, for most ASP.NET Web sites, you bypass IIS authentication in favor of ASP.NET authentication even if only for scalability reasons. ASP.NET uses the authenticated identity to manage authorization.

ASP.NET Authentication Services

ASP.NET includes a great deal of support for authenticating users (outside of IIS support). Most of it comes from the *FormsAuthentication* class. The class includes support for hashing passwords for secure storage, encrypting and decrypting strings, creating authentication cookies, redirecting request following authentication, and managing authentication parameters (such as expiration times).

The *FormsAuthentication* Class

Many ASP.NET authentication services center around the *FormsAuthentication* class. The examples shown in Listings 9-1 and 9-2 show how the rudimentary authentication works by installing an authentication cookie in the response and redirecting the processing back to the originally requested page. This is the primary purpose of *FormsAuthentication. RedirectFromLoginPage*. Some other interesting methods in the *FormsAuthentication* class allow for finer-grained control over the authentication process. For example, you can authenticate users manually, without forcing a redirect, which is useful for creating optional login pages that vary in content based on the authentication level of the client.

FormsAuthentication includes a number of other services as well. Table 9-1 shows some of the useful members of the *FormsAuthentication* class.

TABLE 9-1 Useful *FormsAuthentication* Class Members

FormsAuthentication Method	Description
CookiesSupported	Property indicating whether cookies are supported for authentication
FormsCookieName	Property representing the Forms Authentication cookie name
FormsCookiePath	Property representing the Forms Authentication cookie path
LoginUrl	Redirects URL for logging in
RequireSSL	Property representing whether Secure Sockets Layer is required
SlidingExpiration	Property indicating whether sliding expiration is set
Authenticate	Authenticates the user
Encrypt	Generates an encrypted string representing a Forms Authentication ticket suitable for use in an HTTP cookie
Decrypt	Creates a Forms Authentication ticket from an encrypted Forms Authentication ticket
GetAuthCookie	Creates an authentication cookie for a specific user
GetRedirectUrl	Gets the original URL to which the client was surfing
HashPasswordForStoringInConfigFile	Creates a hashed password suitable for storing in a credential store
RedirectFromLoginPage	Authenticates the user and redirects to the originally requested page
SignOut	Invalidates the authentication ticket

An Optional Login Page

The CD accompanying this book includes an example showing how to authenticate separately. The page in Listing 9-3 uses the same authentication algorithm: three users—Gary, Jay, and Susan—with hard-coded passwords. However, the page authenticates users, and then redirects them back to the same page (OptionalLogin.aspx).

LISTING 9-3 OptionalLogin.aspx

```
<%@ Page language=C# trace="false"%>
<html>
  <script runat=server>

  protected bool AuthenticateUser(String strUserName,
                                  String strPassword)
  {
    if (strUserName == "Gary")
    {
      if(strPassword== "K4T-YYY")
      {
        return true;
      }
    }
    else if(strUserName == "Jay")
    {
      if(strPassword== "RTY!333")
      {
        return true;
      }
    }
    else if(strUserName == "Susan")
    {
      if(strPassword== "erw3#54d")
      {
        return true;
      }
    }
    return false;
  }

  public void OnLogin(Object src, EventArgs e)  {
    if (AuthenticateUser(m_textboxUserName.Text,
                         m_textboxPassword.Text))
    {
     FormsAuthentication.SetAuthCookie(
               m_textboxUserName.Text,
      m_bPersistCookie.Checked);
          Response.Redirect("optionallogin.aspx");
    } else {
       Response.Write("Invalid login: You don't belong here...");
    }
  }
```

```
protected void ShowContent()
{
   if(Request.IsAuthenticated)
   {
      Response.Write("Hi, you are authenticated. <br>" );
      Response.Write("You get special content...<br>" );
   }
   else
   {
      Response.Write("You're anonymous. Nothing special for you... ");
   }
}
</script>
<body><form runat=server>

    <h2>Optional Login Page</h2>

    User name:
    <asp:TextBox id="m_textboxUserName" runat=server/><br>
    Password:
    <asp:TextBox id="m_textboxPassword"
        TextMode="password" runat=server/>
    <br/>
    Remember password and weaken security?:
    <asp:CheckBox id=m_bPersistCookie runat="server"/>
    <br/>
    <asp:Button text="Login" OnClick="OnLogin"
                runat=server/>

    <br/>

    <%ShowContent(); %>
  </form></body>
</html>
```

Notice that the page sets the authentication cookie manually by calling *FormsAuthenticati on.SetAuthCookie*, and then redirects the processing back to the page. Each time the page shows, it calls the *ShowContent* method, which checks the authentication property in the page to decide whether to display content specialized for an authenticated user. Because the page redirects manually after authenticating, the web.config file needs to look a bit different. To make it work, the authentication node should remain, but the authorization node that denies anonymous users needs to be removed. That way, any user can log in to the OptionalLogin.aspx page—they won't be denied—and they can proceed after they are authenticated. The new web.config file is shown in Listing 9-4. The file on the accompanying CD is named Web.ConfigForOptionalLogin. To make it apply to the application, copy the file and name it *web.config*.

LISTING 9-4 A web.config file supporting optional login

```
<configuration>
  <system.web>
    <authentication mode="Forms">
    </authentication>
  </system.web>
</configuration>
```

Figure 9-5 shows how the optional login page appears before the user has been authenticated.

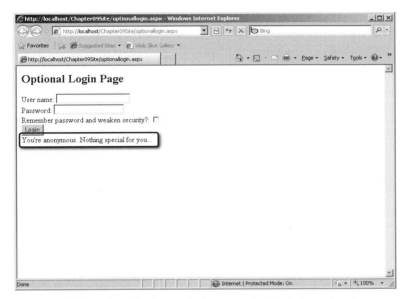

FIGURE 9-5 The optional login page before an authenticated user logs in.

This example shows how to run the optional login page.

Running the optional login page

1. To run the optional login page, create a virtual directory to hold the site. Alternatively, you can use an already existing site and try the optional login page from there.

2. Copy the OptionalLogin.aspx page from the Chapter 9 examples on the accompanying CD into the virtual directory.

3. Copy the Web.ConfigForOptionalLogin from the Chapter 9 examples on the accompanying CD into the virtual directory. Be sure to rename the configuration file *web.config* so that ASP.NET loads the appropriate configuration settings.

4. Try to surf to a page in that virtual directory. ASP.NET should allow you to see the page, but as an unauthenticated user.

5. Type in a valid user name and password. You should see the content tailored for authenticated users. Subsequent requests/responses to and from the site will include an authentication token, so you would always see the special authenticated content.

After the user has been authenticated, the optional login page shows the content tailored to the specific authenticated user. Figure 9-6 shows the page after an authenticated user logs in.

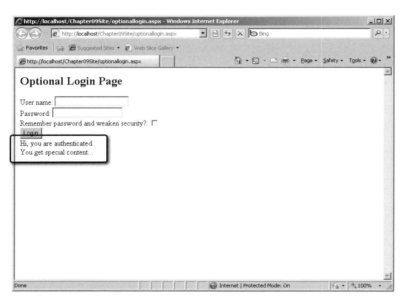

FIGURE 9-6 The optional login page after an authenticated user has logged in.

Managing Users

So far, you can see that the fundamentals of Forms Authentication are easy to manage. In the previous examples, the pages are inaccessible until users prove their identity. The preceding example shows raw authentication for which the user names and passwords are hard-coded into the ASPX file. This is useful for illustration purposes; however, in a production application you'll undoubtedly want to assign identities to the authorized users visiting your site.

ASP.NET and Visual Studio include facilities for managing user identities and roles. The following exercise shows how to set up a secure site in which users are allowed access only after they identify themselves correctly.

Managing user access

1. Create a new Web site named *SecureSite*.

2. Add a label to the Default.aspx page with the text "Congratulations. You made it in." That way, when you get to the default page after logging in, you'll know which page you are looking at in the browser.

3. Open the ASP.NET Web Site Administration Tool by clicking Web Site, ASP.NET Configuration on the main menu. Click the Provider tab. Click the Select A Single Provider For All Site Management Data link. You can click the Test link to test the provider to make sure the connection is working.

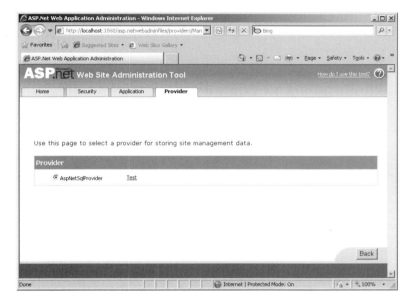

> **Tip** As you recall from Chapter 8, IIS includes ASP.NET configuration facilities as well. If your site has a virtual directory, you can get to the facilities by opening IIS, selecting the virtual directory of interest, and navigating among the Features icons.

4. To ensure that the database is working, click the Security tab and add a user directly from there. This creates the SQL Express database for you. Alternatively, you can run the program aspnet_regsql.exe to create a data store to hold membership information. You can find aspnet_regsql.exe in C:\Windows\Microsoft.NET\Framework\v4.0.20506>.

5. You can change the authentication type by clicking the Security tab. You will see the page shown in the following graphic. Click the Select Authentication Type link. (Visual Studio should have set you up with Forms Authentication.)

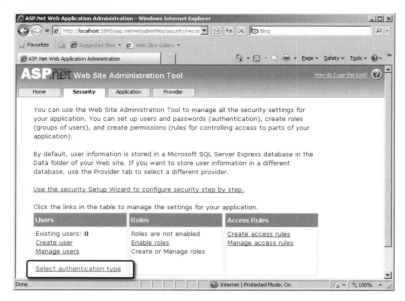

6. Make sure the From The Internet option is selected as the as the access method, as shown in the following graphic. Then, click the Done button. This causes the site to use Forms Authentication.

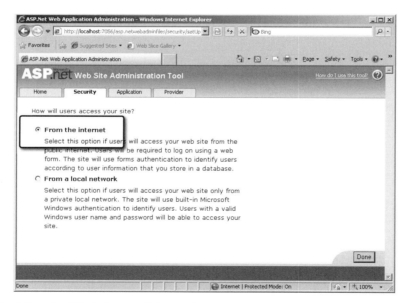

7. Select Enable Roles, and then select Create Or Manage Roles. Add some roles to the site. The example here includes three roles: Admin, JoeUser, and PowerUser. Add these roles now. You assign real users to them shortly.

As you create roles, you'll see each new role on the page:

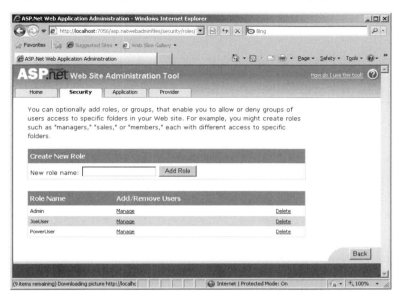

8. In the main Security tab, click the Create User link and add some users. You can assign them to roles now if you wish.

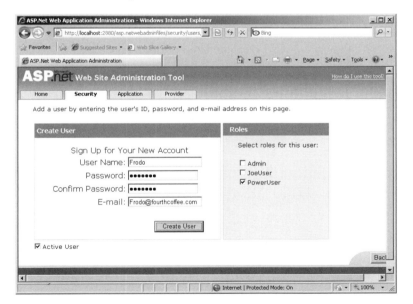

After you've worked with the configuration a bit, web.config should be able to find the authentication settings. (You set up the Authorization node later.)

```xml
<?xml version="1.0"?>
<configuration >
   <!-- other config info -->
   <system.web>


   <!-- other config info -->
   <authentication mode="Forms">
     <forms loginUrl="~/Account/Login.aspx" timeout="2880" />
   </authentication>
   <membership>
     <providers>
       <clear/>
         <add name="AspNetSqlMembershipProvider"
         type="System.Web.Security.SqlMembershipProvider"
          connectionStringName="ApplicationServices"
         enablePasswordRetrieval="false"
         enablePasswordReset="true"
         requiresQuestionAndAnswer="false" requiresUniqueEmail="false"
         maxInvalidPasswordAttempts="5"
         minRequiredPasswordLength="6"
         minRequiredNonalphanumericCharacters="0" passwordAttemptWindow="10"
         applicationName="/" />
     </providers>
   </membership></system.web>
</configuration>
```

9. At this point, you can authenticate users to your site. However, you would probably like to control which parts of your site they may access. To manage authorization, create some access rules by clicking the Create Access Rules link in the Security tab. Deny access for anonymous users, as shown in the following graphic:

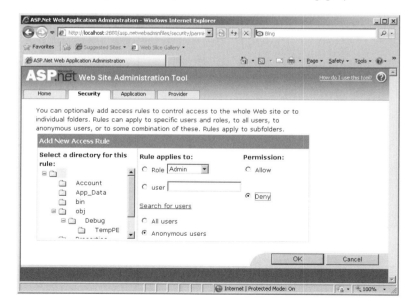

Denying access for anonymous users causes the following changes in web.config. Notice the *authorization* element.

```
<?xml version="1.0" encoding="utf-8"?>
<configuration
>


  <system.web>
    <authorization>
      <deny users="?" />
    </authorization>
    <!-- more config info here -->
  </system.web>
</configuration>
```

10. Now try running the site. ASP.NET should deny you access to the site and direct you to the login page, as shown here:

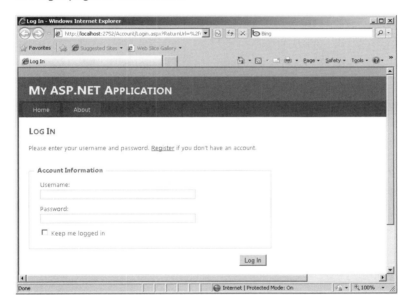

ASP.NET is looking for a way to authenticate the user. Because this is a fresh session with an anonymous user. The Forms Authentication setting is set to *true* and anonymous users are denied access. By default, Visual Studio generates a project that points to a prebuilt login page named login.aspx in the Account folder.

The next section looks at ASP.NET login controls used by the login page created by Visual Studio.

ASP.NET Login Controls

Earlier in this chapter, you handcrafted a couple of different login pages. During the heyday of ASP.NET 1.1, that's exactly what you had to do to get Forms Authentication to work. Later versions of ASP.NET add a number of login controls that perform the most common login scenarios you might need for your site.

These controls include the *Login, LoginView, PasswordRecovery, LoginStatus, LoginName, ChangePassword,* and *CreateUserWizard* controls. Here's a summary of what each control does:

- *Login* The *Login* control is the simplest login control and supports the most common login scenario—signing in using a user name and password. The control includes user name and password text boxes and a check box for users who want to compromise password security by saving their passwords on the computer. The control exposes properties through which you can change its text and appearance. You can also add links to manage registration and password recovery. The *Login* control interacts with the ASP.NET membership component for authentication by default. If you want to manage authentication yourself, you can do so by handling the control's *Authenticate* event.

- *LoginView* The *LoginView* control is very similar to the optional login page discussed earlier. It's useful for managing the content you display for authenticated versus unauthenticated users. The *LoginView* displays the login status through the display templates *AnonymousTemplate* and *LoggedInTemplate*. The control renders a different template depending on the status of the user. With the *LoginView* control, you can also manage text and links in each template.

- *PasswordRecovery* The *PasswordRecovery* control supports Web sites that send user passwords to clients when users forget their passwords. The control collects the user's account name and then follows up with a security question (provided that functionality is set up correctly). The control either e-mails the current password to the user or creates a new one.

- *LoginStatus* The *LoginStatus* control displays whether the current user is logged on. Users who are not logged in are prompted to log in, whereas logged-in users are prompted to log out.

- *LoginName* The *LoginName* control displays the user's login name.

- *ChangePassword* The *ChangePassword* control gives users a chance to change their passwords. An authenticated user can change his or her password by supplying the original password and a new password along with a confirmation of the new password.

- *CreateUserWizard*   The *CreateUserWizard* control collects information from users so that it can set up an ASP.NET membership account for them. Out of the box, the control gathers a user name, a password, an e-mail address, a security question, and a security answer. The *CreateUserWizard* can collect different information from users depending on the membership provider your application uses.

The following exercise illustrates how to write a login page using the login controls.

Working with the login page

1. Visual Studio creates a login page for you by default. So that you can see how the login controls work, create a new login page. Remove the login page from the Accounts folder, and then create a new one by right-clicking the Account folder, clicking New, Add New Item, and selecting Web Form From Master Page. Name it *login.aspx*. Drop a *Login* control into the Content area:

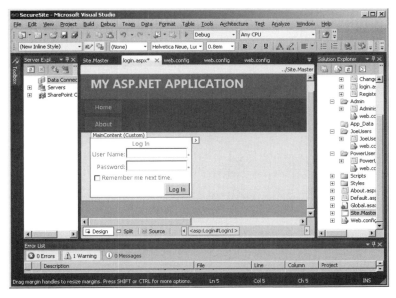

2. Visual Studio generates a site that uses Forms Authentication by default. (Or you can turn on Forms Authentication by selecting Internet access through the ASP.NET Web Site Administration Tool.) The login URL specified in web.config is ~/Account/Login.aspx (which now points to your new login page).

3. Now try to surf to the default page. ASP.NET presents you with the login page. Try typing in a user name and password that you provided in the last example.

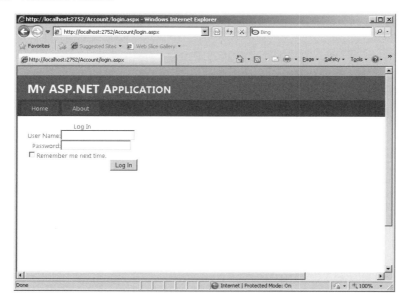

Provided you log in successfully, you next see the default page:

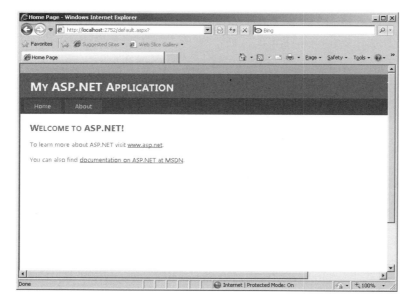

Authentication is an important step in managing the security of your site. The second half of the equation is managing access to your site after users have authenticated themselves. This is known as *authorization*.

Table 9-2 shows the users' names and their passwords for the example included in this chapter.

TABLE 9-2 User Names and Passwords for the Example Code in This Chapter

User Name	Password
George	abc!123
Joe	abc!123
Frodo	abc!123

Authorizing Users

When you authenticate a user, you establish his or her identity. Although that information is sometimes useful by itself, a system becomes more secure when authentication is combined with authorization. Authentication establishes identity, whereas authorization establishes what users can do when they're logged in to your site.

In the previous example, you added user roles to the site. The following example illustrates how to limit access to certain areas of your site based on the user's identity.

Managing authorization

1. Add a folder named Administrators for administrators to access by right-clicking the project node and clicking New Folder. Name the folder *Admin*. Add a Web Form to the folder that contains the label "Administrators Only." Similarly, create a JoeUsers folder and a Web Form for JoeUsers, and create a PowerUsers folder. Add a single default file to each of these directories so that you have something to surf to in each directory. Insert labels on each of the pages with unique text so that you can distinguish each page.

2. Now set up associations between the roles you've defined and these new resources. In the Web Site Administration Tool, add some more users and assign each a role. For example, the example on the CD includes a user named George assigned to the Administrator role, a user named Joe assigned to the JoeUser role, and a user named Frodo assigned to the PowerUser role.

3. After you add the new roles, set up new access roles by clicking the Manage Access Rules link, and then clicking the Add New Access Rule link. You can selectively allow or deny various users or classes of users, as shown in the following graphic. For example, users assigned the Administrators role are given access to the Administrators folder.

After you make these changes, you should see the changes in the web.config file in the Authentication and Authorization nodes in web.config files created for each folder. When you apply access rules, the administration tool will put a Web.config file into the directory for which you're modifying the access rules. The tool should also put a <deny users="*"> node following the allow node:

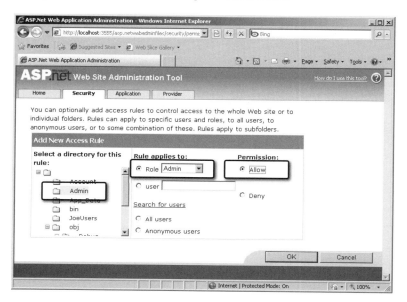

4. So that clients can try to navigate to the various restricted pages, drag three *Hyperlink* controls onto the master page—one for the Administrator page, one for the JoeUser page, and one for the PowerUsers page that you created in step 1. Set the *Text* property of each *Hyperlink* to some meaningful text (for example, the *Text* property for the Administrator.aspx file might be "Go to Administrator Page"). Use the Property pane to set the *NavigationUrl* for each *Hyperlink* to the appropriate page.

5. Run the page. After logging in, you should see the default page, which displays the text "Congratulations. You made it in. This is the default page" and three hyperlinks. Depending on your identity, ASP.NET does or does not allow you to view the pages in the subdirectories. Click the various links to see how ASP.NET permits or restricts page viewing based on roles.

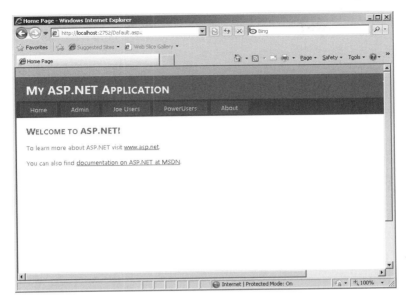

If you logged in successfully as a user assigned the JoeUser role, ASP.NET lets you view the pages in that subdirectory, as shown in the following graphic:

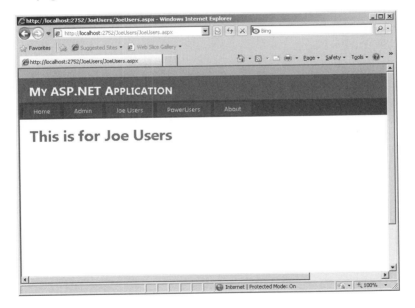

This example only touches on the utility the login controls provide. There is much more to managing a Web site than simply filtering users. For even more robust login scenarios, including password recovery and optional logins, experiment with some of the other login controls.

Chapter 9 Quick Reference

To	Do This
Use Forms Authentication in your application	1. Use the ASP.NET Web Site Administration tool (click Web Site, ASP.NET Configuration).
	2. Click the ASP.NET tab in IIS. Note that the authentication type must be FormsAuthentication.
Configure the security aspects of your Web site	1. Use the ASP.NET Web Site Administration Tool (click Web Site, ASP.NET Configuration).
	2. Click the ASP.NET tab in IIS. From there you can administer users and roles, and assign users to specific roles.
Authenticate a request manually	Use the Set Auth cookie in the *FormsAuthentication* class.
Invalidate an authentication cookie	Call the *SignOut* method in the *FormsAuthentication* class.
Verify the presence of the authentication cookie	Turn on tracing.

Chapter 10
Data Binding

After completing this chapter, you will be able to

- Represent collections using data-bound controls.

- Talk to database providers in ASP.NET.

- Customize data-bound controls.

This chapter covers one of the most useful features of ASP.NET: data binding. A number of controls in ASP.NET have the capability to understand the form and content of a collection and to render the correct tags to represent such user elements as list boxes, radio button lists, and combo boxes. This chapter examines how these controls work and how you can use them on a Web page.

Representing Collections Without Data Binding

One of the most common problems encountered in building any software (and Web sites in particular) is representing collections as user interface (UI) elements. Think about some of the sites you have recently visited. If you ordered something from a commercial site, you no doubt hit a page that asked you to enter your address. What happened when you reached the *State* field? Most Web sites display a drop-down list box from which you could choose a state abbreviation.

How was that drop-down list filled? In HTML, the <select> tag nests several <option> tags that represent the elements to be listed. The state abbreviations probably came from a database or some other well-established source. Somewhere (most likely at the server), some piece of code had to go through the collection of states and render <select> and <option> tags for this hypothetical state selection control.

ASP.NET server-side controls, such as the *ListBox* and the *DropDownList*, include *Items* collections. For example, one way to render a collection as a drop-down list is to declare a drop-down list on your ASP.NET page and add the items individually using the *Items.Add* method like so (of course, this assumes this object's *ToString* method returns something meaningful—not the type, but the contents of the object):

```
protected void BuildDropDownList(IList techList)
{
    for(int i = 0; i < techList.Count; i++)
    {
        this.DropDownList2.Items.Add(techList[i]);
    }
}
```

Because representing collections as UI elements is such a prevalent programming task, it makes a lot of sense to push that down into the framework if possible. ASP.NET includes a number of data-bound controls that are capable of taking collections and rendering the correct tags for you. The following sections describe how this works.

Representing Collections with Data Binding

Each of the data-bound controls in ASP.NET includes properties to attach it to a data source. For simple data binding, these controls include a *DataSource* property to which you can attach any collection that implements the *IEnumerable*, *ICollection*, or the *IListSource* interfaces (which include the *DataSet* and *DataTable* classes that you see shortly). After attaching the collection to the control, you call *DataBind* on the page (or the control) to instruct the control to iterate through the collection.

For more complex data binding, some controls include a property named *DataSourceID*. This new style of data binding is named *declarative data binding*. Instead of simply iterating through a collection, the declarative data binding classes use a separate *DataSource* control to manage data for the data-bound control. You can think of the *DataSource* controls as preconfigured database commands. Instead of littering your code with database commands and queries, the *DataSource* controls perform the commands on your behalf. These data managers support the data-bound controls in implementing standard functionality such as sorting, paging, and editing. Declarative binding greatly simplifies the process of rendering collections. It works by referencing the ID of a *DataSource* control on the page. The .NET Framework includes several of these *DataSource* controls—including one for Microsoft Access databases, one for Microsoft SQL Server, one for wrapping ad hoc collections (the *ObjectDataSource*), one for supporting Language Integrated Query (*LinqDataSource*), and one for supporting XML data access (the *XmlDataSource*). Chapter 11, "Web Site Navigation," looks at the *SiteMapDataSource*. With declarative data binding, calling *DataBind* is optional. The control calls *DataBind* during the *PreRendering* event for you.

ASP.NET includes a number of controls that support at least simple data binding, whereas others support declarative data binding as well. These controls include those based on the *ListControl*, the *CheckBoxList*, the *RadioButtonList*, the *DropDownList*, and the *ListBox*. In addition, the more advanced controls include the *TreeView*, the *Menu*, the *GridView*, the *DataGrid*, the *Repeater*, the *FormView*, and the *DetailsView*.

Here's a rundown of how each control works.

ListControl-Based Controls

The most common data-bound controls are those based on the *ListControl* base class. These controls include the *ListBox*, the *BulletedList*, the *RadioButtonList*, the *CheckBoxList*, and the *DropDownList*. You see these controls in detail in a moment. The names are self-explanatory for the most part. They all have direct analogs in Windows desktop programming as well as standard HTML control tags. The *ListBox* displays a list of strings. The *DropDownList* is similar to a *ComboBox*. The *RadioButtonList* displays a group of mutually exclusive radio buttons. The *CheckBoxList* displays a column of check box controls.

TreeView Control

You saw an example of the *TreeView* in Chapter 6, "Control Potpourri." The *TreeView* control represents hierarchical data. It's perfect for matching up with XML data sources. The *TreeView* features collapsible nodes that users can use to move from abstract data elements to more detailed ones. The *TreeView* supports declarative data binding.

Menu Control

The *Menu* control also handles hierarchical data binding. With the *Menu* control, users can navigate the site in much the same way that they can in desktop applications using menus. The *Menu* supports declarative data binding.

FormView Control

The *FormView* control supports free-form layout for individual controls (such as a *TextBox* or a *ListBox*) that render data from a data source. The *FormView* also supports editing of data in the data source through the controls. The *FormView* supports declarative data binding.

GridView Control

Whereas ASP.NET 1.*x* supported only the *DataGrid* control, later versions of ASP.NET support a *DataGrid* on steroids—the *GridView*. The *GridView* control is what it says it is: It renders collections in a grid with individual columns and rows. Each row in the grid represents an individual record in a collection. Each column in a row represents an individual field in the record. Moreover, the original *DataGrid* required you as a developer to manage paging and sorting of data. The *GridView* control, on the other hand, supports automatic paging and sorting. The *GridView* also supports editing (something that requires hand coding in the *DataGrid*) and declarative data binding.

DetailsView Control

If the *GridView* gives you the whole gestalt of a data source, the *DetailsView* control is for focusing in to display one record at a time. The *DetailsView* is often paired with controls such as the *ListBox*, the *DropDownList*, and the *GridView*. Users select the row using one of these controls and the *DetailsView* shows the associated data. The *DetailsView* supports declarative data binding.

DataList Control

The *DataGrid* and the *GridView* controls display the data in a data source using regular rows and columns, and that is that. However, if you want a little more control over the final rendered format, the *DataList* control displays the records in a data source in a format you determine using template controls.

Repeater Control

The *Repeater* control also displays data from a data source in a format you specify (rather than forcing it into rows and columns). The *Repeater* control uses both raw HTML and server-side controls to display the rows. The *Repeater* control repeats the format you define for each row.

Simple Data Binding

The simplest data binding entails attaching a simple collection to the *DataSource* property of one of the *ListControl*-based controls. If you have a collection, you can simply assign it to the *DataSource* property of one of these controls and it will render the correct tags automatically.

The following example shows how to use some of the data-bound controls by hooking up a *List* to several of the *ListControl*-based controls.

Data binding with a collection

1. Start a new Web site named *DataBindORama*. Make it an empty Web site.

2. Add an App_Code directory to the project by right-clicking the project node in Solution Explorer and clicking Add ASP.NET Folder, and then App_Code. Right-click the App_Code node in the project in Solution Explorer, click Add New Item, and then add a class named *TechnologyDescriptor*. Add two implicit string properties named *TechnologyName* and *Description*. This class will represent a technology name and an accompanying description.

Tip In versions earlier than .NET 3.5 you would have had to create private or protected fields to store the string-based information, and then create public properties to expose the string values for public consumption. .NET 3.5 simplifies this by allowing you to use *implicit properties*. Implicit properties are really nothing more than shortcuts, saving time and unnecessary lines of code when your property is doing nothing more than providing access to private (or protected) fields.

Important Exposing the member variables as properties is important so that the controls will work correctly with data binding. When a control binds to a collection composed of classes, it will look for the fields to expose through their property names. Using the data-binding controls, you can specify a display name (that is, the value that will appear in the control), and you can specify a second hidden value to be associated with the item that was selected. In the case of rendering collections of managed objects, the binding architecture depends on these fields being exposed as properties.

Listing 10-1 shows the *TechnologyDescriptor* that exposes a technology name and description as properties. The class also has a static method that creates a collection of *TechnologyDescriptors*.

LISTING 10-1 Code for the *TechnologyDescriptor*

```
public class TechnologyDescriptor
{
    public string TechnologyName { get; set; }
    public string Description { get; set; }

    public TechnologyDescriptor(string strTechnologyName,
                string strDescription)
    {
        this. TechnologyName = strTechnologyName;
        this. Description = strDescription;
    }

    public static List<TechnologyDescriptor> CreateTechnologyList()
    {

        List<TechnologyDescriptor> lTechnologies =
          new List<TechnologyDescriptor>();

        TechnologyDescriptor technologyDescriptor;

        technologyDescriptor =
          new TechnologyDescriptor("ASP.NET",
          "Handle HTTP Requests");
        lTechnologies.Add(technologyDescriptor);

        technologyDescriptor =
          new TechnologyDescriptor("Windows Forms",
          "Local Client UI technology");
        lTechnologies.Add(technologyDescriptor);
```

```
       technologyDescriptor =
         new TechnologyDescriptor("ADO.NET and Linq",
         "Talk to the database");
       lTechnologies.Add(technologyDescriptor);

       technologyDescriptor =
         new TechnologyDescriptor(".NET CLR",
         "Modern runtime environment for manage code");
       lTechnologies.Add(technologyDescriptor);

       technologyDescriptor =
         new TechnologyDescriptor(".NET IL",
         "Intermediary representation for .NET applications");
       lTechnologies.Add(technologyDescriptor);

       technologyDescriptor =
         new TechnologyDescriptor("WPF",
         "Advanced rendering technology");
       lTechnologies.Add(technologyDescriptor);

       technologyDescriptor =
         new TechnologyDescriptor("Silverlight",
         "Advanced rendering on the Web");
       lTechnologies.Add(technologyDescriptor);

       technologyDescriptor =
         new TechnologyDescriptor(".NET Compact Framework",
         "Modern runtime environment for small devices");
       lTechnologies.Add(technologyDescriptor);

       return lTechnologies;
     }
   }
```

3. Add a new Web Form to the project and name it *Default.aspx*. Be sure the Place Code In Separate File check box is selected. Add four data-bound controls to the default page in the content area: a *ListBox*, a *DropDownList*, a *RadioButtonList*, and a *CheckBoxList*. This example uses absolute positioning to lay out the controls.

4. Underneath each of these controls, place a *Label*. You will use the label to show the value associated with each selected item. Give the labels names so that you can refer to them in the code file. This example uses the names *LabelListBoxSelectedValue*, *LabelDropDownListSelectedValue*, *LabelRadioButtonListSelectedValue*, and *LabelCheckBoxListSelectedValue*.

5. Set the *AutoPostBack* property for the *ListBox*, the *DropDownList*, and the *CheckBoxList* to *true* (the *RadioButtonList* will already be set for you). That way, selecting an item in each of the controls will cause a postback during which the selected item might be interrogated.

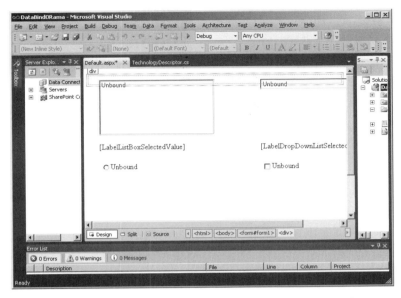

6. Now update the page to instantiate a list of *TechnologyDescriptors* and to attach the collection of *TechnologyDescriptors* to each control. For each control, set the *DataTextField* property to *TechnologyName* (to map it to the *TechnologyName* property of the *TechnologyDescriptor*). This ensures that the technology name appears in the control. Then, set the *DataValueField* for each control to *Description* to map the *Description* property to be the associated value. Listing 10-2 shows how to create a collection of *TechnologyDescriptors* and attach the collection to each of the controls.

7. Add selection handlers for each of the controls by double-clicking them. On receiving the selection events, interrogate the control for the selected item's value. Listing 10-2 also shows the handlers. Except for the labels, the listing uses the default control names generated by Microsoft Visual Studio.

LISTING 10-2 Modifications to Default.aspx.cs to support data binding and control events

```
using System.Collections.Generic;

protected void Page_Load(object sender, EventArgs e)
{

    if (!this.IsPostBack)
    {
        List<TechnologyDescriptor> techList =
            TechnologyDescriptor.CreateTechnologyList();
        this.ListBox1.DataSource = techList;
        this.ListBox1.DataTextField = "TechnologyName";

        this.DropDownList1.DataSource = techList;
        this.DropDownList1.DataTextField = "TechnologyName";

        this.RadioButtonList1.DataSource = techList;
        this.RadioButtonList1.DataTextField = "TechnologyName";
```

```
        this.CheckBoxList1.DataSource = techList;
        this.CheckBoxList1.DataTextField = "TechnologyName";

        this.DataBind();
    }
}
protected void ListBox1_SelectedIndexChanged(object sender, EventArgs e)
{
    this.LabelListBoxSelectedValue.Text = this.ListBox1.SelectedValue;
}
protected void DropDownList1_SelectedIndexChanged(object sender,
  EventArgs e)
{
    this.LabelDropDownListSelectedValue.Text =
      this.DropDownList1.SelectedValue;
}
protected void RadioButtonList1_SelectedIndexChanged(object sender,
  EventArgs e)
{
    this.LabelRadioButtonListSelectedValue.Text =
      this.RadioButtonList1.SelectedValue;
}
protected void CheckBoxList1_SelectedIndexChanged(object sender,
  EventArgs e)


{
    this.LabelCheckboxListSelectedValue.Text =
      this.CheckBoxList1.SelectedValue;
}
```

8. Compile the site and browse to the page:

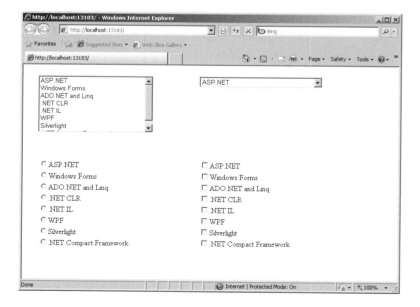

In this example, selecting one of the items in the data-bound controls reveals the related value in the label beneath the control.

In certain programming situations, you might find yourself doing this kind of data binding. For example, simple collections such as states in the United States or short lists (perhaps of employee or contact names) work great with these *ListControl*-based controls. However, very often you'll find yourself dealing with data in a more complex format—beyond a simple standard collection. A number of controls can deal with more complex *DataSets*. However, you first need to understand ADO.NET because it provides the easiest way to reach these more complex data compositions.

Accessing Databases

The previous example shows how to attach an in-memory collection (such as an *ArrayList* and *List*) to a server-side control and have it render the correct tags on the client. Although this is useful, the server-side controls are capable of working with other collections—including ones that come from databases. Before seeing how to render database queries using UI elements, take a quick look at the .NET database story. This chapter covers the fundamentals of using SQL Server with ASP.NET. Chapter 22, "The ASP.NET MVC Framework," demonstrates the new entity framework for creating object models. Later, this chapter discusses Language Integrated Query, or LINQ, as it relates to database access.

The .NET Database Story

Just as .NET includes a library of classes for managing rich client UI (Windows Forms) and for handling HTTP requests (ASP.NET), .NET includes a library for connecting to a wide range of databases. That library is named *ADO.NET*.

ADO.NET is similar to the previous Microsoft database technology named simply ADO. ADO stands for Active Data Objects. Although Microsoft has dropped "Active" from its marketing lexicon, it kept the name ADO and appended ".NET" to name the managed database technology (surely for brand name recognition). ADO represents a set of managed providers that is very similar in function and form to classic ADO. ADO.NET centers around three main units of functionality: connecting to a database, commanding the database, and using the results.

Connections

When you want to talk to a specific database, you usually need to *connect* to it. At the very least, most of the time this involves specifying the location of the database. For many scenarios, connecting also requires managing security (with user names and passwords). More advanced scenarios might also require dealing with such issues as connection pooling and transactions. These are all handled as part of the process of *connecting* to the database. The connection information is usually passed in with a string, the contents of which are used to set various connection parameters when the ADO.NET internals interpret the string.

ADO.NET has classes for making connections to a database. ADO.NET 1.*x* included only two: a connection for Microsoft SQL Server and another for connecting to more generic OLEDB databases. Later versions of ADO.NET add classes specialized for more database types and include a new set of database services using the *provider pattern*.

Working with ADO.NET 1.*x* involved writing most of the data access code using the ADO interfaces (rather than directly instantiating the database classes). By doing so, you could isolate the vendor-specific details in a single place in the code—in the spot where the connection is managed. After that, getting the other parts required for making queries (for example, getting the correct command object) was a matter of asking the connection for it. Although you can still write code to connect to the database using ADO.NET 1.*x*–style code, there's now a better way: using the ADO.NET database provider factories.

The ADO.NET provider pattern offers an improvement in connecting to and using databases. By using the provider pattern, you limit exposing the kind of database you're using to a single call to a *provider factory*. You choose the kind of database in one place and the provider takes care of making sure the correct connection and command objects are used. This was less important in ADO.NET 1.*x*, when ADO.NET divided the database world into two kinds of databases: SQL Server and OLEDB databases. However, with its support of new database types, the provider pattern is a welcome addition.

If you look in machine.config, you'll see providers for the following database technologies:

- ODBC Data Provider
- OLE DB Data Provider
- OracleClient Data Provider
- SqlClient Data Provider
- SQL Server CE Data Provider

The first four of these providers factories are handled by a *DbProviderConfigurationHandler*, while the SQL Server CE provider is handled as a separate component. Listing 10-3 shows a snippet from machine.config illustrating how the provider keys are mapped to provider factories.

LISTING 10-3 Default provider factories defined in machine.config

```
<configuration>
 <configSections>
  <section name="system.data.odbc"
   type="System.Data.Common.DbProviderConfigurationHandler, ..."/>
  <section name="system.data.oledb"
```

```
       type="System.Data.Common.DbProviderConfigurationHandler, ..."/>
     <section name="system.data.oracleclient"
       type="System.Data.Common.DbProviderConfigurationHandler, ..."/>
     <section name="system.data.sqlclient"
       type="System.Data.Common.DbProviderConfigurationHandler, ... "/>
   <configSections />
   <system.data>
      <DbProviderFactories>

        <add name="Microsoft SQL Server Compact Data Provider"
             invariant="System.Data.SqlServerCe.3.5"
             type=" System.Data.SqlServerCe.SqlCeProviderFactory ...    " />
      </DbProviderFactories>
    </system.data>
</configuration>>
```

To get a connection to a database, you ask the runtime for a reference to the right factory,
and then get a connection from the factory, as shown in Listing 10-4. You use the name of
the database type (*System.Data.SqlClient* or *System.Data.SqlServerCe.3.5*, for example). After
getting the right kind of factory, you ask it to create a connection for you.

LISTING 10-4 Obtaining a database provider factory

```
DbConnection GetConnectionUsingFactory()
{
  DbProviderFactory dbProviderFactory =
      DbProviderFactories.GetFactory("System.Data.SqlClient")
  return dbProviderFactory.CreateConnection();
}
```

Once you have a connection, you can use it to connect to the database. Given a SQL Server
database named *AspDotNetStepByStep* is available on your computer, you'd insert a connection string in your web.config. Listing 10-5 shows how this might appear in a web.config file:

LISTING 10-5 Example web.config connection string settings

```
<configuration>
  <connectionStrings>
    <add name="AspDotNetStepByStep"
      connectionString=
        "server=(local);integrated security=sspi;database=AspDotNetStepByStepDB "/>
  </connectionStrings>
</configuration>
```

Once you have a reference to the database connection, you can open the connection and
start commanding the database.

Commands

Once connected, the database is waiting for you to send database commands. These
commands usually include querying the database, updating existing data, inserting new
data, and deleting data. Most databases support Structured Query Language (SQL) to

manage these commands. (Some databases support specialized variations of SQL, so the actual command text might differ from one implementation to another.) Commanding the database usually entails writing SQL statements such as

```
SELECT * FROM DotNetReferences WHERE AuthorLastName = 'Smith'
```

For example, to connect to an SQL database named *AspDotNetStepByStepDB* and query the *DotNetReferences* table for all the references by someone with the last name "Smith," you could use code as shown in Listing 10-6.

LISTING 10-6 Example database query using a data reader

```
class UseDBApp {
    static void Main()
    {
        DbProviderFactory dbProviderFactory =
          DbProviderFactories.GetFactory("System.Data.SqlClient");
        using(DbConnection conn = dbProviderFactory.CreateConnection())
        {
            string s =
              ConfigurationManager.ConnectionStrings["AspDotNetStepByStep"].ConnectionString;
            conn.ConnectionString = s;
            conn.Open();

            DbCommand cmd = conn.CreateCommand();
            cmd.CommandText =
              "SELECT * FROM DotNetReferences WHERE AuthorLastName='Smith'";


            DbDataReader reader = cmd.ExecuteReader();
            // do something with the reader
        }
    }
}
```

Executing the command using *ExecuteReader* sends a query to the database. The results come back by way of an instance of the *IDataReader* interface. The preceding code stops short of using the results. But take a look at how that works in the following section.

Managing Results

Once you've connected to the database and issued a query, you probably need to sift through the data to use it. ADO.NET supports two broad approaches to managing result sets: the *IDataReader* interface and the *DataSet* class.

IDataReader

The preceding example retrieves an *IDataReader* from the query operation. The *IDataReader* interface is useful for iterating through the results of the query. Listing 10-7 shows part of the *IDataReader* interface.

LISTING 10-7 Part of the *IDataReader* interface

```
public interface IDataReader
{
    bool IsClosed {get;}
    int  RecordsAffected {get;}
    void Close();
    bool NextResult();
    bool Read();
    //...
}
```

When iterating through the results of a query, *Read* fetches the next row. *NextResult* fetches the next result set.

Accessing data through *IDataReader* is often termed "fire hose mode" because you have to work your way through the data one row at a time *going forward only*. There's no way to revert back to a previous row except by resetting the reader and starting again. Also, the data rows the reader returns to you are read-only. You can retrieve the data for whatever purpose you need it for, but you can't update the database (insert, update, or delete) using *IDataReader*. An alternative to accessing data through the *IDataReader* interface is to use a *DataSet*.

DataSet

In addition to the *IDataReader*, ADO.NET supports the notion of a disconnected record set—the *DataSet* class in ADO.NET. ADO.NET is primarily designed to help you write large, highly scalable applications. One of the biggest hindrances to scalability is the limits of database connectivity. Databases usually have a limit on the number of active connections available at one time, and if all the connections are in use at any particular time, any piece of code wanting a database connection must wait. If the number of users of a system is about the same as the number of connections available, perhaps that's not a problem. However, if the number of users of a system is greater than the number of database connections, system performance will likely be affected greatly.

To encourage scalability, ADO.NET includes a class named *DataSet* that is designed to give you an easily navigable snapshot of your application's database. The idea behind a database is to get in and get out quickly with a copy of the data. The really good news is that you can insert rows, update columns, and even delete rows using the *DataSet* and later have those changes propagated to the database.

The *DataSet* class is usually filled with data using a *DataAdapter*. A *DataSet* includes a *DataTable* array—one for each selection statement in the query. Once the *DataAdapter* comes back from fetching the data for the *DataSet*, you have the latest snapshot of the queried data in memory. The *DataSet* contains a *DataTable* collection and contains a *DataTable* element for each *SELECT* statement in the query. You can access the *Tables* collection using either ordinal or *String*-type indexes. Once you get to a table, iterating through the rows and columns is a matter of indexing into the table using ordinal indexes for the rows and ordinal or *String*-type indexes for the columns. Listing 10-8 shows an example of using the *SqlDataAdapter* to get a *DataSet*.

LISTING 10-8 Example database query using a *DataSet* and *DataAdapter*

```
class UseDBApp2
{
    static void Main()
    {
        DataSet ds = new DataSet();
        DbProviderFactory dbProviderFactory =
            DbProviderFactories.GetFactory("System.Data.SqlClient");
        using (DbConnection conn = dbProviderFactory.CreateConnection())
        {
            string s =
                ConfigurationManager.ConnectionStrings["AspDotNetStepByStep"].ConnectionString;
            conn.ConnectionString = s;
            conn.Open();

            DbCommand cmd = conn.CreateCommand();
            cmd.CommandText =
                "SELECT * FROM customer; SELECT * FROM country";

            DbDataAdapter adapter = dbProviderFactory.CreateDataAdapter();
            adapter.SelectCommand = cmd;
            adapter.Fill(ds);
        }

        foreach (DataTable t in ds.Tables)
        {
            Console.WriteLine("Table " + t.TableName + " is in dataset");
            Console.WriteLine("Row 0, column 1: " + t.Rows[0][1]);
            Console.WriteLine("Row 1, column 1: " + t.Rows[1][1]);
            Console.WriteLine("Row 2, column 1: " + t.Rows[2][1]);
        }
        ds.WriteXml("dataset.xml");
        ds.WriteXmlSchema("dataset.xsd");


        // Also-may bind to the tables here:
        ;
    }}
```

The code in Listing 10-8 illustrates using a *DataAdapter* and a *DataSet*. The code prints out the second column (that is, column 1) of the first three rows of each table in the *DataSet*. The example in Listing 10-8 indicates that a *DataTable* is valid as a *DataSource* for data-bound controls. The example also shows that the *DataSet* objects also serialize as XML. Both the table schema and the contents can be serialized this way—making it useful for transferring data between systems. Although the *DataSet* is useful for transferring data, it is also heavy-weight. With it, you can transfer the data and the scheme to another system, but with some increase in bandwidth consumption or transfer time. Therefore, use it wisely.

Here's one final note about items in the *DataSet* class: They're disconnected and are not restricted to the "fire hose mode" of data access. You have complete random access to any table, any column, and/or any row in the *DataSet*. In fact, objects in the *DataSet* class are also smart enough to keep track of any data you change inside of them. You can flush the data back to the physical database by using the *CommandBuilder* to prepare the *DataSet* for an *Update* through the *DataAdapter*. A *CommandBuilder* constructs SQL statements on your behalf. This is useful for simple commands and provides a quick and convenient approach for updating a database through a *DataAdapter*.

Given either an *IDataReader* or a *DataSet*, the data-bound controls automatically render themselves appropriately to show the control on the browser. Although you can always connect to the database and fetch the data manually through the standard connection/command architecture, ASP.NET and Visual Studio support an even easier way to render data—declarative data binding.

ASP.NET Data Sources

You just saw how to access data in the raw using ADO.NET, so now look at an easier way. ASP.NET includes some new classes that hide the complexity of managing connections and of gathering data: They're the *DataSource* controls.

DataSource controls abstract the entire connection and command mechanism so that all you need to do is decide on a data source, point the control to that data source, and provide an appropriate query. Visual Studio provides a wizard that guides you through this process. When you have a *DataSource*, you can attach it to a data-bound control that uses it.

The following exercise shows how to make a query and populate controls with the results of the query.

Using a *DataSource* to populate controls with a *DataReader*

1. Add a new form to DataBindORama named *DataBindingWithDB*.

2. The example for this chapter (named DataBindORama), available on the accompanying CD, includes a SQL Server Express database named ASPNETStepByStep4.mdf. First create an App_Data folder by right-clicking the Project node in Solution Explorer and clicking Add, Add ASP.NET Folder, App_Data. Add the database to your project by right-clicking the App_Data node in the project and clicking Add, Existing Item. Locate the ASPNETStepByStep4.mdf file from the CD. Set up a data source control for the database.

   Go to the *Data* controls in the Toolbox. Drag a *SqlDataSource* onto the form. Click Configure Data Source on the context menu displayed by Visual Studio. You'll see a combo box with a list of available databases; the new SQL Server database is the one that will appear, as shown in the following graphic. Click the ASPStepByStep4.mdf file in the combo box to create a connection to the database. Click Next to move to the connection string wizard page. Click Next and accept the connection string that Visual Studio creates for you.

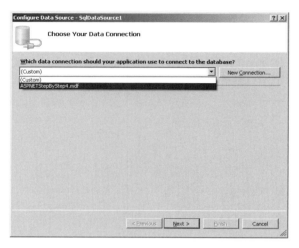

3. Select all the columns and all the rows from the *DotNetReferences* table when configuring the query; that is, select the asterisk (*) to query for all the columns. Click Next.

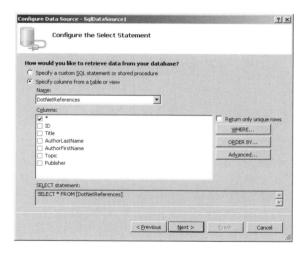

4. If you want to, test the query by clicking the Test Query button, or click Finish:

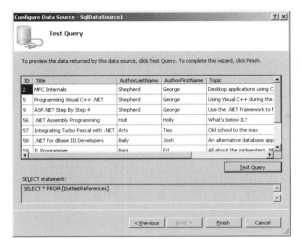

5. Set the *DataSourceMode* property of the data source to *DataReader*. You can do this by clicking the data source control in the Designer, and then modifying the property in the Properties pane.

6. Drag a *ListBox* onto the page. Set the *AutoPostBack* property to *true* by selecting the check box in the Tasks pane. You could also click Choose Data Source in the ListBox Tasks pane. In practice, this is what you would do most likely. However, here add the code to perform the data binding by hand so that you see how it's done in code. In the code view, locate the *Page_Load* method and attach the *ListBox DataSource* property to *SqlDataSource1* like so:

```
protected void Page_Load(object sender, EventArgs e)
{

    if (!this.IsPostBack)
    {
        this.ListBox1.DataSource = this.SqlDataSource1;
        this.ListBox1.DataTextField = "AuthorLastName";
        this.ListBox1.DataValueField = "Title";
        this.ListBox1.DataBind();
    }

}
```

7. Insert a label below the *ListBox* to hold the selected value from the *ListBox*.

8. Double-click *ListBox1* to insert an item changed event handler in your code. In the event handler, set the *Label1* text property to the value field of the selected item.

```
protected void ListBox1_SelectedIndexChanged(object sender,
        EventArgs e)
{
    this.Label1.Text = this. ListBox1.SelectedItem.Value;
}
```

9. Drag a *RadioButtonList* onto the form, as shown in the following graphic. Visual Studio will ask you if you want to configure the control. First, select the *Enable AutoPostBack* check box. Then, click Choose Data Source.

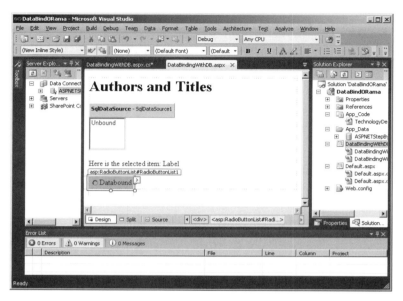

10. Configure the control to use *SqlDataSource1* that you just added:

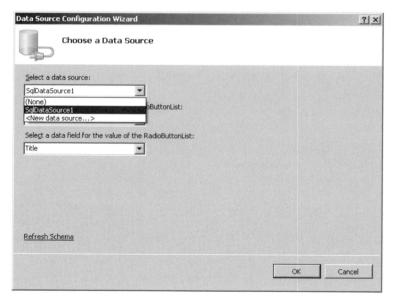

11. Configure the control to use the *AuthorLastName* column for the text field and the *Title* column for the value field. Click OK.

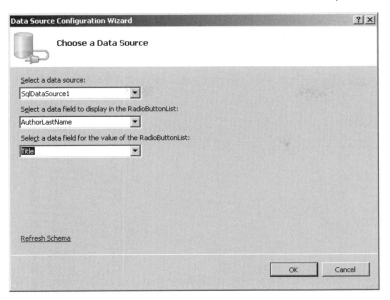

12. Double-click the *RadioButtonList1* object on the form to create a handler for the radio button selection. Handle the selection by updating the *Label1* object with the value associated with the current radio button selection.

```
protected void RadioButtonList1_SelectedIndexChanged(object sender,
        EventArgs e)
{
    this.Label1.Text = this.RadioButtonList1.SelectedItem.Value;
}
```

13. Run the program. The *ListBox* and the *RadioButton* list should show the *AuthorLastName* field, as shown in the following graphic. Selecting one name out of either list will cause a postback and show the title (the associated value) in the label.

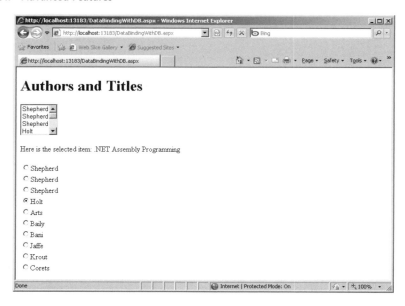

This exercise gives you a taste of how binding to the simple controls works. Although using these controls is common in many scenarios, the utility of data-bound controls doesn't end there. ASP.NET includes other, more complex controls that render data such as complex UI elements as grids and control combinations.

Other Data-Bound Controls

In addition to the simple bound controls, ASP.NET includes several more complex controls. They work very much like the simple bound controls in that you attach a data source to them and they render automatically. However, these controls differ by displaying the data in more elaborate ways. These controls include the *GridView*, the *FormView*, the *DetailsView*, and the *DataList*.

The best way to understand the nature of these controls is to work through a couple of examples. First, the *GridView*.

Using the *GridView*

1. Add a new Web Form to the DataBindORama site. Type in **UseGridView** for the name.

2. Drag a *GridView* from the Toolbox (it's under the *Data* controls) onto the form. Visual Studio will ask you to configure the *GridView*. Under the Choose Data Source option, select New Data Source. Choose a SQL Server database from the options and click OK (it'll use the default name of *SqlDataSource1*). Visual Studio will ask you to specify a connection string. You can use the connection string created in the last exercise (it's in the configuration file). This creates a *SqlDataSource* and puts it on the page for you.

When specifying the query, choose the *DotNetReferences* table and select the asterisk (*) to query for all the columns. Finally, enable paging, sorting, and selection on the *GridView* Configuration menu. After configuring the *GridView*, Visual Studio will show you a design-time representation of the format the query will use when it is rendered to the browser:

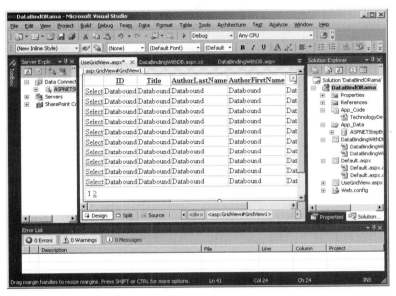

3. Run the program. Try the various options such as paging through the data and sorting to get a feel for how the *GridView* works.

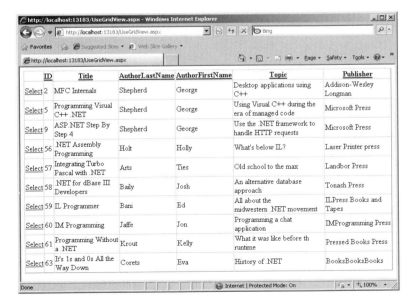

4. Go back to Visual Studio and try formatting the *GridView* to change its appearance. As with all the other ASP.NET controls, the *GridView* includes a number of configurable properties such as the foreground and background colors. Some of the other specialized properties in the *GridView* include *AlternateRowStyle*, *PagerSettings*, and *PagerStyle*. You can, if you like, choose to apply an auto-formatted style, which some ASP.NET controls (including *GridView*) provide for. The following graphic illustrates the UseGridView.aspx page with the *Classic* formatting style applied:

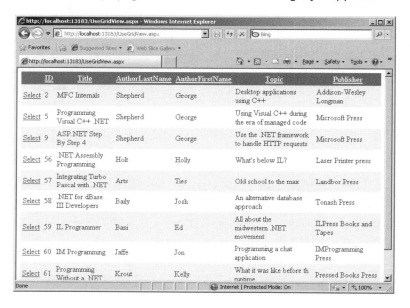

The *GridView* is useful for displaying tables in a format in which you can see all the rows and columns at once. Although the classic *DataGrid* is still available, the *GridView* handles tasks such as selecting rows and sorting by column.

Here's a look at another complex control: the *FormView*.

Using the *FormView*

1. Add a new Web Form to the DataBindORama site named *UseFormView*.

2. Drag a *FormView* from the Toolbox (it's under the *Data* controls) onto the form. Visual Studio will ask you to configure the *FormView*. Under the Choose Data Source option, select New Data Source, make it an SQL database, and click OK. Use the connection that's already available (it'll be listed as "ConnectionString" in the drop-down list) and click Next. When specifying the query, select the asterisk (*) from the *DotNetReferences* table to query for all the columns. Click Next to accept the query and Finish when asked to test the query.

3. Select the *AutoFormat* option on the Configuration menu. Here you have the opportunity to apply a couple of predefined styles to the *FormView*. The example accompanying this text uses the *Classic* formatting style.

4. Enable paging by selecting Enable Paging on the *FormView* Configuration menu. Set the *HeaderText* property (in the Visual Studio Properties pane) to give the *FormView* a title (perhaps something like ".NET Reference Authors and Titles").

5. After configuring the *FormView*, Visual Studio will show you a representation of the format the query will use when it is rendered to the browser:

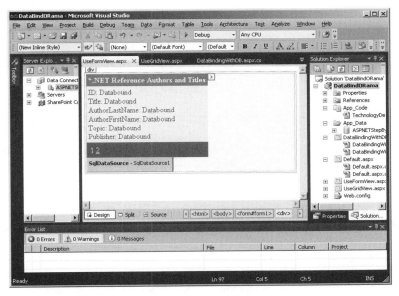

6. Run the program. Try the various options such as paging through the data to get a feel for how the *FormView* works.

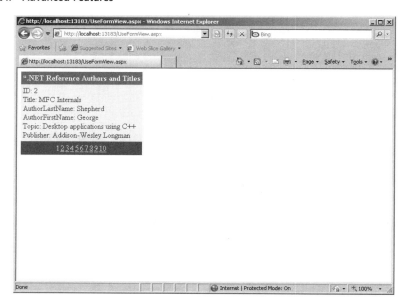

The *FormView* is useful for gathering the information for singular rows in one place. The user navigates between each row, but the focus is always on the current row.

A similar ASP.NET control is the *DetailsView* control. The *DetailsView* control allows you to present row data in a tabular format rather than using the more customizable format that *FormView* allows.

Using the *DetailsView*

1. Add a new Web Form to the DataBindORama site named *UseDetailsView*.

2. Drag a *DetailView* from the Toolbox (it's under the *Data* controls) onto the form. Visual Studio will ask you to configure the *DetailsView*. Under the Choose Data Source option, select New Data Source and configure it similarly to the previous pages. For example, use the same connection string created earlier by Visual Studio. When specifying the query, select the asterisk (*) to select all the columns from the *DotNetReferences* table.

3. Select the *AutoFormat* option on the Configuration menu. As with the previous controls, you have the same opportunity here to apply a couple of predefined styles to the *DetailsView*. The example accompanying this text uses the *Classic* formatting style. In addition, use the *HeaderText* property to give the control a title (I used the header ".NET References").

4. Select the Edit Fields option in the *DetailsView* Tasks pane. Select Auto-Generate Fields in the dialog box if it isn't already selected.

5. Enable paging in the *DetailsView* Tasks pane.

6. After configuring the *DetailsView*, Visual Studio will show you a representation of the format the query will use when it is rendered to the browser:

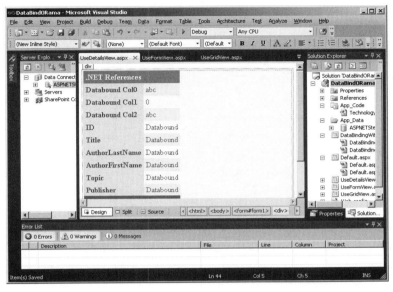

7. Run the program. Try the various options such as paging through the data to get a feel for how the *DetailsView* works.

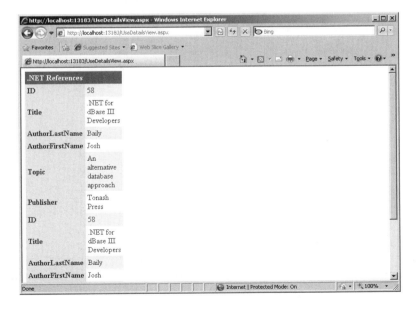

Now for the *DataList*. The *DataList* control has been available since ASP.NET 1.x. It's been updated with later versions of ASP.NET to support declarative data binding. Here's a look at the *DataList*. Like the *DetailsView*, the *DataList* renders the data in a tabular form. Unlike *DetailsView*, *DataList* has no built-in paging capability.

Using the *DataList*

1. Add a new Web Form to the DataBindORama site named *UseDataList*.

2. Drag a *DataList* from the Toolbox (it's under the *Data* controls) onto the form. Visual Studio will ask you to configure the *DataList*. Under the Choose Data Source option, select New Data Source and prepare the data source as in the previous exercises. Use the same connection string created earlier by Visual Studio. When specifying the query, select the asterisk (*) to select all the columns from the *DotNetReferences* table.

3. Select the *AutoFormat* option in the *DataList* Tasks pane. As with the other examples, here you also have the opportunity to apply a couple of predefined styles to the *DataList*. The example accompanying this text uses the *Slate* formatting style.

4. Open the *DataList* Properties dialog box in the *DataList* Tasks pane by selecting Property Builder. If they are not already selected, make sure the Show Header and the Show Footer check boxes are selected:

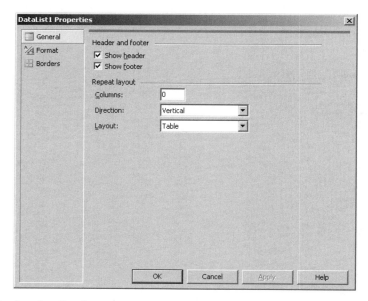

5. Set the *Caption* property to give the *DataList* a title (perhaps something like ".NET References and Titles").

6. After configuring the *DataList*, Visual Studio will show you a representation of the format the query will use when it is rendered to the browser:

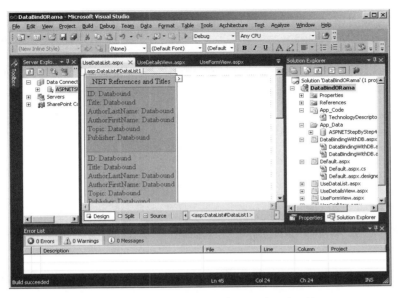

7. Run the program to see how the *DataList* renders itself.

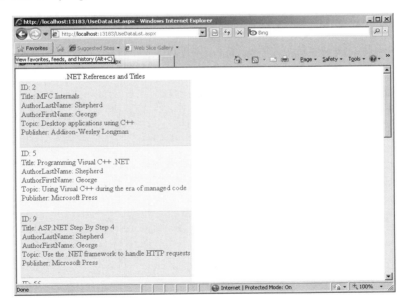

Although the classic data access technologies are here to stay, .NET version 3.0 and later bring a new way to access and manage data—Language Integrated Query. The following section takes a look.

LINQ

New with .NET 3.0 is a database technology named Language Integrated Query (LINQ). LINQ is a set of extensions to the .NET Framework for performing data queries inline. LINQ extends the C# and Visual Basic syntaxes to enable inline queries in the native language syntax (versus SQL or XPath). LINQ doesn't replace existing data access technologies. Instead, LINQ augments existing data query technologies, which makes it easier to perform streamlined queries.

This new technology for making queries is called "language integrated" because you can build queries and use C# (or Visual Basic) language constructs to make selection statements. The following example shows how to develop some queries using LINQ.

Using LINQ

1. Add a new page to the DataBindORama site. Name the page *UseLinq*.

2. Drop a *GridView* onto the page. This will hold the information returned from the LINQ queries.

3. Update the *Page_Load* method to make a LINQ query. Use the *TechnologyDescriptor* collection mentioned earlier in the chapter as the data source for making the query. Set the *DataSource* property of the *DataGrid* to the results of a LINQ query against the *TechnologyDescriptor* collection. The format of the LINQ statement should be as follows:

    from <variable of type held in collection> in <the collection> where <criteria> orderby <criteria> select <property from selected item>

    Select *TechnologyDescriptors* that include ".NET" in the name and order them by length of the *TechnologyName* property. Here is the code that does just that:

```
public partial class UseLinq : System.Web.UI.Page
{
    protected void Page_Load(object sender, EventArgs e)
    {
      if(!this.IsPostBack)
      {
        List<TechnologyDescriptor> techList =
            TechnologyDescriptor.CreateTechnologyList();

        GridView1.DataSource = from technologyDescriptor in techList

        where
        technologyDescriptor.TechnologyName.Contains(".NET") == true

        orderby technologyDescriptor.TechnologyName.Length
```

```
      select technologyDescriptor.TechnologyName.ToUpper();
      GridView1.DataBind();
    }
  }
}
```

4. Run the UseLinq.aspx page to see how the query looks in the *GridView*:

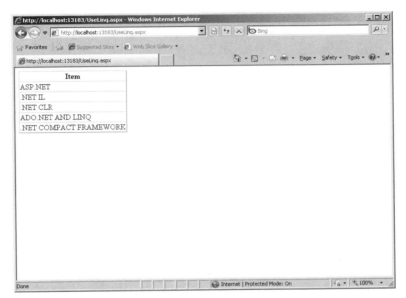

5. Notice how the *GridView* shows only the single property grabbed from each *TechnologyDescriptor*. Now update the query statement to include the whole *TechnologyDescriptor* structure. It should look like this:

```
public partial class UseLinq : System.Web.UI.Page
{
    protected void Page_Load(object sender, EventArgs e)
    {
      if(!this.IsPostBack)
      {
        List<TechnologyDescriptor> techList =
            TechnologyDescriptor.CreateTechnologyList();

        GridView1.DataSource = from technologyDescriptor in techList

        where
        technologyDescriptor.TechnologyName.Contains(".NET") == true

        orderby technologyDescriptor.TechnologyName.Length

        select technologyDescriptor;
        GridView1.DataBind();
      }
    }
}
```

6. Run the page and see how the *GridView* now shows the entire *TechnologyDescriptor*.

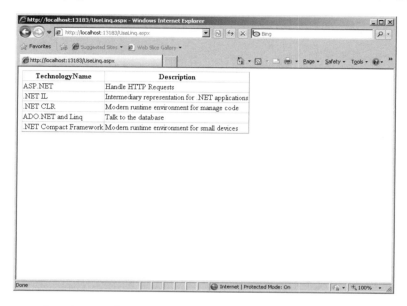

This example only scratches the surface of the power of LINQ. LINQ introduces a very streamlined way to make queries on demand from within your project using the language of your project (Visual Basic, C#, and so forth). You can use the data returned from the queries in any context. In this case, the example shows using the results of a LINQ query in a *GridView*.

Chapter 10 Quick Reference

To	Do This
Bind a collection to a control	Set the control's DataSource property to the collection.
Choose a column to display in the control	Set the control's TextTextField property to the column name for controls that sopport this feature.
Choose a column to use programmatically (that's not displayed in the control)	Set the control's TextValueField property to the column name for controls that sopport this feature.
Display a DataTable as a grid	Use the DataGrid or (preferably) the GridView controls.
Display a DataTable as a formatted, repeating list	Use the DataList.
Make a class's member variables available as DataTextFields and DataValueFields in a control	Expose the members as properties.
Represent data using Master/Detail style presentations	Use the FormView control.

Chapter 11
Web Site Navigation

After completing this chapter, you will be able to

- Understand ASP.NET support for navigation and site maps.

- Implement a site map using an XML data source.

- Use the site map to power the ASP.NET navigation controls.

- Capture and respond to site map navigation events.

One of the major issues facing Web site users is figuring out how to move around sites effectively. Web sites are often hierarchical in nature, and pages are sometimes nested several layers deep. Users can find themselves asking such questions as, "Where am I now?" and "Where can I go from here?" This chapter covers the support that ASP.NET provides for addressing the issue of Web site navigation.

The art of Web site design has progressed far enough that some common navigation idioms are beginning to appear ubiquitously. If you browse a few Web sites hosted on various platforms, you might notice that the sites support a number of different ways to navigate their content. For example, many Web sites include a menu bar across the top of the page that contains links to separate areas on the site. Certain sites include some sort of tree structure to navigate the site. Still others include a "breadcrumb" trail showing users where they are and how to get back to previous pages. ASP.NET supports all these idioms.

ASP.NET Navigation Support

ASP.NET navigation support comes in three parts: navigation controls, site map data source, and site map provider architecture. The *navigation controls* (the *Menu*, the *TreeView*, and the *SiteMapPath*) all can resolve human-readable display names to real URLs to which HTTP requests are sent. The *site map data source* stores information about a site's hierarchical organization. The *site map provider* interprets physical data (often in the form of an XML file) and implements a kind of database cursor representing the current position in a site's hierarchy.

Navigation Controls

ASP.NET includes three server-side controls devoted specifically to site navigation: *SiteMapPath*, *Menu*, and *TreeView*. The *Menu* and *TreeView* controls both maintain collections of display name/URL mappings. You can edit these collections by hand. In addition, these controls can build hierarchical collections of display name/URL mappings based on information in a site map data source. The *SiteMapPath* builds its collection of display name/ URL mappings solely through a site map data source. Table 11-1 summarizes the ASP.NET navigation controls.

TABLE 11-1 The ASP.NET Navigation Controls

Navigation Control	Description
Menu	Interprets the site navigational information contained in the site map XML file and presents it in a menu format. Top-level XML nodes become top-level menu items, with child XML nodes becoming child menu items.
TreeView	Interprets the site navigational information contained in the site map XML file and presents it in a tree format. The top-level site map XML nodes in this case become higher-level branches in the tree, with child nodes represented as child tree nodes.
SiteMapPath	Interprets the site navigational information contained in the site map XML file and presents it in a "breadcrumb" format. In this case, only the current XML node's path is displayed (from the root node to the current child node).

All three controls are useful for navigation, but *Menu* and *TreeView* are useful outside the context of site navigation. *SiteMapPath* is designed strictly for navigating the Web site's site map XML file. The *Menu* control displays items hierarchically and fires events back to the server as the items are selected. The items in the *Menu* control can also be assigned navigation URLs. *TreeView* is useful for displaying any hierarchical data source that implements either the *IHierarchicalDataSource* or the *IHierarchicalEnumerable* interface, and it also can cause redirects to other URLs (that is, it is useful for site navigation). And, as mentioned earlier, *SiteMapPath* is meant specifically to be used for Web site navigation.

For shallow Web sites that will probably change very little over time, building a navigation infrastructure from scratch is easy. However, as the complexity of a site increases, so does the difficulty of managing a navigation structure.

When you organize your site and determine the layout of your pages, it's easy to formalize the layout with a master page that includes a menu linking to other pages. (This is described in Chapter 7, "A Consistent Look and Feel," which discusses master pages.) The work involves creating the menu and adding the links (through the *NavigateUrl* property of the menu item). Implementing the navigation infrastructure by hand is easy enough the first time around. However, as your site grows and becomes more complex, having to update the navigation support repeatedly becomes a problem.

Enter ASP.NET navigation and site map support. The main advantage of using ASP.NET navigation support is that you can establish the layout of the site and then represent it using a hierarchical data structure (such as an XML file or even a database table). The *Menu*, *TreeView*, and *SiteMapPath* controls can all point to a site map data source and use the data source to populate themselves. When you plug the site map data source into the navigation controls, the navigation controls use the data source to create the individual links.

After you have established the site map, updating the navigation links simply requires updating the site map. All controls using the site map data source reflect the changes automatically.

XML Site Maps

ASP.NET includes built-in support for navigation using XML files that describe the layout of the site. These are called *XML site maps*. The ASP.NET default site map support consists of an XML file describing the site layout and the *SiteMapProvider* that reads the XML file and generates *SiteMap* nodes to whatever components are listening (for example, a *Menu* or a *TreeView* control).

The *SiteMapProvider*

The *SiteMapProvider* establishes the base class used by the navigation controls. The ASP.NET default implementation is the *XmlSiteMapProvider*, which reads the XML file named (by default) *web.sitemap*.

Although the default XML site map generally works very well, the ASP.NET navigation controls are perfectly happy using data sources generated from other places (rather than the XML data source). For example, you might decide to implement your own site map provider based on data in a database. The XML site map provides basic raw functionality for navigating a site. However, if you want to do something like manage the site map using a schema different from the default XML schema, that calls for designing a custom provider.

This chapter looks at the default XML site map provider—which is plenty powerful for most circumstances.

The *SiteMap* Class

The main rendezvous point for the ASP.NET navigation infrastructure is the *SiteMap* class. To support the navigation infrastructure, the *SiteMap* class has a set of static methods for managing site navigation. The *SiteMap* class serves as an in-memory representation of the navigation structure for a site, and its functionality is implemented by one or more site map providers. It's an abstract class, so it must be inherited.

The *SiteMap* class performs several functions. First, it serves as the root node of the site navigation hierarchy. Second, it establishes the principal site map provider. Finally, it keeps track of all the provider objects that comprise the site map.

The *SiteMap* contains a hierarchical collection of *SiteMapNode* objects. Regardless of how the site map data is maintained, the *SiteMap* is the interface for accessing a site's navigation information.

The ASP.NET default configuration specifies a default site map. However, as with all things configurable in ASP.NET, you can easily override the default configuration to establish a different provider.

The *SiteMap* class offers only static members. By being static, they enhance performance. In addition, the site map functionality can be accessed at any time in a Web application from a page or even from within a server-side control.

Table 11-2 describes the properties and sole event the *SiteMap* class exhibits.

TABLE 11-2 *SiteMap* Events and Properties

Name	Type	Description
SiteMapResolve	Event	The *SiteMapResolve* event fires when the *CurrentNode* property is accessed. This enables you to implement custom logic when creating a *SiteMapNode* representation of the currently executing page without requiring a custom provider implementation.
CurrentNode	Property	A *SiteMapNode* instance that represents the currently requested page in the navigational hierarchy. If there is no node in the XML site map file, the returned value is null.
Enabled	Property	Returns a Boolean value indicating whether a site map provider is both specified and enabled in the web.config file.
Provider	Property	Returns the default *SiteMapProvider* for the current site map.
Providers	Property	Returns a read-only collection of named *SiteMapProvider* objects that are available to the *SiteMap* class as specified in the web.config file (because you can specify more than one if you wish). Note that only the default provider is used during initialization, however.
RootNode	Property	Returns the *SiteMapNode* that represents the top-level page of the navigation hierarchy for the site.

The *SiteMapNode*

The *SiteMapNode* represents the hierarchical elements of the site map, which is to say, each instance of a *SiteMapNode* represents a page in your Web site. Each node represents an individual page that is located somewhere in the overall Web site navigation hierarchy. When a Web application starts, the *SiteMap* loads the collection of *SiteMapNodes* based on the providers that have been configured in your web.config file for that site.

The *SiteMapNode* includes several useful properties: *ChildNodes*, *Description*, *HasChildNodes*, *Key*, *NextSibling*, *ParentNode*, *PreviousSibling*, *Provider*, *ReadOnly*, *ResourceKey*, *Roles*, *RootNode*, *Title*, and *Url*. It also includes several useful methods: *GetAllNodes*, *GetDataSourceView*, *GetHierarchicalDataSourceView*, *IsAccessibleToUsers*, and *IsDescendentOf*. You see some of these properties being used in later examples. For instance, you will use many of these properties in the example for this chapter when you handle the *SiteMapResolve* event and modify the navigation functionality on the fly.

Using Navigation Controls

When you run Microsoft Visual Studio 2010 and look in the Designer's Toolbox, you can see that ASP.NET includes three controls in the navigation category: *Menu*, *TreeView*, and *SiteMapPath*. This section looks at each in a bit more detail before diving into an example.

The *Menu* and *TreeView* Controls

The *Menu* and *TreeView* controls can bind to hierarchical data sources implementing *IHierarchicalDataSource* or *IHierarchicalEnumerable*. Although they are tailor-made to support site maps, they also work with other data sources. Figure 11-1 shows the *Menu* control in action, and Figure 11-2 shows *TreeView* in action. Both are reading the data from the site map data source to populate themselves.

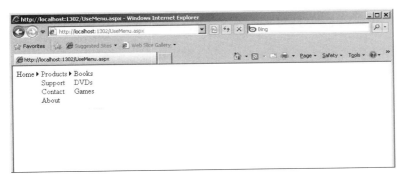

FIGURE 11-1 *Menu* in action.

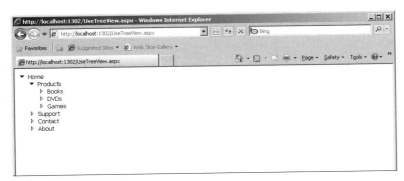

FIGURE 11-2 *TreeView* in action.

The *SiteMapPath* Control

You might have seen user interface (UI) elements similar to the *SiteMapPath* control on other sites—especially online forms that go several layers deep. The *SiteMapPath* control shows a trail indicating where the user is in the Web page hierarchy and shows a path back to the top node (kind of like a trail of breadcrumbs). The *SiteMapPath* is most useful in sites that maintain a very deep hierarchy for which a *Menu* or a *TreeView* control would be overwhelmed.

Although the *SiteMapPath* control is like the *Menu* and the *TreeView* controls (the *SiteMapPath* control reflects the state of the *SiteMap* object), it does deserve special attention. The *SiteMapPath* control and the site map data in the provider are tightly coupled. For example, if you leave a page out of your site map and the user somehow ends up on the page (perhaps through some other navigation method), the user will not see the *SiteMapPath* control on the page. (For this reason, in many cases you find the control embedded in a master page.) Figure 11-3 shows the *SiteMapPath* control in action. The *Menu* underneath the *SiteMapPath* shown in the figure is there so that the user can navigate the page in detail. (The user would not be able to descend the hierarchy without a *Menu* or a *TreeView*.)

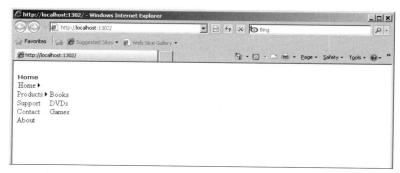

FIGURE 11-3 *SiteMapPath* in action.

Site Map Configuration

The global configuration settings configure ASP.NET sites to use the default *XmlSiteMapProvider*. Listing 11-1 shows the configuration information that is part of the default web.config. Of course, as with all things configurable, you can swap in a different site map provider in your own site by modifying the web.config that goes along with your application.

LISTING 11-1 Default configuration for the site map data

```
<siteMap>
  <providers>
    <add siteMapFile="web.sitemap" name="AspNetXmlSiteMapProvider"
      type="System.Web.XmlSiteMapProvider, System.Web, Version=4.0.0.0, Culture=neutral,
        PublicKeyToken=b03f5f7f11d50a3a" />
  </providers>
</siteMap>
```

In addition to adding the configuration information to web.config, Visual Studio 2010 adds a blank top-level node in the site map, as shown in Listing 11-2.

LISTING 11-2 The default site map that is added by Visual Studio 2010

```xml
<?xml version="1.0" encoding="utf-8" ?>
<siteMap xmlns="http://schemas.microsoft.com/AspNet/SiteMap-File-1.0" >
    <siteMapNode url="" title=""  description="">
        <siteMapNode url="" title=""  description="" />
        <siteMapNode url="" title=""  description="" />
    </siteMapNode>
</siteMap>
```

Once the site map is added, it's easy to update—for example, to add a few new nodes to the site map, simply edit the file as (XML) text. Listing 11-3 shows an XML site map file with a few extra nodes added.

LISTING 11-3 Site map data in XML

```xml
<?xml version="1.0" encoding="utf-8" ?>
<siteMap xmlns="http://schemas.microsoft.com/AspNet/SiteMap-File-1.0" >
 <siteMapNode url=""
  title="Navigation Menu"  description="">
  <siteMapNode url="~/Default.aspx"
    title="Home"  description="" />
  <siteMapNode url="~/Products.aspx"
    title="Products"  description="" />
  <siteMapNode url="~/Support.aspx"
    title="Support" description="" />
  <siteMapNode url="~/Contact.aspx"
    title="Contacts"  description="" />
 </siteMapNode>
</siteMap>
```

Building Navigable Web Sites

Adding navigation support to a Web site is pretty straightforward. Once you establish the hierarchical layout of the site, use the site map XML file to describe the structure. When that's done, just point any navigation controls you put on the page to the new XML site map file. The navigation controls will then populate themselves and render a navigable Web site. The following example shows how to add navigation support to a Web site and use the ASP.NET navigation controls in the application.

Creating a site map

1. Start Visual Studio and create a new ASP.NET Web application project. The example here is called NavigateMeSite.

2. Notice that Visual Studio creates a new Web site complete with a master page ready to populate with controls. In this case, you place some navigation controls on it. Visual Studio also gives you a Default.aspx page and an About.aspx page.

3. The styles created by Visual Studio make it a bit difficult to read the menu and navigation controls. Open the file Site.css and modify the *hideSkiplink* so that the background color is a light gray rather than the dark blue one created by Visual Studio. This example uses #C0C0C0 as the background color for the *hideSkiplink* style, which is used as the style for the menu background on the master page.

4. Add four pages based on the master page: a Default page, a products page, a support page, and a contact page. Visual Studio includes a template for creating a form based on a master page. For each page you add, right-click the project node, click Add New Item, and then click Web Form from the available templates. Be sure the Select Master Page option is selected and click Add. Populate the pages with content so that you know what you're looking at when you run the site (simple text placed directly on the page is fine).

5. Add a new site map to the project by right-clicking the project in Solution Explorer and selecting Add New Item and then choosing Site Map from the available templates. Keep the name Web.sitemap. The following graphic shows the Visual Studio templates with the site navigation template highlighted:

6. Add the following data to the site map (you can change the URLs if the names of the page files are different). Simply edit (or overwrite) the two blank nodes Visual Studio inserted for you:

```xml
<?xml version="1.0" encoding="utf-8" ?>
  <siteMap xmlns="http://schemas.microsoft.com/AspNet/SiteMap-File-1.0" >
    <siteMapNode url="~/Default.aspx" title="Home"
      description="This is the home page">
    <siteMapNode url="~/Products.aspx" title="Products"
      description="This is the products page" />
    <siteMapNode url="~/Support.aspx" title="Support"
      description="This is the support page" />
    <siteMapNode url="~/Contact.aspx" title="Contacts"
      description="This is the contacts page" />
  </siteMapNode>

</siteMap>
```

7. To see how the site map data works with the site, hook up the main menu to the new site map. Open the Site.master file in the Designer and select the navigation menu control (currently it will have links to the Home and About pages). Click the arrow in the upper right-hand corner of the menu to open the menu tasks. Open the drop-down list associated with Choose Data Source, and then click New Data Source. This activates the Data Source Configuration dialog box. There, set the *Menu* data source to the default site map file, and then click OK. The following graphic shows how to select a site map data source for the *Menu* control:

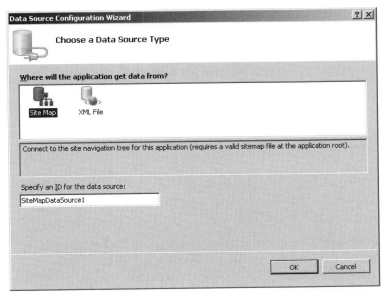

8. Run the site so that you can see the *Menu* in action. Click some pages on the *Menu* and notice how your selections navigate you to the correct places.

9. Next add a *TreeView* to the master page by dragging one from the Toolbox and placing it on the master page. Point the *TreeView* to the default site map data source. Run the application and see what happens.

10. Now add a *SiteMapPath* control to the master page. Apply the XML site map data source to the *DataSource* property of the *SiteMapPath* control.

11. Add two more pages to the project to display two ways to contact the business running this site—one to display the physical address of the business and the other to display other contact information such as e-mail addresses and phone numbers. First, create two new folders, one for each page. Name the folders ContactAddress and ContactEmailPhone. Add the new pages, one per folder. Name the pages ContactAddress.aspx and ContactEmailPhone.aspx. Be sure these pages use the master page. As before, to each page add labels or text describing the page so that you can identify it when the Web application runs.

12. Add two more elements to the site map XML file (web.sitemap) to reflect these new pages. Nest them so that their parent node is the *Contact* node:

```xml
<?xml version="1.0" encoding="utf-8" ?>
<siteMap xmlns="http://schemas.microsoft.com/AspNet/SiteMap-File-1.0" >
  <siteMapNode url="Default.aspx" title="Home"
        description="This is the home page" >
    <siteMapNode url="Products.aspx" title="Products"
        description="This is the products page" />
    <siteMapNode url="Support.aspx" title="Support"
        description="This is the support page"
        ImageURL="supportimage.jpg"/>
    <siteMapNode url="Contact.aspx" title="Contacts"
        description="This is the contacts page" >
      <siteMapNode url="~/ContactAddress/ContactAddress.aspx"
                   title="Contact using physical address"
                   description="This is the first contact page" />
      <siteMapNode url="~/ContactEmailPhone/ContactEmailPhone.aspx"
                   title="Contact by email or phone"
                   description="This is the second contact page" />
    </siteMapNode>
  </siteMapNode>
</siteMap>
```

13. Run the Web site and see what effect the changes have. You should see new navigation options appear in the *Menu* and the *TreeView*, and the new pages should also be reflected in the *SiteMapPath* control.

14. Experiment with the *SiteMapDataSource* properties to see how the *Menu* and *TreeView* are affected. For example, *SiteMapDataSource.ShowStartingNode* turns off the root node (often the "home" page node). *SiteMapDataSource.StartFromCurrentNode* determines the hierarchical position at which the data source begins producing data.

15. Experiment with the *Menu* properties to see how the *Menu* is affected. For example, the *Menu.StaticDisplayLevels* and *MaximumDynamicDisplayLevels* determine how much of the data from *SiteMapDataSource* the *Menu* displays.

16. Notice how easy it is to add navigation capability to your Web site. By using the site map file (and underlying provider-based architecture), you limit the number of places you need to modify to update site navigation.

Trapping the *SiteMapResolve* Event

ASP.NET is full of extensibility points. They're all over the place—and the navigation architecture is no exception. ASP.NET site map support includes an application-wide event that informs listeners (usually the application object) whenever the end user is navigating through the Web site using a control connected to the site map data. Here's an example that shows how to handle that event.

Handling the *SiteMapResolve* event

1. You can add the *SiteMapResolve* handler anywhere in the project. In this example, you add it to the global application object. Open the file Global.asax, which Visual Studio has created for you already.

2. Add a *SiteMapResolve* event handler to the Global.asax file you just added. The handler can do whatever you want it to do. The example here clones the *SiteMapNode* object that's passed in by the event arguments. (By cloning the node, the handler avoids modifying the underlying data structure.) Then, the handler modifies the node's *Title* field to add the phrase "(you are here)." (Note that you see this only if the *Title* field is displayed by your navigation control. The *SiteMapPath* control displays it by default.) After finishing the handler, update *Application_Start* to connect the handler to the *SiteMapResolve* event in the *Application_Start* handler of Global.asax:

```
<%@ Application Language="C#" %>

<script runat="server">

    void Application_Start(object sender, EventArgs e)
    {
        SiteMap.SiteMapResolve +=
          new SiteMapResolveEventHandler(ResolveNode);
    }

    SiteMapNode ResolveNode(object sender,
                            SiteMapResolveEventArgs e)
    {
        SiteMapNode n = e.Provider.CurrentNode.Clone();
        n.Title = n.Title + " (you are here)";
        return n;
    }

    ...
</script>
```

3. Now run the site and navigate through the pages. You should see the title of each *SiteMapNode* change as you page through the site. This is reflected by the display name in the *SiteMapPath* control. The following graphic shows the site map path control with the modified title:

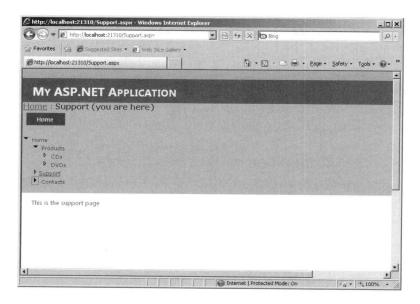

Defining Custom Attributes for Each Node

Another way to extend your Web application's navigation is to define custom attributes for the site nodes in web.sitemap and retrieve them at run time. Imagine that you want to associate a specific image with each page in your site. To accomplish this, just create a new attribute and specify it in the *siteMapNode* element in the site map data.

ASP.NET site map navigation support makes it very easy to add arbitrary attributes to each node. In this example, you add JPEG URLs to the site map nodes. As each page is loaded, the master page shows the JPEG in an *Image* control. The following example shows how to add custom attributes to the site map nodes.

Adding custom attributes to the site map

1. Add six new JPEGs to the project—one to represent each kind of page. For example, produce separate JPEGs for the home page, the products page, the three contact pages, and the support page. Update the web.sitemap file to include an *ImageURL* property in each *siteMapNode* element, like so:

```
<?xml version="1.0" encoding="utf-8" ?>
<siteMap xmlns="http://schemas.microsoft.com/AspNet/SiteMap-File-1.0" >
```

```
<siteMapNode url="~/Default.aspx" title="Home"
   description="This is the home page"
   ImageURL="~/homeimage.jpg">
   <siteMapNode url="~/Products.aspx" title="Products"
      description="This is the products page"
      ImageURL="~/productsimage.jpg" />
   <siteMapNode url="~/Support.aspx" title="Support"
      description="This is the support page"
      ImageURL="~/supportimage.jpg"/>
   <siteMapNode url="~/Contact.aspx" title="Contacts"
      description="This is the contacts page"
      ImageURL="/contactimage.jpg">
      <siteMapNode url="~/ContactAddress/ContactAddress.aspx"
         title="Contact using physical address"
         description="This is the first contact page"
         ImageURL="~/contactPhysicalAddressimage.jpg"/>
      <siteMapNode url="~/ContactEmailPhone/ContactEmailPhone.aspx"
         title="Contact by email or phone"
         description="This is the second contact page"
         ImageURL="~/contactPhoneimage.jpg" />
   </siteMapNode>

   </siteMapNode>
</siteMap>
```

2. Programmatically, the *ImageURL* custom attribute appears as a property of the node when the nodes are accessed. There are many ways to use the new property. Probably the easiest way is to add an *Image* control to the master page and update the *Image* control's *ImageUrl* property with the value from the node in the master page's *Page_Load* method.

```
public partial class SiteMaster: System.Web.UI.MasterPage
{
    protected void Page_Load(object sender, EventArgs e)
    {
        SiteMapNode current = SiteMap.CurrentNode;
        string strImageURL = current["ImageURL"];
        if (strImageURL != null)
        {
            this.Image1.ImageUrl = strImageURL;
        }
    }
}
```

3. Although setting an image during the master page's *Page_Load* method is pretty straightforward, it's not the only way to change the UI based on specific *SiteMapNode* information. For example, you might handle the *OnMenuItemDataBound* event and set

any custom properties there. The following two graphics illustrate how the master page plugs in a new image URL each time a postback is issued:

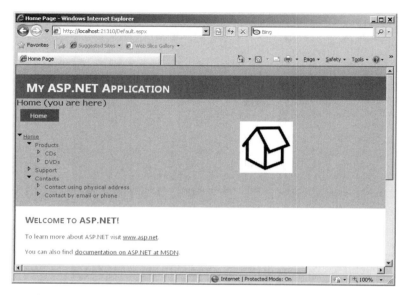

The following graphic shows the products page:

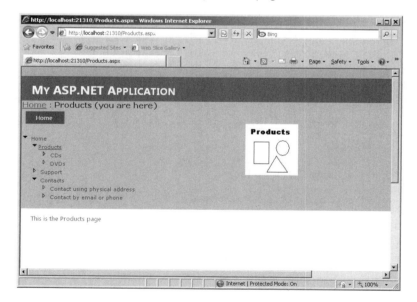

Security Trimming

The ASP.NET navigation support works with the authentication and authorization mechanisms to support security trimming. *Security trimming* means showing only part of the menu based on the role of the current user. Of course, this means that the Web site must somehow authenticate the user. (See Chapter 9, "Logging In.")

To make security trimming work, turn the *securityTrimmingEnabled* attribute on in web.config. The list of roles for which the navigation option is available is a property for each *SiteMapNode*.

For more information about security trimming, see *http://msdn.microsoft.com/en-us/library/ms178428.aspx*.

URL Mapping

Finally, the ASP.NET navigation architecture supports URL mapping. URL mapping is mapping a virtual (or nonexistent) URL to an existing ASPX file in the web.config file using the *urlMappings* element. Setting up URL mappings causes ASP.NET to read the requested URL and uses the handler for the mapped URL. This is done in *HttpApplication* using *HttpContext.RewritePath*.

For example, imagine your Web site includes a single products page containing both CDs and DVDs. However, your UI model requires you to build a menu structure that separates the CD products and the DVD products into two options that appear separately on the menu. URL mapping provides a way of handling this situation.

Here's an exercise showing how to use URL mapping to represent a single page as two separate menu items. In this case, the page's content is distinguished by a URL parameter.

Implementing URL mapping

1. Update the Products page so that it shows different content when the ID parameter is 1 or 2. This example divides the products into CDs and DVDs. The page displays different content based on the value of the ID parameter (whether it's 1 or 2 or something else). Place a *Label* control on the Products page and assign its ID property the value *LabelProductType*. Then, drop a *ListBox* on the page and assign its ID the value

ListBoxProducts. The code-beside file then implements the URL mapping functionality in the *Page_Load* handler, as shown here:

```csharp
public partial class Products : System.Web.UI.Page
{
    protected void AddCDsToListBox()
    {
        this.ListBoxProducts.Items.Add("CD- Snakes and Arrows");
        this.ListBoxProducts.Items.Add("CD- A Farewell To Kings");
        this.ListBoxProducts.Items.Add("CD- Moving Pictures");
        this.ListBoxProducts.Items.Add("CD- Hemispheres");


        this.ListBoxProducts.Items.Add("CD- Permanent Waves");
        this.ListBoxProducts.Items.Add("CD- Counterparts");
        this.ListBoxProducts.Items.Add("CD- Roll the Bones");
        this.ListBoxProducts.Items.Add("CD- Fly By Night");
        this.ListBoxProducts.Items.Add("CD- 2112");
    }

    protected void AddDVDsToListBox()
    {
        this.ListBoxProducts.Items.Add("DVD- A Show Of Hands");
        this.ListBoxProducts.Items.Add("DVD- Exit Stage Left");
        this.ListBoxProducts.Items.Add("DVD- Rush In Rio");
        this.ListBoxProducts.Items.Add("DVD- R30");
    }

    protected void Page_Load(object sender, EventArgs e)
    {
        if (this.Request.Params["ID"] == "1")
        {
            this.LabelProductType.Text = "CDs";
            AddCDsToListBox();
        }
        else if (this.Request.Params["ID"] == "2")
        {
            this.LabelProductType.Text = "DVDs";
            AddDVDsToListBox();
        }
        else
        {
            this.LabelProductType.Text = "All CDs and DVDs";
            AddCDsToListBox();
            AddDVDsToListBox();
        }
    }
}
```

2. Update the web.sitemap file to include the new menu items mapped to virtual files (for example, CDs.aspx and DVDs.aspx). Add this to the Web.site file:

```xml
<?xml version="1.0" encoding="utf-8" ?>
  <siteMap xmlns="http://schemas.microsoft.com/AspNet/SiteMap-File-1.0" >
    <siteMapNode url="~/Default.aspx" title="Home"
      description="This is the home page"
      ImageURL="~/homeimage.jpg">
    <siteMapNode url="~/Products.aspx" title="Products"
      description="This is the products page"
      ImageURL="~/productsimage.jpg">
      <siteMapNode url="~/CDs.aspx" title="CDs"
        description="This is the CDs page"
        ImageURL="~/productsimage.jpg"/>
      <siteMapNode url="~/DVDs.aspx" title="DVDs"
        description="This is the DVDs page"
        ImageURL="~/productsimage.jpg"/>
      </siteMapNode>
    <siteMapNode url="~/Support.aspx" title="Support"
      description="This is the support page"
      ImageURL="~/supportimage.jpg"/>
    <siteMapNode url="~/Contact.aspx" title="Contacts"
      description="This is the contacts page"
      ImageURL="~/contactimage.jpg">
    <siteMapNode url="~/ContactAddress/ContactAddress.aspx"
      title="Contact using physical address"
      description="This is the first contact page"
      ImageURL="~/contactPhysicalAddressimage.jpg"/>
    <siteMapNode url="~/ContactEmailPhone/ContactEmailPhone.aspx"
      title="Contact by email or phone"
      description="This is the second contact page"
      ImageURL="~/contactPhoneimage.jpg" />
    </siteMapNode>
  </siteMapNode>
</siteMap>
```

3. Add this to the web.config file:

```xml
<configuration>
  <system.web>
    <urlMappings enabled="true">
      <add url="~/CDs.aspx" mappedUrl="~/Products.aspx?ID=1"/>
      <add url="~/DVDs.aspx" mappedUrl="~/Products.aspx?ID=2"/>
    </urlMappings>
  </system.web>
</configuration>
```

4. Run the page. Notice that changes occurred and two new items now appear on the Products menu. The site map points these two items to the CDs.aspx file and the DVDs.aspx file. Although the application does *not* include files with these names, users still see a page that works when they redirect using one of these menu items. The web.config file remaps the request back to the Products.aspx page, passing a URL parameter with a specific value. When the Products.aspx page is loaded and the ID parameter is 1 or 2, the page loads the list box with CD titles or DVD titles.

The following graphic shows the CDs Products page being selected from the site map data:

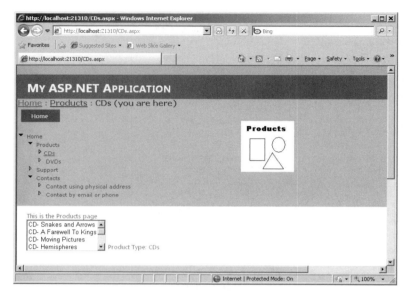

The next graphic shows the DVDs Products page being selected from the site map data:

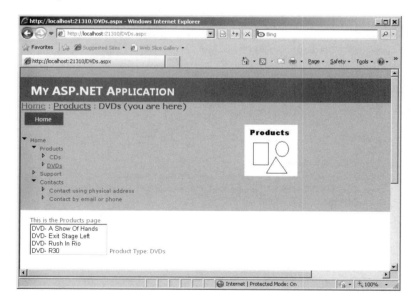

This graphic shows the main Products page being selected from the site map data:

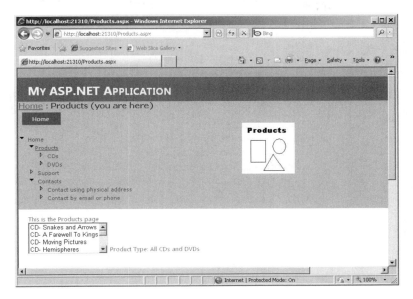

URL mapping is useful in all kinds of situations when you need to represent pages in a navigation control, even when there might not be a physical page to support it.

URL Rewriting

Microsoft Internet Information Services (IIS) 7.0 now includes a URL Rewrite Module that supports the more contemporary technique of URL rewriting. URL rewriting is a much more dynamic technique for redirecting requests than is the simple configuration file *urlMappings* technique used in the last example. For example, you can use URL rewriting to redirect based on various run-time criteria, such as server variables or HTTP headers. You can also set up redirects based on URL rewriting rules.

Chapter 11 Quick Reference

To	Do This
Add an XML site map to the application	Right-click the project name in Solution Explorer. Click Add New Item. Select Site Map from the templates. This is useful for adding an XML-based site map to your site.
Add a navigation control to a page in your site	Open the Navigation controls node in the Toolbox. Select the *Menu*, the *TreeView*, or the *SiteMapPath* control and place it on the page.
	When you place the navigation control on the page, you'll see a small task window asking you to choose the data source. If you already have the appropriate data source on your page, select it. If you've created an XML-based site map for your page, select New Data Source and select SiteMap or XML File, depending on how your navigation data is packaged.
Intercept navigation requests as they occur	Write a handler for the *SiteMapResolve* event in the Global.asax file.
Map virtual nonexistent URLs to real URLs	Add a *urlMappings* section to web.config to map the virtual URLs. Add the virtual URLs to your site map data so that the user can more easily navigate to the given page. (Better yet, look into IIS 7.0 URL rewriting.)

Chapter 12
Personalization

After completing this chapter, you will be able to

- Use ASP.NET personalization.

- Apply personalization to a Web site.

This chapter covers the built-in personalization features of ASP.NET. A major theme throughout ASP.NET is to provide frameworks and support for implementing features most Web sites need. For example, ASP.NET provides support for applying a common look and feel to a site through master pages and themes, as described in Chapter 7, "A Consistent Look and Feel." Chapter 9, "Logging In," describes the new login controls, which are there so that you don't have to hash out yet one more login control. Then, there are authentication and authorization, site maps, and on and on. ASP.NET today is just packed with features to make your site development task easier and faster.

Personalization is another feature that often makes for great Web sites. Prior to ASP.NET 2.0, you had to provide any personalization support for your site. Now these features are rolled into ASP.NET.

This chapter looks at Web personalization.

Personalizing Web Visits

When the Internet and the Web first began gaining popularity, most sites contained only static content. That is, they offered only text, graphics, and perhaps links to other pages. The early Web-surfing community consisted of only the few folks who knew how to use browsers to peer into the contents of those early Web servers.

Until the Web began exploding with interactive sites, there was really no need for Web sites to provide anything but generalized content. However, savvy businesspeople know that tailoring and targeting content to specific individuals are good for business.

For example, the next time you go online to shop or visit a subscription-type site, take note of how much the site knows about you. Very often, if at some point you provided login information, the site will greet you by name. It might even point you to information or products that might interest you. These are examples of how a Web site can be personalized.

In the early days, any personalization of a site resulted from code you wrote, such as code to manage user preferences in cookies or code to store personal information in databases. In addition to simply storing and managing the personal information, you had to integrate the personal information management with the authentication and authorization scheme you decided to use. That is, once you authenticated the user, you then could tailor your pages according to his or her personal information.

ASP.NET now includes services for personalizing a Web site to suit a particular client's taste. There's no reason you can't write your own database and services to provide this functionality. However, as with other services, ASP.NET provides a way to do this with consistency and so that you do not have to write all the code yourself.

Personalization in ASP.NET

Although it might not be surprising to find that the ASP.NET personalization services follow the same provider pattern as do authentication and site mapping, defining a Web site's personalization facilities begins by defining user profiles. This section starts there.

User Profiles

The heart of the new ASP.NET personalization service is the *user profile*. A user profile defines what kind of personal information your Web site needs. For example, you might want to know personal data about users of your Web site, such as name, gender, number of visits to the site, and so forth. User profiles are also handy for storing user preferences for your site. For example, you might include a theme as part of a personal profile so that users can tailor the pages to their particular tastes.

Once the personalization properties are defined in web.config, a component in ASP.NET has to be able to read them and use them. That job is handled by ASP.NET personalization providers.

Personalization Providers

Chapter 8, "Configuration," describes how .NET includes a provider pattern. Providers hide the infrastructural code necessary to support the service, yet they allow you to choose different underlying storage media with little impact on your site. Perhaps you start your site using XML files for storing data but later move to Microsoft SQL Server or you have legacy authentication databases you want to connect to your ASP.NET site. ASP.NET personalization is no different. In fact, ASP.NET includes two personalization providers out of the box: a profile provider for custom user data, and a personalization provider for Web Parts. (Chapter 13, "Web Parts," describes Web Parts in more detail.)

ASP.NET defines the fundamental provider capabilities in an abstract class named *PersonalizationProvider*. Those capabilities include loading and saving personalization properties and managing their relationship to any Web Parts used in a site. ASP.NET provides a default implementation of these capabilities in a concrete class named *SqlPersonalizationProvider*, which is derived from *PersonalizationProvider*.

Using Personalization

Using personalization is straightforward. You define personalization properties in web.config. ASP.NET synthesizes a class for you to use to manage personalization settings. Then, profile information is available in much the same way as session state is available.

Defining Profiles in Web.Config

Your site's profile schema is defined in web.config as name/type pairs. Imagine that in the course of designing your site, you decide you would like to track the following information about a particular user:

- User name (a string)

- Gender (a Boolean value)

- Visit count (an integer)

- Birthday (a date)

Defining these properties is a matter of specifying them in web.config. A definition for the properties just mentioned might look like the following in web.config:

```
<system.web>
   <profile automaticSaveEnabled="true" >
      <properties>
         <add name="NumVisits" type="System.Int32"/>
         <add name="UserName" type="System.String"/>
         <add name="Gender" type="System.Boolean">
         <add name="Birthday" type="System.DateTime">
      </properties>
   </profile>
</system.web>
```

Once defined in the web.config file, you can use the profile in the site through the *Profile* property found in the current *HttpContext* (and also through the *Page* base class).

Using Profile Information

To use the profile in your Web site, you access it in much the same way you might access session state. You see how session state works in Chapter 14, "Session State"—right now it's enough to say that you can access data tied to a specific session by accessing the page's *Session* member. The *Session* member is a name/value dictionary that holds arbitrary information tied to a particular session. Versions 2, 3, and 3.5 of the ASP.NET compiler actually synthesize a profile class based on the schema defined in the web.config file. This is no longer available in ASP.NET 4, where accessing profile state information is done through the *ProfileBase* class using name/value pairs.

The ASP.NET class representing the profile information defined in web.config is named *ProfileBase*. You can access the profile properties using the *GetPropertyValue* and *SetPropertyValue* methods like so:

```
protected void Page_Load(object sender, EventArgs e)
{
  ProfileBase profile = HttpContext.Current.Profile;
  string name = (string)profile.GetPropertyValue("Name");
  if (name != null)
  {
  Response.Write("Hello " + name);
  DateTime dateTime = (DateTime)profile.GetPropertyValue("Birthday");
  Response.Write("Your birthday is " +
dateTime);
  }
}
```

Saving Profile Changes

The preceding code snippet assumes that there is already personalization information associated with the user. To insert profile data for a particular user, simply set the properties of the *Profile* object. For example, imagine a page that includes a handler for saving the profile. It might look something like this:

```
protected void ProfileSaveClicked(object sender, EventArgs e)
{  ProfileBase profile = HttpContext.Current.Profile;
  profile.SetPropertyValue("Name", this.TextBoxName.Text);

  profile.Save();


}
```

The easiest way to ensure that the personalization properties persist is to set *automaticSaveEnabled* to *true*. Personal profile data is then saved automatically by the provider.

Alternatively, you can call *Profile.Save* as necessary to save the personalization properties manually. In addition to saving and loading profiles, you can also delete the profile for a specific user by calling *Profile.DeleteProfile*.

Profiles and Users

Profile information is associated with the current user based on the identity of the user. By default, ASP.NET uses the *User.Identity.Name* in the current *HttpContext* as the key to store data. Because of this, profiles are generally available only for authenticated users.

However, ASP.NET supports anonymous profiles as well. As you might expect, this is also configured in web.config. The default tracking mechanism for anonymous profiles is to use cookies. However, you can direct ASP.NET to use a mangled URL. A *mangled URL* is one in which a key identifying the particular client is embedded in the URL used to post requests back to the server.

The following exercise illustrates using personalization profiles based on the user's login ID.

Using profiles

1. Create a new Web Application project. Name the project *MakeItPersonal*.

2. Microsoft Visual Studio creates a local database including the proper tables to make personalization work.

3. Update web.config to include some profile properties, which should be placed in the existing *<profile>* element. The example here includes a user name, a theme, and a birth date. The following example shows that you can group and nest profile structures in a profile declaration using the *group* element. Visual Studio adds a *<profile>* section to the web.config file. Add the configuration information between the *<properties>* beginning and ending node.

```
<system.web>

    <profile>
      <providers>
        <clear/>
        <add name="AspNetSqlProfileProvider" ... />
      </providers>
      <properties >
        <add name="Theme" type="System.String"/>
        <add name="Name" type="System.String"/>
        <add name="Birthdate" type="System.DateTime"/>
        <group name="Address">
            <add name="StreetAddress" type="System.String"/>
            <add name="City" type="System.String"/>
            <add name="State" type="System.String"/>
            <add name="ZipCode" type="System.String"/>
        </group>
      </properties>
    </profile>

</system.web>
```

> **Note** This example uses the authenticated user name as the key for locating personalization information. However, ASP.NET supports *anonymous* personalization. That is, ASP.NET supports personalization information for anonymous users—but tracks the users with a cookie. You can add support for anonymous personalization tracking by setting the *anonymousIdentification* element to *true* and specifying cookie parameters like this:
>
> ```
> <anonymousIdentification enabled="true"
>     cookieName=".ASPXANONYMOUSUSER"
>     cookieTimeout="120000"
>     cookiePath="/"
>     cookieRequireSSL="false"
>     cookieSlidingExpiration="true"
>     cookieProtection="Encryption"
>     cookieless="UseDeviceProfile" />
> ```
>
> In addition to setting up anonymous access in web.config, you need to set the *[allowAnonymous]* attribute for the properties.
>
> By configuring the site this way and adding the *allowAnonymous* attribute to properties in the profile information, ASP.NET will store the personalization settings based on a cookie it generates when a user first hits the site.

4. Borrow the Default and SeeingRed themes from the MasterPageSite project (Chapter 7). This allows the user to pick the theme. First, add Default and SeeingRed folders to the application's Themes directory. Then, right-click each of the theme folders and click Add Existing Item. Use the file navigation dialog box to navigate to the Chapter 7 directory and select the theme files.

5. Borrow the UseThemes.aspx and .cs files from the MasterPageSite project. If you place them in a separate folder (for example, perhaps a folder named Secured), you can manage access rights to the folder.

6. Update the Default.aspx page. This is where users will enter profile information.

   Add text boxes for the name, address, city, state, and zip code.

   Add a drop-down list box populated with Default and SeeingRed items to be used for selecting the theme.

   Also add a calendar control to pick the birth date.

7. Add a button that the user can click to submit profile information. Add a handler to input these values into the profile. Double-click the button to add the handler.

The input screen should look something like this:

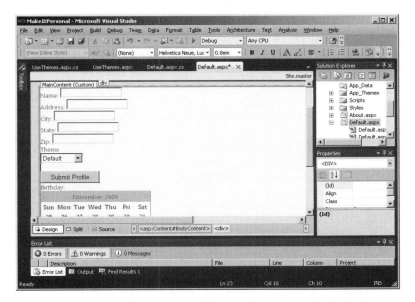

Note This example uses the authenticated user name as the key for storing personalization values. Use the ASP.NET Configuration Utility to apply Forms Authentication to this application (as described in Chapter 8). Also add at least one user so that you have one to personalize. The generated project will give you a login page under the Accounts folder. Add a Login.aspx screen to the site and modify the site's access rules to enforce authentication so that you can see the personalization information being stored and retrieved.

8. Update *Page_Load* to display profile information (if it's there). Grab the profile object and set each of the text boxes and the calendar control.

```
using System.Web.Profile;

public partial class _Default : System.Web.UI.Page
{
  protected void Page_Load(object sender, EventArgs e)
  {
    if (!this.IsPostBack)
    {
      ProfileBase profile = HttpContext.Current.Profile;
      string theme = (string)profile.GetPropertyValue("Theme");
      this.TextBoxName.Text = (string)profile.GetPropertyValue("Name");
      this.TextBoxAddress.Text =
        (string)profile.GetPropertyValue("Address.StreetAddress");
      this.TextBoxCity.Text = (string)profile.GetPropertyValue("Address.City");
```

```
      this.TextBoxState.Text =
        (string)profile.GetPropertyValue("Address.State");
      this.TextBoxZipCode.Text = (string)profile.GetPropertyValue("Address.ZipCode");
      this.DropDownList1.SelectedValue =
        (string)profile.GetPropertyValue("Theme");
      this.Calendar1.SelectedDate = (DateTime)profile.GetPropertyValue("Birthdate");
    }
  }
}
```

9. Update the profile submission handler to store the profile information:

```
public partial class _Default : System.Web.UI.Page
{
  //...
  protected void ButtonSubmitProfile_Click(object sender, EventArgs e)
  {
    if (this.User.Identity.IsAuthenticated)
    {
      ProfileBase profile = HttpContext.Current.Profile;
      profile.SetPropertyValue("Theme", "SeeingRed");
      profile.SetPropertyValue("Name", this.TextBoxName.Text);
      profile.SetPropertyValue("Address.StreetAddress", this.TextBoxAddress.Text);
      profile.SetPropertyValue("Address.City", this.TextBoxCity.Text);
      profile.SetPropertyValue("Address.State", this.TextBoxState.Text);
      profile.SetPropertyValue("Address.ZipCode", this.TextBoxZipCode.Text);
      profile.SetPropertyValue("Theme", this.DropDownList1.SelectedValue);
      profile.SetPropertyValue("Birthdate", this.Calendar1.SelectedDate);
      profile.Save();
    }
  }
}
```

10. Finally, update the UseThemes.aspx page to use the theme. Override the page's
    OnPreInit method. Have the code apply the theme as specified by the profile:

```
protected override void OnPreInit(EventArgs e)
{
  ProfileBase profile = HttpContext.Current.Profile;
  if (profile != null)
  {
    String strTheme = (string)profile.GetPropertyValue("Theme");
    if (strTheme != null &&
      strTheme.Length > 0)
    {
      this.Theme = strTheme;
    }
  }
  base.OnPreInit(e);
}
```

11. Add a *Hyperlink* control to the Default.aspx page. Set the *Text* property to *View Themes*
    and set the *NavigateURL* property to point to the UseThemes.aspx page. When users
    surf to the page, they should be able to enter the profile information and submit it.

After their initial visit, the profile is available whenever they hit the site. The following graphic shows the profile information being displayed in the default page:

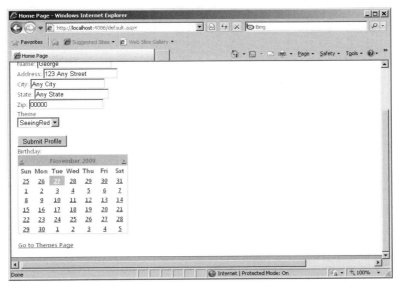

12. When users visit the UseThemes.aspx page, the page should use the theme that each user selected in the profile. The following graphic shows the UseThemes.aspx page using the SeeingRed theme pulled from the profile:

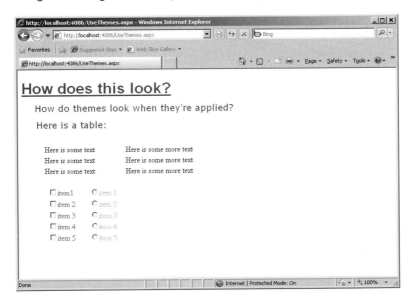

Chapter 12 Quick Reference

To	Do This
Define personalization profile settings	Use the <profile> element in web.config. Define name/type pairs to create the profile schema.
Access the profile properties	Profile properties are available through the current HttpContext. Use the GetPropertyValue and SetPropertyValue methods.
Track anonymous profiles with cookies	Enable anonymousIdentification in web.config and add the allowAnonymous attribute to the profile properties.

Chapter 13
Web Parts

After completing this chapter, you will be able to

- Understand ASP.NET Web Parts.
- Use standard Web Parts in a Web page.
- Create a custom Web Part.
- Use the custom Web Part in a Web page.

Earlier chapters discuss rendered and composite controls and controls available in Microsoft ASP.NET. Because rendering an ASP.NET Web Form is broken down into small, manageable chunks, arbitrarily extending the framework by adding new controls is a straightforward affair. Server-side controls offer very fine-grained control over the HTML rendered by your application.

In this chapter, you get acquainted with Web Parts. The topic of Web Parts could take up an entire book—they represent a whole new level of interaction with Web sites. Web Parts are in many ways like custom controls. They give you a way to customize the HTML coming out of your Web site without requiring you to hard-code the output of your page.

Whereas custom controls derive either from *System.Web.UI.Control* or from *System.Web. UI.WebControl*, Web Parts derive from *Microsoft.SharePoint.WebPartPages.WebPart*. Although *WebPart* does inherit from *System.Web.UI.Control,* it goes beyond the regular control functionality by handling interactions with *WebPartPage* and *WebPartZone* classes to support adding, deleting, customizing, connecting, and personalizing Web Parts on a page.

Probably the largest difference between ASP.NET server-side controls and Web Parts is that Web Parts provide a way for *end users* to configure your site to their liking. By contrast, ASP.NET server-side controls are targeted to ASP.NET developers. In ASP.NET, lower-level developers can build interactive Web pages easily, whereas with Web Parts users of a Web site gain a certain degree of flexibility in managing their view of the site.

Another way to get a good idea of the effectiveness of Web Parts is to consider the wave of social networking sites, such as Windows Live Spaces, that has emerged during the past few years. Although the main thrust of the site is governed at the server, end users can create their own accounts and completely customize the presentation appearing on their screen. End users can add friends and associates, and they can build in links to other sites.

In addition to creating Web sites that are customizable by end users, Web Parts can be very useful to lower-level site developers. Web Parts combine the flexibility of rendered custom controls with the drag-and-drop manageability of user controls. As a developer, you can drag completed Web Parts from Web Parts galleries onto Web Parts zones. You can modify the shared properties of a group of Web Parts and make them persistent. In addition to being a useful way to package user interface (UI) components, Web Parts can connect with each other through standard interfaces.

Web Parts technology is very useful in building portals and collaboration sites. Microsoft SharePoint is an excellent example of this type of site. Rather than building document collaboration and sharing facilities into an application from the ground up, SharePoint already has high-level components that handle those sorts of features. Setting up a portal is about assembling high-level parts into an application.

A Brief History of Web Parts

In the early 2000s, SharePoint emerged as a highly leveraged way for organizations to build portals and collaboration environments. For example, coordinating large teams toward a common goal is an excellent reason for creating a portal. Team endeavors such as software development require systems such as version control and bug tracking. If the team is distributed geographically or is in some other way not part of the office network, the next logical step is to share information over the Web.

Without a framework such as SharePoint, developers would likely duplicate much effort between them. SharePoint introduces some prefabricated components to ease building collaboration sites (rather than building them from scratch). SharePoint Web pages are based on a type of component named *Web Parts*. Web Parts are a way to package information and functionality for users.

Whereas SharePoint is a stand-alone framework dedicated to building collaboration portals, modern ASP.NET represents a broad-spectrum Web development framework that happens to have a built-in portal framework. That is, SharePoint represents a dedicated means to build portals, and ASP.NET includes some classes useful for building portal-like applications. However, even though they're different development environments, they do share a principal concept between them—Web Parts. Although ASP.NET Web Parts and SharePoint Web Parts aren't exactly the same animal, they operate similarly.

What Good Are Web Parts?

WebPart controls are useful for developing portal-type Web sites. Work flow and collaboration management is quickly becoming one of the most important application areas for Web site development. Because portals often have much of the same functionality from one to another, it makes more sense to build portals from a framework than to build them completely from scratch. Much of this functionality includes such items as file transfers, implementing user profiles, and user administration.

ASP.NET offers three distinct Web Parts development scenarios:

- Building regular pages to consume Web Parts controls
- Developing Web Parts controls
- Implementing Web Parts pages and Web Parts in a portal-type application.

Developing Web Parts Controls

Web Parts controls represent a superset of the existing ASP.NET server-side controls (including custom rendered controls, user controls, and composite controls), regardless of who wrote them. For maximum programmatic control of your environment, you can also create custom Web Parts controls that derive from the *System.Web.UI.WebControls.WebParts.WebPart* class.

Web Parts Page Development

Regular Web pages can use Web Parts. Microsoft Visual Studio includes support for creating pages to host *WebPart* controls. Developing a *WebPart* page involves introducing a *WebPartManager* to the page, specifying a number of zones on the page, and then populating them with *WebPart* controls.

Web Parts Application Development

Finally, you can develop entire applications out of *WebPart* controls. For example, you might decide to build a portal. With *WebPart* controls, you can write personalized pages that are customizable. Web Parts are also ideal for building a commonly used application (such as sharing records or documentation) and shipping it as a unit so that it can be deployed on another company's Web site wholesale.

The Web Parts Architecture

The Web Parts architecture serves multiple purposes. Given that the job of Web Parts is to behave as a bigger UI lever, the functional components have been broken down into overall page management and zone management. *WebPart* controls need to be coordinated together. In addition, the different functional areas of a page often need to be handled as a group of controls (for managing layout, for example).

In terms of framework classes, Web Parts are nested in zones, which are managed by a singular *WebPartManager* (or the *ProxyPartManager*) that talks to the application data store. Figure 13-1 illustrates how the parts are related.

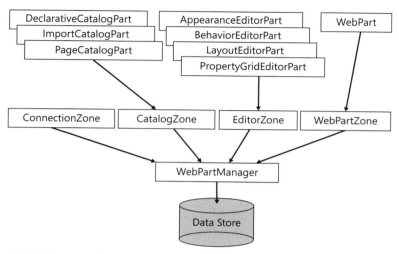

FIGURE 13-1 How Web Parts are managed in zones, which in turn are managed by an instance of *WebPartManager*.

WebPartManager and *WebZones*

As Figure 13-1 illustrates, *WebPartManager* manages each *WebPartZone*, which in turn manages each individual *WebPart*. Any page using at least one *WebPart* needs an instance of *WebPartManager*. The *WebPartManager* is responsible for managing and coordinating the zone(s) and the controls in it. The *WebPartZone* also manages any extra *UI* elements that go with the group of controls.

In the zone, the *ZoneTemplate* contains all Web Parts. If a regular ASP.NET control is in a *ZoneTemplate*, ASP.NET wraps it as a Web Part.

Built-In Zones

Web Parts zones manage the layout for a group of controls. Out of the box, ASP.NET includes four built-in zones. These are as follows:

- *WebPartZone* The *WebPartZone* class represents basic functionality for managing server-side controls in zones on a page. *WebPartZone* controls are responsible for hosting both typical server-side controls and *WebPart* controls. Typical controls are wrapped by the *GenericWebPart* control at run time to add *WebPart* qualities to them.

- *CatalogZone*   The *CatalogZone* zone hosts *CatalogPart* controls. Catalogs generally manage the visibility of parts on a page. The *CatalogZone* control shows and hides its contents based on the catalog display mode. Web Parts catalogs are named such because they act as catalogs of controls from which the end user can select.

- *EditorZone*   The *EditorZone* control represents the means through which end users can modify and personalize Web pages according to their preferences. Personalizing a Web site includes such things as setting up personal information, such as birthdays, gender-specific addressing, number of visits to the site, and so forth. Other kinds of personalization involve setting up color schemes and layouts. The *EditorZone* helps manage this functionality as well as saves and loads those settings so that they are available the next time the user logs on.

- *ConnectionZone*   Web Parts are often more useful when they're connected and communicate dynamically. The *ConnectionZone* manages this functionality.

Built-In Web Parts

In addition to including several zones straight out of the box, ASP.NET provides some ready-to-use *WebPart* controls. The *WebPart* controls fit into various functional categories. Some are for managing catalogs, whereas others are for managing editing. Each specific kind of *WebPart* fits in a particular zone. Here's a rundown of the currently available *WebPart* Toolbox:

- *DeclarativeCatalogPart*   When building a *WebPart* page, you can add parts dynamically or declaratively. Adding parts to a page dynamically means executing code that adds parts to the page at run time. For example, imagine you have a Web Part represented as a class named *MyWebPart* (ultimately derived from *System.Web.UI.Controls.WebParts*). You can add the part to the page by creating an instance of the part and adding it to the *WebPartManager* using *WebPartManager. AddWebPart*. Adding parts to a page declaratively means including tag declarations in the ASPX file representing the *WebPart* page. The *DeclarativeCatalogPart* control manages server-side controls added declaratively to a catalog on a Web page.

- *PageCatalogPart*   One way end users will probably want to customize a site is by opening and closing controls. The *PageCatalogPart* represents a page catalog for holding controls that were previously added to a page that are now closed. By managing the controls in a *PageCatalogPart*, you can make it so that users can add controls back to the page.

- *ImportCatalogPart*   With the *ImportCatalogPart*, users can import a Web Part description from XML data.

- *AppearanceEditorPart*   The *AppearanceEditorPart* is used to edit the appearance properties of an associated *WebPart* or *GenericWebPart*.

- *BehaviorEditorPart*   To support editing the behavior of a *WebPart* or *GenericWebPart*, ASP.NET provides the *BehaviorEditorPart*.

- *LayoutEditorPart*   The *LayoutEditorPart* is for editing the layout properties and associated *WebPart* (or *GenericWebPart* control).

- *PropertyGridEditorPart*   To support users in editing custom properties of *WebPart* controls, ASP.NET provides the *PropertyGridEditorPart* (the other *EditorPart* controls only support editing existing properties from the *WebPart* class, however).

To get a feel for how to use *WebPart* controls, try this example. The following exercise shows how to build a Web page from *WebPart* controls.

> **Note** Web Parts require personalization to be turned on to work. That is, make sure the database is set up with personalization, as was done in Chapter 12, "Personalization." Also, Web Parts require the users be authenticated. Be sure to add at least one user to the site by going to the ASP.NET configuration page and adding a user.

Using Web Parts

1. Create a new Visual Studio Web Application project. Name it *UseWebParts*.

2. In the default page, add a *WebPartManager* by dragging an instance from the Toolbox onto the page.

3. Drag a *WebPartZone* onto the page. Set the ID to **WebPartZoneLinks**. Set the *HeaderText* to **Try These Links**. Set the *HeaderStyle* font *ForeColor* to *Blue* (so that you can see it better later during editing mode). Using the *AutoFormat* editor of the control itself, set the style to Professional. (To access *AutoFormat*, click the caret to the right of the control in the Designer.)

4. Add some *HyperLinks* to the *WebPartZone*, as shown here. Feel free to add any hyperlink you like (these are just examples).

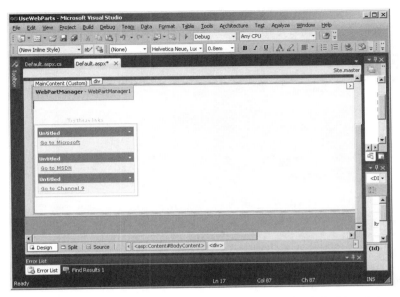

5. Run the page. You should see the links appear on the left side of the page.

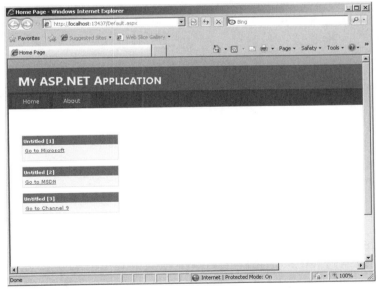

6. Add a *Label* to the page. The text should be **Switch Display Mode**. Add a *DropDownList* to the page. Name it *DropDownListDisplayModes,* and set its *AutoPostBack* property to *true.* This is used to switch the display mode back and forth.

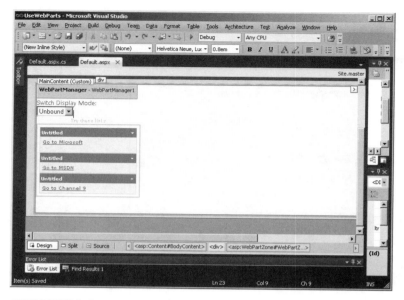

ASP.NET Web Parts support five separate display modes. You add code to support
(some of) these display modes in the next step:

- **BrowseDisplayMode**   This is normal mode. No personalization or editing is
  available here.

- **DesignDisplayMode**   This mode turns on drag-and-drop layout personalization.

- **EditDisplayMode**   This option turns on personalization or customization of
  WebPart properties and permits a user to delete Web Parts that have been added
  to the page dynamically.

- **ConnectDisplayMode**   This mode allows a user to connect Web Parts at run time.

- **CatalogDisplayMode**   This mode allows a user to add Web Parts into a
  WebPartZone at run time.

7. Update the *_Default* class to support switching modes. Visual Studio added a
   WebPartManager to the page. Update the *Page_Init* method to attach an event handler
   to the page's *InitializationComplete* event. In the *InitializationComplete* handler, get the
   current *WebPartManager* and stash the reference in the *WebPartManager1* member, as
   shown in the following code.

```
public partial class _Default : System.Web.UI.Page
{
  protected void Page_Load(object sender, EventArgs e)
  {
    if (!this.IsPostBack)
    {
      String browseModeName = WebPartManager.BrowseDisplayMode.Name;
      foreach (WebPartDisplayMode mode in
        this.WebPartManager1.SupportedDisplayModes)
      {
        String modeName = mode.Name;
        // Make sure a mode is enabled before adding it.
        if (mode.IsEnabled(this.WebPartManager1))
        {
          ListItem item = new ListItem(modeName, modeName);
          DropDownListDisplayModes.Items.Add(item);
        }
      }
    }
  }
}
```

The code listed in the *InitializationComplete* handler interrogates the current *WebPartManager* for the supported display modes and puts them in the *DropDownList*.

8. Add a handler for the *DropDownListDisplayModes* drop-down list when the *SelectedIndexChanged* event occurs. Have the handler switch the *WebPart* page into the selected mode. The following code shows how:

```
protected void
    DropDownListDisplayModes_SelectedIndexChanged(
            object sender, EventArgs e)
{
  string selectedMode = DropDownListDisplayModes.SelectedValue;
  WebPartDisplayMode mode =
    this.WebPartManager1.SupportedDisplayModes[selectedMode];
  if (mode != null)
  {
    this.WebPartManager1.DisplayMode = mode;
  }
}
```

9. Run the site. Make sure at least one user is registered with the site (by using the ASP.NET Configuration utility on the Project menu). Make sure a user is logged in by going to the Login page.

10. You can enter Browse mode and Design mode, as shown in the following graphic:

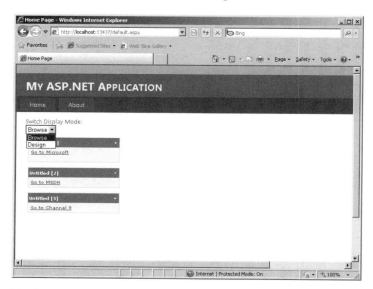

You'll see more modes later as you add more zones. Notice how the title now shows up. You can pick up items on the page and move them around now. For example, you can pick up one of the links and move it around in the Links *WebPartZone*.

11. Now add some more functionality. Add an *EditorZone* to the page. Then, in the *EditorZone*, add an *AppearanceEditorPart*, as shown in the following graphic (the Designer's default layout is to lay out components one after the other—this example shows the *EditorZone* part with an absolute layout style set so that it can be placed anywhere on the form):

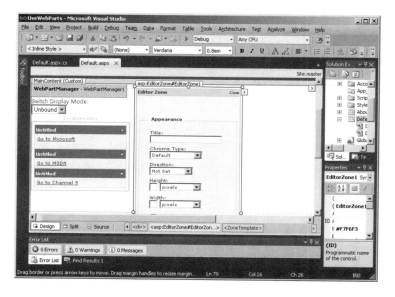

12. Now run the site and log in as a user. You'll see a new option in the Switch Display Mode drop-down list—the Edit mode.

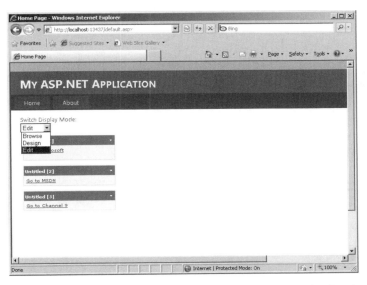

13. Now go back and add a *CatalogZone*. Drop a *DeclarativeCatalogPart* into the new *WebPartZone* and select Edit Templates.

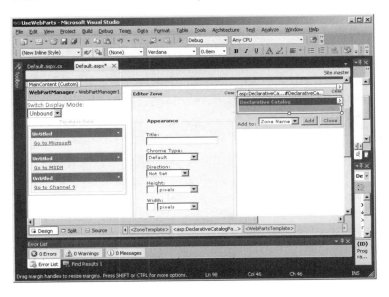

14. While in Template Editing mode, pick up a *TextBox* control from the Toolbox and drop it into the *DeclarativeCatalogPart*. Then, access the page's source view and update the actual markup to add a *Title* attribute, as shown:

```
<ZoneTemplate>
   <asp:DeclarativeCatalogPart
      ID="DeclarativeCatalogPart1" runat="server">
      <WebPartsTemplate>
         <asp:TextBox ID="TextBox1"
            Title="A TextBox"
            runat="server">
         </asp:TextBox>
      </WebPartsTemplate>
   </asp:DeclarativeCatalogPart>
</ZoneTemplate>
```

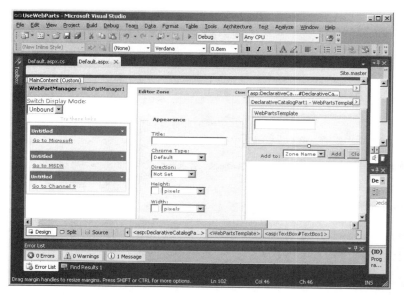

15. Now run the page again. Switch to Catalog mode. Select the A TextBox check box, and click Add to add a *TextBox* to the Try These Links zone. (This might not seem too interesting yet. However, in the next exercise, you write a hyperlink Web Part that you can add to the links page from the catalog—and then update it with your own links and display names.)

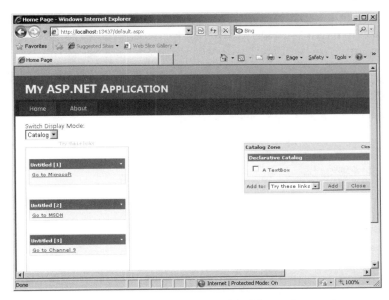

Here is the page with a new *TextBox* added from the catalog:

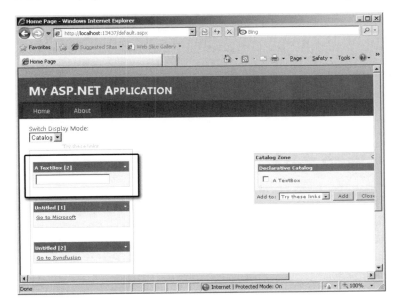

16. Run the page and shift to Edit mode. Select a local menu from one of the hyperlink Web Parts in the Links zone. (You can get to the local "verb" menu by clicking the arrow in the upper right-hand corner of each Web Part.) Select Edit. You should see a collection of controls for editing the Web Part appearing in the Editor Zone, like so:

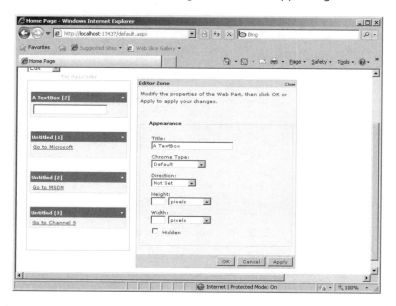

So, there's an example of adding Web Parts zones to a page and then using normal ASP.NET server-side controls as if they were Web Parts (the *HyperLink* controls). Next, take a look at how to develop a real Web Part.

Developing a Web Part

The previous example shows how to use Web Parts in a page and how to switch the page among various modes at run time. The catalog built into the page includes a *TextBox* control that you can add to a *WebPartZone* on the page. The example delivers a glimpse of the flexibility and power of Web Parts. However, simply dropping a *TextBox* onto a *WebPartZone* isn't very interesting. In this example, you build a hyperlink Web Part that you can use to augment the Links *WebPartZone*.

Developing a Web Part is actually fairly straightforward and quite similar to developing a custom control (like the ones in Chapter 4, "Custom Rendered Controls," and Chapter 5, "Composite Controls"). Instead of deriving a class from *System.Web.UI.Controls.WebControl* or *System.Web.UI.Controls.CompositeControl*, you derive a class from *System.Web.UI.WebControls.WebParts.WebPart*. From that point, you have the choice of either rendering HTML or composing a Web Part from other ASP.NET controls. The *WebPart* includes considerable functionality for integrating with the Web Part architecture.

For example, in the next example, the navigation URL and display name properties of the hyperlink Web Part are exposed as properties that the end user can modify through the *PropertyGridEditorPart*.

The following example illustrates how to create a hyperlink Web Part that you can add to the Links *WebPartZone* in the UseWebParts project. Although you could add a regular *HyperLink* control to the catalog, typical controls don't provide the same support for the user to modify the links. For example, when you edited the *HyperLink* controls in the previous example, all you could do was move them around in the Links Web Part. To provide your Web application users with additional properties they can configure, the links need to be represented as Web Parts in their own right.

Developing the *HyperLinkWebPart*

1. Add a new project to the UseWebParts solution. Make it a class library and name the library *WebPartLib*. Visual Studio asks you to name the file, and the name you choose also becomes the name of the first class placed in the library. Name the file *HyperLinkWebPart.cs*. (Visual Studio will name the class *HyperLinkWebPart*.)

2. Make a reference to the *System.Web* assembly in the new child project. Right-click the WebPartLib node in Solution Explorer and click the Add Reference option to add the *System.Web* assembly.

3. Derive the new class from *System.Web.UI.WebControls.WebParts.WebPart* by adding it to the inheritance list, as shown here:

```
using System;
using System.Collections.Generic;

using System.Linq;
using System.Text;
using System.Web;
using System.Web.UI;
using System.Web.UI.WebControls;
using System.Web.UI.WebControls.WebParts;

namespace WebPartLib
{

    public class HyperLinkWebPart : WebPart
    {

    }
}
```

4. Add two string member variables to the *HyperLinkWebPart* class—one to represent the display name of the Web Part and the other to represent the actual URL. Initialize them with reasonable values:

```
using System;
using System.Collections.Generic;
```

```
using System.Text;
using System.Web;
using System.Web.UI;
using System.Web.UI.WebControls;
using System.Web.UI.WebControls.WebParts;

namespace WebPartLib
{

    public class HyperLinkWebPart :
    WebPart
    {

        string _strURL = "http://www.microsoft.com";
        string _strDisplayName = "This is a link";
    }
}
```

5. Add a field of type *HyperLink* to the class. The Web Part uses the existing functionality of the *HyperLink* control. Override *CreateChildControls* to create an instance
   of *HyperLink* and add it to the *HyperLinkWebPart* controls collection. Initialize the
   HyperLink.Text property to the member variable representing the display name.
   Initialize the *HyperLink.NavigateUrl* property to the member variable representing
   the URL:

```
using System;
using System.Collections.Generic;
using System.Text;
using System.Web;
using System.Web.UI;
using System.Web.UI.WebControls;
using System.Web.UI.WebControls.WebParts;

namespace WebPartLib
{

    public class HyperLinkWebPart : WebPart
    {

        HyperLink _hyperLink;

        string _strURL = "http://www.microsoft.com";
        string _strDisplayName = "This is a link";
        protected override void  CreateChildControls()
        {
            _hyperLink = new HyperLink();
            _hyperLink.NavigateUrl = this._strURL;


            _hyperLink.Text = this._strDisplayName;
            this.Controls.Add(_hyperLink);
            base.CreateChildControls();
        }
    }
}
```

6. Finally, expose the URL and the display name as properties so that the Web Parts architecture can understand and work with them. To allow the exposed properties to work with the Web Parts architecture through the *PropertyGridEditorPart* that you add later, be sure to adorn the properties with the attributes *Personalizable*, *WebBrowsable*, and *WebDisplayName*, as shown here:

```
using System;
using System.Collections.Generic;
using System.Text;
using System.Web;
using System.Web.UI;
using System.Web.UI.WebControls;
using System.Web.UI.WebControls.WebParts;

namespace WebPartLib
{

    public class HyperLinkWebPart :
    System.Web.UI.WebControls.WebParts.WebPart
    {

        HyperLink _hyperLink;

        string _strURL = "http://www.microsoft.com";
        string _strDisplayName = "This is a link";
        [Personalizable(), WebBrowsable, WebDisplayName("Display Name")]
        public string DisplayName
        {
            get
            {
                return this._strDisplayName;
            }
            set
            {
                this._strDisplayName = value;
                if (_hyperLink != null)
                {
                    _hyperLink.Text = this.DisplayName;
                }
            }
        }
        [Personalizable(), WebBrowsable, WebDisplayName("URL")]
        public string URL
        {
            get
            {
                return this._strURL;
            }

            set
            {
                this._strURL = value;
```

```
                    if (_hyperLink != null)
                    {
                        _hyperLink.NavigateUrl = this.URL;
                    }


                }
            }

            protected override void  CreateChildControls()
            {
                _hyperLink = new HyperLink();
                _hyperLink.NavigateUrl = this._strURL;
                _hyperLink.Text = this._strDisplayName;
                this.Controls.Add(_hyperLink);
                base.CreateChildControls();
            }
        }
    }
```

7. Compile the WebPartLib project. Note that this adds the new *HyperLinkWebPart* Web Part to the Toolbox. You need that in the next step.

8. Now add the *HyperLinkWebPart* to the catalog. The Web Part should already be in the Toolbox.

9. Put the *CatalogZone* into Edit Templates mode by clicking the small arrow in the Web Template. Then, drag the *HyperLinkWebPart* into the *CatalogZone*, just as you did earlier with the *TextBox*, as shown here:

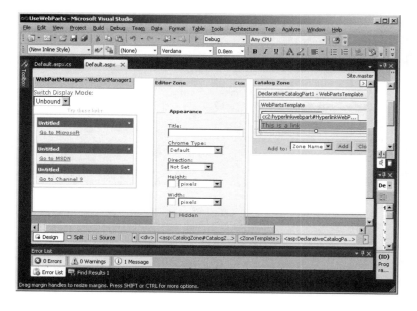

10. Add a title to the new catalog item. Switch to the source code window in Visual Studio. In the markup (in the Source view), add a title to the new control:

```
<ZoneTemplate>
    <asp:DeclarativeCatalogPart
     ID="DeclarativeCatalogPart1" runat="server">
        <WebPartsTemplate>
            <cc1:HyperLinkWebPart
            Title="A HyperLink"
            ID="HyperLinkWebPart1"
            runat="server" />
            <asp:TextBox ID="TextBox1"
            Title="A TextBox"
            runat="server">
            </asp:TextBox>
        </WebPartsTemplate>
    </asp:DeclarativeCatalogPart>
</ZoneTemplate>
```

The *HyperLinkWebPart* should now appear in the catalog with a title, as shown here:

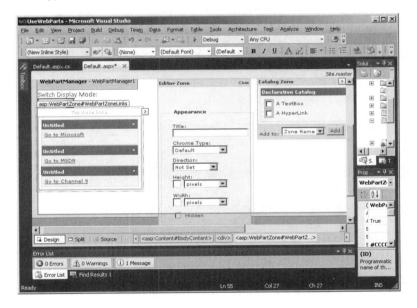

11. Add a *PropertyGridEditorPart* to the *EditorZone* on the page. Just pick one out of the Toolbox and drop it onto the *EditorZone*, as shown in the following graphic:

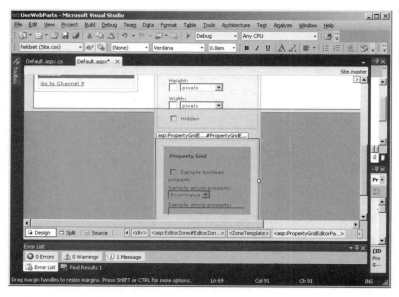

12. Surf to the Web site. Put the page in Catalog mode by selecting Catalog from the Switch Display Mode drop-down list.

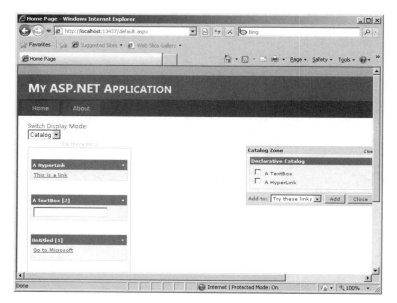

13. Select A Hyper Link in the Catalog Zone, and add it to the Links Web Part Zone.

14. Put the Web Parts Page into Edit mode by selecting Edit from the Switch Display Mode drop-down list. Click the arrow in the upper-right corner of the newly added link.

15. Select Edit to edit this link. You should see the Editor Zone appear, along with the new Property Grid showing text boxes for editing the *DisplayName* and *URL*. The default *DisplayName* and *URL* appear in the text boxes—just type in new values.

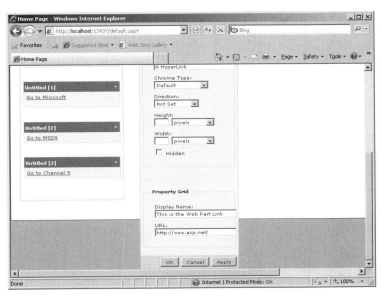

16. Type in a new *DisplayName* and a new *URL*. (The example points to *www.asp.net*.) Select OK. The browser should now show the new properties for the *HyperLinkWebPart*.

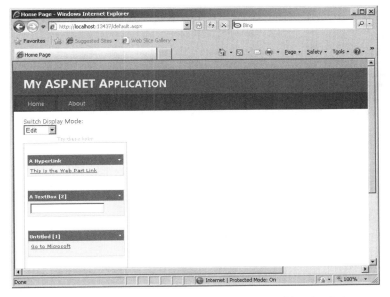

You should be able to surf to the site represented by the link.

Chapter 13 Quick Reference

To	Do This
Enable a Web site to use Web Parts	Run aspnet_regsql against your application's database to make sure Personalization and roles are enabled for the site.
Enable a Web page to use *WebPart* controls	Add a *WebPartManager* to the page on which you wish to use *WebPart* controls.
Add various editing capabilities to a Web Parts page	Add an *EditorZone* to the page.
Add a place in which to position server-side controls to be managed by the Web Part architecture	Add a *WebZone* to the page.
Allow users to dynamically add controls from a collection of controls	Add *CatalogZone* to the page. Add controls to the catalog while in Edit Templates mode.
Create a Web Part	Derive a class from *System.Web.UI.WebControls.WebParts. WebPart,* and then do one of the following: ❑ Render some HTML in the Web Part *Render* method ❑ Create ASP.NET child controls, and add them to the Web Part *Controls* collection for automatic rendering

Part III
Caching and State Management

Chapter 14
Session State

After completing this chapter, you will be able to

- Understand the importance of managing session state in a Web application.

- Use the session state manager (the *Session* object).

- Configure session state.

- Be aware of the different possibilities for storing session state with ASP.NET.

This chapter covers managing session state in your ASP.NET application. Programming Web applications requires that you to be very mindful of how the state of your application is distributed at any moment. One of the most important types of state in a Web application is session state—the state associated with a single particular session. Because Web applications are distributed by nature, and because the nature of the HTTP protocol is stateless, keeping track of any single client has to be done deliberately.

ASP.NET session state support is extensive, reliable, and flexible—offering many advantages over the session state support available in other Web platforms such as classic ASP. For starters, ASP.NET session state is handled by the *Session* object, an object dictionary that's automatically created with each new session (if you have session state enabled). The *Session* object is easily accessible through the *HttpContext* object, which you can reference at any point during the request. The process of associating user state with a particular user's session is handled automatically by ASP.NET. Whenever you want to access session state, you just grab it from the context (it's also mapped into a member variable living on the page). You can choose how ASP.NET tracks session state, and you can even tell ASP.NET where to store session state.

This chapter begins with a look at how various pieces of state are managed by ASP.NET and the gap filled by the session state manager.

Important To install the code samples for this book, you must have Administrator rights on your computer. If you are using your own computer, you probably have Administrator rights. If you are using a computer in an organization and you do not have Administrator rights, please consult your computer support or IT staff. See the "Code Samples" section in the Introduction for more information.

Why Session State?

After you have worked with ASP.NET in the previous chapters, one theme should be emerging. Web-based programming distinguishes itself as a programming idiom in which you try to manage an application serving multiple users distributed over a wide area. What's more, you're doing it over a disconnected (and stateless) protocol.

For example, imagine you're writing some sort of shopping portal. Certain types of application data—such items as inventory and supplier lists—can be kept in a central database.

You know that *System.Web.UI.Page* and server-side controls manage view state. However, when you think about the nature of data in a user's shopping cart, you see that the data clearly belongs elsewhere.

You don't really want to store the data in the page's *ViewState*. Although it's possible for simple applications, storing large chunks of data in view state bogs down your users' experience of the site (the site is much slower) and it poses a security risk by having items travel back and forth with each request. In addition, only serializable types can be stored in view state. Finally, you lose the view state if you redirect to another page.

Unfortunately, a single user's session data doesn't really belong in the application database either. Perhaps if you expected only one user over the lifetime of your application, that might work. However, remember the nature of a Web application is to make your application available to as many clients as possible. Suddenly, it becomes clear that you want to be able to carve out a small data-holding area that persists for the lifetime of a single user's session. This type of data is known as *session state*.

ASP.NET and Session State

Since its inception, ASP.NET has supported session state. When session state is turned on, ASP.NET creates a new *Session* object for each new request. The *Session* object becomes part of the context (and is available through the page). ASP.NET stamps the *Session* object with an identifier (more on that later), and the *Session* object is reconstituted when a request comes through containing a valid session identifier. The *Session* object follows the page around and becomes a convenient repository for storing information that has to survive throughout the session, not simply for the duration of the page.

The *Session* object is a dictionary of name/value pairs. You can associate any Common Language Runtime (CLR)-based object with a key of your choosing and place it in the *Session* object so that it will be there when the next request belonging to that session comes through. Then, you can access that piece of data using the key under which it was stored. For example, if you want to store some information provided by the user in the *Session* object, you can write code like this:

```
void StoreInfoInSession()
{
    String strFromUser = TextBox1.Text;
    Session["strFromUser"] = strFromUser;
}
```

To retrieve the string during the next request, use code like this:

```
void GetInfoFromSession()
{
    String strFromUser = Session["strFromUser"] ; // NOTE: may be null
    TextBox1.Text = strFromUser;
}
```

The brackets on the *Session* object indicate an *indexer*. The indexer is a convenient syntax for expressing keys—both when inserting data into and retrieving data from the *Session* object. Do note, however, that if the key you provide doesn't map to a piece of data in the session dictionary, the *Session* object will return null. In production code, it's always wise to check for a null value and react accordingly.

Managing session state in ASP.NET is extraordinarily convenient. In ASP.NET, session state can live in a number of places, including (1) "in proc"—in the ASP.NET worker process, (2) on a separate state server running a Windows Service process, and (3) in a Microsoft SQL Server database. Because session management follows the provider pattern you saw in earlier chapters, you can replace relatively easily the ASP.NET built-in session state management with an implementation of your own.

First, start by getting a taste of using session state right now.

Introduction to Session State

To understand how session state works, this exercise involves creating a Web site with a page that stores a value as a member variable and as an element of session state. It illustrates the difference between page state during a request and session data that persists beyond a request.

Trying session state

1. Create a new Empty ASP.NET Web Application. Name it *SessionState*.

2. In the default page (Default.aspx), drag a text box to enter a value that will be stored in session state. Add a label to identify the *TextBox*, too, as shown here:

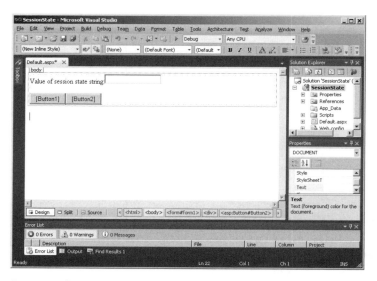

3. Drag two buttons and a label onto the form. The first button is for adding data to the session string. The second is to show the session state. Set the *Text* property of the first button to **Add String To Session State**. Then, give the button the value *AddStringToSessionState* as an ID and double-click it in the Designer to insert an event handler in the code-behind file. This button ultimately adds the string from the text box to the page's session state. Doing so can help you distinguish the buttons later on. It doesn't matter what you name the second button (I used the text "Just Submit" and kept the default ID). The first button submits the string to the server to be saved in a local field (for now), and the other button simply performs a postback. This way, you can see the ephemeral nature of page member variables. Name the label *LabelShowString*. You use it to display the value of the string.

4. Add a *string* variable member to the page named *sessionString*. In the *Page_Load* handler, set the text box on the page to the value of the string. Then, turn your attention to the event handler for the *SubmitString* button. Have the handler take the *Text* property from the *TextBox1* and store it in the page member variable. Then, set the *LabelShowString* label text to the value of the string like so:

```
public partial class _Default : System.Web.UI.Page
{
  string sessionString;
  protected void Page_Load(object sender, EventArgs e)
```

```
   {
     this.LabelShowString.Text = this.sessionString;
   }
   protected void AddStringToSessionState_Click(object sender, EventArgs e)
   {
     this.sessionString = this.TextBox1.Text;
     this.LabelShowString.Text = this.sessionString;
   }
}

   }
```

5. Now run the program. Type a string into the text box and click Add String To Session State. When the post goes to the page, the page will show the string in the label like this:

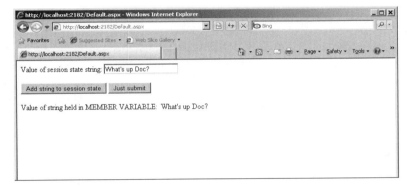

6. Now click the Just Submit button. What happens? Remember, *Page_Load* simply looks at the value of the *sessionString* member variable and stuffs it into the label. Pages (and HTTP handlers in general) are very short-lived objects. They live for the duration of the request and then are destroyed—along with all the data they hold.

The *sessionString* member variable evaporated as soon as the last request finished. A new *sessionString* member variable (which was empty) was instantiated as soon as the page was re-created:

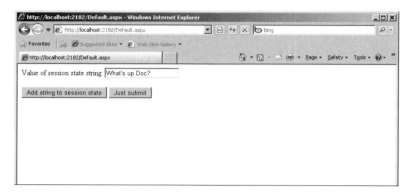

Chapter 4, "Custom Rendered Controls," describes how controls manage their own state. But in this case, you take the data from the text box and store it in a member variable in the *Page* class. The lifetime of the page is very short. The page lives long enough to generate a response, and then it disappears. Any state you store as data members in the page disappears too. That's why, when you click the Just Submit button, you don't see the string displayed. You *do* see the string when you click Add String To Session State because the member variable survives long enough to support the button's *Click* event handler.

7. Using session state is a way to solve this issue. To show this, add a new label named *LabelShowStringAsSessionState* to the page. This one will show the data as retrieved from the *Session* object:

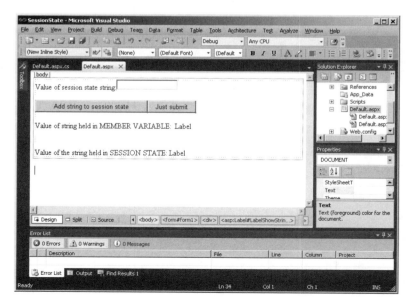

8. Write code to store the string in session state. Have the *AddStringToSessionState* take the text from *TextBox1* and store it in the *Session* object. Then, update the *Page_Load* method to display the value as it came from session state, as shown in bold type in the following code:

```
public partial class _Default : System.Web.UI.Page
{
   string sessionString;

   protected void Page_Load(object sender, EventArgs e)
   {
      this.LabelShowString.Text = this.sessionString;
      this.LabelShowStringAsSessionState.Text =
        (string)this.Session["sessionString"];
   }

   protected void AddStringToSessionState_Click(object sender, EventArgs e)
   {
      // store in member variable
      this.sessionString = this.TextBox1.Text;

      // store in session state
      this.Session["sessionString"] = this.TextBox1.Text;

      // show member variable
      this.LabelShowString.Text = this.sessionString;

      // show session state
      this.LabelShowStringAsSessionState.Text =
        (string)this.Session["sessionString"];
   }
}


   }
```

9. Run the program. Type in a string and click the Add String To Session State button. Both labels should contain data. The *LabelShowString* label holds data because the *SubmitString* handler made the member variable assignment. The *LabelShowStringAsSessionState* label also shows data because the handler stored that text in session state:

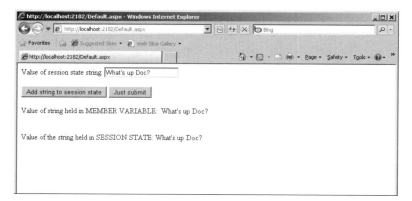

10. Now click the Just Submit button and see what happens:

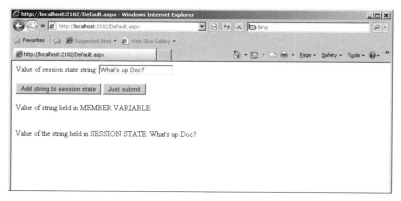

In this case, the page was simply submitted, causing only the *Page_Load* to be executed. *Page_Load* displays both the *sessionString* member variable (which is empty because it lives and dies with the page) and the data from the *Session* object (which lives independently of the page).

As you can see, session state is pretty convenient. However, you wouldn't get very far if all you could do was store simple strings and scalars. Fortunately, the session dictionary stores all manner of CLR objects.

Session State and More Complex Data

The ASP.NET *Session* object can store any (serializable) object running in the CLR. That goes for larger data—not just small strings or other scalar types. One of the most common uses for the *Session* object is for implementing features such as shopping carts or any other data that has to go with a particular client. For example, in a commerce-oriented site where customers can purchase products, you would probably implement a central database representing your inventory. Then, as users sign on, they have the opportunity to select items from your inventory and place them in a temporary holding area associated with the session they're running. In ASP.NET, that holding area is typically the *Session* object.

A number of different collections are useful for managing shopping cart–like scenarios. Probably the easiest to use is the good ole *ArrayList,* an automatically sizing array that supports both random access and the *IList* interface. However, for other scenarios you might use a small *DataTable,* a *DataSet,* or some other more complex type. Keep in mind that *DataTable* and *DataSet* have more features than necessary for some situations, which could lead to bloated session state if you're not careful.

Chapter 10, "Data Binding," takes a quick look at ADO and data access. The next example revisits data-bound controls (the *DataList* and the *GridView*). You also work with the *DataTable* in depth. The example illustrates using ADO.NET objects, data-bound controls, and session state to transfer items from an inventory (represented as a *DataList*) to a collection of selected items (represented as a *GridView*).

Using session state, ADO.NET objects, and data-bound controls

1. Create a new page on the SessionState site named UseDataList.aspx.

   Add *DataList* to the page by copying the following code between the <div> tags on the generated page. The *DataList* will display the elements in the .NET References table from the database shown in Chapter 10.

   ```
   <asp:DataList ID="DataList1"
         runat="server" BackColor="White" BorderColor="#E7E7FF"
         BorderStyle="None" BorderWidth="1px" CellPadding="3"
         GridLines="Horizontal"
         Style="z-index: 100; left: 8px; position: absolute; top: 16px"
         OnItemCommand="DataList1_ItemCommand" Caption="Items in Inventory" >
   <FooterStyle BackColor="#B5C7DE" ForeColor="#4A3C8C" />
   <SelectedItemStyle BackColor="#738A9C"
         Font-Bold="True" ForeColor="#F7F7F7" />
   <AlternatingItemStyle BackColor="#F7F7F7" />
   <ItemStyle BackColor="#E7E7FF" ForeColor="#4A3C8C" />
         <ItemTemplate>
         ID:
         <asp:Label ID="IDLabel"
         runat="server" Text='<%# Eval("ID") %>'></asp:Label><br />
         Title:
   ```

```
                <asp:Label ID="TitleLabel"
                runat="server" Text='<%# Eval("Title") %>'></asp:Label><br />
                AuthorLastName:
                <asp:Label ID="AuthorLastNameLabel"
                runat="server" Text='<%# Eval("AuthorLastName")
                %>'></asp:Label><br />
                AuthorFirstName:
                <asp:Label ID="AuthorFirstNameLabel"
                runat="server" Text='<%# Eval("AuthorFirstName")
                %>'></asp:Label><br />
                Topic:
                <asp:Label ID="TopicLabel" runat="server"
                Text='<%# Eval("Topic") %>'></asp:Label><br />
                Publisher:
                <asp:Label ID="PublisherLabel"
                runat="server"

                Text='<%# Eval("Publisher") %>'></asp:Label><br />
                <br />

            <asp:Button ID="SelectItem"

                runat="server" Text="Select Item" />

                 
            </ItemTemplate>
                <HeaderStyle BackColor="#4A3C8C" Font-Bold="True"
                    ForeColor="#F7F7F7" />
        </asp:DataList>
```

The Microsoft Visual Studio Designer should appear like this when you finish:

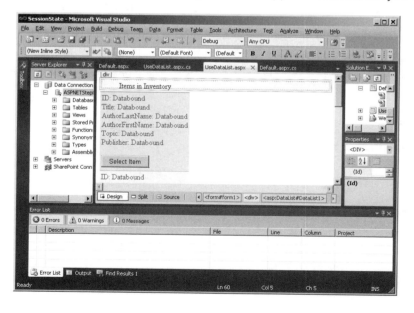

2. Stub out a shell for the Select Item button on the *ItemCommand* handler. Select *DataList1* on the page. Look at the Properties pane in Visual Studio. Click the lightning bolt button to view the available events you can handle. In the edit box next to the *ItemCommand* event, notice the name of the command: *DataList1_ItemCommand*. Double-click inside the edit box and Visual Studio will produce an item command handler. The button's handler will be named *DataList1_ItemCommand* to match the identifier in the *DataList1*. You use it shortly to move items from the inventory to the selected items table.

```
public partial class UseDataList : System.Web.UI.Page
{

    protected void DataList1_ItemCommand(object source,
            DataListCommandEventArgs e)
    {
    }

}
```

3. Go back to the code for the page and add some code to open a database and populate the *DataList*. Name the function *GetInventory*. The example that comes with this book includes a SQL Server database named *AspNetStepByStep4* that will work. Add the database from the Chapter 10 example to the App_Data folder of this project. You can obtain the connection string by viewing the database in Server Explorer after you have added it to the project. You can find the connection string in the Properties pane after you select the database in Server Explorer.

```
using System.Data;
Using System.Data.Common;

public partial class UseDataList : System.Web.UI.Page
{

    protected DataTable GetInventory()
    {
      string strConnection =
        @"Data Source=
        .\SQLEXPRESS;
        AttachDbFilename=|DataDirectory|\ASPNETStepByStep4.mdf;
        Integrated Security=True;
        User Instance=True";

      DbProviderFactory f =
        DbProviderFactories.GetFactory("System.Data.SqlClient");

      DataTable dt = new DataTable();
      using (DbConnection connection = f.CreateConnection())
      {
        connection.ConnectionString = strConnection;
        connection.Open();
        DbCommand command = f.CreateCommand();
```

```
        command.CommandText = "Select * from DotNetReferences";
        command.Connection = connection;

        IDataReader reader = command.ExecuteReader();
        dt.Load(reader);
        reader.Close();
        connection.Close();
      }
      return dt;
    }


    protected DataTable BindToinventory()
    {
      DataTable dt;
      dt = this.GetInventory();
      this.DataList1.DataSource = dt;
      this.DataBind();
      return dt;
    }


      // More goes here...
    }
```

4. Now add a method named *CreateSelectedItemsData*. This is a table into which selected items are placed. The method takes a *DataTable* object that describes the schema of the data in the live database (you see how to get that soon). You can create an empty *DataTable* by constructing it and then adding *Columns* to the column collection. The schema coming from the database will have the column name and the data type.

```
public partial class UseDataList : System.Web.UI.Page
{

  protected DataTable CreateSelectedItemsTable(DataTable tableSchema)
  {

      DataTable tableSelectedItemsData = new DataTable();

      foreach(DataColumn dc in tableSchema.Columns)
      {
          tableSelectedItemsData.Columns.Add(dc.ColumnName,
              dc.DataType);
      }
      return tableSelectedItemsData;


  }
}
```

5. Add code to the *Page_Load* handler. When the initial request to a page is made (that is, if the request is *not* a postback), *Page_Load* should call *BindToInventory*, which returns the *DataTable* snapshot of the *DotNetReferences* table. Use the *DataTable* as the schema on which to base the selected items table. That is, declare an instance of a *DataTable* and assign it the result of *CreateSelectedItemsTable*. Then, store the (now empty) table in the *Session* object using the key *tableSelectedItems*.

```
public partial class UseDataList : System.Web.UI.Page
{
    protected void Page_Load(object sender, EventArgs e)
    {
        if (!IsPostBack)
        {
            DataTable dt = BindToinventory();
            DataTable tableSelectedItems =
                this.CreateSelectedItemsTable(dt);
            Session["tableSelectedItems"] = tableSelectedItems;
        }
    }
}
```

Browse to the Web site to make sure that the database connects. It should look something like this:

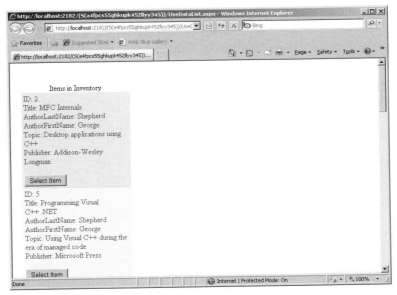

6. Now add a *GridView* to the page. It represents the table of selected items held in session state. Don't bother to give it a data source. You add that shortly. Make sure the

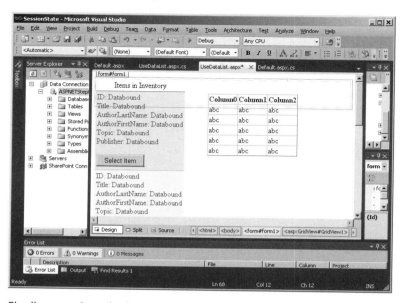

7. Finally, complete the handler for the *SelectItem* button. This method should move items from the inventory to the selected items table. You can get the selected item index from the *DataListCommandEventArgs* coming into the handler. Call *BindToInventory* to set up the *DataList* data source so that you can fetch the selected item. You can access the columns in the selected row using ordinal indices. From the values in each column, construct a new *DataRow* and add it to the selected items table. Store the modified table back in session state. Finally, apply the new selected items table to the *DataSource* in the *GridView1* and bind the *GridView1*.

```
public partial class UseDataList : System.Web.UI.Page
{
    protected void DataList1_ItemCommand(object source,
        DataListCommandEventArgs e)
    {
        int nItemIndex = e.Item.ItemIndex;
        this.DataList1.SelectedIndex = nItemIndex;

        BindToinventory();

        // Order of the columns is:
        // ID, Title, FirstName, LastName, Topic, Publisher

        DataTable dt = (DataTable)DataList1.DataSource;
        String strID = (dt.Rows[nItemIndex][0]).ToString();
        String strTitle = (dt.Rows[nItemIndex][1]).ToString();
        String strAuthorLastName = (dt.Rows[nItemIndex][2]).ToString();
        String strAuthorFirstName = (dt.Rows[nItemIndex][3]).ToString();
```

```
        String strTopic = (dt.Rows[nItemIndex][4]).ToString();
        String strPublisher = (dt.Rows[nItemIndex][5]).ToString();

        DataTable tableSelectedItems;
        tableSelectedItems = (DataTable)Session["tableSelectedItems"];

        DataRow dr = tableSelectedItems.NewRow();
        dr[0] = strID;
        dr[1] = strTitle;
        dr[2] = strAuthorLastName;
        dr[3] = strAuthorFirstName;
        dr[4] = strTopic;
        dr[5] = strPublisher;

        tableSelectedItems.Rows.Add(dr);

        Session["tableSelectedItems"] = tableSelectedItems;

        this.GridView1.DataSource = tableSelectedItems;
        this.GridView1.DataBind();
    }
}
```

8. Run the site. When the page first appears, you should see only the inventory list on the left side of the page. Click the Select Item button on some of the items. You should see your browser post back to the server and render the *DataList* and the *GridView* with each newly added selected item.

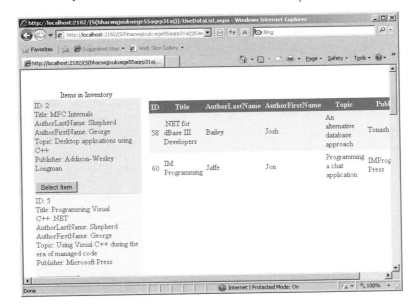

Now you have a working application that uses session state. Next, look at the different ways in which you can configure ASP.NET session state.

Configuring Session State

ASP.NET gives you several choices for managing session state. You can turn it off completely, you can run session state in the ASP.NET worker process, you can run it on a separate state server, or you can run it from a SQL Server database. Here's a rundown of the options available:

- **Don't use it at all.**   By disabling session state, your application performance will increase because the page doesn't need to load the session when starting, and neither does it need to store session state when it's going away. On the other hand, you won't be able to associate any data with a particular user between page invocations.

- **Store session state "in proc."**   This is how session state is handled by default. In this case, the session dictionaries (the *Session* objects) are managed in the same process as the page and handler code. The advantage of using session state in process is that it's very fast and convenient. However, it's not durable. For example, if you restart Internet Information Services (IIS) or somehow knock the server down, all session state is lost. In some cases, this might not be a big deal. However, if the shopping cart contains sizable orders, losing that might be a big deal. In addition, the in-process session manager is confined to a single computer, meaning you can't use it in a Web farm. (A *Web farm* is a group of servers tied together to serve Web pages as a single application.)

- **Store session state in a state server.**   This option tells the ASP.NET runtime to direct all session management activities to a separate Windows Service process running on a particular computer. With this option, you have the advantage of running your server in a Web farm. The ASP.NET session state facilities support Web farms explicitly. To run in a Web farm, you direct all your applications to go to the same place to retrieve session information. The downside of this approach is that it does impede performance somewhat—applications need to make a network round-trip to the state server when loading or saving session information. To reduce the overall size of the stored information, when storing session data in the state server, with ASP.NET 4 you now have the option of using compression to reduce the amount of data being transferred. Just include the *compressionEnabled=true* setting in the *sessionState* section of web.config.

- **Store session state in a database.**   Configuring your application to use a SQL Server database for state management causes ASP.NET to store session information in a SQL Server database somewhere on your network. Use this option when you want to run your server from in a Web farm when you want session state to be durable and safe. As with the state server approach, when storing session data in the SQL Server database, you have the option of using compression to reduce the amount of data being transferred. Again just include the *compressionEnabled=true* setting in the *sessionState* section of web.config.

When you configure ASP.NET session state during development, you can edit the configuration file directly. After your site is deployed, you might prefer to configure session state through the session state configuration page in IIS:

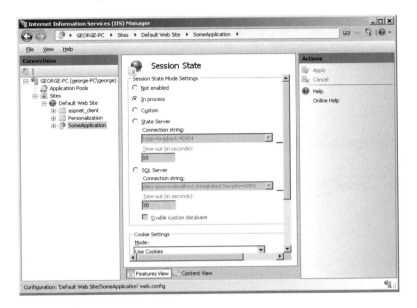

Turning Off Session State

The ASP.NET session state configuration tool available through IIS touches your Web site's web.config file and inserts the right configuration strings to enforce the settings you choose. To turn off session state completely, select Off from the session state mode control.

Storing Session State *InProc*

To store session state in the ASP.NET worker process, select *InProc* from the session state mode control. Your application will retrieve and store session information very quickly, but the session state information is available to your application only on the particular server on which the session information was originally stored. (That is, the session information is not available to other servers that might be working together on a Web farm.)

Storing Session State in a State Server

To have ASP.NET store session state on another server on your network, select *StateServer* from the *SessionState* mode control. When you select this item, the *Connection String* text box and the network *Timeout* text box become available. Insert the protocol, IP address, and port for the state server in the *Connection String* text box. For example, the string

```
tcpip=loopback:42424
```

will store the session state on the local computer over port 42424. If you want to store the session state on a computer other than your local server, simply provide its IP address in place of *loopback*. Before session state is stored on a server, you need to make sure the ASP.NET state service is running on that computer. You can get to it using the Services icon in Control Panel and Administration Tools, as shown in the following graphic, which shows the Services control panel:

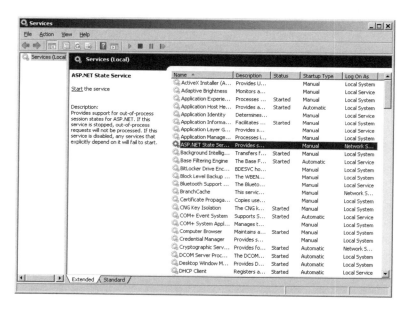

Storing Session State in a Database

The final option for storing session state is to use a SQL Server database. Select *SQLServer* from the ASP.NET session state mode combo box. You are asked to enter the connection string to the SQL Server state database. Here's the string provided by default:

```
data source=localhost;Integrated Security=SSPI
```

You can configure ASP.NET so that it references a database on another server. Of course, you need to have SQL Server installed on the target server to make this work. In addition, you can find some SQL scripts to create the state databases in your .NET system directory (C:\WINDOWS\Microsoft.NET\Framework\v2.0.50727 on my computer at the time of this writing). The aspnet_regsql.exe tool sets up the databases for you.

Tracking Session State

Because Web-based applications rely on HTTP to connect browsers to servers and HTML to represent the state of the application, ASP.NET is essentially a disconnected architecture. When an application needs to use session state, the runtime needs a way of tracking the origin of the requests it receives so that it can associate data with a particular client. ASP.NET offers three options for tracking the session ID—by cookies, the URL, or device profiles.

Tracking Session State with Cookies

This is the default option for an ASP.NET Web site. In this scenario, ASP.NET generates a hard-to-guess identifier and uses it to store a new *Session* object. You can see the session identifier come through the cookie collection if you have tracing turned on. Notice how ASP.NET stores the session ID in a request cookie. The tracing information also reveals the names and the values of the session variables. The following graphic shows the session ID in the request details section of the trace:

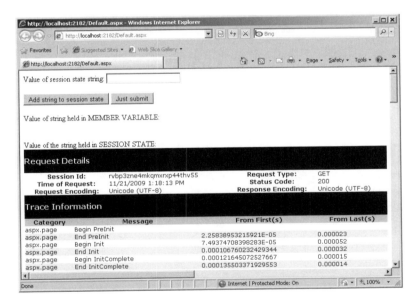

The following graphic shows tracing information, indicating the session ID is just another cookie:

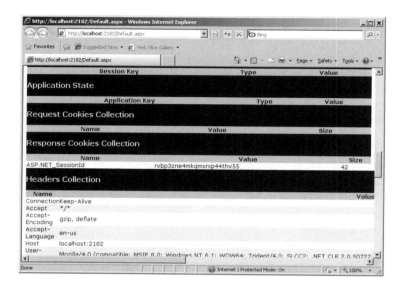

Tracking Session State with the URL

The other main option is to track session state by embedding the session ID as part of the request string. This is useful if you think your clients will turn off cookies (thereby disabling cookie-based session state tracking). Notice that the navigation URL has the session ID embedded in it:

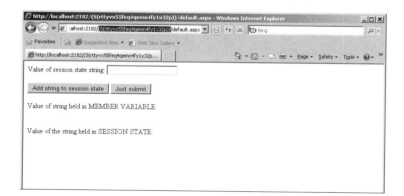

Using *AutoDetect*

When you use *AutoDetect*, the ASP.NET runtime determines whether the client browser has cookies turned on. If cookies are turned on, the session identifier is passed around as a cookie. If not, the session identifier is stored in the URL.

Applying Device Profiles

The *UseDeviceProfile* option tells ASP.NET to determine whether the browser supports cookies based on the *SupportsRedirectWithCookie* property of the *HttpBrowserCapabilities* object set up for the request. Requests that flip this bit to *true* cause session identifier values to be passed as cookies. Requests that flip this bit to *false* cause session identifiers to be passed in the URL.

Session State Timeouts

The *timeout* configuration setting manages the lifetime of the session. The lifetime of the session is the length of time in minutes a session can remain idle before ASP.NET abandons it and renders the session ID invalid. The maximum value is 525,601 minutes (one year), and the default is 20.

Other Session Configuration Settings

ASP.NET supports some other configuration settings not available through the IIS configuration utility. These are values you need to type into the web.config file directly.

If you don't like the rather obvious name of the session ID cookie made up by ASP.NET (the default is SessionID), you can change it using the *cookieName* setting. You might want to rename the cookie as a security measure to hamper hackers in their attempts to hijack a session ID key.

If you want to replace an expired session ID with a new one, set the *regenerateExpiredSessionId* setting to *true*. This is only for cookieless sessions.

If you don't like the SQL Server database already provided by ASP.NET to support session state, you can use your own database. The *allowCustomSqlDatabase* setting turns this feature on.

When you use SQL Server to store session data, ASP.NET has to act as a client of SQL Server. Usually, the ASP.NET process identity is impersonated. You can instruct ASP.NET to use the user credentials supplied to the *identity* configuration element in web.config by setting the *mode* attribute to *Custom*. By setting the *mode* attribute to *SQLServer,* you tell ASP.NET to use a trusted connection.

Use the *stateNetworkTimeout* for setting the number of seconds for the idle time limits of the TCP/IP network connection between the Web server and the state server, or between the SQL Server and the Web server. The default is 10.

Finally, you can instruct ASP.NET to use a custom provider by setting the name of the provider in the *custom* element. For this to work, the provider must be specified elsewhere in web.config (specifically in the *providers* element).

The *Wizard* Control: An Alternative to Session State

One of the most common uses for session state is to keep track of information coming from a user even though the information is posted back through several pages. For example, scenarios such as collecting mailing addresses, applying for security credentials, or purchasing something on a Web site introduce this issue.

Sometimes the information to be gathered is minimal and can be done through only one page. However, when collecting data from users requires several pages of forms, you need to keep track of that information between posts. For example, most commercial Web sites employ a multistage checkout process. After a users places a bunch of items in the shopping cart, he or she clicks *Check Out* and the site redirects to a checkout page. From there, the user is usually required to perform several distinct steps: set up a payment method, confirm the order, and receive an order confirmation.

Although you could code something like this in ASP.NET 1.*x*, later versions of ASP.NET include a *Wizard* control to deal with multistage data collection.

If you were to develop a multistage input sequence, you'd need to build in the navigation logic and keep track of the state of the transaction. The *Wizard* control provides a template that performs the basic tasks of navigating through multiple input pages while you provide the specifics. The *Wizard* control logic is built around specific steps and includes facilities for managing these steps. The *Wizard* control supports both linear and nonlinear navigation.

This example shows how to use the *Wizard* control to gather several different pieces of information from the client: a name and address, what kinds of software he or she uses, and the kind of hardware he or she uses. For example, this might be used to qualify users for entry into a certain part of the Web site or perhaps to qualify them for a subscription.

Using the *Wizard* control

1. Create a new page in the SessionState project named UseWizard.aspx.

2. Drop a *WizardControl* from the Toolbox onto the page.

3. When the Wizard Tasks window appears in the Designer, click the small arrow near the top right corner of the *Wizard*. Click Auto Format to style the *Wizard*. The example here uses the Professional style.

   The example here also uses a *StartNavigationTemplate* and a *SidebarTemplate* so that you have greater control over the look of these aspects of the *Wizard*. Although they are not used explicitly in the example, they are shown here to illustrate how they fit into the *Wizard* control. Using these templates, you can define how these parts of the *Wizard* look by introducing controls to them. To convert these areas to templates, click the small arrow in the upper right corner of the *Wizard* and select Convert To

StartNavigationTemplate. Then, click the small arrow in the upper right corner of the *Wizard* again, and click Convert To SideBarTemplate.

Click the arrow again and select Add/Remove Wizard Steps to open the WizardStep Collection Editor dialog box. Visual Studio adds two samples steps for you. Delete them, as the following graphic shows:

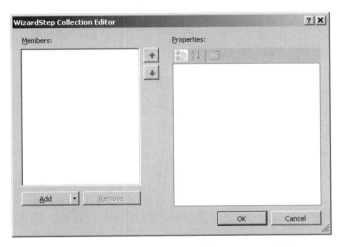

4. Add an Intro step, a Name and Address step, a Software step, a Hardware step, and a Submit information step. That is, click the Add button to open the dialog box where you can enter steps. "Name," "Address," "Software," "Hardware," and "Submit Information" are the *Titles* for these pages. Make sure Intro uses a *StepType* of Start.

5. Make sure the Submit information step has its *StepType* set to *Finish*, as shown in the following graphic. With all of the steps in place, click OK.

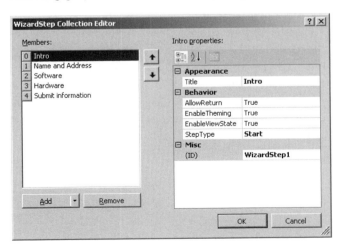

6. Add controls to the steps. First, select the *Wizard* in the Designer, and then select Set Position on the Format menu. Select Absolute. Now you can resize the *Wizard*. Set the *Height* to 240 px and the *Width* to 650 px. Navigate to the step by selecting the small arrow that appears on the upper right corner of the *Wizard* control. Select the *Intro* step. The *Intro* step gets a label that describes what the user is entering:

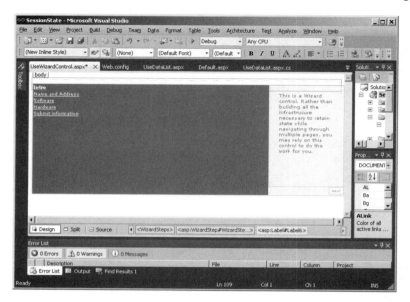

7. The *Name and Address* step should include labels and text boxes to get personal information. As you add these controls, select *Absolute* positioning for each one by selecting *Set Position* on the Format menu. This lets you change the height and width. Drop the name *Label* onto the pane on the right side of the *Wizard*. Below that, add the name *TextBox*. Below that, drop the address *Label* on the pane followed below by the address *TextBox*. Underneath that, add the city *Label* followed by the city *TextBox*. Drop the state and postal code *Label*s next, followed by the state and postal code *TextBox*es on that line. Be sure to give usable IDs to the text boxes. The name *TextBox* should have the ID *TextBoxName*. The address *TextBox* should have the ID *TextBoxAddress*. The city *TextBox* should have the ID *TextBoxCity*. The state *TextBox* should have the ID *TextBoxState*, and the postal code *TextBox* should have the ID *TextBoxPostalCode*. You'll need them during the submission step:

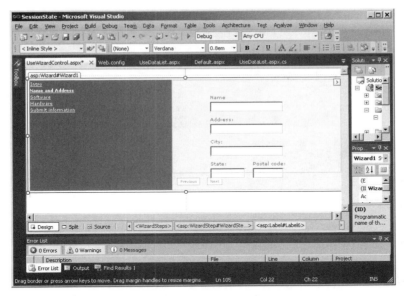

8. Select the *Software* step and modify it. The *Software* step should include several check boxes listing common software types. Add a *CheckBoxList* with the ID *CheckBoxListSoftware* and fill it with the values you see here:

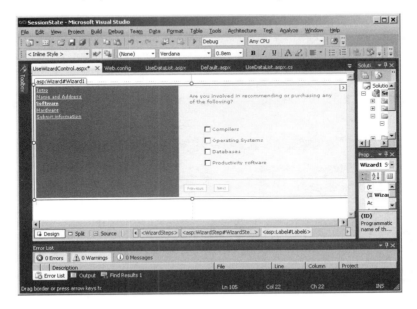

9. The *Hardware* step should include several check boxes listing common hardware types. Add a *CheckBoxList* with the ID *CheckBoxListHardware* and fill it with the values you see here:

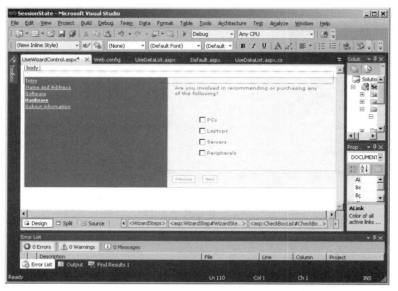

10. The *Submit Information* step (which you can use to show information before submitting) should include a multiline *TextBox* that summarizes the information collected. Give the *TextBox* the ID *TextBoxSummary* so that you can use it to display the summary:

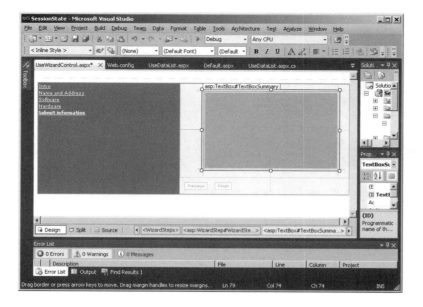

11. Finally, edit the *Page_Load* method as shown in the following snippet to collect the information from each of the controls in the *Wizard*. The controls are actually available as member variables on the page. This information is loaded every time the page is loaded. However, it is hidden from view until the user selects the step. Double-click the *Wizard* control to add a handler for the *Finish* button that you can use to harvest the information gathered by the wizard.

```
protected void Page_Load(object sender, EventArgs e)
{
    StringBuilder sb = new StringBuilder();
    sb.Append("You are about to submit. \n");

    sb.Append(" Personal: \n");
    sb.AppendFormat("  {0}\n", this.TextBoxName.Text);
    sb.AppendFormat("  {0}\n", this.TextBoxAddress.Text);
    sb.AppendFormat("  {0}\n", this.TextBoxCity.Text);
    sb.AppendFormat("  {0}\n", this.TextBoxState.Text);
    sb.AppendFormat("  {0}\n", this.TextBoxPostalCode.Text);
    sb.Append("\n Software: \n");
     foreach (ListItem listItem in CheckBoxListSoftware.Items)
     {
         if (listItem.Selected)
         {
             sb.AppendFormat("  {0}\n", listItem.Text);
         }
     }

        sb.Append("\n Hardware: \n");
     foreach (ListItem listItem in CheckBoxListHardware.Items)
     {
         if (listItem.Selected)
         {
             sb.AppendFormat("  {0}\n", listItem.Text);
         }
     }
     this.TextBoxSummary.Text = sb.ToString();
}
protected void Wizard1_FinishButtonClick(object sender,
    WizardNavigationEventArgs e)
{
    // Do something with the data here
}
```

12. Now run the page and go through the steps. You should see each step along the way and then finally a summary of the information collected. If the wizard on your page doesn't start with the first step (*Intro*), it's probably because you're running the page in the debugger and a wizard step other than *Intro* is selected in the Designer. Simply select Intro in the Designer and rerun the page. The following graphic shows the intro step in the Designer:

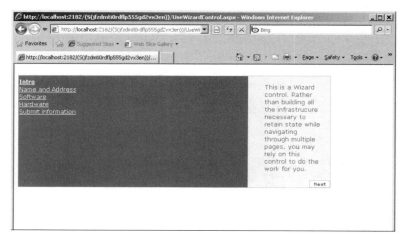

Here's the name and address step.

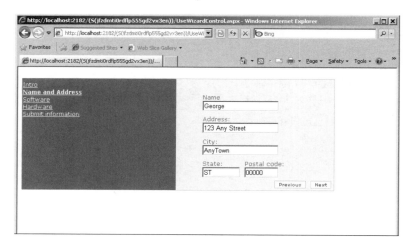

Here's the software step:

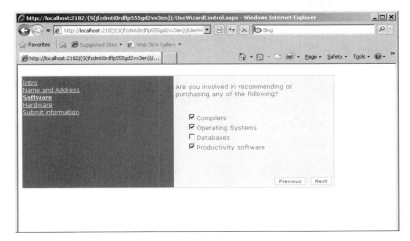

Here's the hardware step.

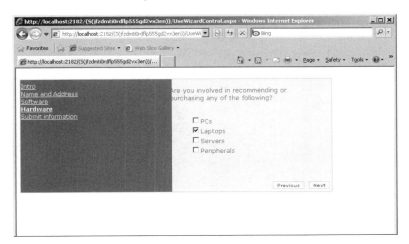

Here's the final step.

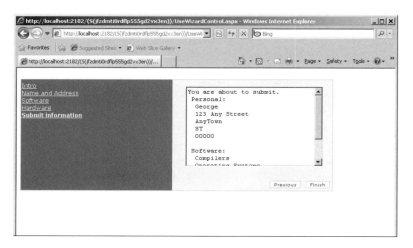

Chapter 14 Quick Reference

To	Do This
Access the current client's session state	Use the *Page.Session* property. Use the current context's *HttpContext.Session* property.
Access a specific value in the current client's session state	Session state is a set of key/value pairs. Access the data with the string-based key originally used to insert the data in the cache.
Store session state in proc	Edit the *sessionState* attributes in web.config. Set mode to *InProc*.
Store session state in a state server	Edit the *sessionState* attributes in web.config. Set *mode* to *StateServer*. Be sure to include a *stateConnectionString*.
Store session state in SQL Server	Set the *sessionState* attributes in web.config. Set mode to *SQLServer*. Be sure to include a *sqlConnectionString*.
Disable session state	Set the *sessionState* attributes in web.config. Set mode to *Off*.
Use cookies to track session state	Set the *sessionState* attributes in web.config. Set cookieless to *false*.
Use URL to track session state	Set the *sessionState* attributes in web.config. Set cookieless to *true*.
Set session state timeout	Set the *sessionState* attributes in web.config. Set *timeout* to a value (representing minutes).

Chapter 15
Application Data Caching

After completing this chapter, you will be able to

- Improve the performance of your application by using the application data cache.
- Avoid unnecessary round-trips to the database.
- Manage items in the application data cache.

This chapter covers built-in data-caching features in ASP.NET. Caching is a long-standing means of improving the performance of any software system. The idea is to place frequently used data in quickly accessed media. Even though access times for mass storage continue to improve, accessing data from a standard hard disk is *much* slower than accessing it in memory. By taking often-used data and making it available quickly, you can improve the performance of your application dramatically.

The ASP.NET runtime includes a dictionary (key/value map) of Common Language Runtime (CLR) objects. The *Cache* lives with the application and is available through the *HttpContext* and *System.Web.UI.Page*. Using the cache is very much like using the *Session* object. You can access items in the cache using an indexer. In addition, you can control the lifetime of objects in the cache and even set up links between the cached objects and their physical data sources. This chapter starts by examining a case in which using the cache is justified.

Getting Started with Caching

ASP.NET's caching facility is extremely easy to use. In addition, it's also configurable in the sense that you can tell ASP.NET to apply expirations to cached items and you can set up callback methods so that your application knows when items have been removed from the cache. The following exercise shows how using the cache can benefit your application.

Making an application that benefits from caching

1. Create a new project. Make it an Empty ASP.NET Web Application. Call it *UseDataCaching*. (If you prefer, you can use the project from Chapter 14, "Session State," because this project uses the same database.)

2. Look at the UseDataList page. If you created a new Web site, borrow the *UseDataList* code from the example in Chapter 14. To bring it into your new project, right-click the project in Solution Explorer and click Add Existing Item. Navigate to the location of the code from Chapter 14. Grab the UseDataList.aspx, UseDataList.aspx.cs, and UseDataList.aspx.designer.cs files from Chapter 14. Click Add to copy them into this new project.

The code you imported refers to the database in the *SessionState* example. That's okay. If you want to, you can change it to the database in this application's *App_Data* directory, but that is not strictly necessary as long as the path points to an available database somewhere on your system.

3. Examine in particular the *GetInventory*, the *BindToInventory*, and the *Page_Load* methods. Listing 15-1 shows the code.

LISTING 15-1 Inventory binding code

```
protected DataTable CreateSelectedItemsTable(DataTable tableSchema)
{
    DataTable tableSelectedItemsData = new DataTable();

    foreach (DataColumn dc in tableSchema.Columns)
    {
        tableSelectedItemsData.Columns.Add(dc.ColumnName,
            dc.DataType);
    }
    return tableSelectedItemsData;
}


protected DataTable GetInventory()
{
    DataTable dt = null;

    dt = new DataTable();
    string strConnection =
    @"Data Source=
    .\SQLEXPRESS;
    AttachDbFilename=|DataDirectory|\ASPNETStepByStep4.mdf;
    Integrated Security=True;
    User Instance=True";
    DbProviderFactory f =
        DbProviderFactories.GetFactory("System.Data.SqlClient");
        using (DbConnection connection = f.CreateConnection())
        {
            connection.ConnectionString = strConnection;
            connection.Open();
            DbCommand command = f.CreateCommand();
            command.CommandText = "Select * from DotNetReferences";
            command.Connection = connection;

            IDataReader reader = command.ExecuteReader();
            dt.Load(reader);
            reader.Close();
            connection.Close();
        }
        return dt;
        }
protected DataTable BindToInventory()
{
```

```
        DataTable dt;
        dt = this.GetInventory();
        this.DataList1.DataSource = dt;
        this.DataBind();
        return dt;
    }
    protected void Page_Load(object sender, EventArgs e)
    {   if (!IsPostBack)

        {
            DataTable dt = BindToInventory();
            DataTable tableSelectedItems =
                this.CreateSelectedItemsTable(dt);
                Session["tableSelectedItems"] = tableSelectedItems;
        }
    }
```

4. Run the application to make sure it works. That is, it should connect to the *DotNetReferences* table and bind the *DataList* to the table from the database.

The *GetInventory* and *BindToInventory* methods are called by the *Page_Load* method. How often is *Page_Load* called? Every time a new page is created—which happens for every single HTTP request destined for the UseDataList page. In the case of running this application on a single computer with one client (in a testing situation), perhaps connecting to the database for every request isn't a big deal. However, for applications that are expected to serve thousands of users making frequent requests, repeated database access actually becomes a very big deal. Accessing a database is a very expensive operation. As you see shortly, it can take a long time (on the computer time scale) simply to connect to this database and read the several rows contained in the *DotNetReferences* table. Data access can only get more expensive as the size of the tables in the database grows. A half second in the computer processing time scale is eons to the program.

Now think about the nature of the inventory table. Does it change often? Of course, not in the case of this simple application. However, think about how this might work in a real application. The items carried in an inventory might not change as often as other data sets might (and such changes might occur at regular, predictable intervals). If that's the case, why does the application need to hit the database each time a page is loaded? Doing so is certainly overkill. If you could take those data elements and store them in a medium that offers quicker access than the database does (for example, the computer's internal memory), your site could potentially serve many more requests than if it had to make a round-trip to the database every time it loads a page. This is a perfect opportunity to cache the data. (The caveat here is that if the inventory data set begins fluctuating quickly, for example, every 5 seconds, it becomes a poor candidate for caching.)

Using the Data Cache

Using the data cache in the simplest and most naive way supported by ASP.NET is very much like accessing the *Session* object. Remember, accessing the *Session* object involves using an indexer (the square bracket syntax) and a consistent index to store and retrieve data. The data cache works in exactly the same way (although it has some other features for managing items in the cache).

The strategy for caching a piece of data usually involves these steps:

1. Look in the cache for the data element.

2. If it's there, use it (bypassing the expensive database round-trip).

3. If the data element is unavailable in the cache, make a round-trip to the database to fetch it.

4. If you had to fetch the data, cache the data element so that it is available next time around.

The next example modifies the UseDataList page so that it stores the data item in the cache after acquiring it for the first time. Although the first time *Page_Load* is called it might take a while (on a computer's time scale), subsequent calls are much faster.

Using the cache

1. Open the UseDataList.aspx.cs file and go to the *GetInventory* method.

2. Modifying the method to use the cache is fairly straightforward. The following listing highlights the changes. First, check to see whether the item is in the cache. If searching the cache for the *DataSet* turns up a valid object reference, you can bypass the database lookup code and return the referenced *DataSet*. If searching the cache turns up a null object reference, go ahead and make the round-trip to the database. When the database lookup finishes, you'll have a good *DataSet* (provided the query succeeds). Cache it before returning the reference to the caller. If you include the *Trace* statements, you can see exactly how big an impact caching can make. The changes you need to make are shown in bold type:

```
protected DataTable GetInventory()
{
  DataTable dt = null;

  Trace.Warn("Page_Load", "looking in cache");
  dt = (DataTable)Cache["InventoryDataTable"];
  Trace.Warn("Page_Load", "done looking in cache");
  if (dt == null)
  {
    Trace.Warn("Page_Load", "Performing DB lookup");
    dt = new DataTable();
```

```
        string strConnection =
          @"Data Source=
          .\SQLEXPRESS;
          AttachDbFilename=|DataDirectory|ASPNETStepByStep4.mdf;
          Integrated Security=True;
          User Instance=True";
        DbProviderFactory f =
          DbProviderFactories.GetFactory("System.Data.SqlClient");

        using (DbConnection connection = f.CreateConnection())
        {
          connection.ConnectionString = strConnection;
          connection.Open();
          DbCommand command = f.CreateCommand();
          command.CommandText = "Select * from DotNetReferences";
          command.Connection = connection;

          IDataReader reader = command.ExecuteReader();
          dt.Load(reader);
          reader.Close();
          connection.Close();
        }
        Cache["InventoryDataTable"] = dt;
        Trace.Warn("Page_Load", "Done performing DB lookup");
      }
    return dt;
}
```

This code significantly reduces the cost of loading the page (after the data is loaded in the cache, of course). Next time the page is loaded, it uses the cached version—available through *Cache* at a tremendously reduced cost. How much is the cost savings? It's huge, as you can see by looking at the trace pages for the application, as described in the following section.

Impact of Caching

If you included the *Trace* statements in the *GetInventory* method, you can surf to the trace page to see the effect of caching. The UseDataCaching application included here has the *Trace* attribute turned off in the page but has *application tracing* turned on. That is, the web.config includes the following section:

```
<configuration>
    <system.web>
    <trace enabled="true" />
    <system.web>
</configuration>
```

You can see the trace information by surfing to the virtual directory with a file name of Trace.axd. Instead of surfing to the UseDataList.aspx file, surf to the Trace.axd file in the same directory.

Figure 15-1 shows the trace statements produced by accessing the page for the first time. The column farthest to the right indicates the time elapsed since the previous trace statement. The trace statement shows that more than 0.016 seconds has elapsed during the page loading time.

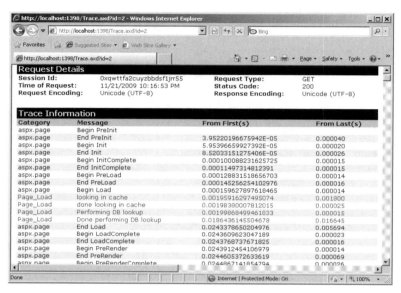

FIGURE 15-1 Hitting the database takes more than half a second in this scenario.

Make a few more posts to the page (for example, add some items from the inventory to the selected items grid). Then, go back and look at the tracing information for the subsequent postbacks. Figure 15-2 shows some examples of trace statements. Fetching from the *Cache* is dramatically faster than hitting the database—by several orders of magnitude! Again, you might not notice the difference with just one client surfing the page every once in a while. However, when multiple clients are surfing to the same page simultaneously, they'll get their responses much more quickly than if the page had to make a round-trip to the database.

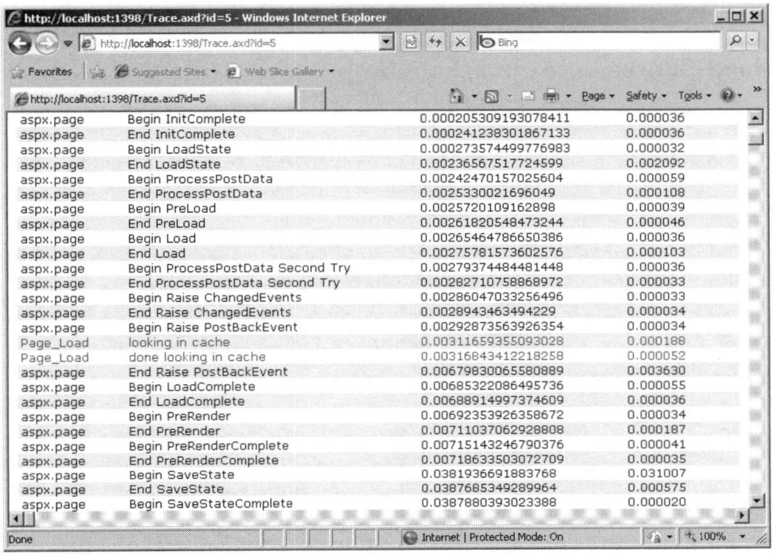

FIGURE 15-2 Fetching data from the cache takes 0.000040 seconds.

Managing the Cache

The last example cached items in the most naive way possible. They were simply placed in the cache and given an index. However, at times you might need a bit more control over the items in the cache. For example, what if the physical source backing one of the items you cache changes? If getting accurate information out to your users is important, you might want to know about the change so that you can handle it (perhaps by reloading the new information into the cache). As another example, what if you knew that the data in your cache would become invalid after a certain period of time or on a certain date? You'd want to make sure that the data in the cache is invalidated and the cache is appropriately refreshed with new data.

In addition to placing items in the cache using the indexer, the *Cache* object implements a parameterized method named *Insert* that you can use to control many aspects of the cached item. The ways in which you can control cache entries include the following:

- Setting up an absolute expiration time

- Setting up a sliding expiration time

- Setting up dependencies between cached items and their backing sources (for example, database, file, or directory dependencies, or even dependencies on other cache entries)

- Managing a relative invalidation priority of cached items

- Setting up callback functions to be called when items are removed

The *Cache*'s *insert* method includes four overloads. Table 15-1 enumerates them.

TABLE 15-1 Overloads for the *Cache.Insert* Method

Insert Overload	Description
Insert (*String, Object*)	Directly corresponds to the indexer version. Blindly places the object in the *Cache* using the string key in the first parameter.
Insert (*String, Object, CacheDependency*)	Inserts an object into the *Cache* and associates it with a dependency.
Insert (*String, Object, CacheDependency, DateTime, TimeSpan*)	Inserts an object into the *Cache*, associating it with a dependency and an expiration policy.
Insert (*String, Object, CacheDependency, DateTime, TimeSpan, CacheItemPriority, CacheItemRemovedCallback*)	Inserts an object into the *Cache*. Associates a dependency and expiration and priority policies. Also associates the *Cache* entry with a delegate for a callback to notify the application when the item is removed from the cache.

The following example illustrates some of these settings and how they work. In addition, the forthcoming examples illustrate another way to get *DataTables* and *DataSets*. You can actually create them programmatically. The next few examples use a *DataTable* that is created in memory rather than being fetched from a database. Although the impact of caching isn't quite as dramatic when using the in-memory *DataTable*, it is still appreciable—and you can see this other approach to managing data. The following section also shows how the *DataTable* serializes as XML as well (which is useful for examining cached items with file dependencies).

DataSets in Memory

Chapter 10, "Data Binding," looks at making a round-trip to the database to gather data suitable to bind to a control. The previous chapter looks at maintaining data between requests by using the *Session* object. The *Session* object holds any serializable .NET CLR object—even a *DataReader*. However, it's not a good idea to hold on to a *DataReader* for long periods of time because that means holding a connection open. Having too many open connections ultimately slows your site to a crawl. A better approach is to make single round-trips to the database and hold on to a *DataTable* or a *DataSet*.

In addition to fetching them from databases, you can synthesize a *DataTable* programmatically. Doing so involves constructing a *DataTable* and adding *DataRows* to describe the schema. After constructing a *DataTable*, you can use it to create columns with the correct "shape," populate them, and then add them to the table's columns collection. Listing 15-2 shows an example of creating a *DataTable* in memory. (Note that you also saw basic table creation in Listing 15-1 and in the previous chapter, but I didn't call your attention to it at the time so that I could save the discussion for this section.) The table is a collection of famous quotes and their originators that will be useful in the next examples.

LISTING 15-2 The *QuotesCollection* object

```
public class QuotesCollection : DataTable
{
    public QuotesCollection()
    {

        //
        // TODO: Add constructor logic here
        //
    }

    public void Synthesize()
    {
        // Be sure to give a name so that it will serialize as XML
        this.TableName = "Quotations";
        DataRow dr;

        Columns.Add(new DataColumn("Quote", typeof(string)));
        Columns.Add(new DataColumn("OriginatorLastName",
            typeof(string)));
        Columns.Add(new DataColumn("OriginatorFirstName",
            typeof(string)));


        dr = this.NewRow();
        dr[0] = "Imagination is more important than knowledge.";
        dr[1] = "Einstein";
        dr[2] = "Albert";
        Rows.Add(dr);

        dr = this.NewRow();
        dr[0] = "Assume a virtue, if you have it not";
        dr[1] = "Shakespeare";
        dr[2] = "William";
        this.Rows.Add(dr);

        dr = this.NewRow();
        dr[0] = @"A banker is a fellow who lends you his umbrella
            when the sun is shining, but wants it back the
            minute it begins to rain.";
        dr[1] = "Twain";
        dr[2] = "Mark";
        this.Rows.Add(dr);

        dr = this.NewRow();
        dr[0] = @"A man cannot be comfortable without his own
            approval.";
        dr[1] = "Twain";
        dr[2] = "Mark";
        this.Rows.Add(dr);
```

```
      dr = this.NewRow();
      dr[0] = "Beware the young doctor and the old barber";
      dr[1] = "Franklin";
      dr[2] = "Benjamin";
      this.Rows.Add(dr);

      dr = this.NewRow();
      dr[0] = @"Reality is merely an illusion, albeit a
                   very persistent one.";
      dr[1] = "Einstein";
      dr[2] = "Albert";
      this.Rows.Add(dr);

      dr = this.NewRow();
      dr[0] = "Beer has food value, but food has no beer value";
      dr[1] = "Sticker";
      dr[2] = "Bumper";
      this.Rows.Add(dr);

      dr = this.NewRow();
      dr[0] = @"Research is what I'm doing when I don't know
                   what I'm doing";
      dr[1] = "Von Braun";
      dr[2] = "Wernher";
      this.Rows.Add(dr);


      dr = this.NewRow();
      dr[0] = "Whatever is begun in anger ends in shame";
      dr[1] = "Franklin";
      dr[2] = "Benjamin";
      this.Rows.Add(dr);

      dr = this.NewRow();
      dr[0] = "We think in generalities, but we live in details";
      dr[1] = "Whitehead";
      dr[2] = "Alfred North";
      this.Rows.Add(dr);

      dr = this.NewRow();
      dr[0] = "Every really new idea looks crazy at first.";
      dr[1] = "Whitehead";
      dr[2] = "Alfred North";
      this.Rows.Add(dr);

      dr = this.NewRow();
      dr[0] = @"The illiterate of the 21st century will not be
            those who cannot read and write, but
            those who cannot learn,
            unlearn, and relearn.";
      dr[1] = "Whitehead";
      dr[2] = "Alfred North";
      this.Rows.Add(dr);

    }
  }
```

Building a *DataTable* in memory is straightforward—it's mostly a matter of defining the column schema and adding rows to the table. This class is available on the CD accompanying this book, so you don't need to type the whole thing. You can just import it into the next examples.

The next section looks at managing items in the cache.

Cache Expirations

The first way to manage cached items is to give them expiration thresholds. In some cases, you might be aware of certain aspects of your cached data that allow you to place expiration times on it. The *Cache* supports both absolute expirations and sliding expirations.

Placing absolute expirations

1. To try out absolute expirations, add a new page to the UseDataCaching site named CacheExpirations.aspx.

2. Use Website, Add Existing Item to bring the QuoteCollection.cs file from the CD accompanying this book and make it part of this project.

3. Drag a *GridView* onto the CacheExpirations page, as shown in the following graphic. Don't bind it to a data source yet. You handle that in the *Page_Load* method.

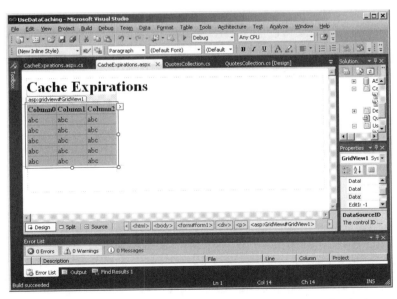

4. In the *Page_Load* method of the CacheExpirations page, check the cache to see whether there's already an instance of the *QuotesCollection* object (just as in the previous example). If the data set is not available from the cache, create an instance of the

QuotesCollection class and call the *Synthesize* method to populate the table. Finally, add it to the cache using the overloaded *Insert* method. You can use the *DateTime* class to generate an absolute expiration. Bind the *QuotesCollection* object to the *GridView*. The caching policy should be *Cache.NoSlidingExpiration*. Set up some trace statements so that you can see how the expiration times affect the lifetime of the cached object.

```
protected void Page_Load(object sender, EventArgs e)
{
        QuotesCollection quotesCollection;

        DateTime dtCurrent = DateTime.Now;
        Trace.Warn("Page_Load",
           "Testing cache at: " +
           dtCurrent.ToString());
        quotesCollection = (QuotesCollection)Cache["QuotesCollection"];

        if (quotesCollection == null)
        {           quotesCollection = new QuotesCollection();
            quotesCollection.Synthesize();

            DateTime dtExpires = new DateTime(2008, 5, 31, 23, 59, 59);
            dtCurrent = DateTime.Now;

            Trace.Warn("Page_Load",
               "Caching at: " +
               dtCurrent.ToString());
            Trace.Warn("Page_Load",
               "This entry will expire at: " +
               dtExpires);
            Cache.Insert("QuotesCollection",
                    quotesCollection,
                    null,
                    dtExpires,
                    System.Web.Caching.Cache.NoSlidingExpiration,
                    System.Web.Caching.CacheItemPriority.Default,
                    null);
        }

        this.GridView1.DataSource = quotesCollection;
        this.DataBind();

}
```

5. Experiment with changing the dates and times to see how setting the expiration time forces a reload of the cache.

An absolute expiration time applied to the cached item tells ASP.NET to flush the item from the cache at a certain time. Now try using a different kind of expiration technique—the *sliding expiration*. Using a sliding expiration tells ASP.NET to keep the data in the cache as long as it has been accessed within a certain period of time. Items that have not been accessed within that time frame are subject to expiration.

Placing sliding expirations

1. To set a sliding expiration for the cached data, modify the *Page_Load* method in the CacheExpirations page. Getting a sliding expiration to work is simply a matter of changing the parameters of the *Insert* method. Make up a time span after which you want the cached items to expire. Pass *DateTime.MaxValue* as the absolute expiration date and the *TimeSpan* as the final parameter like so:

```
protected void Page_Load(object sender, EventArgs e)
{
        QuotesCollection quotesCollection;

        DateTime dtCurrent = DateTime.Now;
        Trace.Warn("Page_Load",
                "Testing cache: " + dtCurrent.ToString());

         quotesCollection =
                (QuotesCollection)Cache["QuotesCollection"];

        if (quotesCollection == null)
        {
                quotesCollection = new QuotesCollection();
                quotesCollection.Synthesize();

                TimeSpan tsExpires = new TimeSpan(0, 0, 15);
                dtCurrent = DateTime.Now;

                Trace.Warn("Page_Load",
                        "Caching at: " + dtCurrent.ToString());
                Trace.Warn("Page_Load",
                        "This entry will expire in: " +
                        tsExpires.ToString());
                Cache.Insert("QuotesCollection",
                        quotesCollection,
                            null,
                            DateTime.MaxValue,
                            tsExpires);
        }

        this.GridView1.DataSource = quotesCollection;
        this.DataBind();
}
```

2. Surf to the page. You should see the cache reloading if you haven't accessed the cached item within the designated time frame.

Cache dependencies represent another way to manage cached items. Look at how they work next.

Cache Dependencies

In addition to allowing objects in the cache to expire by duration, you can set up dependencies for the cached items. For example, imagine your program loads some data from a file and places it into the cache. The backing file (that is, the source of the cached information) might change, making the data in the cache invalid. ASP.NET supports setting up a dependency between the cached item and the file so that changing the file invalidates the cached item. The conditions under which the cached items may be flushed include when a file changes, a directory changes, another cache entry is removed, or data in a table in Microsoft SQL Server changes (this is an often requested feature available since ASP.NET 2.0).

Here's an example that illustrates setting up cache dependencies.

Setting up cache dependencies

1. Add a new page to the UseDataCache site. Name it CacheDependencies.aspx.

2. Place a button on the page that you can use to post a request to the page to generate an XML file from the *QuotesCollection*. Use *ButtonSaveAsXML* as its ID. Also, drag a *GridView* onto the page like so:

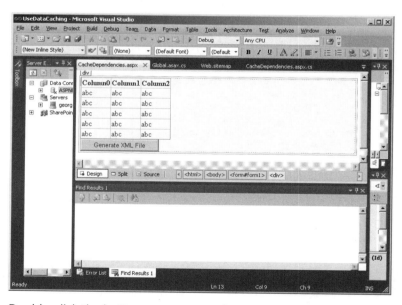

3. Double-click the button to generate a handler for the button that will save the XML Schema and the XML from the *DataTable* to XML and XSD files in the *App_Data* directory.

4. In the handler, instantiate a *QuotesCollection* object and call *Synthesize* to generate the
data. In the page, you have a reference to the *Server* object. Call the *MapPath* method
in the *Server* object to get the physical path for saving the file. Then, use that path to
create an XML file and a schema file. The *DataTable* will do this for you automatically by
calling the *WriteXmlSchema* and *WriteXml* methods, respectively.

```
protected void ButtonSaveAsXML_Click(object sender, EventArgs e)
{
    QuotesCollection quotesCollection = new QuotesCollection();
    quotesCollection.Synthesize();
    String strFilePathXml =

    Server.MapPath(Request.ApplicationPath +
    "\\App_Data\\QuotesCollection.xml");
    String strFilePathSchema =
    Server.MapPath(Request.ApplicationPath +
    "\\App_Data\\QuotesCollection.xsd");
    quotesCollection.WriteXmlSchema(strFilePathSchema);
    quotesCollection.WriteXml(strFilePathXml);
}
```

5. Now write a method to load the XML into the *QuotesCollection* object and cache the
data. You can use the file path to the XML file to create a dependency on the file. When
it changes, ASP.NET will empty the cache. Turn off the absolute expiration and the sliding expiration by passing in *Cache.NoAbsoluteExpiration* and *Cache.NoSlidingExpiration*.
If you put trace statements in, you can see the effect of updating the file after it's been
loaded in the cache. Finally, make sure to bind the *GridView* to the *QuotesCollection*.

```
protected void CacheWithFileDependency()
{
    QuotesCollection quotesCollection;

    Trace.Warn("Page_Load", "Testing cache ");
    quotesCollection = (QuotesCollection)Cache["QuotesCollection"];

    if (quotesCollection == null)
    {
        Trace.Warn("Page_Load", "Not found in cache");
        quotesCollection = new QuotesCollection();

        String strFilePathXml =
            Server.MapPath(Request.ApplicationPath +
            "\\App_Data\\QuotesCollection.xml");
        String strFilePathSchema =
            Server.MapPath(Request.ApplicationPath +
            "\\App_Data\\QuotesCollection.xsd");

        quotesCollection.ReadXmlSchema(strFilePathSchema);
        quotesCollection.ReadXml(strFilePathXml);
```

```
                    System.Web.Caching.CacheDependency cacheDependency =
                         new System.Web.Caching.CacheDependency(strFilePathXml);

              Cache.Insert("QuotesCollection",
                              quotesCollection,
                              new
                              System.Web.Caching.CacheDependency(strFilePathXml),
                              System.Web.Caching.Cache.NoAbsoluteExpiration,
                              System.Web.Caching.Cache.NoSlidingExpiration,
                              System.Web.Caching.CacheItemPriority.Default,
                                 null);
         }

         this.GridView1.DataSource = quotesCollection;
         this.DataBind();
      }
```

6. Call the *CacheWithFileDependency()* in the *Page_Load* method.

```
protected void Page_Load(object sender, EventArgs e)
{
    if (!IsPostBack)
    {
        ButtonSaveAsXML_Click(null, null);
    }
    CacheWithFileDependency();
}
```

7. Now run the page. It should load the XML and schema into the *QuotesCollection*, save the *QuotesCollection* in the cache, and then show the data in the grid. Clicking the Save Table As XML button refreshes the XML file (on which a cache dependency was made). Because the file on the disk changes, ASP.NET will flush the cache. Next time you load the page, the cache will need to be reloaded.

Next, look at the final cache dependency: the SQL Server dependency.

The SQL Server Dependency

ASP.NET 1.0 had a huge gap in its cache dependency functionality. The most useful type of dependency was completely missing—that is, a dependency between a cached item coming from SQL Server and the physical database. Because so many sites use data provided by SQL Server to back their *DataGrids* and other controls, establishing this dependency is definitely a most useful way to manage cached data.

For the SQL Server dependency to work, you first configure SQL Server using the program aspnet_regsql.exe. The dependency is described in the configuration file, whose name is passed into the *SqlCacheDependency* constructor. The *SqlCacheDependency* class monitors the table. When something causes the table to change, ASP.NET will remove the item from the *Cache*.

Listing 15-3 shows a configuration file with a dependency on SQL Server.

LISTING 15-3 Configuration settings for SQL Server cache dependency

```
<caching>
 <sqlCacheDependency enabled="true" >
   <databases >
      <add name="DBName" pollTime="500"
          connectionStringName="connectionString"/>
   </databases>
 </sqlCacheDependency>
</caching>
```

Listing 15-4 shows an ASP.NET page that loads the data from the SQL Server database and establishes a dependency between the database and the cached item.

LISTING 15-4 Page using *SqlCacheDependency*

```
<%@ Page Language="C#" %>
<%@ Import namespace="System.Data" %>
<%@ Import namespace="System.Data.SqlClient" %>
<script runat="server">
    protected void Page_Load(Object sender, EventArgs e)
    {
        DataSet ds = null;
        ds = (DataSet)Cache["SomeData"];
        if (ds == null)
        {
            string connectionString =
                ConfigurationManager.ConnectionStrings["connectionString"].
                    ConnectionString;
                SqlDataAdapter da =
                    new SqlDataAdapter("select * from DBName.tableName",
                    connectionString);
                ds = new DataSet();
                da.Fill(ds);
                SqlCacheDependency sqlCacheDependency =
                    new SqlCacheDependency("DBName", "tableName");
            Cache.Insert("SomeData",
                            ds,
                            sqlCacheDependency);
        }
        GridView1.DataSource = ds;
        DataBind();
    }
</script>
<html><body>
    <form id="form1" runat="server">
        <asp:GridView ID="GridView1" runat="server">
        </asp:GridView>
    </form>
</body></html>
```

Once items are in the cache and their lifetimes are established through expirations and cached item dependencies, one other cache administrative task remains—reacting when items are removed.

Clearing the Cache

As you can see from the previous examples, ASP.NET clears the cache on several occasions, as follows:

- Removing items explicitly by calling *Cache.Remove*
- Removing low-priority items because of memory consumption
- Removing items that have expired

One of the parameters to one of the *Insert* overloaded methods is a callback delegate so that ASP.NET can tell you that something's been removed from the cache. To receive callbacks, you simply need to implement a method that matches the signature, wrap it in a delegate, and then pass it when calling the *Insert* method. When the object is removed, ASP.NET will call the method you supply.

The next example illustrates setting up a removal callback function.

Setting up a removal callback

1. One of the main tricks to getting the removal callback to work is finding an appropriate place to put the callback. What happens if you make the callback a normal instance member of your *Page* class? It won't work. The callback will become disconnected after the first page has come and gone. The callback has to live in a place that sticks around. (You could make the callback a static method, however.) The perfect class for establishing the callback is in the global application class. Chapter 18, "The *HttpApplication* Class and HTTP Modules," describes the application class and its services in more detail. For now, add a global application class to your application. Select Website, Add New Item. Select the Global Application Class template, and click Add to insert it into the project. Microsoft Visual Studio adds a new file named Global.asax to your application.

2. Global.asax.cs includes application-wide code. Write a method to handle the callback in the Global.asax.cs file. In this case, the response will be to set a flag indicating the cache is dirty. Then, the code will simply place the data back into the cache during the *Application_BeginRequest* handler. The code for doing so looks very much like the code in the *CacheWithFileDependency* method shown earlier. You can get a reference to the cache through the current *HttpContext*.

```
using System;
using System.Collections.Generic;
using System.Linq;
using System.Web;
```

```
using System.Web.Security;
using System.Web.SessionState;
using System.Web.Caching;

namespace UseDataCaching
{
  public class Global : System.Web.HttpApplication
  {
    bool _bReloadQuotations = false;
    public void OnRemoveQuotesCollection(string key, object val,
      CacheItemRemovedReason r)
    {
      // Do something about the dependency Change
      if (r == CacheItemRemovedReason.DependencyChanged)
      {
        _bReloadQuotations = true;
      }
    }

    protected void ReloadQuotations()
    {
      QuotesCollection quotesCollection = new QuotesCollection();
      String strFilePathXml =
        Server.MapPath(HttpContext.Current.Request.ApplicationPath +
        "\\App_Data\\QuotesCollection.xml");
        String strFilePathSchema =
        Server.MapPath(HttpContext.Current.Request.ApplicationPath +
        "\\App_Data\\QuotesCollection.xsd");
      quotesCollection.ReadXmlSchema(strFilePathSchema);
      quotesCollection.ReadXml(strFilePathXml);

      System.Web.Caching.CacheDependency
        cacheDependency =
          new System.Web.Caching.CacheDependency(strFilePathXml);

      HttpContext.Current.Cache.Insert("QuotesCollection",
        quotesCollection,
        cacheDependency,
        System.Web.Caching.Cache.NoAbsoluteExpiration,
        System.Web.Caching.Cache.NoSlidingExpiration,
        System.Web.Caching.CacheItemPriority.Default,
        this.OnRemoveQuotesCollection);

    }

    protected void Application_BeginRequest(object sender, EventArgs e)
    {
      if (_bReloadQuotations == true)
      {
        ReloadQuotations();
        _bReloadQuotations = false;
      }
    }
  // VS-provided code
  }

}
```

3. Update the *CacheWithFileDependency* method to use the callback method when establishing the *QuotesServer* in the cache. You can access the callback method through the page's *Application* member.

```
protected void CacheWithFileDependency()
{
  QuotesCollection quotesCollection;
  Trace.Warn("Page_Load", "Testing cache ");
  quotesCollection = (QuotesCollection)Cache["QuotesCollection"];

  if (quotesCollection == null)
  {
    Trace.Warn("Page_Load", "Not found in cache");
    quotesCollection = new QuotesCollection();

    string strFilePathXml =
      Server.MapPath(Request.ApplicationPath +
      "\\App_Data\\QuotesCollection.xml");
    string strFilePathSchema =
    Server.MapPath(Request.ApplicationPath +
      "\\App_Data\\QuotesCollection.xsd");
    quotesCollection.ReadXmlSchema(strFilePathSchema);
    quotesCollection.ReadXml(strFilePathXml);

    System.Web.Caching.CacheDependency cacheDependency =
      new System.Web.Caching.CacheDependency(strFilePathXml);

    Global global = HttpContext.Current.ApplicationInstance as Global;
    Cache.Insert("QuotesCollection",
      quotesCollection,
      cacheDependency,
      System.Web.Caching.Cache.NoAbsoluteExpiration,
      System.Web.Caching.Cache.NoSlidingExpiration,
      System.Web.Caching.CacheItemPriority.Default,
      global.OnRemoveQuotesCollection);
  }
  this.GridView1.DataSource = quotesCollection;
  this.DataBind();
}
```

When you surf to the page, you should never see the *Page_Load* method refreshing the cache. That's because when the XML file is overwritten, ASP.NET immediately calls the *ReloadQuotations* method—which loads the cache again.

Chapter 15 Quick Reference

To	Do This
Access the data cache	The data cache is available as ❏ the *Cache* property in the page ❏ the *Cache* proper in the current *HttpContext*
Insert an item in the cache	Use the indexer notation to add an object and a value to the cache.
Insert an item in the cache with a dependency	Create a *CacheDependency* object and add the object to the cache using the overloaded *Cache.Insert* method.
Insert an item in the cache with an expiration time	Create a *DateTime* object and add the object to the cache using the overloaded *Cache.Insert* method.
Delete an item from the cache	Call the cache's *Cache.Remove* method.
Be notified that an item is being removed from the cache	Include a callback delegate when inserting an item in the cache.

Chapter 16
Caching Output

After completing this chapter, you will be able to

- Cache page content.

- Improve the performance of Web applications by using output caching.

- Manage the cached content through the *OutputCache* directive.

- Manage the cached content through the *HttpCachePolicy* class.

This chapter covers ASP.NET support for caching output. Chapter 15, "Application Data Caching," demonstrates what an impact data caching could make on your application. By avoiding round-trips to the database, you can make parts of your Web site run much faster than they otherwise would. In addition to data caching, however, ASP.NET supports *output caching*.

Now, after spending a bit of time watching the entire page-rendering process, you know it can be pretty involved. A lot happens between the time a page loads and the time when the final closing tag is sent to the browser. For example, the page might require database access. It might have a number of controls declared on it. Furthermore, perhaps some of those controls are the more complex controls such as the *DataList* or the *GridView* whose rendering process is expensive. All of these items usually take time to process.

Just as you can bypass recurring round-trips to a database by caching data in memory, you can configure ASP.NET to bypass the entire page-rendering process and send back content that's already been rendered once. This is called *output caching*.

Caching Page Content

As you surf the Web, you see all manner of pages. Some sites update their content very often, whereas others change much less often. Some pages have portions that change while other portions of the page remain static. If you have a page whose content changes infrequently, you can cache the output instead of regenerating it every time a request comes in.

At the outset, turning on output caching is easy. To set up caching, place the *OutputCache* directive on the page. It's a separate directive, like the *Page* directive, that enables caching and provides certain control over caching behavior. The following exercise introduces caching output.

Creating a cacheable page

1. Create a new project. Make it an Empty ASP.NET Web Application named *OutputCaching*.

2. Add a new Web Form to the project. Name it Default.aspx. Microsoft Visual Studio opens the file for you after you create it. Insert the *OutputCache* directive near the top, immediately after the *Page* directive. For now, set the *Trace* attribute to *false*. (You turn it on later when you cache user controls.) At the very least, the *OutputCache* directive needs two things: (1) the *Duration* attribute to be set and (2) the *VaryByParam* attribute set to *none*. The *Duration* attribute specifies how long the content should be cached. The *VaryByParam* attribute is for managing the caching of multiple versions of the page. You learn more about these attributes shortly. The following code shows the syntax of the *OutputCache* directive. This example caches the page's content for 15 seconds. The code following the output directive was generated by Visual Studio:

```
<%@ Page Language="C#" AutoEventWireup="true"
CodeFile="Default.aspx.cs" Inherits="_Default" Trace="false"%>
<%@ OutputCache Duration="15" VaryByParam="none" %>

<!DOCTYPE html PUBLIC
"...">

<html xmlns="http://www.w3.org/1999/xhtml" >
<head runat="server">
    <title>Untitled Page</title>
</head>
<body>
    <form id="form1" runat="server">
    <div>
    </div>
    </form>
</body>
</html>
```

3. Update the *Page_Load* method to print the date and time that this page was generated, like so:

```
public partial class _Default : System.Web.UI.Page
{
    protected void Page_Load(object sender, EventArgs e)
    {
        Response.Write("This page was generated and cached at: " +
            DateTime.Now.ToString());
    }
}
```

The first time the content is produced, the *Page_Load* method runs and produces the following output:

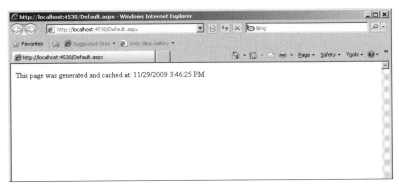

No matter how many times you refresh the browser (you can do this by pressing F5 while running Windows Internet Explorer within 15 seconds of first accessing the page), ASP.NET will grab the cached content and display that. When 15 seconds has expired, ASP.NET runs the page in the usual way, calling *Page_Load*, regenerating the content, and caching it again. The following graphic illustrates the new page accessed just moments (no longer than 15 seconds) after the first hit. The date and time are the same as the previous page, even though it's a completely new request (I promise these are two separate requests):

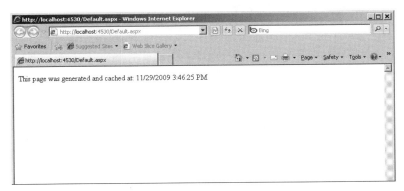

4. To get an idea about how caching content might improve performance, add a small amount of code to the *Page_Load* method to put the executing thread to sleep for perhaps 10 seconds (this is to simulate an expensive content-generating routine). Use the *System.Threading* namespace to access the threading functions:

```
using System;
using System.Collections.Generic;
using System.Linq;
using System.Web;
```

```
using System.Web.UI;
using System.Web.UI.WebControls;
using System.Threading;

namespace OutputCache
{
  public partial class _Default : System.Web.UI.Page
  {
    protected void Page_Load(object sender, EventArgs e)
    {
      Thread.Sleep(10000);
      Response.Write("This page was generated and cached at: " +
        DateTime.Now.ToString());
    }
  }
}
```

5. Surf to the page. Notice how long the page takes to load (about 10 seconds).
    Immediately refresh the page. Notice that the browser displays the content right
    away—without the long wait time. Most pages don't take quite as long to load, but you
    get the idea of how caching content might improve the performance of your Web ap-
    plication. For pages that are expensive to generate and that don't change very often,
    caching the content represents an enormous performance boost for your Web site,
    especially as the number of clients increases.

Managing Cached Content

In some cases, it's enough to blindly cache the content of certain pages by simply putting
the *OutputCache* directive in the page. However, sometimes you need a bit more control
over what's happening in the output cache. ASP.NET supports a number of parameters
you can use to manage the way the cache functions. You can control the output caching
behavior by either changing the parameters in the *OutputCache* directive or tweaking the
HttpCachePolicy property available through the *Response* object.

Modifying the *OutputCache* Directive

It's often very useful to be able to govern output caching. For example, some pages present
exactly the same content to all the users who access the page. In that case, caching a single
version of the content is just fine. However, there are other circumstances in which sending
the same content to everyone is inappropriate. The easiest way to control the behavior of
output caching is to modify the *OutputCache* directive.

One obvious case in which controlling the cache is important is while caching different versions of content for different browsers making requests. Different browsers often
have different capabilities. If you send content that requires a feature not supported by all
browsers, some browsers making requests will get a response that they're unable to handle

adequately. With the *VaryByCustom* parameter in the *OutputCache* directive, you can cache different content based on different browsers.

Controlling the output caching is also important when your page renders content based on the parameters that are sent in the query string. For example, imagine you have a page through which a user has identified him- or herself by typing a name in a text box. The browser inserts that name in a parameter inside the query list. You can instruct the output cache to cache different versions based on parameters in the query string. For example, users who identify themselves as "John Doe" can get a different version of cached content than can users who identify themselves as "Jane Smith." The *VaryByParam* attribute controls this behavior.

Table 16-1 shows a summary of these parameters.

TABLE 16-1 Summary of *OutputCache* Parameters

Attribute	Option	Description
CacheProfile	A string	Name of a profile (found in web.config) to control output cache settings. Default is an empty string.
Duration	*number*	Number of seconds the page or control is cached (required).
NoStore	*true* *false*	Specifies that the "no store" cache control header is sent (or not). Not available to user controls. Default value is *false*.
Location	*Any* *Client* *Downstream* *Server* *None*	Manages which header and metatags are sent to clients to support caching; here are their meanings: *Any*—page can be cached anywhere (default). *Client*—cached content remains at browser. *Downstream*—cached content is stored both downstream and on the client. *Server*—content cached on the server only. *None*—disables caching.
Shared	*true* *false*	Determines whether user control output can be shared with multiple pages.
SqlDependency	A string representing a database/table name pair	Identifies a set of database and table name pairs on which a page's or control's output cache depends.
VaryByContentEncoding	*encodings*	Specifies a list of encoding strings separated by commas used to vary the output cache.

Attribute	Option	Description
VaryByCustom	*browser* *custom string*	Tells ASP.NET to vary the output cache by browser name and version or by a custom string; must be handled by an override of *GetVaryByCustomString* in Global.asax.
VaryByHeader	* header names	A semicolon-delimited list of strings specifying headers that might be submitted by a client. Not available to user controls. Default value is an empty string (no headers).
VaryByParam	*None* * param name	A semicolon-delimited list of strings specifying query string values in a GET request or variables in a POST request (required).

The following exercise illustrates creating separate versions of cached content based on how the user identifies himself or herself.

Varying cached content by query string parameters

1. Returning to the OutputCache Web application, add a *TextBox* and a *Button* to the default.aspx page. Give the *TextBox* an ID of *TextBoxName* and the *Button* an ID of *ButtonSubmitName*. The *TextBox* will hold the client's name and will serve as the parameter controlling the number of cached versions of the page.

2. Double-click the button to add a *Click* event handler. In the handler, respond to the user's request by displaying a greeting using the contents of the text box. Also, modify the processing time of the page loading by reducing the amount of time the current thread sleeps (or by commenting out that line):

```
public partial class _Default : System.Web.UI.Page
{
    protected void Page_Load(object sender, EventArgs e)
    {
        Thread.Sleep(0);
        Response.Write("This page was generated and cached at: " +
            DateTime.Now.ToString());


    }
    protected void ButtonSubmitName_Click(object sender, EventArgs e)
    {
        Response.Write("<br><br>");
        Response.Write("<h2> Hello there, " +
        this.TextBoxName.Text + "</h2>");
    }
}
```

3. Increase the time that the content will be cached (this example uses 1 minute) so that you have time to change the contents of the *TextBox* to view the effects of caching. Also, include *TextBoxName* as the parameter by which to vary the content in the *OutputCache* directive.

```
<%@ Page Language="C#" AutoEventWireup="true"
CodeFile="Default.aspx.cs" Inherits="_Default"
Trace="false"%>

<%@ OutputCache Duration="60" VaryByParam="TextBoxName" %>
```

4. Add a *Substitution* control to the page following the *TextBox* and the *Button*. You can just drag one from the Toolbox onto the page. Use the *Substitution* control to display the time of the request to compare it with the time displayed by the cached page. *Substitution* controls call back to a method on the code beside that displays arbitrary strings. Write a method in the code-beside class to handle the substitution.

```
public partial class _Default : System.Web.UI.Page
{
    // Existing code ...
    protected static string SubstituteDateAndTime(HttpContext c)
    {
        return "Request occurred at :" + DateTime.Now;
    }
}
```

5. Set the *MethodName* attribute of the *Substitution* control to the *SubstituteDateAndTime* method in the ASPX file, like this:

```
<asp:Substitution ID="Substitution1" MethodName="SubstituteDateAndTime"
    runat="server" />
```

6. Surf to the page and type in a name. Click the button to submit the form and note the time stamp of the page. Type a second name in the *TextBox* and click the button to submit the form. Note the time stamp. Then, type the same name you typed the first time. Click the button to submit the form. If you do all of this within the 60-second window, you should see the cached versions of the page, which you can discern using the time stamp displayed as part of each page. The following three graphics illustrate the caching varying by the value of the *TextBoxName* parameter. The first graphic shows the original request using a particular name in the *TextBox*. Notice that the request time shown by the *Substitution* and the time shown by the *Page_Load* method are the same.

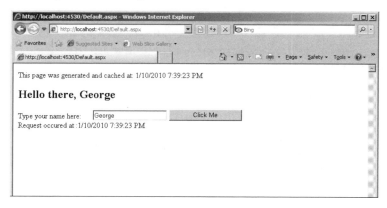

The second graphic shows a request with a new value for the *TextBoxName* parameter. Notice that the request time shown by the *Substitution* and the time shown by the *Page_Load* method are the same this time as well:

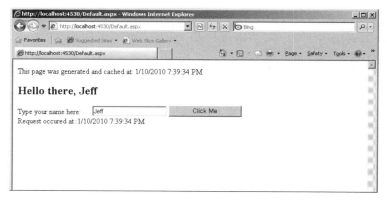

The third graphic shows making a request to the page using the same name as the original request. Notice that the request time shown by the *Substitution* and the time shown by the *Page_Load* method are different. The request time is earlier than the time shown during the *Page_Load* method, meaning the page content was cached:

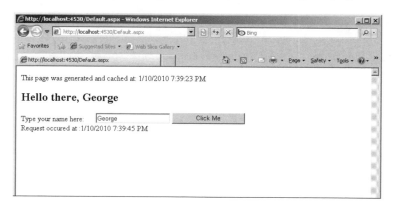

There are other ways to modify the *VaryByParam* attribute. One way is to use the word *none*, which means ASP.NET will cache only one version of the page for each type of request (for example, GET, POST, and HEAD). Using an asterisk (*) for *VaryByParam* tells ASP.NET to cache as many different versions of the page as there are query string or POST body requests. The previous example caches as many different versions of the page as there are unique names typed by users into the name text box.

Using *VaryByHeader* in the *OutputCache* directive tells ASP.NET to generate a separate cache entry for each new header string that comes down. (For example, *UserAgent* and *UserLanguage* represent HTTP headers that can be sent by the client.)

You will cache a user control shortly. With the *VaryByControl* attribute, you can cache separate content versions for each page that has a user control with unique properties.

Finally, *VaryByCustom* tells ASP.NET to manage separate cache entries dependent on a couple of factors. The first factor is the browser types and versions. Alternatively, you can provide a custom *GetVaryByCustomString* method in Global.asax that tells ASP.NET to create separate cached versions of a page based on a custom defined string.

The *HttpCachePolicy*

The second way to manage the output cache is through the *HttpCachePolicy*, which is available from the *Response* class. Table 16-2 shows a portion of the *HttpCachePolicy* class.

TABLE 16-2 The *HttpCachePolicy* Class

Member	Description
AppendCacheExtension	Appends specified text to the Cache-Control HTTP header
SetCacheability	Sets the Cache-Control HTTP header, which controls how documents are to be cached on the network
SetETag	Sets the ETag HTTP header to the specified string
SetExpires	Sets the Expires HTTP header to an absolute date and time
SetLastModified	Sets the Last-Modified HTTP header to a specific date and time
SetMaxAge	Sets the Cache-Control: max-age HTTP header to a specific duration
SetRevalidation	Sets the Cache-Control HTTP header to either the must-revalidate or the proxy-revalidate directives
SetValidUntilExpires	Determines whether the ASP.NET cache should ignore HTTP Cache-Control headers sent by the client for invalidating the cache
SetVaryByCustom	Specifies a custom text string for managing varying cached output responses
VaryByHeaders	Parameter list of all HTTP headers that will be used to vary cache output
VaryByParam	Parameter list received by a GET (query string) or POST (in the body of the HTTP request) that affects caching

When you set up an *OutputCache* directive, you tell ASP.NET to populate this class during the *Page* class's *InitOutputCache* method. The *Response* object makes the *HttpCachePolicy* available through its *Cache* property. The name *Cache* is unfortunate because you might easily confuse it with the application data cache. Perhaps *CachePolicy* would have been a better name for the property to avoid such confusion. In any case, you can use the *HttpCachePolicy* class to control the behavior of server-side output caching as well as the headers used for content caching. You can also use the *OutputCache* directive to control some of the same aspects as the *HttpCachePolicy* class. However, some features, such as sliding the expiration date or changing the "last modified" stamp for a page, are available only through the *HttpCachePolicy* class.

For example, Listing 16-1 shows a page fragment ensuring that all origin-server caching for the current response is stopped. It also sets the last modified date to the current date and time.

LISTING 16-1 Manipulating the output cache policy

```
public partial class _Default : System.Web.UI.Page
{
    protected void Page_Load(object sender, EventArgs e)

    {
      Thread.Sleep(0);
      Response.Write("This page was generated and cached at: " +
          DateTime.Now.ToString());

      Response.Cache.SetNoServerCaching();
      Response.Cache.SetLastModified(DateTime.Now);
    }
}
```

Caching Locations

In addition to varying the number of cached versions of a page, you can tell ASP.NET where to cache the content. This is controlled through either the *Location* attribute in the *OutputCache* directive or by using the *HttpCachePolicy* class's *SetCacheability* method.

ASP.NET supports several output caching locations that you can specify using the *OutputCache* directive:

- *Any*   Page can be cached by the browser, a downstream server, or on the server.
- *Client*   Page should be cached on the client browser only.
- *Downstream*   Page should be cached on a downstream server and the client.
- *Server*   Page will be cached on the server only.
- *None*   Disable caching.

With the *HttpCachePolicy*, you can also determine the location of the cached content programmatically. This is done through the *HttpCachePolicy.SetCacheability* method (or the *HttpResponse.CacheControl* property), which takes a parameter of the *HttpCacheability* enumeration. The enumeration is a bit easier to read than the attributes used in the *OutputCache* directive are. They include the following:

- **NoCache**   Disable caching.

- **Private**   Only cache on the client.

- **Public**   Cache on the client *and* the shared proxy.

- **Server**   Cache on the server.

- **ServerAndNoCache**   Specify that the content is cached at the server but all others are explicitly denied the ability to cache the response.

- **ServerAndPrivate**   Specify that the response is cached at the server and at the client but nowhere else; proxy servers are not allowed to cache the response.

Output Cache Dependencies

Chapter 15 explains how ASP.NET supports data caching. The contents of the application data cache in ASP.NET can be flushed because of various dependencies. The same is true of ASP.NET output caching. The response object has a number of methods for setting up dependencies based on cached content. For example, you might want to set up a page that renders data from a text file. You can set up a *CacheDependency* on that text file so that when the text file is changed, the cached output is invalidated and reloaded.

Caching Profiles

One of the problems associated with using the *OutputCache* directive directly is that the values become hard-coded. Changing the caching behavior means going in and changing the source code of the page. A feature added to ASP.NET 2.0 and later versions is the ability to add caching profiles. That way, setting the caching behavior variables is offloaded to the configuration file, and output caching becomes an administration issue and not a programming issue (as it should be).

The web.config file can include an *outputCacheSettings* section that contains a list of *outputCacheProfiles*. The *outputCacheProfiles* are simply key/value pairs whose keys are the output caching variables (such as *Duration*). When you mention the profile name in the *OutputCache* directive, ASP.NET simply reads the values out of the configuration file and applies them to the *OutputCache* directive.

The following exercise illustrates how to set up a cache profile instead of hard coding the values into the page.

Setting up a cache profile

1. Add a cache profile to the site's web.config file. If web.config isn't already there, go ahead and add one to the project. Then, add a cache profile to web.config nested between the system.web opening and closing tags. Name the cache profile *profile*.

```xml
<configuration>
  <system.web>
    <caching>
      <outputCacheSettings>
        <outputCacheProfiles>
          <add name="profile"
            duration="60"
            varyByParam="TextBoxName" />
        </outputCacheProfiles>
      </outputCacheSettings>
    </caching>
  </system.web>
</configuration>
```

2. Change the *OutputCache* directive in the Default.aspx page to use the new profile:

```
<%@ Page Language="C#" AutoEventWireup="true"
CodeFile="Default.aspx.cs" Inherits="_Default"
trace="false"%>

<%@ OutputCache CacheProfile="profile" %>
```

3. Surf to the page. It should work exactly as it did before when the caching values were hard-coded. That is, run the page, type a name, and note the date and time stamp. Type a new name and note the date and time stamp. Type the original name, submit it, and you should see the original cached page appear (as long as you complete the post within the specified time window).

Caching User Controls

Just as whole pages can be cached, ASP.NET supports caching *UserControls* as well. Imagine your job is to create a sizable Web site that allows users to navigate through information using various navigation controls (menus, hyperlinks, and so forth). For example, imagine a part of your page shows links or other navigation controls that lead users to the most recent news, summary information, and other places. The actual content might change, but the links probably don't. If the links don't change very often and the cost of generating that section of the page is expensive, it makes sense to move the functionality into a *UserControl* and apply the *OutputCache* directive to the *UserControl*. Doing so causes ASP.NET to cache the portion of the page represented by the control.

The *OutputDirective* can be applied to the ASCX file that makes up a *UserControl*. The *OutputDirective* for a *UserControl* can also use the *Shared* property to tell ASP.NET to cache one version of the control for all pages that use it, resulting in potentially even higher performance over the span of many hits (the default is *false*).

The following exercise illustrates how to cache the output of a *UserControl*.

Caching the output of user controls

1. Create a simple *UserControl* for the OutputCaching project. Navigation controls are perfect for caching, so create a control that has a menu. Name the control *SiteMenu.ascx*. Drag a *Menu* control onto the *UserControl*, as shown here:

Add some menu items, as shown in this graphic:

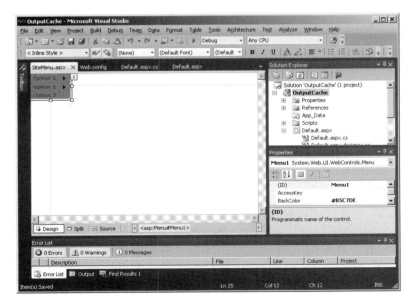

2. Add the *OutputCache* directive with the following parameters in the control source, like so:

```
<%@ Control Language="C#" AutoEventWireup="true"
CodeFile="SiteMenu.ascx.cs" Inherits="SiteMenu" %>
<%@ OutputCache Duration="60" VaryByParam="none" %>
```

3. Create a new page in the project. Name it *UseSiteMenuControl.aspx*.

4. Drag the *SiteMenu UserControl* from Solution Explorer onto the UseSiteMenuControl page. When ASP.NET loads and runs your Web page, ASP.NET caches the *UserControl* because the *UserControl* mentions the *OutputDirective*.

5. Make sure tracing is turned on in the UseSiteMenuControl.aspx file. (That is, set the *Trace="true"* attribute in the *Page* directive.) Surf to the page. The first time you surf to the page, you'll see the following information in the control tree section of the *Trace* output:

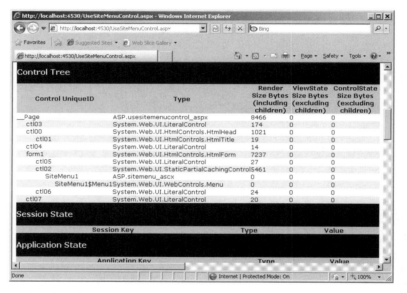

Notice that the entire control tree was rendered. Press the refresh key (F5 in Internet Explorer) while looking at UseSiteMenuControl.aspx. Examine the control tree portion of the *Trace* output again. Notice that ASP.NET uses the cached control instead of rerendering the entire *SiteMenu* control.

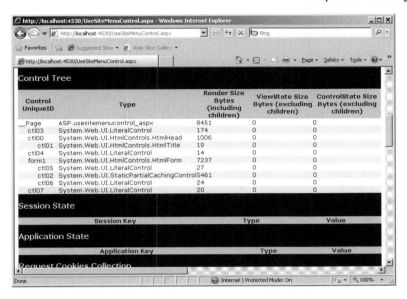

When Output Caching Makes Sense

As with other caching techniques, one of the most effective strategies is to turn on output caching for those pages that are accessed frequently but yet are expensive to generate. Also, be sure to cache only those pages that don't change frequently (otherwise, you might be better off simply *not* using output caching).

For example, pages full of controls that render a great deal of HTML are probably expensive. Imagine a page including a *DataGrid* displaying an employee directory. This is a perfect candidate for caching for several reasons. First, a database access (or even an in-memory cache hit) is required. Second, a *DataGrid* is pretty expensive to render—especially if it needs to figure out the schema of the employee directory table on the fly. Finally, an employee directory probably doesn't change very often. By caching it once, you can avoid spending a great deal of unnecessary cycles.

A related issue here is to be careful when typing asterisks into the output caching parameters such as *VaryByParam*. Using *VaryByParam*=* tells ASP.NET to generate a new page for every single request in which *any* query string parameter has changed. That's almost the same as *not* caching altogether—with the added cost of the memory consumed by the output cache. However, this might make sense for Web sites with limited audiences where the parameter variance between requests remains limited.

In addition, be wary of how caching might affect the appearance of your page on different browsers. Much of the time, content will appear the same regardless of the browser. However, if you cache some content that depends on a specific browser feature (such as dynamic HTML), clients whose browsers don't understand the feature might see some very weird behavior in the browser.

Tuning the behavior of the output cache is also important. Effective caching is always a matter of balance. Although you can potentially speed up your site by employing output caching, the cost is memory consumption. Using instrumentation tools can help you balance performance against cost.

Finally, user controls often represent a prime output caching opportunity—especially if they don't change frequently. Wrapping the portion of a page that *doesn't* change in an output-cached user control usually enhances the perceived performance of your application at a minimal cost because only the user control content is cached.

Other Cache Providers

ASP.NET 4 now includes a new feature for output caching: the ability to store output in places other than memory. You can now specify alternate providers through which ASP.NET manages page output caching. This is especially useful for implementing alternate scaling strategies such as cloud computing.

Custom output cache providers derive from *OutputCacheProvider*. At the very least, the provider must override *Add*, *Get*, *Remove*, and *Set*. *Add* is called by ASP.NET to insert a new item into the cache. *Get* is called by ASP.NET to retrieve a specific entry from the cache. ASP.NET calls *Remove* to delete an item from the cache. Finally, ASP.NET calls *Set* to replace an already-existing item in the cache.

After writing the custom cache provider, just mention it in the *cache* section of the web.config file. The following listing specifies a custom cache provider class named *CacheWithFileBackingProvider* found in an assembly named *MyCacheLibrary*.

```
<caching>
  <outputCache defaultProvider="CacheWithFileBacking">
    <providers>
      <add name="CacheWithFileBacking"
        type=
          "MyCacheLibrary,
            CacheWithFileBackingProvider"/>
    </providers>
  </outputCache>
</caching>
```

Once the cache provider is available through the web.config file, ASP.NET uses the new provider when you decide to cache a specific page.

Chapter 16 Quick Reference

To	Do This
Cache a page's output	Add the *OutputCache* directive to the page.
Store multiple versions of a page based on varying query string parameters	Use the *VaryByParam* attribute of the *OutputCache* directive.
Store multiple versions of a page based on varying headers	Use the *VaryByHeader* attribute of the *OutputCache* directive.
Store multiple versions of a page based on varying browsers	Use the *VaryByCustom* attribute of the *OutputCache* directive, selecting *browser* as the value.
Specify the location of the cached content	Specify the *Location* attribute in the *OutputCache* directive.
Access caching attributes programmatically	Use the *Cache* property of the *Response* object, which is an instance of the *HttpCachePolicy* class.
Offload output caching configuration to the web.config file	Add *outputCacheProfile* elements to your web.config file. Use them as necessary.
Cache a user control	Apply the *OutputCache* directive to the control's .ascx file.

Part IV
Diagnostics and Plumbing

Chapter 17
Diagnostics and Debugging

After completing this chapter, you will be able to

- Turn on page tracing.

- Insert custom trace messages in the page trace.

- Turn tracing on for an entire application.

- Manage custom error pages.

- Manage exceptions in your applications.

Even with all the software architecture methodologies and development practices available these days, software development is still very much a craft. Software libraries such as ASP.NET and Windows Forms go a long way toward making development more standardized and predictable (good things in software practice). However, inevitably there are times when you need to figure out what's wrong with an application that decides to behave differently from how you expect it to act.

This chapter covers the support provided by ASP.NET for troubleshooting your ASP.NET applications. As you can imagine, debugging Web applications introduces a whole new set of challenges. Remember, HTTP is basically connectionless, and the only output the client really gets to see is a snapshot of the application. This chapter shows you how to watch your applications as they run and how to trace the state of any particular request. It also covers managing error pages and trapping application exceptions in ASP.NET.

Page Tracing

The first place to start with debugging is to examine ASP.NET page tracing. The *Page* class has a property named *Trace*. When *Trace* is turned on, it tells the ASP.NET runtime to insert a rendering of the entire context of the request and response at the end of the HTML sent to the client.

You have already seen page tracing to some extent. When you examined the ASP.NET server-side control architecture, the page trace was invaluable in understanding the structure of the page. Remember, a rendered page is composed of a number of server-side controls collected in a hierarchical tree. A *Page* nests several controls, and the controls themselves might nest other controls (they can be nested several levels deep, as a matter of fact). The page trace includes a section displaying the composition of the page in terms of server-side controls.

Tracing

Turning on tracing is easy. Simply set the *Trace* property of the page to *true*. You can turn on tracing either by modifying the ASPX code directly or by setting the *Trace* property using the Properties window in the Visual Studio Designer. Here's the *Trace* property being turned on directly in the ASPX code as part of the page directive:

```
<%@ Page Language="C#" AutoEventWireup="true" CodeFile="TraceMe.aspx.cs"
Inherits="TraceMe" Trace="true" %>
```

As soon as you turn on tracing and surf to the page, you'll see tracing information appear at the end of the HTML stream. Listing 17-1 shows some code from the DebugORama example that is included on the CD accompanying this book. The TraceMe.aspx page builds a table of strings as they're entered on the site. The list of strings is kept in session state and refreshes the table every time a new string is submitted.

LISTING 17-1 Code that builds a table on loading

```csharp
public partial class TraceMe : System.Web.UI.Page
{
    ArrayList alTableEntries = null;

    protected void Page_Load(object sender, EventArgs e)
    {
        alTableEntries = (ArrayList)this.Session["TableEntries"];
        if (alTableEntries == null)
        {
            alTableEntries = new ArrayList();
        }
        AssembleTable();
    }

    protected void AssembleTable()
    {
        this.Table1.Rows.Clear();
        foreach (string s in alTableEntries)
        {
            TableRow row = new TableRow();
            TableCell cell = new TableCell();
            cell.Text = s;
            row.Cells.Add(cell);
            this.Table1.Rows.Add(row);
        }
    }

    protected void Button1_Click(object sender, EventArgs e)
    {
        alTableEntries.Add(this.TextBox1.Text);
        this.Session["TableEntries"] = alTableEntries;
        AssembleTable();
    }
}
```

Figure 17-1 shows how the page appears with tracing turned on.

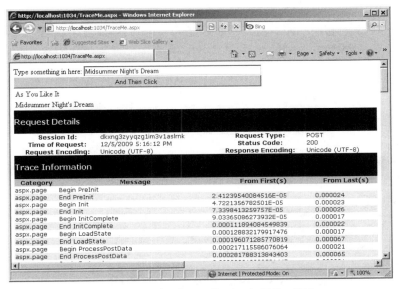

FIGURE 17-1 Tracing turned on for the application in Listing 17-1.

A bit farther down the tracing output, you can see the control tree (as shown in earlier chapters). The control tree for this page is shown in Figure 17-2.

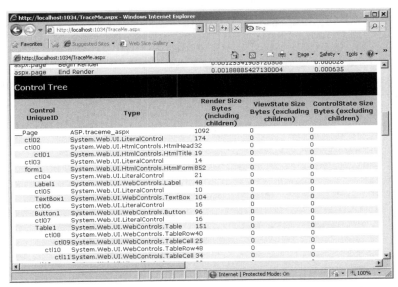

FIGURE 17-2 Tracing turned on for the application in Listing 17-1. Notice the control tree.

Finally, scroll down a bit more and you start seeing some of the context information associated with the request. Figures 17-3 and 17-4 show some of this context information. This application uses session state to save the array of strings. Notice that the session state tracing shows the contents of the session state dictionary. You also get to see other context information. For example, the tracing section shows the session ID and the URL used to surf to this page.

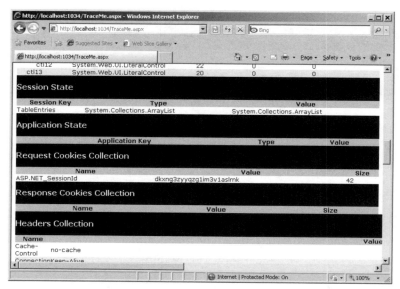

FIGURE 17-3 Tracing turned on for the application in Listing 17-1. Note the detailed information about the context of the request.

Of course, much of this information becomes more useful when there's a problem with your Web site. For example, the table might stop building itself because you somehow removed the session state item holding the list of strings. You could detect that by examining the page trace. If users begin to complain about layout issues with your site, you can look at the user agent coming down with the request and learn that the client is using a browser that your application does not accommodate.

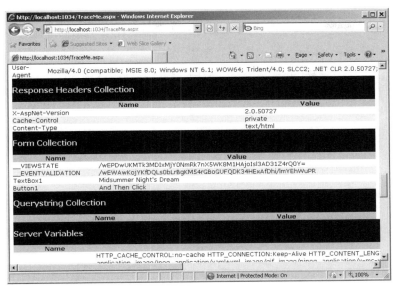

FIGURE 17-4 Tracing turned on for the application in Listing 17-1. This figure shows the page a bit farther down where there are even more details.

Trace Statements

In addition to all the request context information included with the HTML stream, the page trace also includes specific statements printed out during execution. If you scroll to the Trace Information block on the page, you can see these trace statements, as shown in Figure 17-5.

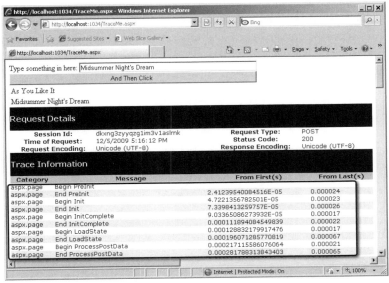

FIGURE 17-5 Tracing turned on for the application in Listing 17-1. These Trace Information statements track the execution of the page.

The ASP.NET framework produces the statements that appear in Figure 17-5. You can see the execution of the page progressing through the various events such as *PreInit*, *Init*, *LoadState*, and so forth.

Not only do you get tracing information from ASP.NET itself, but you can also insert your own tracing information. The *Page* class's *Trace* object provides a means of tracing page execution. Here's an exercise that shows you how to do this.

> **Important** To install the code samples for this book, you must have Administrator rights on your computer. If you are using your own computer, you probably have Administrator rights. If you are using a computer in an organization and you do not have Administrator rights, please consult your computer support or IT staff. See the "Code Samples" section in the Introduction for more information.

Adding tracing statements

1. Create a new Web site called *DebugORama* (it can be a File System–based Web site). Add a new page called *TraceMe.aspx*.

2. Open the TraceMe.aspx page and add the *Label* (which says "Type something in here:"), the *TextBox*, the *Button*, and the *Table* as they appear in the previous figures. Double-click the *Button* to add a handler for the *Click* event. Add the code from Listing 17-1 (the code that builds the table during the *Page*'s *Load* event). Enable tracing by including *Trace="true"* in the *Page* directive. Run the page to ensure that page tracing occurs.

3. Add tracing statements in strategic places through the page's *Trace* object. For example, you might want to monitor the table as it's being built. Do this by calling either *Trace.Write* or *Trace.Warn* in the page. *Trace.Write* renders the string in black, whereas *Trace.Warn* renders the tracing string in red. The first parameter is a category string you can use to help distinguish the statements you write when they finally render. You can add whatever you want to the category string.

```
public partial class TraceMe : System.Web.UI.Page
{
    ArrayList alTableEntries = null;

    protected void Page_Load(object sender, EventArgs e)
    {
        alTableEntries = (ArrayList)this.Session["TableEntries"];
        if (alTableEntries == null)
        {
            Trace.Warn("Page_Load", "alTableEntries is null");
            alTableEntries = new ArrayList();
        }
        AssembleTable();
```

```
    }

    protected void AssembleTable()
    {
        this.Table1.Rows.Clear();

        foreach (String s in alTableEntries)
        {
            Trace.Write("AssembleTable", "String found: " + s);
            TableRow row = new TableRow();
            TableCell cell = new TableCell();
            cell.Text = s;
            row.Cells.Add(cell);
            this.Table1.Rows.Add(row);
        }
    }

    protected void Button1_Click(object sender, EventArgs e)
    {
        Trace.Write("Button1_Click", "Adding string: " + this.TextBox1.Text);
        alTableEntries.Add(this.TextBox1.Text);
        this.Session["TableEntries"] = alTableEntries;
        AssembleTable();
    }
}
```

4. Compile the program and run the Web site. You should see your trace statements appearing in the output (as long as tracing is turned on). The tracing will appear red on your computer screen—although it appears as gray in the following graphics. The first graphic shows the string indicating *alTableEntries* is null.

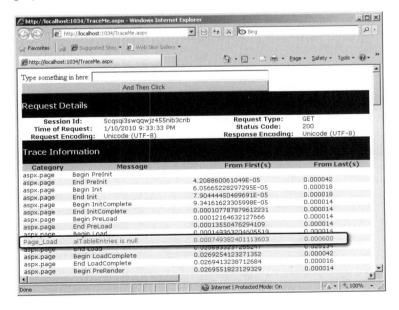

The second graphic shows the tracing statement indicating when a string is added to the table.

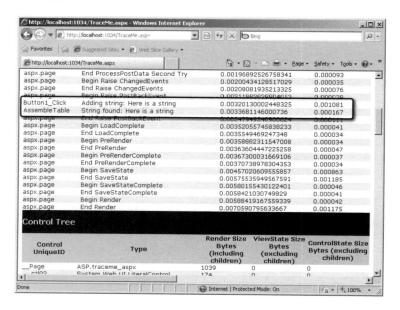

Application Tracing

Although single page tracing is useful (especially for quick spot checks for problems), it has a major downside in that it litters the page with lots of garbage at the end. You can use application tracing to get around that. Application tracing shows you exactly the same details as page tracing, except they're held in memory and made available rendered as a different page and through a special HTTP handler that ASP.NET provides.

To turn on tracing, you need to enable tracing in web.config like so:

```
<configuration>
  <system.web>
    <trace enabled="true"/>
  </system.web>
</configuration>
```

This simply turns on tracing. You can actually control several aspects of page tracing. For example, you could have tracing available on the host computer only (in case you don't want clients getting to your trace information). You might also want to control the number of responses that are held in memory.

Table 17-1 shows the possible values that can go in the configuration file to support tracing.

TABLE 17-1 Web.config Settings Supporting Tracing

Key	Possible Values	Meaning
Enabled	*true* *false*	Enable or disable application-level tracing.
localOnly	*true* *false*	Specify whether to show trace output only on local host or everywhere.
mostRecent	*true* *false*	Specify whether to recycle traces once *requestLimit* is met or to keep the first *N* (up to the *requestLimit* threshold).
pageOutput	*true* *false*	Specify whether to display trace output on individual pages in addition to caching application-level traces.
requestLimit	Decimal number	Specify how many traces to store in memory before removing earlier traces (default is 10).
traceMode	*SortByTime* *SortByCategory*	Specify the order in which to display trace information.
writeToDiagnosticsTrace	*true* *false*	Specify whether the trace data is also piped to *System.Diagnostics.Trace*.

The following exercise demonstrates how application-level tracing works and how to navigate around the results.

Using application-level tracing

1. Open the DebugORama project. Open the TraceMe.aspx page. Turn off tracing in the page by ensuring the *Page* class's *Trace* property is set to *false*.

2. Ensure that application-level tracing is turned on in web.config. That is, open web.config and add a *trace* element, as shown earlier. If the application doesn't yet have a configuration file, you can add one by selecting Add New Item from the local project menu.

3. Surf to the TraceMe.aspx page a few times by pressing Ctrl+F5, and then adding a few strings to the table.

4. In the URL that appears in the address box, make the endpoint *Trace.axd*, as shown in the following graphic. This name in the URL redirects request processing through a special handler that renders the tracing results being kept in memory.

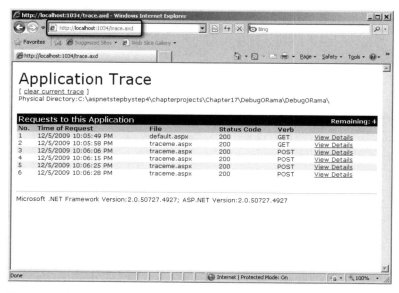

5. You should be able to see a list of requests. You can see individual requests and the request details, as shown in the following graphic, by clicking the View Details link.

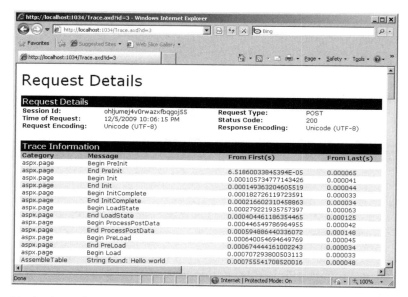

Notice how the output is exactly the same as the output of the earlier page tracing example. However, now the tracing information stands alone without cluttering up the Web page.

Enabling Tracing Programmatically

Although much of the time you will enable tracing through the Designer, at times you might find it useful to manage tracing during run time (programmatically). For example, you might have regular clients receive normal content; however, when someone with specific credentials appears, you might want to enable tracing for that individual. You might also decide to modify tracing when a certain parameter comes through the request.

The DebugORama site includes a page named EnableTracing.aspx that illustrates how to control the tracing programmatically. If the user types the correct password, the tracing is turned on. The page also shows how to enable and disable tracing programmatically.

```csharp
public partial class EnableTracing : System.Web.UI.Page
{
    protected void Page_Load(object sender, EventArgs e)
    {
    }
    protected void Button1_Click(object sender, EventArgs e)
    {


        if (this.TextBoxSecretCode.Text == "password")
        {
            this.Trace.IsEnabled = true;
        }
    }
    protected void Button2_Click(object sender, EventArgs e)
    {
        this.Trace.IsEnabled = false;
    }
}
```

The *TraceFinished* Event

The tracing context includes an interesting event named *TraceFinished* that gives you a last chance opportunity to log the tracing information or deal with it in some other way. The *TraceFinished* event is raised by the *Trace* object after all request information is gathered.

To subscribe to the event, simply set up the handler during the *Page_Load* event. The DebugORama example includes a page named TraceFinished.aspx that shows how the trace information was gathered and written to the debug console using *System.Diagnostics.Debug*.

```csharp
public partial class TraceFinished : System.Web.UI.Page
{
    protected void Page_Load(object sender, EventArgs e)
    {
        Trace.TraceFinished +=
            new TraceContextEventHandler(TracingFinished);
    }
```

```
void TracingFinished(object sender, TraceContextEventArgs e)
{
  foreach (TraceContextRecord traceContextRecord in e.TraceRecords)
  {
    System.Diagnostics.Debug.WriteLine(traceContextRecord.Message);
  }
}
}
```

Piping Other Trace Messages

In the last example, tracing messages were logged manually to the debug console by setting up the *TraceFinished* event handler in the *Trace* context. *System.Diagnostics.Debug* is a standard .NET type that's helpful for managing tracing and debugging information. Since version 2.0, ASP.NET has had the ability to plug in the *WebPageTraceListener* type so that calls to *System.Diagnostics.Trace* are also inserted into the ASP.NET trace. Setting it up is simply a matter of inserting a line in web.config (note the *writeToDiagnosticsTrace* option in Table 17-1). A case in which this is useful is for logging compiler output. To do this, set the *writeToDiagnosticsTrace* option to *true*, and then turn on compiler tracing. Compiler tracing is another setting you can set in web.config, but notice that this lies outside the typical *System.web* section of web.config.

```
<system.codedom>
    <compilers>
        <compiler compilerOptions="/d:TRACE" />
    </compilers>
</system.codedom>
```

Debugging with Visual Studio

The tracing support built into ASP.NET works really well and is a great way to debug your application—especially once it is deployed. However, when you're in development mode, having to plant tracing messages in your page and then run it to see what happens is cumbersome and sometimes not the most efficient way of debugging. Microsoft Visual Studio provides excellent debugging support through the environment, and you can use it to watch your code execute and to step through the code one line at a time. In fact, you have access to all of the Visual Studio debugging facilities, even though you're developing Web applications.

Remember, ASP.NET and Visual Studio work in concert to make you feel like you're doing desktop application development, even though you are developing Web applications. That goes for the debugger as well. The following exercise familiarizes you with the Visual Studio debugging environment.

Debugging an application

1. Open the DebugORama Web site. To support debugging, web.config needs to include the correct setting. You can type the debugger setting manually if you wish; however, Visual Studio will insert it for you once you start debugging.

    ```
    <system.web>
        <compilation debug="true"/>
    </system.web>
    ```

2. Open the TraceMe.aspx page and insert breakpoints in *Page_Load*, *AssembleTable*, and *Button1_Click*. You can insert breakpoints by highlighting a line in the editor window and pressing the F9 key. You can also click Debug, Toggle Breakpoint on the main menu or simply click the light gray ribbon to the left of the text in the code editor (where the breakpoints are indicated). Visual Studio will show a big red dot to the left of the breakpoint lines, as shown in the following graphic:

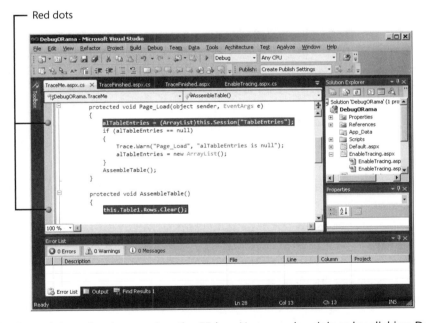

3. Start debugging by pressing the F5 key. You can also debug by clicking Debug, Start Debugging on the main menu. If debugging is *not* turned on in the web.config file, Visual Studio will ask you before it sets the debugging attribute. Visual Studio will start running the site. When it comes to your breakpoints, Visual Studio will stop execution and highlight the current line in yellow in the window, as shown here:

Code line background is yellow

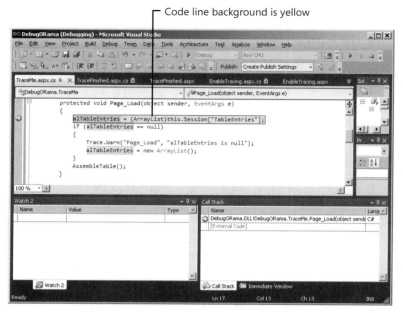

4. In this example, *Page_Load* is the first breakpoint Visual Studio encounters. At this point, you can start stepping through the code. Press F10 to step *over* methods, and press F11 to step *into* methods. Alternatively, you can click Debug, Step Over and Debug, Step Into on the main menu or use the corresponding toolbar buttons.

5. Rest the mouse pointer on any variables you see. Notice how Visual Studio displays the value of the variable in a tooltip.

6. Press F5 to resume the program. Visual Studio runs until it hits another breakpoint. Run through all the breakpoints.

7. Next, post back to the server using the button. Notice the breakpoints are hit again. Also notice that first the *Page_Load* is hit, and then the *Button_Click* handler. This highlights the ephemeral nature of a Web page. A new page is being created for each request that comes in.

8. Finally, try out a couple of the debug windows. You can monitor various aspects of your program by clicking Debug, Window on the main menu and selecting the window. Here is the Locals window, showing those variables in local scope:

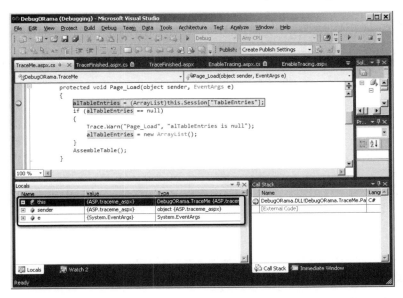

9. The Call Stack window, as depicted in the following graphic, shows how execution finally arrives at this spot. You can trace through and follow the entire program execution up to this point.

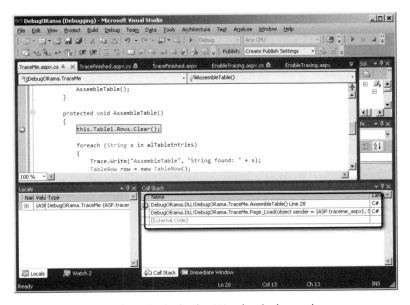

Other notable windows include the Watch window, where you can examine any variable you want, and the *Threads* window, where you can see how many threads are running, what their thread IDs are, and so forth.

Error Pages

As you have seen throughout the tour of ASP.NET, one of the main goals is to incorporate as much of the management of Web development as possible in ASP.NET. At this point, Microsoft Internet Information Services (IIS) is really only a middle manager in the overall scheme. ASP.NET now handles many facilities previously handled exclusively by IIS (although IIS brings many ASP.NET features under its auspices with version 7.0 running in Integrated mode). One of those facilities is managing custom error pages. In ASP.NET, you can introduce custom error pages instead of allowing the client to be bombarded with ASP.NET error messages.

You can tell ASP.NET, on encountering errors anywhere in your application, to display a particular page by tweaking the web.config file. Table 17-2 shows the custom error attributes for web.config.

TABLE 17-2 **Web.config Values for Setting Error Pages**

Attribute	Description
defaultRedirect	Direct users here in the event of an exception.
on/off	on = Display custom pages. off = Display ASP.NET error pages.
remoteOnly	Display custom errors to client, display ASP.NET errors locally.

The following example illustrates how to work with custom error pages. In this example, you add some error pages to your application and see what conditions cause them to appear.

Working with error pages

1. Open the DebugORama project.

2. Add a new Web Form named *ThrowErrors.aspx* to the DebugORama application.

3. Add two buttons: one to throw 404 errors (the nearly ubiquitous "object not found" error) and one to throw other exceptions. Set the 404 button's ID to *ButtonThrow404* and set the other button's ID to *ButtonThrowOther*.

4. Add two HTML pages to your application to act as custom error pages. Name one page *404Error.htm* and the other *SomethingBadHappened.htm*. (This example uses straight

HTML pages, although you can use ASPX files here.) The following graphic shows the 404Error.htm file being added to the Web solution.

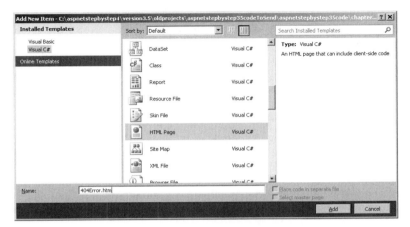

Here is the SomethingBadHappened.htm page being added:

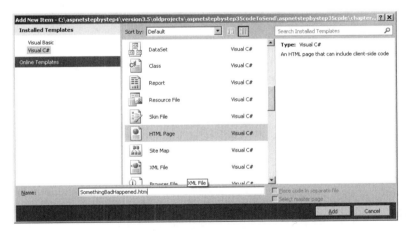

5. Add some content to the error pages. The 404 error handler here displays an error message in haiku. The other error page simply displays a label saying "Something bad happened."

6. Tell ASP.NET to use the error pages by adding the *customErrors* section to web.config, like so:

```
<configuration>
  <system.web>
    <customErrors
       defaultRedirect="SomethingBadHappened.htm" mode="On">
         <error statusCode="404"
            redirect="404Error.htm"/>
    </customErrors>
  </system.web>
</configuration>
```

This tells ASP.NET to show the 404Error.htm page when a file isn't found. ASP.NET will show SomethingBadHappened.htm for any other type of error.

7. Now add handlers to generate the errors. Handle the 404 error button by directing the client to a nonexistent page: In this example, there is no page named NonExistent.aspx, so redirecting to it will cause a 404 error. Handle the second error generator by throwing a random exception.

```csharp
public partial class ThrowErrors : System.Web.UI.Page
{
    protected void Page_Load(object sender, EventArgs e)
    {
    }

    protected void ButtonThrow404_Click(object sender, EventArgs e)
    {
        this.Response.Redirect("NonExistent.aspx");
    }

    protected void ButtonThrowOther_Click(object sender, EventArgs e)


    {
        throw new Exception();
    }
}
```

When you try to redirect to a nonexistent file, the "object not found" error page shows:

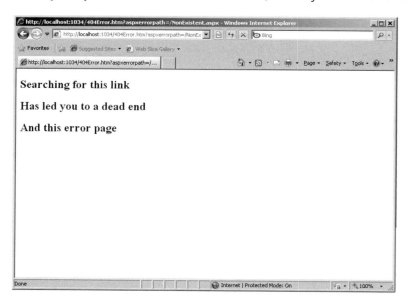

Throwing a generic exception causes the other page to show:

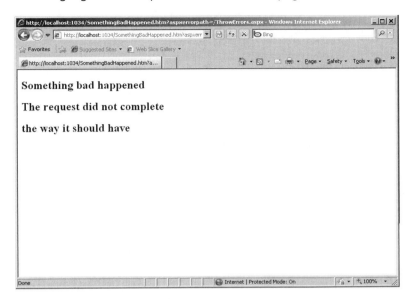

If you're running the example in the debugger, the debugger breaks as soon as it encounters an exception. To continue and show the error page after Visual Studio reports the exception, press F5.

In this example, the error pages don't really help the end user because the pages do not provide any detailed information about the exception. Your own error pages should provide a bit more information, perhaps even a way to contact someone for assistance. Before leaving debugging and diagnostics, take a look at how you can trap unhandled exceptions more gracefully.

Unhandled Exceptions

In the last example page that threw an exception, ASP.NET responded by redirecting to the default error page. In ASP.NET, you also can trap exceptions by setting up a handler for *Error* events fired by *HttpApplication* so that you can handle them more appropriately.

The easiest way to accomplish this is to define a handler in your *HttpApplication*-derived class in Global.asax.cs. With the handler connected to the event, your application will receive notifications whenever something bad happens, and you can deal with it gracefully. For example, you might log the error or show it on the debug console before redirecting the user to an error page. The following example redirects the exception to an error page:

```csharp
public class Global : System.Web.HttpApplication
{
  protected void Application_Error(object sender, EventArgs e)
  {
    Exception ex = Server.GetLastError();
    // display the exception
    System.Diagnostics.Debug.WriteLine("Error in app: " + ex);
    // display the exception
    System.Diagnostics.Debug.WriteLine("Error in app: " + ex);
    if (ex is HttpUnhandledException)
    {
      Context.ClearError();
      Server.Transfer("somethingbadhappened.htm");
    }
    else
    {}
  }
}
```

The preceding code traps the exception before the redirection happens. This gives you the opportunity to log the exception (or, as in this example, to show it in the *System.Diagnostics.Debug* context). The following graphic shows the exception details listed in the Output tab in Visual Studio.

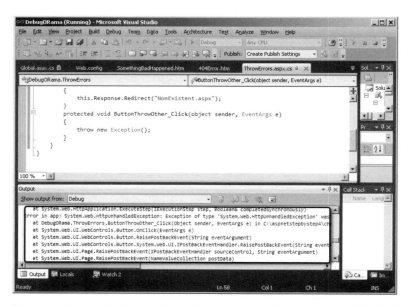

You can also redirect users to a different page if you want to hijack the exception handling before ASP.NET redirects to the page specified in web.config. Be sure to call *Context.ClearError* first to clear the error so that ASP.NET won't generate its standard error page.

Chapter 17 Quick Reference

To	Do This
Prepare a Web site for debugging	Include the following in web.config: ``` <system.web> <compilation debug="true"/> </system.web> ```
Enable tracing for an entire application	Include the following in web.config: ``` <system.web> <trace enabled="true"/> </system.web> ```
Enable tracing for your page	Set the *Page* class's *trace* attribute to *true* either by using the Properties pane in Visual Studio or declaring *Trace="true"* in the page directive.
Debug a Web application in Visual Studio	Ensure that the debug attribute is turned on in web.config. Start the program running in debug mode by 1. Clicking Debug, Start Debugging on the main menu or 2. Pressing the F5 key.

Set up breakpoints in an application in Visual Studio	Place the cursor on the line where you'd like to stop execution and
	1. Click Debug, Toggle Breakpoint
	   or
	2. Press the F9 key
	   or
	3. Toggle the breakpoint by clicking the gray ribbon to the left of the text in the code editor.

Execute a line of source code in the Visual Studio debugger	While the debugger is running and execution has stopped at the line you'd like to execute, 1. Click Debug, Step Over on the main menu or 2. Press the F10 key.
Step into a line of source code in the Visual Studio debugger	While the debugger is running and execution has stopped at the line you'd like to execute, 1. Click Debug, Step Into on the main menu or 2. Press the F11 key.
Instruct ASP.NET to show a particular page when a specific HTTP error occurs	Assign the error-handling page to the specific error in the *<customErrors>* section of web.config.
Trap specific .NET exceptions or deal with general unhandled exceptions in ASP.NET	Handle exceptions, including otherwise uncaught exceptions, within the *Application_Error* handler in Global.asax. Usually, you can then redirect to a specific page. (Note that specific errors are assigned as the *InnerException* of the *HttpUnhandledException*!)

Chapter 18

The *HttpApplication* Class and HTTP Modules

After completing this chapter, you will be able to

- Use *HttpApplication* as a rendezvous point for your application.

- Manage data in the *HttpApplication* object.

- Manage events in the *HttpApplication* object.

- Work with HTTP modules.

This chapter covers working with *application state* and *application-wide events* in your ASP.NET application. In typical desktop applications, the notion of a global meeting place for various parts of an application is well understood. For example, Microsoft Foundation Class (MFC), a C++ class library supporting low-level Windows development, includes a class named *CWinApp* that holds state that is useful throughout the program. This state includes such items as a handle to the current instance of the application, a handle to the main window, and the parameters that were passed in when the application started. The *CWinApp* class also runs the message loop—something that can be done only within the global scope of a Windows application. A running Windows application contains one and only one instance of the *CWinApp* class, and it is universally available from anywhere in the application.

Both Windows Forms and the Windows Presentation Foundation—the .NET libraries that support Windows desktop applications—have a similar class named *Application*. Each includes the same sort of state: access to command-line parameters, a top-level window, other state required by the program. Their *Application* classes also run the message loop. In fact, Microsoft Silverlight employs a model to WPF by including an *Application* object.

Web development also requires the same sort of "global space" that a desktop application requires. Having a global space in a Web application makes implementing features such as data caching and session state possible. This chapter looks at how ASP.NET implements a global space for Web applications.

The Application: A Rendezvous Point

As you have seen so far, one of the most distinctive aspects of Web-based development is the requirement that you must be very mindful of the state of your application. By itself, raw Web application development includes no support for dealing with state. After all,

Web requests are made over a disconnected protocol and much of the state of a request evaporates as soon as it hits an endpoint.

Chapter 4, "Custom Rendered Controls," examines the notion of view state in an ASP.NET Web Forms application. ASP.NET server-side controls have the option of supporting view state. View state is embedded in the data transmitted between the browser and the server and is used (most of the time) to keep the user interface (UI) appearing as though the browser and the server are connected continually. For example, without view state (or some special coding in the server application), UI elements such as drop-down lists lose their state between posts, causing the first item in the list always to show as the selected item—even if it is not really the item selected.

As its title indicates, Chapter 14, "Session State," discusses *session state*, the data accompanying a specific session. Session state is useful for items such as shopping carts for which the application has to associate data with a particular client.

Finally, Chapter 15, "Application Data Caching," discusses how you can cache state to avoid unnecessary round-trips to a data source. Loading data from memory is usually much faster than is loading it from a database or regenerating it. To store data that all parts of your application can access, the data must be stored somewhere else besides view state and session state. The cache is available from virtually anywhere in the application by way of the *HttpContext* object. *HttpContext* includes a reference to an instance of the *HttpApplication* object. In addition to being a holding place for the cache, the application object has its own dictionary that serves as a useful place to hold data. It works in very much the same way that the *Cache* does. However, there are some subtle yet important differences between the *Cache* and the dictionary held by *HttpApplication*.

Keeping a dictionary and a data cache available for the rest of the application isn't the only good reason to implement a central application object. Another reason is to have a mechanism for handling application-wide events. You know that the *Page* class handles events for a request specifically. However, think about how the entire ASP.NET pipeline works. Some useful events aren't part of the page processing or request processing mechanism. Implementing those involves code working outside the usual page processing mechanism.

For example, as mentioned, Chapter 14 looks at session state. When a request first comes through a site where session state is enabled, when should the session object be set up? Certainly, you want it set up before the page-specific processing begins. Chapter 9, "Logging In," discusses the ASP.NET security model. When should authentication and authorization be handled? You want those things to happen outside the context of the typical request processing, too. A final example is output caching, as discussed in Chapter 16, "Caching Output." For output caching to work, ASP.NET needs to intercept the request when it first enters the pipeline so that it can bypass the whole page creation process and render the cached content instead.

The ASP.NET *HttpApplication* object can manage these sorts of operations. When running, the *HttpApplication* object represents a rendezvous point for all the parts of your entire Web application. The *HttpApplication* most closely represents the *singleton* software pattern in ASP.NET. You treat it as a single instance of an object in your application. A reference to it is accessible at any point in time through the *HttpContext* class using the *Current* property.

Overriding *HttpApplication*

Overriding the *HttpApplication* to include your own state and event handling is a matter of adding a global application object to your site. If you ask Microsoft Visual Studio to create a normal Web site for you (that is, click File, New, Website, ASP.NET Web Site in Visual Studio), Visual Studio throws a singular global.asax file into your project. Global.asax includes a server-side script block to hold any code you want to add to the application object.

If you ask Visual Studio to create an ASP.NET Web Application Project (that is, click File, New Project, ASP.NET Web Application in Visual Studio), Visual Studio adds a pair of files, Global.asax and Global.asax.cs, to your application. Global.asax and Global.asax.cs have the same relationship to each other as an ASPX file and its accompanying CS file have. In fact, you can use Visual Studio to add the global application object to your application if it wasn't precreated for you. When you add a Global.asax/Global.asax.cs file pair to your application, the application is set up and ready to handle a few application-wide events. Remember that the *Page* files include the *Page* directive at the top of the file. The Global.asax file includes a similar directive. The *Application* directive tells the runtime compiling machinery that this file is meant to serve as the application object. Unlike pages, there can be only one Global.asax file in your application.

Listing 18-1 shows an example of the Global.asax.cs file deriving from *HttpApplication* that Visual Studio generates for you when you click File, New, Project, ASP.NET Web Application. The Global.asax.cs provided by Visual Studio handles the *Application_Start*, *Application_End*, *Application_Error*, *Begin_Request*, *Authenticate_Request*, *Session_Start*, and *Session_End* events.

LISTING 18-1 Global.asax.cs file and stubbed-out application event handlers

```
public class Global : System.Web.HttpApplication
{
  protected void Application_Start(object sender, EventArgs e){}
  protected void Session_Start(object sender, EventArgs e){}
  protected void Application_BeginRequest(object sender, EventArgs e){}
  protected void Application_AuthenticateRequest(object sender, EventArgs e){}
  protected void Application_Error(object sender, EventArgs e){}
  protected void Session_End(object sender, EventArgs e){}
  protected void Application_End(object sender, EventArgs e){}
}
```

To get an idea of how these events work, the following exercise illustrates placing a piece of data in the application's dictionary and retrieving it later when the page loads.

Managing application state

1. Create a new Web application project named *UseApplication* (that is, click File, New, Project, Empty ASP.NET Web Application in Visual Studio).

2. Drag a *GridView* onto the default page. Don't assign a data source to it yet. In later steps, you populate it with data that is stored with the application.

3. Add a Global.asax/Global.asax.cs file pair to the site by right-clicking the project in Project Explorer (or clicking Web Site, Add New Item on the main menu). Select the Global Application Class template, as shown here:

4. After you add the two files, Global.asax and Global.asax.cs, to your application, you can see that the *Application_Start* event is already handled (although it does nothing right now).

5. To have some data to store with the application object, import the *QuotesCollection* data and code files from Chapter 15. The project name is UseDataCaching. If you haven't generated the XML and XSD files, you do so by running the UseDataCaching project. The XML and schema files are generated when you click the Generate XML File button on the CacheDependencies.aspx page. Click Web Site, Add Existing Item on the main menu and find the file QuotesCollection.cs. In addition to importing the QuotesCollection.cs file, grab the QuotesCollection.xml and QuotesCollection.xsd files from the UseDataCaching\App_Data directory.

6. Add some code to the *Application_Start* event to load the quotes data and place it in the application dictionary. *Server.MapPath* gives you the path from which the application is executing so that you can load the XML and XSD files. Storing the data in the dictionary is very much like adding it to the cache:

```
void Application_Start(Object sender, EventArgs e) {
    QuotesCollection quotesCollection = new QuotesCollection();

    String strAppPath = Server.MapPath("");

    String strFilePathXml =
            strAppPath  + "\\app_data\\QuotesCollection.xml";
    String strFilePathSchema = strAppPath +
            "\\app_data\\QuotesCollection.xsd";
    quotesCollection.ReadXmlSchema(strFilePathSchema);
    quotesCollection.ReadXml(strFilePathXml);

    Application["quotesCollection"] = quotesCollection;
}
```

7. Update the *Page_Load* method in the Default.aspx page to load the data from the application's dictionary. The application state is available through the page's reference to the *Application* object. Accessing data in the dictionary is a matter of indexing it correctly. After loading the data from the dictionary, apply it to the *DataSource* property in the *GridView* and bind the *DataGrid*:

```
protected void Page_Load(object sender, EventArgs e)
{
  QuotesCollection quotesCollection =
      (QuotesCollection)Application["quotesCollection"];

  GridView1.DataSource = quotesCollection;
  GridView1.DataBind();
}
```

Application State Caveats

As you can see, the application state and the application data cache seem to overlap in functionality. Indeed, they're both available from similar scopes (from any point in the application), and getting the data in and out involves using the right indexer. However, the application state and the cache are different in a couple of significant ways.

First, items that go into the application state stay there until you remove them explicitly. The application data cache implements more flexibility in terms of setting expirations and other removal/refresh conditions.

In addition, putting many items into the application state dictionary inhibits the scalability of your application. To make the application state thread safe, the *HttpApplicationState* class includes a *Lock* method that you can use to make the global state thread safe. Although using the *Lock* method ensures that the data is not corrupted, locking the application frequently greatly reduces the number of requests it can handle.

Ideally, data going into the application state should be read only once when it is loaded and should be changed very infrequently, if at all. As long as you're aware of these issues, the application state can be a useful place to store information required by all parts of your application.

Handling Events

The other useful aspect of the application object is its ability to handle application-wide events. As you can see in the previous example, the Global.asax.cs file is the place to insert global event handlers. Visual Studio will insert a few for you when you simply add one to your application. The events for which Visual Studio generates stub handlers inside Global.asax.cs include *Application_Start*, *Application_End*, *Application_Error*, *Application_BeginRequest*, *Application_AuthenticateRequest*, *Session_Start*, and *Session_End*. A rundown of these events follows.

Application_Start

Application_Start happens when the application is first initialized—that is, when the first request comes through. Because *Application_Start* happens first (and only once) during the lifetime of an application, the most common response for the event is to load and initialize data at the start of the application (as with the previous example).

Application_End

The ASP.NET runtime raises *Application_End* as the application is shutting down. This is a useful place to clean up any resources that require special attention for disposal.

Application_Error

Unfortunately, bad things sometimes happen inside Web applications. If something bad has happened in one of your existing applications, you might already have seen the standard pale yellow and red ASP.NET error page. Once you deploy your application, you probably don't want clients to see this sort of page. Intercept this event (*Application_Error*) to handle the error. Sometimes, an exception can be managed locally. Exceptions that cannot be handled locally can be handled here.

Application_BeginRequest

The *Application_BeginRequest* event occurs every time a user makes a request to the application. This is a good place to handle anything that needs to occur before the request starts in earnest.

Application_AuthenticateRequest

The *Application_AuthenticateRequest* event occurs after ASP.NET confirms the identity of the user making a request. You know who is making the request after this event is fired.

Session_Start

The *Session_Start* event occurs when a user makes an initial request to the application, which initializes a new session. This is a good place to initialize session variables (if you want to initialize them before the page loads).

Session_End

This event occurs when a session is released. Sessions end when they time out or when the *Abandon* method is called explicitly. This event happens only for applications whose session state is being held in-process.

HttpApplication Events

The events listed previously are implemented in the Visual Studio default *HttpApplication* override (either Global.asax or Global.asax/Global.asax.cs depending on the project type). The application object can fire a number of other events. Table 18-1 shows a summary of all the events pumped through the application object. Some of these events are handled only through Global.asax, whereas the others are handled in *HttpModules*.

TABLE 18-1 Application-wide Events

Event	Reason	Order	Only in Global.asax?
Application_Start	Application is starting up.	Start of app	Yes
Application_End	Application is ending.	End of app	Yes
Session_Start	Session is starting.		Yes
Session_End	Session is ending.		Yes
BeginRequest	A new request has been received.	1	No
AuthenticateRequest/ PostAuthenticateRequest	The user has been authenticated— that is, the security identity of the user has been established.	2	No

Event	Reason	Order	Only in Global.asax?
AuthorizeRequest/ PostAuthorizeRequest	The user has been authorized to use the requested resource.	3	No
ResolveRequestCache/ PostResolveRequestCache	Occurs between authorizing the user and invoking the handler. This is where output caching is handled. If content is cached, the application can bypass the entire page-rendering process.	4	No
AcquireRequestState/ PostAcquireRequestState	Occurs when session state needs to be initialized.	5	No
PreRequestHandlerExecute	Occurs immediately before request is sent to the handler. This is a last-minute chance to modify the output before it heads off to the client.	6	No
PostRequestHandlerExecute	Occurs following the content being sent to the client.	7	No
ReleaseRequestState/ PostReleaseRequestState	Occurs following request handling. This event occurs so that the system can save state used if necessary.	8	No
UpdateRequestCache/ PostUpdateRequestCache	Occurs following handler execution. This is used by caching modules to cache responses.	9	No
EndRequest	Fires after the request is processed.	10	No
Disposed	Occurs before the application shuts down.	End of app	No
Error	Fires when an unhandled application error occurs.	When an exception occurs	No
PreSendRequestContent	Fires before content is sent to the client.		No
PreSendRequestHeaders	Fires before HTTP headers are sent to the client.		No

The following example shows how to time requests by intercepting the *BeginRequest* and the *EndRequest* events in Global.asax.

Timing requests

1. Open Global.asax.cs in the UseApplication Web application.

2. Look for the *Application_BeginRequest* handler. Notice that Visual Studio includes one. However, *Application_EndRequest* is not stubbed out, so you need to type that one in:

```
protected void Application_BeginRequest(object sender, EventArgs e)
{

}protected void Application_EndRequest(object sender, EventArgs e)
{

}
```

3. Implement the *Application_BeginRequest* handler by getting the current date and time and storing them in the *Items* property of the current *HttpContext*. The *Items* property is a name/value collection that you can index in the same way that you index the cache, the session state, and the *HttpApplication* dictionary. Implement the *EndRequest* handler by comparing the time stamp obtained from the beginning of the request to the current date and time. Print out the amount of time taken to process the request using *Response.Write*.

```
protected void Application_BeginRequest(object sender, EventArgs e)
{
    DateTime dateTimeBeginRequest = DateTime.Now;

    HttpContext ctx = HttpContext.Current;
    ctx.Items["dateTimeBeginRequest"] = dateTimeBeginRequest;
}



protected void Application_EndRequest(object sender, EventArgs e)
{
    DateTime dateTimeEndRequest = DateTime.Now;

    HttpContext ctx = HttpContext.Current;
    DateTime dateTimeBeginRequest =
        (DateTime)ctx.Items["dateTimeBeginRequest"];

    TimeSpan duration = dateTimeEndRequest - dateTimeBeginRequest;

    Response.Write("<b>From Global.asax: This request took " +
        duration.ToString() + "</b></br>");
}
```

You should see the duration printed in the response returned to the browser.

HttpModules

Managing global events in Global.asax.cs is a very convenient way to manage data and events in an application. Visual Studio generates a Global.asax.cs and even stubs out the more important events for you. However, using Global.asax.cs isn't the only way to store state and handle application-wide events. The other way is to write an HTTP module.

HTTP modules serve very much the same purpose that Internet Server Application Programming Interface (ISAPI) filters served for classic ASP—as a place to insert functionality in the request processing. HTTP modules plug into the ASP.NET processing chain to handle application-wide events in the same way that Global.asax handles application-wide events. In fact, many ASP.NET features are implemented through HTTP modules. One thing to keep in mind as a caveat before we proceed is that plugging too much into the request chain can start to reduce performance. However, with that in mind modules are a great place to take advantage of the flexibility of ASP.NET.

Existing Modules

ASP.NET employs HTTP modules to enable features such as output caching and session state. To get an idea of which features are implemented through HTTP modules, take a look at the master configuration file for your computer (that is, go to the Windows directory, look in the Microsoft.NET directory, and navigate to the configuration directory for the most current release). The master web.config file mentions several modules in the *httpModules* section of the configuration, as shown in Listing 18-2. For brevity, this list does not include entire strong names of the assemblies, but it gives you an idea of which modules are already part of the ASP.NET pipeline.

LISTING 18-2 Excerpt from the master web.config file indicating configured *HttpModules*

```
<httpModules>
  <add name="OutputCache" type="System.Web.Caching.OutputCacheModule" />
  <add name="Session" type="System.Web.SessionState.SessionStateModule" />
  <add name="WindowsAuthentication" type="System.Web.Security.WindowsAuthenticationModule"
/>
  <add name="FormsAuthentication" type="System.Web.Security.FormsAuthenticationModule" />
  <add name="PassportAuthentication" type="System.Web.Security.PassportAuthenticationModule"
/>
  <add name="RoleManager" type="System.Web.Security.RoleManagerModule" />
  <add name="UrlAuthorization" type="System.Web.Security.UrlAuthorizationModule" />
  <add name="FileAuthorization" type="System.Web.Security.FileAuthorizationModule" />
  <add name="AnonymousIdentification" type="System.Web.Security.
AnonymousIdentificationModule" />
  <add name="Profile" type="System.Web.Profile.ProfileModule" />
  <add name="ErrorHandlerModule"
    type="System.Web.Mobile.ErrorHandlerModule, System.Web.Mobile, Version=4.0.0.0,
    Culture=neutral, PublicKeyToken=b03f5f7f11d50a3a" />
  <add name="ServiceModel"
    type="System.ServiceModel.Activation.HttpModule, System.ServiceModel.Activation,
```

```
Version=4.0.0.0,
    Culture=neutral, PublicKeyToken=31bf3856ad364e35" />
  <add name="UrlRoutingModule-4.0" type="System.Web.Routing.UrlRoutingModule" />
  <add name="ScriptModule-4.0"
    type="System.Web.Handlers.ScriptModule, System.Web.Extensions, Version=4.0.0.0,
    Culture=neutral, PublicKeyToken=31bf3856ad364e35"/>

</httpModules>
```

The *httpModules* section mentions the name of a module, followed by a fully specified type that implements the feature. The following features are handled by modules:

- Output caching

- Session state

- Windows authentication

- Forms authentication

- Passport authentication

- Role manager

- URL authorization

- File authorization

- Anonymous identification

- Profile

- ErrorHandlerModule

- ServiceModule-4.0

- ScriptModule-4.0

Chapter 2, "ASP.NET Application Fundamentals," includes a short summary of the ASP.NET pipeline. The modules fit into the processing chain and take effect prior to being processed by the *HttpApplication* object. In fact, Microsoft Internet Information Services (IIS) 7.0 uses modules extensively—especially when running in Integrated mode. Although the features themselves can require extensive code to implement (for example, imagine all the work that went into the session state manager), the basic formula for hooking a module into your application is pretty straightforward. Creating a module involves the following four steps:

1. Writing a class implementing *IHttpModule*

2. Writing handlers for the events you want handled

3. Subscribing to the events

4. Configuring the module in web.config

Implementing a Module

Here's an example illustrating how HTTP modules work. The previous example in this chapter demonstrates how to time requests by handling events in Global.asax. It shows time stamping the beginning of a request, storing the time stamp in the current *HttpContext*, and examining the time stamp as the request finishes.

The following example performs the same functionality. However, this example uses an HTTP module to handle the events.

Using a timing module

1. To implement a timing module, open the Web application solution file for this chapter—UseApplication. To work, the module needs to exist in an assembly. It's easiest to write a completely separate assembly for the module. Add a project to the solution by clicking File, Add, New Project on the main menu. Make the project a Class Library and name the project *TimingModule*.

2. Visual Studio will add a class to the library named *Class1*. (The name of the file generated by Visual Studio is *Class1.cs* and the name of the class generated by Visual Studio is *Class1*.) Change the name of the file to *Timer.cs* and the name of the class to *Timer*. Place the code in the *TimingModule* namespace.

3. The module as generated by Visual Studio doesn't understand the ASP.NET types. Add a reference to *System.Web* to make the ASP.NET types available.

4. Add handlers for the beginning and ending of the request. You can borrow the code from Global.asax if you want. The signatures for the event's handlers are such that the methods have the return type of *void* and accept two arguments: an *object* and *EventArgs*.

```
using System;
using System.Collections.Generic;
using System.Linq;
using System.Text;
using System.Web;

/// <summary>
/// Summary description for Timer
/// </summary>
namespace TimingModule {
    public class Timer
    {
        public Timer()
        {
        }
```

```
public void OnBeginRequest(object o, EventArgs ea)
{
        DateTime dateTimeBeginRequest = DateTime.Now;


    HttpContext ctx;
    ctx = HttpContext.Current;
    ctx.Items["dateTimeBeginRequest"] = dateTimeBeginRequest;
}

public void OnEndRequest(object o, EventArgs ea)
{
    DateTime dateTimeEndRequest = DateTime.Now;

    HttpContext ctx;
    ctx = HttpContext.Current;
    DateTime dateTimeBeginRequest =
        (DateTime)ctx.Items["dateTimeBeginRequest"];

    TimeSpan duration = dateTimeEndRequest - dateTimeBeginRequest;

    ctx.Response.Write("<b>From the TimingModule: This request took " +
        duration.ToString() + "</b></br>");
    }
  }
}
```

5. Add *IHttpModule* to the class's inheritance list. Add implementations for the methods *Init* and *Dispose* by right-clicking *IHttpModule* in the editor and clicking Implement Interface. The job performed by *Init* is to subscribe to events. The job performed by *Dispose* is to release any resources used by the module. (*Dispose* doesn't need to do anything in this example.)

```
public class Timer
        : IHttpModule
{
    public Timer()
    {
    }

    public void Init(HttpApplication httpApp)
    {
        httpApp.BeginRequest +=
            new EventHandler(this.OnBeginRequest);

        httpApp.EndRequest +=
            new EventHandler(this.OnEndRequest);
    }
    public void Dispose() { }

// ...
}
```

6. The Web site needs to know about the new module. Add a project-level reference (a reference to the new module) to the UseApplication Web application project so that you can use it from the page code. Right-click the UseApplication node in Solution Explorer and click Add Reference. In the Add Reference dialog box, click the Project tab and select TimingModule from the list, and then click OK. The following graphic shows the Add Reference dialog box:

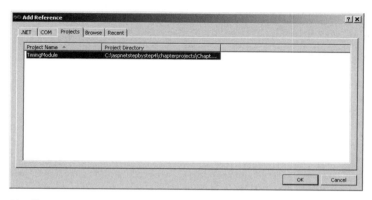

7. Finally, mention the *TimingModule* in the web.config file. It needs to appear in the *httpModules* section, nested within the *system.web* section, like so:

```
<configuration>
 <system.web>
    <httpModules>
     <add name="TimingModule"
          type="TimingModule.Timer, TimingModule" />
        </httpModules>
 </system.web>
 </configuration>
```

As long as the *TimingModule* assembly is available to your application (that is, it's in the *Bin* subdirectory of your virtual directory), it will be linked into the processing chain. When you run the page, you'll see the timing information coming from both the Global.asax.cs file and the timing module.

Seeing Active Modules

Many ASP.NET features are implemented through modules. Although you can see the modules listed in the master configuration file, you can also see the list of available modules at run time. They're available through the current application instance. The following exercise illustrates how to view the active modules.

Listing the modules

1. Add a button to the Default.aspx page of the UseApplication solution, as shown in the following graphic. Assign its *ID* to be *ButtonShowmodules*. This button will list the attached modules, so set its *Text* property to *Show Modules*. Also, add a list box to the page that will show the modules.

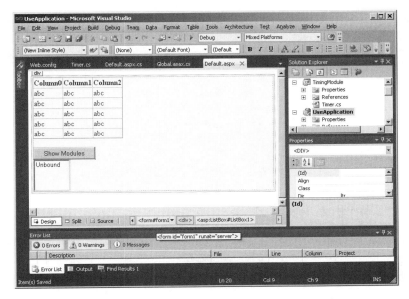

2. Double-click the button to add a *Click* event handler to the page.

3. Handle the button event by grabbing the list of modules from the application instance. The list comes back as a collection that you can apply to the list box's *DataSource* property. Calling *DataBind* on the *ListBox* will put the names of all the modules in the *ListBox*.

```
protected void ButtonShowmodules_Click(object sender, EventArgs e)
{
    HttpApplication httpApp = HttpContext.Current.ApplicationInstance;
    HttpModuleCollection httpModuleColl = httpApp.Modules;

    Response.Write("<br>");
    String[] rgstrModuleNames;
    rgstrModuleNames = httpModuleColl.AllKeys;

    this.ListBox1.DataSource = rgstrModuleNames;
    this.ListBox1.DataBind();
}
```

Run the page and click the Show Module button to fill the list box with a list of modules plugged into the application, as shown in the following graphic. Check out the *TimingModule* entry in the list.

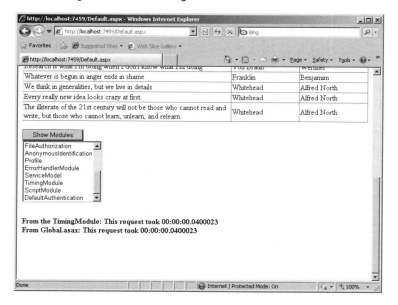

Storing State in Modules

HTTP modules are also very handy places to store global state for your application. The following example shows how to track the average request duration, which requires storing the duration of each request as part of application state.

Tracking average request duration

1. Before inserting the functionality into the module, think about how to use the information about the average request duration. You might use it to profile and to find bottlenecks in your application. Although sending the information out to the client browser is always useful, there might be times when you want to use the information programmatically. To retrieve the information from the module, you need to add one or more methods (above and beyond the *Init* and *Dispose* methods) to the *TimingModule*. The best way to do that is to define an interface that has functions you can use to talk to the module. The following code defines an interface for retrieving the average request duration. Create a file named *ITimingModule.cs* and add it to the TimerModule subproject:

```
public interface ITimingModule
{
    TimeSpan GetAverageLengthOfRequest();
}
```

2. Implement the *ITimingModule* interface in the *Timer* class. Include an *ArrayList* in the *Timer* class to hold on to durations of the requests. (You need to add the *System.Collections* namespace to the list of *using* directives.) Store the duration of the request at the end of each request in the *OnEndRequest* handler. Use clock ticks as the measurement to make it easier to compute the average duration. Finally, implement *GetAverageLengthOfRequest* (the method defined by the *ITimingModule* interface) by adding all the elements in the *ArrayList* and dividing that number by the size of the *ArrayList*. Create a *TimeSpan* using the result of the calculation and return that to the client.

```
using System.Collections;

public class Timer : IHttpModule, ITimingModule
{
    public Timer()
    {
    }

    protected ArrayList _alRequestDurations = new ArrayList();
    public void Init(HttpApplication httpApp)
    {
        httpApp.BeginRequest +=
            new EventHandler(this.OnBeginRequest);
        httpApp.EndRequest +=
            new EventHandler(this.OnEndRequest);
    }
    public void Dispose() { }

    public void OnBeginRequest(object o, EventArgs ea)
    {
        DateTime dateTimeBeginRequest = DateTime.Now;

        HttpContext ctx;
        ctx = HttpContext.Current;
        ctx.Items["dateTimeBeginRequest"] = dateTimeBeginRequest;
    }

    public void OnEndRequest(object o, EventArgs ea)
    {
        DateTime dateTimeEndRequest = DateTime.Now;

        HttpContext ctx;
        ctx = HttpContext.Current;
        DateTime dateTimeBeginRequest =
            (DateTime)ctx.Items["dateTimeBeginRequest"];

        TimeSpan duration =
                dateTimeEndRequest - dateTimeBeginRequest;

        ctx.Response.Write("<b> From the TimingModule: this request took " +
        duration.Duration().ToString() + "</b></br>");
        _alRequestDurations.Add(duration);
    }
```

```
public TimeSpan GetAverageLengthOfRequest()
{
  long lTicks = 0;
  foreach (TimeSpan timespanDuration in this._alRequestDurations)
  {
      lTicks += timespanDuration.Ticks;
  }

  long lAverageTicks = lTicks / _alRequestDurations.Count;
  TimeSpan timespanAverageDuration = new TimeSpan(lAverageTicks);
  return timespanAverageDuration;
}
}
```

3. Now add some code in the Default.aspx page to examine the average time taken to process each request. Add a button to fetch the average duration, and add a label to display the average duration. Give the button the *Text* value *Show Average Duration Of Requests*, as shown in the following graphic, and the ID *ButtonShowAverageDurationOfRequests*. The label should have an empty *Text* value and the ID *LabelAverageDurationOfRequests*. Also, include a reference to the *TimingModule* in the Default.aspx page so that the page code has access to the interface.

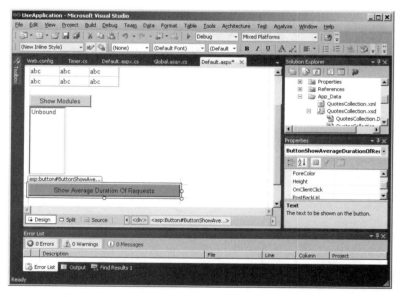

4. Double-click the Show Average Duration Of Requests button in Visual Studio to add a *Click* event handler. Handle the event by fetching the *TimingModule* from the collection of modules. You can fetch it by name because the collection is indexed by module name (as specified in web.config).

```
using TimingModule;

...

protected void
    ButtonShowAverageDurationOfRequests_Click(
        object sender,
        EventArgs e)
{
   HttpApplication httpApp =
        HttpContext.Current.ApplicationInstance;

   HttpModuleCollection httpModuleColl = httpApp.Modules;
   IHttpModule httpModule =
      httpModuleColl.Get("TimingModule");
   ITimingModule TimingModule =
        (ITimingModule)httpModule;

   TimeSpan timeSpanAverageDurationOfRequest =
      TimingModule.GetAverageLengthOfRequest();
   LabelAverageDurationOfRequests.Text =
      timeSpanAverageDurationOfRequest.ToString();
}
```

The object you get back by accessing the module collection is an *HttpModule*. To be able to talk to it using the *ITimingModule* interface, you need to cast the reference to the module. After you do that, you can call *GetAverageLengthOfRequest* and display it in the label, as shown in the following graphic:

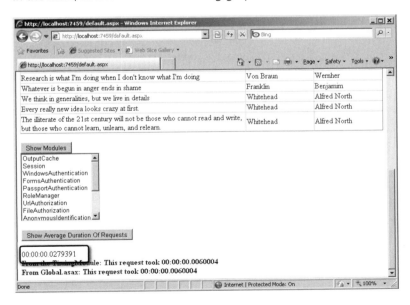

Global.asax vs. *HttpModules*

The application object expressed through Global.asax and the one offered through HTTP modules offer a rendezvous point for your application. You can use both of them to store global state between requests as well as to respond to application-wide events. When choosing one over the other, remember that Global.asax really goes with your application; Global.asax is intended to manage state and events specific to your application. HTTP modules exist as completely separate assemblies; they're not necessarily tied to a particular application, and they might even be signed and deployed in the global assembly cache. That makes modules an ideal vehicle for implementing generic functionality that's useful between different applications.

Chapter 18 Quick Reference

To	Do This
Create a custom module assembly	Create a new class implementing *IHttpModule*. Implement *Init*. Implement *Dispose*.
Insert the module into the processing chain	Configure the module in the *httpModule* node of the application's web.config file.
Handle application events in the module	Write a handler (in the module) for every event you want to handle. During the *Init* method, subscribe to the events by attaching the event handlers to the events.
Override the application object in the Global.asax file	Click Web site, Add New Item. Select Global Application Class from the templates. Insert your own code for responding to the application-wide events.
Use the application's dictionary	Access the application object (it's always available from the current *HttpContext*). Use the indexer notation to access the dictionary.

Chapter 19
HTTP Handlers

After completing this chapter, you will be able to

- Recognize the role of custom handlers in ASP.NET.
- Write custom handlers.
- Write just-in-time compiled custom handlers.
- Configure your site to include your custom handler.

This chapter covers writing custom HTTP handlers. Chapter 2, "ASP.NET Application Fundamentals," describes the ASP.NET pipeline. Remember that the endpoint of all requests handled by ASP.NET is always an implementation of *IHttpHandler*.

ASP.NET includes several classes capable of handling requests in the most common ways. For example, the *Page* class handles requests by interpreting the query strings and returning meaningful user interface (UI)-oriented HTML. The *Service* class interprets incoming query strings as method calls and processes them accordingly. So far, this book has focused on a single handler—*System.Web.UI.Page*. However, at other times it is appropriate to tweak the processing or even handle it in a completely different way. You might find yourself needing to handle a request in a way not already provided through the *System.Web.UI.Page* or the *System.Web.Services.Service* classes. What do you do then? ASP.NET supports custom HTTP handlers for just such occasions.

ASP.NET Request Handlers

So far, most attention has focused on the *Page* class. The *Page* class is responsible primarily for managing the UI aspects of an application. Because UI processing is very involved (and much of it is boilerplate-type code), the *Page* class has a great deal of functionality built into it. The *Page* class can solve the majority of user interface needs that require UI processing.

Although you haven't come across Web services yet, the *WebService* class implements the details required to interpret HTTP requests as method calls. Clients call Web services by packaging method calls in an XML format formalized as SOAP.

 Note Formerly, the acronym SOAP stood for Simple Object Access Protocol, but as of SOAP 1.2 the spelled-out version has been dropped to avoid confusion—SOAP isn't about objects and it isn't necessarily simple, at least to implement.

Clients call Web services in the same way they make HTTP requests for Web pages—through the HTTP GET and POST requests. When the request reaches the server, it becomes the server's job to unpack the parameters, place them on a real or virtual call stack, and finally invoke the correct method. Most of the work required to make a method call through HTTP is well understood and consistent and can be pushed down into the *WebService* class.

As discussed in Chapter 2, the endpoint for all HTTP requests destined for ASP.NET is a class implementing *IHttpHandler*. *IHttpHandler* is a simple interface, including a mere two methods. However, any class implementing that interface qualifies to participate in the HTTP pipeline as an HTTP handler. This chapter describes the interface in detail shortly.

HTTP handlers are simply classes that implement *IHttpHandler* (just as HTTP modules are classes implementing *IHttpModule*). Handlers are listed inside web.config. As with the HTTP modules, ASP.NET comes out of the box with several HTTP handlers (for implementing features such as tracing and preventing access to sensitive files on the site). ASP.NET comes with these HTTP handlers already registered in the master web.config configuration file, which resides alongside machine.config in the main configuration directory.

So far, ASPX, ASAX, and ASCX files have seemed to work magically in ASP.NET. For example, you saw earlier that simply surfing to an ASPX file causes ASP.NET to compile the file just in time and to synthesize a class based on *System.Web.UI.Page*. The reason the ASPX files work that way is that ASP.NET includes handlers for that functionality.

ASP.NET HTTP handlers are specified in web.config in much the same way as HTTP modules. The format of the handler elements includes four items. First, they include a file name and/ or extension to which the handler applies. This is done through the *add* attribute. Remember, all HTTP requests come to the server as resource requests—the HTTP protocol is built around the idea that requests contain resource names. The second part of the handler specification, *verb*, is a list of verbs to which this handler applies. These verbs correspond to the HTTP specification. For example, you might want a handler to apply only to GET and not to POST requests. Or you might wish to have a handler apply to all requests. The third element, *type*, is the name of the .NET type assigned to handle the request. Finally, the last attribute, *validate*, specifies whether ASP.NET should load the class at startup immediately or wait until a matching request is received.

Listing 19-1 includes a smattering of the HTTP handlers already installed as part of the ASP.NET master web.config file.

LISTING 19-1 Excerpt from the master web.config file

```
<httpHandlers>
  <add path="trace.axd" verb="*"
    type="System.Web.Handlers.TraceHandler" validate="True" />
  <add path="WebResource.axd" verb="GET"
    type="System.Web.Handlers.AssemblyResourceLoader" validate="True" />
  <add verb="*" path="*_AppService.axd"
    type="System.Web.Script.Services.ScriptHandlerFactory,
```

```
      System.Web.Extensions, Version=4.0.0.0, Culture=neutral,
      PublicKeyToken=31bf3856ad364e35" validate="False" />
    <add verb="GET,HEAD" path="ScriptResource.axd" type="System.Web.Handlers.
ScriptResourceHandler,
      System.Web.Extensions, Version=4.0.0.0, Culture=neutral,
      PublicKeyToken=31bf3856ad364e35" validate="False"/>
    <add path="*.axd" verb="*" type="System.Web.HttpNotFoundHandler" validate="True" />
    <add path="*.aspx" verb="*" type="System.Web.UI.PageHandlerFactory" validate="True" />
    <add path="*.ashx" verb="*" type="System.Web.UI.SimpleHandlerFactory" validate="True" />
    <add path="*.asmx" verb="*"
      type="System.Web.Script.Services.ScriptHandlerFactory, System.Web.Extensions,
      Version=4.0.0.0, Culture=neutral, PublicKeyToken=31bf3856ad364e35" validate="False" />
    <add path="*.rem" verb="*"
      type="System.Runtime.Remoting.Channels.Http.HttpRemotingHandlerFactory,
      System.Runtime.Remoting, Version=4.0.0.0, Culture=neutral,
      PublicKeyToken=b77a5c561934e089" validate="False" />
    <add path="*.soap" verb="*"
      type="System.Runtime.Remoting.Channels.Http.HttpRemotingHandlerFactory,
      System.Runtime.Remoting, Version=4.0.0.0, Culture=neutral,
      PublicKeyToken=b77a5c561934e089" validate="False" />
    <add path="*.asax" verb="*" type="System.Web.HttpForbiddenHandler"
      validate="True" />
    <add path="*.ascx" verb="*" type="System.Web.HttpForbiddenHandler" validate="True" />
    <add path="*.master" verb="*" type="System.Web.HttpForbiddenHandler" validate="True" />
    <add path="*.skin" verb="*" type="System.Web.HttpForbiddenHandler" validate="True" />
    <add path="*.browser" verb="*" type="System.Web.HttpForbiddenHandler" validate="True" />
    <add path="*.sitemap" verb="*" type="System.Web.HttpForbiddenHandler" validate="True" />
    <add path="*.dll.config" verb="GET,HEAD" type="System.Web.StaticFileHandler"
validate="True" />
<!-More handlers follow... -->
</httpHandlers>
```

The following sections look at a couple of specific handlers—the *Trace* handler and the *Forbidden* handler—to show how having a separate request handling facility (that is, one that is not tied specifically to UI or to Web services) can be useful.

The Built-in Handlers

One of the best examples of custom handling is the *Trace* handler built into ASP.NET. Chapter 17, "Diagnostics and Debugging," describes tracing. You turn tracing on in the web.config file by inserting the trace element, *<trace enabled=true />*. This instructs the ASP.NET runtime to store summaries of the requests going through the site so that they can be viewed for diagnostic purposes.

ASP.NET caches the tracing output in memory. To view the trace results, you surf to the virtual directory managing the site and ask for a specific resource: Trace.axd. Take a look at Listing 19-1 and you'll see the first entry among all the standard HTTP handlers is for a re-source named *Trace.axd*. The tracing functionality behind ASP.NET falls outside of normal UI processing, so it makes sense that tracing is handled by a custom handler.

When you surf to the Trace.axd resource, the handler renders HTML that looks like the output shown in Figure 19-1. The processing for this handler is very specific—the handler's job is to render the results of the last few requests.

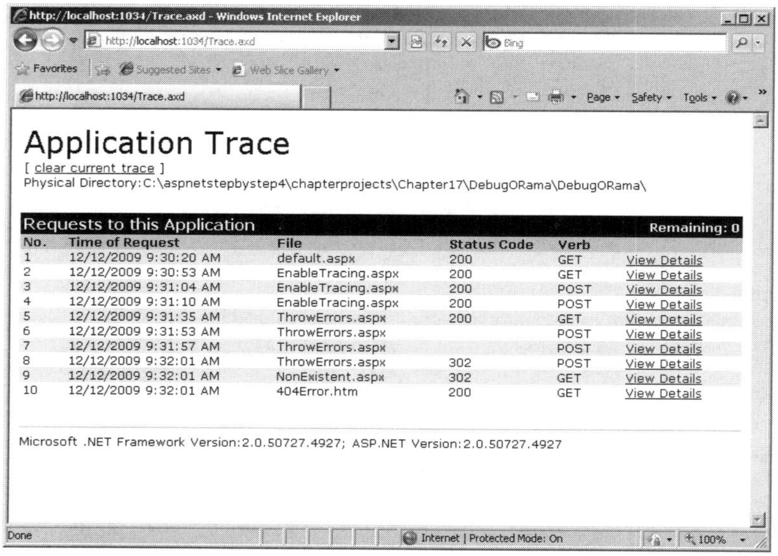

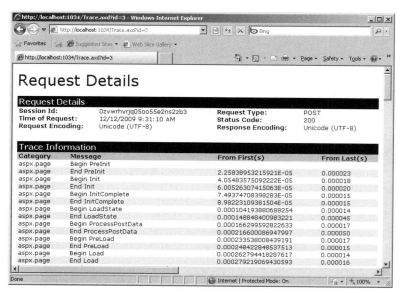

FIGURE 19-1 The output of the Trace.axd handler.

As shown in Figure 19-2, clicking the View Details link resubmits the request with a parameter *id=3* in the query string. This causes the handler to render the details of the third request.

FIGURE 19-2 The output of the Trace.axd handler focused on a specific request summary.

Figure 19-3 shows the Microsoft Internet Information Services (IIS) file mapping for files with the .axd extension. Although you won't really see this aspect until deployment time, it's interesting to observe because it shows how ASP.NET is very versatile in the kinds of requests it can handle. IIS handles Trace.axd requests the same way as any other ASP.NET request. That means IIS will pass requests for resources with an extension of .axd on to ASP.NET. Once inside the ASP.NET pipeline, the web.config file tells ASP.NET to handle the request with the *Trace* handler.

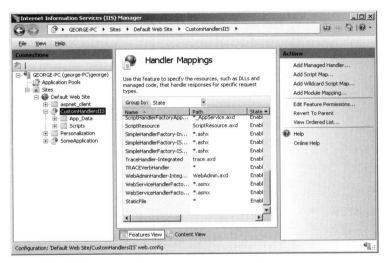

FIGURE 19-3 IIS has a handler mapping for Trace.axd.

If you look through the default web.config file a bit more, you'll see some other critical ASP.NET handlers. As you might expect, source code is banned explicitly from normal clients by default. Notice that files such as *.cs, *.config, and *.vb are handled by the *Forbidden* handler. If you try to look at source code in a Web browser, ASP.NET returns the page shown in Figure 19-4 by default.

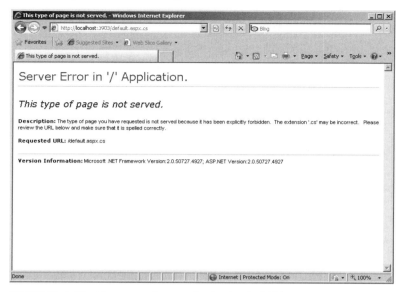

FIGURE 19-4 What happens when you try to view forbidden content.

Remember that ASP.NET's configuration is very malleable and that you can choose to let clients see your source code by one of two means. You can remove the source code extension to ASP.NET mappings in IIS. Alternatively, you can write your own source code viewer handlers and declare them in your application's web.config file.

These handlers plug into the pipeline by implementing *IHttpHandler*. The next section describes this key interface.

Handlers and *IHttpHandler*

Here it is. Shield your eyes while you look at Listing 19-2 (just kidding—it's not a very big interface).

LISTING 19-2 The *IHttpHandler* interface

```
public interface IHttpHandler
{
  void ProcessRequest(HttpContext ctx);
  bool IsReusable {get;}
}
```

There's really not much to it, is there? The interface includes a method named *ProcessRequest* and a property named *IsReusable*. If the handler instance can be used multiple times,

IsReusable should return *true*. If the handler generally returns static content, it's probably reusable. If the content is dynamic, it's probably not reusable. The heart of the handler is the *ProcessRequest* method that includes a single parameter: the current *HttpContext*.

When a request finally arrives at the handler (through the *ProcessRequest* method), *ProcessRequest* can literally do anything to respond to the request. The Trace.axd handler responds to a GET request by listing the requests being tracked by the runtime. The forbidden handler responds by tossing a roadblock in the processing pipeline so that the client can't see the forbidden resource. A custom Web service might respond to the request by parsing the XML payload, constructing a call stack, and making a call to an internal method.

Implementing *IHttpHandler* is simple—at least from the architectural standpoint. The *ProcessRequest* method takes a single parameter—the current *HttpContext*. However, the code inside *ProcessRequest* is free to do just about anything, possibly making the internal processing quite complex! The following example illustrates taking over the entire form-rendering process to display a list of choices in a combo box, allowing the end client to select from the choices, and finally rendering the chosen item.

Writing a custom handler

1. Create a new, empty Web project named *CustomHandlers*.

2. Add a new class library subproject to the CustomHandlers solution (just as you did when you created an HTTP module). Name the project *CustomFormHandlerLib*. The name of the class it generates for you is *Class1*. Rename the file *CustomFormHandler.cs* and the class *CustomFormHandler*.

3. The library generated by Microsoft Visual Studio comes without any knowledge of the ASP.NET framework and classes. Add a reference to the *System.Web* assembly.

4. To turn the *CustomFormHandler* class into an eligible handler, add the *IHttpHandler* interface to the inheritance list and implement *ProcessRequest*. Add a method named *ManageForm* that takes a parameter of type *HttpContext*. *ManageForm* should write out <html>, <body>, and <form> tags through *Response.Write*. Write the question "Hello there. What's cool about .NET?" followed by a line break. Next, write a <select> tag and set the *name* attribute to "Feature." Then, write several .NET features surrounded by <option> tags. This will produce a drop-down list box on the client's browser. Write out an <input> tag. The tag's *type* attribute should be *submit*, its *name* attribute should be "Lookup," and its *value* attribute should be "Lookup." Next, look up the new value for the "Feature" selection tag in the *HttpContext Request.Params* collection. If the value is not *null*, the end user selected something. Write the value provided by the

"Feature" selection tag. Finally, write out closing tags. That is, </form>, </body>, and </html> tags.

Have the *ProcessRequest* method call the *ManageForm* method like so:

```csharp
using System;
using System.Collections.Generic;
using System.Text;
using System.Web;
public class CustomFormHandler : IHttpHandler
{
    public void ProcessRequest(HttpContext ctx)
    {
        ManageForm(ctx);
    }

    public void ManageForm(HttpContext context)
    {
        context.Response.Write("<html><body><form>");

        context.Response.Write(
           "<h2>Hello there. What's cool about .NET?</h2>");

        context.Response.Write(
            "<select name='Feature'>");
        context.Response.Write(
           "<option> Strong typing</option>");
        context.Response.Write(
           "<option> Managed code</option>");
        context.Response.Write(
           "<option> Language agnosticism</option>");

        context.Response.Write(
           "<option> Better security model</option>");
        context.Response.Write(
           "<option> Threading and async delegates</option>");
        context.Response.Write(
           "<option> XCOPY deployment</option>");
        context.Response.Write(
           "<option> Reasonable HTTP handling framework</option>");
        context.Response.Write("</select>");
        context.Response.Write("</br>");

        context.Response.Write(
           "<input type=submit name='Lookup' value='Lookup'></input>");
        context.Response.Write("</br>");

        if (context.Request.Params["Feature"] != null)
        {
            context.Response.Write("Hi, you picked: ");
            context.Response.Write(
               context.Request.Params["Feature"]);
```

```
        context.Response.Write(
            " as your favorite feature.</br>");
    }

    context.Response.Write("</form></body></html>");
}

public bool IsReusable {
    get
    {
        return true;
    }
}
}
```

The code in the *ProcessRequest* will render a *form* element and a *select* element that render a form that can be submitted by the browser. When the form is submitted back to the server, the parameter collection will contain a *Features* element. The code examines the parameter collection to see whether it references a feature, and it displays the feature if it's been selected.

5. The class library you just created deposits its output in the project directory. For ASP.NET to use the page, the resulting executable needs to live in the application directory's *bin* subdirectory. You can do this by adding the CustomHandlerLib.dll as a project reference to the Web site. Right-click the Web site project in Solution Explorer and add a new project reference. Select the *CustomFormHandlerLib* project and click *OK*.

6. Now update web.config so that it uses the handler when clients request the *CustomFormHandler* resource. If you don't already have a web.config in the project, add one. Then, insert an *httpHandlers* section that points requests for the *CustomFormHandler* to the new *CustomFormHandler* class.

```
<configuration >
<system.web>
    <httpHandlers>
        <add path="*.cstm" verb="*"
            type="CustomFormHandlerLib.CustomFormHandler, CustomFormHandlerLib"
            validate="true" />
    </httpHandlers>
</system.web>
</configuration>
```

Note If this site were running under IIS, you would need to tell IIS about the new file types to be handled by the *CustomFormHandler*. If you decide to run this application under IIS (instead of the Visual Studio Web server), you can configure IIS to run your handler by editing config.sys directly, if you know the correct settings, or by doing the following:

1. Open IIS and navigate to the virtual directory for the site.

2. Open the Features View and locate the Handler Mappings icon, as shown in the following graphic.

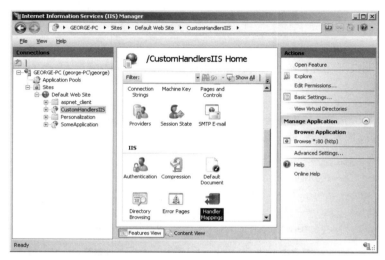

3. Double-click the Handler Mappings icon to open the Handler Mappings page:

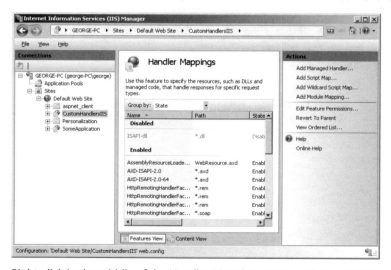

Right-click in the middle of the Handler Mappings page, and click Add Managed Handler. Type in an extension you'd like to have mapped to the custom handler, as shown in the following graphic. Then, assign a handler. IIS will look at all the handlers available to your application (including the ones local to your application). Select the handler from the drop-down list, give the handler an alias, and you'll be able to surf to that file type to invoke the handler.

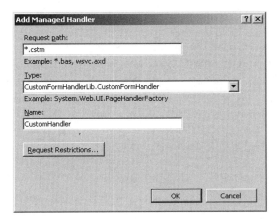

7. Finally, add a blank text file named *CustomHandler.cstm* to your project. You can use the file with that extension to surf to the handler.

8. Surf to the customhandler.cstm resource, and ASP.NET will invoke the custom handler you just created, as shown in this graphic:

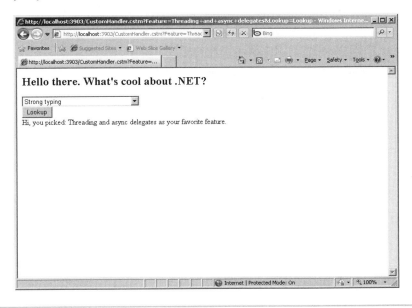

Of course, most of this processing could be handled more easily by setting up a Web Form. However, this example shows the flexibility of the ASP.NET handler architecture. It should also give you more appreciation for the Web Form and custom controls machinery in ASP.NET.

Handlers and Session State

Chapter 14, "Session State," discusses, as its title implies, session state. Session state works automatically in the context of *System.Web.UI.Page*. However, custom handlers need to turn on the ability to use session state deliberately.

The .NET architecture uses an interesting idiom known as *marker interfaces*. Marker interfaces are empty interfaces (without any methods or properties defined). Their sole purpose is to signal the runtime about various aspects of the application. For example, the ASP.NET runtime often uses them to turn on and off various features. When the runtime detects a marker interface as part of an object's class hierarchy, the runtime can bring into play certain features.

For a handler to use session state, it must have the *System.Web.SessionState.IRequiresSessionState* interface in its inheritance list. That way the runtime will know to load and store session state at the beginning and end of each request.

Listing 19-3 shows a handler with session state enabled.

LISTING 19-3 Example HTTP handler that accesses session state

```
using System;
using System.Collections.Generic;
using System.Text;
using System.Web;
using System.Web.SessionState;

public class HandlerWithSessionState : IHttpHandler, IRequiresSessionState
{
    public void ProcessRequest(HttpContext ctx)
    {
        string strData = (string)ctx.Session["SomeSessionData"];

        if (String.IsNullOrEmpty(strData))
        {
            strData = "This goes in session state";
            ctx.Session["SomeSessionData"] = strData;
        }
        ctx.Response.Write("This was in session state: " + strData);
    }


    public bool IsReusable {
        get
        {
            return true;
        }
    }
}
```

Generic Handlers (ASHX Files)

Just as ASPX files can be compiled on the fly ("just in time"), so can handlers. Generic handlers have an extension of ASHX. They're equivalent to custom handlers written in C# or Visual Basic in that they contain classes that fully implement *IHttpHandler*. They're convenient in the same way ASPX files are convenient. You simply surf to them and they're compiled automatically.

The following example illustrates the *CustomFormHandler* implemented as a "generic handler."

Writing a generic handler

1. Add a "generic" handler to the Web site. In Solution Explorer, right-click the CustomHandler Web site node and click Add New Item. Select Generic Handler from the templates. Name the handler *CustomFormHandler.ashx*.

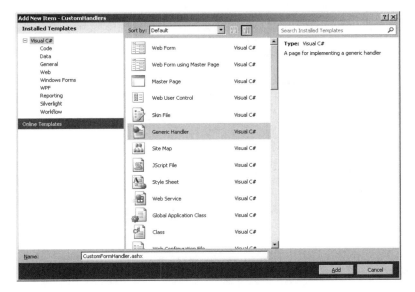

2. Visual Studio generates a handler that includes a stubbed-out *ProcessRequest* method and a completed *IsReusable* property. Open the handler's code-beside file (named CustomFormHandler.ashx.cs) and write a function to emit the form-handling code (you can borrow it from the last exercise). Call the method from inside *ProcessRequest*. Replace the stubbed-out method and property with real implementations.

```
using System;
using System.Collections.Generic;
using System.Linq;
using System.Web;
```

```
namespace CustomHandlers
{
  public class CustomFormHandler : IHttpHandler
  {
    public void ProcessRequest(HttpContext context)
    {
      ManageForm(context);
    }

    public void ManageForm(HttpContext context)
    {
      context.Response.Write("<html><body><form>");
      context.Response.Write(
        "<h2>Hello there. What's cool about .NET?</h2>");
      context.Response.Write("<select name='Feature'>");
      context.Response.Write("<option> Strong typing</option>");
      context.Response.Write("<option> Managed code</option>");
      context.Response.Write("<option> Language agnosticism</option>");
      context.Response.Write("<option> Better security model</option>");
      context.Response.Write(
        "<option> Threading and async delegates</option>");
      context.Response.Write("<option> XCOPY deployment</option>");
      context.Response.Write(
        "<option> Reasonable HTTP handling framework</option>");
      context.Response.Write("</select>");
      context.Response.Write("</br>");
      context.Response.Write(
        "<input type=submit name='Lookup' value='Lookup'></input>");
      context.Response.Write("</br>");
      if (context.Request.Params["Feature"] != null)
      {
        context.Response.Write("Hi, you picked: ");
        context.Response.Write(context.Request.Params["Feature"]);
        context.Response.Write(" as your favorite feature.</br>");
      }

      context.Response.Write("</form></body></html>");
    }

    public bool IsReusable
    {
      get {return true; }
    }
  }
}
```

3. Browse to the CustomFormHandler.ashx file. It should work in just the same way as the handler implemented in the *CustomFormHandler* class that you wrote in the first example.

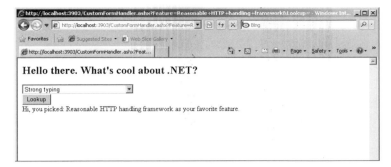

The advantage of using the generic handler is twofold. First, it's usually much more convenient to generate a simple handler than it is to create a whole new assembly to handle the
request. Second, you don't need to configure either web.config or IIS (when it comes time to
deploy). That is, ASP.NET and IIS already understand what to do when encountering resource
requests with the extension of .ashx. Installing ASP.NET places those when mapping to IIS.

However, ASHX files have the same limitations as ASPX and ASCX files in terms of their place
in an ASP.NET project. Simple generic handlers go with the project. That is, for the handler to
work, it must accompany the whole project. Alternatively, custom handlers deployed as separate assemblies you can deploy and share throughout the enterprise as global assemblies
(that is, strongly named assemblies placed in the global assembly cache).

Chapter 19 Quick Reference

To	Do This
Create a custom handler assembly	Create a new class implementing *IHttpHandler*. Implement the *IsReusable* property. Implement *ProcessRequest*.
Assign a file mapping to the handler in ASP.NET	Configure the handler in the *httpHandler* segment of the application's web.config file.
Assign a file mapping to the handler in IIS	Right-click the virtual directory. Select Properties. Click the Configure button. Click the Add button. Add a new extension and map it to aspnet_isapi.dll.
Create a simple handler	Select Web site, Add New Item. Select Generic Handler from the templates. Insert your own code for responding to the request.

Part V
Dynamic Data, XBAP, MVC, AJAX, and Silverlight

Chapter 20
Dynamic Data

After completing this chapter, you will be able to

- Understand the problems Dynamic Data solves.

- Understand how Dynamic Data works.

- Create a functional Web site using the Dynamic Data feature.

- Customize the default appearance of a Dynamic Data site.

- Apply validation to a Dynamic Data site.

Now, more than a decade into the evolution of ASP.NET, it's becoming clear that ASP.NET makes usability and ease of development priorities. For example, ASP.NET master pages make developing a common look and feel very doable in practice, relieving the need instead for developers to handcraft some sort of inheritance mechanism. ASP.NET authentication and authorization support makes security manageable. The validation controls make for convenient data validation. ASP.NET data source controls make data sources available through the Designer. ASP.NET 4 includes another major usability feature: Dynamic Data. Dynamic Data extends the ASP.NET *GridView* and *DetailsView* controls with a rich framework, making data-driven sites much more approachable. (Although it has been around for a while, only now is Dynamic Data available officially through Microsoft Visual Studio.)

Chapter 10, "Data Binding," discusses data binding. In ASP.NET, some controls bind directly to a data source (for example, the *DataGrid*). Data source controls are convenient because you can display data easily without having to write a lot of code manually to make the data appear for end users. Although the *DataGrid* can take a data source and display whatever data you send it, that's the extent of its functionality. Many developers would love an easy way to add validation infrastructure to the *DataGrid*. Unfortunately, validation is not part of *DataGrid* functionality. However, with ASP.NET Dynamic Data, you can build data-driven sites because Dynamic Data supports just this type of facility.

Here's another way to think about ASP.NET Dynamic Data features: As a developer, you need to know (basically, a priori) what your site will look like. You have an idea of the data model, and your job is to create a visual representation of the data (for example, a presentation suitable for humans). The *DataGrid* can infer the data structure using reflection and display a reasonable presentation for the end user. However, the grid's data presentation is often just a fragment of the page. ASP.NET Dynamic Data facilities take things a step further, enabling you to build a whole site based on a data model.

This chapter starts by looking at the Dynamic Data controls.

Dynamic Data Controls

The ASP.NET Dynamic Data framework provides six controls that specifically support Dynamic Data. These controls make up the core of ASP.NET Dynamic Data functionality. Here's a run-down of the Dynamic Data controls:

- **DynamicControl** The *DynamicControl* control displays content defined in templated data-bound controls (such as the ones described in Chapter 10) using ASP.NET Dynamic Data features.

- **DynamicDataManager** The *DynamicDataManager* is a nonvisual control that manages the dynamic behavior of the controls that support Dynamic Data.

- **DynamicEntity** The *DynamicEntity* control represents an entity for use by ASP.NET Dynamic Data.

- **DynamicFilter** The *DynamicFilter* control displays the user interface (UI) for filtering table rows using a specified column.

- **DynamicHyperLink** The *DynamicHyperLink* control displays links to table actions such as edit, delete, and insert.

- **DynamicValidator** The *DynamicValidator* control manages exception handling and error message display for those exceptions thrown in a data model.

These controls fit into the ASP.NET infrastructure—just like the rest of the server-side controls. The following exercise illustrates how to develop a Dynamic Data Web site.

Developing a Dynamic Data site

1. Start Visual Studio. Create a new ASP.NET Project using the ASP.NET Dynamic Data LINQ To SQL template. Name the project *DynamicDataLinqToSQLSite*, as shown here:

2. Visual Studio generates a Web Project primed to use Dynamic Data. Look at the items in Solution Explorer. (A few of these items are described throughout the rest of the chapter.)

3. Borrow the ASPNETStepByStep4.mdf file from the Chapter 10 project. Right-click the App_Data folder in Solution Explorer, and click Add, Existing Item. Navigate to the Chapter 10 project and pick up ASPNETStepByStep4.mdf from the App_Data folder.

4. Build a data model for the application. Right-click the project node from within Solution Explorer, and click Add, New Item. Select the Linq To SQL Classes template from the Installed Templates (Data node). Name the Linq To SQL class (to be generated by Visual Studio) *DotNetReferences*, as shown in the following graphic:

5. Open Server Explorer and expand the ASPNETStepByStep4 database under the Data Connections node. Open the Tables node and find the *DotNetReferences* table. Visual Studio will display the Object Relational Designer surface automatically. Drag the *DotNetReferences* table from Server Explorer into the Object Relational Designer, as shown here (Visual Studio is showing that it will create a class named *DotNetReference*):

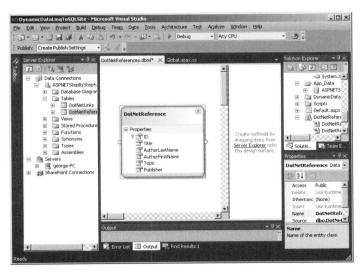

6. Visual Studio adds a file named DotNetReferences.dbml to your project (along with some useful classes). Save this file.

7. Open the Global.asax file. Find the code that registers the data context with the default data model. It will be commented out. Uncomment the line and have the *DefaultModel* register the *DotNetReferencesDataContext* (which was generated by Visual Studio), as shown in the following code. Also set the *ScaffoldAllTables* parameter to *true*.

```
public static void RegisterRoutes(RouteCollection routes)
{
  DefaultModel.RegisterContext(typeof(DotNetReferencesDataContext),
    new ContextConfiguration() { ScaffoldAllTables = true});
  // more registration code...
}
```

8. Now run the site. The default page will appear like this:

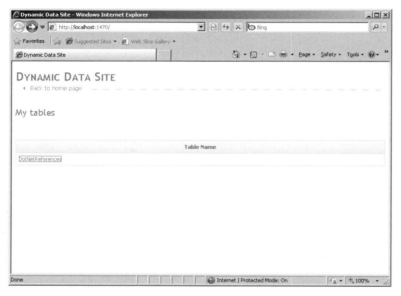

9. Click the DotNetReferences link that appears under the My Tables banner. Visual Studio reflected on the data in the data model and populated a *GridView* based on the data. (In fact, if you read the source code of Default.aspx, you can see only a *GridView*—you see the source code in the next step.) You should this in your browser when you click the DotNetReferences link:

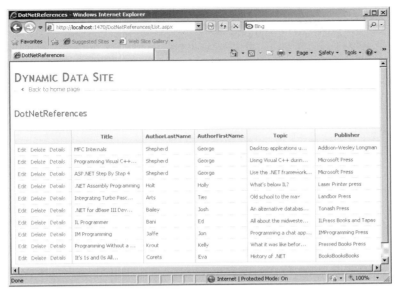

10. Open the Default.aspx file and look at what Visual Studio produced for you:

```
<asp:GridView ID="Menu1" runat="server" AutoGenerateColumns="false"
  CssClass="DDGridView" RowStyle-CssClass="td" HeaderStyle-CssClass="th"
  CellPadding="6">
  <Columns>
    <asp:TemplateField HeaderText="Table Name" SortExpression="TableName">
      <ItemTemplate>
        <asp:DynamicHyperLink ID="HyperLink1"
          runat="server"><%# Eval("DisplayName") %>
        </asp:DynamicHyperLink>
      </ItemTemplate>
    </asp:TemplateField>
  </Columns>
</asp:GridView>
```

11. This code generates a table of hyperlinks based on the default data model (which is made up of a single table right now). When you click the link, ASP.NET directs the request to a file named List.aspx. You can find List.aspx in the DynamicData\ PageTemplates node of the project in Solution Explorer. ASP.NET substitutes the display name (the DotNetReferences) in the URL and uses the data to produce a listing of the contents of the *DotNetReferences* table. If you open the List.aspx file, you also find a *GridView*—this *GridView* in List.aspx produces the listing of the table contents.

Dynamic Data Details

At this point, you might be looking at the preceding example and wondering what the big deal is. After all, if you point the *GridView* toward a data source, the *GridView* automatically reflects the data source columns and creates a bunch of columnar representations. However, the columns for the *GridView* shown so far are bound columns that use the *BoundField* server-side control. Once the GridView is rendered—that's all the end user sees, and there is no easy way to customize the behavior. ASP.NET Dynamic Data features change that: The Dynamic Data features are built around the *DynamicControl* and the *DynamicField* controls.

The *DynamicControl* is used in the *ListView* and the *FormView* data controls. Using the *DynamicControl* causes ASP.NET to render a UI based on schema from the database. You use the *DynamicField* in the *GridView* and *DetailsView* (instead of the *BoundField)* to render the UI. The *DynamicField* relies on the *DynamicControl* internally, so produces the same sort of data-driven UI in the context of the *GridView* and the *DetailsView*.

When you use the *DynamicControl* (either explicitly or implicitly), ASP.NET renders data entry forms generated directly from the tables of your database, and you can substitute other controls to render the UI (rather than relying on the default provided by ASP.NET). This lets you use a wide variety of controls easily in the *GridView*, *ListView*, *FormView*, and *DetailsView*.

For example, imagine you want to allow users to enter a Social Security number using the *DataGrid*. If you do *not* use Dynamic Data, the *GridView* uses the standard *TextBox* control to render the editing UI, and there's no easy way to inject any other control. Now imagine you want to use a different control during editing: the *MaskedTextBoxExtender* from the AJAX toolkit. By applying the *MaskedTextBoxExtender* to the *TextBox*, you can ensure that the user enters the number in the correct format (three digits, a hyphen, two digits, another hyphen, and then four more digits). Up until now, it has not been feasible to extend the *GridView* in this way. But now you can with the *DynamicControl* or *DynamicField*. The Dynamic Data scaffolding produced by Visual Studio includes well-delineated places where you can substitute different, nondefault controls. In addition, Dynamic Data supports automatic validation. For example, by using the Dynamic Data features of ASP.NET, you can avoid having to recode all those validators over and over again because the database schema can inform how the data validation works for a particular column.

The next example illustrates how to extend the application to show more tables and to use the automatic validation supplied by the scaffolding.

Extending the application

1. Open the DotNetReferences.dbml file. Visual Studio should display the Object Relational Designer. Open Server Explorer. Find the *DotNetLinks* table and drag it into the Object Relational Designer. Rebuild the application and you will see links for the

DotNetLinks table (as well as the *DotNetReferences* table). Click the DotNetLinks hyper-link. You should see the *DotNetLinks* table represented in the browser as follows:

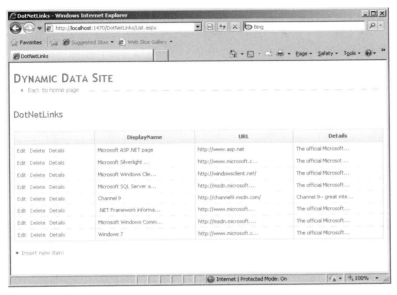

2. Close the browser and open the file List.aspx; it is in Solution Explorer under the Project node: Open the Dynamic Data node, and then open the Page Templates node. After you open List.aspx, switch to Design mode if not already displayed as such. You should see the *GridView* in Design mode:

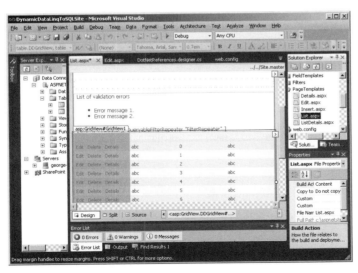

3. This page is just like any other Web form at this point. If you would like to format the *GridView*, you can by clicking the SmartTag for the grid (the angle bracket (>) in the box in the upper right corner of the control). For example, you can auto format the

GridView to give it a more colorful appearance. You can also edit the control to have alternating row styles, as shown in Chapter 10. The example here skins the *GridView* using the Classic format. Here's the DotNetLinks *GridView* following the reformat:

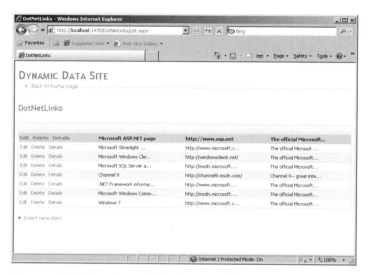

4. Now update the Linq to SQL data model to support regular expression validation. The file created by Visual Studio is named DotNetReferences.Designer.cs, and you can edit it by expanding the DotNetReferences.dbml file in Solution Explorer. Find the URL property in the *DotNetLink* class and add the *RegularExpression* attribute to it. The regular expression shown here is borrowed from the *RegularExpressionValidator*'s *ValidationExpression* dialog box:

```
[global::System.Data.Linq.Mapping.ColumnAttribute(Storage="_URL",
  DbType="NVarChar(100) NOT NULL", CanBeNull=false)]
[System.ComponentModel.DataAnnotations.RegularExpression
                    ("http(s)?://([\\w-]+\\.)+[\\w-]+(/[\\w- ./?%&=]*)?")]
public string URL
{
  get
  {
    return this._URL;
  }
  set
  {
    if ((this._URL != value))
    {
      this.OnURLChanging(value);
      this.SendPropertyChanging();
      this._URL = value;
      this.SendPropertyChanged("URL");
      this.OnURLChanged();
    }
  }
}
```

5. Run the site. Go to the DotNetLinks page and try to edit one of the links. You are presented with the DotNetLinks edit page. Type an invalid URL in the edit box. Click the Update link and watch the built-in regular expression validator fire, just as shown in Chapter 6, "Control Potpourri," and as illustrated in the following graphic. This happens because the *URL* property in the data model throws an exception when a value not matching the regular expression defined in the attribute is set.

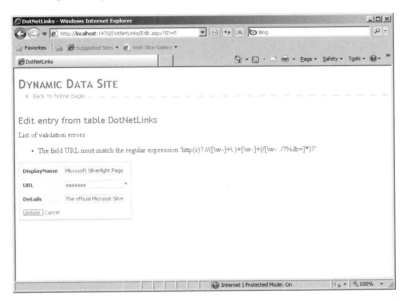

6. To see where the built-in *RegularExpressionValidator* is set up, open the file Text_Edit.ascx, which is in the DynamicData\FieldTemplates folder in Server Explorer. You'll see the following code:

```
<%@ Control Language="C#" CodeBehind="Text_Edit.ascx.cs"
  Inherits="DynamicDataLinqToSQLSite.Text_EditField" %>

<asp:TextBox ID="TextBox1" runat="server"
  Text='<%# FieldValueEditString %>' CssClass="DDTextBox"></asp:TextBox>

<asp:RequiredFieldValidator runat="server"
  ID="RequiredFieldValidator1" CssClass="DDControl DDValidator"
  ControlToValidate="TextBox1"
  Display="Dynamic" Enabled="false" />
<asp:RegularExpressionValidator runat="server"
  ID="RegularExpressionValidator1" CssClass="DDControl DDValidator"
  ControlToValidate="TextBox1" Display="Dynamic" Enabled="false" />

<asp:DynamicValidator runat="server"
  ID="DynamicValidator1"
  CssClass="DDControl DDValidator"
  ControlToValidate="TextBox1" Display="Dynamic" />
```

Voila! The editing facilities of the page are controlled by a user control!

As you can see, there is nothing hidden or magical about the ASP.NET Dynamic Data feature. In fact, if you peruse the files generated by Visual Studio, you can see a host of common ASP.NET idioms and features that you have explored in earlier chapters of this book. The power of Dynamic Data is that you can use it to tailor a site that is driven by the data model rather than spending a lot of time creating a UI to match the data model. This is especially powerful if you expect your data model to change in the future.

Chapter 20 Quick Reference

To	Do This
Create a Dynamic Data-enabled Web site	Use Visual Studio's Dynamic Data Linq To SQL template or Dynamic Data Entity template.
Create a Linq to SQL data model	Use Visual Studio's Linq to SQL Classes template to create dbml and class files for you. Drag the table(s) you want represented in your data model onto the Object Relational Designer surface.
Include the scaffolding in the request routing chain	Call *DefaultModel.RegisterContext* passing in the correct data context type (produced by Visual Studio).
Apply validation to the data model	Annotate the property to validate with one of the validation attributes (for example, *RegularExpression* or the *Required* attributes).
Modify the look and field of the generated source code	Open the DynamicData\PageTemplates node in Solution Explorer. The generated code is in the aspx files located there (for example, List.aspx, ListDetails.aspx, Details.aspx, Edit.aspx, and Insert.aspx).

Chapter 21
ASP.NET and WPF Content

After completing this chapter, you will be able to

- Understand the benefits of Windows Presentation Foundation (WPF) over traditional Windows user interfaces.

- Create an XAML-based browser application (XBAP) site.

- Add WPF-based content to an ASP.NET site.

The last 20 chapters demonstrate how ASP.NET makes Web development approachable by pushing most HTML rendering to the ASP.NET *Control* class and its descendents. In addition, the ASP.NET pipeline hides many of the details of a Web request so that you can focus on your part in development. The next few chapters show alternative paths for producing content for the end user, including information on ASP.NET support for AJAX, its implementation of the Model-View-Controller pattern, and how Microsoft Silverlight works. This chapter starts by discussing how you can render Extensible Application Markup Language (XAML)-based content to the browser.

Improving Perceived Performance by Reducing Round-Trips

Throughout the history of the Web, one main way developers have improved end-user experience has been to reduce the number of round-trips to the server. For a long time, the only way to do this was to employ client-side scripting in a Web page. That way, certain parts of the application were executed on the client's browser, which is usually much faster than making an entire round-trip.

Chapter 23, "AJAX," discusses AJAX, which represents a major improvement in Web-based user interfaces (UIs). AJAX adds many elements to Web-based user interfaces that have been available previously only to desktop applications. For example, the AJAX *AutoComplete* extender allows users typing text into a *TextBox* to select from options generated dynamically from a Web service. With the *ModalPopupExtender,* you can provide content in a pane that behaves like a standard Windows modal dialog box at run time.

However, scripting isn't the only way to push functionality to the browser. AJAX still relies fundamentally on HTML, and although HTML includes a huge set of tags that render to standard user interface elements that run in the browser, it stops there. Being able to run WPF content on a site changes that. WPF represents a new way to add rich user interfaces to a site, and it turns standard Web-based (and Windows-based) user interface programming on its head. In this chapter, you see how WPF works and how it relates to the Internet and to browser applications. You revisit some of this when you look at Silverlight, a similar technology. For now, first look at WPF.

What Is WPF?

Windows-based user interface programming is based on an architecture that has remained fundamentally unchanged for more than a quarter century. Since back in the early 1980s through today, all applications have had the same basic underpinnings: The main application runs a message loop, picks up Windows messages off of the message queue, and deposits them into a window handler. Every window is responsible for rendering its own presentation—that is, every window, from the top-level window of the application to the most minor control in the window.

Nearly all Windows-based applications today use the Win32 application programming interface (API) at the lowest level. The classic Win32 API has worked well for a long time. However, its design is beginning to show its age. Because every window and control is responsible for its own rendering using the Win32 Graphics Device Interface (GDI, or the GDI+ interface, in the case of Windows Forms), fundamental user interface limitations are built into the design of the Windows operating system. The GDI and GDI+ interfaces have a huge array of functions. However, it takes a lot of work to do much more than basic drawing and text rendering. That is, special effects such as transformations, transparency, and video play integration are difficult to accomplish using the current Windows graphics interface. Windows does support a richer graphics-based interface named Direct X; however, using it is often beyond the scope of most Windows-based applications and is typically reserved for use by game programmers.

The limitations of the classic Windows API prompted Microsoft to develop a new programming interface: the Windows Presentation Foundation (WPF). With WPF, programming special effects for Windows-based applications (including presenting Web content, as described later) is very approachable. The WPF libraries are made up of a number of classes that work together very much like the Windows Forms classes do (on the surface at least; underneath the goings-on are very different from Windows Forms).

WPF represents a very rich programming interface for developing a user interface. Here's a short list of the kinds of features available through WPF (this is a broad summary and is not exhaustive):

- User interface elements that you can modify in all kinds of ways much more easily than you can using Win32 and subclassing
- Paths, shapes, and geometries for drawing two-dimensional presentations

- Transforms (scaling, translating, rotation, and skewing) that allow consistent and uniform modifications to all user interface elements

- Ability to manage the opacity of individual elements

- Built-in layout panels

- Brushes—image, video, and drawing brushes for filling areas on the screen

- Animations

WPF applications arrange the UI elements using layout panels. Rather than relying on absolute positioning (as is the case for Win32 applications) or flow layout (as is the case for ASP.NET pages), WPF introduces a number of layout options including the following:

- *Grid*   Elements are placed in a table.

- *StackPanel*   Elements are stacked vertically or horizontally.

- *Canvas*   Elements are positioned absolutely.

- *DockPanel*   Elements are positioned against the sides of the host.

- *WrapPanel*   Elements are repositioned to fit when the host is resized.

The example that follows later uses the *Canvas*.

You craft a typical WPF application from files in very much the same way that you create an ASP.NET application. A stand-alone WPF application includes a main application object that runs the message loop and one or more windows, which are browser-based WPF applications made up of pages. WPF application components are typically composed from a markup file, just like ASP.NET pages are. WPF layouts are defined using Extensible Application Markup Language (XAML).

XAML files describe a WPF layout's logical tree, the collection of WPF user interface elements. A WPF application is made up of Common Language Runtime (CLR) classes underneath the façade of markup language, very much like the ASP.NET object model is. XAML files represent instructions for constructing a logical tree of visual elements. In the case of a stand-alone Windows application, the logical tree exists in a top-level window. In the case of a browser-based application, the logical tree exists in a browser pane. The following is a short XAML listing that displays "Hello World" in a button hosted in a browser pane:

```
<Page
  xmlns="http://schemas.microsoft.com/winfx/2006/xaml/presentation"
  xmlns:sys="clr-namespace:System;assembly=mscorlib"
  xmlns:x="http://schemas.microsoft.com/winfx/2006/xaml" >
  <Button Height="100" Width="100">Hello World</Button>
</Page>
```

The preceding code doesn't do a whole lot, but it is an example of the fundamental structure of a WPF page as expressed in XAML. When run, the XAML you see listed starts a browser session and displays a button with the string "Hello World" as its content (provided the XAML plug-in is installed). In a real application, instead of containing a single button with a string, the top-level WPF node can contain elaborate layouts using the different layout panels available in WPF. You see an example of this soon.

How Does WPF Relate to the Web?

What does all this mean for Web applications? Windows Internet Explorer and other browsers running under the Windows operating system are based on the classic Windows architecture. Browsers are responsible for rendering HTML using the graphic interface available to Windows: the Graphics Device Interface (GDI). Consequently, accomplishing special effects in browsers (and typical HTML) is just as difficult as it is with traditional Windows programs.

Web programming is based on submitting HTTP requests to a server, processing the requests, and sending back responses to the client. In that sense, any user interface–specific responses are constrained to whatever can be expressed in HTML. The Web is dynamic, and HTML is basically a document technology.

Is there another markup language that provides more than just simple tags that can be interpreted by an HTML browser? Yes, that's what XAML is when used in the context of a Web application.

Remember the previous code example? If the contents of the file are saved in an ASCII text file named HelloWorld.xaml, and you double click it in Windows Explorer, Internet Explorer loads and parses the XAML content. Figure 21-1 shows how it appears in Internet Explorer when you load the XAML file into the browser. Simply double-click the file name in Windows Explorer to see the application.

When adding WPF-style content directly to a Web site, you have three options: presenting the content through loose XAML files, creating an XAML-based browser application (XBAP), or using Silverlight. (Silverlight is described in more detail in Chapter 24, "Silverlight and ASP.NET.")

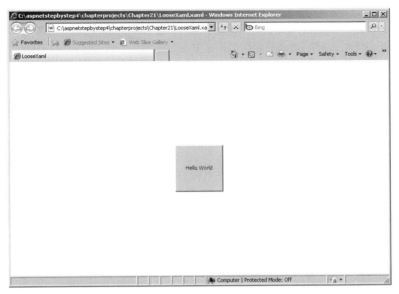

FIGURE 21-1 A button rendered as specified by XAML.

Loose XAML Files

As just shown, if you place a properly formatted XAML file in your site and make it available through a Web server, any browser capable of using the XAML plug-in (such as Internet Explorer) can pick it up and render it. This is one option for presenting WPF-based content from a Web site. This technique is useful for rendering semidynamic content—that is, for rendering anything expressible using pure XAML files.

The WPF programming model marries XAML layout instructions with accompanying code modules in very much the same way that ASP.NET does. Events generated from user interface elements are handled in the accompanying code. Deploying s as loose XAML files precludes adding event handlers and accompanying code.

However, WPF elements are dynamic in the sense that they can be animated, and user interface elements can be tied together using only XAML. That's why WPF content expressed only through XAML is semidynamic. You can hook up some interactive elements using only XAML, but there's a limit. For example, all through XAML you can render a list of names of images in a list box and allow users to select an image to zoom. You can attach slider controls to user interface elements so that the end user can change various aspects of the elements through the slider. However, you cannot implement event handlers for controls; that requires deploying a WPF application as an XBAP application.

XBAP Applications

XBAPs are another way to deploy WPF content over the Web. They're a bit more complex than loose XAML files are. In addition to expressing layout, XBAPs support accompanying executable code for each page. When you deploy a WPF application over the Web, the client receives the WPF visual layout and the accompanying code is downloaded to the client computer. Events occurring in the XBAP are handled on the client side.

The upside of deploying an application as an XBAP is that it works in very much the same way that a Windows-based desktop application works (though with greatly reduced permissions and tightened security). For example, the application can handle mouse click events and can respond to control events all on the client side.

Although XBAPs are not related directly to ASP.NET, XBAP content can be hosted in ASP.NET-served pages in the same way that loose XAML content can be served. That is, you can make redirects to XBAP files or host XBAP files from within <iframe> HTML elements.

Microsoft Visual Studio includes a wizard for generating XBAPs that can present WPF content. In addition, the user interface elements contained in the WPF content can respond to events and messages the same way as any other desktop application can. When browsers surf to your XBAPs (which are ultimately deployed through Internet Information Services), they will have a very desktop-like experience in terms of user interface rendering and responsiveness, even though the application is running in a browser. The following exercise illustrates how to create an XBAP.

Creating an XBAP

1. Start Visual Studio and click File, New Project. Go to the Windows application templates and select WPF Browser Application. Name the Application *XBAPORama*, as shown here:

2. Visual Studio should have created for you a new XBAP that includes a page and an application XAML file set. The file names are Page1.xaml/Page1.xaml.cs and App.xaml/ App.xaml.cs. This is very similar to the ASP.NET Web Form application structure in that there is a markup file that contains the bulk of the UI and a code file that implements functionality to be run on the client. Visual Studio should show the Page1.xaml file, which contains a *Grid* layout panel.

3. Change the layout panel from a *Grid* to a *StackPanel* so that it is simpler to work with. With a *StackPanel*, you can drop in controls and not worry about creating grid columns and rows:

```
<Page x:Class="XBAPORama.Page1"
   xmlns="http://schemas.microsoft.com/winfx/2006/xaml/presentation"
   xmlns:x="http://schemas.microsoft.com/winfx/2006/xaml"
   xmlns:mc="http://schemas.openxmlformats.org/markup-compatibility/2006"
   xmlns:d="http://schemas.microsoft.com/expression/blend/2008"
   mc:Ignorable="d"
   d:DesignHeight="300" d:DesignWidth="300"
   Title="Page1">
   <StackPanel>
   </StackPanel>
</Page>
```

4. Modify the XAML a bit more. Change the *FontSize* property for the *Page* to **16**. Nest the following controls in the *StackPanel*: a *TextBox*, a *ListBox*, and a *Button*. WPF works very similarly to ASP.NET in that you can name controls in the markup file (the XAML file) and they will appear as programmatic elements in the code behind. Set the *Name* property for the *TextBox* to "theTextBox" and set the *Name* property of the *ListBox* to "theListBox" so that you can refer to them in the code files. Finally, set the *Height* property of the *ListBox* to 100 so that it will show up even if it is empty:

```
<Page x:Class="XBAPORama.Page1"
   xmlns="http://schemas.microsoft.com/winfx/2006/xaml/presentation"
   xmlns:x="http://schemas.microsoft.com/winfx/2006/xaml"
   xmlns:mc="http://schemas.openxmlformats.org/markup-compatibility/2006"
   xmlns:d="http://schemas.microsoft.com/expression/blend/2008"
   mc:Ignorable="d"
   d:DesignHeight="300" d:DesignWidth="300"
   Title="Page1" FontSize="16">
   <StackPanel>
     <TextBox Name="theTextBox"></TextBox>
     <ListBox Name="theListBox" Height="100"></ListBox>
     <Button>Click to Add Items</Button>
   </StackPanel>
</Page>
```

The Designer should show all the controls in the *StackPanel* like this:

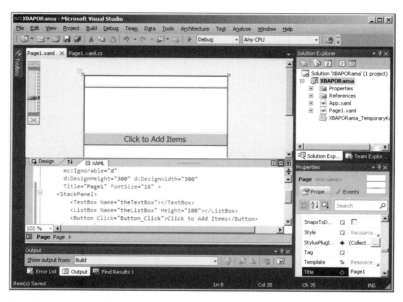

5. Double-click the button to add a handler. Visual Studio creates a handler for the button click. You can find the handler in the code file for the page. Because you didn't name the *Button*, Visual Studio gave the handler a default name of *Button_Click*. The method looks very much like the ASP.NET button click handlers except the second argument is a *RoutedEventArg* instead of the .NET typical *EventArg*.

6. Implement the handler by adding whatever is in the *TextBox* to the *ListBox*. It should feel almost like you are programming a Web Form—the code model is very similar:

```
using System;
using System.Collections.Generic;
using System.Linq;
using System.Text;
using System.Windows;
using System.Windows.Controls;
using System.Windows.Data;
using System.Windows.Documents;
using System.Windows.Input;
using System.Windows.Media;
using System.Windows.Media.Imaging;
using System.Windows.Navigation;
using System.Windows.Shapes;

namespace XBAPORama
{
/// <summary>
/// Interaction logic for Page1.xaml
/// </summary>
  public partial class Page1 : Page
```

```
  {
    public Page1()
    {
      InitializeComponent();
    }
    private void Button_Click(object sender, RoutedEventArgs e)
    {
      this.theListBox.Items.Add(this.theTextBox.Text);
    }
  }
}
```

7. Press Ctrl+F5 from within Visual Studio to run the application in the browser. When you type text into the *TextBox* and click the *Button*, the code running on the client side will add the contents of the *TextBox* to the *ListBox*, as follows (notice the .xbap extension at the end of the file name in the URL):

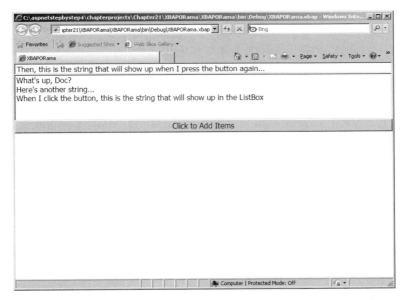

Although this example does not strictly run in ASP.NET, it does show an alternative way of producing content. When you compiled the application, Visual Studio created a few files including XBAPORama.xbap and XBAPORama.exe. You can include this content as part of an ASP.NET site by including the XBAP, the EXE, and the manifest files that resulted from the compilation in a folder in an ASP.NET application. You do that shortly.

WPF Content and Web Applications

You can serve WPF content from an ASP.NET application in much the same way that ASP.NET serves other content. You can include loose XAML files in a Web application, or you can host some specific WPF content in an <iframe> HTML element.This exercise illustrates how you can use WPF content in an ASP.NET application.

Adding XAML content to a site

1. Create a new Empty ASP.NET Web Application project in Visual Studio. Name the project *XAMLORama*.

2. Use Visual Studio to add a new text file to the project. Right-click the XAMLORama project node in Visual Studio, and click Add, New Item. Select a text file type from the templates.

3. Rename the file so that it has an .xaml extension. This file shows a paper airplane drawing, so name the file *PaperAirplane.xaml*. The Visual Studio XAML designer might show an error right away because there's no content yet. This is not a problem because you add content in the next step.

4. Add some XAML content to the file, starting by defining the top-level layout node. Include the following XML namespaces and make the window 750 units wide:

```
<Page xmlns="http://schemas.microsoft.com/winfx/2006/xaml/presentation"
      xmlns:x="http://schemas.microsoft.com/winfx/2006/xaml" Width="750">

</Page>
```

All WPF layouts begin with a top-level node. In this case, the node is a *Page* so that it will show up in the client's browser.

5. Add a *Grid* to the page, and add two row definitions and two column definitions:

```
<Page xmlns="http://schemas.microsoft.com/winfx/2006/xaml/presentation"
      xmlns:x="http://schemas.microsoft.com/winfx/2006/xaml" Width="750">
    <Grid>
        <Grid.RowDefinitions>
            <RowDefinition/>
            <RowDefinition Height="100"/>
        </Grid.RowDefinitions>
        <Grid.ColumnDefinitions>
            <ColumnDefinition/>
            <ColumnDefinition Width="25"/>
        </Grid.ColumnDefinitions>
    </Grid>
</Page>
```

6. Add WPF elements to the grid. Add a *Canvas* to the upper left corner of the *Grid*, and make the *Background SkyBlue*. Add two *Slider* controls to the *Grid*, too. The first *Slider* controls the X position of the airplane. Name the *Slider sliderX*. Put the slider into

row 1, and use the *ColumnSpan* to stretch the *Slider* across two columns. The maximum value of this slider should be 500. Orient the second *Slider* vertically and configure it to occupy column 1 in the *Grid*. Use the *RowSpan* to stretch the *Slider* across both rows. This slider controls the rotation of the airplane. Name this *Slider* *sliderRotate*. Its maximum value should be 360.

```
<Page xmlns="http://schemas.microsoft.com/winfx/2006/xaml/presentation"
      xmlns:x="http://schemas.microsoft.com/winfx/2006/xaml" Width="750">
    <Grid
        <!-- Grid column and row definitions are here... -->
        <Canvas Background="SkyBlue" Grid.Row="0"
                Grid.Column="0">
        </Canvas>
        <Slider x:Name="sliderRotate" Orientation="Vertical"
                Grid.Row="0"
                Minimum="0" Maximum="360"
                Grid.Column="1"></Slider>
        <Slider x:Name="sliderX" Maximum="500"
                Grid.Column="0" Grid.Row="1"
                Grid.ColumnSpan="2"></Slider>
    </Grid>
</Page>
```

7. Add the airplane and connect it to the sliders using XAML data binding. Here's how: Create the airplane drawing using a WPF *Path*. The *Path* draws a series of line segments using a specific pen. Make the *Stroke* Black and set the the *StrokeThickness* to 3. The *Path* data should connect the following points. Move the cursor to 0,0, and then draw a line to 250,50, and then to 200,75 to 0,0. Then, move the cursor to 200,75 and draw a line to 190,115 and another line to 180,85 to 0,0. Next, move the cursor to 180,85 and draw a line to 140,105 and then to 0,0. Finally, move the cursor to 190,115 and draw a line to 158,93. Set the *Path*'s relationship to the *Top* of the *Canvas* as 200. Bind the *Path*'s relationship to the *Left* of the *Canvas* to *sliderX*'s *Value*. Finally, add a *RenderTransform* to the *Path* and include a *RotateTransform*. Bind the *RotateTransform*'s *Angle* to *sliderRotate*'s *Value*. Set the *Path*'s *RenderTransformOrigin* to .5, .5. Here's the *Path* code:

```
<Page xmlns="http://schemas.microsoft.com/winfx/2006/xaml/presentation"
      xmlns:x="http://schemas.microsoft.com/winfx/2006/xaml" Width="750">

    <Grid>
        <!-- Grid column and row definitions are here... -->
        <Canvas Background="SkyBlue" Grid.Row="0"
                Grid.Column="0">
            <Path Stroke="Black" StrokeThickness="2" Fill="White"
                Data="M0,0 L250,50 L200,75 L0,0 M200,75 L190,115 L180,85
                      L0,0 M180,85 L140,105 L0,0 M190,115 L158,93"
                RenderTransformOrigin=".5, .5"
                Canvas.Top="200"
                Canvas.Left="{Binding ElementName=sliderX,Path=Value}" >
```

```
                        <Path.RenderTransform>
                            <RotateTransform Angle=
                                "{Binding ElementName=sliderRotate,Path=Value}"/>
                        </Path.RenderTransform>
                    </Path>
                </Canvas>
                <!-Sliders go here... -->
            </Grid>
        </Page>
```

After setting up the *Canvas*, the *Path*, and the *Slider*s in the grid, you should see it appear in Visual Studio.

8. Add these references to the project: *WindowsBase*, *PresentationCore*, and *PresentationFramework* by right-clicking the References node in Solution Explorer and clicking Add Reference. Look in the .NET tab of the Add Reference dialog box to find these assemblies. Run the page. Because Visual Studio doesn't allow you to run loose XAML files directly, you need to navigate from another page. Add a new page to the application. Name it *Default.aspx*. Add a *Hyperlink* to the Default.aspx page and set the *NavigationUrl* property to *PaperAirplane.xaml*. Surf to the default page and click the hyperlink that loads the XAML file in the browser. It should appear like this:

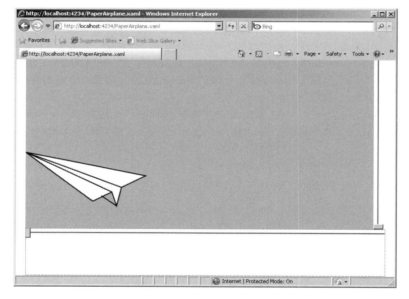

9. Experiment by moving the sliders. Because the vertical slider controls the angle of rotation, moving it up causes the airplane to spin in a clockwise direction. Because the horizontal slider is connected to the *Path*'s *Canvas.Left* property, moving the horizontal slider moves the plane along the x-axis, like this:

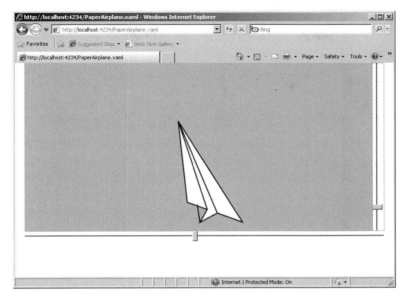

10. Integrate the new WPF content with some HTML. Add a new Page to the XAMLORama file by right-clicking the XAMLORama node in Solution Explorer and adding a new Web page. Name the page *PaperAirplane.aspx*. Add an <iframe> tag to the page in between the <div> tags that Visual Studio provides. Set the <iframe> *height* to **500** and the *width* to **750**. Finally, set the <iframe> *src* to **PaperAirplane.xaml**.

```
<%@ Page Language="C#" AutoEventWireup="true" CodeFile="PaperAirplane.aspx.cs"
    Inherits="PaperAirplane" %>

<!DOCTYPE html PUBLIC "...">

<html xmlns="http://www.w3.org/1999/xhtml">
<head runat="server">
    <title>Untitled Page</title>
</head>
<body>
    <form id="form1" runat="server">
    <div>

        <iframe height="500"
            width="750"
            src="paperairplane.xaml"></iframe> <br />
    </div>
    </form>
</body>
</html>
```

11. Run the page. The PaperAirplane.xaml content appears in a frame in the page. The XAML content has the same functionality in the frame as it did when it was run in the browser:

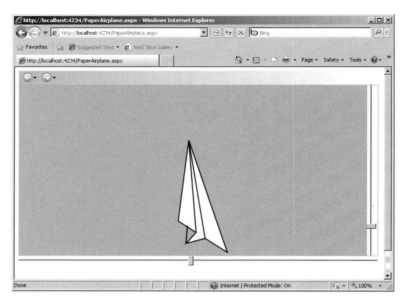

Because this is rendered from a typical ASP.NET page, you could include ASP.NET server controls along with the WPF content.

12. Add the XBAP content from the previous example to this site. First, create a new folder under the Project node in Solution Explorer. Name the folder *XBAPContent*. Right-click the new folder and click Add, Exiting Item. Navigate to the previous example's bin directory (on my computer, it is C:\aspnetstepbystep4\chapterprojects\Chapter21\ XBAPORama\XBAPORama\bin\Debug). Add XBAPORama.xbap, XBAPORama.exe, and XBAPORama.exe.manifest to this XAMLORama ASP.NET project.

13. Add a new link to the Default.aspx page. Set the *NavigationUrl* property to the XBAPORama.xbap file in the XBAPContent folder. Run the application and click the link that redirects to the XBAP content. You will see the XBAPORama.xbap content in the browser. The Web server downloads the XBAP content (you can see a little status bar in the browser, as shown in the following graphic). Try adding some items to the list box to ensure that it works.

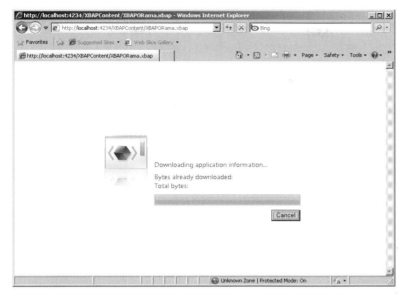

Here is the XBAP content running from in the ASP.NET site.

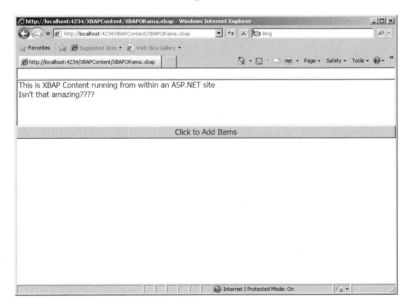

This example illustrates how it is possible to integrate HTML with XAML-based content. You also saw that it is possible to include XBAP content in an ASP.NET site. Although these techniques lie somewhat outside of the usual ASP.NET pipeline, XBAP-based and XAML-based WPF content is still useful in many cases. A full investigation of WPF is beyond the scope of this book. WPF and XAML offer entirely new ways to present content to the end user. Because it is such new technology, the different ways it can be exploited are only now being invented and discovered.

What About Silverlight?

As a Web developer, you have probably been unable to avoid hearing the buzz about Silverlight. Until now, the only effective way to produce dynamic Web content has been through Macromedia Flash. Flash is a plug-in for rendering dynamic content over the Web (that is, animations). However, with the advent of WPF and its dynamic content capabilities, now there is a markup technology that rivals Flash in raw capability if you can find a way to deliver it to the browser. Although other dynamic content technologies certainly have worked, they have had some serious shortcomings for developers. Silverlight changes this.

Silverlight is a platform-independent WPF rendering engine. Without Silverlight, the only way to render WPF content in a browser is to run Internet Explorer or the Firefox browser with the XAML plug-in. Silverlight is packaged as an ActiveX Control for the Microsoft environment. For example, the Apple Safari browser is supported by Silverlight. Visual Studio 2010 includes full support for Silverlight applications. You visit Silverlight in Chapter 24.

Chapter 21 Quick Reference

To	Do This
Add an XAML file to your site	Right-click the project node in the Visual Studio Solution Explorer. Click Add New Item. Select Text File from the available templates. Be sure to name the file with an .xaml extension.
Declare a Page within the XAML file	At the top of the file, add a beginning *<Page>* tag and an ending *</Page>* tag. Using WPF within XAML requires the standard WPF namespace "http://schemas.microsoft.com/winfx/2006/xaml/presentation" and the keywords namespace "http://schemas.microsoft.com/winfx/2006/xaml" (which is often mapped to "x").
Add a *Canvas* to the *Page*	Use the *<Canvas>* opening tag and the *</Canvas>* closing tag. Nest objects you'd like displayed in the canvas between the opening and closing tags.
Add content to the *Canvas*	Nest objects you'd like to appear on the canvas between the *<Canvas>* opening tag and the *</Canvas>* closing tag. Assign positions within the canvas using the *Canvas.Top* and *Canvas.Right* properties.
Add a *Grid* to a *Page*	Declare a *<Grid>* opening tag and a *</Grid>* closing tag on the page. Use the Grid's *RowDefinitions* and the Grid's *ColumnDefinitions* properties to define the rows and columns.
Add content to the *Grid*	Nest objects you'd like to appear on the canvas between the *<Grid>* opening tag and the *</Grid>* closing tag. Assign positions within the grid using the *Grid.Row* and *Grid.Column* properties.
Create an XAML-based browser application	Select File, New Project in Visual Studio. From the Windows application templates, choose WPF Browser Application. Visual Studio will create an XBAP application for you, starting with a simple page. Add WPF controls and handlers to the page. If you want to run the XBAP contront from an ASP.NET site, just make sure the XBAP,exe, and manifest files are available to the ASP.NET Web Project.

Chapter 22
The ASP.NET MVC Framework

After completing this chapter, you will be able to

- Understand the software patterns behind Model-View-Controller (MVC).

- Understand how ASP.NET implements the MVC pattern.

- Create a functional MVC-based Web site.

As many aspects of ASP.NET have stabilized and matured over the years, some interesting new features have appeared. Of the new features, ASP.NET application of the classic Model-View-Controller (MVC) software development pattern has probably received the most attention of all.

The ASP.NET MVC framework represents an alternative to the ASP.NET Web Forms environment. Web Forms offers a structured, controls-based framework for generating Web pages. Using Web Forms can make it feel like you're developing a desktop or rich client application even though the application UI is built upon HTML transmitted over a disconnected protocol. The basis of a Web Forms page is a collection of server-side controls—each one dedicated to emitting some HTML toward the output stream that eventually ends up at the client. Web Forms offers developers great leverage through its ability to handle view state and its event model. The Microsoft Visual Studio Designer has extensive support for Web Forms. You can develop entire pages and not have to deal with much, if any, raw HTML.

By contrast, the MVC framework works "closer to the metal." That is, as a developer, you're on the hook to work with some raw HTML. However, rather than leaving you in the wild to concoct a framework to manage the main application concerns (data and the UI), the MVC framework incorporates an industry-recognized software pattern for coordinating the two concerns. The MVC model draws strict distinctions between an application's data, its rendering, and its request processing. Each of these concerns is handled by a separate software component, and together they operate in concert with each other to handle HTTP requests.

This chapter covers how to use the ASP.NET MVC framework to create Web pages.

The Model-View-Controller (MVC) Architecture

Modern software is complex. As you've seen so far, even developing Web applications using a framework that hides as much detail as ASP.NET does can become fairly involved. Many times, the complexity comes down to a problem of managing multiple concerns. For example, a typical ASP.NET application involves dealing with a data source (often a database), making sure the HTML rendered by the application is in sync with the application state, and managing the incoming and outgoing message traffic.

By itself, ASP.NET has separate components for managing these concerns. ADO, LINQ, and the entity framework work well for talking to a database. ASP.NET data binding and the data-bound controls help to keep the client view of the data current. Together with the ASP.NET pipeline, the ASP.NET control architecture hides the details of managing incoming and outgoing message traffic. Although these features of ASP.NET make Web development very approachable, there are other approaches to Web development. MVC offers an alternative means for handling HTTP requests.

The MVC pattern is tailor-made for Web applications. MVC divides the three main concerns of a typical Web application (managing data, keeping the visual aspect of an application in sync with its internal state, managing message traffic) and handles each through three separate components: a model, a view, and a controller. The model handles data access and management and application state, the view handles the visual representation of the application state, and the controller manages message traffic.

The MVC model component is responsible for maintaining application state, as well as sometimes hosting code not tied directly to the view. Application state is often managed through a persistent database. In an MVC-based application, the model encapsulates low-level database access. For example, the model for a human resources application might include an *Employee* class that represents rows from a table of employee information in a human resources database. It might also include a collection of *Employee* classes in an in-memory structure.

MVC view components render the application's user interface. This might include some controls (for example, to display and edit data). These controls are usually tied to the model data. For instance, an application might display separate views for showing employee data and for editing employee data. The details view might simply render the details in read-only form, while the editing view might include controls for editing the employee information fields.

Finally, MVC controller components manage interactions with the end user. Although the view component is responsible for rendering, rendering remains distinct from user interaction. Within the context of ASP.NET, managing user interaction means managing Web traffic, updating the model (the application state), and ultimately managing the UI (that is, emitting the correct HTML).

Figure 22-1 illustrates the relationships between all three components. Notice that the controller talks to the model and the view. That is, the controller updates the model as necessary, and it also interacts with the view when rendering. The view talks with the model to make sure it's displaying the most current application state.

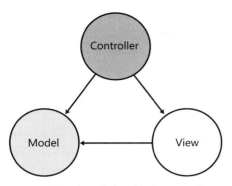

FIGURE 22-1 The relationship between the model, the view, and the controller.

Software Design Patterns

The MVC architecture is composed of several software *patterns*. Before exploring the ASP.NET version of MVC, it's worthwhile to make a short side trip to see how MVC uses software design patterns.

> *At the moment when a person is faced with an act of design, he does not have time to think about it from scratch.*
>
> —*Christopher Alexander, architect*

These words written by architect Christopher Alexander were intended originally to apply to building architecture. However, as any software developer can tell you, these words apply equally well to software development. It makes no sense to design something from scratch if there are some already established and reliable methodologies or components to help you get your software out the door sooner.

Seasoned software developers might remember the Patterns movement from the mid-1990s. It really began to take flight around the end of 1993. The idea of software design patterns is borrowed from work on building architecture patterns by Christopher Alexander. As a building architect, Christopher Alexander noticed many recurring themes in buildings that "worked." The results of his investigation into architectural patterns resulted in two renowned books on the subject: *A Pattern Language* and *The Timeless Way of Building*.

In 1995, four computer scientists collaborated to create a similar work within the software world—*Design Patterns: Elements of Reusable Object-Oriented Software*, written by Erich Gamma, Richard Helm, Ralph Johnson, and John Vlissides, and published by Addison Wesley. *Design Patterns* catalogues a number of software design patterns (approaches) for solving common software problems.

Software design patterns represent a formal way to document a solution to a design problem. Software patterns generally describe solutions from a broad perspective and usually avoid spelling out a specific implementation. A written pattern describes the intent behind a pattern, the problem to be solved, and some specific applications of the pattern. Patterns come with descriptive names such as the Command pattern. The idea behind the Command pattern is to encapsulate a request as an object. This lets you parameterize clients with different requests, queue requests, and support operations that might be undone. Microsoft Message Queuing (MSMQ) is a great real-world example of the Command pattern.

One of the most well known software architectures is the Model-View-Controller architecture (MVC, for short). The MVC architecture combines several patterns to form a foundation suitable for creating applications. In general, the MVC pattern incorporates the Composite, Observer, and Strategy patterns. The Composite pattern partitions software concerns (in this case, the database, user interface rendering, and interaction concerns). The Observer pattern describes a publish/subscribe relationship between software components. Finally, the Strategy pattern is used for selecting program behavior at run time.

ASP.NET and MVC

MVC came to ASP.NET fairly recently. You can think of ASP.NET as a very loosely coupled set of classes working together to handle requests. ASP.NET includes a pipeline that acts as a substrate with different kinds of handlers hooked on to it. The pipeline is configured so that requests for various file types go to their correct handlers.

As useful as ASP.NET is for handling Web requests, ASP.NET is not quite a true framework. ASP.NET Web Forms mingles the concerns of the Web developer. MVC distinguishes itself as a framework by drawing a clear separation between the concerns of Web developers. Remember, models handle application state, views handle rendering, and controllers handle interactions with the end user.

The ASP.NET MVC framework coexists with the other parts of ASP.NET. The framework operates independently of the standard .aspx and .ascx files, master pages, and Global.asax files. MVC also works with the ASP.NET Forms Authentication and the standard membership and roles providers. MVC has complete access to the existing data cache and output cache, as well as the existing data providers. Developers can mix and match any of these other features of ASP.NET with the MVC framework.

To support MVC's coexistence with ASP.NET, MVC looks to flexibility as a primary design goal. MVC is intended to be customizable all around. For example, the code generated by

Visual Studio for an MVC-based application includes a standard routing table for helping the application figure out how to handle requests. Although the out-of-the-box routing mechanism works fairly well most of the time, it might not be the best for all situations. Changing the routing policy is relatively straightforward in an MVC application.

By moving all of the MVC routing architecture into the controller, you can easily swap routing policies. This leads to some distinct advantages over typical ASP.NET development. For example, the MVC URL mapping keeps strange URLs hidden from the end user. URL mappings are pushed into the framework, so you can spare your users from seeing messy URL names. Strange URLs, such as */contacts/edit/3256*, can be mapped cleanly and internally. At first glance, this might seem like a small feature. However, it does help clean up Web UIs when long, ugly URLs can be stashed away, making room for some very clever routing scenarios. For example, applications using the MVC framework do not need to include extensions, which makes it easy for MVC to support naming schemes for Search Engine Optimization (SEO) and Representational State Transfer (REST) for services.

The MVC framework still uses existing ASP.NET file types, such as .aspx files, .ascx files, and .master files. MVC uses these markup files as *view templates*. They support the same inline coding syntax (that is, <%= %> snippets). However, rather than each interaction posting back to the server directly, MVC routes interactions to a *Controller* class. This makes MVC applications much easier to test in the general sense, and to use specifically with test-driven design (TDD) techniques if you prefer. Classic ASP.NET Web Forms by their very nature cannot directly support automated unit testing.

Finally, all the other features of ASP.NET remain intact while using MVC: The cache is still there, output caching is available, session state still works, the provider architecture is still there, and configuration works the same.

ASP.NET MVC vs. Web Forms

The ASP.NET MVC framework is fundamentally different from ASP.NET Web Forms. MVC makes a very clear distinction between data sources, program interaction with the data, and the presentation of data. MVC enforces a separation of concerns, whereas that sort of separation is something you'd have to build into an ASP.NET Web Forms application explicitly.

MVC eschews some of the other features of standard Web Forms. For example, ASP.NET MVC does not support view state directly (that feature really stems from server-side controls). As a result, you won't see any hidden fields showing up in pages rendered by the MVC framework.

One of the most prominent places you'll notice that MVC differs from Web Forms is in the area of handling postback events. In MVC, events are routed through a routing table rather than through the singular server-side controls. With Web Forms, however, routing typically occurs through specific event handlers placed on a page.

The MVC framework distinguishes between data, presentation, and program logic, allowing for more isolation between components. This leads to easier testing and debugging. In fact, the ASP.NET MVC framework supports test-driven development very well. This becomes a huge advantage for projects built and supported by large teams.

Because MVC does not rely on certain features, such as view state and server-based controls, more onus is placed on the developer to produce correct HTML. Although this means more responsibility for the developer, it also gives developers much more direct control over how the HTML is rendered.

Finally, ASP.NET Web Forms and server-side controls handle specific events, making it difficult to follow the execution path of a Web Forms–based application. MVC differs significantly because all requests pass through a single point in the application—the routing table. With use of a routing table, developers can control request routing at a single point rather than at ad-hoc points on the page (that is, the event handlers).

MVC and Testing

The MVC framework's separation of functionality into specific areas of responsibility makes testing MVC applications much easier than is testing of Web Forms applications. Although the Web Forms model clearly improved the Web programming paradigm for Microsoft developers by separating the concerns of presentation (user interface) and program logic, the Web Forms model still mixes several other concerns. Data access is usually mixed right in with the rest of the program code. For example, if you code your own authentication scheme, you might perform a user lookup directly when a postback occurs because the user clicked the login button. The lookup code is usually right there in the code-beside file. As another example, requests are routed directly back to the .aspx file that's in play. Without MVC, there's no way to perform any alternate routing.

The MVC framework separates these other concerns, making for a much more modular architecture that accommodates unit testing. Testing typical ASP.NET programs usually means clicking through all the controls and UI elements on a page to make sure they work. Then, when something doesn't work, you need to track it down and fix it. The MVC framework supports test-driven development where you define the requirements of code first, and even write test cases prior to writing the code. At that point, you can run user interactions in the MVC framework individually without running the entire application. With this capability, you can unit test individual parts of the application using any of the currently available testing frameworks, such as MS Test and NUnit.

How MVC Plays with ASP.NET

When building a new Web site, it's usually best to decide up front whether you want to use MVC. Although ASP.NET standard parts work independently of the MVC framework, having Visual Studio create the Web application for you can save some headaches. Visual Studio wires up a few components to make MVC work in your application. For example, the routing mechanism must be hooked in so that HTTP requests can be handled by the correct controller method. Visual Studio inserts the correct code into the *Application_Start* event in the application's Global.asax file. Here's an example:

```
protected void Application_Start()
{
  RegisterRoutes(RouteTable.Routes);
}
public static void RegisterRoutes(RouteCollection routes)
{
  routes.IgnoreRoute("{resource}.axd/{*pathInfo}");
  routes.MapRoute(
    "Default",                                   // Route name
    "{controller}/{action}/{id}",                // URL with parameters
    new { controller = "Home", action = "Index", id = "" }  // Parameter defaults
  );

}
```

The MVC framework includes a class named *RouteTable* that holds a number of entries that tell the MVC framework how requests should be handled. Visual Studio generates a single entry for the *RouteTable* that maps the URL to a specific method name in a specific controller, along with parameters necessary to handle the request. The Visual Studio–generated route map defaults to a method in the home controller named *Index* with an empty parameter. Usually, the *Index* method displays some default information for the site and represents a starting point for the user. You are free to add as many entries to the *RouteTable* as you need to support your own routing scenarios.

In addition to adding the *RouteTable* setup to the Global.asax file, the Visual Studio–generated code throws in a slightly modified Default.aspx file. This file is necessary—in fact, Visual Studio throws in a comment warning you never to delete it. A quick look at the Default.aspx *Page_Load* handler reveals that it hooks up the MVC *HttpHandler* to intercept incoming MVC-based requests.

Following the Request Path

With all the MVC framework pieces in place, the application is ready to start processing requests. Requests come to the Web site in a typical fashion. For the first request, ASP.NET fires up an instance of the application (represented by Global.asax). After that, the first access to Default.aspx hooks up the MVC handler so that requests are routed correctly. Figure 22-2 illustrates the request path as it travels through the system.

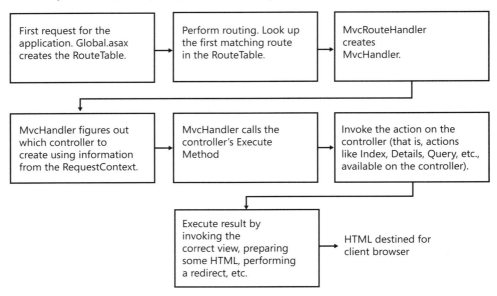

| First request for the application. Global.asax creates the RouteTable. | → | Perform routing. Look up the first matching route in the RouteTable. | → | MvcRouteHandler creates MvcHandler. |

| MvcHandler figures out which controller to create using information from the RequestContext. | → | MvcHandler calls the controller's Execute Method | → | Invoke the action on the controller (that is, actions like Index, Details, Query, etc., available on the controller). |

| Execute result by invoking the correct view, preparing some HTML, performing a redirect, etc. | → | HTML destined for client browser |

FIGURE 22-2 The path of a request through the MVC framework.

The following procedure shows how you can create an MVC-based site to see how it all works.

Creating an MVC site

1. Start Visual Studio. Select New Project on the File menu. Select ASP.NET MVC Site from the available templates, as shown in the following graphic, and name the site *MVCORama*. Visual Studio will ask you whether you want to create some unit tests for the application; click OK. Visual Studio will create the site for you.

2. When it finishes, Visual Studio will have created a full ASP.NET project for you to build around the MVC framework. Look in Solution Explorer and notice the MVC folders: Controllers, Models, and Views.

3. Run the application to see how it looks.

4. To see how MVC integrates with the rest of ASP.NET, open the master page under the Views\Shared folder in the Designer. The master page file name is Site.master. You can see some typical HTML, as well as some HTML helpers doing some work as inline code. (You look at the HTML helpers a bit later in the chapter.) For example, inside the master page, you can also see that the application uses something called the *LogOnUserControl*. For now, change the heading text of the page from My MVC Application to **Dot Net References**.

5. You can change the styles and colors of the master page, too. The main CSS file is in the Content folder and is named Site.css. To change the body style, right-click inside the body style description in the code, and click Build Style on the shortcut menu. You can change the background color, as well as any other style elements, by using the Style Builder dialog box. After changing some of the elements, run the Web site by pressing Ctrl+F5 from within Visual Studio. You should be able to see that the style elements have changed for the pages.

6. To start you off, Visual Studio creates an *AccountController* and a *HomeController* along with the files to support the accompanying views. The Home controller/ view includes the text Welcome To ASP.NET MVC. To change this text, open the HomeController.cs file under the Controllers\Home folder. The *Index* method prints out the greeting—change the *Index* method to emit **Welcome to the Dot Net References Site**. Then, open the Index.aspx file under the Views\Home folder. Change the text from the following:

```
To learn more about ASP.NET MVC visit
<a href="http://asp.net/mvc"
title="ASP.NET MVC Website">http://asp.net/mvc</a>
```

to this:

```
To learn more about Dot Net, visit
<a href="http://msdn.microsoft.com/en-us/netframework/default.aspx"
title="Dot Net Framework Development Center"> Dot Net Information </a>
```

7. When you run the site, you'll see that the new text appears, and the link should take you to the Microsoft main .NET Framework Development Center:

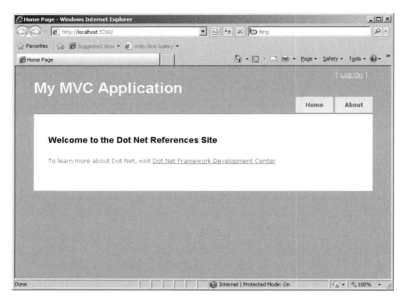

8. Next, create the data model for the application. Borrow the ASPNETStepByStep4.mdf file from the solution for Chapter 22 on the accompanying CD. This is a Microsoft SQL Server database file containing two tables. The first table includes some .NET book references. The second table includes some HTTP links to .NET developer Web sites. You can use these tables as the basis for the models for the MVC-based application. To put the ASPNETStepByStep4.mdf file in your App_Data directory, right-click App_Data in Solution Explorer and click Add Existing Item. Locate the database file on the accompanying CD and bring it into the project.

9. Once the database is available to your application, create some helper classes to access the data. The easiest way to do this is to create some LINQ to SQL wrapper classes. In Solution Explorer, right-click the Models folder. Click Add New Item on the shortcut menu. Select Data from the left-hand side of the Add New Item dialog box. Select LINQ To SQL in the panel on the right. Name the file *DotNetReferences.dbml*. This will create a Database Markup Language (DBML) source file that Visual Studio will add to the project. Next, drag the *DotNetReferences* table from the Server Explorer to the Designer surface. Visual Studio will create a wrapper class named *DotNetReference* that represents a single row from the table. You'll use this class shortly.

10. The *DotNetReference* class is useful but operates only in the context of a live database. When Visual Studio created the *DotNetReference* class, it also created a class named *DotNetReferencesDataContext* that represents the *DotNetReferences* table. Rather than accessing the database directly, you can use LINQ and a database

manager class to work with the data easily. In Solution Explorer, right-click the Model folder, and add a new class. Name this class *DotNetReferencesManager*. The *DotNetReferencesManager* class will wrap the *DotNetReferencesDataContext*, so have the *DotNetReferencesManager* create an instance of the *DotNetReferencesDataContext* class. Then, add a method named *GetAllReferences* to the *DotNetReferencesDataContext* class. It should return *IQueryable<DotNetReference>*. You can use the *DotNetReferencesDataContext* to fetch all the rows like so:

```csharp
using System;
using System.Collections.Generic;
using System.Linq;
using System.Web;
namespace MVCORama.Models
{
  public class DotNetReferencesManager
  {
    DotNetReferencesDataContext dataContext =
      new DotNetReferencesDataContext();

    public IQueryable<DotNetReference> GetAllReferences()
    {
      return dataContext.DotNetReferences;
    }
  }
}
```

11. Create a view for the *DotNetReferences* model. Right-click the View folder. Create a new View folder and name it *DotNetReferences* by right-clicking the project's Views folder and clicking New Folder. Right-click the new folder and click Add and then View on the shortcut menu. Visual Studio will then display the Add View dialog box for configuring the view. Visual Studio will name the view Index. Make it strongly typed based on the *DotNetReferences* class (it will be available in the dialog box). Leave the master as is. Finally, Visual Studio will generate the following view code for you by using reflection against the *DotNetReferences* model:

```
<%@ Page Title=""
  Language="C#"
  MasterPageFile="~/Views/Shared/Site.Master"
 Inherits="System.Web.Mvc.ViewPage<IEnumerable<MVCORama.DotNetReference>>" %>

<asp:Content ID="Content1" ContentPlaceHolderID="TitleContent" runat="server">
  Index
</asp:Content>
<asp:Content ID="Content2" ContentPlaceHolderID="MainContent" runat="server">
    <h2>Index</h2>
    <table>
        <tr>
            <th></th>
            <th>ID</th>
            <th>Title</th>
```

```
            <th>AuthorLastName</th>
            <th>AuthorFirstName</th>
            <th>Topic</th>
            <th>Publisher</th>
        </tr>
    <% foreach (var item in Model) { %>
        <tr>
            <td>
                <%= Html.ActionLink("Edit", "Edit", new { id=item.ID }) %> |
                <%= Html.ActionLink("Details", "Details", new { id=item.ID })%>
            </td>
            <td>
                <%= Html.Encode(item.ID) %>
            </td>
            <td>
                <%= Html.Encode(item.Title) %>
            </td>
            <td>
                <%= Html.Encode(item.AuthorLastName) %>
            </td>
            <td>
                <%= Html.Encode(item.AuthorFirstName) %>
            </td>
            <td>
                <%= Html.Encode(item.Topic) %>
            </td>
            <td>
                <%= Html.Encode(item.Publisher) %>
            </td>
        </tr>
    <% } %>
    </table>
    <p>
        <%= Html.ActionLink("Create New", "Create") %>
    </p>
</asp:Content>
```

12. Notice that the Index.aspx file is based on typical ASP.NET syntax. The *Page* directive appears at the top of the file followed by the ASP.NET *Content* control (so as to coordinate content placement with the master page). The view is tied to a model based on the *DotNetReferences* class. If you examine the code-beside class, you can see the *Index* iterates through each *Item* in the model and displays it. In this case, each *Item* represents a row in the *DotNetReferences* class. To show the view correctly, you just need to add a controller to the model and view for the edit scenario.

13. Create a controller to handle requests pertaining to the *DotNetReferences* model. Right-click the Controllers folder and select Add, Controller. When the Add Controller dialog box appears, name your new controller *DotNetReferencesController*. Visual Studio will create a class based on the MVC framework *Controller* class. Add an instance of the *DotNetReferencesManager* to the controller. Look for the method named *Index* that returns an *ActionResult*. Instantiate a *var* in the *Index* method and use the

DotNetReferencesManager.GetAllReferences method to populate it. The *var* type is a typeless collection useful for managing a collection of things—for when you don't know the type of objects in the collection ahead of time. The code you should add is in bold type in the following example:

```
using System;
using System.Collections.Generic;
using System.Linq;
using System.Web;
using System.Web.Mvc;
using System.Web.Mvc.Ajax;
using MVCORama.Models;

namespace MVCORama.Controllers
{
  public class DotNetReferencesController : Controller
  {
    DotNetReferencesManager dotNetReferencesManager =
      new DotNetReferencesManager();

    public ActionResult Index()
    {
      var dotNetReferences =
        dotNetReferencesManager.GetAllReferences().ToList();
          return View("Index", dotNetReferences);
    }
  }
}
```

14. When you navigate to the *DotNetReferences* page, the MVC framework is set up to show the DotNetReferences view. But to do this, you will need to add a tab to the master page to navigate to the *DotNetReferences* page as shown:

```
<%@ Master Language="C#" Inherits="System.Web.Mvc.ViewMasterPage" %>
<!DOCTYPE html PUBLIC "-//W3C//DTD XHTML 1.0 Strict//EN"
"http://www.w3.org/TR/xhtml1/DTD/xhtml1-strict.dtd">
<html xmlns="http://www.w3.org/1999/xhtml">
<head runat="server">
    <title><asp:ContentPlaceHolder ID="TitleContent" runat="server" /></title>
    <link href="../../Content/Site.css" rel="stylesheet" type="text/css" />
</head>
<body>
    <div class="page">
        <div id="header">
            <div id="title">
                <h1>My MVC Application</h1>
            </div>
            <div id="logindisplay">
                <% Html.RenderPartial("LogOnUserControl"); %>
            </div>
</body>
```

```
        <div id="menucontainer">
            <ul id="menu">
                <li><%= Html.ActionLink("Home", "Index", "Home")%></li>
                <li><%= Html.ActionLink("DotNetReferences", "Index",
                    "DotNetReferences")%></li>
                <li><%= Html.ActionLink("About", "About", "Home")%></li>
            </ul>
        </div>
    </div>

    <div id="main">
        <asp:ContentPlaceHolder ID="MainContent" runat="server" />
        <div id="footer">
        </div>
    </div>
    </div>
</body>
</html>
```

15. Go ahead and compile the application, and then press Ctrl+F5 to execute it. Once the default page is displayed, navigate to the *DotNetReferences* page using the new tab. You should see the application display the contents of the DotNetReferences database:

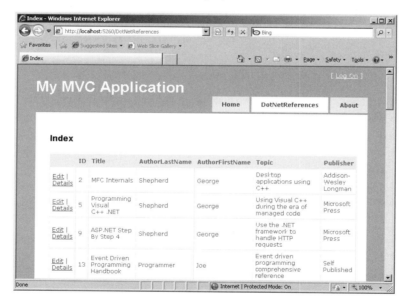

In the next procedure, you create a more fully featured MVC-based section in the application that is more interactive. This example illustrates how to display item details as well as edit, delete, and create entries.

Implementing scenarios for adding, deleting, and updating scenarios

1. Open the MVCORama application that you created in the preceding example. In this procedure, you use the other table from the database—the *DotNetLinks* table. The previous example listed only the contents of the model.

2. Create a model for the *DotNetLinks* table. As in the last exercise, add a LINQ to SQL class for the *DotNetLinks* table. Right-click the Models folder, and click Add New Item. In the Visual Studio Add New Item dialog box, click the Data tab and select LINQ To SQL. Name the LINQ to SQL class *DotNetLinks*. Drag the *DotNetLinks* table from Server Explorer onto the design surface of the LINQ to SQL class. Visual Studio will create a wrapper class named *DotNetLink*.

3. As with the *DotNetReferences*, create a data manager for the *DotNetLinks* table. Right-click the Models folder, and click Add New Item. Select Class from the palette and name the class *DotNetLinksManager*. Visual Studio will create the class for you.

4. Add an instance of the *DotNetLinksDataContext* to the *DotNetLinksManager* class. Add methods to get all the rows from the table, to find a *DotNetLink* in the *DotNetLinksDataContext*, to add a *DotNetLink* to the *DotNetLinksDataContext*, and to delete a *DotNetLink* from the *DotNetLinksDataContext*. Finally, add a method to commit the changes to the underlying table. You exercise these methods through the controller:

```
public class DotNetLinksManager
{
  DotNetLinksDataContext dataContext =
    new DotNetLinksDataContext();

  public IQueryable<DotNetLink> GetAllLinks()
  {
    return dataContext.DotNetLinks;
  }

  public DotNetLink Find(int id)
  {
    DotNetLink dotNetLink;

    dotNetLink =
      dataContext.DotNetLinks.SingleOrDefault(l => l.ID == id);

    return dotNetLink;
  }

  public void Add(DotNetLink dotNetLink)
  {
    dataContext.DotNetLinks.InsertOnSubmit(dotNetLink);
  }
```

```
public void Delete(DotNetLink dotNetLink)
{
  dataContext.DotNetLinks.DeleteOnSubmit(dotNetLink);
}

public void Save()
{
  dataContext.SubmitChanges();
}
}
```

5. Add a *DotNetLinks* controller to the Controllers folder. Right-click the Controllers folder, and click Add, Controller. Visual Studio will create the controller class for you. Add an instance of the *DotNetLinksManager* class as a member variable of the controller and instantiate it.

```
public class DotNetLinksController : Controller
{
  DotNetLinksManager dotNetLinksManager =
    new DotNetLinksManager();

  // more code
}
```

6. Add a new folder to the Views folder and name it *DotNetLinks*. Add a new view to that folder named Index.aspx by right-clicking the Views\DotNetLinks folder and clicking Add, View. Make it strongly typed to the *DotNetLink* class, and have it display the links as a list.

7. Now go back to the *DotNetLinksController* and have the *Index* action method create a new index view based on a list of all the available links (call the *DotNetLinksManager.GetAllLinks* method to do this). Note that this method catches all exceptions so that it runs cleanly. Another strategy is to let the exception propagate through the pipeline:

```
public ActionResult Index()
{
  try {
    var dotNetLinks =
      dotNetLinksManager.GetAllLinks().ToList();
    return View("Index", dotNetLinks);
  }
  catch (Exception ex) {
    System.Diagnostics.Debug.WriteLine(ex.Message);
    return View();
  }
}
```

8. Open the Index.aspx file and tailor the presentation to show the URLs as links that can be navigated. Changing this code causes the page to display the URL as a functional link. Locate the code that displays the URL column and change it from the following:

```
<td>
    <%= Html.Encode(item.URL) %>
</td>
```

to this:

```
<td>
    <a href="<%= item.URL %>" > <%= Html.Encode(item.DisplayName) %> </a>
</td>
```

9. Open the master page and add a new tab to the menu in the Site.Master file to show the *DotNetLinks* information:

```
<ul id="menu">
  <li><%= Html.ActionLink("Home", "Index", "Home")%></li>
  <li><%= Html.ActionLink("DotNetReferences",
  "Index", "DotNetReferences")%></li>
  <li><%= Html.ActionLink("Dot Net Links", "Index", "DotNetLinks")%></li>  <li><%=
Html.ActionLink("About", "About", "Home")%></li>
</ul>
```

10. Run the program and navigate to the DotNetLinks page. You should now see the links displayed as typical, functional HTTP links, as shown in the following graphic:

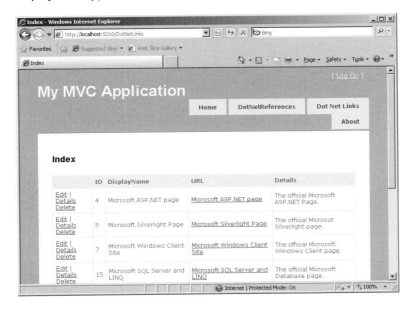

11. Now handle the details scenario—where the user can see some more detailed information about the link. Add the Details view by right-clicking the DotNetLinks\Views folder and clicking Add, View. Use the Add View dialog box to configure a strongly typed view based on the *DotNetLink* class, and select Details from the View Content combo box. Visual Studio will create a view based on the *DotNetLink* class. Make sure the name of the view file is Details.aspx.

12. Now you need to tell MVC how to respond to requests for the details of a particular link. Add a public method to the *DotNetLinksController* class to return a view to the details of a single link. Call the *DotNetLinksManager.Find* method using the ID passed in to the method. The *ID* parameter is actually passed as a URL parameter and packaged into a managed type by the MVC framework. The index view generated by Visual Studio includes a Details navigation link for items displayed in the model. After finding the specific link in the *DotNetLinksManager,* call the controller's *View* method, passing in the string "Details" as the first parameter and the *DotNetLink* as the second parameter:

```
// Get the details for a single link and show them:
public ActionResult Details(int id)
{
  try {
    DotNetLink dotNetLink = dotNetLinksManager.Find(id);
    if (dotNetLink != null)
    {
      return View("Details", dotNetLink);
    } else {
        return View();
    }
  }
  catch(Exception ex)
  {
    System.Diagnostics.Debug.WriteLine(ex.Message);
    return View();
  }
}
```

13. Use the new tab to navigate to the *DotNetLinks* index page, and select one of the links
to show the details. You should see the following in the browser:

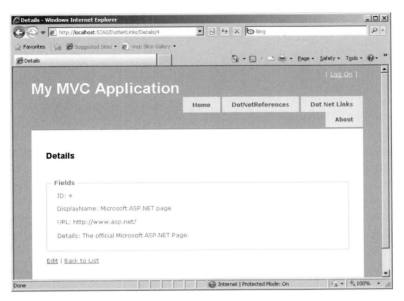

14. Now handle adding new entries to the database. Start by adding a new strongly typed
view to the Views\DotNetLinks folder. Right-click the Views\DotNetLinks folder and
click Add, View. Use the resulting dialog box to configure a strongly typed view based
on the *DotNetLink* class. Then, select Create from the View Content combo box. Name
the view **Create**.

15. Now add some methods to the controller to support adding entries. First, write a method named *Create*. It should simply display the default view. The following code displays
the default Create view with text boxes awaiting input for the *DotNetLink* properties:

```
public ActionResult Create()
{
  return View();
}
```

16. Add a static helper method named *DotNetLinkFromFormsCollection* that takes a single *FormCollection* as a parameter and have it return a *DotNetLink*. The *FormCollection* class is a name/value collection representing the contents of a postback. Use it to populate the *DotNetLink*:

```
private static DotNetLink DotNetLinkFromFormsCollection(FormCollection collection)
{
  DotNetLink dotNetLink = new DotNetLink();
  dotNetLink.DisplayName = collection["DisplayName"];
  dotNetLink.URL = collection["URL"];
  return dotNetLink;
}
```

17. Add a method named *Create* that takes a *FormCollection* as the first parameter and returns an *ActionResult*. Apply the *AcceptVerbs* attribute using the *HttpVerbs. Post* enumeration. This helps the MVC framework to process the postback. The MVC framework will populate the *FormCollection* using the results of the postback. Use the *DotNetLinkFromFormsCollection* helper method to populate an instance of the *DotNetLink* class. Use the *DotNetLinksManager.Add* method to add the *DotNetLink* to the collection, and then call the *DotNetLinksManager.Save* method to commit the change to the underlying database. Note that this is not production code, and doesn't validate user input. A production application probably should check input to avoid bad input that might cause errors or even security attacks:

```
// Create scenario
[AcceptVerbs(HttpVerbs.Post)]
public ActionResult Create(FormCollection collection)
{
  try {
    DotNetLink dotNetLink =
      DotNetLinkFromFormsCollection(collection);    if (dotNetLinksManager.
Find(dotNetLink.ID) == null)

    {

      dotNetLinksManager.Add(dotNetLink);

      dotNetLinksManager.Save();

    }
    return RedirectToAction("Index");
  }
  catch(Exception ex) {
    System.Diagnostics.Debug.WriteLine(ex.Message);
    return View();
  }
}
```

18. Run the application and try adding a new link to the collection of *DotNetLinks*. For example, try clicking the Create New link. When the Create page opens, type in a display name such as **MSDN**. Then, type **http://msdn.microsoft.com** in the URL field and some comments in the information field.

19. Now create a view to handle the edit scenario. Right-click the Views\DotNetLinks folder and add a new strongly typed view based on the *DotNetLink* class. Select Edit in the View Content combo box. Visual Studio will generate a new view useful for editing existing entries.

20. Add a method to the controller for handling editing. It should take a single integer parameter representing the ID of the item to edit. The MVC framework will call this method in the controller when you navigate to the Edit page (you can do this by go-ing to the DotNetLinks home page and clicking the Edit link for one of the entries). Use the *DotNetLinksManager.Find* method to get the DotNetLink specified by the ID. Then, call the controller *View* method, passing the string "Edit" (to invoke the Edit view) and a reference to the DotNetLink retrieved from the DotNetLinksManager:

```
// handle editing...
public ActionResult Edit(int id)
{
  try {
    DotNetLink dotNetLink =
      dotNetLinksManager.Find(id);
    if (dotNetLink != null)
    {
      return View("Edit", dotNetLink);
    }
    return View();
  }
  catch (Exception ex) {
    System.Diagnostics.Debug.WriteLine(ex.Message);
    return View();
  }
}
```

21. Add a method to the controller for handling the postback. Name the method *Edit* and have it take two parameters: an integer specifying the ID of the link being ed-ited, and a *FormCollection*. Have the *Edit* method return an *ActionResult* and use the *AcceptVerbs* attribute to specify this method is a response to a postback. Use the *DotNetLinksManager.Find* method to get the DotNetLink specified by the *ID*. Use the controller's base class method named *UpdateModel* to populate the *DotNetLink* from the collection (*UpdateModel* is part of the framework and automatically updates the

model). Then, call the *DotNetLinkManager.Save* method to save the information to the database:

```
[AcceptVerbs(HttpVerbs.Post)]
public ActionResult Edit(int id, FormCollection collection)
{
  try {

    DotNetLink dotNetLink = dotNetLinksManager.Find(id);
    UpdateModel(dotNetLink);
    dotNetLinksManager.Save();
    return RedirectToAction("Index");
  }
  catch (Exception ex) {
    System.Diagnostics.Debug.WriteLine(ex.Message);
    return View();
  }
}
```

22. Finally, handle the delete scenario. Add a strongly typed view based on the *DotNetLinks* class to the Views\DotNetLinks folder and name it **Delete**. Make it empty by selecting Empty in the View Content combo box. This will be the confirmation page. Add some text to the content area that asks the user to confirm that the record should be deleted. Add an HTML form to the page by calling *Html.BeginForm*. Include a Submit button in the form. Clicking this button will cause a postback:

```
<%@ Page Title="" Language="C#" MasterPageFile="~/Views/Shared/Site.Master"
Inherits="System.Web.Mvc.ViewPage<MVCORama.Models.DotNetLink>" %>

<asp:Content ID="Content1" ContentPlaceHolderID="TitleContent" runat="server">
  Delete
</asp:Content>

<asp:Content ID="Content2" ContentPlaceHolderID="MainContent" runat="server">

    <h2>
        Confirm Delete
    </h2>
    <div>
        <p>Do you want to delete this link?:
        <i> <%=Html.Encode(Model.DisplayName) %>? </i> </p>
    </div>
    <% using (Html.BeginForm()) { %>
        <input name="confirmButton" type="submit" value="Delete" />
    <% } %>

</asp:Content>
```

23. Open the Index.aspx page (the index view for the DotNetLinks). Locate the section of code that iterates through the items and include a *Delete* action (put it along with the existing links to get the item's details and to edit the item):

```
<% foreach (var item in Model) { %>

  <tr>
    <td>
      <%= Html.ActionLink("Edit", "Edit", new { id=item.ID }) %> |
      <%= Html.ActionLink("Details", "Details", new { id=item.ID })%> |
      <%= Html.ActionLink("Delete", "Delete", new { id=item.ID})%>
    </td>
    <td>
      <%= Html.Encode(item.DisplayName) %>
    </td>
    <td>
      <a href="<%= item.URL %>" > <%= Html.Encode(item.DisplayName) %> </a>
    </td>
  </tr>
<% } %>
```

24. Now add some methods to the controller for deleting a specific DotNetLink record. First, add a single method named *Delete* that takes a single parameter of type integer. The method should return an *ActionResult*. This is the method for responding to the delete GET request. Use the *DotNetLinksManager.Find* method to get a reference to the DotNetLink represented by the ID. Then, call the controller's *View* method, passing in the string "Delete" and the reference to the DotNetLink. This will show the delete confirmation page:

```
// Methods for deleting
public ActionResult Delete(int id)
{
  try {
    DotNetLink dotNetLink =
      dotNetLinksManager.Find(id);

    if (dotNetLink != null)
    {
      return View("Delete", dotNetLink);
    }
    else
    {
      return View();
    }
  }
  catch (Exception ex) {
    System.Diagnostics.Debug.WriteLine(ex.Message);
    return View();
  }
}
```

25. Finally, add a method named *Delete* to the controller that takes an integer and a *FormCollection*. Adorn the method using the *AcceptVerbs* attribute and pass in the

HttpVerbs.Post enumeration so that this method is called during postbacks. This method will be called when users click the delete confirmation button. Use the *DotNetLinksManager.Find* method to locate the specific DotNetLink based on the ID passed in to the controller. Then, call the *DotNetLinksManager.Delete* and the *DotNetLinksManager.Save* methods to remove the record from the database. Use the controller's *RedirectToAction* method to show the index view:

```
[AcceptVerbs(HttpVerbs.Post)]
public ActionResult Delete(int id,
  FormCollection formsCollection)
{
  try {
    DotNetLink dotNetLink =
      dotNetLinksManager.Find(id);

    if (dotNetLink != null)
    {
      dotNetLinksManager.Delete(dotNetLink);
      dotNetLinksManager.Save();
      return RedirectToAction("Index");
    }
    else
    {
      return View();
    }
  }
  catch (Exception ex) {
    System.Diagnostics.Debug.WriteLine(ex.Message);
    return View();
  }
}
```

26. Now run the program and try deleting one of the links.

Chapter 22 Quick Reference

To	Do This
Create a new MVC Web site	Select the MVC template when creating a new Web application project.
Create wrapper classes for a table in a database to support the model	Right-click the Model folder and click Add, New Item. Select LINQ To SQL from the Data templates. Drag the database table for which you want classes from the Server Explorer onto the design surface.
Add a view to the project	Create a new folder under the Views folder to hold views of a specific type. Right-click the specific folder. Click Add, View. Select a strongly typed view if you'd like Visual Studio to reflect the table and produce a typed view. Select the Create, Update, Details, or List view for standard scenarios. Select Empty view for other scenarios.
Add a controller to the project	Right-click the Controllers folder and click Add, Controller.
Add HTML tags to a view	In the view's .aspx file, type HTML tags directly. Alternatively, you can use the HTML helpers.

Chapter 23
AJAX

After completing this chapter, you will be able to

- Understand the problem AJAX solves.

- Understand ASP.NET support for AJAX.

- Write AJAX-enabled Web sites.

- Take advantage of AJAX as necessary to improve the user's experience.

This chapter covers AJAX, possibly the most interesting feature added to ASP.NET recently. AJAX stands for Asynchronous JavaScript and XML, and it promises to produce an entirely new look and feel for Web sites throughout the world.

Rich Internet Applications

Software evolution always seems to happen in this typical fashion: Once a technology is grounded firmly (meaning the connections between the parts work and the architecture is fundamentally sound), upgrading the end user's experience becomes a much higher priority. Application technology is in this stage, and the general term for this kind of application is a Rich Internet Application (RIA). AJAX is one means of producing Rich Internet Applications. (Microsoft Silverlight is another popular means of creating RIAs.)

The primary reason for the existence of AJAX is to improve the standard HTTP GET/POST idiom with which Web users are so familiar. That is, the standard Web protocol in which entire forms and pages are sent between the client and the server is getting a whole new addition.

Although standard HTTP is functional and well understood by Web developers, it does have certain drawbacks—the primary one is that the user is forced to wait for relatively long periods while pages refresh. This has been a common problem in all event-driven interfaces. (The Windows operating system is one of the best examples.) AJAX introduces technology that shields end users from having to wait for a whole page to post.

Think back to the way HTTP typically works. When you make a request (using GET or POST, for example), the Web browser sends the request to the server, but you can do nothing until the request finishes. That is, you make the request and wait—watching the little progress indicator in the browser. When the request returns to the browser, you can begin using the application again. The application is basically useless until the request returns. In some cases, the browser's window even goes completely blank. Web browsers have to wait for Web sites to finish an HTTP request in much the same way that Windows-based programs have to wait for message handlers to complete their processing. (Actually, if the client browser uses a multithreaded user interface such as Windows Internet Explorer, users can usually cancel the request—but that's all they can really do.) You can easily demonstrate this problem by introducing a call to *System.Threading.Thread.Sleep* inside the *Page_Load* method of an ASPX page. By putting the thread to sleep, you force the end user to wait for the request to finish.

The AJAX solution to this problem is to introduce some way to handle the request asynchronously. What if there were a way to introduce asynchronous background processing into a Web site so that the browser would appear much more responsive to the user? What if (for certain applications) making an HTTP request didn't stall the entire browser for the duration of the request, but instead seemed to run the request in the background, leaving the foreground unhindered and changing only the necessary portion of the rendered page? The site would present a much more continuous and smooth look and feel to the user. As another example, what if ASP.NET included some controls that injected script into the rendered pages that modified the HTML Document Object Model, providing more interaction from the client's point of view? Well, that's exactly what ASP.NET AJAX support is designed to do.

What Is AJAX?

AJAX formalizes a style of programming meant to improve the UI responsiveness and visual appeal of Web sites. Many AJAX capabilities have been available for a while now. AJAX consolidates several good ideas and uses them to define a style of programming and extends the standard HTTP mechanism that is the backbone of the Internet. Like most Web application development environments, ASP.NET takes advantage of HTTP capabilities in a very standard way. The browser usually initiates contact with the server using an HTTP GET request, followed by any number of POSTs. The high-level application flow is predicated upon sending a whole request and then waiting for an entire reply from the server. Although the ASP.NET server-side control architecture greatly improves back-end programming, users still get their information a whole page at a time. It operates almost like the mainframe/terminal model popular during the 1970s and early 1980s. However, this time the terminal is one of many modern sophisticated browsers and the mainframe is replaced by a Web server (or Web farm).

The standard HTTP round-trip has been a useful application strategy, and the Web grew up using it. While the Web was developing in the late 1990s, browsers had widely varying degrees of functionality. For example, browsers ranged all the way from the rudimentary

America Online Browser (which had very limited capabilities) to cell phones and personal digital assistants (PDAs), to more sophisticated browsers such as Internet Explorer and Netscape Navigator, which were rich in capability. For instance, Internet Explorer supports higher level features such as JavaScript and Dynamic HTML. This made striking a balance between usability of your site and the reach of your site very difficult prior to the advent of ASP.NET.

However, the majority of modern computing platforms can run a decent browser that can process client-side scripting. These days, most computing environments run a modern operating system, such as the Windows Vista or Windows 7 operating systems, or even Macintosh OS X. These environments run browsers fully capable of supporting XML and JavaScript. With so many Web client platforms supporting this functionality, it makes sense to take advantage of the capabilities. As you see later in this chapter, AJAX makes good use of these modern browser features to improve the user experience.

In addition to extending standard HTTP, AJAX is also a very clever way to use the Web service idiom. Web services are traditionally geared toward enterprise-to-enterprise business communications. However, Web services are also useful on a smaller scale for handling Web requests out of band. ("Out of band" simply means making HTTP requests using other methods instead of the standard page posting mechanism.) AJAX uses Web services behind the scenes to make the client UI more responsive than it is for traditional HTTP GETs and POSTs. This chapter describes how this works, especially in the section titled "Extender Controls" later in the chapter, which describes the ASP.NET AJAX Control Toolkit extender controls.

ASP.NET and AJAX

One of the primary changes AJAX brings to Web programming is that it depends on the browser taking an even more active role in the process. Instead of the browser simply rendering streams of HTML and executing small custom-written script blocks, AJAX includes some new client-script libraries to facilitate the asynchronous calls back to the server. AJAX also includes some basic server-side components to support these new asynchronous calls coming from the client. There's even a community-supported AJAX Control Toolkit available for the ASP.NET AJAX implementation. Figure 23-1 shows the organization of ASP.NET AJAX support.

Client Side **Server Side**

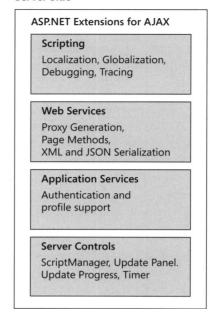

FIGURE 23-1 The conceptual organization of ASP.NET AJAX support layers.

Reasons to Use AJAX

If traditional ASP.NET development is so entrenched and well established, why would you want to introduce AJAX? At first glance, AJAX seems to introduce some new complexities into the ASP.NET programming picture. In fact, it seems to reintroduce some programming idioms that ASP.NET was designed to deprecate (such as overuse of client-side script). However, AJAX promises to produce a richer experience for the user. Because ASP.NET support for AJAX is nearly seamless, the added complexities are well mitigated. When building a Web site, there are a few reasons you might choose to enable your ASP.NET site for AJAX:

- AJAX improves the overall efficiency of your site by performing, when appropriate, parts of a Web page's processing in the browser. Instead of waiting for the entire HTTP protocol to get a response from the browser, you can push certain parts of the page processing to the client to help the client to react much more quickly. Of course, this type of functionality has always been available—as long as you're willing to write the code to make it happen. ASP.NET AJAX support includes a number of scripts so that you can get a lot of browser-based efficiency by simply using a few server-side controls.

- ASP.NET AJAX introduces to a Web site UI elements usually found in desktop applications, such as rectangle rounding, callouts, progress indicators, and pop-up windows that work for a wide range of browsers (more browser-side scripting—but most of it has been written for you).

■ AJAX introduces partial-page updates. By refreshing only the parts of the Web page that have been updated, the user's wait time is reduced significantly. This brings Web-based applications much closer to desktop applications with regard to perceived UI performance.

■ AJAX is supported by most popular browsers—not just Internet Explorer. It works for Mozilla Firefox and Apple Safari, too. Although it still requires some effort to strike a balance between UI richness and the ability to reach a wider audience, the fact that AJAX depends on features available in most modern browsers makes this balance much easier to achieve.

■ AJAX introduces a huge number of new capabilities. Whereas the standard ASP.NET control and page-rendering model provides great flexibility and extensibility for programming Web sites, AJAX brings in a new concept—the extender control. Extender controls attach to existing server-side controls (such as the *TextBox*, *ListBox*, and *DropDownList*) at run time and add new client-side appearances and behaviors to the controls. Sometimes extender controls can even call a predefined Web service to get data to populate list boxes and such (for example, the *AutoComplete* extender).

■ AJAX improves on ASP.NET Forms Authentication and profiles and personalization services. ASP.NET support for authentication and personalization provides a great boon to Web developers—and AJAX just sweetens the offerings.

These days, when you browse different Web sites, you run into many examples of AJAX-style programming. Here are some examples:

■ Colorado Geographic: *http://www.coloradogeographic.com/*

■ Cyber Homes: *http://www.cyberhomes.com/default.aspx*

■ Component Art: *http://www.componentart.com/*

Real-World AJAX

Throughout the 1990s and into the mid-2000s, Web applications were nearly a throwback to 1970s mainframe and minicomputer architectures. However, instead of a single large computer serving dumb terminals, Web applications consist of a Web server (or a Web farm) connected to smart browsers capable of fairly sophisticated rendering capabilities. Until recently, Web applications took their input from HTTP forms and presented output in HTML pages. The real trick in understanding standard Web applications is to see the disconnected and stateless nature of HTTP. Classic Web applications can show only a snapshot of the state of the application.

As this chapter describes, Microsoft supports standard AJAX idioms and patterns in the ASP.NET framework. However, AJAX is more a style of Web programming involving out-of-band HTTP requests than any specific technology.

You've no doubt seen sites engaging the new interface features and stylings available through AJAX programming. Examples include Microsoft.com, Google.com, and Yahoo.com. Very often while browsing these sites, you'll see modern features such as automatic page updates that do not require you to generate a postback explicitly. Modal-type dialog boxes that require your attention appear until you dismiss them. These are all features available through AJAX-style programming patterns and the ASP.NET extensions (for example, a rich set of AJAX server-side controls and extensions) for supporting AJAX.

If you're a long-time Microsoft environment Web developer, you might be asking yourself whether AJAX is something really worthwhile or whether you might be able to get much of the same type of functionality using a tried and true technology such as DHTML.

AJAX in Perspective

Any seasoned Web developer targeting Internet Explorer as the browser is undoubtedly familiar with Dynamic HTML (DHTML). DHTML is a technology that runs at the browser for enabling Windows desktop-style UI elements in the Web client environment. DHTML was a good start, and AJAX brings the promise of more desktop-like capabilities to Web applications.

AJAX makes available wider capabilities than DHTML does. With DHTML, primarily you can change the style declarations of an HTML element through JavaScript. However, that's about as far as it goes. DHTML is very useful for implementing such UI features as having a menu open when the mouse pointer rests on it. AJAX expands on this idea of client-based UI using JavaScript as well as out-of-band calls to the server. Because AJAX is based on out-of-band server requests (rather than relying *only* on a lot of client script code), AJAX has the potential for much more growth in terms of future capabilities than does DHTML.

ASP.NET Server-Side Support for AJAX

Much of ASP.NET support for AJAX resides in a collection of server-side controls responsible for rendering AJAX-style output to the browser. Recall from Chapter 3, "The Page Rendering Model," that the entire page-rendering process of an ASP.NET application is broken down into little bite-sized chunks. Each individual bit of rendering is handled by a class derived from *System.Web.UI.Control*. The entire job of a server-side control is to render output that places HTML elements in the output stream so that they appear correctly in the browser. For example, *ListBox* controls render a <select/> tag. *TextBox* controls render an

<input type="text" /> tag. ASP.NET AJAX server-side controls render AJAX-style script and HTML to the browser.

ASP.NET AJAX support consists of these server-side controls along with client code scripts that integrate to produce AJAX-like behavior. The following subsections describe the most frequently used AJAX-oriented ASP.NET server controls: *ScriptManager*, *ScriptManagerProxy*, *UpdatePanel*, *UpdateProgress*, and *Timer*.

ScriptManager Control

The *ScriptManager* control manages script resources for the page. The *ScriptManager* control's primary action is to register the AJAX Library script with the page so that the client script can use type system extensions. The *ScriptManager* also makes possible partial-page rendering and supports localization as well as custom user scripts. The *ScriptManager* assists with out-of-band calls back to the server. Any ASP.NET site wishing to use AJAX must include an instance of the *ScriptManager* control on any page using AJAX functionality.

ScriptManagerProxy Control

Scripts on a Web page often require a bit of special handling in terms of how the server renders them. Typically, the page uses a *ScriptManager* control to organize the scripts at the page level. Nested components such as content pages and user controls require the *ScriptManagerProxy* to manage script and service references to pages that already have a *ScriptManager* control.

This is most notable in the case of master pages. The master page typically houses the *ScriptManager* control. However, ASP.NET throws an exception if a second instance of *ScriptManager* is found in a given page. So, what would content pages do if they needed to access the *ScriptManager* control that the master page contains? The answer is that the content page should house the *ScriptManagerProxy* control and work with the true *ScriptManager* control through the proxy. Of course, as mentioned, this also applies to user controls as well.

UpdatePanel Control

The *UpdatePanel* control supports partial-page updates by tying together specific server-side controls and events that cause them to render. The *UpdatePanel* control causes only selected parts of the page to be refreshed instead of the whole page (as happens during a typical HTTP postback).

UpdateProgress Control

The *UpdateProgress* control coordinates status information about partial-page updates as they occur in *UpdatePanel* controls. The *UpdateProgress* control supports intermediate feedback for long-running operations.

Timer Control

The *Timer* control issues postbacks at defined intervals. Although the *Timer* control will perform a typical postback (posting the whole page), it is especially useful when coordinated with the *UpdatePanel* control to perform periodic partial-page updates.

AJAX Client Support

ASP.NET AJAX client-side support is centered around a set of JavaScript libraries. The following layers are included in the ASP.NET AJAX script libraries:

- The browser compatibility layer assists in managing compatibility across the most frequently used browsers. Whereas ASP.NET by itself implements browser capabilities on the server end, this layer handles compatibility on the client end (the browsers supported include Internet Explorer, Mozilla Firefox, and Apple Safari).

- The ASP.NET AJAX core services layer extends the usual JavaScript environment by introducing classes, namespaces, event handling, data types, and object serialization that are useful in AJAX programming.

- The ASP.NET AJAX base class library for clients includes various components, such as components for string management and for extended error handling.

- The networking layer of the AJAX client-side support manages communication with Web-based services and applications. The networking layer also handles asynchronous remote method calls.

The pièce de résistance of ASP.NET AJAX support is the community-supported Control Toolkit. Although all the features mentioned previously provide solid infrastructure for ASP.NET AJAX, AJAX isn't very compelling until you add a rich tool set.

ASP.NET AJAX Control Toolkit

The ASP.NET AJAX Control Toolkit is a collection of components (and samples showing how to use them) encapsulating AJAX capabilities. When you browse through the samples, you can get an idea of the kind of user experiences available through the controls and extenders.

The Control Toolkit also provides a powerful software development kit for creating custom controls and extenders. You can download the ASP.NET AJAX Control Toolkit from the ASP.NET AJAX Web site.

The AJAX Control Toolkit is a separate download and not automatically included with Microsoft Visual Studio 2010. The latest version is 3.0, which was made available at the end of September 2009. See *http://asp.net/ajax/ajaxcontroltoolkit/* for details. You can download the binaries or the source code. If you aren't interested in the source code, you only need to make a reference to the AjaxControlToolkit.dll assembly in your project.

If you want to build the toolkit yourself, follow these steps:

1. Download the toolkit source code.

2. After unzipping the Toolkit file, open the AjaxControlToolkit solution file in Visual Studio.

3. Build the AjaxControlKit project.

4. The compilation process produces a file named AjaxControlToolkit.dll in the AjaxControlToolkit\bin directory.

5. Right-click the Toolbox in Visual Studio, and click Choose Items on the menu. Browse to the AjaxControlToolkit.dll file in the AjaxControlToolkit\bin directory and include the DLL. This brings all the new AJAX controls from the toolkit into Visual Studio so that you can drop them in forms in your applications.

Note You can find a wealth of AJAX-enabled server-side controls and client-side scripts available through a community-supported effort. Although they are not quite officially part of the Microsoft AJAX release, the support includes the ASP.NET AJAX community-supported controls (mentioned previously) as well as support for client declarative syntax (XML script) and more. Go to *http://www.asp.net/ajax/* for more information. This site includes links to download the ASP.NET AJAX Control Toolkit, links to some interesting AJAX-enabled sites, video tutorials, and other useful downloads.

AJAX Control Toolkit Potpourri

A number of other extenders and controls are available through a community-supported effort. You can find a link to the AJAX Control Toolkit at *http://www.asp.net/ajax/*. This chapter discusses a few of the controls available from the toolkit. Table 23-1 lists the controls and extenders available through this toolkit.

TABLE 23-1 The ASP.NET Control Toolkit

Component	Description
Accordion	This extender is useful for displaying a group of panes one pane at a time. It's similar to using several *CollapsiblePanels* constrained to allow only one to be expanded at a time. The *Accordion* is composed of a group of *AccordionPane* controls.
AlwaysVisibleControl	This extender is useful for pinning a control to the page so that its position remains constant while content behind it moves and scrolls.
Animation	This extender provides a clean interface for animating page content.
AsyncFileUpload	This control is for uploading a file asynchronously in the background.
AutoComplete	This extender is designed to communicate with a Web service to list possible text entries based on what's already in the text box.
Calendar	This extender is targeted for the *TextBox* control providing client-side date-picking functionality in a customizable way.
CascadingDropDown	This extender is targeted toward the *DropDownList* control. It functions to populate a set of related *DropDownList* controls automatically.
CollapsiblePanel	This extender is targeted toward the *Panel* control for adding collapsible sections to a Web page.
ConfirmButton	This extender is targeted toward the *Button* control (and types derived from the *Button* control) and is useful for displaying messages to the user. The scenarios for which this extender is useful include those requiring confirmation from the user (for example, where linking to another page might cause the end user to lose state).
DragPanel	This is an extender targeted toward *Panel* controls for adding the capability for users to drag the *Panel* around the page.
DropDown	This extender implements a Microsoft SharePoint–style drop-down menu.
DropShadow	This extender is targeted toward the *Panel* control that applies a drop shadow to the *Panel*.
DynamicPopulate	This extender uses an HTML string returned by a Web service or page method call.
FilteredTextBox	This extender is used to ensure that an end user enters only valid characters in a text box.
HoverMenu	This extender is targeted for any *WebControl* that has an associated pop-up window for displaying additional content. The pop-up window is activated when the user rests the mouse pointer on the targeted control.

Component	Description
ListSearch	This extender searches items in a designated *ListBox* or *DropDownList* based on keystrokes as they're typed by the user.
MaskedEdit	This extender is targeted toward *TextBox* controls to constrain the kind of text that the *TextBox* will accept by applying a mask.
ModalPopup	This extender mimics the standard Windows modal dialog box behavior. With the *ModalPopup*, a page can display content of a pop-up window that focuses attention on itself until it is dismissed explicitly by the end user.
MutuallyExclusiveCheckBox	This extender is targeted toward the *CheckBox* control. The extender groups *CheckBox* controls using a key. When a number of *CheckBox* controls all share the same key, the extender ensures that only a single check box will appear selected at a time.
NoBot	This control attempts to provide CAPTCHA (Completely Automated Public Turing test to tell Computers and Humans Apart)-like bot/spam detection and prevention without requiring any user interaction. Although a noninteractive approach might be bypassed more easily than one requiring actual human interaction can be, this implementation is invisible.
NumericUpDown	This extender is targeted toward the *TextBox* control to create a control very similar to the standard Windows Edit control with the Spin button. The extender adds "up" and "down" buttons for incrementing and decrementing the value in the *TextBox*.
PagingBulletedList	This extender is targeted toward the *BulletedList* control. The extender enables sorted paging on the client side.
PasswordStrength	This extender is targeted toward the *TextBox* control to help when end users type passwords. Whereas the typical *TextBox* hides only the actual text, the *PasswordStrength* extender also displays the strength of the password using visual cues.
PopupControl	This extender is targeted toward all controls. Its purpose is to open a pop-up window for displaying additional relevant content.
Rating	This control renders a rating system from which end users rate something using images to represent their choice (stars are common).
ReorderList	This ASP.NET AJAX control implements a bulleted, data-bound list with items that can be reordered interactively.
ResizableControl	This extender works with any element on a Web page. Once the *ResizableControl* is associated with an element, the user can resize that control. The *ResizableControl* puts a handle on the lower right corner of the control.
RoundedCorners	The *RoundedCorners* extender can be applied to any Web page element to turn square corners into rounded corners.

Component	Description
Seadragon	The *Seadragon* control renders an image along with buttons for zooming in and out, going to full screen, and panning,
Slider	This extender is targeted to the *TextBox* control. It adds a graphical slider that the end user can use to change the numeric value in the *TextBox*.
SlideShow	This extender controls and adds buttons users can use to move between images individually and to play the slide show automatically.
Tabs	This server-side control manages a set of tabbed panels for managing content on a page.
TextBoxWatermark	*TextBoxWatermark* extends the *TextBox* control to display a message while the *TextBox* is empty. When the *TextBox* contains some text, the *TextBox* appears as a typical *TextBox*.
ToggleButton	This extender extends the *CheckBox* to show custom images reflecting the state of the *CheckBox*.
UpdatePanelAnimation	This extender provides a clean interface for animating content associated with an *UpdatePanel*.
ValidatorCallout	*ValidatorCallout* extends the validator controls (such as *RequiredFieldValidator* and *RangeValidator*). The callouts are small pop-up windows that appear near the UI elements containing incorrect data to direct user focus to them.

Getting Familiar with AJAX

Here's a short example to help get you familiar with AJAX. It's a very simple Web Forms application that shows behind-the-scenes page content updates with the *UpdatePanel* server-side control. In this exercise, you create a page with labels showing the date and time that the page loads. One label is outside the *UpdatePanel*, and the other label is inside the *UpdatePanel*. You can see how partial-page updates work by comparing the date and time shown in each label.

Implementing a simple partial-page update

1. Create a new Web site project named *AJAXORama*. Make it an empty, file system-based Web site. Visual Studio 2010 creates AJAX Enabled projects right from the start. Make sure the default.aspx file is open.

2. Add a *ScriptManager* control to the page by dragging one from the Toolbox onto the page. (It is under the *AJAX Extensions* tab in the Toolbox instead of the normal control tab.) Using the AJAX controls requires a *ScriptManager* to appear prior to any other AJAX controls on the page. By convention, the control is usually placed outside the DIV

Visual Studio creates for you. After placing the script manager control on your page, the <body> element in the *Source* view should look like this:

```
<body>
    <form id="form1" runat="server">
    <asp:ScriptManager ID="ScriptManager1" runat="server">
    </asp:ScriptManager>
    <div>

    </div>
    </form>
</body>
```

3. Drag a *Label* control onto the Default.aspx form. In the Properties pane, give the *Label* control the name *LabelDateTimeOfPageLoad*. Then, drop a *Button* on the form as well. Give it the text *Click Me*. Open the code-beside file (default.aspx.cs) and update the *Page_Load* handler so that the label displays the current date and time:

```
using System;
using System.Data;
using System.Configuration;
using System.Web;
using System.Web.Security;
using System.Web.UI;
using System.Web.UI.WebControls;
using System.Web.UI.WebControls.WebParts;
using System.Web.UI.HtmlControls;

public partial class _Default : System.Web.UI.Page
{
    protected void Page_Load(object sender, EventArgs e)
    {
        this.LabelDateTimeOfPageLoad.Text = DateTime.Now.ToString();
    }
}
```

4. Run the page and generate some postbacks by clicking the button a few times. Notice that the label on the page updates with the current date and time each time you click the button.

5. Add an *UpdatePanel* control to the page. (You can find this control alongside the *ScriptManager* control in the AJAX node in the Visual Studio *Toolbox*.) Then, drop another *Label* from the Toolbox into the content area of the *UpdatePanel*. Name the label *LabelDateTimeOfButtonClick*.

6. Add some code to the *Page_Load* method so that the label shows the current date and time:

```
using System;
using System.Data;
using System.Configuration;
```

```
using System.Web;
using System.Web.Security;


using System.Web.UI;
using System.Web.UI.WebControls;
using System.Web.UI.WebControls.WebParts;
using System.Web.UI.HtmlControls;

public partial class _Default : System.Web.UI.Page
{
    protected void Page_Load(object sender, EventArgs e)
    {
        this.LabelDateTimeOfPageLoad.Text = DateTime.Now.ToString();
        this.LabelDateTimeOfButtonClick.Text =
            DateTime.Now.ToString();
    }
}
```

The following graphic shows the *UpdatePanel*, *Button*, and *Labels* as displayed in the Visual Studio Designer (there are some line breaks in between so that the page is readable):

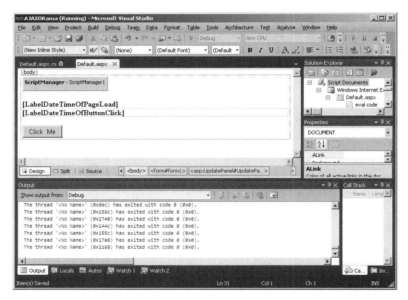

7. Run the page and generate some postbacks by clicking the button. Both labels should be showing the date and time of the postback (that is, they should show the same time). Although the second label is inside the *UpdatePanel*, the action causing the postback is happening outside the *UpdatePanel*.

The following graphic shows the Web page running without the *Button* being associated with the *UpdatePanel:*

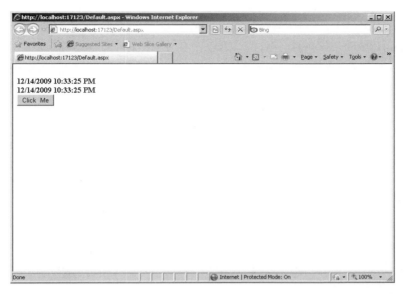

8. Now delete the current button from the form and drop a new button into the *UpdatePanel1* control. Add a *Label* to the *UpdatePanel1* as well. Name the new label *LabelDateTimeOfButtonPress*. Look at the Default.aspx file to see what was produced:

```
<%@ Page Language="C#" AutoEventWireup="true"
CodeFile="Default.aspx.cs" Inherits="_Default" %>

<!DOCTYPE html PUBLIC
"-//W3C//DTD XHTML 1.1//EN"
"http://www.w3.org/TR/xhtml11/DTD/xhtml11.dtd">
<html xmlns="http://www.w3.org/1999/xhtml">
<head runat="server">
    <title>Untitled Page</title>
</head>
<body>
    <form id="form1" runat="server">
        <asp:ScriptManager
         ID="ScriptManager1" runat="server" /><br/>
        <asp:Label ID="LabelDateTimeOfPageLoad"
         runat="server"></asp:Label> <br/>
        <asp:UpdatePanel ID="UpdatePanel1" runat="server">

            <ContentTemplate>
             <asp:Label ID="LabelDateTimeOfButtonPress"
                 runat="server">
             </asp:Label><br/>
```

```
            <asp:Button ID="Button1"
                runat="server" Text="Click Me" />
        </ContentTemplate>
    </asp:UpdatePanel>
</form>
</body>
</html>
```

The new *Button* should now appear nested inside the *UpdatePanel* along with the new *Label*.

9. Run the page and generate some postbacks by clicking the button. Notice that only the label showing the date and time enclosed in the *UpdatePanel* is updated. This is known as a *partial-page update* because only part of the page is actually updated in response to a page action, such as clicking the button. Partial-page updates are also sometimes referred to as *callbacks* rather than postbacks. The following graphic shows the Web page running with the *Button* being associated with the *UpdatePanel*:

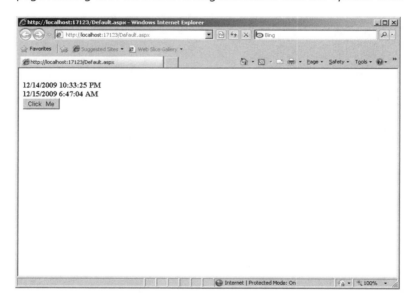

10. Add an *UpdatePanel* trigger. Because the second label and the button are both associated with the single *UpdatePanel*, only the second *Label* is updated in response to the postback generated by the button. If you could set up partial-page updates based only on elements tied to a single *UpdatePanel*, that would be fairly restrictive. As it turns out, the *UpdatePanel* supports a collection of triggers that generate partial-page updates. To see how this works, you need to first move the button outside the *UpdatePanel* (so that the button generates a full normal postback). The easiest way is simply to drag a button onto the form, making sure it lands outside the *UpdatePanel*.

Because the button is outside the *UpdatePanel* again, postbacks generated by the button are no longer tied solely to the second label, and the partial-page update behavior you saw in step 9 is again nonfunctional.

11. Update the *UpdatePanel's Triggers* collection to include the *Button's Click* event. With the Designer open, select the *UpdatePanel*. Go to the properties Window and choose *Triggers*.

12. Add a trigger and set the control ID to the button's *ID* and the event to *Click* as shown in the following graphic:

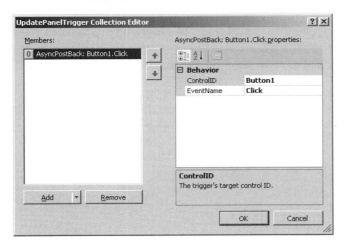

(Note that the handy drop-down lists for each property assist you with this selection.) Run the page. Clicking the button should now generate a callback (causing a partial-page update) in which the first label continues to show the date and time of the original page load and the second label shows the date and time of the button click. Pretty cool!

Async Callbacks

As you know by now, standard Web pages require the browser to instigate post-backs. Many times, postbacks are generated by clicking a *Button* control (in ASP.NET terms). However, you can enable most ASP.NET controls to generate postbacks as well. For example, if you'd like to receive a postback whenever a user selects an item in a *DropDownList*, just flip the *AutoPostBack* property to *true*, and the control will generate the normal postback whenever the selected item changes.

In some cases, an entire postback is warranted for events such as when the selected item changes. However, in most cases generating postbacks is distracting for users and leads to very poor performance of your page. That's because standard postbacks refresh the whole page.

ASP.NET AJAX support introduces the notion of the *asynchronous* postback by using JavaScript running inside the client page. The *XMLHttpRequest* object posts data to the server—making an end run around the normal postback. The server returns data as XML, JSON, or HTML and has to refresh only part of the page. The JavaScript running in the page replaces old HTML in the Document Object Model with new HTML based on the results of the asynchronous postback.

If you've done any amount of client-side script programming, you can imagine how much work doing something like this can be. Performing asynchronous postbacks and updating pages usually requires a lot of JavaScript.

The *UpdatePanel* control you just used in the preceding exercise hides all of the client-side code and also the server-side plumbing. Also, because of the well-architected server-side control infrastructure in ASP.NET, the *UpdatePanel* maintains the same server-side control model you're used to seeing in ASP.NET.

The Timer

In addition to causing partial-page updates through an event generated by a control (such as a button click), AJAX includes a timer to cause regularly scheduled events. You can find the *Timer* control alongside the other standard AJAX controls in the Toolbox. By dropping a *Timer* on a page, you can generate automatic postbacks to the server.

Some uses for the *Timer* include a "shout box"—like an open chat where a number of users type in messages and they appear near the top like a conversation. Another reason you might like an automatic postback is if you wanted to update a live Web camera picture or to refresh some other frequently updated content.

The *Timer* is very easy to use—simply drop it on a page that hosts a *ScriptManager*. The default settings for the timer cause the timer to generate postbacks every minute (every 60,000 milliseconds). The *Timer* is enabled by default and begins firing events as soon as the page loads.

Here's an exercise using the *Timer* to write a simple chat page that displays messages from a number of users who are logged in. The conversation is immediately updated for the user typing in a message. However, users who have not refreshed since the last message don't get to see it—unless they perform a refresh. The page uses a *Timer* to update the conversation automatically. At first, the entire page is refreshed. Then, the chat page uses an *UpdatePanel* to update only the chat log (which is the element that changes).

Using the *Timer* to create a chat page

1. Open the AJAXORama application if it's not already open. The first step is to create a list of chat messages that can be seen from a number of different sessions. Add a global application class to the project by right-clicking in Solution Explorer and clicking Add New Item. Choose Global Application Class as the type of file to add. This adds files named Global.asax and Global.asax.cs to your Web site.

2. Update the *Application_Start* method in Global.asax.cs to create a list for storing messages and add the list to the application cache.

```
using System;
using System.Collections.Generic;
using System.Linq;
using System.Web;
using System.Web.Security;
using System.Web.SessionState;

namespace AJAXORama
{
  public class Global : System.Web.HttpApplication
{
  protected void Application_Start(object sender, EventArgs e)
  {
    // Code that runs on application startup
    List<string> messages = new List<string>();
    HttpContext.Current.Cache["Messages"] = messages;
  }
  // other generated code is here...
}


}
```

3. Create a chat page by adding a new page to the Web site and calling it *GroupChat.aspx*. This will hold a text box with messages as they accumulate, and it also gives users a means of adding messages.

4. When the messages are coming in, it would be very useful to know who sent which messages. This page forces users to identify themselves first; then, they can start adding messages. First, type in the text **Group Chatting...** after the *ScriptManager*. Give it a large font style with block display so that it's on its own line. After that, type in the text **First, give us your name:**. Then, drag a *TextBox* control from the Toolbox onto the page. Give the *TextBox* the ID *TextBoxUserID*. Drop a *Button* on the page so that the user can submit his or her name. Give it the text *Submit ID* and the ID *ButtonSubmitID*.

5. Drop another *TextBox* onto the page. This one will hold the messages, so make it large (800 pixels wide by 150 pixels high should do the trick). Set the *TextBox*'s *TextMode* property to *MultiLine*, and set the *ReadOnly* property to *True*. Give the *TextBox* the ID *TextBoxConversation*.

6. Drop one more *TextBox* onto the page. This one will hold the user's current message. Give the *TextBox* the ID *TextBoxMessage*.

7. Add one more *Button* to the page. This one enables the user to submit the current message and should include the text *Add Your Message*. Be sure to give the button the ID value *ButtonAddYourMessage*. The following graphic shows a possible layout of these controls:

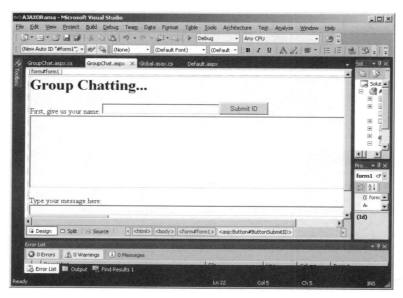

8. Open the code-beside file GroupChat.aspx.cs for editing. Add a method that retrieves the user's name from session state:

```csharp
using System;
using System.Collections.Generic;
using System.Linq;
using System.Web;
using System.Web.UI;
using System.Web.UI.WebControls;


public partial class GroupChat : System.Web.UI.Page
{
    protected void Page_Load(object sender, EventArgs e)
    {
    }

    protected string GetUserID()
    {
        string strUserID =
          (string) Session["UserID"];
        return strUserID;
    }
}
```

9. Add a method to update the UI so that users may type messages only after they've identified themselves. If the user has not been identified (that is, the session variable is not there), *disable* the chat conversation UI elements and *enable* the user identification UI elements. If the user has been identified, *enable* the chat conversation UI elements and *disable* the user identification UI elements:

```
using System;
using System.Collections.Generic;
using System.Linq;
using System.Web;
using System.Web.UI;
using System.Web.UI.WebControls;


public partial class GroupChat : System.Web.UI.Page
{
    protected void Page_Load(object sender, EventArgs e)
    {
    }
    // other code goes here...
    void ManageUI()
    {
        if (GetUserID() == null)

        {
            // if this is the first request, then get the user's ID
            TextBoxMessage.Enabled = false;
            TextBoxConversation.Enabled = false;
            ButtonAddYourMessage.Enabled = false;

            ButtonSubmitID.Enabled = true;
            TextBoxUserID.Enabled = true;
        }
        else
        {
            // if this is the first request, then get the user's ID
            TextBoxMessage.Enabled = true;
            TextBoxConversation.Enabled = true;
            ButtonAddYourMessage.Enabled = true;

            ButtonSubmitID.Enabled = false;
            TextBoxUserID.Enabled = false;
        }
    }
}
```

10. Add a *Click* event handler for the *Button* that stores the user ID (*ButtonSubmitID*). The method should store the user's identity in session state and then call *ManageUI* to enable and disable the correct controls:

```
using System;
using System.Collections.Generic;
using System.Linq;
using System.Web;
```

```csharp
using System.Web.UI;
using System.Web.UI.WebControls;

public partial class GroupChat : System.Web.UI.Page
{
    protected void Page_Load(object sender, EventArgs e)
    {
    }
    // other page code goes here...
    protected void ButtonSubmitID_Click(object sender, EventArgs e)
    {
        Session["UserID"] = TextBoxUserID.Text;
        ManageUI();
    }
}
```

11. Add a method to the page for refreshing the conversation. The code should look up the message list in the application cache and build a string that shows the messages in reverse order (so the most recent is on top). Then, the method should set the conversation *TextBoxConversation*'s *Text* property to the new string (that is, the text property of the *TextBox* showing the conversation):

```csharp
using System;
using System.Collections.Generic;
using System.Linq;
using System.Web;
using System.Web.UI;
using System.Web.UI.WebControls;

public partial class GroupChat : System.Web.UI.Page
{
    // other page code goes here...
    void RefreshConversation()
    {
        List<string> messages = (List<string>)Cache["Messages"];
        if (messages != null)
        {
            string strConversation = "";

            int nMessages = messages.Count;

            for(int i = nMessages-1; i >=0; i--)
            {
                string s;

                s = messages[i];
                strConversation += s;
                strConversation += "\r\n";
            }

            TextBoxConversation.Text =
                strConversation;
        }
    }
}
```

12. Add a *Click* event handler for adding your message by double-clicking the *Button* for adding your message (the lower button on the form) and adding a *Click* event handler to respond to the user submitting his or her message (*ButtonAddYourMessage*). The method should grab the text from the user's message *TextBoxMessage*, prepend the user's ID to it, and add it to the list of messages held in the application cache. Then, the method should call *RefreshConversation* to make sure the new message appears in the conversation *TextBox*:

```
using System;
using System.Collections.Generic;
using System.Linq;
using System.Web;
using System.Web.UI;
using System.Web.UI.WebControls;

public partial class GroupChat : System.Web.UI.Page
{
    // Other code goes here...
    protected void ButtonAddYourMessage_Click(object sender,
                                              EventArgs e)
    {
        // Add the message to the conversation...
        if (this.TextBoxMessage.Text.Length > 0)
        {
            List<string> messages = (List<string>)Cache["Messages"];
            if (messages != null)
            {
                TextBoxConversation.Text = "";

                string strUserID = GetUserID();

                if (strUserID != null)
                {
                    messages.Add(strUserID +
                        ": " +
                        TextBoxMessage.Text);
                    RefreshConversation();
                    TextBoxMessage.Text = "";
                }
            }
        }
    }
}
```

13. Update the *Page_Load* method to call *ManageUI* and *RefreshConversation*:

```
using System;
using System.Collections.Generic;
using System.Linq;
using System.Web;
using System.Web.UI;
using System.Web.UI.WebControls;

using System.Xml.Linq;
using System.Collections.Generic;

public partial class GroupChat : System.Web.UI.Page
{
    // Other code goes here...
    protected void Page_Load(object sender, EventArgs e)
    {
        ManageUI();
        RefreshConversation();
    }
}
```

14. Now run the page to see how it works. After you've identified yourself, you can start typing in messages—and you'll see them appear in the conversation *TextBox*. Try browsing the page using two separate browsers. Do you see an issue? The user typing a message gets to see the message appear in the conversation right away. However, other users involved in the chat don't see any new messages until after they submit messages of their own. You can solve this issue by dropping an AJAX *Timer* onto the page.

15. Drag a *ScriptManager* from the AJAX controls onto the page. Then, drag a *Timer* from the AJAX controls onto the page. Although the AJAX *Timer* starts generating postbacks automatically, the default interval is 60,000 milliseconds, or once per minute. Set the *Timer*'s *Interval* property to something more reasonable, such as 10,000 milliseconds (or 10 seconds).

Now run both pages and see what happens. You should see the pages posting back automatically every 10 seconds. However, there's still one more issue with this scenario. If you watch carefully enough, you'll see that the whole page is refreshed—even though the user name is not changing. During the conversation, you're really only interested in seeing the conversation *TextBox* updated. You can fix this by putting in an *UpdatePanel*.

16. Drag an *UpdatePanel* from the AJAX controls onto the page. Position the *UpdatePanel* so that it can hold the conversation text box. Move the conversation text box so that it's positioned in the *UpdatePanel*. Modify the *UpdatePanel*'s triggers so that it includes the *Timer*'s *Tick* event. Now run the chat pages, and you should see only the conversation text box being updated on each timer tick. The following graphic shows the new layout of the page employing the *UpdatePanel*:

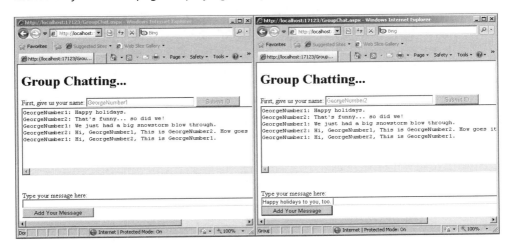

The ASP.NET AJAX *Timer* is useful whenever you need regular, periodic posts back to the server. You can see here how it is especially useful when combined with the *UpdatePanel* to do periodic partial-page updates.

Updating Progress

A recurring theme when programming any UI environment is keeping the user updated about the progress of a long-running operation. If you're programming Windows Forms, you can use the *BackgroundWorker* component and show progress updating using the *Progress* control. Programming for the Web requires a slightly different strategy. ASP.NET AJAX support includes a component for this—the ASP.NET AJAX *UpdateProgress* control.

UpdateProgress controls display during asynchronous postbacks. All *UpdateProgress* controls on the page become visible when any *UpdatePanel* control triggers an asynchronous postback.

Here's an exercise for using an *UpdateProgress* control on a page.

Using the *UpdateProgress* control

1. Add a new page to the AJAXORama site named *UseUpdateProgressControl.aspx*.

2. Drag a *ScriptManager* from the Toolbox onto the page.

3. Drag an *UpdatePanel* onto the page. Give the panel the ID *UpdatePanelForProgress* so that you can identify it later. Add the text **This is from the update panel**, and then add a *Button* to the update panel that will begin a long-running operation. Give it the ID *ButtonLongOperation* and the text *Activate Long Operation*.

4. Add a *Click* event handler for the button. The easiest way to create a long-running operation is to put the thread to sleep for a few seconds, as shown here. By introducing a long-running operation, you have a way to test the *UpdateProgress* control and see how it works when the request takes a long time to complete.

```
public partial class UseUpdateProgressControl : System.Web.UI.Page
{
    protected void Page_Load(object sender, EventArgs e)
    {

    }

    protected void
        ButtonLongOperation_Click(object sender,
                                  EventArgs e)
    {
        // Put thread to sleep for five seconds
        System.Threading.Thread.Sleep(5000);
    }
}
```

5. Now add an *UpdateProgress* control to the page. An *UpdateProgress* control must be tied to a specific *UpdatePanel*. Set the *UpdateProgress* control's *AssociatedUpdatePanelID* property to the *UpdatePanelForProgress* panel you just added. Note that you can simply use the provided droplist to select this ID. Also change the *DisplayAfter* value to be 100 (indicating the progress indication should begin 100 milliseconds after the refresh begins).

6. Add a *ProgressTemplate* to the *UpdateProgress* control—this is where the content for the update display is declared. Add a *Label* to the *ProgressTemplate* so that you can see it when it appears on the page:

```
<asp:UpdateProgress ID="UpdateProgress1"
    runat="server"
    AssociatedUpdatePanelID="UpdatePanelForProgress"
    DisplayAfter="100">
    <ProgressTemplate>
        <asp:Label ID="Label1" runat="server"
         Text="What's happening? This takes a long time...">
        </asp:Label>
    </ProgressTemplate>
</asp:UpdateProgress>
```

7. Run the page to see what happens. When you click the button that executes the long-running operation, you should see the *UpdateProgress* control show its content automatically. This graphic shows the *UpdateProgress* control in action:

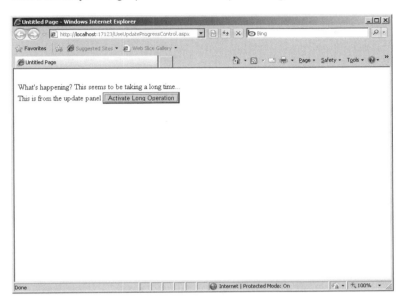

8. Finally, no asynchronous progress updating UI technology is complete without a means to cancel the long-running operation. If you wish to cancel the long-running opera-tion, you can do so by inserting a little of your own JavaScript into the page. You need to do this manually because there's no support for this using the wizards. Write a client-side script block and place it near the top of the page—inside the <head> tag. The script block should get the instance of the *Sys.WebForms.PageRequestManager.* The *PageRequestManager* class is available to the client as part of the script injected by the ASP.NET AJAX server-side controls. The *PageRequestManager* has a method named *get_isInAsyncPostBack()* that you can use to figure out whether the page is in the middle of an asynchronous callback (generated by the *UpdatePanel*). If the page is in the middle of an asynchronous callback, use the *PageRequestManager*'s *abortPostBack()* method to quit the request. Add a *Button* to the *ProgressTemplate* and assign its *OnClientClick* property to make a call to your new *abortAsyncPostback* method. In addition to setting the *OnClientClick* property to the new abort method, insert *return false;* immediately after the call to the abort method, as shown in the following code. (Inserting *return false;* prevents the browser from issuing a postback.)

```
<%@ Page Language="C#"
 AutoEventWireup="true"
CodeFile="UseUpdateProgressControl.aspx.cs"
Inherits="UseUpdateProgressControl" %>
```

```html
<!DOCTYPE html PUBLIC
"...">

<html xmlns="http://www.w3.org/1999/xhtml">
<head runat="server">
   <title></title>

<script type="text/javascript">
  function abortAsyncPostback()
  {
    var obj =
        Sys.WebForms.PageRequestManager.getInstance();
    if(obj.get_isInAsyncPostBack())
    {
        obj.abortPostBack();
    }
  }
</script>

</head>
<body>
    <form id="form1" runat="server">
    <div>

        <asp:ScriptManager ID="ScriptManager1" runat="server">
        </asp:ScriptManager>

    </div>
    <asp:UpdateProgress ID="UpdateProgress1"
        runat="server"
        AssociatedUpdatePanelID="UpdatePanelForProgress"
        DisplayAfter="100">
        <ProgressTemplate>
            <asp:Label ID="Label1" runat="server"
             Text="What's happening? This takes a long time...">
            </asp:Label>
            <asp:Button ID="Cancel" runat="server"
              OnClientClick="abortAsyncPostback(); return false;"
              Text="Cancel" />
        </ProgressTemplate>
    </asp:UpdateProgress>
    <asp:UpdatePanel ID="UpdatePanelForProgress" runat="server">
        <ContentTemplate>
            This is from the update panel
            <asp:Button ID="ButtonLongOperation"
              runat="server"
              onclick="ButtonLongOperation_Click"
              Text="Activate Long Operation" />
        </ContentTemplate>
    </asp:UpdatePanel>

    </form>
</body>
</html>
```

> **Caution** *Caveat Cancel:* As you can see, canceling an asynchronous postback is completely a client-side affair. Canceling a long-running operation on the client end is tantamount to disconnecting the client from the server. Once the client is disconnected from the server, the client will never see the response from the server.
>
> Also, although the client is happy that it could cancel the operation, the server might *never know* that the client canceled. So, the big caveat here is to plan for such a cancelation by making sure you program long-running blocking operations carefully so that they don't spin out of control. Although Microsoft Internet Information Services (IIS) 6 and IIS 7 should eventually refresh the application pool for such runaway threads, it's better to depend on your own good programming practices to make sure long-running operations end reasonably nicely.

ASP.NET AJAX support provides a great infrastructure for managing partial-page updates and for setting up other events such as regular timer ticks. The next section looks at the ASP.NET AJAX extender controls.

Extender Controls

The *UpdatePanel* provides a way to update only a portion of the page. That's pretty amazing. However, AJAX's compelling features have a very broad reach. One of the most useful features is the extender control architecture.

Extender controls target existing controls to extend functionality in the target. Whereas controls such as the *ScriptManager* and the *Timer* do a lot in terms of injecting script code into the page as the page is rendered, the extender controls often manage the markup (HTML) in the resulting page.

The following subsections discuss the ASP.NET AJAX extender controls. The first one is the *AutoComplete* extender.

The *AutoComplete* Extender

The *AutoComplete* extender attaches to a standard ASP.NET *TextBox*. As the end user types text in the *TextBox*, the *AutoComplete* extender calls a Web service to look up candidate entries based on the results of the Web service call. The following example borrows a component from Chapter 15, "Application Data Caching"—the quotes collection containing a number of famous quotes by various people.

Using the *AutoComplete* extender

1. Add a new page to AJAXORama. Because this page will host the *AutoComplete* extender, name it *UseAutocompleteExtender*.

2. Add an instance of the *ScriptManager* control to the page you just added.

3. Borrow the *QuotesCollection* class from Chapter 15. Remember, the class derives from *System.Data.Table* and holds a collection of famous quotes and their originators. You can add the component to AJAXORama by right-clicking the project node, selecting Add Existing Item, and locating the QuotesCollection.cs file associated with the UseDataCaching example in Chapter 15.

4. Add a method to retrieve the quotes based on the last name. The method should accept the last name of the originator as a string parameter. The *System.Data.DataView* class you use for retrieving a specific quote is useful for performing queries on a table in memory. The method should return the quotes as a list of strings. There might be none, one, or many, depending on the selected quote author. You use this function shortly.

```csharp
using System;
using System.Data;
using System.Configuration;
using System.Web;
using System.Web.Security;
using System.Web.UI;
using System.Web.UI.WebControls;
using System.Web.UI.WebControls.WebParts;
using System.Web.UI.HtmlControls;
using System.Collections.Generic;

/// <summary>
/// Summary description for QuotesCollection
/// </summary>
public class QuotesCollection : DataTable
{
    public QuotesCollection()
    { }

    public void Synthesize()
    {
        this.TableName = "Quotations";
        DataRow dr;

        Columns.Add(new DataColumn("Quote", typeof(string)));
        Columns.Add(new DataColumn("OriginatorLastName", typeof(string)));
        Columns.Add(new DataColumn(@"OriginatorFirstName",
                typeof(string)));

        dr = this.NewRow();
        dr[0] = "Imagination is more important than knowledge.";
        dr[1] = "Einstein";

        dr[2] = "Albert";
        Rows.Add(dr);
```

```
        // Other quotes added here...
    }

    public string[]
    GetQuotesByLastName(string strLastName)
    {
        List<string> list = new List<string>();

        DataView dvQuotes = new DataView(this);
        string strFilter = String.Format("OriginatorLastName = '{0}'", strLastName);
        dvQuotes.RowFilter = strFilter;

        foreach (DataRowView drv in dvQuotes)
        {
            string strQuote =
                drv["Quote"].ToString();

            list.Add(strQuote);
        }

        return list.ToArray();
    }
}
```

5. Add a class named *QuotesManager* to the project. The class manages caching. The caching example from which this code is borrowed stores and retrieves the *QuotesCollection* during the *Page_Load* event. Because the *QuotesCollection* will be used within a Web service, the caching has to happen elsewhere. To do this, add a public static method named *GetQuotesFromCache* to retrieve the *QuotesCollection* from the cache:

```
using System;
using System.Collections.Generic;
using System.Linq;
using System.Web;


/// <summary>
/// Summary description for QuotesManager
/// </summary>
public class QuotesManager
{
    public QuotesManager()
    {
    }


    public static QuotesCollection GetQuotesFromCache()
    {
        QuotesCollection quotes;
```

```
        quotes =
            (QuotesCollection)HttpContext.Current.Cache["quotes"];

        if (quotes == null)
        {
            quotes = new QuotesCollection();
            quotes.Synthesize();
        }
        return quotes;
    }
}
```

6. Add an XML Web Service to your application. Right-click the project and add an ASMX file to your application. Name the service *QuoteService*. You can remove the *WebService* and *WebServiceBinding* attributes, but be sure to adorn the XML Web Service class with the *[System.Web.Script.Services.ScriptService]* attribute by uncommenting it (Visual Studio put it in for you). That way, it is available to the *AutoComplete* extender later on. The *AutoCompleteExtender* uses the XML Web Service to populate its drop-down list box.

7. Add a method to get the last names of the quote originators—that's the method that populates the drop-down box. The method should take a string representing the text already typed in as the first parameter, an integer representing the maximum number of strings to return. Grab the *QuotesCollection* from the cache using the *QuoteManager*'s static method *GetQuotesFromCache*. Use the *QuotesCollection* to get the rows from the *QuotesCollection*. Finally, iterate through the rows and add the originator's last name to the list of strings to be returned if it starts with the prefix passed in as the parameter. The Common Language Runtime (CLR) *String* type includes a method named *StartsWith* that's useful to figure out whether a string starts with a certain prefix. Note that you also have to add *using* statements for generic collections and data as shown:

```
using System;
using System.Linq;
using System.Web;
using System.Collections.Generic;
using System.Linq;
using System.Web;
using System.Web.Services;

using System.Data;


[System.Web.Script.Services.ScriptService]
public class QuoteService : System.Web.Services.WebService
{
```

```
[WebMethod]
public string[]
GetQuoteOriginatorLastNames(string prefixText,
                            int count)


{
    List<string> list = new List<string>();

    QuotesCollection quotes =
        QuotesManager.GetQuotesFromCache();

    prefixText = prefixText.ToLower();

    foreach (DataRow dr in quotes.Rows)
    {
        string strName =
            dr["OriginatorLastName"].ToString();

        if (strName.ToLower().StartsWith(prefixText))
        {
            if (!list.Contains(strName))
            {
                list.Add(strName);
            }
        }
    }

    return list.GetRange(0,
        System.Math.Min(count, list.Count)).ToArray();
}
}
```

8. Now drop a *TextBox* on the UseAutocompleteExtender page to hold the originator's last name to be looked up. Give the *TextBox* an ID of *TextBoxOriginatorLastName*.

9. Drag an *AutoCompleteExtender* from the AJAX Toolbox and add it to the page. Set its ID to be *AutoCompleteExtenderForOriginatorLastName*. Point the *AutoComplete TargetControlID* to the *TextBox* holding the originator's last name, *TextBoxOriginatorLastName*. Make the *MinimumPrefix* length *1*, the *ServiceMethod GetQuoteOriginatorLastNames*, and the *ServicePath quoteservice.asmx*. This wires up the *AutoComplete* extender so that it takes text from the *TextBoxOriginatorLastName TextBox* and uses it to feed the XML Web Service *GetQuoteOriginatorLastNames* method.

```
<cc1:AutoCompleteExtender
    ID="AutoCompleteExtenderForOriginatorLastName"
    TargetControlID="TextBoxOriginatorLastName"
    MinimumPrefixLength="1"
    ServiceMethod="GetQuoteOriginatorLastNames"
    ServicePath="quoteservice.asmx"
    runat="server">
</cc1:AutoCompleteExtender>
```

10. Add a *TextBox* to the page to hold the quotes. Name the *TextBox TextBoxQuotes*.

11. Update the *Page_Load* method. It should look up the quotes based on the name in the text box by retrieving the *QuotesCollection* and calling the *QuotesCollection GetQuotesByLastName* method:

```
using System;
using System.Collections.Generic;
using System.Linq;
using System.Web;
using System.Web.UI;
using System.Web.UI.WebControls;
using System.Text;

public partial class UseAutocompleteExtender :
System.Web.UI.Page
{
    protected void Page_Load(object sender, EventArgs e)
    {
        QuotesCollection quotes =
            QuotesManager.GetQuotesFromCache();
        string[] quotesArray =
            quotes.GetQuotesByLastName(TextBoxOriginatorLastName.Text);

        if (quotesArray != null && quotesArray.Length > 0)
        {
            StringBuilder str = new StringBuilder();
            foreach (string s in quotesArray)
            {
                str.AppendFormat("{0}\r\n", s);
            }
            this.TextBoxQuotes.Text = str.ToString();
        }
        else
        {
            this.TextBoxQuotes.Text = "No quotes match your request.";
        }
    }
}
```

12. To make the page updates more efficient, drop an *UpdatePanel* onto the page. Put the *TextBox* for holding the quotes in the *UpdatePanel*. This causes only the *TextBox* showing the quotes to be updated instead of performing a whole-page refresh. Add a button following the originator's last name *TextBox* with the ID *ButtonFindQuotes*.

13. Add two *asynchPostBack* triggers to the *UpdatePanel*. The first trigger should connect the *TextBoxOriginatorLastName TextBox* to the *TextChanged* event. The second trigger should connect the *ButtonFindQuotes* button to the button's *Click* event.

The following graphic shows the layout of the page using the *AutoCompleteExtender* in action:

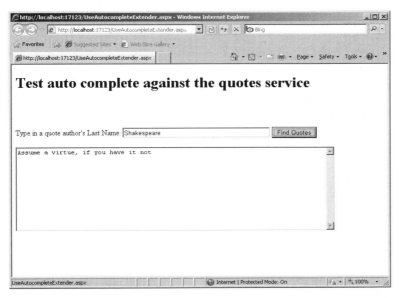

14. Run the page. As you type originator names into the *TextBox*, you should see a drop-down list appear containing candidate names based on the *QuotesCollection*'s contents.

The *AutoComplete* extender is an excellent example of the capabilities that ASP.NET AJAX support includes. Internet Explorer has had an autocomplete feature built in for quite a while. Internet Explorer remembers often-used names of HTML input text tags and recent values that have been used for them. For example, when you go online to buy an airline ticket and then go back to buy another one later, watch what happens as you type in the Web address. The Internet Explorer autocomplete feature makes available a drop-down list below the address bar that shows the last few addresses you've typed in that begin with the same text you began typing in the text box.

The ASP.NET *AutoComplete* extender works very much like this. However, the major difference is that the end user sees input candidates generated by the Web site rather than simply a history of recent entries. Of course, the Web site could mimic this functionality by tracking a user's profile identity and store a history of what a particular user has typed in to a specific input field on a page. The actual process of generating autocomplete candidates is completely up to the Web server, giving a whole new level of power and flexibility in programming user-friendly Web sites.

A Modal Pop-up Dialog-Style Component

AJAX provides another interesting feature that makes Web applications appear more like desktop applications: the *ModalPopup* extender. Historically, navigating a Web site involves users walking down the hierarchy of a Web site and climbing back out. When users provide inputs as they work with a page, the only means available to give feedback about the quality of the input data has been the validation controls. In addition, standard Web pages have no facility to focus users' attention while they type in information.

Traditional desktop applications usually employ modal dialog boxes to focus user attention when gathering important information from the end user. The model is very simple and elegant: The end user is presented with a situation in which he or she must enter some data and then click OK or Cancel before moving on. After dismissing the dialog box, the end user sees exactly the same screen he or she saw right before the dialog box appeared. There's no ambiguity and no involved process where the end user must walk up and down some arbitrary page hierarchy.

This example shows how to use the pop-up dialog extender control. You create a page with some standard content and then have a modal dialog-style pop-up window appear right before the page is submitted.

Using a *ModalPopup* extender

1. Add a new page to AJAXORama to host the pop-up extender. Call it *UseModalPopupExtender*.

2. As with all the other examples using AJAX controls, drag a *ScriptManager* from the Toolbox onto the page.

3. Add a title to the page (the example here uses "ASP.NET Code of Content"). Give the banner some prominence by surrounding it with <h1> and </h1> tags. You can simply replace the existing <div> tag with the <h1> tag.

4. Drag a *Panel* from the Toolbox onto the page to hold the page's normal content.

5. Add a *Button* to the *Panel* for submitting the content. Give the *Button* the ID *ButtonSubmit* and the text *Submit* and create a button *Click* event handler. You need this button later.

6. Place some content on the panel. The content in this sample application uses several check boxes that the modal dialog pop-up examines before the page is submitted.

```
<h1 >ASP.NET Code Of Conduct </h1>

<asp:Panel ID="Panel1" runat="server"
    style="z-index: 1;left: 10px;top: 70px;
    position: absolute;height: 213px;width: 724px;
    margin-bottom: 0px;">
```

```
<asp:Label ID="Label1" runat="server"
    Text="Name of Developer:"></asp:Label>
     <asp:TextBox ID="TextBox1"
    runat="server"></asp:TextBox>

<br />
<br />
<br />
As an ASP.NET developer, I promise to
<br />
<input type="checkbox" name="Check" id="Checkbox1"/>
<label for="Check1">Use Forms Authentication</label>
<br />
<input type="checkbox" name="Check" id="Checkbox2"/>
<label for="Check2">Separate UI From Code</label>
<br />
<input type="checkbox" name="Check" id="Checkbox3"/>
<label for="Check3">Take Advantage of Custom Controls</label>
<br />
<input type="checkbox" name="Check" id="Checkbox4"/>
<label for="Check4">Use AJAX</label>
<br />
<input type="checkbox" name="Check" id="Checkbox5"/>
<label for="Check5">Give MVC a try</label>
<br />
<input type="checkbox" name="Check" id="Checkbox6"/>
<label for="Check6">Give Silverlight a try</label>
<br />

<asp:Button ID="ButtonSubmit" runat="server" Text="Submit"
        onclick="ButtonSubmit_Click" />
<br />
</asp:Panel>
```

7. Add another *Panel* to the page to represent the pop-up. Give this *Panel* a light yellow background color so that you'll be able to see it when it comes up. It should also have the ID *PanelModalPopup*.

8. Add some content to the new *Panel* that's going to serve as the modal pop-up. At the very least, the pop-up should have *OK* and *Cancel* buttons. Give the *OK* and *Cancel* buttons the ID values *ButtonOK* and *ButtonCancel*. You need them a bit later, too.

```
<asp:Panel ID="PanelModalPopup" runat="server"
    BorderColor="Black"
    BorderStyle="Solid"
    BackColor="LightYellow" Height="72px"
    Width="403px">
    <br />
    <asp:Label
        Text="Are you sure these are the correct entries?"
        runat="server">
    </asp:Label>
        
```

```
<asp:Button ID="ButtonOK"
    runat="server"
    Text="OK" />
  
<asp:Button ID="ButtonCancel"
runat="server" Text="Cancel" />
<br />
</asp:Panel>
```

9. Add a script block to the ASPX file. You need to do this by hand. Write functions to handle the *OK* and *Cancel* buttons. The example here examines check boxes to see which ones have been selected and then displays an alert to show which features have been chosen. The *Cancel* handler simply displays an alert indicating that the *Cancel* button was clicked:

```
<script type="text/javascript">

    function onOk() {
        var optionsChosen;
        optionsChosen = "Options chosen: ";

        if($get('Checkbox1').checked)
        {
          optionsChosen =
            optionsChosen.toString() +
            "Use Forms Authentication ";
        }

        if($get('Checkbox2').checked)
        {
          optionsChosen =
            optionsChosen.toString() +
            "Separate UI From Code ";
        }

        if($get('Checkbox3').checked)
        {
          optionsChosen =
            optionsChosen.toString() +
            "Take Advantage of Custom Controls ";
        }

        if($get('Checkbox4').checked)
        {
          optionsChosen =
            optionsChosen.toString() +
            "Give AJAX a try ";
        }
        alert(optionsChosen);
    }

    function onCancel() {
        alert("Cancel was pressed");
    }
</script>
```

10. Drag the *ModalPopup* extender from the Toolbox onto the page.

11. Add the following markup to the page to set various properties on the new
ModalPopup extenders.s This sets the *OkControlID* property to *ButtonOK* and
the *CancelControlID* property to *ButtonCancel*. It also sets the *OnCancelScript*
property to *onCancel()* (the client-side Cancel script handler you just wrote). Set
OnOkScript="onOk()" (the client-side OK script handler you just wrote). Finally, the
following markup sets the *TargetControlID* property to *ButtonSubmit*:

```
<cc1:ModalPopupExtender
    ID="ModalPopupExtender1"
    runat="server"
    OkControlID="ButtonOK"
    CancelControlID="ButtonCancel"
    OnCancelScript="onCancel()"
    OnOkScript="onOk()"
    TargetControlID="ButtonSubmit"
    PopupControlID="PanelModalPopup"
    runat="server"
    DynamicServicePath="" Enabled="True">
</cc1:ModalPopupExtender>
```

This graphic shows the layout of the page using the *ModalPopup* extender in Visual
Studio 2010:

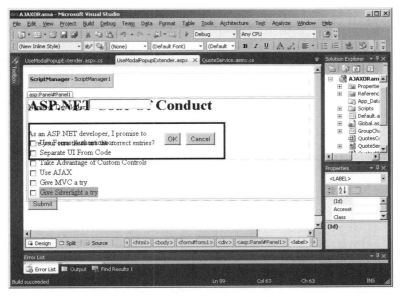

12. Run the page. When you click the Submit button, the *Panel* designated to be the modal
pop-up window is activated. (Remember, the Submit button is the *TargetControlID* of
the *ModalPopup* Extender.) When you dismiss the pop-up window by clicking OK or

Cancel, you should see the client-side scripts being executed. The following graphic image shows the *ModalPopup* extender displaying the modal pop-up window:

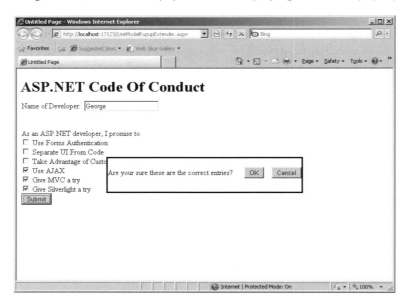

Chapter 23 Quick Reference

To	Do This
Enable a Web site for AJAX	Normal Web sites generated by Visual Studio 2010's template are AJAX-enabled by default. However, you must add a *ScriptManager* to a page before using any of the AJAX server-side controls.
Implement partial page updating in your page	From within an ASP.NET project, select an *UpdatePanel* from the toolbox. Controls that you place in the *UpdatePanel* will trigger updates for only that panel, leaving the rest of the page untouched.
Assign arbitrary triggers to an *UpdatePanel* (that is, trigger partial page updates using controls and events not related to the panel)	Modify an *UpdatePanel*'s trigger collection to include the new events and controls. Highlight the *UpdatePanel* from within the Visual Studio designer. Select the *Triggers* property from within the property editor. Assign triggers as appropriate.
Implement regularly timed automatic posts from your page	Use the AJAX *Timer* control, which will cause a postback to the server at regular intervals.
Use AJAX to apply special UI nuances to your Web page	After installing Visual Studio 2008, you can create AJAX-enabled sites, and use the new AJAX-specific server-side controls available in the AJAX toolkit. Select the control you need. Most AJAX server-side controls may be programmed completely from the server. However, some controls require a bit of JavaScript on the client end.

Chapter 24
Silverlight and ASP.NET

After completing this chapter, you will be able to

- Understand the importance of Microsoft Silverlight.

- Create a Silverlight application.

- Add Silverlight content to Web pages.

- Understand the "Silverlight way."

- Work with Silverlight layout.

- Work with Silverlight animations.

Chapter 21, "ASP.NET and WPF Content," covers integrating Windows Presentation Foundation–based content into a site using XAML-based browser applications (XBAP). Using XBAP is an alternate way to get content out to the client's browser. Rather than simply emitting some HTML tags that turn into controls when they hit the browser, WPF XBAP applications allow for much richer content, including sophisticated layout schemes, deep and varied colors, and even two-dimensional and three-dimensional graphics and transformations.

Although XBAP goes a long way toward producing rich content for your site, it does have a few associated drawbacks. The primary drawback is that XBAP works only with the Windows operating system. Sites providing XBAP content won't work on Macintosh pure clients unable to support the Microsoft .NET Framework version 3.0 (or later) runtime. The second drawback is that integrating usual Web content and Windows Presentation Foundation (WPF) content can be tricky. One option for adding XBAP content is to create a separate page to which clients can navigate. Another option is to use the <iframe /> tag to host the XBAP content within other HTML.

To help overcome these obstacles, Microsoft introduced Silverlight as a tool for creating Rich Internet Applications (RIAs). RIAs are characterized by the inclusion of content you'd expect to see as part of desktop applications. The main advantage of Silverlight is that it works on computers running Windows and Windows Internet Explorer (or Firefox) and Macintoshes running the Safari browser. Because these two platforms constitute the bulk of online consumers, Silverlight makes such WPF-style content available to a majority of Web users.

This chapter shows you how to get started using Silverlight, including the following:

- Some reasons why you might want to include Silverlight content on your site

- How to create a Silverlight application

- How to develop Silverlight-based content

- How to integrate Silverlight content with the rest of your site's pages

First, consider the reason Silverlight even exists.

Web Applications Mature

At this point, you're familiar with the way a typical Web application works—the browser issues an HTTP request to the server, and the server responds with *something*. Most of the time, the response is composed mostly of some HTML that represents a user interface (UI) or data representation on the end user's browser. As you've seen, Microsoft ASP.NET responses are typically built from the ASP.NET *Page* class and its server-side control architecture. A *Page* contains a collection of server-side controls, and the server-side controls are responsible for emitting HTML into the response stream. The browser turns the response stream into the visual representation displayed by the browser.

The earliest Web pages were typically just some formatted text with images sprinkled about and normal HTTP links for navigating around the site. There was usually nothing fancy about these sites: no pop-up menus using Dynamic HTML (DHTML), no interactive graphics, and no pop-up windows (using Asynchronous JavaScript and XML, or AJAX). As various Web technologies have grown and matured, these desktop-like user interface features began to appear in more and more sites. In fact, you can track the evolution of many of these features by going to a Web site archive named "The Wayback Machine" at *http://www.archive.org*. After entering a URL, you can track the evolution of a specific company's site—often all the way back to 1996 or 1997.

Some Web technologies such as DHTML and AJAX have moved much of the UI and interactive processing to the client end—enabled through script. For example, the earliest pop-up menus (the kind that appear when the mouse pointer rests on a single menu item) were often implemented using DHTML. Developers were left to roll them by hand. An early version of an ASP.NET server-side control toolkit made available through the Microsoft Developer Network (MSDN) simplified the task for developers using ASP.NET.

For richer content, many developers relied on a product named Flash (originally produced by Macromedia and now produced by Adobe). Until recently, Flash was the primary tool enabling rich graphics and animations for Web developers. The Flash player was implemented as an ActiveX control for Windows-based computers and as a browser plug-in for other operating systems. Near the end of the 1990s and into the 2000s, most animated and graphic content appeared by way of Flash. The latest rich content tool available from Adobe is named Flex.

With so much of this type of content appearing courtesy of Flash and Flex, you might ask why Microsoft would even venture into producing a Web tool that could be perceived simply as a competitor of a product that already has a foothold in the RIA space.

The most compelling answer is that Silverlight provides the same kind of rich content features as existing products—but it's geared specifically for the Microsoft developer. As a site developer, I've always found it difficult to move from the beautiful, clean .NET programming model to a programming model that is scripted—and comes with all the issues brought on by scripting. For example, writing script is often difficult because it's not type safe. Sometimes scripts don't perform well because they're interpreted rather than compiled into native code. In addition, the tools for developing scripts are as mature as the tools for developing .NET code.

Enter Silverlight.

What Is Silverlight?

Silverlight is Microsoft's foray into the RIA arena. The idea of the RIA has been gaining ground. More and more features closely associated with desktop applications have been moving into browser-hosted applications implemented through client-side scripting, AJAX, or browser plug-ins. Silverlight enables rich, client-style features for PC clients running the Windows operating system and Internet Explorer and Firefox, and Macintosh clients using Safari.

Silverlight has gone through several permutations over the last few years, moving from Silverlight version 1.0 to 2 and now 3. Whereas Silverlight 1.0 and 2 are completely different from each other, Silverlight 3 builds upon the foundations of Silverlight 2.

Silverlight 1.0 was more of an Extensible Application Markup Language (XAML) rendering engine than anything else. Though you could interact with browser content and handle events, it was all done through scripting. Silverlight 2 is actually a subset of the .NET common language runtime (CLR) and WPF-style rendering technology running on the client. When you develop content using Silverlight 2 or 3, you program it using a syntax that is compiled into Intermediate Language. It is compiled just in time (JIT) and runs similarly to how typical desktop .NET applications run. Silverlight offers many of the same development features as typical .NET development. However, some features are missing because they either do not fit the scope of Silverlight, or they don't make sense to implement within what is basically a browser-based platform.

Here are some of the features available through Silverlight:

- With Silverlight, you can plant an island of rich, interactive content in a Web page. Although much of a page might be composed of HTML rendered by a browser, Silverlight content is run within a miniature CLR. The .NET programming model remains largely intact, replete with the usual .NET event handlers, .NET collections, and the .NET control and event model.

- Silverlight includes a rich and ever-growing library of controls. From a development perspective, these controls are much like typical Windows controls or ASP.NET controls. That is, *Button*, *ListBox*, *RadioButton*, *Label*, and *TextBox* controls are part of the control canon. They support many of the same properties and events as the classic Windows and ASP.NET controls do. For example, the *Button* control supports properties such as *Foreground* and *Background* as well as events like *Click*. *ListBoxes* include a source to which collections are bound as well as events like *SelectionChanged*.

- Silverlight supports rich graphics. Traditionally, the only way to get drawings up to the browser has been to draw them in a design tool and ship them to the client as JPG files or PNG files. Silverlight has a programmatic drawing API that you can use to render figures on the client computer. Because Silverlight allows programmatic access to your drawings, the drawings become active content that can be changed on the fly and that responds to user-generated events.

- Silverlight includes controls that provide media services, making it easy to embed video and audio in your Web pages.

- Silverlight integrates well with the HTML Document Object Model. You can access HTML elements from within Silverlight code, and you can access Silverlight code from JavaScript code.

- Silverlight is targeted to the .NET developer. Silverlight is actually a miniature .NET runtime that downloads onto the client computer as an ActiveX control (for Windows-based computers) or as a plug-in for the Safari browser (for Macs). Although other Rich Internet Application tools have been available for some time, they all require their own scripting syntax to make the content interactive. .NET developers can step right into Silverlight development because they can program Silverlight using the .NET programming model.

- Tool support for Silverlight is unsurpassed. Microsoft Visual Studio 2010 fully supports Silverlight development from programming and debugging points of view. Those with design skill can use Microsoft Expression Blend to help develop the visual appearance of applications independently of the programming and logic of the applications. Microsoft Expression Design is a high-end vector graphics drawing tool, and Microsoft Expression Encoder is for supporting media.

Silverlight takes many architecture and design cues from WPF. In many ways, Silverlight is like the younger sibling of WPF. As in WPF, the visual appearance of a Silverlight UI is usually expressed using XAML, an XML dialect useful for expressing object models (such as the one that represents the Silverlight visual tree). The program logic is expressed using a .NET language.

Next, dive right in and see how a Silverlight application works.

Creating a Silverlight Application

Before getting into the details of Silverlight, consider how it fits in with the rest of the project types available through Visual Studio. Creating a Silverlight application is like creating other types of applications using Visual Studio. Visual Studio includes a template that creates the Silverlight content. Visual Studio also gives you the option to include one of the following:

- A simple HTML test page on which to exercise the Silverlight content
- An entire ASP.NET site so that you can exercise the Silverlight content in an ASP.NET-type setting

From there, developing a Silverlight component follows much the same programming model as the rest of .NET: You develop the Silverlight portion, and then exercise it using the HTML page or the ASP.NET project. In fact, when you start debugging, Visual Studio starts up the Web development server and your browser of choice—just as it does with typical Web application development. If you set any breakpoints in your Silverlight code, Visual Studio will stop there so that you can watch your code execute.

This first exercise shows the steps necessary for creating a simple Silverlight application. The purpose here is just to get started. You'll see Silverlight's capabilities in more detail soon.

Creating a Silverlight application

1. Begin by starting Visual Studio. Select File, New, Project. Under Project Type, select Silverlight Application. Name the project *SilverlightSite*:

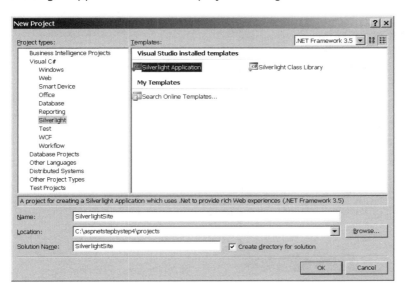

2. Visual Studio asks you whether you'd like to create a single HTML page for testing or an entire ASP.NET site for testing. The default is to create an entire site, as shown in the following graphic. Select this option, and click OK. If you have not yet installed all the necessary Silverlight development tools (the Silverlight SDK in this case), Visual Studio reminds you to do so. In fact, Visual Studio will not let you proceed until the SDK is downloaded.

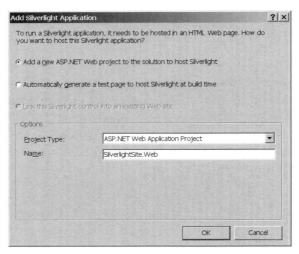

3. Visual Studio generates a solution with two projects. The first project contains the Silverlight content. The second project is a Web Application project. Here is Solution Explorer after creating the Silverlight application:

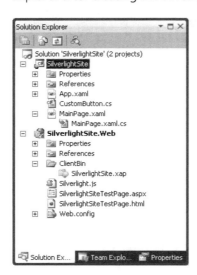

The first node in the solution represents the project holding the Silverlight content. Notice the normal Properties folder, which includes a version of AssemblyInfo.cs with assembly-wide information. You also see the familiar References folder, which contains references to other assemblies. The assemblies to which this project is linked are actually the Silverlight versions of the .NET system assemblies. There are also MainPage.xaml and App.xaml nodes. You dig into those in the section titled "Architecture" later in this chapter.

The second project in the solution is the ASP.NET site that you can use to exercise the content. In many ways, it looks like any typical ASP.NET site. There is a Default.aspx folder, an App_Data folder, and the usual Properties and References folders. There are a few new folders and files here, as well. First, there are two files named SilverlightSiteTestPage—a raw HTML version and an ASPX version. These illustrate alternate ways to host the Silverlight content in your site. You take a closer look at these in the section titled "Adding Silverlight Content to a Web Page" later in this chapter. The Silverlight.js file includes some script utilities you might find useful—most notably a scripting function useful for instantiating the Silverlight content dynamically from script. Finally, notice the ClientBin directory—this is the folder into which the final Silverlight content will be compiled so that the client browser can fetch it as the browser loads the page.

4. Open the Page.xaml file and type the following tag so that the page renders a *Button*. Doing so places a *Button* control in the Silverlight display area so that you can see the Silverlight content when you run the application. Whatever string you assign to the *Content* property becomes the text the *Button* displays:

```
<UserControl x:Class="SilverlightSite.MainPage"
  xmlns="http://schemas.microsoft.com/winfx/2006/xaml/presentation"
  xmlns:x="http://schemas.microsoft.com/winfx/2006/xaml"
  xmlns:d="http://schemas.microsoft.com/expression/blend/2008"
  xmlns:mc="http://schemas.openxmlformats.org/markup-compatibility/2006"
  mc:Ignorable="d"
  d:DesignHeight="300" d:DesignWidth="400">

  <Grid x:Name="LayoutRoot" Background="White">
    <Button Content="Hello World!"></Button>
  </Grid>
d</UserControl>
```

5. Build the program and run it by pressing Ctrl+F5. Because you created the solution to use an ASP.NET project as the test project, Visual Studio starts the Web development browser and uses the ASP.NET test page. (There's actually an ASP.NET server-side control that will host Silverlight—you see that in just a minute.) Notice that without the *Height* and *Width* properties defined, the button takes up the entire area allotted to Silverlight.

6. To make the Silverlight content interactive, add an event handler to the button. Before you add the handler, it's usually best to name the control because Visual Studio uses the control name to generate the handler method name. That makes it easier to track the handlers later on. Add the *Name* attribute to the <Button> tag, followed by a *Click* handler. When you start typing the word *Click*, Visual Studio offers to write the event handler for you. This is what you see when you look at the code:

```
<UserControl x:Class="SilverlightSite.MainPage"
 xmlns="http://schemas.microsoft.com/winfx/2006/xaml/presentation"
 xmlns:x="http://schemas.microsoft.com/winfx/2006/xaml"
 xmlns:d="http://schemas.microsoft.com/expression/blend/2008"
 xmlns:mc="http://schemas.openxmlformats.org/markup-compatibility/2006"
 mc:Ignorable="d"
 d:DesignHeight="300" d:DesignWidth="400">
 <Grid x:Name="LayoutRoot" Background="White">
  <Button Content="Hello World!"
        x:Name="theButton"
        Click="theButton_Click"
        >
  </Button>
 </Grid>
</UserControl>
```

7. Now add some code to handle the button click. Open the file MainPage.xaml.cs and locate the new handler. If you allowed Visual Studio to create the handler code for you, the handler method will be named *theButton_Click*. The handler takes two arguments (like most other .NET handlers). The first parameter is the sender—in this case, a reference to the button that was clicked. The second parameter is of the type

RoutedEventArgs. The *RoutedEventArgs* is similar to the typical .NET *EventArgs* in that it contains information about the event. However, Silverlight manages its own message routing scheme (routed events), so the event information argument type is slightly enhanced.

Modify the *Click* handler to update the content of the button, increase the font size, and change the *Foreground* color to red. To do so, add the code you see here in bold type:

```
private void theButton_Click(object sender,
    RoutedEventArgs e)
{
 Button button = sender as Button;
 button.Content =
   "The button was clicked";
 button.FontSize = 22;
 button.Foreground =
   new SolidColorBrush(Colors.Red);
}
```

8. Run the program to ensure that it works. Visual Studio opens a browser and shows the ASP.NET test page. When you click the button, you should see the font size increase and the font color change, and the button should show new content.

Architecture

Now that you've seen Silverlight in action, here's how it works. The architecture of a Silverlight component is pretty straightforward. It consists of an instance of the *Application* object (represented by the Application.xaml and the Application.xaml.cs files) and a visual component (represented by the MainPage.xaml and MainPage.xaml.cs files). Silverlight divides its presentation code and its logic/behavior code into separate concerns—just like ASP.NET does. The ASP.NET code-beside model involves ASPX/C# or Visual Basic file pairings. Silverlight uses XAML/C# or Visual Basic pairings. The XAML files usually express the user interface, and the C# or Visual Basic files support the behavior.

The *Application* object is there to provide a rendezvous point for the component. It's a place where you can store any component-wide state, and it has startup and shutdown events to which you can subscribe. If you open the Application.xaml.cs file, you can see that Visual Studio has stubbed out some of those events and wired them up for you already.

The *Application* object is available at all times (in the same way the ASP.NET *HttpApplication* object is always available). In addition to supporting global events, the *Application* object maintains global state.

Part of the *Application* bootstrapping is to set up the application's *RootVisual* property. The *RootVisual* property tells the Silverlight rendering engine what to present. The *RootVisual* derives from a class named *UserControl*. It represents the backplane onto which visual content is placed. By taking a closer look at the *UserControl* you can get a good idea about how XAML works.

XAML

XAML stands for eXtensible Application Markup Language. XAML is a dialect of XML invented primarily for constructing object graphs declaratively. Although it was originally developed to support WPF, it's found its way into other uses—most notably Windows Workflow Foundation. Silverlight presentations are described through XAML.

Silverlight uses XAML to build the visual tree. Take another look at the *MainPage* class from the last example:

```
<UserControl x:Class="SilverlightSite.MainPage"
 xmlns="http://schemas.microsoft.com/winfx/2006/xaml/presentation"
 xmlns:x="http://schemas.microsoft.com/winfx/2006/xaml"
 xmlns:d="http://schemas.microsoft.com/expression/blend/2008
     xmlns:mc="http://schemas.openxmlformats.org/markup-compatibility/2006"
   mc:Ignorable="d"
 d:DesignHeight="300" d:DesignWidth="400">
  <Grid x:Name="LayoutRoot" Background="White">
    <Button Content="Hello World!"
      x:Name="theButton"
      Click="theButton_Click"></Button>
  </Grid>
</UserControl>
```

The XAML constructs an instance of the *UserControl* class, associates it with the class named *SilverlightSite.MainPage*, and initializes the *DesignWidth* property to 400 and the *DesignHeight* property to 300. Next, the XAML constructs an instance of the *Grid* class, assigns the name *LayoutRoot* to the *Grid*, and sets the *Background* to white. Finally, the XAML constructs an instance of the *Button* class, names it *theButton*, assigns the string "Hello World!" to the *Content* property, and then sets up the *Click* event so that it's handled by the *theButton_Click* method (which is a member of the *SilverlightSite.MainPage* class). After spending some time with ASP.NET, this should look awfully familiar—this is how the ASP.NET *Page* class builds its control tree. The major difference here is really between the ASPX syntax and the XAML syntax.

Constructing the Visual Tree

The role of XAML in Silverlight is to construct the Silverlight component's visual tree. This happens in the *MainPage* constructor. Notice that the code produced by Visual Studio contains a call to the method *InitializeComponent*. *InitializeComponent* parses the XAML to create the objects composing the visual tree and initializes the properties mentioned in the XAML. For example, the previous snippet and the following snippet produce the same visual tree:

```
Page ConstructVisualTreeProgrammatically()
{
  Page page = new Page();

  Grid grid = new Grid();
  Button button = new Button();
  button.Click += this.theButton_Click;
  button.Content = "Hello World!";
  grid.Children.Add(button);

  return page;
}
```

XAML and Namespaces

Near the top of the XAML in the earlier example, you can see four XML namespaces defined, the first two of which I discuss here (they're most important). The default namespace is assigned to be "http://schemas.microsoft.com/winfx/2006/xaml/presentation". This namespace scopes the typical Silverlight features and the control canon. For example, by making this the default namespace, you can simply use the <Button /> tag without any prefixes. The second namespace, "x", is assigned to "http://schemas.microsoft.com/winfx/2006/xaml". This namespace defines Silverlight keywords such as *Name* (used to name XAML elements to make them available programmatically) and *Key* (used to assign key/value pairs within Silverlight resource dictionaries).

You can add other namespaces as necessary. For example, if you want to make any types you define in the SilverlightSite assembly available within XAML, you could add a namespace. For example, if the Silverlight component assembly has a type named *CustomButton* in it, and you'd like to include it as part of the visual presentation, you could add the namespace as follows, and then use the component from within the XAML as shown in the following bold text:

```
<UserControl x:Class="SilverlightSite.MainPage"
 xmlns="http://schemas.microsoft.com/winfx/2006/xaml/presentation"
 xmlns:x="http://schemas.microsoft.com/winfx/2006/xaml"
 xmlns:d="http://schemas.microsoft.com/expression/blend/2008"
 xmlns:mc="http://schemas.openxmlformats.org/markup-compatibility/2006"

 xmlns:my="clr-namespace:SilverlightSite"

 mc:Ignorable="d"
 d:DesignHeight="300" d:DesignWidth="400">
  <Grid x:Name="LayoutRoot" Background="White">
```

```
<my:CustomButton
 Content="Hello World!"
 x:Name="theButton"
 Click="theButton_Click"></my:CustomButton>

    </Grid>
</UserControl>
```

Compiling the Silverlight Application

To compile the Silverlight application from within Visual Studio, select Build, Debug from the main menu, or press F6. When you build the SilverlightSite solution, Visual Studio compiles the Silverlight component into a regular .NET assembly (though the references are to the Silverlight system assemblies rather than the normal .NET assemblies). Afterward, Visual Studio creates a XAP (pronounced "zap") file containing the Silverlight component and any external resources (images, graphics, fonts, and so forth) you want to have available when the component finally ends up at the client browser.

The XAP file is a typical zip-compressed file. In fact, you can open it with any standard zip compression utility to view the contents. Compressing the Silverlight content this way cuts down on page loading time for pages using the component.

Finally, Visual Studio copies the XAP file into the ClientBin directory managed by the ASP.NET project.

Adding Silverlight Content to a Web Page

You can add Silverlight content to a Web page in three ways. The first is to use the traditional <object> tag embedded in HTML. Second, you can use the ASP.NET server-side control for hosting Silverlight content. Finally, you can add Silverlight content dynamically using some JavaScript. Begin by adding content using the <object> tag.

Using the Object Tag

The first way to add Silverlight content is by using the standard <object> tag (the one that loaded ActiveX controls on pages written in the late 1990s!). In fact, Visual Studio creates an HTML page for you that loads the Silverlight content using the <object> tag.

```
<body>
 <!-Run-time errors from Silverlight will be displayed here. -->
 <!-- This will contain debugging information and should be removed -->
 <!-- or hidden when debugging is completed -->
 <div id='errorLocation' style="font-size: small;color: Gray;"></div>
```

```
<div id="silverlightControlHost">
 <object data="data:application/x-silverlight-2,"
  type="application/x-silverlight-2" width="100%" height="100%">
  <param name="source" value="ClientBin/SilverlightSite.xap"/>
  <param name="onerror" value="onSilverlightError" />
  <param name="background" value="white" />
  <param name="minRuntimeVersion" value="2.0.31005.0" />
  <param name="autoUpgrade" value="true" />
  <a href="http://go.microsoft.com/fwlink/?LinkID=124807"
   style="text-decoration: none;">
   <img src="http://go.microsoft.com/fwlink/?LinkId=108181"
    alt="Get Microsoft Silverlight" style="border-style: none"/>
  </a>
 </object>
 <iframe style='visibility:hidden;height:0;width:0;border:0px'>
 </iframe>
 </div>
</body>
```

Silverlight is implemented as an ActiveX control for Windows clients and as a Safari browser plug-in for Macintosh clients. The <object> tag looks up the Silverlight implementation on the client computer, and then fetches the appropriate XAP file from the server and hosts it. Notice how parameters can be passed to Silverlight. The ones listed previously are predefined, but you can define your own parameters to be passed into Silverlight when it loads.

Using the ASP.NET Silverlight Server-Side Control

The second way to include Silverlight content on your page is to use the ASP.NET server-side control that generates the object tag for you when it renders. Visual Studio creates a page using the ASP.NET *Silverlight* control.

```
<%@ Page Language="C#" AutoEventWireup="true" %>
<%@ Register Assembly="System.Web.Silverlight"
    Namespace="System.Web.UI.SilverlightControls"
    TagPrefix="asp" %>
<!DOCTYPE html PUBLIC "-//W3C//DTD XHTML 1.0 Transitional//EN"
 "http://www.w3.org/TR/xhtml1/DTD/xhtml1-transitional.dtd">
<html xmlns="http://www.w3.org/1999/xhtml" style="height:100%;">
<head runat="server">
<title>SilverlightORama</title>
</head>
<body style="height:100%;margin:0;">
<form id="form1" runat="server" style="height:100%;">
 <asp:ScriptManager ID="ScriptManager1" runat="server"></asp:ScriptManager>
 <div   style="height:100%;">
  <asp:Silverlight ID="Xaml1" runat="server"
   Source="~/ClientBin/SilverlightSite.xap"
   MinimumVersion="2.0.31005.0" Width="100%"
   Height="100%" />
 </div>
 </form>
</body>
</html>
```

The *Silverlight* control works much the same way as all of the other server-side controls work. They end up in the page's control tree and send HTML to the browser. The Silverlight control emits the HTML necessary to allow the client browser to load Silverlight and host the content in it.

Using the JavaScript Function

Visual Studio also includes a JavaScript library with a helper function— *Silverlight.createObjectEx*. You can find it in the Silverlight.js file included as part of the ASP.NET test project produced by Visual Studio. Call *Silverlight.createObjectEx* from within the HTML page and pass in the path to the XAP file, the events, and any other parameters important to the Silverlight control. Although this is less convenient than is using the server-side control, it offers you the ability to invoke Silverlight content dynamically—for example, by way of a JavaScript event.

Controls and Events

Because you are well versed in the controls available through ASP.NET, there's a lot to say about the way Silverlight controls work. Silverlight includes nearly all the same controls available as ASP.NET server-side controls (*Button*, *ListBox*, *RadioButton*, *TextBox*, *Label*, and so forth).

Whereas the job of an ASP.NET server-side control is to emit a tag to be interpreted by the browser eventually, Silverlight controls are rendered directly on the client by the Silverlight engine. ASP.NET control events are usually handled on the server by server-side event handlers, while Silverlight control events are handled on the client side within the Silverlight component.

Routed Events

Silverlight control events look much like typical .NET events. The event handlers all use an object as the first parameter (always the sender). Following the sender parameter, the handlers include some permutation of the standard event arguments. To manage events Silverlight uses routed events, which are like typical .NET events in that handlers for routed events can be attached directly to the controls that produce them (for example, the *Button* control exposes a *Click* event). However, routed events are different because you can attach handlers for events at various places up and down the Silverlight visual tree. That is, you do not need to attach the handlers directly to the controls. This can be useful in various scenarios. For example, imagine you want to trap the left mouse down event for all elements in a layout panel (within a *Grid*, for instance). Rather than attaching singular event handlers to each element in the panel, you could attach the handler to the layout panel itself and intercept the event there.

Silverlight Controls and Class Members

Just as ASP.NET tags that are given IDs in the ASPX file have corresponding members in the code-beside class, XAML tags that are given names also end up as members in the code-beside class. For example, the following XAML produces *Grid* and *Button* member variables named *LayoutRoot* and *theButton* that you can access from the code-beside accompanying the Silverlight application:

```
<UserControl x:Class="SilverlightSite.MainPage"
 xmlns="http://schemas.microsoft.com/winfx/2006/xaml/presentation"
 xmlns:x="http://schemas.microsoft.com/winfx/2006/xaml" xmlns:d="http://schemas.microsoft.
com/expression/blend/2008"
 xmlns:mc="http://schemas.openxmlformats.org/markup-compatibility/2006"
 mc:Ignorable="d"
 d:DesignHeight="300" d:DesignWidth="400">
   <Grid x:Name="LayoutRoot" Background="White">
      <Button Content="Hello World!"
       x:Name="theButton"
       Click="theButton_Click"></Button>
   </Grid></UserControl>
```

Expression Blend

Although Visual Studio does contain a designer that you can use to see basically what your finished content will look like, Visual Studio is better for programming and debugging. For more intricate design tasks, Microsoft provides Expression Blend. You should consider using Expression Blend to design and modify the visual elements of an application. Expression Blend is too complex to discuss in detail in this chapter, but Visual Studio and Expression Blend share the same solution and project file formats. You can create Silverlight applications using Visual Studio and open them with Expression Blend, and you can create Silverlight applications using Expression Blend and open them with Visual Studio.

As mentioned, extensive coverage of Expression Blend is beyond the scope of this book, but it's worthwhile for you to learn about this application. Expression Blend provides a perspective of the visual aspect of a Silverlight component different from the perspective provided by Visual Studio. For more information about Expression Blend, see the Microsoft Silverlight page at *http://www.microsoft.com/expression/products/ Blend_Overview.aspx.*

Silverlight and Layout

As mentioned earlier in the chapter, *MainPage* (derived from *UserControl*) is the main presentation area for the Silverlight content. The *UserControl* is a *ContentControl* that can contain a single piece of content. Although you could put any control (such as a *TextBlock* or a *Button*) on the page, you'd be left with no more room to put anything else. This was the case with the SilverlightSite application you saw earlier in the chapter.

Rather than forcing a singular layout scheme (for example, absolute *x* and *y* positioning), Silverlight supports various layout schemes available through layout panels. By using these panels, you can add many controls as well as dictate their positioning in the final user interface. Out of the box, Silverlight supports the *Canvas*, the *Grid*, and the *StackPanel*.

When you place a *Canvas* layout panel inside the *MainPage*, it positions elements at absolute *x* and *y* locations. The *Grid* positions elements in rows and columns. The *StackPanel* stacks elements either vertically or horizontally. Here is an exercise to illustrate how Silverlight layout works.

Working with Silverlight layout

1. Create a new Silverlight application named *SilverlightLayout*. Have Visual Studio create an ASP.NET test project for you.

2. Examine the MainPage.xaml file generated by Visual Studio. Make the *UserControl* width 600.

3. Visual Studio gives you a grid as the layout. Turn on grid lines and add two grid columns. The *Grid ShowGridLines* property is a simple Boolean. However, the *Grid* column definitions are a little trickier. Defining columns requires using the rich property syntax:

```
<UserControl x:Class="SilverlightLayout.MainPage"
 xmlns="http://schemas.microsoft.com/winfx/2006/xaml/presentation"
 xmlns:x="http://schemas.microsoft.com/winfx/2006/xaml"
 xmlns:d="http://schemas.microsoft.com/expression/blend/2008"
 xmlns:mc="http://schemas.openxmlformats.org/markup-compatibility/2006"
 mc:Ignorable="d"

 DesignWidth="600" DesignHeight="300">
 <Grid x:Name="LayoutRoot" Background="White"
  ShowGridLines="True">
  <Grid.ColumnDefinitions>
   <ColumnDefinition ></ColumnDefinition>
   <ColumnDefinition ></ColumnDefinition>
  </Grid.ColumnDefinitions>
 </Grid>
</UserControl>
```

4. Add a *Canvas* to the grid, name the *Canvas theCanvas* so that you can refer to it programmatically later on. Put it in column 0. Add some content to the *Canvas*. The following example shows how you can draw a few shapes and locate them within the *Canvas* using the *Canvas.Left* and *Canvas.Right* attached properties. Notice that shapes have *Stroke* and *StrokeThickness* that define the color and thickness of each shape's border. There's also a *Fill* property with which you can define the color used to fill a shape. Finally, set the opacity of each of these shapes to 60 percent. You can use this property to add some mouse interactivity to the shapes.

```
<UserControl x:Class="SilverlightLayout.MainPage"
 xmlns="http://schemas.microsoft.com/winfx/2006/xaml/presentation"
 xmlns:x="http://schemas.microsoft.com/winfx/2006/xaml"
 xmlns:d="http://schemas.microsoft.com/expression/blend/2008"
 xmlns:mc="http://schemas.openxmlformats.org/markup-compatibility/2006"
 mc:Ignorable="d"

DesignWidth="600" DesignHeight="300">
    <Grid x:Name="LayoutRoot" Background="White"
          ShowGridLines="True">
        <Grid.ColumnDefinitions>
            <ColumnDefinition ></ColumnDefinition>
            <ColumnDefinition ></ColumnDefinition>
        </Grid.ColumnDefinitions>

        <Canvas Grid.Column="0" x:Name="theCanvas">
            <Rectangle Width="100" Height="100"
                       Fill="LightBlue" Stroke="Black"
                       StrokeThickness="2"
                       Canvas.Top="75" Canvas.Left="150"
                       Opacity=".6">
            </Rectangle>
            <Ellipse Width="150" Height="100"
                     Fill="Green" Stroke="Yellow"
                     StrokeThickness="3"
                     Canvas.Left="50"
                     Canvas.Top="175"
                     Opacity=".6">
            </Ellipse>
            <Rectangle Width="150" Height="150"
                       Fill="Red"
                       Stroke="Maroon"
                       StrokeThickness="3"
                       Canvas.Left="30"
                       Canvas.Top="45"
                       Opacity=".6">
            </Rectangle>
        </Canvas>
    </Grid>
</UserControl>
```

5. Now add some mouse interactivity to the shapes on the *Canvas*. First, set up mouse enter and leave handlers to increase the opacity of the shapes in the *Canvas* when the pointer rests on them. To do this, open the MainPage.xaml.cs file and implement event handlers for the *MouseEnter* and the *MouseLeave* events. The event handlers are going to be attached to the shapes themselves, so the sender of these events is going to be the shapes. For each implementation, cast the first argument (the sender) to be of type *Shape*. This is necessary to access its *Opacity* property. The *MouseEnter* handler should then assign the *Opacity* property to be 100 percent (the number 1, that is). The *MouseLeave* handler should reduce the *Opacity* property to 60 percent (the number 0.6, that is). After implementing the *MouseEnter* and *MouseLeave* handlers, in the *Page* constructor, wire up the event handlers to the *MouseEnter* and *MouseLeave* events of every element on the *Canvas*, as shown in bold text in the following XAML:

```
public partial class MainPage : UserControl
{
  private void theCanvas_MouseEnter(object sender, MouseEventArgs e)
  {
    Shape shape = sender as Shape;
    if (shape != null)
    {
      shape.Opacity = 1;
    }
  }
  private void theCanvas_MouseLeave(object sender, MouseEventArgs e)
  {
    Shape s = sender as Shape;
    if (s != null)
    {
      s.Opacity = .6;
    }
  }

  public MainPage()
  {
    InitializeComponent();
    foreach (Shape s in theCanvas.Children)
    {
      s.MouseEnter += this.theCanvas_MouseEnter;
      s.MouseLeave += this.theCanvas_MouseLeave;
    }
  }
}
```

6. Run the application. At first, you should be able to see the outlines of all the shapes because they start out with an opacity of 60 percent, as shown in the following graphic:

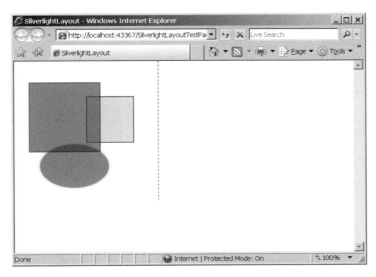

7. Then, when you move the pointer over one of the shapes, you should see it become opaque:

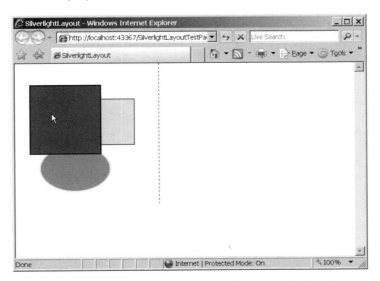

In this case, when the pointer rests on the rectangle that is topmost in the Z-order, the rectangle blocks full view of the other rectangle and ellipse behind it.

8. Now add a *StackPanel* to the grid and place it in the second column. Add a *Button* to the *StackPanel*, followed by a *ListBox* with some contained items. Following the first *ListBox*, nest another *StackPanel* in the outer *StackPanel*—orient this one horizontally by setting the *Orientation* property to *Horizontal*. Place two more *ListBoxes* in the nested *StackPanel*:

```
<UserControl x:Class="SilverlightLayout.MainPage"
xmlns="http://schemas.microsoft.com/winfx/2006/xaml/presentation"
 xmlns:x="http://schemas.microsoft.com/winfx/2006/xaml"
 xmlns:d="http://schemas.microsoft.com/expression/blend/2008"
 xmlns:mc="http://schemas.openxmlformats.org/markup-compatibility/2006"
 mc:Ignorable="d"

DesignWidth="600" DesignHeight="600">
    <Grid x:Name="LayoutRoot" Background="White"
          ShowGridLines="True">
        <Grid.ColumnDefinitions>
            <ColumnDefinition ></ColumnDefinition>
            <ColumnDefinition ></ColumnDefinition>
        </Grid.ColumnDefinitions>

        <!-- Canvas goes here... -->

        <StackPanel Grid.Column="1">
            <Button Content="Button1"></Button>
            <ListBox Height="75">
                <ListBoxItem Content="Item 1"></ListBoxItem>
                <ListBoxItem Content="Item 2"></ListBoxItem>
                <ListBoxItem Content="Item 3"></ListBoxItem>
                <ListBoxItem Content="Item 4"></ListBoxItem>
                <ListBoxItem Content="Item 5"></ListBoxItem>
            </ListBox>
            <StackPanel Orientation="Horizontal">
                <ListBox Height="75">
                    <ListBoxItem Content="Item 1"></ListBoxItem>
                    <ListBoxItem Content="Item 2"></ListBoxItem>
                    <ListBoxItem Content="Item 3"></ListBoxItem>
                    <ListBoxItem Content="Item 4"></ListBoxItem>
                    <ListBoxItem Content="Item 5"></ListBoxItem>
                </ListBox>
                <ListBox Height="75">
                    <ListBoxItem Content="Item 1"></ListBoxItem>
                    <ListBoxItem Content="Item 2"></ListBoxItem>
                    <ListBoxItem Content="Item 3"></ListBoxItem>
                    <ListBoxItem Content="Item 4"></ListBoxItem>
                    <ListBoxItem Content="Item 5"></ListBoxItem>
                </ListBox>
            </StackPanel>
        </StackPanel>
    </Grid>
</UserControl>
```

The layout should appear like this when you're finished:

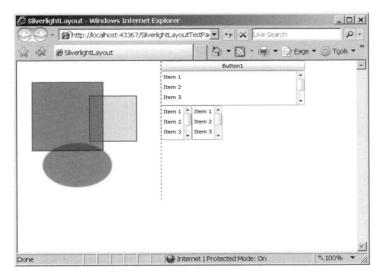

This example shows that you can nest Silverlight layout panels arbitrarily. In addition to the three panels available as part of the official control set, you can write your own custom panel by deriving from the *Panel* class.

Integrating with HTML

Silverlight offers two paths for integrating with traditional Web content (that is, HTML). First, Silverlight components can access the Document Object Model (DOM). Second, JavaScript within a Web page can access Silverlight components.

To access HTML elements from within Silverlight, use the *System.Windows.Browser. HtmlDocument* class. The *HtmlDocument* class is loaded with the HTML Document Object Model of the currently loaded Web page. It's available through the static *Document* member of *System.Windows.Browser.HtmlPage*. You can find elements identified in the HTML document using *HtmlDocument.GetElementByName* or *HtmlDocument.GetElementById*. From there, you can access the data within the tags and use the data programmatically. In addition, you can attach managed events to the HTML elements (for example, to input buttons) and handle the events from managed code rather than from JavaScript.

For example, take a look at the following code, which shows some HTML with the tags identified through the *ID* attribute:

```
<input id="input" type="text" />
<input id="submit" type="button" value="Submit" />
<div   id="output" />
```

Accessing the DOM is straightforward. In the Silverlight component code, declare separate *HtmlElements* for each tag you want to access within the DOM. You find the *HtmlElement* definition in the *System.Windows.Browser* namespace. The *HtmlDocument* class (available through the *HtmlPage* class) gives you access to the tags. The most useful methods of the *HtmlElement* class are *GetProperty*, *SetProperty*, and *AttachEvent*. The following code illustrates how to access the identified tags through the *HtmlDocument* class. It also shows how to get and set properties within the tag and how to attach events (for example, how to attach a click handler to the button tag). The HTML DOM helper classes are in the *System. Windows.Browser* namespace.

```
namespace UseDOM
{
    public partial class MainPage : UserControl
    {
        HtmlElement _input;
        HtmlElement _output;
        HtmlElement _submit;

        public MainPage()
        {
            InitializeComponent();

            HtmlDocument document = HtmlPage.Document;
            _input = document.GetElementById("input");
            _output = document.GetElementById("output");
            _submit = document.GetElementById("submit");

            _submit.AttachEvent("onclick", OnSubmit);
        }

        void OnSubmit(object sender, HtmlEventArgs ea)
        {
            string input = (string)_input.GetProperty("value");
            string output = "you typed: " + input;
            _output.SetProperty("innerHTML", output);
        }
    }
}
```

So that you can access managed code from within JavaScript, Silverlight includes the *[ScriptableType]* attribute that you use to mark entire types as scriptable and the *[ScriptableMember]* attribute that you use to mark individual type members as scriptable. The *System.Windows.HtmlPage* class includes two methods for registering managed types to make them available to script: *RegisterCreatableType* allows fresh instances of the type to be created from within script, and *RegisterScriptableObject* allows access to already-existing instances of the type. From there, use the Silverlight plug-in's content member to create the type or look up the existing instance. Then, you can use the type from within script code and treat it as though it was a normal JavaScript object.

Animations

One of the most compelling features of Silverlight is how it gives you the ability to incorporate animations in the content space. Silverlight provides a uniform and consistent means of animating UI elements within a visual tree.

To understand how Silverlight animation works, you need to understand a bit about Silverlight *dependency properties*. Many Silverlight classes expose their properties as dependency properties, which work this way. As a concrete example, think about the *Button* control. Instead of storing properties such as *Height* and *Width* as actual data members within the *Button* class, Silverlight stores the actual data for these properties in a backing store managed by Silverlight. *Backing store* is simply a term that means that the underlying class or infrastructure provides the memory for the property data storage.

Each class gets its own storage for data members, and the values are keyed to the class instance identities. This might seem like an odd way to approach storing data members, but it provides the developer two important features. First, storing data this way can save a lot of instance data, which helps performance (for example, by reducing garbage collections). Another main feature is that when the values change (for any reason), Silverlight can trigger events—for example, telling the scene to rearrange (and redraw) itself. This eliminates the need to write all those painting event handlers when any (from a possible multitude) of values change.

Animations best illustrate the value of dependency properties. All Silverlight animations generally work the same way:

1. Choose the property you wish to animate (only dependency properties can be animated).

2. Choose from a number of animation drivers (there's one for most data types, including double, integer values, Boolean values, colors, and so on).

3. Connect the animation driver to the property.

4. Create a storyboard to hold the animation and add the animation.

5. Start the storyboard.

When the storyboard starts, it uses the animation drivers to modify the target properties. Because the target properties are dependency properties, changes become immediately apparent. For example, if you animate the *Width* property of a button, you literally see the width of the button change.

Silverlight animations are configurable in many ways. For example, you can configure the following factors:

- The duration of an animation

- Whether an animation reverses automatically

- The acceleration curve of an animation

- How many times or how long an animation repeats

Finally, Silverlight offers more complex animations, as well. For example, Silverlight offers key frame animations and spline animations for nonlinear animation effects.

Following is an exercise that shows how Silverlight animations work. This example shows how you can animate a set of images so that they grow in height and width, become more opaque, and then reset to their original state. The example illustrates several concepts, including how to work with animations within the code beside, transform UI elements visually and animate the transform, and how binary resources are packed in the Silverlight XAP container.

Animating the *RenderTransform* and *Opacity* properties of an image

1. Create a new Silverlight application named *SilverlightAnimations*. Have Visual Studio create an ASP.NET Web Project.

2. Add 5 *ColumnDefinitions* and 10 *RowDefinitions* to the *Grid* that is the *LayoutRoot*. This is all the XAML code you add in this example. The rest of the code lives in the code beside.

```
<UserControl x:Class="SilverlightAnimation.MainPage"
 xmlns="http://schemas.microsoft.com/winfx/2006/xaml/presentation"
 xmlns:x="http://schemas.microsoft.com/winfx/2006/xaml"
 xmlns:d="http://schemas.microsoft.com/expression/blend/2008"
 xmlns:mc="http://schemas.openxmlformats.org/markup-compatibility/2006"
 mc:Ignorable="d"

 DesignWidth="600" DesignHeight="300">
    <Grid x:Name="LayoutRoot"
          Background="White">
        <Grid.RowDefinitions>
            <RowDefinition></RowDefinition>
            <RowDefinition></RowDefinition>
            <RowDefinition></RowDefinition>
            <RowDefinition></RowDefinition>
            <RowDefinition></RowDefinition>
            <RowDefinition></RowDefinition>
            <RowDefinition></RowDefinition>
            <RowDefinition></RowDefinition>
            <RowDefinition></RowDefinition>
            <RowDefinition></RowDefinition>
        </Grid.RowDefinitions>
```

```
<Grid.ColumnDefinitions>
    <ColumnDefinition></ColumnDefinition>
    <ColumnDefinition></ColumnDefinition>
    <ColumnDefinition></ColumnDefinition>
    <ColumnDefinition></ColumnDefinition>
    <ColumnDefinition></ColumnDefinition>
</Grid.ColumnDefinitions>
    </Grid>
</UserControl>
```

3. Add some images of the state flags so that there's something to animate. Go to the final solution (included on the CD that accompanies this book) and borrow the JPGs of the 50 state flags. From Solution Explorer, right-click the SilverlightAnimation project and click Add, Folder. Name the Folder *Images*. Right-click the Images folder and click Add, Existing Items. Navigate to the solution for Chapter 24 on the CD accompanying the book (the directories are named by chapter), and select all 50 images from the Images folder. These images are JPEG images of all 50 state flags. Including them as part of the project makes them available to be loaded as images. The normal build action for these images is to include them as resources. They will be transported to the client computer.

4. Add a class to manage all the state flags. Notice that the names of the flag images follow the pattern <state abbreviation>.jpg. This new class simply contains a list of all the state abbreviations. Right-click the SilverlightAnimation project and click Add, New Item, and then select Class (so that Visual Studio generates the code for a new class). Name the class *States*. Visual Studio opens the code in the editor for you.

5. Derive the *State* class from the generic *List* class, and provide *string* as the type argument. Then, add the abbreviations for all the states. (If you'd like, you can borrow this code from the solution rather than typing in all the state abbreviations.)

```
class States : List<string>
{
 public States()
 {
   Add("AL");
   Add("AK");
   Add("AZ");
   Add("AR");
   Add("CA");
   Add("CO");
   // more states…
   Add("WA");
   Add("WV");
   Add("WI");
   Add("WY");
 }
}
```

6. Open the file MainPage.xaml.cs, add code to *MainPage* constructor to load the images, and mark each cell with a *TextBlock* naming the state. Create an instance of the *States* class so that you can look up the state abbreviations. Iterate through all the columns and rows within the *LayoutRoot*. For each cell within the grid, create a *TextBlock* to show the state abbreviation. Get the state abbreviation from the instance of the *States* class and set the *Text* property to the state abbreviation. You can set various properties such as the *FontSize* and *FontFamily* to dress up the *TextBlock*. Add the *TextBlock* to the children collection of *LayoutRoot*. Use the *TextBlock.SetRow* and *SetColumn* static methods to position the *TextBlock* in the grid.

Next, create an instance of the *Image* class. Add a *ScaleTransform* to the *Image*. You animate that a bit later. Use the current state abbreviation to create a URI indicating the image containing the state flag (it is in the Images folder). Finally, set the *Opacity* of the *Image* to a little less than half, add the *Image* to the *LayoutRoot*, and position it in the current row and column.

```
public MainPage()
{
  InitializeComponent();

  States states = new States();
  int stateNumber = 0;

  for (int column = 0; column < 5; column++)
  {
    for (int row = 0; row < 10; row++)
    {
      // get the state abbrev
      string stateAbbrev = states[stateNumber];

      TextBlock theTextBlock = new TextBlock();
      theTextBlock.FontSize = 22;
      theTextBlock.Text = stateAbbrev;
      theTextBlock.TextAlignment = TextAlignment.Center;
      theTextBlock.VerticalAlignment = VerticalAlignment.Center;
      LayoutRoot.Children.Add(theTextBlock);
      Grid.SetRow(theTextBlock, row);
      Grid.SetColumn(theTextBlock, column);

      // Add an image control to the grid
      Image theImage = new Image();
      ScaleTransform st = new ScaleTransform();
      st.ScaleX = 1; st.ScaleY = 1;
      theImage.RenderTransform = st;
      Uri uri =
      new Uri("Images/" +
        stateAbbrev + ".jpg", UriKind.Relative);

      theImage.Source = new BitmapImage(uri);
      theImage.Margin = new Thickness(10);
      theImage.Opacity = .4;
```

```
      LayoutRoot.Children.Add(theImage);

      // then position it
      Grid.SetRow(theImage, row);
      Grid.SetColumn(theImage, column);

      stateNumber++;
    }
  }
}
```

7. Run the application. It should look something like this:

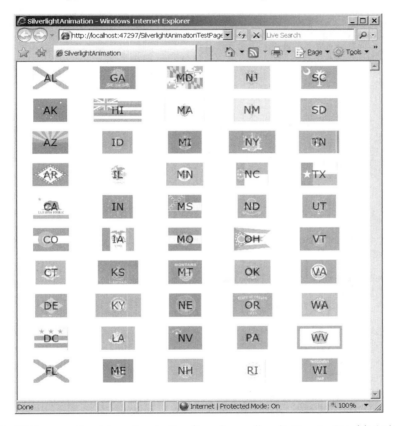

8. Write a method to animate the flags by scaling it. Create *DoubleAnimation*s for the *ScaleTransform ScaleX* and *ScaleY* properties, and another for the *Image Opacity* property. Set the *From* properties of the *ScaleTransform* animations to 1, and the *To* properties to 5. Set the *From* property of the *Opacity* animation to .4 and the *To* property to 1. Set the *AutoReverse* properties of the three *DoubleAnimations* to true so that they roll back after they are finished. Create a *Storyboard* to hold the animations.

Associate the animations with their targets within the *Storyboard* by using the *StoryBoard SetTarget* and *SetTargetProperty* methods. Finally, add the animations to the *Storyboard*.

Putting this all within a *try/catch* block can help you debug any errors when this executes.

```
public partial class MainPage : UserControl
{
 void AnimateImage(Image image)
 {
  try
  {
   DoubleAnimation scaleXAnimation = new DoubleAnimation();
   scaleXAnimation.AutoReverse = true;
   DoubleAnimation scaleYAnimation = new DoubleAnimation();
   scaleYAnimation.AutoReverse = true;
   DoubleAnimation opacityAnimation = new DoubleAnimation();
   opacityAnimation.AutoReverse = true;

   scaleXAnimation.From = 1;
   scaleXAnimation.To = 5;
   scaleYAnimation.From = 1;
   scaleYAnimation.To = 5;
   opacityAnimation.From = .4;
   opacityAnimation.To = 1;

   Storyboard sb = new Storyboard();
   Storyboard.SetTarget(scaleXAnimation, image.RenderTransform);
   Storyboard.SetTargetProperty(scaleXAnimation,
     new PropertyPath("ScaleX"));

   Storyboard.SetTarget(scaleYAnimation, image.RenderTransform);
   Storyboard.SetTargetProperty(scaleYAnimation,
     new PropertyPath("ScaleY"));

   Storyboard.SetTarget(opacityAnimation, image);
   Storyboard.SetTargetProperty(opacityAnimation,
     new PropertyPath("Opacity"));

   sb.Children.Add(scaleXAnimation);
   sb.Children.Add(scaleYAnimation);
   sb.Children.Add(opacityAnimation);
```

```
    sb.Begin();
  }
  catch (Exception ex)
  {
    System.Diagnostics.Debug.WriteLine(ex.Message);
  }
 }
}
```

9. Add a handler for the *OnMouseLeftButtonDown* event to the *MainPage* class that animates the image. This will be hooked up to the images directly, so the sender is the image. Just cast the sender as an *Image* and call the *Animate* method, passing in the image:

```
public partial class MainPage : UserControl
{
 void OnMouseLeftButtonDown(object sender, MouseButtonEventArgs ea)
 {
   Image image = sender as Image;
   AnimateImage(image);
 }
}
```

10. Finally, connect the *MouseLeftButtonDown* event of each *Image* to the handler:

```
public MainPage()
{
  // other initialization code
  for (int column = 0; column < 5; column++)
  {
   for (int row = 0; row < 10; row++)
    {
      // other code...
      Image theImage = new Image();

      theImage.MouseLeftButtonDown += OnMouseLeftButtonDown;

      // other code.
    }
  }

 }
```

11. Click one of the flags. It should animate. You should see it grow by five times its original height and width, become more opaque, and then recede back to its original state.

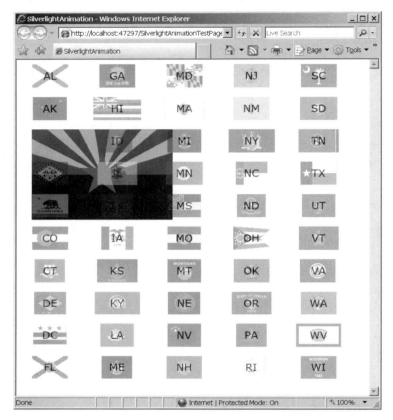

WCF Services and Silverlight

As you might have noticed by now, Silverlight presents an entirely new programming model for Web sites. ASP.NET programming traditionally involves managing a collection of ASP.NET controls that emit HTML to the client. ASP.NET has a whole infrastructure for managing session state and view state (necessary for HTML over HTTP).

Silverlight content is generally disconnected from the rest of the Web site. Ways exist to integrate with the HTML on the client side through the Document Object Model, and you can pass parameters into your Silverlight content before sending it off to the client. However, support for connecting with the rest of the Web site is not built-in as much. To communicate with the rest of the Web site, Silverlight usually uses Windows Communication Foundation (WCF) services provided by the Web site.

Here's an exercise that shows how Silverlight works with WCF. This example shows how you can add a Silverlight-enabled WCF service to your Silverlight Web site. The Web site exposes a collection of products through a Web service. The Silverlight control queries the service for a list of products, and then looks them up one at a time when the end user selects a product from a list box. This exercise illustrates how to create a WCF service, expose data through the WCF service, and data bind to a *ListBox* and a *TextBlock*.

Using Silverlight with ASP.NET and WCF

1. Create a new Silverlight application named *SilverlightAndWCF*. Have Visual Studio create an ASP.NET Web Project along with the Silverlight application.

2. Add a Silverlight-enabled WCF service. Name it *ProductsService*.

3. Create a *ProductInfo* class in the Web project to hold individual products. Right-click the SilverlightAndWCF project in Solution Explorer and click Add, New Item. Select Class from the available templates. Name the class *ProductInfo*. It should include properties for the name of the product, a description of the product, and the price of the product. It's important that these members be exposed as properties be-cause the Silverlight client will use data binding to connect to the properties. Use the *DataContract* and *DataContractFormat* attributes to enable this class to be exposed through the WCF service. Use the *DataMember* attribute before each property so that the members show up as properties in the proxy (to be produced for use on the cli-ent). You need to use the *System.Runtime.Serialization* and the *System.ServiceModel* namespaces to resolve the attributes. Remember, this is still in the Web Service project.

```
[DataContract]
[DataContractFormat]
public class ProductInfo
{
    string product;
    [DataMember]
    public string Product
    {
        get { return product; }
        set { product = value; }
    }

    string description;

    [DataMember]
    public string Description
    {
        get { return description; }
        set { description = value; }
    }

    double price;

    [DataMember]
    public double Price
    {
        get { return price; }
        set { price = value; }
    }
}
```

4. Create a collection of *ProductInfo*s (derive from the generic *List* class). You can
either have Visual Studio create the class for you, or you could add it directly to the
ProductInfo.cs file. Write a constructor that adds some *ProductInfo* objects to the
collection. They can be any kind of products. I'm a guitar enthusiast, so I added a
guitar to the product list you see here:

```
public class Products: List<ProductInfo>
{
 public Products()
 {
  ProductInfo productInfo = new ProductInfo();

  productInfo = new ProductInfo();
  productInfo.Product = "Solidbody";
  productInfo.Description = @"Flame maple top " +
      "mahogany body. Rosewood fingerboard. " +
      "One piece mahogany neck. Two humbucking " +
      "pickups. With case.";
  productInfo.Price = 2500.00;
  Add(productInfo);
  // add more products...
 }
}
```

5. Open the file ProductsService.svc.cs (remember—this is all going in the Web Service
project right now). Add a static instance of the *Products* class. Add two methods to
the service: one to get the entire list of *ProductInfos*, and one to look up a particular
product. The *ServiceContract* attribute usually stipulates a namespace. I left it out in this
case for the sake of brevity. You also need to use the *System.ServiceModel.Activation*
namespace.

```
[ServiceContract(Namespace = "")]
[AspNetCompatibilityRequirements
    (RequirementsMode =
    AspNetCompatibilityRequirementsMode.Allowed)]
public class ProductsService
{
    static Products products = new Products();

    [OperationContract]
    public Products GetProducts()
    {
        return ProductsService.products;
    }

    [OperationContract]
    ProductInfo GetProduct(string key)
    {
        return ProductsService.products.Find(
            delegate(ProductInfo productInfo)
            {
```

```
                    if (productInfo.Product == key)
                    {
                        return true;
                    }
                    else
                    {
                        return false;
                    }
                }
            );
        }
    }
```

6. Edit the MainPage.xaml XAML file to produce a layout. Add four rows to the *LayoutRoot*. The first three rows should resize to their content (that is, the *RowDefinition*s should use *Auto* as the *Height*). Add three columns. The first column should size automatically (that is, the *ColumnDefinition* should use *Auto* as its *Width*).

```
<Grid x:Name="LayoutRoot"
 Background="White">
    <Grid.RowDefinitions>
        <RowDefinition  Height="Auto"/>
        <RowDefinition Height="Auto"/>
        <RowDefinition Height="Auto"/>
        <RowDefinition Height="*"/>
    </Grid.RowDefinitions>
    <Grid.ColumnDefinitions>
        <ColumnDefinition Width="Auto"/>
        <ColumnDefinition />
        <ColumnDefinition />
     </Grid.ColumnDefinitions>

</Grid>
```

7. Now add content to the grid.

   a. Add a *TextBlock* to the top row and first column (row 0, column 0) to serve as a header for the Details section. It should span two columns.

   b. Add a *TextBlock* to the first row, third column to serve as a header for the list box.

   c. Add three *TextBlocks* down the first column to serve as labels. The *TextBlock* in row 2 should say "Product:", the *TextBlock* in row 3 should say "Price:", and the *TextBlock* in row 4 should say "Description:".

   d. Add three *TextBlocks* down the second column to display the product info. The *TextBlock* in row 2 should use the *Binding* markup extension to bind the *Text* property to the *ProductInfo Product* property. That is, assignment of the *Text* property should look like this: *Text =" {Binding Product}"*. The *TextBlock* in row 3 should bind its *Text* property to the *ProductInfo Price* property, and the *TextBlock* in row 4 should bind its *Text* property to the *ProductInfo Description* property using the same binding statement as the one used for binding the *Product* property.

e. Finally, add a *ListBox* to row 1, column 2. Make it span three rows. Name it "theListBox". Assign a handler to the *SelectionChanged* event. When you type **SelectionChanged** in the tag, Visual Studio stubs one out for you. Assign the *DisplayMemberPath* property the string "Product". That way, when the collection of *ProductInfos* is bound to the *ListBox*, the *ListBox* will show the *Product* property.

```
<Grid x:Name="LayoutRoot"
  Background="White">
  <!-grid row and column definitions are here  -->
  <TextBlock Grid.Row="0"
   Grid.Column="0"
   Grid.ColumnSpan="2"
   FontSize="24"
   Text="Details:"/>

  <TextBlock Grid.Row="0"
   Grid.Column="2"
   FontSize="24"
   Text="Select Product:"/>

  <TextBlock Grid.Row="1"
   Grid.Column="0"
   FontSize="18"
   Text="Product:" />

  <TextBlock Grid.Row="2"
   Grid.Column="0"
   FontSize="18"
   Text="Price:" />

  <TextBlock Grid.Row="3"
   Grid.Column="0"
   FontSize="18"
   Text="Description:" />

  <TextBlock Grid.Row="1"
   Grid.Column="1"
   FontSize="14"
   Text="{Binding Product}"
   Margin="5"/>

  <TextBlock Grid.Row="2"
   Grid.Column="1"
   FontSize="14"
   Text="{Binding Price}"
   Margin="5"/>

  <TextBlock Grid.Row="3"
   Grid.Column="1"
   FontSize="14"
   Margin="5"
```

```
        TextWrapping="Wrap"
        Text="{Binding Description}"/>

    <ListBox x:Name="theListBox"
      Grid.Row="1"
      Grid.Column="2"
      Grid.RowSpan="3"
      DisplayMemberPath="Product"
      SelectionChanged=
      "theListBox_SelectionChanged">
    </ListBox>
  </Grid>
```

8. Run the application. It should look something like this:

9. Add a service reference for the WCF service to the SilverlightAndWCF project. Right-click the SilverlightAndWCF project in Solution Explorer, and click Add Service Reference. Visual Studio will display the following dialog box to get information about the service. Click the Discover button in the upper right-hand corner. Visual Studio will find the *ProductsService* service for you.

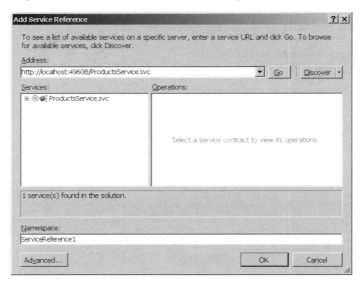

10. Click the expansion symbol next to the ProductsService.svc service to expand the node so that you can see details about the service. Click OK (leave the namespace the same: *ServiceRefernce1*). Visual Studio will write a proxy for you to use in the Silverlight control.

11. Include a *using* clause to scope the new service reference. Declare an instance of the *ProductsServiceClient* class as a member of the *MainPage* class. Create an instance of the client so that the *MainPage* can talk to the Web site. You use the proxy to issue calls to the service to get all the products and to look up singular products.

```
using SilverlightAndWCF.ServiceReference1;

public partial class Page : UserControl
{
  ProductsServiceClient productsService =
   new ProductsServiceClient();

  public MainPage()
  {
    InitializeComponent();
  }
}
```

Silverlight-enabled WCF proxies work asynchronously. When you call the *GetProducts* and the *GetProduct* methods, they run on a different thread. You need to add event handlers to the service client to harvest the results when the service call is finished. Write a method named *GetProductsCompleted* to harvest the collection of products. The first argument is of type *object* (the sender) and the second argument is a *GetProductsCompletedEventArgs* (defined within the proxy code generated by Visual Studio). *GetProductsCompletedEventArgs* includes a *Result* property representing the collection. *GetProductsCompleted* should assign that collection to the *ListBox ItemsSource* property. Because the *ListBox DisplayMemberPath* property is set to "Product", the *ListBox* displays the *Product* property of each *ProductInfo* in the collection.

In addition, add a method named *GetProductCompleted* to harvest the results of the singular product lookup. The method should take an *object* (the sender) as the first parameter and a *GetProductCompletedEventArgs* (also generated by Visual Studio) as the second parameter. *GetProductCompletedEventArgs* holds the selected product in its *Result* property. Set the *LayoutRoot DataContext* property to the *ProductInfo* returned by the service. Because the *TextBox* controls in the *Grid* are bound to the *Product*, *Price*, and *Description* properties, this data appears in the *TextBlocks* automatically.

```
public partial class MainPage : UserControl
{
public MainPage()
 {
  InitializeComponent();
 }

 void GetProductscompleted(object sender,
   GetProductsCompletedEventArgs ea)
 {
  if (ea.Error == null)
  {
   this.theListBox.ItemsSource = ea.Result;
  }
  else
  {
   System.Diagnostics.Debug.WriteLine(ea.Error.InnerException);
   this.theListBox.Items.Add("Gibson Les Paul Standard");
  }
 }

 void GetProductCompleted(object sender,
  GetProductCompletedEventArgs ea)
 {
  ProductInfo pi = ea.Result as ProductInfo;
  if (pi != null)
  {
   this.LayoutRoot.DataContext = pi;
  }
 }
}
```

12. Connect the *GetProductCompleted* and *GetProductsCompleted* handlers to the *ProductsService* proxy in the *MainPage* constructor, and then call *ProductsService. GetProducts* to fetch the collection of products.

    Implement the *ListBox SelectionChanged* handler. Get the *SelectedItem* property from the *ListBox* and use it when calling the proxy's *GetProduct* method (that is, pass the currently selected item as the key). When the service completes its work, the result ends up in the *GetProductCompleted* method.

```
public partial class MainPage : UserControl
{
public MainPage()
 {
  InitializeComponent();

  productsService.GetProductsCompleted +=
              GetProductscompleted;

  productsService.GetProductCompleted +=
              this.GetProductCompleted;

  productsService.GetProductsAsync(this);
 }

 // Asynchronous handlers here...

 private void theListBox_SelectionChanged(object sender,
  SelectionChangedEventArgs e)
 {
  string key =
   (theListBox.SelectedItem as ProductInfo).Product;

  productsService.GetProductAsync(key, this);
 }
}
```

13. Run the program. When the browser opens, you can see a collection of products on the right-hand side. When you select a product, the details appear on the left-hand side.

Chapter 24 Quick Reference

To	Do This
Generate a Silverlight application	Click File, New, Project from the main menu. Select the Silverlight Application template.
Manage layout in a Silverlight component	Choose a layout panel as a *UserControl* for the *RootVisual*. The *Grid* positions visual elements into rows and columns. The *StackPanel* positions visual elements on top of each other (when aligned vertically) or next to each other (when aligned horizontally). With the *Canvas*, you can position visual elements absolutely using *x* and *y* coordinates.
Change the properties of controls on a page	Make sure the page editor is in Design mode. Highlight the control whose property you want to change. Select the property to edit in the *Properties* window.
Use the HTML Document Object Model in a Silverlight component	Follow these steps: 1. Name the HTML elements using the *ID* attribute. 2. Use the *HtmlPage.Document* property to retrieve the *HtmlElements*. Call the *GetElementById* to fetch the element. 3. Use the *HtmlElement GetProperty* and *SetProperty* methods to modify the elements. 4. Use the *HtmlElement AttachEvent* to connect managed event handlers to the elements.
Access managed code from within JavaScript	Use the *ScriptableType* attribute to mark an entire type as scriptable. Use the *ScriptableMember* attribute to mark individual type members as scriptable. Use the *HtmlPage.RegisterCreatableType* to create fresh instances from within script. Use *HtmlPage.RegisterScriptableObject* to allow access to already-existing instances of the type. From there, access the methods and properties using the Silverlight plug-in.
Access the ASP.NET site programmatically	Add a Silverlight-enabled WCF service to the Web site. Use the proxy created by Visual Studio to access the service methods easily.

Part VI
Services and Deployment

Chapter 25
Windows Communication Foundation

After completing this chapter, you will be able to

- Understand the motivation behind Windows Communication Foundation (WCF).

- Understand the WCF architecture.

- Implement a WCF-based server.

- Build a client to use the WCF server.

Distributed Computing Redux

Released in 2006, the Windows Communication Foundation (WCF) is one of three main pillars of Microsoft .NET Framework version 3 and later. The other two specific, highly advantageous technological pillars are Windows Workflow Foundation and Windows Presentation Foundation. Each redefines programming within a certain idiom. Windows Workflow Foundation unifies the business work flow model. Windows Presentation Foundation redefines user interface development for Windows-based desktop applications and for the Web (using Microsoft Silverlight). And Windows Communication Foundation unifies the distributed programming model for the Microsoft environment. Clearly uniting these fragmented programming models is the main theme of .NET 3.5.

To get an idea of how fragmented the distributed computing solutions are, think back to the earliest ways computers were connected. At one point, you could program in a standard way only the old venerable RS232 serial connection or through a modem. Over the years, distributed computing in the Microsoft environment has grown to encompass many different protocols. For example, the Microsoft Windows NT operating system supported a Remote Procedure Call (RPC) mechanism that was eventually wrapped using the Distributed Component Object Model (DCOM). The Windows operating system also supports sockets programming. Near the turn of the twenty-first century, Microsoft released Microsoft Message Queuing (MSMQ) to support disconnected queuing-style distributed applications. When it became apparent that DCOM was running into some dead-ends, Microsoft introduced .NET remoting. (The dead-ends that DCOM implemented are mainly its requirement to contact client objects periodically to remain assured of a connection, which limits scalability; its complex programming model; its difficult configuration needs; and its Internet-unfriendly security architecture.) Finally, to help supplement a wider reach for distributed programming, Microsoft introduced an XML Web Service framework in ASP.NET represented by the ASMX files you looked at earlier in Chapter 23, "AJAX."

A Fragmented Communications API

Each of the older technologies mentioned previously has its own specific advantages—especially when you consider the periods in computing history in which they were introduced. However, having so many different means of writing distributed computing applications has led to a fragmented application programming interface (API). Which technology to use has always been a decision that must be made early in development. Earlier distributed technologies often tied applications to a specific transport protocol. If you made the wrong architectural decision or later simply wanted to migrate to a newer technology, doing so was often difficult, if not nearly impossible. Even if it could be done, it was usually an expensive proposition in terms of application redevelopment and end-user acceptance and deployment.

When you rely on these older technologies, a number of programming and configuration issues are involved. Earlier connection technologies coupled multiple auxiliary factors, those not directly required for communicating data, with the communication process itself. For example, earlier distributed computing systems forced decisions such as how to format data in the early stages of design, as well as in the implementation of a distributed system. To make DCOM Remote Procedure Calls, an application was required to be tied to the DCOM connection protocol and wire format. This forced administrators to open port 135, the DCOM object discovery port, leading to immense security risks. With the .NET Framework, you can choose the transports and wire formats: Out of the box, you can choose to use HTTP or TCP as the connection protocol, and you can use either SOAP or the .NET binary format as the wire format. However, even with the choices provided, applications using classic .NET remoting are often fated to use a single connection protocol and wire format once the configuration is set. You can swap out connection protocols and wire formats, but it's not easy. At best, significant code changes are required. At worst, entire application architectures need revision.

In addition to tying wire formats and connection protocols to the implementation of a distributed system, many more issues arise when you try to connect two computers together. Right off you have to think about issues such as transactions, security, reliability, and serialization—these issues inevitably become embedded in the application code (instead of being added later as necessary). In addition, earlier communication technologies don't lend themselves to the currently in-vogue service-oriented architectures (SOAs) where interoperability is key, although in practice interoperability is tricky to achieve.

WCF for Connected Systems

The main job of WCF is to unify the previously fragmented Windows communication APIs and provide applications with a single programming model. At the same time, WCF aims to decouple the process of communicating over a distributed system from the applications themselves. When you work with WCF, you see that the distinctions between contracts, transports, and implementation are enforced rather than just offered as a good idea. In addition, because Microsoft is attuned to the needs of existing applications, it designed WCF to accommodate partial or complete migrations from earlier communication technologies (.NET remoting or XML Web Services) to WCF-based computing.

SOA is becoming an important design influence in modern software development. SOA is an architectural philosophy that encourages building large distributed systems from loosely coupled endpoints that expose their capabilities through well-known interfaces. WCF adheres to standard SOA principles, such as setting explicit boundaries between autonomous services, having services be contract and policy based (rather than class based), having business processes be the focal point of the services (rather than the services themselves), and accommodating fluctuating business models easily. WCF is designed for both high performance and maximum interoperability.

WCF represents a communication *layer*, so introduces a level of indirection between a distributable application and the means by which that application is distributed. As an independent layer, WCF makes implementing and configuring a distributed application simpler by providing a consistent interface for managing such aspects as security, reliability, concurrency, transactions, throttling (throughput limitations for callers or methods), serialization, error handling, and instance management.

Whereas WCF is capable of communicating with XML Web Services using SOAP (a standard for many existing Web services), you can also configure and extend it to communicate using messages based on non-SOAP formats, such as custom XML and Really Simple Syndication (RSS).

WCF is smart enough to know whether both endpoints are WCF based, in which case it uses optimized wire encoding. The structures of the messages are the same—they're just encoded in binary form. WCF includes other services often required by distributed systems. For example, WCF includes built-in queued messaging.

WCF Constituent Elements

WCF is composed of a few separate elements: endpoints, channels, messages, and behaviors. Whereas earlier communication technologies tended to couple these concepts, WCF distinguishes them as truly separate entities. Here's a rundown of the elements of WCF.

Endpoints

Endpoints define the originators and recipients of WCF communications. Microsoft devised a clever acronym for defining endpoints: *ABC*. That is, WCF endpoints are defined by an *address*, a *binding*, and a *contract*.

Address

The address identifies the network location of the endpoint. WCF endpoints use the addressing style of the transport moving the message. WCF addressing supports the use of both fully qualified addresses and relative addresses. For example, a fully qualified Internet protocol address looks like the following:

http://someserver/someapp/mathservice.svc/calculator

WCF supports relative addressing by using a base address and then a relative address. Base addresses are registered with the service, and WCF can find services relative to the base address. For example, a whole address of an endpoint might comprise a base address such as *http://*someserver/someapp/*mathservice.svc* and a relative address of *calculator.*

Binding

WCF bindings specify *how* messages are transmitted. Rather than being identified simply by a coupled transport and wire format (à la DCOM), WCF bindings are composed from a stack of binding elements, which at a minimum include a protocol, a transport, and an encoder.

Contract

The final element defining an endpoint is the contract. The contract specifies the primary agreement between the client and the service about what the service can do for the client. The contract specifies the information to be exchanged during a service call.

WCF expresses a service contract as a .NET interface adorned with the *ServiceContract* attribute. Methods in the WCF contract interface are annotated with the *OperationContract* attribute. WCF interfaces can pass data structures as well. Data members in the structures are exposed as properties and adorned with the *DataMember* attribute.

Channels

WCF channels represent the message transmission system. WCF defines *protocol channels* and *transport channels*. Protocol channels add services such as security and transactions independently of transport. Transport channels manage the physical movement of bytes between endpoints (for example, WCF uses protocols such as MSMQ, HTTP, P2P (Point-to-Point), TCP, and Named Pipes). WCF uses a factory pattern to make channel creation consistent.

Behaviors

In WFC, the service contract defines *what* the service will do. The service contract implementation specifies exactly *how* the service contract functionality works. However, one of the hallmarks of a distributed system is that it usually requires some add-on functionality that might not necessarily be tied to contract implementation. For example, when securing a Web service, authenticating and authorizing the client might be necessary, but it's usually not part of the service contract. WCF implements this kind of add-on functionality through *behaviors*. Behaviors implement the SOA higher-order notion of policy and are used to customize local execution.

Behaviors are governed by attributes—the main two of which are the *ServiceBehavior* and the *OperationBehavior*. The *ServiceBehavior* and *OperationBehavior* attributes control the following aspects of the service execution:

- Impersonation
- Concurrency and synchronization support
- Transaction behavior
- Address filtering and header processing
- Serialization behavior
- Configuration behavior
- Session lifetime
- Metadata transformation
- Instance lifetimes

Applying these attributes to modify the server execution is easy. Just adorn a service or operation implementation with the appropriate attribute and set the properties. For example, to require that callers of an operation support impersonation, adorn a service operation with the *OperationBehavior* attribute and set the *Impersonation* property to *ImpersonationOption. Require*.

Messages

The final element of WCF is the actual message. WCF messages are modeled on SOAP messages. They are composed of an envelope, a header, a body, and addressing information. Of course, messages also include the information being exchanged. WCF supports three message exchange patterns: one way, request–response, and duplex. One-way messages are passed from the transmitter to the receiver only. Messages passed using the request–response pattern are sent from the transmitter to the receiver, and the receiver is expected to send a reply back to the originator. Messages using the request–response pattern block until the receiver sends a response to the originator. In duplex messaging, services can call back to the client while executing a service requested by the client. The default message exchange pattern is request–response.

How WCF Plays with ASP.NET

Although WCF applications can be hosted by manually written servers, ASP.NET makes a perfectly good host. You can either write your own Windows Service to act as a host, or you can take advantage of a readily available Windows Service, Internet Information Services (IIS), and consequently ASP.NET. WCF and ASP.NET can coexist on a single computer in two different modes: side-by-side mode and ASP.NET compatibility mode. Here's a rundown of these two modes.

Side-by-Side Mode

When running in side-by-side mode, WCF services hosted by IIS are colocated with ASP.NET applications composed of ASPX files and ASMX files (and ASCX and ASHX files when necessary). ASP.NET files and WCF services reside inside a single, common application domain (AppDomain). When run this way, ASP.NET provides common infrastructure services such as AppDomain management and dynamic compilation for both WCF and the ASP.NET HTTP runtime. WCF runs in side-by-side mode with ASP.NET by default.

When running in side-by-side mode, the ASP.NET runtime manages only ASP.NET requests. Requests intended for a WCF service go straight to the WCF-based service. Although the ASP.NET runtime does not participate in processing the requests, there are some specific ramifications of running in side-by-side mode.

First, ASP.NET and WCF services can share AppDomain state. This includes such items as static variables and public events. Although it shares an AppDomain with ASP.NET, WCF runs independently—some features you might count on when working with ASP.NET become unavailable. Probably the major restriction is that there's no such thing as a current *HttpContext* from within a WCF service (despite the architectural similarity of WCF to the ASP.NET runtime pipeline). Architecturally speaking, WCF can communicate over many different protocols, including but not limited to HTTP, so an HTTP-specific context might not even make sense in many scenarios.

Second, authentication and authorization can get a bit tricky. For example, a client might be authenticated on an ASP.NET site using Forms Authentication, and then suddenly require reauthentication to accommodate a service call if the service call requires a different authentication scheme. In this case, the site might need to support two authentication and authorization schemes.

Even though WCF applications do not interfere with ASP.NET applications, WCF applications can access various parts of the ASP.NET infrastructure such as the application data cache. In fact, this chapter's example shows one approach to accessing the cache.

ASP.NET Compatibility Mode

WCF is designed primarily to unify the programming model over a number of transports and hosting environments. However, there are times when a uniform programming model with this much flexibility is not necessary and the application might desire or even require some of the services provided by the ASP.NET runtime. For those cases, WCF introduces the ASP.NET compatibility mode. With ASP.NET compatibility mode, you can run your WCF application as a full-fledged ASP.NET citizen, complete with all the functionality and services available through ASP.NET.

WCF services that run using ASP.NET compatibility mode have full access to the ASP.NET pipeline and execute through the entire ASP.NET HTTP request life cycle. In ASP.NET compatibility mode, WCF includes an implementation of *IHttpHandler* that wraps WCF services and moves them through the ASP.NET HTTP pipeline. In effect, a WCF service running in ASP.NET compatibility mode looks, tastes, and feels just like a standard ASP.NET Web service (that is, an ASMX file).

WCF applications running under ASP.NET compatibility mode get a current *HttpContext* with all its contents—the session state, the *Server* object, the *Response* object, and the *Request* object. WCF applications running as ASP.NET-compatible applications can implement security by associating Windows access control lists (ACLs) to the service .svc file. In this manner, only specific Windows users could use the WCF service. ASP.NET URL authorization also works for WCF applications running as ASP.NET-compatible applications. The pipeline remains arbitrarily extensible for WCF applications running as ASP.NET applications because service requests are not intercepted as they are with the general-purpose side-by-side mode—they're managed by ASP.NET for the entire request life cycle.

You can turn on WCF ASP.NET compatibility mode at the application level through the application's web.config file. You can also apply ASP.NET compatibility to a specific WCF service implementation.

Writing a WCF Service

Here's an example of a WCF service to help illustrate how WCF works. Recall the XML Web Service example application from Chapter 23, the QuoteService that doled out pithy quotes to any client wishing to invoke the service. The example here represents the same service—but using a WCF-based Web site instead of an ASMX-based Web service. This way, you can see what it takes to write a WCF-based service and client, and you can see some of the differences between WCF-based services and ASMX-based services (there are a couple of distinct differences).

Building the QuotesService as a WCF service

1. Create a Web Application project that uses WCF. This example takes you through the details of developing a working WCF application that can be accessed from any client anywhere. Start Microsoft Visual Studio 2010. Click File, New, Project and select WCF Service Application from the available templates. Name the site *WCFQuotesService*. The following graphic shows the New Project dialog box:

2. Examine the files created by Visual Studio. Visual Studio generated several files: IService1.cs, Service1.svc, and Service1.svc.cs. These files are placeholders representing the WCF contract (as a .NET interface type) and a class implementing the contract.

3. Tweak the files produced by Visual Studio. Name the code files representing the service: *IService.cs* should become *IQuotesService.cs*, and *Service1.svc* should become *QuotesService.svc*. When you rename the SVC file, Visual Studio will rename the corresponding C# file, too.

4. Change the service interface name from *IService1* to *IQuotesService*, and change the service class name from *Service1* to *QuotesService*. Use the Visual Studio refactoring facilities to do this. That is, highlight the identifier you want to change, right-click in the text editor, and click Rename on the Refactoring menu. Visual Studio will make sure the change is propagated through the entire project.

5. Borrow the *QuotesCollection* object from the project for Chapter 15, "Application Data Caching" (that is, add the QuotesCollection.cs file to the WCFQuotesService project). You can get the QuotesCollection.cs file from Chapter 15's project, UseDataCaching, by right-clicking the Project node in Solution Explorer and clicking Add Existing Item. Navigate to the UseDataCaching project from Chapter 15 (you can use the one that comes with the CD). Select the file QuotesCollection.cs. The QuotesCollection.cs file will be copied into your WCF solution and added to the project.

6. Borrow the QuotesCollection.xml and QuotesCollection.xsd from the Web service example. Right-click the *App_Data* node in the WCFQuotesService project, and click Add Existing Item. Go to the Web services project and pick up the XML and XSD files.

7. Now that the data and the data management code are in place, the service needs a way to expose itself. It's time to develop a contract for the service. First, create a structure for passing quotes back and forth. Open the file IQuotesService.cs to add the data and operation contracts by deleting the *CompositeType* class that Visual Studio placed there for you as an example. In its place, type in the following code for the *Quote* structure. The *Quote* structure should contain three strings—one to represent the quote text, and separate strings to represent the originator's first and last names. Expose the strings as properties adorned with the *DataMember* attribute:

```
[DataContract]
public struct Quote
{
    private String _strQuote;

    [DataMember]
    public String StrQuote
    {
        get { return _strQuote; }
        set { _strQuote = value; }
    }

    private String _strOriginatorLastName;

    [DataMember]
    public String StrOriginatorLastName
    {
        get { return _strOriginatorLastName; }
        set { _strOriginatorLastName = value; }
    }

    private String _strOriginatorFirstName;

    [DataMember]
    public String StrOriginatorFirstName
    {
        get { return _strOriginatorFirstName; }
        set { _strOriginatorFirstName = value; }
    }

    public Quote(String strQuote,
                 String strOriginatorLastName,
                 String strOriginatorFirstName)
    {
        _strQuote = strQuote;
        _strOriginatorLastName = strOriginatorLastName;
        _strOriginatorFirstName = strOriginatorFirstName;
    }
}
```

8. Develop a service contract for the service. In the IQuotesService.cs file, update the interface to include methods to get a single quote, add a quote, and get all the quotes:

```
using System.Data; // must be added to identify DataSet

[ServiceContract]
public interface IQuotesService
{
    [OperationContract]
    Quote GetAQuote();

    [OperationContract]
    void AddQuote(Quote quote);

    [OperationContract]
    DataSet GetAllQuotes();
}
```

9. Implement the service contract. Open the file QuotesService.svc.cs to add the implementation. Start by implementing a method that loads the quotes into memory and stores the collection and the ASP.NET cache. Although this application is an ASP.NET application, ASP.NET handles WCF method calls earlier in the pipeline than it does typical ASP.NET requests, and because of that there's no such thing as a current *HttpContext* object. You can still access the cache through the *HttpRuntime* object, which is available in the context of WCF. The *HttpRuntime.AppDomainAppPath* property includes the path to the application that's useful for setting up a cache dependency for the XML file containing the quotes. Make sure to add *using* statements for the *system.Web*, *system.Web.Caching*, and *system.Data* namespaces.

```
using System;
using System.Collections.Generic;
using System.Linq;
using System.Runtime.Serialization;
using System.ServiceModel;
using System.ServiceModel.Web;
using System.Text;
using System.Web;
using System.Web.Caching;
using System.Data;

namespace WCFQuotesService
{
    // NOTE: You can use the Rename command on the
    // Refactor menu to change the class name "Service1" in code, svc, and config file
together.
    public class QuotesService : IQuotesService
    {
        QuotesCollection LoadQuotes()
        {
            QuotesCollection quotesCollection;
            quotesCollection =
            (QuotesCollection)
```

```
    HttpRuntime.Cache["quotesCollection"];
    if (quotesCollection == null)
    {
      quotesCollection = new QuotesCollection();
      string strAppPath;
      strAppPath = HttpRuntime.AppDomainAppPath;
      string strFilePathXml =
        string.Format("{0}\\App_Data\\QuotesCollection.xml", strAppPath);
      string strFilePathSchema =
        string.Format("{0}\\App_Data\\QuotesCollection.xsd", strAppPath);
      quotesCollection.ReadXmlSchema(strFilePathSchema);
      quotesCollection.ReadXml(strFilePathXml);
      CacheDependency cacheDependency =
        new CacheDependency(strFilePathXml);
      HttpRuntime.Cache.Insert("quotesCollection",
        quotesCollection,
        cacheDependency,
        Cache.NoAbsoluteExpiration,
        Cache.NoSlidingExpiration,
        CacheItemPriority.Default,
        null);
    }
    return quotesCollection;
  }
  // more code will go here...
  }
}
```

10. Implement the *GetAQuote* method in the *QuotesService* class. Call *LoadQuotes* to get the *QuotesCollection* object. Generate a random number between 0 and the number of quotes in the collection and use it to select a quote in the collection. Create an instance of the *Quote* structure and return it after populating it with the data from the stored quote.

```
public class QuotesService : IQuotesService
{
    // LoadQuotes here...

    public Quote GetAQuote()
    {
        QuotesCollection quotesCollection = this.LoadQuotes();
        int nNumQuotes = quotesCollection.Rows.Count;

        Random random = new Random();
        int nQuote = random.Next(nNumQuotes);
        DataRow dataRow = quotesCollection.Rows[nQuote];
        Quote quote = new Quote((String)dataRow["Quote"],
                        (String)dataRow["OriginatorLastName"],
                        (String)dataRow["OriginatorFirstName"]);
        return quote;
    }
    // more code will go here...
}
```

11. Implement *AddAQuote*. Call *LoadQuotes* to get the *QuotesCollection*. Create a new row in the *QuotesCollection* and populate it with information coming from the client (that is, the *Quote* parameter). Use the *HttpRuntime.AppDomainAppPath* to construct the path to the QuotesCollection.xml file and use the *QuotesCollection*'s *WriteXml* method to reserialize the XML file. *WriteXml* is available from the *QuotesCollection* class because *QuotesCollection* derives from *System.Data.DataTable*. Because it was loaded in the cache with a file dependency, the cache is invalidated and the new quotes collection is loaded the next time around.

```
public class QuotesService : IQuotesService
{
    // LoadQuotes here...
    // GetAQuote here

    public void AddQuote(Quote quote)
    {
        QuotesCollection quotesCollection = this.LoadQuotes();

        DataRow dr = quotesCollection.NewRow();
        dr[0] = quote.StrQuote;
        dr[1] = quote.StrOriginatorLastName;
        dr[2] = quote.StrOriginatorFirstName;
        quotesCollection.Rows.Add(dr);

        string strAppPath;
        strAppPath = HttpRuntime.AppDomainAppPath;

        String strFilePathXml =
            String.Format("{0}\\App_Data\\QuotesCollection.xml", strAppPath);
        String strFilePathSchema =
            String.Format("{0}\\App_Data\\QuotesCollection.xsd", strAppPath);

        quotesCollection.WriteXmlSchema(strFilePathSchema);
        quotesCollection.WriteXml(strFilePathXml);
    }
}
```

12. Implement the *GetAllQuotes* operation. Create a new *DataSet*, load the quotes, and add the *QuotesCollection* to the data set as the first table. Then, return the *DataSet*.

```
public class QuotesService : IQuotesService
{
    // LoadQuotes here
    // GetAQuote here
    // AddQuote here

    public DataSet GetAllQuotes()
    {
        QuotesCollection quotesCollection = LoadQuotes();
        DataSet dataSet = new DataSet();
        dataSet.Tables.Add(quotesCollection);
        return dataSet;
    }
}
```

13. Examine the web.config file. ASP.NET 4 simplifies WCF Web Service configuration considerably. Earlier versions of ASP.NET (for example, version 3.5) require you to add information about the endpoints manually. You can still tweak the bindings and add service behaviors (for example, to manage security for the service). In this example, the default provided by Visual Studio works just fine.

That is how you build a WCF service hosted through ASP.NET that can be called from anywhere in the world (where Internet service is available, that is). In many ways, it is very similar to writing a classic ASP.NET Web service. However, because this service runs in ASP.NET side-by-side mode, there's no such thing as a current *HttpContext* (as is available in typical ASP.NET applications). In many cases, this might not be necessary. You can get to many of the critical ASP.NET run-time services (for example, the cache) through the *HttpRuntime* object. If you need full ASP.NET support (such as for session state if the WCF service you write depends on session data), WCF supports ASP.NET Compatibility mode.

Building a WCF Client

A WCF service is useless without any clients to employ it. This section illustrates how to build a client application that consumes the Quotes service. Here, you can see how Visual Studio makes it very easy to create a reference to a service. You see how to make WCF service calls both synchronously and asynchronously.

Building the QuotesService client

1. Start Visual Studio 2010. Open the WCFQuotesService solution and add a new Console Application project named *ConsumeQuotesService* to it. The following graphic illustrates adding the Console Application project to the solution:

2. Create a reference to the WCFQuotesService application by right-clicking the ConsumeQuotesService Project tree node in Solution Explorer and clicking Add Service Reference. In the Add Service Reference dialog box, click the Discover button. Select the Service.svc file from this project and expand its associated tree node. After a minute, the dialog box displays the service contracts that are available through the service. Expand the Services tree in the left pane to make sure you see the *IQuotesService* contract. Notice the namespace given by the dialog box: *ServiceReference1. Do not* click OK yet. The following graphic shows adding the service reference:

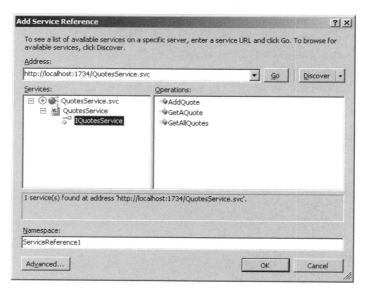

3. Click the Advanced button. Select the Generate Asynchronous Operations option so that Visual Studio generates the asynchronous versions of the proxy methods.

4. Click the OK button to add the service reference. Visual Studio produces a new directory named ServiceReferences in the ConsumeQuotesService project directory. Visual Studio generates information about the service in the form of XML files, XSD files, and a WSDL file (among others). You also get source code for a proxy class that will call the service on your behalf (by default, the proxy lands in a file named Reference.cs).

5. Try calling the *GetAQuote* operation. Calling the proxy methods generated for the WCF service calls can be a bit verbose from time to time, but they are effective and it's much better than setting everything up manually by yourself. First, create an instance of the *QuotesServiceClient*, available from the *ServiceReference* you just created. Create an instance of the *ServiceReference1.Quote* structure to receive the results of calling *GetAQuote*. Call *GetAQuote* from the *QuotesServiceClient*, and print the result on the console.

```
using System;
using System.Collections.Generic;
```

```
using System.Linq;
using System.Text;

namespace ConsumeQuotesService
{
    class Program
    {
        static void Main(string[] args)
        {
            // Get a single random quote
            ServiceReference1.QuotesServiceClient quotesServiceClient =
                new ServiceReference1.QuotesServiceClient();

            ServiceReference1.Quote quote = quotesServiceClient.GetAQuote();

            Console.WriteLine("Getting a single quote: " + quote.StrQuote);
            Console.WriteLine();
        }
    }
}
```

6. Now try calling *AddAQuote*. This is very much like calling *GetAQuote*. However, this time the request requires some parameters. Create an instance of the *Quote* (available from the *ServiceReference*). Find a pithy quote somewhere (or make one up) and plug it into the *Quote* object along with the first and last names of the originator. You can use the same instance of the *QuotesServiceClient* to call *AddAQuote*, passing the *Quote* object in. The next call to *GetAllQuotes* reveals that the quote was added to the quotes collection (which you see in a minute).

```
using System;
using System.Collections.Generic;
using System.Linq;
using System.Text;
namespace ConsumeQuotesService
{
    class Program
    {
        static void Main(string[] args)
        {
            // Get a single random quote
            ...

            // Now add a quote
            ServiceReference1.Quote newQuote = new ServiceReference1.Quote();
            newQuote.StrQuote = "But to me nothing - the negative, the empty" +
                "- is exceedingly powerful.";
            newQuote.StrOriginatorFirstName = "Alan";
            newQuote.StrOriginatorLastName = "Watts";

            quotesServiceClient.AddQuote(newQuote);

            Console.WriteLine("Added a quote");
            Console.WriteLine();
        }
    }
}
```

7. Now try calling *GetAllQuotes*. By now you should know the pattern pretty well. Use the *QuotesServiceClient* to call *GetAllQuotes*. *GetAllQuotes* returns a *DataSet* object that contains a collection of all the quotes, so declare one of those, too. Use the *QuotesServiceClient* object to call *GetAllQuotes*. When the call returns, use the *DataSet* object to print the quotes to the console. Be sure to include the *System.Data* namespace so that the compiler understands the *DataSet*.

```
using System;
using System.Collections.Generic;
using System.Linq;
using System.Text;
using System.Data;

namespace ConsumeQuotesService
{
    class Program
    {
        static void Main(string[] args)
        {
            // Get a single random quote

            // Now add a quote

            // Now get all the quotes
            DataSet dataSet = quotesServiceClient.GetAllQuotes();
            DataTable tableQuotes = dataSet.Tables[0];


            foreach (DataRow dr in tableQuotes.Rows)
            {
                System.Console.WriteLine(dr[0] + " " +
                dr[1] + "   " + dr[2]);
            }
        }
    }
}
```

8. Try calling *GetAQuote* asynchronously. The proxy created by Visual Studio supports asynchronous invocation if you ask it to generate the asynchronous methods. To call *GetAQuote* asynchronously, you need to implement a callback method that WCF will call when the method is finished executing. Add a static method named *GetAQuoteCallback* to your *Program* class. Have the method return void, and take *IAsyncResult* as a parameter. When WCF calls back into this method, the *IAsyncResult* parameter will be an instance of the class originating the call—an instance of *QuotesServiceClient*. Declare an instance of the *ServiceReference1.QuotesServiceClient* class and assign it by casting the *IAsyncResult* parameter's *AsyncState* property to the *ServiceReference1.QuotesServiceClient* type. Then, declare an instance of the *Quote* class and harvest the quote by calling *QuotesServiceClient.EndGetAQuote*, passing the *AsyncResult* parameter. Finally, write the quote out to the console.

```
using System;
using System.Collections.Generic;
using System.Linq;
using System.Text;
using System.Data;

namespace ConsumeQuotesService
{
    class Program
    {
        static void Main(string[] args)
        {
            // Get a single random quote

            // Now add a quote

            // Now get all the quotes
        }

        static void GetAQuoteCallback(IAsyncResult asyncResult)
        {
            ServiceReference1.QuotesServiceClient quotesServiceClient =
                (ServiceReference1.QuotesServiceClient)
                asyncResult.AsyncState;

            ServiceReference1.Quote quote =
                quotesServiceClient.EndGetAQuote(asyncResult);

            Console.WriteLine(quote.StrQuote);
        }
    }
}
```

9. Make the asynchronous call to *GetAQuote*. This is easy—just call the
   QuotesServiceClient's *BeginGetAQuote* method from the *Program* class's *Main* method.
   Pass in the *GetAQuoteCallback* method you just wrote as the first parameter and the
   QuotesServiceClient object as the second parameter. Add a call to *System.Console*
   .*ReadLine* to pause the main thread so that the asynchronous call has time to execute.

```
using System;
using System.Collections.Generic;
using System.Linq;
using System.Text;
using System.Data;

namespace ConsumeQuotesService
{
    class Program
    {
        static void Main(string[] args)
        {
            // Get a single random quote
```

```
            // Now add a quote

            // Now get all the quotes

            // Now call GetAQuote asynchronously
            System.Console.WriteLine(
                "Now fetching a quote asynchronously");
            Console.WriteLine();

            quotesServiceClient.BeginGetAQuote(GetAQuoteCallback,
                quotesServiceClient);

            Console.WriteLine("Press enter to exit...");
            Console.ReadLine();
        }

        static void GetAQuoteCallback(IAsyncResult asyncResult)
        {
            // implementation removed for clarity
        }
    }
}
```

10. Run the program to watch the console application call the WCFQuotesService. You should see the following output:

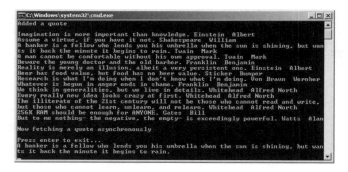

Chapter 25 Quick Reference

To	Do This
Create a WCF-enabled Web site	In Visual Studio, choose File, New, Web Site and select WCF Service from the available templates. This will produce a WCF-enabled Web site for you and will stub out a default contract and implementation that you may change to fit your needs.
Create a service contract	Service contracts are defined as .NET interfaces. The entire interface should be adorned with the *[ServiceContract]* attribute. Interface members meant to be exposed as individual services are adorned with the *[OperationContract]* attribute. Data structures may be passed through the interface. Structure members meant to be visible through the interface are adorned with the *[DataContract]* attribute.
Implement the service contract	Create a class that derives from the interface defining the service contract and implement the members.
Expose the WCF service as an ASP.NET application	Make sure that the web.config file mentions the service contract and the implementation.
Create a client to consume the WCF service	Use the Add Service Reference menu item found in the project's context menu (exposed from Visual Studio Solution Explorer) to discover and locate the service metadata. Alternatively, use the ServiceModel Metadata Utility Tool (packaged as an assembly named *Svcutil.exe*).
Customize the service's local execution, managing execution aspects such as security, instance lifetime, and threading	Apply the *ServiceBehaviorAttribute* and *OperationBehaviorAttribute* attributes as necessary to control the following aspects of the service execution: instance lifetimes, concurrency and synchronization support, configuration behavior, transaction behavior, serialization behavior, metadata transformation, session lifetime, address filtering and header processing, and impersonation.
Access the ASP.NET application cache from a standard WCF application (one not configured to run in ASP.NET compatibility mode)	Use the *HttpRuntime.Cache* property.

Chapter 26
Deployment

After completing this chapter, you will be able to

- Understand Microsoft Visual Studio support for deploying Web Applications.

- Create a deployment package using Visual Studio.

The first 25 chapters of this book focus on how the various features of ASP.NET work. A major theme in ASP.NET is to solve the most common use cases of Web site development. The preceding chapters have discussed the following aspects of ASP.NET:

- Rendering model, which breaks down page rendering into small manageable pieces using server-side controls

- Support for data binding, easing the task of rendering collections

- Login controls that cover the most common login scenarios

- Session state, which makes tracking users manageable

- Navigation and site map support

- XML Web Services as well as Windows Communication Foundation (WCF)-based Web site service support

- Support for creating a common look and feel for an application through master pages and themes

- Support for rich content using Microsoft Silverlight

- Support for AJAX-style programming

After you build a feature-rich application that streamlines your company operations or drives customers to your business, you need to be able to deploy it and manage it effectively. That's the topic of this chapter—how the various Visual Studio models affect your deployment strategy. In addition, this chapter looks at building a Web setup project.

 Important This chapter's code samples on the companion CD require IIS support to execute. See the "Code Samples" section in the Introduction for important information on running the examples for this chapter.

Visual Studio Web Sites

The Visual Studio File, New menu includes an entry for creating new ASP.NET projects and another entry for creating new Web sites. Most of this book focuses on creating new ASP.NET projects; this chapter focuses on deploying ASP.NET projects. Before discussing deployment, this chapter takes a quick look at the Visual Studio Web site templates that you can use to develop and deploy directly to various platforms (for example, to a file system, to an FTP site, or to Internet Information Services (IIS)).

HTTP Web Sites

In Visual Studio, when you click File, New, Web Site, and then select HTTP in the Web Location combo box in the New Web Site dialog box, you get a project that is much like the very first ASP.NET project development model available in Visual Studio (that is, in versions earlier than Visual Studio 2005). For the HTTP Web site model, Visual Studio creates a virtual directory under IIS and uses IIS to intercept requests during development time. Under this model, the solution file (.sln file) resides in a directory specified under the Visual Studio project settings directory. The source code for the project is stored in the IIS virtual directory (that is, \Inetpub\wwwroot).

Although this is not the preferred development model for most companies, the option is still available for some fringe scenarios, for example, individual developers creating sites. You might use this option if you want to work as closely as possible with IIS. With an IIS Web site during development, you can test the entire request path because it will run in production (not just the path through the Visual Studio–integrated Web server).

FTP Web Sites

The Visual Studio New Web Site template also includes a facility for creating an FTP Web Site. To create an FTP site, select FTP in the Web Location combo box in the New Web Site dialog box. This option was introduced in 2005 for projects that you want to manage remotely through an FTP server. For example, using an FTP project is a good option if you employ a remote hosting service to host your Web site. The FTP site option represents a reasonable means of getting files from your development environment to the hosting site.

For this type of site, Visual Studio can connect to any FTP server for which you have file and directory Read and Write access. You then use Visual Studio to manage the content on the remote FTP server.

File System Web Sites

The File System Web Site is the most developer-oriented Web site option. To create a File System Web Site, click File, New Web Site, and then select File System in the Web Location combo box in the New Web Site dialog box. File System Web Sites rely on the Web server integrated with Visual Studio to run Web sites during development. When you specify a File System Web Site, you can tell Visual Studio to put it anywhere on your file system or in a shared folder on another computer.

If you don't have access to IIS, or you don't have administration rights to the system on which you're developing, you can create a File System–based Web site project. The site runs locally but independently of IIS. The most common scenario in this case is to develop and test a Web site on the file system. Then, when it is time to expose your site, you can simply create an IIS virtual directory and point it to the pages in the file system Web site.

Another aspect of developing ASP.NET Web applications, aside from selecting the proper project type, is deciding whether to *precompile* your Web app. By default, Visual Studio does *not* precompile your Web application. After you have developed a site using Visual Studio, you can decide to precompile it for performance reasons. The next section looks at this option.

Precompiling

The earliest versions of Visual Studio automatically built ASP.NET applications when you selected Build, Build Solution on the main menu. All the source code (the .vb and the .cs files) was compiled into a resulting assembly with the same name as the project. This precompiled assembly went into the project's bin directory and became part of the files used for deployment. ASP.NET still precompiles an application for you. However, now you have two choices with regard to precompilation—using a virtual path (for applications already defined in IIS) and using a physical path (for sites that live on the file system). In addition, you must be deliberate about precompiling. The two precompilation options are precompile for performance and precompile for deployment. Precompiling a Web site involves using command-line tools.

Precompiling for Performance

The first option is also known as "precompiling in place." This is useful for existing sites for which you want to enhance performance. When you precompile the source code behind your site, the primary benefit is that ASP.NET does not have to run that initial compilation when the site is hit for the first time. If your site requires frequent updates to the code base, you might see a small amount of performance improvement.

To precompile an IIS-based site in place, open a Visual Studio command window. Navigate to the .NET directory on your computer (probably Windows\Microsoft.Net\ Framework\<*versionnumber*>). In that directory is a program named aspnet_compiler. Execute the aspnet_compiler program, with the name of the Web site as known by IIS following the –*v* switch. For example, if IIS has a virtual directory named *MySite*, the following command line will build it:

```
aspnet_compiler -v MySite
```

The precompiled application ends up in the Temporary ASP.NET Files directory under your current .NET directory.

If the Web site is a file system Web site without an IIS virtual directory, use the –*p* command-line parameter to specify the physical path. This compilation option precompiles the code and places it in the bin directory for the application.

Precompiling for Deployment

Compiling for deployment involves compiling the code for a site and directing the output to a special directory from which it can be copied to the deployment computer or used in a setup project (as you see momentarily). In this case, the compiler produces assemblies from all ASP.NET source files that are typically compiled at run time. That includes the code for the pages, source code in the App_Code directory, and resource files.

To precompile a site for deployment, open a Visual Studio command window. Navigate to the .NET directory. Run the aspnet_compiler command-line program, specifying the source as either a virtual path or a physical path. Provide the target folder following the input directory. For example, the following command builds the code in the *MySite* virtual directory and puts the resulting compiled version in C:\MySiteTarget:

```
aspnet_compiler -v MySite c:\MySiteTarget
```

If you add a –*u* command-line parameter at the end of the command line, the compiler will compile some of the code and leave the page code files to be compiled just in time.

Visual Studio 2010 Deployment Support

For many developers, deploying an ASP.NET application is a far-off activity that they have to simply take care of at the end of the development cycle. However, it turns out that deploying and redeploying an application is a big deal—especially with the advent of cloud computing where you might not have direct access to your servers. The deployment task is the one task to which Visual Studio has been only partially suited. That is, up until now.

Visual Studio includes several new features that make Web site deployment much more manageable than before. These features include the following:

- Web packaging

- Transforming web.config files for deployment (for example, by substituting development-time connection strings with production-time connection strings)

- Database deployment/redeployment

- One-Click Publish for Web applications

These new Visual Studio 2010 deployment features address a long-neglected phase of ASP.NET application development—getting your code to a place where users can browse to it. Before these features were available, the best deployment option was usually to create an install package to distribute to those administering a Web farm. Although creating an install package is definitely preferable to simply copying files to a Web server, the install package mechanism didn't take care of everything. For example, database schema changes were often a big problem during site redeployment. The ASP.NET debug/release Web.config file mechanism is completely unaccounted for by the Web install project. The ASP.NET new Web packaging feature solves these problems. Using the Web packaging feature, you can create either a ZIP file or a folder containing all the content and support files necessary to deploy the project onto a Web server. The following items are included in a Web package:

- The content—such as Web Form pages, user controls, and HTML files

- Microsoft SQL Server database schemas and data, if desired

- IIS settings such as error page settings and application pooling information

- Other pieces required to support the project, such as components to be installed in the global assembly cache, security certificates, and registry setting information

Once created, you can either copy the Web package to a server and install it manually (using IIS Manager), or you can install it using command-line programs or the deployment APIs (useful for automated deployment scenarios).

The best way to understand these features is to set up an ASP.NET site for deployment.

Packaging an ASP.NET project for deployment

1. Create a new Empty ASP.NET Web Application project named *DeployThisApplication*.

2. Add some content to this site so that you can see it when it's deployed. At the very least, include a Default.aspx page, and include a *Button* named *ButtonShowApplicationSetting* and a *Label* named *LabelShowApplicationSetting*. These illustrate how the web.config transforms work. The example included with this book also has a Default.aspx page, Page1.aspx, and Page2.aspx.

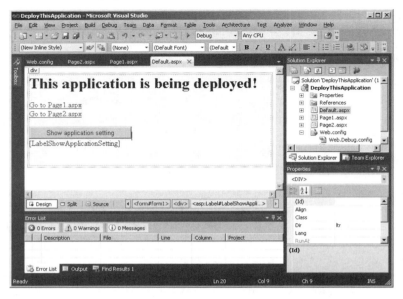

3. The application created by Visual Studio comes in two flavors: Debug and Release. You want to create a new configuration named Staging that might require some slightly different settings once the application is running on the Web servers. Right-click the Solution node in Solution Explorer, and then select Configuration Manager. Visual Studio displays this dialog box:

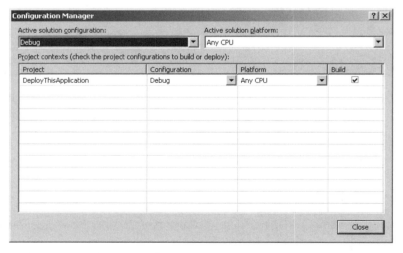

4. In the Active Solution Configuration combo box, select *<New...>*. Visual Studio will display the New Solution Configuration dialog box, as shown in the following graphic. Name the new configuration Staging, and copy the settings from the Release configuration, like so. Click OK to save the new configuration.

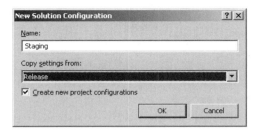

5. Now that there's a staging configuration, add a transform for web.config to handle any configuration changes that might occur between development and deployment. To see how this works, start by adding an application setting to the web.config file. Use the ASP.NET Configuration tool to add an application setting to this project's configuration file (you can find it under Project, ASP.NET Configuration). This example has a setting whose key is *ApplicationSetting* and whose value is This ApplicationSetting was created at development time, as shown here:

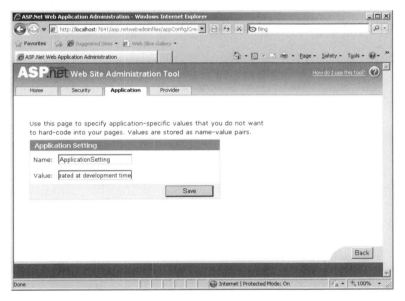

6. Create a button handler by double-clicking the button in the Designer. Write a handler that looks up the application setting and displays it in the label, like so:

```
protected void ButtonShowApplicationSetting_Click(object sender, EventArgs e)
{
  string applicationSetting =
    System.Configuration.ConfigurationManager.AppSettings["ApplicationSetting"];
  this.LabelShowApplicationSetting.Text = applicationSetting;
}
```

It should appear something like this when you run the page and click the button:

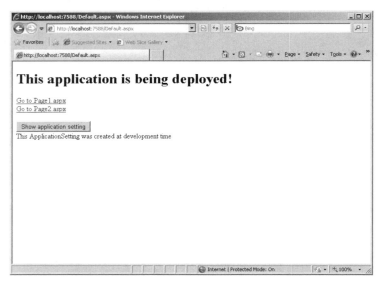

7. Now set up a version of the configuration file to be used during deployment. To do this, right-click the Web.config node in Solution Explorer and select Add Configuration Transform. Visual Studio will create a Web.Staging.config for you automatically. You can see it in Solution Explorer along with Web.Debug.config and Web.Release.config:

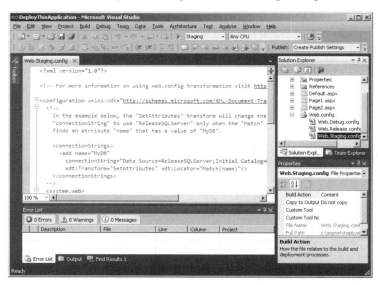

8. Open the main web.config file and copy the application settings section to the Clipboard. Then, open the Web.Staging.config file and paste the application settings section into it. Now the development and deployment application settings can differ—and Visual Studio will make sure the deployment settings are in the deployment web.config file.

9. Modify the Web.Staging.config file to include a different setting. Change the setting to reflect that it is coming from the staging configuration. Also, add two XML Document Transform attributes, *xdt:Transform* and *xdt:Locator,* so that the setting will be substituted correctly when the application is transformed for deployment. Visual Studio will read the attributes when the package is created and will replace the application setting string in the Web.Staging.config file.

```
<appSettings>
  <add key="ApplicationSetting"
    value="This ApplicationSetting was created at DEPLOYMENT time"
    xdt:Transform="Replace"
    xdt:Locator="Match(key)"
  />
</appSettings>
<system.web>
</system.web>
```

10. Have Visual Studio create the deployment package for you. Make sure Staging is the active configuration. First, open the Package/Publish Settings for the project by right-clicking the project in Solution Explorer and clicking Package/Publish Settings. Clear the Create Web Package As A ZIP File check box so that the files will be deployed into a directory structure you can later examine. Click the Save button on the toolbar to save your new setting.

11 Right-click the project node in Solution Explorer and click Create Package. Visual Studio will create a directory structure with everything needed to deploy the application. You can find it in the project's directory structure under obj\Staging\Package\PackageTmp, like so:

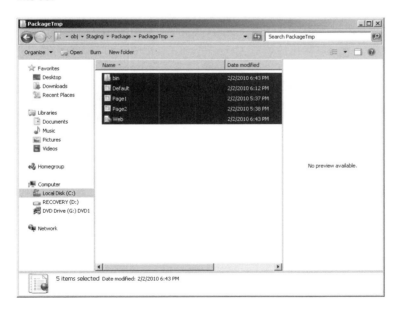

12. Copy the contents of the package directory into a directory on your root directory that you can use as a virtual directory for IIS. This example assumes that the content is copied into C:\deploythisapplication. Use IIS to create a new Web Application under the Default Web Site by right-clicking the Default Web Site node in IIS and selecting Add Application as you did in Chapter 2, "ASP.NET Application Fundamentals." Provide IIS with the directory containing the new content, like this:

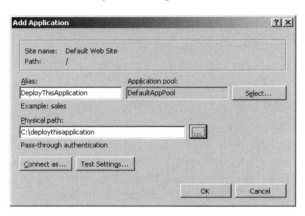

13. Open the content pane for the new site and notice the deployed content is visible to IIS:

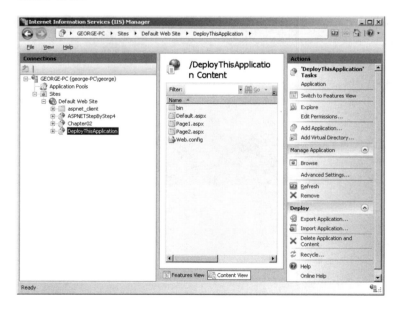

14. Right-click the Default.aspx page and browse to the Default page. Click the button and notice that the DEPLOYMENT version of the application setting is displayed:

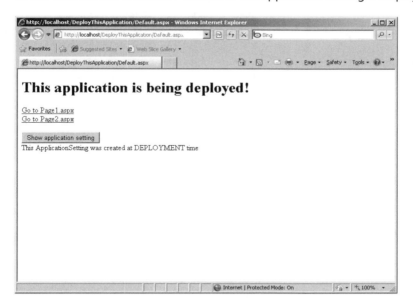

Chapter 26 Quick Reference

To	Do This
Work on a Web site locally without going through IIS	Create a File System Web site.
Work on a Web site using IIS	Create an HTTP Web site.
Work on a Web site by copying files over to the server FTP	Create an FTP site.
Precompile for performance or for deployment	Use the aspnet_compiler utility to precompile the code or publish it using Visual Studio.
Publish a Web application	Use the Build, Publish option in Visual Studio. Visual Studio will push the files to the directory you specify (which can be an IIS virtual directory).
Create an installer for your Web application	Add a second project to your solution. Make it a Web Setup project. Add the necessary files to the project to make it work. Build the installer.

To	Do This
Create a new configuration for deployment	Right mouse click on the Solution node in Solution Explorer. Select Configuration Manager. Under the Active solution configuration, select <new configuration>. Name the configuration and copy it from an existing configuration.
Create a new Web.config file to transform	After creating a new configuration, right mouse click on the Web.config file in Solution Explorer. Select Add Config Transforms.
Create a Web Package	Right mouse click on the Project node in Solution Explorer. Select Create Package.

Index

Symbols

404 errors, 378

<% and %> tags, 19, 31

<body> tag, 147

<Canvas>/</Canvas> tags, 448

[DataContract] attribute, 573

<deny users="*"> node, 204

<form>/</form> tags, 9–11
  action attribute, 10
  method attribute, 10–11

<Grid>/</Grid> tags, 448

<iframe> element, 442, 445

<img /> tag, 128

<input type=image /> tag, 129

<object> tags, 524–525

[OperationContract] attribute, 573

<option> tag, 207

<Page>/</Page> tags, 448

[ScriptableMember] attribute, 534

[ScriptableType] attribute, 534

<select>and </select> tags, 9, 207

[ServiceContract] attribute, 573

A

ABC endpoints definition, 557

abortPostBack() method, 499

absolute expirations, for cached data, 331–333

absolute positioning, 77, 150

AcceptVerbs attribute, 469, 471

access
  managing, 181. *See also* security
  speeds of, 321

access rules, 198
  creating, 203–204

Accordion extenders, 482

AccountController, 457

action attribute, 10

ActionResult, 460, 469

Active Data Objects (ADO), 215

Active Server Pages (ASP), 18–21
  code processing, 46
  control state, loss of, 97
  dynamic content support, 60, 61
  execution model, 25
  locked files in, 42

Response object, 32
  script blocks, 31

ActiveViewIndex property, 137

ActiveX controls, for Web-based GUIs, 62

Add Application Setting dialog box, 178

add attribute, 406

Add Connection String dialog box, 177

Add New Access Rule link, 203

Add New Item dialog box, 53

Add Reference dialog box, 398

Add Service Reference command, 547

Add Service Reference dialog box, 568

Add Style Rule dialog box, 156–157

administrators, user access control, 182

ADO (Active Data Objects), 215

ADO.NET, 215–221
  database connection classes, 216
  database provider factories, 216–217
  database scalability and, 219
  result set management, 218–221

ADO.NET objects, data-bound controls, session state and, 299–305

AJAX (Asynchronous Java and XML), 433, 474–475
  AJAX-style programming examples, 477
  ASP.NET and, 475–478
  async callbacks, 489–490
  authentication support, 477
  AutoComplete extender, 433, 501–507
  base class library, 480
  benefits of, 476–477
  browser compatibility layer, 480
  browser support, 477
  client-side support, 480–484
  core services layer, 480
  vs. DHTML, 478

extender control architecture, 477, 501–512
  ModalPopup extender, 433, 508–512
  networking layer, 480
  partial-page updates, 477, 484–489
  personalization support, 477
  progress updating, 497–501
  in the real world, 477–478
  RIAs, creating with, 473
  server-side support, 478–480
  style of programming, 474–475
  Web service idiom use, 475
  Web sites, enabling for, 512
  for Web UIs, 62

AJAX Control Toolkit, 475, 480–481
  building, 481
  community-supported effort, 481
  controls and extenders, 482–484

AJAX Library scripts, registering with page, 479

AJAX script libraries, 480

Alexander, Christopher, 451

allowAnonymous attribute, 262, 266

allowCustomSqlDatabase setting, 311

AlternateRowStyle property, 228

AlternateText property, 130

AlwaysVisibleControl extenders, 482

Animation extenders, 482

animations
  rendering, 448
  in Silverlight, 535–542

Anonymous Authentication mode, 183

anonymousIdentification element, 262, 266

anonymous personalization, 262

anonymous profiles, 261
  tracking, 266

AnonymousTemplate template, 200

About the Author

George Shepherd is a software consultant who specializes in Microsoft .NET technologies. As an instructor for DevelopMentor, George delivers short seminars that cover .NET, ASP.NET, and WPF. George is the author and co-author of several other books on software development, including *MFC Internals* (Addison-Wesley) and *Programming with Microsoft Visual C++ .NET* (Microsoft Press). He has served as contributing editor for MSDN Magazine and Dr. Dobb's Journal and is a contributing architect for Syncfusion's Essential .NET toolset.